Lecture Notes in Artificial Intelligence 1650

Subseries of Lecture Notes in Computer Science
Edited by J. G. Carbonell and J. Siekmann

Lecture Notes in Computer Science
Edited by G. Goos, J. Hartmanis and J. van Leeuwen

Springer

Berlin
Heidelberg
New York
Barcelona
Hong Kong
London
Milan
Paris
Singapore
Tokyo

Klaus-Dieter Althoff Ralph Bergmann
L. Karl Branting (Eds.)

Case-Based Reasoning Research and Development

Third International Conference
on Case-Based Reasoning, ICCBR-99
Seeon Monastery, Germany, July 27-30, 1999
Proceedings

Springer

Series Editors

Jaime G. Carbonell, Carnegie Mellon University, Pittsburgh, PA, USA
Jörg Siekmann, University of Saarland, Saarbrücken, Germany

Volume Editors

Klaus-Dieter Althoff
Fraunhofer Institute for Experimental Software Engineering (IESE)
Sauerwiesen 6, D-67661 Kaiserslautern, Germany
E-mail: althoff@iese.fhg.de

Ralph Bergmann
University of Kaiserslautern, Department of Computer Science
P.O. Box 3049, D-67653 Kaiserslautern, Germany
E-mail: bergmann@informatik.uni-kl.de

L. Karl Branting
University of Wyoming, Department of Computer Science
P.O. Box 3682, Laramie, WY 82072, USA
E-mail: karl@uwyo.edu

Cataloging-in-Publication data applied for

Die Deutsche Bibliothek - CIP-Einheitsaufnahme

Case based reasoning research and development : proceedings / Third International Conference on Case Based Reasoning, ICCBR-99, Seeon Monastery, Germany, July 27 - 30, 1999. Klaus-Dieter Althoff ... (ed.). - Berlin ; Heidelberg ; New York ; Barcelona ; Hong Kong ; London ; Milan ; Paris ; Singapore ; Tokyo : Springer, 1999
(Lecture notes in computer science ; Vol. 1650 : Lecture notes in artificial intelligence)
ISBN 3-540-66237-5

CR Subject Classification (1998): I.2, J.4, J.1, F.4.1

ISBN 3-540-66237-5 Springer-Verlag Berlin Heidelberg New York

Printed in Germany

Typesetting: Camera-ready by author
SPIN 10703943 06/3142 – 5 4 3 2 1 0 Printed on acid-free paper

Preface

The biennial International Conference on Case-Based Reasoning (ICCBR) series, which began in Sesimbra, Portugal, in 1995, was intended to provide an international forum for the best fundamental and applied research in case-based reasoning (CBR). It was hoped that such a forum would encourage the growth and rigor of the field and overcome the previous tendency toward isolated national CBR communities.

The foresight of the original ICCBR organizers has been rewarded by the growth of a vigorous and cosmopolitan CBR community. CBR is now widely recognized as a powerful and important computational technique for a wide range of practical applications. By promoting an exchange of ideas among CBR researchers from across the globe, the ICCBR series has facilitated the broader acceptance and use of CBR.

ICCBR-99 has continued this tradition by attracting high-quality research and applications papers from around the world. Researchers from 21 countries submitted 80 papers to ICCBR-99. From these submissions, 17 papers were selected for long oral presentation, 7 were accepted for short oral presentation, and 19 papers were accepted as posters. This volume sets forth these 43 papers, which contain both mature work and innovative new ideas.

In addition to a technical session of invited talks, presentations, and posters, ICCBR-99 included an Industry Day, where the focus was on mature technology and applications in industry. Papers describing these "industrial-strength" applications are contained in a separate volume. Information on this volume is available at the ICCBR-99 home page, `www.iccbr.org/iccbr99`. The ICCBR-99 program also included four half-day workshops, also described in the ICCBR-99 home page.

The program chairs of ICCBR-99 were Klaus-Dieter Althoff, of the Fraunhofer Institute for Experimental Software Engineering, and L. Karl Branting, of the University of Wyoming. The conference chair was Ralph Bergmann, of the University of Kaiserslautern. The chairs would like to thank the program committee and the additional reviewers for their thoughtful and rigorous reviewing during the paper selection process.

The chairs gratefully acknowledge the generous support of ICCBR-99's sponsors, the American Association for Artificial Intelligence (AAAI), AcknoSoft, BSR Consulting, DaimlerChrysler, the Fraunhofer Institute for Experimental Software Engineering, the German Society for Computer Science (Gesellschaft für Informatik, GI), Inference, Interactive Multimedia Systems, tec:inno, the University of Kaiserslautern, and the University of Wyoming. We would also like to thank Christine Harms for her assistance in making the local arrangements for the conference.

May 1999

Klaus-Dieter Althoff
Ralph Bergmann
L. Karl Branting

Program Chairs

Klaus-Dieter Althoff, Fraunhofer IESE, Germany
L. Karl Branting, University of Wyoming, USA

Conference Chair

Ralph Bergmann, University of Kaiserslautern, Germany

Industrial Chairs

Brigitte Bartsch-Spörl, BSR Consulting, Germany
Wolfgang Wilke, tec:inno GmbH, Germany

Workshop Chairs

Sascha Schmitt, University of Kaiserslautern, Germany
Ivo Vollrath,University of Kaiserslautern, Germany

Program Committee

Agnar Aamodt	Norwegian University of Science and Tech.
Robert Aarts	Nokia Telecommunications, Finland
David Aha	Office of Naval Research, USA
Klaus-Dieter Althoff	Fraunhofer IESE, Germany
Kevin Ashley	University of Pittsburgh, USA
Paolo Avesani	IRST Povo, Italy
Ralph Barletta	Inference Corporation, USA
Brigitte Bartsch-Spörl	BSR Consulting, Germany
Ralph Bergmann	University of Kaiserslautern, Germany
Carlos Bento	University of Coimbra, Portugal
L. Karl Branting	University of Wyoming, USA
Michael Brown	Siemens, Germany
Hans-Dieter Burkhard	Humboldt University Berlin, Germany
Michael Cox	Wright State University, Dayton, USA
Pádraig Cunningham	Trinity College Dublin, Ireland
Boi Faltings	EPFL Lausanne, Switzerland
Ashok Goel	Georgia Institute of Technology, USA
Andrew Golding	MERL Cambridge, USA
Kris Hammond	Northwestern University, USA
Mark Keane	University College Dublin, Ireland
Janet Kolodner	Georgia Institute of Technology, USA
David Leake	Indiana University, USA
Brian Lees	University of Paisley, UK
Ramon López de Mántaras	IIIA-CSIC, Spain
Robert Macura	Medical College of Georgia, USA
Mary Lou Maher	University of Sydney, Australia
Michel Manago	AcknoSoft, France

Héctor Muñoz-Avila	University of Maryland, USA
Bart Netten	Delft University of Technology, NL
Enric Plaza	IIIA-CSIC, Spain
Pearl Pu	EPFL Lausanne, Switzerland
Francesco Ricci	IRST Povo, Italy
Michael M. Richter	University of Kaiserslautern, Germany
Edwina Rissland	University of Massachusetts, USA
Hideo Shimazu	NEC, Japan
Barry Smyth	University College Dublin, Ireland
Gerhard Strube	University of Freiburg, Germany
Brigitte Trousse	INRIA Sophia Antipolis, France
Manuela Veloso	Carnegie Mellon University, USA
Ian Watson	Salford University, UK
Stefan Wess	tec:inno GmbH, Germany
Qiang Yang	Simon Fraser University, Canada

Additional Reviewers

Vincent Aleven	Mario Lenz
Kati Börner	Cindy Marling
Derek Bridge	Mirjam Minor
Roger Carasso	Petri Myllymäki
Stefanie Brüninghaus	Petra Perner
Werner Dubitzky	Frank Puppe
Dieter Ehrenberg	Rainer Schmidt
Michael Fagan	Sascha Schmitt
Paulo Gomes	Alexander Seitz
Christiane Gresse von Wangenheim	Armin Stahl
Conor Hayes	Adelinde Uhrmacher
André Hübner	Ivo Vollrath
Jacek Jarmulak	David C. Wilson

Conference Support

ICCBR-99 was organized by the German Society for Computer Science (Gesellschaft für Informatik, GI) and supported by the American Association for Artificial Intelligence (AAAI), AcknoSoft, BSR Consulting, DaimlerChrysler, the Fraunhofer Institute for Experimental Software Engineering, Inference, Interactive Multimedia Systems, tec:inno, the University of Kaiserslautern, and the University of Wyoming.

Table of Contents

Research Papers

Application Papers

Affect-Driven CBR to Generate Expressive Music

Josep Lluís Arcos, Dolores Cañamero, and Ramon López de Mántaras

IIIA, Artificial Intelligence Research Institute
CSIC, Spanish Council for Scientific Research
Campus UAB, 08193 Bellaterra, Catalonia, Spain.
Vox: +34-93-5809570, Fax: +34-93-5809661
{arcos, lola, mantaras}@iiia.csic.es
http://www.iiia.csic.es

Abstract. We present an extension of an existing system, called *SaxEx*, capable of generating expressive musical performances based on Case-Based Reasoning (CBR) techniques. The previous version of *SaxEx* did not take into account the possibility of using affective labels to guide the CBR task. This paper discusses the introduction of such affective knowledge to improve the retrieval capabilities of the system. Three affective dimensions are considered—tender-aggressive, sad-joyful, and calm-restless—that allow the user to declaratively instruct the system to perform according to any combination of five qualitative values along these three dimensions.

1 Introduction

In recent years, many researchers in human emotions have rejected the idea of emotion as something irrational. Emotion is now seen as fundamental to reasoning and this new view has raised a number of theories. One theory that fits musical experience particularly well is the so called "discrepancy theory" [13] which regards emotion as a reaction to unexpected experience. Music indeed sets up anticipations and then satisfies them. For example, in a chord cadence (the resolution of a harmonic progression back toward a tonal center), listeners anticipate the pleasing resolving chord (tonal center) that brings the listener from tension to repose. It is possible (and good music always does so) to satisfy very pleasingly the anticipation by withholding the resolution and therefore hightening the anticipation. When music goes out of its way to violate the expectations we call it expressive. Musicians breathe feeling into a performance by means of suitable deviations not only in timing (rubato) and loudness (dynamics) but also in vibrato, articulation and the attack of notes. With too much deviation, music becomes too incoherent and with too little deviation becomes cold, mechanical and boring. This phenomenon has also a neurological basis [15]. Like most neurons, auditory neurons fire constantly but are the changes in firing rates that are significant. Some neurons answer to raw frequency information but most are concerned with changes in sound. Firing rates change when frequency or intensity varies. Furthermore, some 85 percent of primary auditory neurons exhibit the phenomenon of habituation: the longer they are stimulated, the less they respond. It can be said that the brain is mainly interested in change. This is why typical computer-generated music in which tempo and loudness are always constant, pitch is perfect (no vibrato at all) and in which the attack of the notes is always the same is rejected by the musically sensitive. The work described in this paper addresses the automatic generation of expressive music endowing the resulting piece with the expressivity that characterizes human performances. Following musical rules, whatever sophisticated and complete they are, is not enough to achieve this expressivity, and indeed music generated in this way usually sounds monotonous and mechanical. The main problem here is to grasp the performer's "personal touch", the knowledge brough about when performing a score and that is absent from it. This knowledge concerns not only "technical" features (use of musical resources) but also the affective aspects implicit in music. A large part of this knowledge is tacit and therefore very difficult to generalize and verbalize, although it is not inaccessible. Humans acquire it through a long process of observation, imitation, and experimentation [11]. For this reason, AI approaches based on declarative knowledge representations have serious limitations. An alternative approach, much closer to the observation-imitation-experimentation process observed in humans, is that of directly using the knowledge implicit in examples from recordings of human performances.

In order to achieve this we have extended *SaxEx* [2], a case-based reasoning (CBR) system for generating expressive performances of melodies based on examples of human performances (for the moment *SaxEx* is limited to jazz ballads). CBR is appropriate for problems where (a) many examples of solved problems can be obtained—like in our case where multiple examples can be easily obtained from recordings of human performances; and (b) a large part of the knowledge involved in the solution of problems is tacit, difficult to verbalize and generalize.

We have improved *SaxEx* allowing the user to control the degree and type of expressivity desired in the output by means of qualitative affective labels along three orthogonal affective dimensions (tender-aggressive, sad-joyful, and calm-restless). This enables the user to ask the system to perform a phrase according to a specific affective label or a combination of them.

2 SaxEx elements

In this section, we briefly present some of the elements underlying *SaxEx* which are necessary to understand the system (see Figure 1).

2.1 SMS

Sound analysis and synthesis techniques based on spectrum models like Spectral Modeling and Synthesis (SMS) are useful for the extraction of high level parameters from real sound files, their transformation, and the synthesis of a modified version of these sound files. *SaxEx* uses SMS in order to extract basic information related to several expressive parameters such as dynamics, rubato,

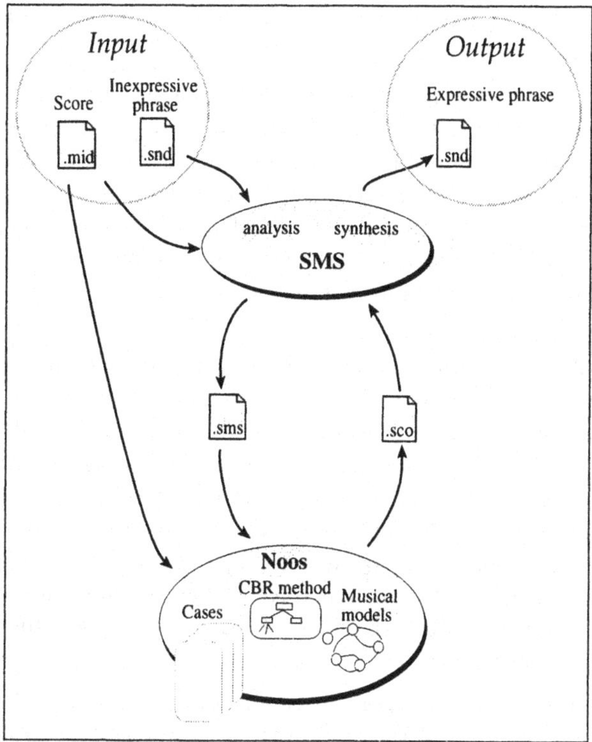

Fig. 1. General view of *SaxEx* blocks.

vibrato, and articulation. The SMS synthesis procedure allows the generation of expressive reinterpretations by appropriately transforming an inexpressive sound file.

The SMS approach to spectral analysis is based on decomposing a sound into sinusoids plus a spectral residual. From the sinusoidal plus the residual representation we can extract high level attributes such as attack and release times, formant structure, vibrato, and average pitch and amplitude, when the sound is a note or a monophonic phrase of an instrument. These attributes can be modified and added back to the spectral representation without loss of sound quality.

This sound analysis and synthesis system is ideal as a preprocessor, giving to *SaxEx* high level musical parameters, and as a post-processor, adding the transformations specified by the case-based reasoning system to the inexpressive original sound.

2.2 Noos

SaxEx is implemented in *Noos* [4,3], a reflective object-centered representation language designed to support knowledge modeling of problem solving and learning. Modeling a problem in Noos requires the specification of three different types of knowledge: domain knowledge, problem solving knowledge, and metalevel knowledge.

Domain knowledge specifies a set of concepts, a set of relations among concepts, and problem data that are relevant for an application. Concepts and relations define the domain ontology of an application. For instance, the domain ontology of *SaxEx* is composed by concepts such as notes, chords, analysis structures, and expressive parameters. Problem data, described using the domain ontology, define specific situations (specific problems) that have to be solved. For instance, specific inexpressive musical phrases to be transformed into expressive ones.

Problem solving knowledge specifies the set of tasks to be solved in an application. For instance, the main task of *SaxEx* is to infer a sequence of expressive transformations for a given musical phrase. Methods model different ways of solving tasks. Methods can be elementary or can be decomposed into subtasks. These new (sub)tasks may be achieved by other methods. A method defines an execution order over subtasks and an specific combination of the results of the subtasks in order to solve the task it performs. For a given task, there can be multiple alternative methods that may solve the task in different situations. This recursive decomposition of a task into subtasks by means of a method is called task/method decomposition.

The metalevel of Noos incorporates, among other types of (meta-)knowledge, *Preferences*, used by *SaxEx* to rank cases, and *Perspectives*, used in the retrieval task. *Preferences* model decision making criteria about sets of alternatives present in domain knowledge and problem solving knowledge. For instance, preference knowledge can be used to model criteria for ranking some precedent cases over other precedent cases for a task in a specific situation.

Perspectives [1], constitute a mechanism to describe declarative biases for case retrieval that provides a clear and flexible way to express retrieval mechanisms in complex-real applications that use structured representations of cases. Our research on perspectives, presented in [1], is based on the observation that, in complex tasks, the identification of the relevant aspects for retrieval in a given situation may involve the use of knowledge intensive methods and requires dynamical decisions about the relevant aspects of a problem. Then, a system capable of solving complex tasks can be forced to work with non predefined retrieval indexes in the memory of cases.

Perspectives are used by *SaxEx* to guide its decisions about the relevant aspects of an input musical phrase. *SaxEx* incorporates two types of declarative biases in the perspectives. On the one hand, metalevel knowledge to assess similarities among scores using the analysis structures built upon the IR and GTTM musical models. On the other hand, (metalevel) knowledge to detect affective intention in performances and to assess similarities among them.

Once a problem is solved, Noos automatically memorizes (stores and indexes) that problem. The collection of problems that a system has solved is called the episodic memory of Noos. The problems solved by Noos are accessible and retrievable. This introspection capability of Noos is the basic building block for integrating learning, and specifically CBR, into Noos.

2.3 Backgound musical knowledge

SaxEx incorporates two theories of musical perception and musical understanding that constitute the background musical knowledge of the system: Narmour's implication/realization (IR) model [17] and Lerdahl and Jackendoff's generative theory of tonal music (GTTM) [16].

Narmour's implication/realization model proposes a theory of cognition of melodies based on eight basic structures. These structures characterize patterns of melodic implications that constitute the basic units of the listener perception. Other parameters such as metric, duration, and rhythmic patterns emphasize or inhibit the perception of these melodic implications. The use of the IR model provides a musical analysis based on the structure of the melodic surface.

Examples of IR basic structures are the `P` process (a melodic pattern describing a sequence of at least three notes with similar intervals and same ascending or descending registral direction) and the `ID` process (a sequence of at least three notes with same intervals and different registral directions).

On the other hand, Lerdahl and Jackendoff's generative theory of tonal music (GTTM) offers a complementary approach to understanding melodies based on a hierarchical structure of musical cognition. GTTM proposes four types of hierarchical structures associated with a piece.

Examples of GTTM analysis structures are **`prolongational-reduction`**—a hierarchical structure describing tension-relaxation relationships among groups of notes—and **`time-span-reduction`**—a hierarchical structure describing the relative structural importance of notes within the heard rhythmic units of a phrase. Both are tree structures that are directly represented in *Noos* because of the tree-data representation capabilities of the language.

The goal of using both, IR and GTTM models, is to take advantage of combining the IR analysis of melodic surface with the GTTM structural analysis of the melody. These are two complementary views of melodies that influence the execution of a performance.

2.4 Affective descriptions

The use of affective adjectives to characterize different aspects of musical performance has a long tradition. In baroque music, each piece or movement had an "affect" associated with it that was intended to have "the soul exert control over the body and fill it with passions that were strongly expressed" [8]. Many lists of affective adjectives have been proposed by different theorists, e.g., Castiglioni, Galilei, Rousseau, Quantz, Mattheson, or more recently Cooke [7]. The main problems with the use of affective adjectives for musical purposes are that their meaning might vary over time, they are highly subjective and usually redundant or overlapping, and it is very difficult to assess what are the relationships between different labels. In order to avoid these problems, we decided not to use isolated adjectives, but rather to rank affective intentions along three orthogonal dimensions: tender-aggressive, sad-joyful, and calm-restless. To come out with these dimensions, we drew inspiration from the experiments conducted by [5], where sonological analysis of jazz recordings and the listeners' perception of them showed that a broad set of affective adjectives (16 in the experiments reported there) could be clustered into a few main dimensions. In addition, these dimensions relate to semantic notions, such as activity, tension versus relaxation, brightness, etc., although a one-to-one correlation cannot be neatly established.

3 SaxEx system

An input for *SaxEx* is a musical phrase described by means of its musical score (a MIDI file), a sound, and specific qualitative labels along affective dimensions. Affective labels can be partially specified, i.e. the user does not have to provide labels for every dimension.

The score contains the melodic and the harmonic information of the musical phrase. The sound contains the recording of an inexpressive interpretation of the musical phrase played by a musician. Values for affective dimensions will guide the search in the memory of cases. The output of the system is a new sound file, obtained by transformations of the original sound, and containing an expressive performance of the same phrase.

Solving a problem in *SaxEx* involves three phases: the analysis phase, the reasoning phase (performed by the CBR-method), and the synthesis phase (see Figure 1). Analysis and synthesis phases are implemented using SMS sound analysis and synthesis techniques. The reasoning phase is performed using CBR techniques and implemented in Noos and is the main focus of this paper.

The development of *SaxEx* involved the elaboration of two main models: the domain model and the problem-solving model. The domain model contains the concepts and structures relevant for representing musical knowledge. The problem-solving model consists mainly of a CBR method for inferring a sequence of expressive transformations for a given musical phrase.

3.1 Modeling musical knowledge

Problems solved by *SaxEx*, and stored in its memory, are represented in *Noos* as complex structured cases (see Figure2) embodying three different kinds of musical knowledge: (1) concepts related to the score of the phrase such as notes and chords, (2) concepts related to background musical theories such as implication/realization structures and GTTM's time-span reduction nodes, and (3) concepts related to the performance of musical phrases. Affective labels belong to this third type.

A score is represented by a melody, embodying a sequence of notes, and a harmony, embodying a sequence of chords. Each note holds in turn a set of features such as its pitch (C5, G4, etc), its position with respect to the beginning of the phrase, its duration, a reference to its underlying harmony, and a reference

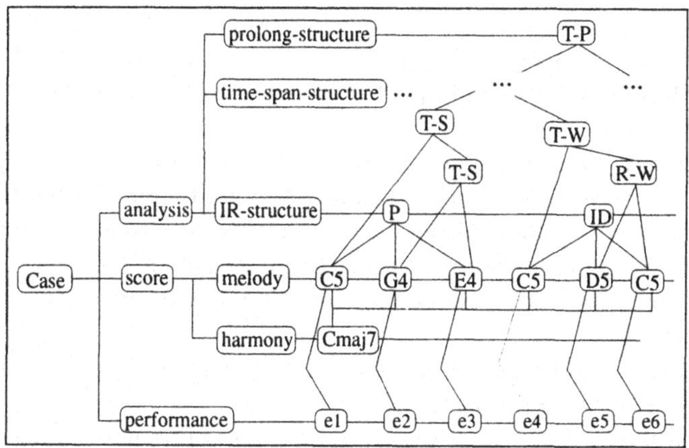

Fig. 2. Overall structure of the beginning of an 'All of me' case.

to the next note of the phrase. Chords hold also a set of features such as name (Cmaj7, E7, etc), position, duration, and a reference to the next chord.

The musical analysis representation embodies structures of the phrase inferred using Narmour's and GTTM background musical knowledge. The analysis structure of a melody is represented by a process-structure (embodying a sequence of IR basic structures), a time-span-reduction structure (embodying a tree describing metrical relations), and a prolongational-reduction structure (embodying a tree describing tensing and relaxing relations). Moreover, a note holds the metrical-strength feature, inferred using GTTM theory, expressing the note's relative metrical importance into the phrase.

The information about the expressive performances contained in the examples of the case memory, is represented by a sequence of *affective regions* and a sequence of *events*, one for each note, (extracted using the SMS sound analysis capabilities), as explained below.

Affective regions group (sub)-sequences of notes with common affective expressivity. Specifically, an affective region holds knowledge describing the following affective dimensions: *tender-aggressive*, *sad-joyful*, and *calm-restless*. These affective dimensions are described using five qualitative labels as follows. The middle label represents no predominance (e.g. neither tender nor aggressive), lower and upper labels represent, respectively predominance in one direction (e.g. absolutely calm is described with the lowest label). For instance, a jazz ballad can start very tender and calm and continue very tender but more restless. Such different nuances are represented in *SaxEx* by means of different affective regions.

There is an *event* for each note within the phrase embodying information about expressive parameters applied to that note. Specifically, an event holds information about dynamics, rubato, vibrato, articulation, and attack. These expressive parameters are described using qualitative labels as follows:

• Changes in dynamics are described relative to the average loudness of the phrase by means of a set of five ordered labels. The middle label represents average loudness and lower and upper labels represent respectively increasing or decreasing degrees of loudness.

• Changes in rubato are described relative to the average tempo also by means of a set of five ordered labels. Analogously to dynamics, qualitative labels about rubato cover the range from a strong accelerando to a strong ritardando.

• The vibrato level is described using two parameters: frequency and amplitude. Both parameters are described using five qualitative labels from no-vibrato to highest-vibrato.

• The articulation between notes is described using again a set of five ordered labels covering the range from legato to staccato.

• Finally, *SaxEx* considers two possibilities regarding note attack: (1) reaching the pitch of a note starting from a lower pitch, and (2) increasing the noise component of the sound. These two possibilities were chosen because they are characteristic of saxophone playing but additional possibilities can be introduced without altering the system.

3.2 The SaxEx CBR task

The task of *SaxEx* is to infer a set of expressive transformations to be applied to every note of an inexpressive phrase given as input problem. To achieve this, *SaxEx* uses a CBR problem solver, a case memory of expressive performances, and background musical knowledge. Transformations concern the dynamics, rubato, vibrato, articulation, and attack of each note in the inexpressive phrase.

The cases stored in the episodic memory of *SaxEx* contain knowledge about the expressive transformations performed by a human player given specific labels for affective dimensions. Affective knowledge is the basis for guiding the CBR problem solver.

For each note in the phrase, the following subtask decomposition (Figure 3) is performed by the case-based problem solving method implemented in Noos:

- *Retrieve*: The goal of the retrieve task is to choose, from the memory of cases (pieces played expressively), the set of notes—the cases—most similar to the current one—the problem. This task is decomposed in three subtasks:
  - *Identify*: its goal is to build retrieval perspectives using the affective values specified by the user and the musical background knowledge integrated in the system. Affective labels are used to determine a first declarative retrieval bias: we are interested in notes with affective labels close to affective labels required in the current problem.

    Musical knowledge gives two possible declarative retrieval biases: a first bias based on Narmour's implication/realization model, and a second bias based on Lerdahl and Jackendoff's generative theory. These perspectives guide the retrieval process by focusing it on the most relevant aspects of the current problem.

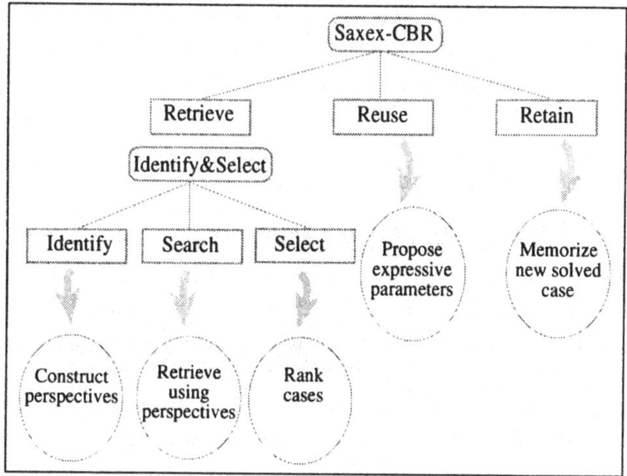

Fig. 3. Task decomposition of the *SaxEx* CBR method.

For instance, using the Narmour's IR criterion that determines as relevant the role that a given note plays in a IR structure, the user can instruct identification task to build perspectives such as 'look for notes that are the first note of a P structure'.

- *Search*: its goal is to search cases in the case memory using Noos retrieval methods and some previously constructed Perspective(s). As an example, let us assume that, by means of a Perspective, we declare that we are interested in notes belonging to calm and very tender affective regions. Then, the Search subtask will search for notes in the expressive performances that, following this criterion, belong to either "calm and very tender" affective regions (most preferred), or "calm and tender" affective regions, or "very calm and very tender" affective regions (both less preferred).

- *Select*: its goal is to rank the retrieved cases using Noos preference methods. Preference methods use criteria such as similarity in duration of notes, harmonic stability, or melodic directions. For instance, given a problem note belonging to a descending melody group and given several retrieved cases belonging to either ascending or descending melody groups, the melodic direction preference criterion will select those cases belonging to descending melody groups.
- *Reuse*: its goal is to choose, from the set of more similar notes previously selected, a set of expressive transformations to be applied to the current note. The first criterion used is to adapt the transformations of the most similar note. When several notes are considered equally similar, the transformations are selected according to the majority rule. Finally, in case of a tie, one of them is selected randomly.

– *Retain*: the incorporation of the new solved problem to the memory of cases is performed automatically in Noos. All solved problems will be available for the reasoning process in future problems.

4 Results

We are studying the issue of musical expression in the context of tenor saxophone interpretations. We have done several recordings of a tenor sax performer playing several Jazz standard ballads ('All of me', 'Autumn leaves', 'Misty', and 'My one and only love') with different degrees of expressiveness, including an inexpressive interpretation of each piece. These recordings were analyzed, using the SMS spectral modeling techniques, to extract basic information related to the expressive parameters. Moreover, the different affective regions in recordings were manually identified and codified with their affective labels for the three affective dimensions.

The set of experiments conducted with the new version of *SaxEx* were influenced by previously conducted experiments. These previous experiments were intended to use examples of expressive performances of some pieces in order to generate expressive reinterpretations of different inexpressive pieces. More concretely, using three different expressive performances of a piece having about fifty notes as cases in order to generate expressive reinterpretations of about thirty-note inexpressive phrases of a different piece. These experiments revealed that the use of perspectives in the retrieval step allows to identify situations such as long notes, ascending or descending melodic lines, etc—such situations are also usually identified by a human performer. Nevertheless, because of such experiments did not take into account the expression of affects, *SaxEx* was no able to discriminate situations where the same note was played by human performers with different affective intention. This implied that the solutions provided by *SaxEx* were conservative.

Current experiments wanted to demonstrate two main goals: i) given the same problem input phase and different affective labels as input, *SaxEx* is able to generate different expressive performances as ouput, and ii) these different outputs are perceived by listeners in terms of the affective labels. To carry out the current experiments we have used the same examples used in previous experiments including the information of their affective labels for the three affective dimensions.

Let us now illustrate some of the expressive transformations applied by *SaxEx* to the first phrase of the 'All of Me' theme (see the score in Figure 4b) imitating precedent cases of the 'Autumn Leaves' theme (see the score in Figure 4a) with two different combinations of affective labels: joyful and restless (J-R), or tender and calm (T-C). When listening the different human expressive performances of 'Autumn Leaves' one can notice that, first of all, in (J-R) performances the dynamics range is broader than in (T-C) performances and the average is higher in (J-R); moreover, (J-R) performances tend to emphasize notes that are important according to the musical structures of the phrase while in (T-C) this expressive

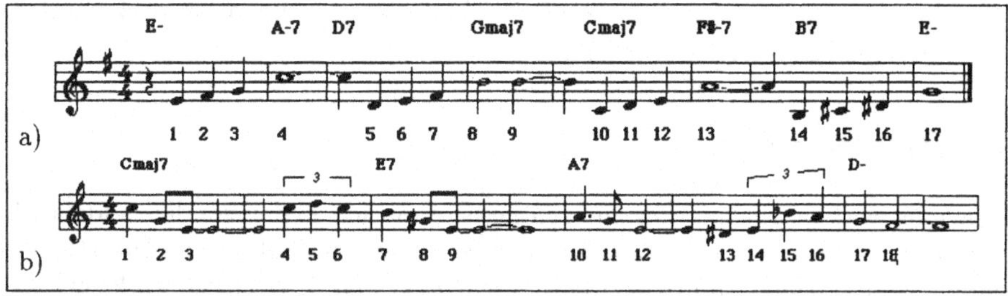

Fig. 4. a) First phrase from the 'Autumn Leaves' theme. b) First phrase from the 'All of Me' theme.

resource is not used. Concerning rubato, the main perception between (J-R) and (T-C) performances is that in (J-R) the beat is increased and in (T-C) is decreased. Vibrato is mainly applied to (J-R) and (T-C) over notes with long duration combined with a dynamics decay (for instance, over the fourth note in Figure 4a). The main difference between (J-R) and (T-C) is that vibrato frequency is higher in (J-R). Articulation is perceived in (J-R) close to staccato and in (T-C) close to legato. Finally, the attack in (J-R) consisted in reaching the first notes of subphrases–like fourth note (C in Figure 4a) or eight and ninth notes (B in Figure 4a)—starting from a lower pitch. In (T-C) the attacks for these same notes are treated in an explosive way, that is, high dynamics, high noise and playing directly the right pitch.

The experiments performed with *SaxEx* have demonstrated that the system is able to identify the relevant parts of the 'Autumn Leaves' cases in the case memory and imitate the expressive transformations stored in those cases to generate the performances of 'All of me'. Specifically, concerning the changes of dynamics, while in (J-R) descending melodic progressions are transformed using diminuendo and emphasizing the first note, in (T-C) the dynamics is equally lowered in all notes. For instance, the first note (C) of 'All of me' starts forte and the dynamics is successively decreased yielding to piano. Concerning rubato, the beat in (J-R) is increased and in (T-C) is decreased. Nevertheless, these changes are not equally applied in all notes. For instance, in (J-R) the duration of the fourth note (C in Figure 4b) is expanded and the the two following notes (D and C) are reduced. Vibrato is applied in both, (J-R) and (T-C) performances, over notes with long duration and dynamics decay (note examples are third and ninth of Figure 4b). Finally, regarding the imitation of the attack transformations, in (J-R) notes such as then first (C) or then seventh note (B)—are attacked starting from a lower pitch—while in (T-C) the attacks for these same notes are explosive.

All these expressive transformations applied to the initially inexpressive version of 'All of me' are clearly consistent with the examples of the 'Autumn Leaves' performances previously described. Moreover, the use of affective knowledge in the retrieval phase of the *SaxEx* CBR-method was revealed as a crucial factor that has improved the quality of the solutions generated by the system.

The reader can visit the *SaxEx* website at 'www.iiia.csic.es/Projects/music/Saxex.html' for sound examples.

5 Related work

Previous work on the analysis and synthesis of musical expression has addressed the study of at most two parameters such as rubato and vibrato [6] [10] [12], or rubato and articulation by means of an expert system [14]. Other work such as in [9] is focalized on the study of how musician's expressive intentions influence the performances.

To the best of our knowledge, the only previous work addressing the issue of learning to generate expressive performances based on examples is that of Widmer [18], who uses explanation-based techniques to learn rules for dynamics and rubato in the context of a MIDI electronic piano. In our approach we deal with additional expressive parameters in the context of an expressively richer instrument. Furthermore, this is the first attempt to deal with this problem using case-based techniques as well as the first attempt to cover the full cycle from an input sound file to an output sound file going in the middle through a symbolic reasoning and learning phase.

6 Conclusion and future work

The integration of affective labels allows to improve the performance of *SaxEx* in several ways. From the perspective of users, a more friendly interaction with the system is possible. On the one hand, users can work in a more intuitive way, without needing formal musical knowledge. On the other hand, it is possible to generate a wider range of expressive intentions by combining affective labels in multiple ways.

Affective knowledge also enhances the reasoning of the system. In particular, affective labels constitute an additional criterion to discriminate among the several candidate performances of a same phrase.

The experiments we are currently carrying on were designed using already existing recordings that had been made without the purpose of communicating affects. As a next step, we plan to incorporate into the system additional recordings in which the performer will be required to play according to affective labels. This will allows us to obtain a richer case memory and to better assess how the affect that the musician intends to communicate is perceived by the listeners. This will also ease the task of relating affective labels with expressive parameters—done by hand in the current experiments. This analysis could be used in the future to have *SaxEx* learn automatically associations of labels and the use of expressive parameters for situations appearing recurrently in the cases. Finally, it would be interesting to discriminate situations where expressive variations are used because of the logical structure of the score, as opposed to situations where these variations come from the affective intentions of the musician.

Acknowledgements

The research reported in this paper is partly supported by the ESPRIT LTR 25500-COMRIS *Co-Habited Mixed-Reality Information Spaces* project. We also acknowledge the support of ROLAND Electronics de España S.A. to our AI and Music project.

References

1. Josep Lluís Arcos and Ramon López de Mántaras. Perspectives: a declarative bias mechanism for case retrieval. In David Leake and Enric Plaza, editors, *Case-Based Reasoning. Research and Development*, number 1266 in Lecture Notes in Artificial Intelligence, pages 279–290. Springer-Verlag, 1997.
2. Josep Lluís Arcos, Ramon López de Mántaras, and Xavier Serra. Saxex : a case-based reasoning system for generating expressive musical performances. *Journal of New Music Research*, 27 (3):194–210, 1998.
3. Josep Lluís Arcos and Enric Plaza. Inference and reflection in the object-centered representation language Noos. *Journal of Future Generation Computer Systems*, 12:173–188, 1996.
4. Josep Lluís Arcos and Enric Plaza. Noos: an integrated framework for problem solving and learning. In *Knowledge Engineering: Methods and Languages*, 1997.
5. Sergio Canazza and Nicola Orio. How are the players perceived by listeners: analysis of "how high the moon" theme. In *International workshop Kansei Technology of Emotion (AIMI'97)*, 1997.
6. Manfred Clynes. Microstructural musical linguistics: composers' pulses are liked most by the best musicians. *Cognition*, 55:269–310, 1995.
7. D. Cooke. *The Language of Music*. New York: Oxford University Press, 1959.
8. Mary Cyr. *Performing Baroque Music*. Portland, Oregon: Amadeus Press, 1992.
9. Giovani De Poli, Antonio Rodà, and Alvise Vidolin. Note-by-note analysis of the influence of expressive intentions and musical structure in violin performance. *Journal of New Music Research*, 27 (3):293–321, 1998.
10. P. Desain and H. Honing. Computational models of beat induction: the rule-based approach. In *Proceedings of IJCAI'95 Workshop on AI and Music*, pages 1–10, 1995.
11. W. Jay Dowling and Dane L. Harwood. *Music Cognition*. Academic Press, 19986.
12. H. Honing. The vibrato problem, comparing two solutions. *Computer Music Journal*, 19 (3):32–49, 1995.
13. Carroll E. Izard, Jerome Kagan, and Robert B. Zajonc. *Emotions, Cognition, and Behavior*. Cambridge University Press, 1984.
14. M.L. Johnson. An expert system for the articulation of Bach fugue melodies. In D.L. Baggi, editor, *Readings in Computer-Generated Music*, pages 41–51. IEEE Computes Society Press, 1992.
15. Robert Jourdain. *Music, the Brain, and Ecstasy*. Avon Books, 1997.
16. Fred Lerdahl and Ray Jackendoff. An overview of hierarchical structure in music. In Stephan M. Schwanaver and David A. Levitt, editors, *Machine Models of Music*, pages 289–312. The MIT Press, 1993. Reproduced from Music Perception.
17. Eugene Narmour. *The Analysis and cognition of basic melodic structures : the implication-realization model*. University of Chicago Press, 1990.
18. Gerhard Widmer. Learning expressive performance: The structure-level approach. *Journal of New Music Research*, 25 (2):179–205, 1996.

Probability Based Metrics for Nearest Neighbor Classification and Case-Based Reasoning

Enrico Blanzieri and Francesco Ricci*

Istituto per la Ricerca Scientifica e Tecnologica (ITC-IRST)
38050 Povo (TN)
Italy
blanzier@irst.itc.it - ricci@sodalia.it

Abstract. This paper is focused on a class of metrics for the Nearest Neighbor classifier, whose definition is based on statistics computed on the case base. We show that these metrics basically rely on a probability estimation phase. In particular, we reconsider a metric proposed in the 80's by Short and Fukunaga, we extend its definition to an input space that includes categorical features and we evaluate empirically its performance. Moreover, we present a novel probability based metric, called Minimum Risk Metric (MRM), i.e. a metric for classification tasks that exploits estimates of the posterior probabilities. MRM is optimal, in the sense that it optimizes the finite misclassification risk, whereas the Short and Fukunaga Metric minimizes the difference between finite risk and asymptotic risk. An experimental comparison of MRM with the Short and Fukunaga Metric, the Value Difference Metric, and Euclidean–Hamming metrics on benchmark datasets shows that MRM outperforms the other metrics. MRM performs comparably to the Bayes Classifier based on the same probability estimates. The results suggest that MRM can be useful in case-based applications where the retrieval of a nearest neighbor is required.

1 Introduction

Nearest Neighbor (NN) algorithms are a well-known and intensively studied class of techniques for the solution of Classification and Pattern Recognition problems. Nowadays NNs are widely exploited for the retrieval phase in the majority of Case Based Reasoning (CBR) systems. In CBR, even if cases are not explicitly classified into a set of finite groups (classes), often the solution space can be clustered into a collection of sets each of them containing similar solutions. When such a set of similar solution is labelled with a class tag, it is natural to match the retrieval step in a CBR system with the nearest neighbor search in a NN classifier [3]. In this framework, for example, Bellazzi et al. [4] have shown that the performance of a CBR system can be improved by driving the retrieval with the information about the same relevant classification in the case space, i.e. reducing the retrieval problem to a classification task. In this

* Current Address: Sodalia S.p.A., 38100 Trento, Italy

perspective, improving the classification accuracy for NN algorithms becomes important for CBR.

The NN classification procedure is straightforward: given a set of classified examples, which are described as points in an input space, a new unclassified example is assigned to the known class of the nearest example. The "nearest" relation is computed using a (similarity) metric defined on the input space. Many researchers [22–24, 10, 1, 2, 13, 12, 19, 20, 6, 26] focused their attention on the use of local metrics, i.e. metrics that vary depending on the position of the points in the input space. Conversely, more traditional global metrics assume that similarity evaluation should be independent from the area of the input space the cases to be compared are taken from. There are pros and cons in using local metrics. On the one hand local metrics generate classifiers that are more sensitive to the local changes of the data and hence more accurate. On the other hand global metrics have fewer parameters and consequentially the classifiers are computationally lighter and less prone to the effect of noisy data. The critical point seems to be the grade of locality of the metric: choosing the 'right' locality in different areas of the input space should lead to better descriptions of the separating surfaces.

Some of the proposed local metrics rely for their effectiveness on the optimization of a given criterion and ultimately on the estimation of some probabilities. In this direction Short and Fukunaga [23] presented a seminal work constrained to a multidimensional numerical input space. They proposed to minimize the expected value of the difference between the misclassification error of a two-classes NN classifier with a finite number of samples and the misclassification error hypothetically achievable with an infinite sample. They expressed the optimal local metric in terms of a linear estimation of posterior probabilities. More recently in the instance based learning context, many proposals of nominal feature metrics also involve probability estimation [24, 10, 8, 25]. In these cases the probability estimation is performed computing frequencies of value occurrences. Finally, in the work by Wilson and Martinez [27] the estimation of probabilities provides an unifying framework for treating both linear (continuous or discrete) and nominal features. Their heterogeneous distances, wich extend the VDM metric [24], deal uniformly with both categorical and numerical features. On a different perspective and in the Bayesian framework, Kontaken et al. [15] proposed a matching function explicitly based on probabilistic considerations.

In spite of the centrality of the probability estimation issue in the metrics briefly described above, there is no unifying description in the literature of the impact of different approaches to the solution of this issue (with a notable exception in [14]). Furthermore, little or no attempt has been made to exploit the advanced nonparametric density estimation techniques developed by the applied statistics community [21] and their possible extensions to nominal features.

In this paper we describe a couple of techniques for probability estimation and their use inside two metrics based on this estimation (Short and Fukunaga and Minimum Risk Metric). From our point of view the approach of constructing metrics via combination of well-known probability estimators and optimal metrics presents several advantages.

- *The metrics have a clear analytical expression and motivation.* For example the metric proposed by Short and Fukunaga minimizes the difference between asymptotic and finite risk. That makes these metrics amenable to analytical study.
- *The metrics can be computed using standard density estimation techniques.* Advances in that area can be reused here. For example, the choice of the right degree of locality can rely on the solutions proposed for the choice of the bandwidth in the nonparametric density estimation models.
- *The metrics can be defined uniformly on data sets with both numeric and nominal attributes.* This point is extremely important for CBR applications. Combining different metrics on the categorical and numerical features usually lead to poor performances [27].

Regarding the last item described above, in real world case bases both continuous and nominal features can be useful to describe cases. That poses a new problem: how to sum contributions to the distance evaluation that come from the comparison of pairs of categorical values together with pairs of real numbers? This problem can be tackled in different ways:

- *Ordering.* Ordering and numbering the values of the nominal features and applying a numerical metric like the Euclidean one. In general this approach introduces artificial neighborhood.
- *Discretization.* Discretizing the numeric features and applying a nominal metric to them, e.g. Hamming or Value Difference Metric [24]. With discretization some information is inevitably lost and parameters of the discretization can be critical.
- *Combination.* This is the most common approach in CBR, it consists of combining two metrics, a nominal and a numeric, each one used on the corresponding part of a case. A very common example of a metric in this class is that obtained by combining the Euclidean and Hamming metric. Combined metrics are hard to adapt in a consistent way and perform poorly, as Wilson and Martinez have shown [27].

Conversely, metrics based on probability estimation provide a natural unifying framework for dealing with both kind of features. The same probability estimation technique is used for both type of features. Furthermore, the optimality evaluation that can be done with this type of metric is impossible when the metric is obtained by combination.

Among the metrics based on probability estimation the one proposed by Short and Fukunaga has a strong theoretical foundation. The original definition was applicable only to cases described uniquely by numeric features. In this paper we extend its definition to the most general situation, i.e., with both type of features, by considering different and more general probability estimators than those exploited by the authors. We call this metric SF2.

Experimental results presented in this paper show that SF2 outperforms more standard metrics but only when we explicitly restricting the scope of application of the metric (locality) or cross–validating the estimator. The analysis of SF2 leads us to a deeper evaluation of the optimality condition underlying the Short and Fukunaga metric and eventually to the definition of an alternative metric.

We propose here another metric, called Minimum Risk Metric (MRM), that relies its effectiveness on a different and simpler optimality condition than that suggested by Short and Fukunaga. In fact MRM minimizes directly the finite misclassification risk. In order to test the effectiveness of the approach we run experiments on 29 benchmark datasets and compare the classification accuracies of Short and Fukunaga Metric and MRM with the performances of other metrics available in the literature.

The work is organized as follows: Section 2 describes the metrics studied in this paper, in particular Subsection 2.4 briefly presents the Minimum Risk Metric and its optimality criterium. Section 3 describes the adopted probability estimators. Section 4 presents the experimental results and finally Section 5 draws conclusions and future directions.

2 Metrics

In this Section we will briefly present four families of metrics studied in this work. The first was introduced by Short and Fukunaga in the 80's [23] and is not well know in CBR mostly because athe original definition seemed confined to cases with only numerical features. The second family originates from the well known Value Difference Metric (VDM) of Stanfill and Waltz [24] and has stemmed a number of other metrics, most notably those introduced by Wilson and Martinez [27]. Third, we recall the very common metric that combines the Euclidean and the Hamming distances. Fourth, we introduce our novel metric called Minimum Risk Metric (MRM).

2.1 Short and Fukunaga Metric (SF2)

Short and Fukunaga [23] were among the first to derive a NN optimal metric relying on probabilistic considerations. In their work they consider a two-class pattern recognition task. Let $x = (x_1, \dots, x_n), y = (y_1, \dots, y_n)$ be two examples in $[0,1]^n$. Let, $p(c_1|x)$ be the probability that the example x be in class c_1. Then $r(x,y) = p(c_1|x)p(c_2|y) + p(c_2|x)p(c_1|y)$ is the finite 1-nearest neighbor error rate at x (i.e., the probability of misclassifying x by the 1-nearest neighbor rule given that the nearest neighbor of x using a particular metric is y) and $r^*(x) = 2p(c_1|x)p(c_2|x)$ is the asymptotic 1-nearest neighbor error rate (i.e., the probability of misclassifying x by the 1-nearest neighbor rule, given a hypothetically infinite design set [9]). Short and Fukunaga show that minimizing the expectation $E[(r(x,y) - r^*(x))^2]$ is equivalent to minimizing $E[(p(c_1|x) - p(c_1|y))^2]$, so the best local metric is:

$$\mathrm{SF2}(x,y) = |p(c_1|x) - p(c_1|y)| \tag{1}$$

We shall call this metric SF2. Short and Fukunaga approximate at the first order $|p(c_1|x) - p(c_1|y)| \simeq |\nabla p(1|x)^T(x-y)|$ and therefore their metric in the original formulation can be applied only to numeric features and in a local restriction.

Myles and Hand in [18] generalize that metric to a multiclass problem and introduce the following two:

$$\mathrm{SF2}(x,y) = \sum_{i=1}^{m} |p(c_i|x) - p(c_i|y)| \tag{2}$$

$$\mathrm{SFM}(x,y) = \sum_{i=1}^{m} p(c_i|x)|p(c_i|x) - p(c_i|y)| \tag{3}$$

where the classes c_i are numbered from 1 to m. We shall still call the first metric SF2, and SFM the second. It is easy to prove that on a two classes classification problem SF2 and SFM coincide. Myles and Hand use the same technique introduced by Short and Fukunaga to approximate $|p(c_i|x) - p(c_i|y)|$.

2.2 Value Difference Metric (VDM)

Another very common metric based on probabilistic consideration is VDM introduced by Stanfill and Waltz [24] and used exclusively on input spaces with nominal attributes. Let $x = (x_1, \ldots, x_n)$ and $y = (y_1, \ldots, y_n)$ be two examples in $\prod_{j=1}^{n} F_j$, and $|F_j|$ is finite. The VDM metric is defined as follow:

$$\mathrm{VDM}(x,y) = \sum_{j=1}^{n} \sqrt{\sum_{i=1}^{m} \left(\frac{N(x_j,c_i)}{N(x_j)}\right)^2 \sum_{i=1}^{m} \left(\frac{N(x_j,c_i)}{N(x_j)} - \frac{N(y_j,c_i)}{N(y_j)}\right)^2} \tag{4}$$

where $N(x_j, c_i)$ is the number of examples that have value x_j for the j-th attribute and are in class c_i, and $N(x_j)$ is the number of examples that have value x_j for the j-th attribute. If probabilities are estimated with frequency counts then VDM can also be written in the following form:

$$\mathrm{VDM}(x,y) = \sum_{j=1}^{n} \sqrt{\sum_{i=1}^{m} (p(c_i|x_j))^2 \sum_{i=1}^{m} (p(c_i|x_j) - p(c_i|y_j))^2} \tag{5}$$

VDM has no clear justification and seems to assume attribute independence. It is easy to conceive an ill-formed dataset where all the $p(c_i|x_j)$ are equal (for example the parity bit class) and therefore VDM is not able to distinguish among the classes. Nevertheless VDM, and a set of modified versions [10, 8, 27], works quite well on real data sets.

Wilson and Martinez extended VDM to instances with numeric attributes [27]. They essentially discretize the numeric attributes (DVDM) and then smooth the histogram estimation of $p(c_i|x_j)$ by averaging. The metric obtained with that procedure is called IVDM. They also suggest a heterogeneous VDM that combines an Euclidean metric for numeric features with a VDM, called HVDM. The version of VDM, and the correspondig metrics IVDM and HVDM, we adopted in our experiments is the version without weighting factors and with the absolute values:

$$\mathrm{VDM}(x,y) = \sum_{j=1}^{n} \sum_{i=1}^{m} |p(c_i|x_j) - p(c_i|y_j)| \tag{6}$$

An empirical study [7] has shown that this version of VDM (IVDM and DVDM) behaves better than the others.

2.3 Combined Euclidean–Overlap Metric (HEOM)

The metric HEOM was introduced by Wilson and Martinez [27] and it is the combination of the Euclidean and Hamming metric. Basically HEOM is an heterogeneous distance function that uses different attributes distance functions on different kinds of attributes. If $x = (x_1, \ldots, x_n)$ and $y = (y_1, \ldots, y_n)$ are two examples then $heom(x,y) = \sqrt{\sum_{j=1}^{n} d_j(x_j,y_j)^2}$ where $d_j(x_j,y_j)$ is the Hamming distance if the j-th feature is nominal and the Euclidean distance if numeric. The numeric features are normalized using the range.

2.4 Minimum Risk Metric

Minimum Risk Metric (MRM) is a very simple metric that directly minimizes the risk of misclassification.

Given an example x in class c_i and a nearest neighbor y the finite risk of misclassifying x is given by $p(c_i|x)(1 - p(c_i|y))$. The total finite risk is the sum of the risks extended to all the different classes and is given by $r(x,y) = \sum_{i=1}^{m} p(c_i|x)(1 - p(c_i|y))$. The approach of Short and Fukunaga and followers is to subtract the asymptotic risk $r^*(x,y)$ and minimize $E(r(x,y) - r^*(x,y))$. Instead we propose to minimize directly the risk $r(x,y)$ and that leads to the metric:

$$\mathrm{MRM}(x,y) = r(x,y) = \sum_{i=1}^{m} p(c_i|x)(1 - p(c_i|y)). \tag{7}$$

We observed in some experiments not shown here, that the application of MRM inside a Nearest Neighbor classifier leads to a classifier comparable to the Bayes rule, i.e., "assign x to the class that maximizes $p(c_i|x)$". That points out that the key element in MRM is the estimation of $p(c_i|x)$. This point is dealt with in the next Section.

3 Probability Distribution Estimation

The presence of the conditional probabilities $p(c_i|x)$ in both the SF2 metric and MRM requires consistent estimates $\hat{p}(c_i|x)$ and this section illustrates the probability estimation techniques used in the experiments.

We must note that, a classification problem would be solved if the probabilities $p(c_i|x)$ were known. In fact the Bayes optimal classification rule says to choose the class c_i that maximizes $p(c_i|x)$. All the classification methods explicitly or implicitly follow this rule and the estimation of $p(c_i|x)$ is not simpler than computing an optimal metric for NN. For that reason the estimation of the quantities $p(c_i|x)$ is a key issue. Notwithstanding that, we will show that even if many of the metrics here presented are based on the same estimation of the quantities $p(c_i|x)$ the definition of the metric is relevant and different performances can be obtained.

The estimates of $p(c_i|x)$ can be done directly or applying the Bayes theorem

$$p(c_i|x) = \frac{p(x|c_i)p(c_i)}{p(x)} = \frac{p(x|c_i)p(c_i)}{\sum_{k=1}^{|C|} p(x|c_k)p(c_k)} \tag{8}$$

therefore reducing to the problem of estimating $p(x|c_k)$.

In the present work we carried out experiments with two different estimators. The first is the Naive Bayes Estimator that is the estimator that is implicit in the Naive Bayes Classifier. It is a natural estimator for nominal feature and it can be extended to the numeric ones by discretization. The second is the Gaussian Kernel Estimator, a non-parametric density estimator that in its original formulation uses the Euclidean metric. In order to extend the density estimation technique to nominal features the Euclidean metric is simply substituted by HEOM and the densities are assumed to replace the probabilities in the expressions of the metrics.

3.1 Naive Bayes Estimator

The simplest probability estimates are based on frequency counts. In this way it is possible to estimate $p(c_i)$ with $\hat{p}(c_i) = \frac{N(c_i)}{N}$ where $N(c_i)$ is the number of cases that are in the c_i class and N is the sample size. Unfortunately, probability estimates based on frequencies perform poorly if the sample size is small (basically the probabilities are understimated) and so they can be improved adopting the Laplace–corrected estimate or equivalently incrementing artificially the sample size [17]. Following the first possibility leads to the estimate $\hat{p}(c_i) = \frac{N(c_i)+f}{N+fn_j}$ where n_j is the number of values of the j-th attribute and $f = 1/N$ is a multiplicative factor [11].

Assuming features' independence and adopting the same notation introduced in 2.2, lead to the estimates:

$$\hat{p}(x|c_i) = \prod_{j=1}^{n} \hat{p}(x_j|c_i) = \prod_{j=1}^{n} \frac{N(x_j, c_i) + f}{N(c_i) + fn_j}$$

which, substituted in the equation (8) gives the estimates that are used in the Naive Bayes Classifier approach.

$$\hat{p}(c_i|x) = \frac{\prod_{j=1}^{n} \frac{N(x_j,c_i)+f}{N(c_i)+fn_j} \frac{N(c_i)+f}{N+fn_j}}{\sum_{k=1}^{|C|} \prod_{j=1}^{n} \frac{N(x_j,c_k)+f}{N(c_k)+fn_j} \frac{N(c_k)+f}{N+fn_j}} \tag{9}$$

3.2 Gaussian Kernel Estimator

The second type of estimates used in this paper belongs to a broad class of nonparametric density estimators represented by the multivariate fixed kernel [21]:

$$\hat{f}(x) = \frac{1}{N} \sum_{l=1}^{n} \frac{1}{h(x, x_l)^n} K\left(\frac{x - x_l}{h(x, x_l)}\right) \tag{10}$$

where n is the dimension of the input space, h is the bandwidth and $K(t)$ is the kernel function.

The bandwidth $h(x, x_l)$ can be constant on the input space or it can vary. In relation to the bandwidth h's dependency on the probe point x or on the sample point x_l, the estimator is called *balloon* or *sample point* respectively.

The Gaussian Kernel Estimator is an example of a *sample point* estimator with fixed bandwidth.

$$\hat{f}(x) = \frac{1}{N(2\pi)^{n/2}} \sum_{l=1}^{N} \frac{\sqrt{|W|}}{h^n} e^{-\frac{1}{2}\left(\frac{\| x - x_l \|_W}{h}\right)^2} \tag{11}$$

where W is a positive definite diagonal matrix, and

$$\| x - x_l \|_W = \sqrt{(x - x_l) W (x - x_l)^T} = \sqrt{\sum_{j=1}^{n} w_{jj} (x_j - x_{lj})^2}$$

$$\sqrt{|W|} = \prod_{j=1}^{n} w_{jj}$$

$\| \cdot \|_W$ is an Euclidean weighted metric and $w_{jj} = \frac{1}{\hat{\sigma}_j}$ where $\hat{\sigma}_j$ is an estimate of the variance on the j–th dimension of the input space. In this case the optimal bandwidth is $h = \left(\frac{4}{n+2}\right)^{\frac{1}{n+4}} N^{-\frac{1}{n+4}}$.

4 Experimental Results

The metrics presented in Section 2 were tested on 27 databases taken from from the Machine Learning Databases Repository at UCI [16] and on two new databases (Derma and Opera). Derma contains data of images for the diagnosis of melanoma collected in Santa Chiara Hospital in Trento, Italy and Opera contains the results of a cognitive pragmatics experiment [5]. The 29 databases contain continuous, nominal and mixed features. The main characteristics of the databases are presented in Table 1. We extended to mixed feature databases the estimate of the Naive Bayes Estimator by discretizing the numeric features and the estimate of the Gaussian Kernel Estimator by substituting the Euclidean Metric with HEOM. We normalized the numeric features with their range and used ten intervals for all the discretizations. The unknown values were simply ignored during the computation. The experimental technique is a 10-fold cross-validation and as a significance test we adopted the paired t-test ($p < 0.05$).

Table 1. The databases used in the experimentation.

Data Set	Instances	Classes	Features		Unknown
			Number	Cont/Symb	Attributes
Annealing	798	6	38	9C 29S	yes
Audiology(standardized)	200	24	69	69S	yes
Breast-cancer	286	2	9	4C 5S	yes
Bridges	108	6	11	9C 2S	yes
Bridges(discretized)	108	6	11	11S	yes
Credit Screening	690	2	15	6C 9S	yes
Derma	152	2	44	44C	no
Flag	194	8	28	10C 18S	no
Glass	214	7	9	9C	no
Hepatitis	155	2	19	6C 13S	yes
Horse-Colic	300	2	27	7C 20S	yes
House-Votes-84	435	2	16	16S	yes
Ionosphere	351	2	34	34C	no
Iris	150	3	4	4C	no
Led+17noise	200	10	24	24S	no
Led	200	10	7	7S	no
Liver Disorders	345	2	6	6C	no
Monks-1	432	2	6	6S	no
Monks-2	432	2	6	6S	no
Monks-3	432	2	6	6S	no
Opera	1216	5	9	9S	no
Pima	768	2	8	8C	no
Post-operative	90	3	8	1C 7S	yes
Promoters	106	2	57	57S	no
Sonar	208	2	60	60C	no
Soybean(large)	307	19	35	35S	yes
Soybean(small)	47	4	35	35S	no
WDBC	569	2	32	32C	no
zoo	101	7	16	16S	no

The experiments presented here measure the classification accuracies of the 1-NN algorithm with SF2 metric (Eq. (2)) and MRM (Eq. (7)) obtained using Naive Bayes Estimator (Eq. (9)) and the Gaussian Kernel Estimator (Eq. (11)). The accuracies are compared to those of DVDM (Eq. (6)) and HEOM (Section 2.3).

The application of SF2 can be restricted to h neighbors with respect to the metric HEOM. This means that when searching for the SF2 nearest neighbor of an example x only the set of h HEOM neighbors of x are considered (e.g. when the metrics are computed on the whole training set $h = N$ holds).

Some of the experiments are conducted adopting as h the cross-validated value h_{CV}. In some cases, we also cross-validate the choice of the estimator. When this is the case the estimator is indicated as Est_{CV}. Both the cross-validations are carried out with a 10-fold cross-validation on each training partition.

4.1 HEOM and Value Difference Metrics results

Table 2. Classification accuracies for different metrics. Significant differences ($p < 0.05$) are shown: for instance, IVDM performs significatively better than DVDM on the sonar dataset.

Data Set	IVDM (I)	HVDM (H)	DVDM (D)	HEOM (E)
annealing	$97.4 \pm 1.33 > E$	$99.1 \pm 1.03 > I, E$	$98.4 \pm 0.98 > I, E$	95.4 ± 2.59
audiology	$80.5 \pm 7.24 > E$	$80.5 \pm 5.98 > E$	$80.5 \pm 5.98 > E$	72.5 ± 11.3
breast-cancer	66.4 ± 6.92	68.2 ± 8.21	64.3 ± 10.0	65.4 ± 8.54
bridges1	61.1 ± 7.97	59.3 ± 11.1	62.3 ± 16.9	$65.9 \pm 13.9 > H$
bridges2	62.1 ± 20.0	59.3 ± 19.0	59.3 ± 19.0	55.5 ± 17.2
crx	79.7 ± 2.36	80.5 ± 5.21	79.5 ± 4.06	81.7 ± 3.36
derma	80.0 ± 12.6	73.0 ± 12.6	74.8 ± 13.4	78.1 ± 10.6
flag	57.4 ± 12.3	$66.6 \pm 8.75 > I, E$	$64.0 \pm 8.34 > I, E$	55.8 ± 12.9
glass	$72.5 \pm 12.5 > D$	$69.7 \pm 9.32 > D$	62.1 ± 11.1	$71.1 \pm 11.8 > D$
hepatitis	82.6 ± 10.1	80.0 ± 9.94	82.0 ± 10.8	80.7 ± 11.8
horse-colic	85.6 ± 5.67	85.6 ± 7.70	86.6 ± 7.53	84.6 ± 4.76
house-votes-84	93.7 ± 3.10	93.0 ± 2.45	93.0 ± 2.45	92.3 ± 3.82
ionosphere	$87.4 \pm 3.38 > H$	35.9 ± 4.75	$88.8 \pm 4.75 > H$	$87.1 \pm 2.81 > H$
iris	94.6 ± 5.25	96.6 ± 4.71	92.6 ± 4.91	95.3 ± 5.48
led	66.5 ± 13.5	66.5 ± 13.5	66.5 ± 13.5	68.0 ± 12.9
led17	$57.5 \pm 12.5 > E$	$59.5 \pm 11.8 > E$	$59.5 \pm 11.8 > E$	39.0 ± 9.06
liver	63.9 ± 8.07	59.4 ± 11.5	64.3 ± 8.22	63.7 ± 7.82
monks-1	78.0 ± 13.4	78.0 ± 13.4	78.0 ± 13.4	71.5 ± 7.54
monks-2	$92.6 \pm 8.39 > E$	$92.6 \pm 8.39 > E$	$92.6 \pm 8.39 > E$	57.1 ± 7.21
monks-3	$100. \pm 0.00 > E$	$100. \pm 0.00 > E$	$100. \pm 0.00 > E$	79.3 ± 8.43
opera	49.0 ± 4.78	49.0 ± 4.78	49.0 ± 4.78	49.0 ± 4.84
pima-indians-diabetes	70.5 ± 4.47	68.4 ± 4.28	70.8 ± 3.31	$71.7 \pm 3.15 > H$
post-operative	63.3 ± 14.8	63.3 ± 13.9	62.2 ± 14.9	57.7 ± 22.7
promoters	$89.7 \pm 10.1 > E$	$89.7 \pm 8.17 > E$	$89.7 \pm 8.17 > E$	80.1 ± 9.42
sonar	$85.0 \pm 8.84 > D$	81.6 ± 6.42	76.9 ± 6.15	$87.0 \pm 7.19 > D$
soybean-large	92.1 ± 4.08	90.2 ± 5.80	90.2 ± 5.80	91.1 ± 5.13
soybean-small	$100. \pm 0.00$	$100. \pm 0.00$	$100. \pm 0.00$	$100. \pm 0.00$
wdbc	95.2 ± 2.19	95.7 ± 2.50	94.9 ± 3.02	95.2 ± 2.34
zoo	95.0 ± 7.00	95.0 ± 7.00	95.0 ± 7.00	96.0 ± 5.16

In the first series of experiments we evaluate the metrics HEOM, DVDM, IVDM and HVDM. These metrics will represent a baseline for SF2 and MRM. Accuracy results are reported in Table 2. In this Table, when on a given dataset, a metric m performs significantly better than another one m', the symbol $> m'$ appear in the column of m. All the metrics of the VDM family seem to outperform the HEOM but there is not a clear winner among them. This results seem to partially contradict the observation by Wilson and Martinez [27] that a better aproximation of the probabilities $p(c_i|x_j)$ for numerical features, would lead to a better metric. Moreover, HVDM, the combined Euclidean and VDM metric, performs well even though it simply sums the heterogeneous contributions of the two metrics.

IVDM is more sophisticated than DVDM. In IVDM the estimate of $p(c_i|x_j)$ obtained by discretizing the j-th numerical featue is smoothed by interpolation. But this approach seems not to improve DVDM to a great extent. For this reason, in the following experiments we compare SF2 and MRM only with DVDM.

4.2 Short and Fukunaga Metric

Table 3. Classification accuracies of the metrics SF2 with Naive , Kernel and cross-validated estimator with different localities. Significant differences ($p < 0.05$) are shown: for instance, Naive $h = h_{CV}$ performs significatively better than Kernel $h = h_{CV}$ on led17 dataset.

Data Set	Naive $h = h_{CV}$ (N)	Kernel $h = h_{CV}$ (K)	Est_{CV} $h = h_{CV}$ (E^*_{CV})
annealing	97.9 ± 1.88	97.9 ± 1.47	97.9 ± 1.88
audiology	77.5 ± 8.57	76.0 ± 10.2	75.5 ± 10.1
breast-cancer	63.5 ± 9.48	64.3 ± 8.65	62.8 ± 9.85
bridges1	64.9 ± 9.95	60.9 ± 12.7	64.0 ± 8.55
bridges2	71.4 ± 19.2	66.7 ± 19.1	70.5 ± 20.8
crx	80.4 ± 2.57	82.4 ± 4.75	80.8 ± 2.88
derma	78.1 ± 13.1	73.5 ± 11.8	77.5 ± 14.2
flag	59.8 ± 10.1	58.9 ± 8.16	59.8 ± 10.1
glass	69.2 ± 11.9	$73.0 \pm 10.9 > E^*_{CV}$	68.7 ± 11.4
hepatitis	88.5 ± 8.72	83.9 ± 7.93	88.5 ± 8.72
horse-colic	83.6 ± 6.74	84.3 ± 6.85	83.3 ± 7.20
house-votes-84	93.0 ± 3.78	93.9 ± 3.67	93.7 ± 3.44
ionosphere	86.5 ± 3.35	$92.5 \pm 4.50 > N, E^*_{CV}$	89.4 ± 4.28
iris	95.3 ± 5.48	94.6 ± 6.88	95.3 ± 5.48
led	68.5 ± 15.4	71.5 ± 17.9	69.0 ± 14.4
led17	$58.0 \pm 8.23 > K$	43.5 ± 7.83	$58.0 \pm 8.23 > K$
liver	66.6 ± 10.7	59.4 ± 12.7	62.3 ± 12.5
monks-1	76.1 ± 10.5	$100. \pm 0.00 > N$	$98.1 \pm 3.40 > N$
monks-2	$91.1 \pm 7.33 > K$	56.4 ± 7.68	$91.1 \pm 7.33 > K$
monks-3	$100. \pm 0.00$	99.7 ± 0.73	$100. \pm 0.00$
opera	48.4 ± 4.41	48.5 ± 4.78	48.6 ± 4.74
pima-indians-diabetes	70.3 ± 3.55	70.3 ± 3.17	70.3 ± 3.55
post-operative	56.6 ± 18.4	53.3 ± 17.9	55.5 ± 16.5
promoters	88.5 ± 7.81	83.8 ± 12.4	88.5 ± 7.81
sonar	87.0 ± 7.19	89.3 ± 5.57	86.0 ± 7.74
soybean-large	92.4 ± 4.94	90.5 ± 5.64	92.4 ± 4.94
soybean-small	$100. \pm 0.00$	$100. \pm 0.00$	$100. \pm 0.00$
wdbc	95.4 ± 2.36	$96.3 \pm 2.53 > E^*_{CV}$	94.7 ± 2.01
zoo	96.0 ± 5.16	96.0 ± 5.16	96.0 ± 5.16

Preliminary results showed a substantial equivalence between SF2 and SFM and therefore we chose the simpler one. Table 3 presents the classification accuracies of SF2 metric with different estimators (Naive , Gaussian Kernel, and the cross–validated one). Moreover the grade of locality is also cross–validated. This means that in the computation of the SF2 nearest neighbor of an example x, the SF2 distance from this example is only taken with examples in a subset of the case base. This subset contains the h nearest neighbors of x with respect to the HEOM metric. In fact, the locality of the SF2 metrics appears to be critical. In a set of results not showed here we noted that an unrestricted application of the metric leads to poor results when compared with DVDM and HEOM.

In Table 4 we show how the SF2 metric based on cross–validation outperforms significatively DVDM and HEOM. In particular the metric with both estimator and locality cross-validated is never worse of them and outperforms DVDM in 4 datasets and HEOM in 8 datasets. However, in a set of experiments not reported here we noted that SF2 often performs worse than the Bayes Classifier based on the same estimation.

Table 4. Classification accuracies of the SF2 with a cross-validated estimator, DVDM and HEOM. Significant differences ($p < 0.05$) are shown.

Data Set	SF2 Est_{CV} $h = h_{CV}$ (E^*_{CV})	DVDM (D)	HEOM (E)
annealing	$97.9 \pm 1.88 > E$	98.4 ± 0.98	95.4 ± 2.59
audiology	75.5 ± 10.1	80.5 ± 5.98	72.5 ± 11.3
breast-cancer	62.8 ± 9.85	64.3 ± 10.0	65.4 ± 8.54
bridges1	64.0 ± 8.55	62.3 ± 16.9	65.9 ± 13.9
bridges2	$70.5 \pm 20.8 > D, E$	59.3 ± 19.0	55.5 ± 17.2
crx	80.8 ± 2.88	79.5 ± 4.06	81.7 ± 3.36
derma	77.5 ± 14.2	74.8 ± 13.4	78.1 ± 10.6
flag	59.8 ± 10.1	64.0 ± 8.34	55.8 ± 12.9
glass	$68.7 \pm 11.4 > D$	62.1 ± 11.1	71.1 ± 11.8
hepatitis	$88.5 \pm 8.72 > E$	82.0 ± 10.8	80.7 ± 11.8
horse-colic	83.3 ± 7.20	86.6 ± 7.53	84.6 ± 4.76
house-votes-84	93.7 ± 3.44	93.0 ± 2.45	92.3 ± 3.82
ionosphere	89.4 ± 4.28	88.8 ± 4.75	87.1 ± 2.81
iris	95.3 ± 5.48	92.6 ± 4.91	95.3 ± 5.48
led	69.0 ± 14.4	66.5 ± 13.5	68.0 ± 12.9
led17	$58.0 \pm 8.23 > E$	59.5 ± 11.8	39.0 ± 9.06
liver	62.3 ± 12.5	64.3 ± 8.22	63.7 ± 7.82
monks-1	$98.1 \pm 3.40 > D, E$	78.0 ± 13.4	71.5 ± 7.54
monks-2	$91.1 \pm 7.33 > E$	92.6 ± 8.39	57.1 ± 7.21
monks-3	$100. \pm 0.00 > E$	$100. \pm 0.00$	79.3 ± 8.43
opera	48.6 ± 4.74	49.0 ± 4.78	49.0 ± 4.84
pima-indians-diabetes	70.3 ± 3.55	70.8 ± 3.31	71.7 ± 3.15
post-operative	55.5 ± 16.5	62.2 ± 14.9	57.7 ± 22.7
promoters	$88.5 \pm 7.81 > E$	89.7 ± 8.17	80.1 ± 9.42
sonar	$86.0 \pm 7.74 > D$	76.9 ± 6.15	87.0 ± 7.19
soybean-large	92.4 ± 4.94	90.2 ± 5.80	91.1 ± 5.13
soybean-small	$100. \pm 0.00$	$100. \pm 0.00$	$100. \pm 0.00$
wdbc	94.7 ± 2.01	94.9 ± 3.02	95.2 ± 2.34
zoo	96.0 ± 5.16	95.0 ± 7.00	96.0 ± 5.16

4.3 Minimum Risk Metric

In this Section we evaluate the Minimum Risk Metric introduced in Section 2.4. In this case we used the Naive Bayes estimator, that in a set of experiments not shown here seems to work best for this metric. In Table 5 MRM is compared with the DVDM metric and HEOM metric. MRM compares very favourably with the exception of the monks datasets. These datasets appear to be a hard task probably as a consequence of the assumption of the independence among features that underlies the Naive Estimator. MRM outperforms DVDM and

Table 5. Classification accuracy of the Minimum Risk Metric with the Naive Estimator, DVDM and HEOM. Significant differences ($p < 0.05$) are shown.

Data Set	MRM $h = N$ Naive (M_N)	DVDM	HEOM
annealing	$97.6 \pm 1.61 > E$	98.4 ± 0.98	95.4 ± 2.59
audiology	76.5 ± 7.47	80.5 ± 5.98	72.5 ± 11.3
breast-cancer	$73.4 \pm 7.16 > D, E$	64.3 ± 10.0	65.4 ± 8.54
bridges1	63.0 ± 11.0	62.3 ± 16.9	65.9 ± 13.9
bridges2	$69.6 \pm 19.0 > D, E$	59.3 ± 19.0	55.5 ± 17.2
crx	$83.9 \pm 1.73 > D$	79.5 ± 4.06	81.7 ± 3.36
derma	77.4 ± 17.9	74.8 ± 13.4	78.1 ± 10.6
flag	61.8 ± 7.83	64.0 ± 8.34	55.8 ± 12.9
glass	66.8 ± 13.6	62.1 ± 11.1	71.1 ± 11.8
hepatitis	87.1 ± 7.88	82.0 ± 10.8	80.7 ± 11.8
horse-colic	83.6 ± 7.44	86.6 ± 7.53	84.6 ± 4.76
house-votes-84	90.5 ± 4.30	93.0 ± 2.45	92.3 ± 3.82
ionosphere	$91.1 \pm 3.42 > E$	88.8 ± 4.75	87.1 ± 2.81
iris	95.3 ± 5.48	92.6 ± 4.91	95.3 ± 5.48
led	72.5 ± 14.5	66.5 ± 13.5	68.0 ± 12.9
led17	$67.0 \pm 9.18 > D, E$	59.5 ± 11.8	39.0 ± 9.06
liver	$71.3 \pm 9.85 > D, E$	64.3 ± 8.22	63.7 ± 7.82
monks-1	66.2 ± 15.0	$78.0 \pm 13.4 > M_N$	71.5 ± 7.54
monks-2	$67.1 \pm 7.49 > E$	$92.6 \pm 8.39 > M_N$	57.1 ± 7.21
monks-3	$97.2 \pm 2.40 > E$	$100. \pm 0.00 > M_N$	79.3 ± 8.43
opera	$58.0 \pm 3.70 > D, E$	49.0 ± 4.78	49.0 ± 4.84
pima-indians-diabetes	$75.1 \pm 4.76 > D, E$	70.8 ± 3.31	71.7 ± 3.15
post-operative	$64.4 \pm 17.9 > E$	62.2 ± 14.9	57.7 ± 22.7
promoters	$90.4 \pm 6.38 > E$	89.7 ± 8.17	80.1 ± 9.42
sonar	78.3 ± 8.15	76.9 ± 6.15	$87.0 \pm 7.19 > M_N$
soybean-large	92.5 ± 4.62	90.2 ± 5.80	91.1 ± 5.13
soybean-small	$100. \pm 0.00$	$100. \pm 0.00$	$100. \pm 0.00$
wdbc	93.8 ± 2.22	94.9 ± 3.02	95.2 ± 2.34
zoo	96.0 ± 5.16	95.0 ± 7.00	96.0 ± 5.16

HEOM more convincingly than SF2 and without any local restriction. This is obviously an important feature as it greatly simplifies the computation of the metric.

5 Conclusions

In this paper we have introduced two new metrics for nearest neighbor classification that are based on probability estimation. The first, SF2, was originally introduced by Short and Fukunaga [23]. We extended its definition to input spaces with nominal features and introduced a different estimate for the density probability used in this metric. The second, the Minimum Risk Metric (MRM) is very similar to SF2 but optimizes a different criterion, the risk of misclassification. Among the main advantages of these types of metrics is the possibility to manage both nominal and numerical features in an uniform way and the fact that these metrics can be analytically studied.

The experiments show that the metric SF2 works only if locally restricted, i.e., examples used for the SF2 nearest neighbor computation are taken from a set of Euclidean nearest neighbors. This is surprising given the theoretical optimality of the metric and further investigations are required to clarify this point. In fact, in the original formulation of Short of Fukunaga the locality is not necessary for the optimality argument but only because they adopt a linear approximation of the probability. Nevertheless the combination of cross–validated locality and cross-validated estimator leads to a metric that outperforms VDM and HEOM.

The Minimum Risk Metric does not require any local restriction, its performances are comparable to the Bayes rule with the same probability estimates, its analytical form is simple and well founded, and finally, equipped with a simple Naive Estimator, it outperforms the other metrics. Even if the metric does not improve the performance of the Naive Bayes Classifier (i.e. a quite good classifier) the choice of MRM appears to be relevant whenever the retrieval of a neighbor is required. For this reasons MRM seems particularly suitable for Case Based Reasoning applications when a relevant classification of the cases is available.

Futher work is required to address in depth the relation between MRM and the Bayes rule, to explore the performances of the metrics not only in 1-NN but also in k-NN and their sensitivity to noisy data.

6 Acknowledgements

We would like to thank M. Cazzani for her contribution to the implementation of CBET, the C++ library used in the experimental evaluation of the metrics presented in this paper.

References

1. D. W. Aha and R. L. Goldstone. Learning attribute relevance in context in instance-based learning algorithms. In *Proceedings of the Twelfth Annual Conference of the Cognitive Science Society*, pages 141–148, Cambridge, MA, 1990. Lawrence Earlbaum.
2. D. W. Aha and R. L. Goldstone. Concept learning and flexible weighting. In *Proceedings of the Fourteenth Annual Conference of the Cognitive Science Society*, pages 534–539, Bloomington, IN, 1992. Lawrence Earlbaum.
3. P. Avesani, A. Perini, and F. Ricci. Interactive case-based planning for forest fire management. *Applied Artificial Intelligence*, 1999. To appear.
4. R. Bellazzi, S. Montani, and L. Portinale. Retrieval in a prototype-based case library: A case study in diabetes therapy revision. In *European Workshop on Case Based Reasoning*, 1998.
5. E. Blanzieri, M. Bucciarelli, and P. Peretti. Modeling human communication. In *First European Workshop on Cognitive Modeling*, Berlin, 1996.
6. C. Cardie and N. Howe. Improving minority class prediction using case-specific feature weight. In *Proceedings of the Fourteenth International Conference on Machine Learning*, pages 57–65. Morgan Kaufmann Publishers, 1997.
7. M. Cazzani. Metriche di similaritá eterogenee per il problema di recupero nei sistemi di ragionamento basato su casi: studio sperimentale. Master's thesis, Univ. of Milano, 1998.
8. S. Cost and S. Salzberg. A weighted nearest neighbor algorithm for learning with symbolic features. *Machine Learning*, 10:57–78, 1993.

9. T. M. Cover and P. E. Hart. Nearest neighbor pattern classification. *IEEE Transaction on Information Theory*, 13:21–27, 1967.
10. R. H. Creecy, B. M. Masand, S. J. Smith, and D. L. Waltz. Trading MIPS and memory for knowledge engineering. *Communication of ACM*, 35:48–64, 1992.
11. P. Domingos and M. J. Pazzani. On the optimality of the simple bayesian classifier under zero-one loss. *Machine Learning*, 29:103–130, 1997.
12. J. H. Friedman. Flexible metric nearest neighbour classification. Technical report, Stanford University, 1994. Available by anonymous FTP from playfair.stanford.edu.
13. T. Hastie and R. Tibshirani. Discriminant adaptive nearest neighbour classification. In U.M.Fayad and R.Uthurusamy, editors, *KDD-95: Proceedings First International Conference on Knowledge Discovery and Data Mining*, 1995.
14. P. Kontkanen, P. Myllymäki, T. Silander, and H. Tirri. Bayes optimal instacebased learning. *Lecture Notes in Computer Science*, 1398:77–88, 1998.
15. P. Kontkanen, P. Myllymäki, T. Silander, and H. Tirri. On Bayesian case matching. *Lecture Notes in Computer Science*, 1488:13–24, 1998.
16. C. J. Merz and P. M. Murphy. *UCI Repository of Machine Learning Databases.* University of California, Department of Information and Computer Science, Irvine, CA, 1996.
17. T. M. Mitchell. *Machine Learning.* McGraw-Hill, 1997.
18. J. P. Myles and D. J. Hand. The multi-class metric problem in nearest neighbour discrimination rules. *Pattern Recognition*, 23(11):1291–1297, 1990.
19. F. Ricci and P. Avesani. Learning a local similarity metric for case-based reasoning. In *International Conference on Case-Based Reasoning (ICCBR-95), Sesimbra, Portugal, Oct. 23-26*, 1995.
20. F. Ricci and P. Avesani. Data compression and local metrics for nearest neighbor classification. *IEEE Transactions on Pattern Analysis and Machine Intelligence*, 1999. To appear.
21. D. W. Scott. *Multivariate Density Estimation: Theory , Practice, and Visualization.* John Wiley, New York, 1992.
22. R. D. Short and K. Fukunaga. A new nearest neighbour distance measure. In *Proceedings of the 5th IEEE International Conference on Patter Recognition*, pages 81–86, Miami beach, FL, 1980.
23. R. D. Short and K. Fukunaga. The optimal distance measure for nearest neighbour classification. *IEEE Transactions on Information Theory*, 27:622–627, 1981.
24. C. Stanfill and D. Waltz. Toward memory-based reasoning. *Communication of ACM*, 29:1213–1229, 1986.
25. D. Wettschereck and T. G. Dietterich. An experimental comparison of the nearest neighbor and nearest hyperrectangle algorithms. *Machine Learning*, 19:5–28, 1995.
26. D. Wettschereck, T. Mohri, and D. W. Aha. A review and empirical comparison of feature weighting methods for a class of lazy learning algorithms. *AI Review Journal*, 11:273–314, 1997.
27. D. R. Wilson and T. R. Martinez. Improved heterogeneous distance functions. *Journal of Artificial Intelligence Research*, 11:1–34, 1997.

Active Exploration in Instance-Based Preference Modeling

L. Karl Branting

Department of Computer Science
University of Wyoming
P.O. Box 3682
Laramie, WY 82972, USA
karl@uwyo.edu

Abstract. Knowledge of the preferences of individual users is essential for intelligent systems whose performance is tailored for individual users, such as agents that interact with human users, instructional environments, and learning apprentice systems. Various memory-based, instance-based, and case-based systems have been developed for preference modeling, but these system have generally not addressed the task of selecting examples to use as queries to the user. This paper describes *UGAMA*, an approach to learning preference criteria through active exploration. Under this approach, Unit Gradient Approximations (UGAs) of the underlying quality function are obtained at a set of reference points through a series of queries to the user. Equivalence sets of UGAs are then merged and aligned (MA) with the apparent boundaries between linear regions. In an empirical evaluation with artificial data, use of UGAs as training data for an instance-based ranking algorithm (1ARC) led to more accurate ranking than training with random instances, and use of UGAMA led to greater ranking accuracy than UGAs alone.

1 Introduction

Knowledge of the preferences of individual users is essential for intelligent systems whose performance is tailored for individual users, such as advisory agents and self-customizing systems. While some simple preferences are easily elicited (e.g., the preference for one soft-drink over another), more complex preference criteria may be difficult or extremely inconvenient for users to articulate (e.g., preferences among designs, schedules, plans, or other configurations).

A variety of approaches to automated preference acquisition are possible, varying in the attentional cost, or cognitive load, that they impose on the user. At one extreme is *a priori* knowledge, such as group membership, stereotypes, and default models, which can be determined at no attentional cost to the user. For example, collaborative filtering systems typically base their preference models on easily-obtained group membership information [GNOT92]. A second approach that has no attentional cost is *passive observation*, simply recording the user's choices.

A more active approach is the "candidate/revision" or "learn-on-failure" approach, under which the system makes suggestions based on its current model and revises the model whenever a suggestion is rejected. This approach has been applied to text retrieval [HGBSO98], telescope observing schedules [BB94], acquisition of "interface agents" [MK93], calendar management [DBM+92], and information filtering [Mae94].

At the opposite end of the spectrum of demands on the user from passive learners are approaches involving queries posed to the user. One approach to querying the user is *criteria elicitation*, in which the user's preference criteria are explicitly elicited through an extended interview process [KR93]. The attentional and time costs of explicit criteria elicitation make it infeasible for most automated systems. However, *exploration*, querying the user with pairs to be ranked (or larger collections from which the best instance should be selected) can potentially lead to faster acquisition of preference models than passive observation with less burden on the user than explicit criteria elicitation.

The choice among the methods for acquisition of user-specific information depends on the relative importance of the accuracy of the preference model and the cognitive load on the user. If the burden on the user is unimportant and accuracy of the preference model is of paramount importance, then a lengthy elicitation process should be followed. If, by contrast, no queries of any sort are permitted, then only *a priori* information and passive observations are available.

If, as is more typically the case, a small number of elicitations, such as candidates or queries, are permitted, the timing and contents of the elicitations are critical for maximizing the trade-off between ranking accuracy and cognitive load.

This paper describes *UGAMA*, an approach to acquiring instances for learning preference criteria through active exploration. The next section defines the preference learning task and describes previous approaches to preference learning by passive observation. Section 3 describes UGAMA, and Section 4 sets forth an empirical evaluation showing that for many target quality functions UGAMA leads to much faster acquisition of preference criteria than learning with an equal number of random observations. The scope of the results and its implications for representation design are described in the last section.

2 The Preference Learning Task

The preference learning task arises in many domains—typified by design and configuration problems—in which the relevant characteristics of problem-solving states can be identified by users or by experts, but users differ as to or are unable to articulate evaluation criteria for problem solving states in terms of these attributes.

For example, in the task of modeling individual preferences for two-dimensional designs, experts in design can identify the characteristics of designs that determine their quality, such as symmetry, contrast, and balance. Moreover, each of these characteristics can be expressed as a numerical or symbolic feature. But the precise manner in which these characteristics combine to determine the overall effectiveness of a design varies with each individual and is quite difficult for a given individual to articulate. Similarly, in the personal scheduling task, the relevant characteristics of schedules may be easy to identify, but their relative importance and interaction may both vary among individuals and be difficult for each individual to articulate.

A preference of user u is a binary relation, P_u such that $P_u(S_1, S_2)$ is satisfied whenever user u prefers S_1 to S_2. Various approaches have been taken to representing such relations. One approach rests on the assumption that a value function, $v_u(S)$, expressing the quality of state S, underlies P_u [KR93]. Thus, $P_u(S_1, S_2)$ is satisfied whenever $v_u(S_1) > v_u(S_2)$. A second approach subsumes preference model acquisition under supervised concept acquisition by viewing the problem of determining whether state S_1 is preferred to state S_2 as equivalent to determining whether the concatenation of S_1 with S_2, $concat(S_1, S_2)$, is an instance of the category "is-preferred-to." Under this approach each ranked pair $< S_1, S_2 >$ for which $P_u(S_1, S_2)$ is converted into a pair of training instances: $concat(S_1, S_2) \in$ "is-preferred-to" and $concat(S_1, S_2) \notin$ "is-preferred-to". For example, perceptron learning and decision-tree induction were applied to preference acquisition in [US87], [UC91], and [CFR91].

A third, intrinsically instance-based, approach represents preference pairs as arcs in feature space and ranks new pairs through nearest-neighbor algorithms, such as 1ARC or CIBL [BB94,BB97]. For example, the set of ranked pairs $\{P_u(A, B), P_u(C, D), P_u(E, F)\}$ can be represented as shown in Figure 1 by the preference arcs $\overleftarrow{AB}$, $\overleftarrow{CD}$, and $\overleftarrow{EF}$ (where $\overleftarrow{AB} \equiv P_u(A, B)$).

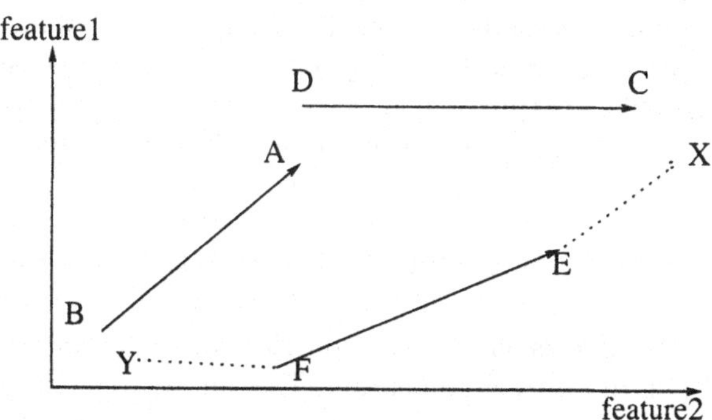

Fig. 1. X is ranked higher than Y by 1ARC because of the match between hypothesis $\overleftarrow{XY}$ and preference arc $\overleftarrow{EF}$. The dissimilarity between $\overleftarrow{XY}$ and $\overleftarrow{EF}$ is the sum of the Euclidean distances represented by dotted lines.

In the 1ARC algorithm, a new pair of objects, X and Y is ranked by determining whether $\overleftarrow{XY}$ or $\overleftarrow{YX}$ has the better match to a ranked pair in the training set. The dissimilarity between a hypothesis, e.g., $\overleftarrow{XY}$, and a ranked pair is measured by the sum of the Euclidean distances between (1) Y and the tail of the ranked pair and (2) X and the head of the preference pair. In Figure 1, for example, the ranked pair $\overleftarrow{EF}$ best matches $\overleftarrow{XY}$ with a dissimilarity of $dist(Y,F)+dist(X,E)$, represented by the sum of the lengths of the dotted lines. The best match for the alternative hypothesis $\overleftarrow{YX}$ is determined in the same way. In this case, $\overleftarrow{XY}$ matches ranked pair $\overleftarrow{EF}$ more strongly than $\overleftarrow{YX}$ matches any ranked pair, so $P_u(X,Y)$ is predicted.

Common to all these previous approaches to preference predicate acquisition is the assumption that the learning algorithm has no control over the choice of instances.

3 UGAMA

This section explores the implications of relaxing the assumption that a preference learning is not permitted to choose instances to learn from, proposing an approach based on two ideas: acquisition of Unit Gradient Approximations (UGAs); and merging and alignment of UGAs with respect to inflections (*i.e., changes in derivative sign* in the underlying quality function (UGAMA).

3.1 Unit Gradient Approximations

An estimation of the gradient of a quality function at a single point in feature space can be obtained as follows. Let R be a point (termed a *reference point*) in feature space. For each dimension d, create a pair $< R_{-d}, R_{+d} >$ by subtracting (respectively, adding) a small increment δ from (to) the value of R in the d dimension. If the user ranks $< R_{-d}, R_{+d} >$ as equal, the d dimension is irrelevant at R. If R_{-d} is ranked better than R_{+d}, Q has negative slope with respect to d at R; if R_{+d} is preferred, the slope is positive at R. For example, Figure 2 shows how points P1 and P2 are δ larger and smaller, respectively, than reference point R in dimension 1, and points P3 and P4, are δ larger and smaller, respectively, than R in dimension 2. If user ranks $P_u(P2,P1)$ and $P_u(P4,P3)$, the UGA has a slope of $< 1, -1 >$.

If there are n dimensions, then n queries are sufficient to determine the relevance and polarity of each dimension. This information can be expressed in a single pair, $\overleftarrow{HT}$, called a *unit gradient approximation* (UGA), in which H and T are identical to R in irrelevant dimensions, H is δ greater than and T δ less than R in dimensions with positive slope, and H is δ less than and T δ greater than R in dimension with negative slope.

If the quality function happens to be a linear function whose coefficients are all either k, $-k$, or 0, for some constant k, then the UGA will be parallel to the gradient of the function.[1] Under these circumstances, a single UGA is a sufficient

[1] For example, suppose that the quality function $Q(x_1, x_2, x_3, x_4) = 2x_1 - 2x_3 + 2x_4$, the reference point is $< .5, .5, .5, .5 >$, and $\delta = .1$. Under these circumstances, the UGA

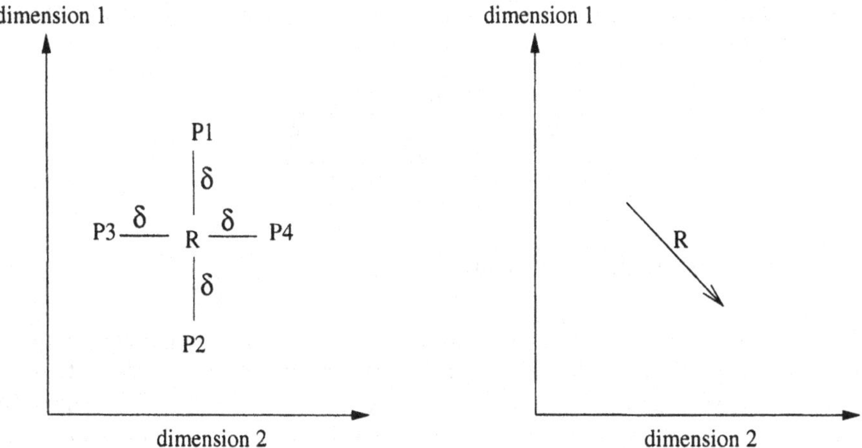

Fig. 2. Determining the relevance and polarity of each dimension, and forming a UGA. If user ranks $P_u(P2, P1)$ and $P_u(P4, P3)$, the UGA has a slope of $< 1, -1 >$

training set for 1ARC to achieve perfect accuracy, that is, correctly rank all pairs (see Theorem 1, Appendix). As shown in Table 1, ranking accuracy given a 4-dimensional linear function defined on $[0, 1]^4$ with 50% irrelevant features is 100% for both perceptron and 1ARC with a single UGA as training data, as compared to only 69.9% for 1ARC and 71.1% for perceptron with a training set consisting of 4 random instances (in 10 trials of 128 random test cases each).

Table 1. Ranking accuracy with linear quality function in 4 dimensions, two of which are irrelevant and two of which have identical weights.

	1ARC	Perceptron
Random	69.9	71.1
UGA	100	100

Of course, if the coefficients of the underlying quality function differ by factors other than 1, -1, or 0, the UGA will no longer be parallel to the gradient and will therefore no longer guaranteed to rank new pairs correctly. For example, given quality function $Q(x_1, \ldots, x_n) = \sum_{i=1}^{n} 2^i x_i$, the ranking accuracy with a single UGA is considerably lower than with unit weights. However, as shown in Table 2, the ranking accuracy is still higher than with an equal number of random instances (4 dimensions, 10 trials of 128 test cases each). In practice, such extreme variations in the weight of relevant attributes coefficients (*i.e.*, in the coefficients of the quality function) seem unlikely.

---

will be ($< .6, .5, .4, .6 >< .4, .5, .6, .4 >$). The slope of this instance is $< .2, 0, -.2, .2 >$, which is parallel to the gradient of Q, $< 2, 0, -2, 2 >$.

Table 2. Ranking accuracy with linear quality function in 4 dimensions with coefficient 2^d for dimension d.

	1ARC	Perceptron
Random	67.6	72.2
UGA	79.9	80.0

3.2 Inflected Quality Functions

The nature of the quality function underlying a person's preferences depends both on the preferences themselves and on the representation of the attributes used to characterize the instances. A quality function may be linear when defined on an optimal set of attributes, but nonlinear when defined on suboptimal attributes. Ideally, a preference learning task should be defined in such a way that user's quality functions defined on those attributes should be linear. But in practice it seems unlikely that a representation guaranteed to lead to linear quality functions for all users can be found for all domains.

For example, the width-to-height ratio of two-dimensional designs is a factor that affects many peoples' preferences for designs. Some people may prefer a width-to-height ratio near the "golden mean," $(1+\sqrt{5})/2$, while others may prefer a unit width-to-height ratio. If the width-to-height ratio attribute of designs were replaced with a distance-from-golden-mean attribute, the function would become linear in the attribute for people in the first group, but the unit width-to-height ratio would be indistinguishable from $\sqrt{5}$ (since both are an equal distance from $(1+\sqrt{5})/2$). Similarly, if a distance-from-unit-ratio attribute were used, the golden mean could no longer be distinguished from $2-(1+\sqrt{5})/2$. Thus, width-to-height ratio itself must be used as a feature if both preferences are to be precisely expressible. However, if the width-to-height ratio is used, then there will be an inflection in the quality function at the golden-mean for people in the first group and at 1 for people in the second group. This example shows that it may not always be feasible to devise a representation that is linear in all attributes because users may differ as to the values of an attribute that they consider optimal.

Clearly, a single UGA is not sufficient to represent a preference predicate based on a nonlinear quality function. If the quality function has inflections, then multiple UGAs must be obtained. Only if at least one UGA has been obtained for each linear region is an accurate preference model possible. Since each UGA requires n queries, where n is the number of dimension, the user's patience is likely to be exhausted if the number of dimensions and linear regions is high. Therefore, it appears that the key condition under which an algorithm for preference acquisition through exploration must work is when the number of inflections in the users' quality function is greater than zero but not too large.

A single perceptron is not capable of expressing nonlinear concepts. However, the 1ARC algorithm is capable of modeling nonlinear quality functions provided that there is at least one ranked pair per linear region. This suggests the strategy of eliciting a set of UGAs at random points and using them as the training set for 1ARC.[2]

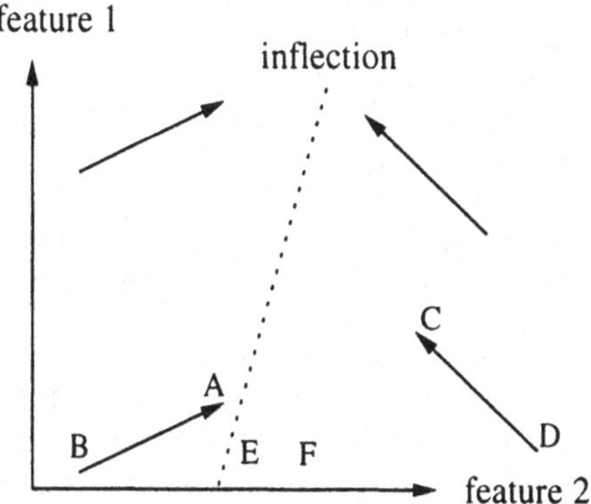

Fig. 3. The pair $< E, F >$, for which $Q(E) > Q(F)$, is misranked because $\overleftarrow{FE}$ matches $\overleftarrow{AB}$ more closely than $\overleftarrow{EF}$ matches $\overleftarrow{CD}$.

The limitation of this approach is that because 1ARC is a nearest-neighbor algorithm, the position of the UGAs within each linear region affects ranking accuracy. An example is illustrated in Figure 3, in which the dotted line represents the inflection between two linear regions. Since $\overleftarrow{AB}$ is much nearer to the inflection than $\overleftarrow{CD}$, the $\overleftarrow{FE}$ matches $\overleftarrow{AB}$ more closely than $\overleftarrow{EF}$ matches $\overleftarrow{CD}$. As a result, the pair $< E, F >$ is misranked.

3.3 Merging and Aligning UGAs

Merging and alignment is a procedure to reduce this effect. As set forth in Figure 4 and illustrated in Figure 5, UGAs with identical slopes that are closer to each other than to UGAs with different slopes are merged. Merging a set S of arcs consists of forming the arc $\overleftarrow{H_m, T_m}$, where H_m is the mean of the heads of the arcs in S and T_m is the mean of the tails of the arcs in S. The merged UGAs from adjacent regions are then displaced, without changing their slope, until their heads (or tails, if the tails are closer to each other than the heads) coincide at the midpoint between their original positions. The purpose of this displacement is to align the endpoints of the UGAs so as to coincide as closely as possible with the inflection in the quality function. Choosing the midpoint of the heads (or tails) is simply a heuristic for estimating the position of the inflection. As shown in Theorem 2, Appendix, if two arcs each parallel to the

[2] Of course, if domain knowledge exists from which one point per linear region can be selected, this knowledge should be used to create the minimal set of UGAs. However, in the general case it is not known how many linear regions there are.

```
Procedure MERGE-AND-ALIGN(UGASET)
Input:  UGASET is a list of UGAs
Output: UGAMASET is list of merged and aligned UGAs
1. Let MERGERS and UGAMASET be {}
2. Let ECLASSES be a partition of UGASET into sets with equal slope
3. For each class C in ECLASSES do
  a. Let SC be a partition of C into the largest sets such that every
     member of SC is closer to some other member of SC than to any member
     of UGASET with a different slope.
  b. For every partition P in SC do
       Add the arc M consisting of mean of every arc in P to MERGERS
4. For each pair of arcs (A1, A2), where A1, A2 are in MERGERS
    LET M be the mean of A1 and A2.
    IF A1 and A2 have different slopes AND M is closer
    to A1 [equivalently, A2] than to any other arc in MERGERS
    THEN {IF the heads of A1 and A2 are closer to each other than the tails
          THEN {Let A1' and A2' be the result of displacing A1 and A2 so that
          their heads coincide at the mean of the heads' original positions}
          ELSE {Let A1' and A2' be the result of displacing A1 and A2 so that
          their tails coincide at the mean of the tail's original positions}
          Add A1' and A2' to UGAMASET.}
5. Return UGAMASET
```

Fig. 4. The merge-and-adjust algorithm.

gradient are symmetric around a single inflection and share a common endpoint, 1ARC will correctly rank all pairs, given the two arcs as a training set. The entire procedure of forming UGAs through successive queries, then merging and aligning the UGAs is termed *UGAMA*.

4 Experimental Evaluation

Theorem 2's guarantee of ranking correctness does not extend to functions with multiple inflections. How well does UGAMA perform with functions with multiple inflections, which are likely to be more typical of actual user quality functions? To answer this question, an evaluation was performed with a set of artificial quality functions.

The experiments were performed on a 4-dimensional feature space, $[0,1]^4$ with 6 artificial quality functions intended to resemble human quality functions. The first quality function, `independent`, shown in Figure 6, is linear in even-numbered dimensions and inflected at 0.5 in odd-numbered dimensions. This corresponds to a domain, like 2-dimensional design, where some dimensions (e.g., width-to-height ratio) are inflected and others (e.g., balance) are not. In `dependent` the quality function is inflected in the sum of successive pairs of dimensions, e.g., for 2 dimensions if $d1 + d2 < 1$, $Q(d1, d2) = d1 + d2$, otherwise $Q(d1, d2) = 2 - (d1 + d2)$. This corresponds to a quality function

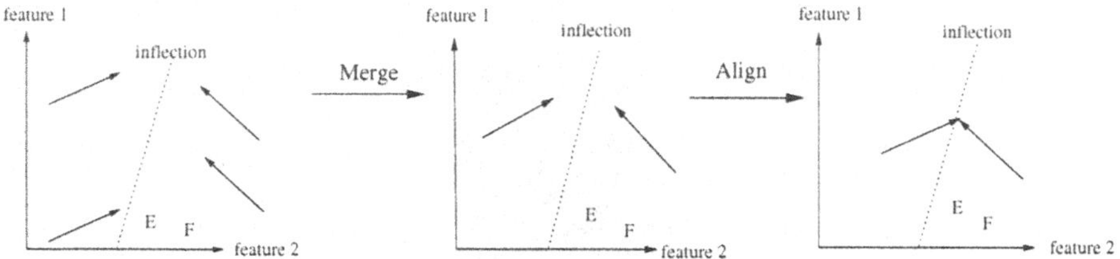

Fig. 5. An example of merging and aligning UGAs. The pair $< E, F >$, incorrectly ranked by the original UGAs, is correctly ranked by the merged and adjusted UGAs

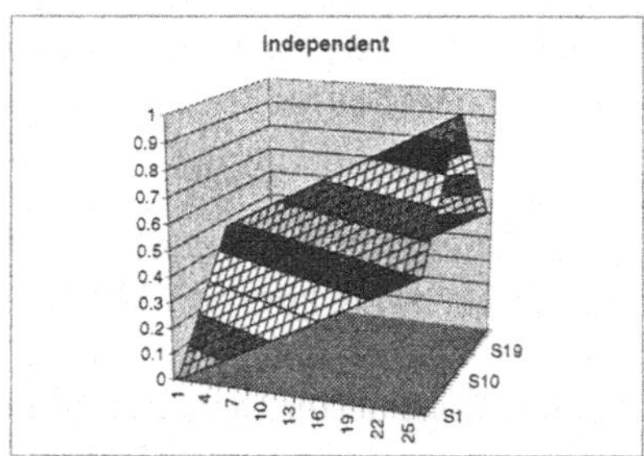

Fig. 6. The 2-dimensional analog of quality function `independent`. The vertical axis represents quality as a function of two features.

with pairwise interactions between dimensions. In `sinusoid .5`, Q is the sine of the sum of the dimensions normalized to range from $[0..\pi]$. `Exponential` is $Q(d1, d2, d3, d4) = 1 - e^{\sqrt{(d1^2+d2^2+d3^2+d4^2)/4}}$. In `double fold`, shown in Figure 7, Q consists of 4 linear regions with inflections perpendicular to the line d1 = d2 = d3 = d4, and `pyramid` consists of 4 linear regions intersecting at (0.5,0.5,0.5,0.5).

In each test, 8 random reference points were selected to create 8 UGAs (through 32 queries to the test function). The accuracy in ranking randomly selected pairs using the UGAs both before and after merging and alignment was compared to accuracy using 32 random instances. Each function was tested with 10 repetitions of 128 random testing instances each.

Figure 8 sets forth the results using 1ARC as the learning mechanism. For each function, UGAs resulted in higher ranking accuracy than did the random training instances, and merging and alignment produced an additional improvement in every function except `exponential`. Merging and alignment produces no improvement in `exponential` because merging results in a single arc.

Non-instance-based learning methods are benefited relatively little by the UGAMA approach. Briefly, perceptron performs at the chance level on inflected quality functions. UGAMA does not improve the performance of decision-tree in-

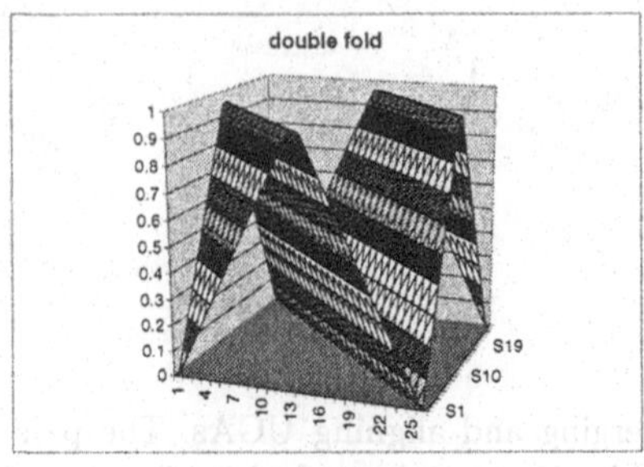

Fig. 7. The 2-dimensional analog of quality function `double-fold`. The vertical axis represents quality as a function of two features.

duction (ID3) or backpropagation, which perform with random instances, UGAs, and UGAMA at approximately the same level as 1ARC given random instances. This result is consistent with previous research, which has shown that instance-based learning methods tend to work better than greedy generalizers when there is a very small number of training instances [BB97,Aha92], such as result from the elicitation of UGAs. Identification of exploration techniques that are appropriate for these alternative preference-learning methods is an open question.

5 Conclusion

This paper has presented an approach for acquiring instance-based preference models through active exploration. The empirical evaluation showed that UGAMA lead to more rapid acquisition of preference predicates than training sets of random instances. The results with *independent* showed that a ranking accuracy of over 80% can be obtained on a quality function with inflections in 2 different dimensions after 32 queries.

The next step in research in acquisition of preference predicates through exploration should be testing with human subjects. The actual complexity of human preference criteria in representative domains is unknown. The performance requirements for preference acquisition algorithms will be better understood when there are well-analyzed sets of human preference data. A second issue in human preference testing is the number of queries that users will tolerate. This probably depends on the complexity of the instances being ranked and on the level of useful assistance that can be expected from the investment of users' effort. A third issue is the amount of noise or inconsistency in human preference rankings. This factor determines the extent to which preference learning algorithms must be noise tolerant.

In view of the dramatic effect that quality function complexity has on the number of instances needed to learn a preference model, design of representations

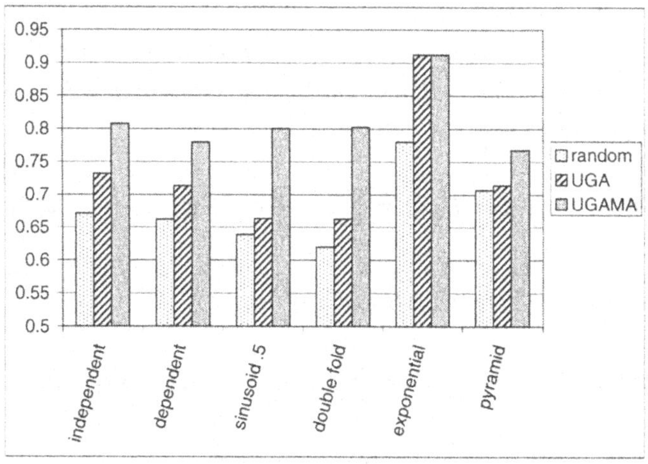

Fig. 8. A comparison of the ranking accuracy of 1ARC using random instances, UGAs, and UGAMA on 6 quality functions.

for which users' quality functions are as nearly linear as possible is clearly essential. However, in many domains some nonlinearity appears to be unavoidable. The UGAMA approach may therefore be a valuable tool for active preference predicate acquisition for such domains.

Acknowledgments

This research was supported in part by a German-American Fulbright Commission Senior Scholars grant, a University of Wyoming Flittie sabbatical award, and the University of Kaiserslautern Center for Learning Systems and Applications.

Appendix

Theorem 1.
With a training set consisting of a single preference instance parallel to the gradient of a linear quality function, 1ARC correctly ranks all pairs with respect to the quality function.

Proof.
Let $Q(x_1, \ldots, x_n) = \sum_{i=1}^{n} a_i x_i$ be a linear quality function of n features. The gradient of Q is the vector G=$< a_1, \ldots, a_n >$. A ranked pair parallel to G in feature space must be of the form

$$P_Q(A, B) \equiv (< u_1 + ca_1, \ldots, u_n + ca_n >< u_1, \ldots, u_n >) \qquad (1)$$

where c is a positive constant.

Let (W,Z) $\equiv$ ($< w_1, \ldots, w_n >< z_1, \ldots, z_n >$) be a testing pair. 1ARC ranks W and Z by finding whether $\overleftarrow{AB}$ more closely matches $\overleftarrow{WZ}$ or $\overleftarrow{ZW}$. The distance between $\overleftarrow{AB}$ and $\overleftarrow{WZ}$ is

$$dist(A,W) + dist(B,Z) = \sum_{i=1}^{n} [(u_i + ca_i - w_i)^2 + (u_i - z_i)^2] \tag{2}$$

Similarly, the distance between $\overleftarrow{AB}$ and $\overleftarrow{ZW}$ is

$$dist(A,W) + dist(B,Z) = \sum_{i=1}^{n} [(u_i + ca_i - z_i)^2 + (u_i - w_i)^2] \tag{3}$$

Thus, 1ARC will rank W as preferable to Z only if

$$\sum_{i=1}^{n} [(u_i + ca_i - w_i)^2 + (u_i - z_i)^2] < \sum_{i=1}^{n} [(u_i + ca_i - z_i)^2 + (u_i - w_i)^2] \tag{4}$$

However, this inequality can be simplified to

$$\sum_{i=1}^{n} w_i a_i > \sum_{i=1}^{n} z_i a_i \tag{5}$$

which is equivalent to $Q(W) > Q(Z)$.
Similarly, 1ARC will rank Z as preferable to W only if

$$\sum_{i=1}^{n} [(u_i + ca_i - w_i)^2 + (u_i - z_i)^2] > \sum_{i=1}^{n} [(u_i + ca_i - z_i)^2 + (u_i - w_i)^2] \tag{6}$$

which can be simplified to

$$\sum_{i=1}^{n} w_i a_i < \sum_{i=1}^{n} z_i a_i \tag{7}$$

which is equivalent to $Q(W) < Q(Z)$. Thus, the single training pair P_Q(A,B) correctly ranks all testing pairs with respect to Q.

Theorem 2.
Let Q be a piecewise linear function symmetrical around a single linear inflection, that is, let the components of the slope on both sides of the inflection have the same magnitude, but let at least one component differ in sign. Then with a training set consisting of two ranked pairs that (1) share a common endpoint, (2) are reflections of one another across the inflection, and (3) are each parallel to the gradient of the quality function, 1ARC correctly ranks all pairs with respect to Q.

Proof.
Assume without loss of generality that the shared endpoint is the preferred point, as pictured in Figure 9 for training pairs $\overleftarrow{E_1E_2}$ and $\overleftarrow{E_1E_3}$ (an analogous argument can be made if the shared endpoint is the less-preferred point). Any two

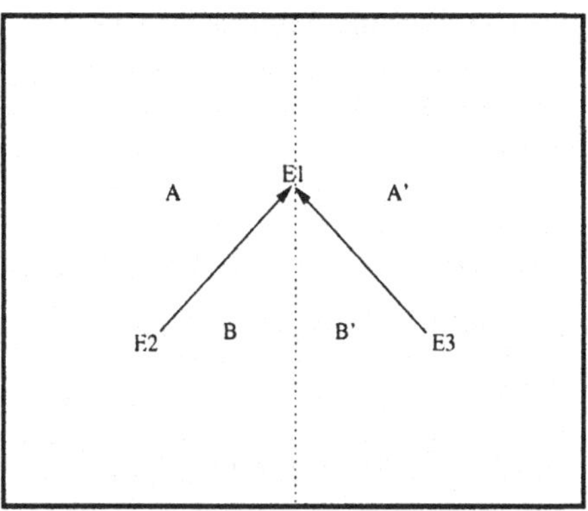

Fig. 9. The inflection between two linear regions is indicated by the dotted line.

pairs to be ranked must either both be on the same side of the inflection or they must be on different sides of the inflection.

(a) Same side
Let A and B be points to be ranked, and suppose that their actual ranking is $\overleftarrow{AB}$, i.e., Q(A) > Q(B) (if not, rename the points). Under Theorem 1,

$$dist(A, E_1) + dist(B, E_2) < dist(A, E_2) + dist(B, E_1) \tag{8}$$

That is, $\overleftarrow{AB}$ is correctly ranked by $\overleftarrow{E_1E_2}$. Thus, $\overleftarrow{AB}$ could be misranked only if

$$dist(A, E_3) + dist(B, E_1) < dist(A, E_1) + dist(B, E_2) \tag{9}$$

However, since E_2 and E_3 are symmetrical across the inflection, the inflection represents the set of points equidistance from E_2 and E_3. Any point on the same side of the inflection as E_2 is closer to E_2 than to E_3. Therefore, $dist(A, E_3) > dist(A, E_2)$, so

$$dist(A, E_2) + dist(B, E_1) < dist(A, E_3) + dist(B, E_1) \tag{10}$$

Inequalities 8 and 10 together imply that:

$$dist(A, E_1) + dist(B, E_2) < dist(A, E_3) + dist(B, E_1) \tag{11}$$

which contradicts inequality 9. Therefore, $\overleftarrow{AB}$ will be correctly ranked by $\overleftarrow{E_1E_2}$.

(b) Different sides
Let A and B' be points to be ranked, and again suppose without loss of generality that their actual ranking is $\overleftarrow{AB'}$.

$\overleftarrow{AB'}$ could not be incorrectly ranked unless either

$$dist(A, E_2) + dist(B', E_1) < dist(A, E_1) + dist(B', E_3) \tag{12}$$

or

$$dist(A, E_3) + dist(B', E_1) < dist(A, E_1) + dist(B', E_3) \tag{13}$$

Let B be the reflection of B' across the inflection and let A' be the reflection of A across the inflection. Then

$$dist(B, E_2) = dist(B', E_3). \tag{14}$$

and

$$dist(A, E_1) = dist(A', E_1) \tag{15}$$

Theorem 1 implies that

$$dist(A, E_1) + dist(B, E_2) < dist(A, E_2) + dist(B, E_1) \tag{16}$$

and

$$dist(A', E_1) + dist(B', E_3) < dist(A', E_3) + dist(B', E_1) \tag{17}$$

Substituting $dist(B', E_3)$ for $dist(B, E_2)$ in 16 we obtain:

$$dist(A, E_1) + dist(B', E_3) < dist(A, E_2) + dist(B, E_1) \tag{18}$$

which contradicts 12. Moreover, substituting $dist(A, E_1)$ for $dist(A', E_1)$, and $dist(A', E_3)$ for $dist(A, E_2)$ in 17 we obtain:

$$dist(A, E_1) + dist(B', E_3) < dist(A, E_3) + dist(B', E_1) \tag{19}$$

which contradicts 13.

Since, $dist(A, E_1) + dist(B', E_3)$ is less than either $dist(A, E_2) + dist(B', E_1)$ or $dist(A, E_3) + dist(B', E_1)$, $\overleftarrow{AB'}$ will be correctly ranked by $\overleftarrow{E_1E_3}$.

References

[Aha92] D. Aha. Generalizing from case studies: A case study. In *Proceedings of the Ninth International Workshop on Machine Learning*, pages 1–10, 1992.

[BB94] P. Broos and K. Branting. Compositional instance-based learning. In *Proceedings of the Twelfth National Conference Conference on Artificial Intelligence (AAAI-94)*, Seattle, Washington, July 31–August 4, 1994.

[BB97] K. Branting and P. Broos. Automated acquisition of user preferences. *International Journal of Human-Computer Studies*, 46:55–77, 1997.

[Bra99] K. Branting. Learning user preferences by exploration. In *The Sixteenth International Conference on Machine Learning*, 27–30 June 1999 1999. Under review.

[CFR91] J. Callan, T. Fawcett, and E. Rissland. Adaptive case-based reasoning. In *Proceedings of the Third DARPA Case-Based Reasoning Workshop*, pages 179–190. Morgan Kaufmann, May 1991.

[DBM+92] L. Dent, J. Boticario, J. McDermott, T. Mitchell, and D. Zabowski. A personal learning apprentice. In *Proceedings of Tenth National Conference on Artificial Intelligence*, pages 96–103, San Jose, CA, July 12–16 1992. AAAI Press/MIT Press.

[GNOT92] D. Goldberg, D. Nichols, B. Oki, and D. Terry. Using collaborative filtering to weave an information tapestry. *Communications of the ACM*, 35(12):61–70, 1992.

[HGBSO98] Ralf Herbirch, Thore Graepel, Peter Bollmann-Sdorra, and Klaus Obermayer. Learning preference relations for information retrieval. In *Proceedings of the AAAI-98 Workshop on Learning for Text Categorization.* AAAI Press, July 26–27 1998.

[KR93] R. Keeney and H. Raiffa. *Decisions with Multiple Objectives: Preferences and Value Tradeoffs.* Cambridge University Press, second edition, 1993.

[Mae94] P. Maes. Agents that reduce work and information overload. *Communications of the ACM*, 37(7):31–40, 1994.

[MK93] P. Maes and R. Kozierok. Learning interface agents. In *Proceedings of Eleventh National Conference on Artificial Intelligence*, pages 459–466, Washington, D.C., July 11–15 1993. AAAI Press/MIT Press.

[UC91] P. Utgoff and J. Clouse. Two kinds of training information for evaluation function learning. In *Proceedings of Ninth National Conference on Artificial Intelligence*, pages 596–600, Anaheim, July 14–19 1991. AAAI Press/MIT Press, Menlo Park, California.

[US87] P. Utgoff and S. Saxena. Learning a preference predicate. In *Proceedings of the Fourth International Workshop on Machine Learning*, pages 115–121, 1987.

A Multiple-Domain Evaluation of Stratified Case-Based Reasoning

L. Karl Branting and Yi Tao
Department of Computer Science
University of Wyoming
Laramie, WY, USA
karl@uwyo.edu

Abstract. Stratified case-based reasoning (SCBR) is a technique in which case abstractions are used to assist case retrieval, matching, and adaptation. Previous work has shown that SCBR can significantly decrease the computational expense required for retrieval, matching, and adaptation under a variety of different problem conditions. This paper extends this work to two new domains: a problem in combinatorial optimization, sorting by prefix reversal; and logistics planning. An empirical evaluation in the prefix-reversal problem showed that SCBR reduced search cost, but severely degraded solution quality. By contrast, in logistics planning, use of SCBR as an indexing mechanism led to faster solution times and permitted more problems to be solved than either hierarchical problem solving (by ALPINE) or ground level CBR (by SPA) alone. The primary factor responsible for the difference in SCBR's performance in these two domains appeared to be that the *optimal-case utility* was low in the prefix-reversal task but high in logistics planning.

1 Introduction

Human problem solvers exhibit great flexibility in reasoning both with specific cases and with abstractions derived from one or more cases [13]. A number of case-based reasoning systems have modeled an important aspect of this flexibility: use of case abstractions to guide case indexing, matching, and adaptation. Termed *stratified case-based reasoning* (SCBR) in [4], this approach has been used for planning [3], [12], design of control software [16], and route planning [4], [5]. A comparative analysis of various approaches to using abstraction in CBR is set forth in [2].

Systematic empirical analyses set forth in [4] and [5] compared the performance of heuristic search (A*), *Refinement* [11] (*i.e.*, hierarchical problem solving), ground-level CBR, and SCBR as a function of (1) number of levels of abstraction, (2) the size of the case library, (3) resemblance among cases, and (4) whether the abstraction hierarchy satisfies the downward-refinement property [1]. However, this evaluation was limited to a route-finding domain in which there was a high liklihood, for typical problems and case libraries, that the case library would contain a case that could be adapted to a solution to the problem as good as would be obtained through *ab initio* problem solving. This liklihood, which depends on both the adaptation method and the case library coverage, is termed the *optimal-case utility* of the library and adaption method.

This paper describes two sets of experiments in which SCBR was applied to alternative domains. Section 2 describes the application of SCBR to a problem in combinatorial optimization, sorting by prefix reversal. Section 3 describes a prototype application of SCBR to logistics planning. These experiments suggest that optimal-case utility is a key factor in the applicability of SCBR.

2 SCBR for Combinatorial Optimization

2.1 The Prefix-Reversal Problem

Sorting by reversals is the task of determining the minimum number of subsequence reversals necessary to transform one sequence into another. This task, which arises in molecular biology [15], has been shown to be NP-hard in the general case [6]. *Sorting by prefix reversals* is a special case of this problem in which all reversals must be of sequence prefixes. Bounds for sorting by prefix reversals were derived in [8].

A prefix-reversal problem is given by specifying start and goal states, each represented as a list of elements. An n-prefix-reversal problem is a prefix-reversal problem involving permutations of an n-element sequence. For example, a 7-prefix-reversal problem is as follows:

Start: (D G C E A F B)

Goal: (A B C D E F G)

A solution is a sequence of operations, where each operator represents the length of the prefix being reversed. For example, the solution to the problem above is (3 6 4 5 7 4 5):

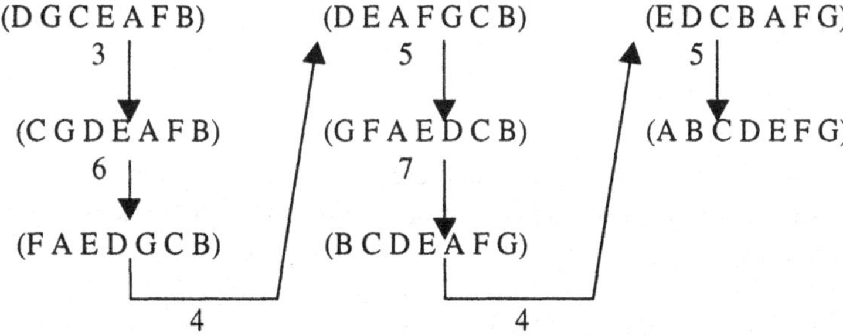

2.2 Abstraction for Prefix Reversal

A simple abstraction mechanism for the prefix-reversal problem is to simply drop from the representation the object that occurs last in the goal state, thereby aggregating all states that differ only in the position of this object into a single state. A solution to the original problem can't be any shorter than the solution to an abstraction of that problem, so the solution length of the abstraction is an admissible distance heuristic, h*, for A*. Moreover, if a solution is obtained for the abstract problem, then at most 4 additional operations are required to solve the original problem. This is because if there are n objects, the operations (p, n, n-1, p-1) will move the pth object to last place without altering the position of any other objects.

Refinement search [11] can be performed using this abstraction hierarchy by solving an abstraction of the original problem, then using this solution as a heuristic for search at the next lower level of abstraction. This process is repeated until the ground level is reached. A very strong alternative heuristic for this problem counts the number for pairs adjacent in the goal state that are not adjacent in the current state. This *adjacent-pairs* heuristic is also admissible, because a prefix reversal can reduce the number of such pairs by at most one.

2.3 Algorithms

To evaluate the effectiveness of SCBR at reducing search in this domain, four different approaches were compared: A*, using the adjacent-pairs heuristic; refinement; ground-level CBR (GRCL), which adapts every case in the library and returns the one with the shortest adapted solution; and Reuse-Closest (RCL), an SCBR algorithm that starts with the most specific matching cases (or the most abstract cases, if no cases match), finds the refinements of each case, adapts each refinement (using A* to find the shortest adaptation paths from the start and goal positions to the solution path at that level of abstraction), and selects the refinements having the shortest adapted solution paths. All four algorithms are described in detail in [4].

As in the route-finding problem described in [4], adaptation in RCL consisted of using A* to find the shortest paths from the start and goal positions to the solution path at the current level of abstraction to form a solution consisting of these paths concatenated with a reused segment of the old solution. Thus, an adapted solution must include a portion of the original solution.

2.4 Experimental Evaluation

The dependent variables of interest were search cost, as measured by the number of nodes expanded by A*, and the solution quality, as measured by solution length. The independent variables were:

- The number of abstraction levels (1,2,3,4)
- The size of case library (1,5,10,50,100,500,1000)

Experiments were performed with 8-prefix-reversal, and results were based on 1000 random test cases.

Varying the number of abstraction levels In the first experiment, the number of cases in case library was fixed at 100 and the number of abstraction levels was varied from 1 to 4. As shown in Figure 1, the number of nodes expanded by A* and GRCL remained constant since these algorithms do not make use of the abstraction hierarchy. Refinement performed slightly better than A*, indicating that abstract solution length is a good heuristic in this domain. RCL expands the smallest number of nodes, given 3 or more abstraction levels.

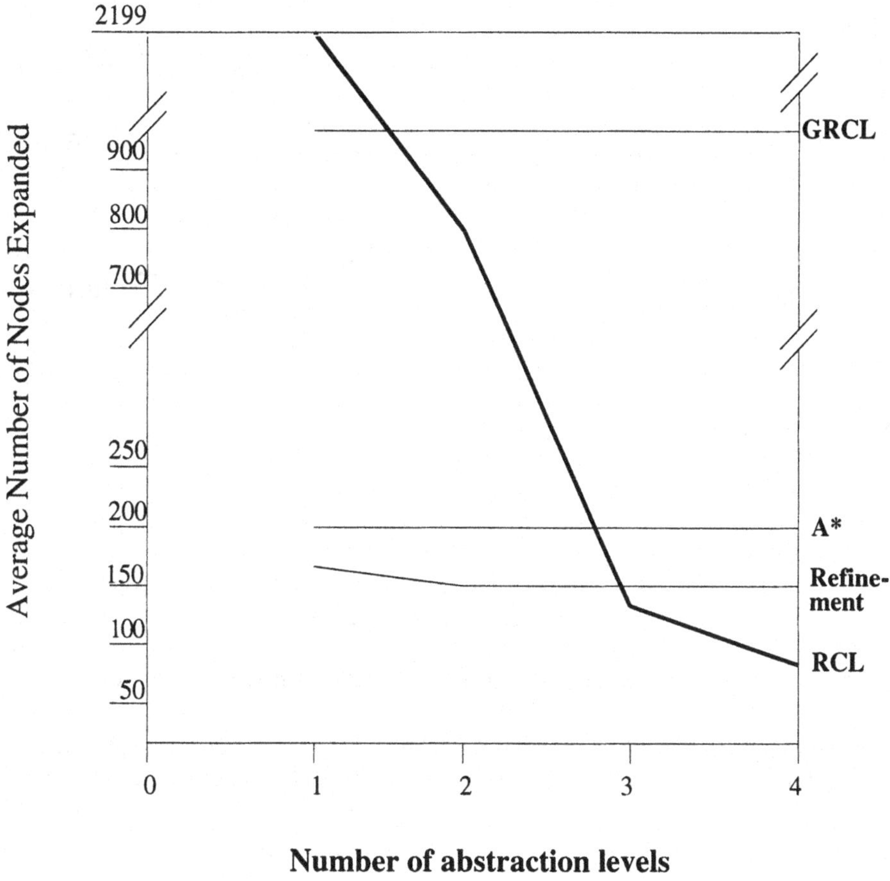

Fig. 1. Mean nodes expanded in 8-prefix-refersal as a function of the number of abstraction levels.

Varying the Case Library Size Figure 2 shows the effect of varying the size of the case library. The number of nodes expanded by A* and Refinement remained constant, because these algorithms do not use cases. The number of nodes expanded climbed steadily for GRCL, but was relatively constant for RCL. Unfortunately, the smallest number of nodes was expanded by GRCL with a case library consisting of a single case. Evidently, a case library consisting of a single case reduces search by converting the original problem of searching for a path to a single state into two easier problems, each consisting of a search for a solution path consisting of, on average, about 7.7 states.

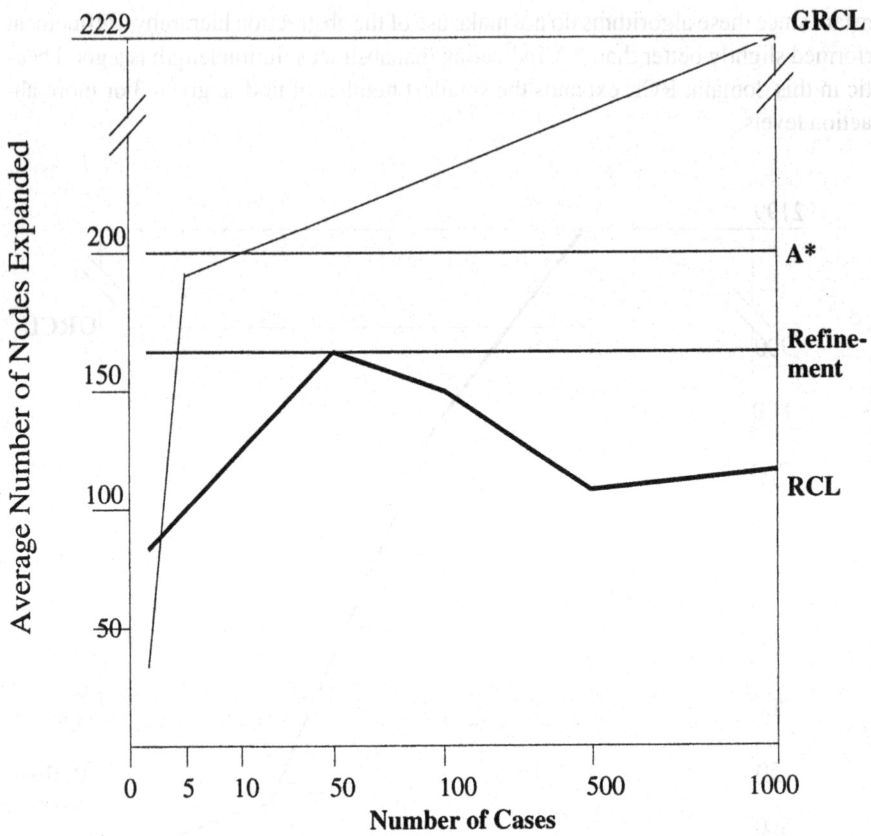

Fig. 2. Mean nodes expanded in 8-prefix-refersal as a function of the number of cases.

Solution Length Tables 1 and 2 show mean solution lengths as a function of abstraction levels (100-case library) and case library size (3 levels of abstraction), respectively.

Table 1. Mean Solution Lengths for 8-prefix-reversal as a function of the number of abstract levels

	A*	HSOLVE	GRCL	RCL
1 abstract level	7.7	7.7	9.3	9.5
2 abstract levels	7.7	7.7	9.3	10.1
3 abstract levels	7.7	7.7	9.3	9.9
4 abstract levels	7.7	7.7	9.3	10.0

Since the adjacent-pairs heuristic is admissible, A* always finds a shortest solution path. Moreover, Refinement also always finds the shortest path because it uses A* at every level, and the length of the next more abstract solution is itself an admissible heuristic. GRCL is guaranteed to return the case requiring the least adaptation. However, the consistent value of 9.3 for the mean solution length obtained by GRCL indicates that the adaptation available to GRCL and RCL (splicing paths onto a reused portion of the old solution) leads to decreased solution quality, even when applied to the most adaptable case in the case library. This is because both problems and solutions are uniformly distributed through state-space in the prefix-reversal problem, so the likelihood that an optimal solution to a new problem will involve reuse of a segment of an old solution is quite low, even if the number of cases is high.

Table 2. Mean Solution lengths for 8-prefix-reversal as a function of the number of cases

	A*	HSOLVE	GRCL	RCL
1 case	7.7	7.7	10.5	10.5
5 cases	7.7	7.7	10.0	10.0
10 cases	7.7	7.7	10.1	10.1
50 cases	7.7	7.7	9.5	10.0
100 cases	7.7	7.7	9.3	9.9
500 cases	7.7	7.7	8.9	10.0
1000 cases	7.7	7.7	8.7	9.6

Since RCL can produce solutions no better than those produced by GRCL, the weakness of the adaptation method guarantees that RCL cases are suboptimal as well. Moreover, while RCL's use of abstract cases to guide retrieval was much less expensive than GRCL's exhaustive matching, the higher mean solution length for RCL means that it did not always find the case leading to the shortest solution.

2.5 Summary

The prefix-reversal experiment illustrated that SCBR can reduce search in a combinatorial optimization problem. However, the experiment also illustrated that SCBR cannot compensate for a weak adaptation method that is incapable of producing solutions as good as those found through *ab initio* problem solving.

3 Logistics Planning

The utility of using case abstractions for indexing and adaptation has been demonstrated in planning domains characterized by task-decomposition abstraction hierarchies [3], [12]. However, development of task-decomposition hierarchies is, in general, a difficult and time-consuming task. The second experiment was designed to explore the feasibility of using SCBR as an indexing technique using inexpensive 'off-the-shelf' abstraction hierarchies. In the early 1990s, several Ph.D. projects developed techniques for automated creation of abstraction hierarchies in the STRIPS formalism, *e.g.*, [8], [14]. One such system, ALPINE, is available to researchers as part of the PRODIGY [7] release version 4 (www.cs.cmu.edu/afs/cs/project/ai-repository/). Alpine is guaranteed to produce abstraction hierarchies with the *ordered monotonicity property* [14], a weaker condition than the downward refinement property shown in [5] to contribute to (although not to be essential to) the effectiveness of SCBR.

An evaluation of the relative contribution of hierarchical problem solving and CBR to SCBR would have the most information value if it involved an ablation of each component, that is, if the hierarchical problem solving, ground-level CBR, and ground-level *ab initio* problem solving components were tested both in isolation and in combination. However, writing a planning system that embodied every combination of these factors was a task beyond the scope of this exploratory project. We therefore selected SPA ([10], a least-commitment generative planner with very simple and general case-retrieval and adaptation mechanisms, as our main planning engine. SPA has no mechanism for hierarchical problem solving, however, so we used ALPINE as our hierarchical problem solver.

The logistics problem domain, taken from the PRODIGY version 4.0 release, includes 14 predicates and 6 operators in STRIPS notation. Problems in this domain involve transportation of objects between various locations through a combination of truck and airplane operations. A logistics transportation problem is given by initial state and a goal state specification. The description of an initial (or any other) state is composed of a list of objects and their corresponding types together with a set of instantiated predicates (i.e. literals) that describes the configuration of those objects. For example, Problem 5 in our test set can be depicted graphically as follows:

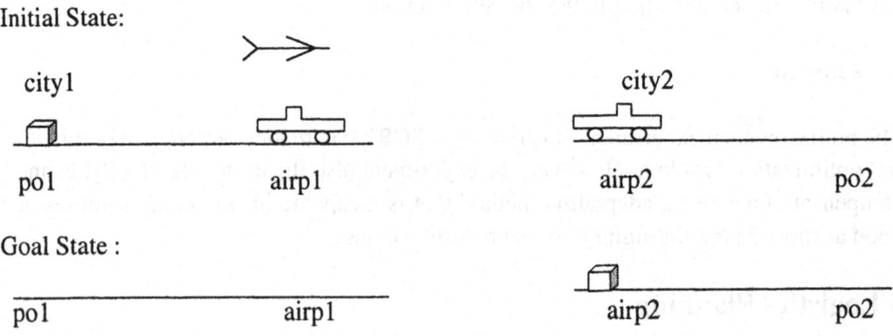

Fig. 3. A Logistics Transportation problem

In STRIPS notation, the problem is as follows:

```
(init
          '((object o1)
          (pos-office po1)
          (pos-office po2)
          (airplane p1)
          (truck t1)
          (truck t2)
          (airport airp1)
          (airport airp2)
          (city c1)
          (city c2)
          (loc-at airp1 c1)
          (loc-at po1 c1)
          (part-of t1 c1)
          (loc-at airp2 c2)
          (loc-at po2 c2)
          (part-of t2 c2)
          (same-city airp1 po1)
          (same-city po1 airp1)
          (same-city airp2 po2)
          (same-city po2 airp2)
          (at-obj o1 po1)
          (at-truck t1 airp1)
          (at-truck t2 airp2)
          (at-airplane p1 airp1)))
(goal '( (at-obj o1 airp2)))
```

One plan for this problem is :

```
          (DRIVE-TRUCK T1 AIRP1 PO1)
          (LOAD-TRUCK O1 T1 PO1)
          (DRIVE-TRUCK T1 PO1 AIRP1)
          (UNLOAD-TRUCK O1 T1 AIRP1)
          (LOAD-AIRPLANE O1 P1 AIRP1)
          (FLY-AIRPLANE P1 AIRP1 AIRP2)
          (UNLOAD-AIRPLANE O1 P1 AIRP2)
```

3.2 Abstraction Hierarchy Creation

ALPINE's problem-independent abstraction hierarchy creating algorithm, described in [14], was applied to various sets of logistics problems. Unfortunately, most resulted in hierarchies with only a single abstraction level. This illustrates a general pitfall of techniques, like SCBR, that used abstraction hierarchies: techniques for automated creation of abstraction hierarchies are still in their infancy. Eventually, however, a set of 9 training cases and 14 testing cases were selected for which ALPINE created a 4-level abstraction hierarchy:

```
(Abstraction
  (Static = loc-at same-city)
  (Level-2 = at-obj
             inside-truck
             inside-airplane)
  (Level-1 = at-airplane)
  (Level-0 = at-truck)
  :order
  (Level-2 > Level-1 Level-0))
```

3.3 Case-Library Creation

Ground level cases for the case library were created using the SPA function *plan-from-scratch*..Abstract cases were then created bottom-up by the following algorithm:

```
Function AbstractCases (initial, goal, levels, hierarchies)
  cases := nil;
  plan := plan-from-scratch (initial, goal);
  case := make-case(initial, goal, plan);
  push(case, cases);
  for i:=1 to levels-1 do
     initial := drop-literals(initial,first(hierarchies));
     goal    := drop-literals(goal,first(hierarchies));
     plan    := fit-plan (initial, goal plan);
     case    := make-case(initial, goal, plan);
     push(case, cases);
     pop(hierarchies);
  Return cases;
```

As in the route-finding domain, logistics cases with initial and goals that are distinct at one level of abstraction may have identical initial and goal states at higher levels of abstraction. The case library may therefore be organized as a forest as described in [4] and illustrated in Figure 4. Note that abstraction is over states, and that abstract plans are formed by adapting lower-level plans to solve the abstract problem.

3.4 Case Retrieval

In SCBR, the retrieval process starts at the most abstraction level of the case library. After the best-matching of the most abstract cases is determined, the matching process is repeated with the children of the best case until the ground level is reached. In this

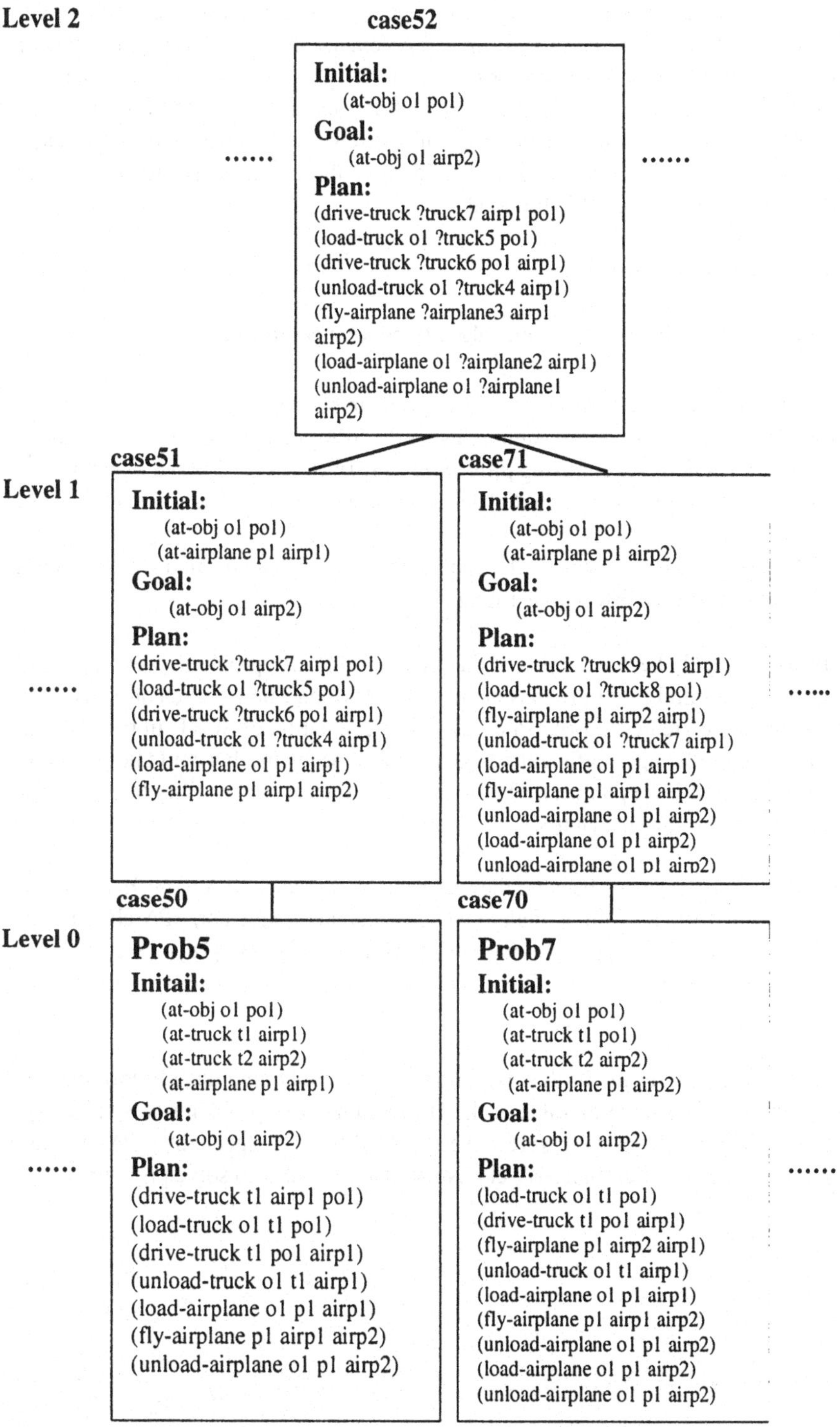

Level 2

case52

Initial:
(at-obj o1 po1)
Goal:
(at-obj o1 airp2)
Plan:
(drive-truck ?truck7 airp1 po1)
(load-truck o1 ?truck5 po1)
(drive-truck ?truck6 po1 airp1)
(unload-truck o1 ?truck4 airp1)
(fly-airplane ?airplane3 airp1 airp2)
(load-airplane o1 ?airplane2 airp1)
(unload-airplane o1 ?airplane1 airp2)

Level 1

case51

Initial:
(at-obj o1 po1)
(at-airplane p1 airp1)
Goal:
(at-obj o1 airp2)
Plan:
(drive-truck ?truck7 airp1 po1)
(load-truck o1 ?truck5 po1)
(drive-truck ?truck6 po1 airp1)
(unload-truck o1 ?truck4 airp1)
(load-airplane o1 p1 airp1)
(fly-airplane p1 airp1 airp2)

case71

Initial:
(at-obj o1 po1)
(at-airplane p1 airp2)
Goal:
(at-obj o1 airp2)
Plan:
(drive-truck ?truck9 po1 airp1)
(load-truck o1 ?truck8 po1)
(fly-airplane p1 airp2 airp1)
(unload-truck o1 ?truck7 airp1)
(load-airplane o1 p1 airp1)
(fly-airplane p1 airp1 airp2)
(unload-airplane o1 p1 airp2)
(load-airplane o1 p1 airp2)
(unload-airplane o1 p1 airp2)

Level 0

case50

Prob5
Initail:
(at-obj o1 po1)
(at-truck t1 airp1)
(at-truck t2 airp2)
(at-airplane p1 airp1)
Goal:
(at-obj o1 airp2)
Plan:
(drive-truck t1 airp1 po1)
(load-truck o1 t1 po1)
(drive-truck t1 po1 airp1)
(unload-truck o1 t1 airp1)
(load-airplane o1 p1 airp1)
(fly-airplane p1 airp1 airp2)
(unload-airplane o1 p1 airp2)

case70

Prob7
Initial:
(at-obj o1 po1)
(at-truck t1 po1)
(at-truck t2 airp2)
(at-airplane p1 airp2)
Goal:
(at-obj o1 airp2)
Plan:
(load-truck o1 t1 po1)
(drive-truck t1 po1 airp1)
(fly-airplane p1 airp2 airp1)
(unload-truck o1 t1 airp1)
(load-airplane o1 p1 airp1)
(fly-airplane p1 airp1 airp2)
(unload-airplane o1 p1 airp2)
(load-airplane o1 p1 airp2)
(unload-airplane o1 p1 airp2)

Fig. 4. Case Library Structure

application of SCBR to planning, the retrieval procedure at a given abstraction level consists of two steps. First, the goals of new problem are matched against the goals of each of the set of cases, and the case or cases with the greatest number of matches are identified. If there are several cases whose goals match equally well, the SPA procedure *fit-plan* is applied to each, and the candidate with the fewest open conditions is chosen as the best. The process is repeated for the children of the current best match until the ground level is reached. See [18] for details.

3.5 Experimental Procedure

In this experiment, 6 different planning algorithms were compared.

- **ALPINE**. ALPINE performs hierarchical problem solving.
- **SPA.** Ground-level, *ab initio* planning using the SPA procedure *plan-from-scratch.*
- **SPA-cbr.** Ground-level cbr using *plan-from-library,* SPA's case-based planner.
- **SPA-cbr-cascading**. SPA-cbr with learning, i.e., each new case is added to the case library.
- **SCBR**. Uses the procedure described above for indexing and *fit-plan* for adaptation
- **SCBR-cascading**. SCBR with learning.

Solvability It quickly became apparent that many of logistics problems were not solvable by all the algorithms within a reasonable time (less than 2 hours) even on a large lisp server (indeed, the greatest barrier to an empirical evaluation of SCBR in this domain was simply accumulating a sufficiently large corpus of problems that could be solved by an *ab initio*, ground-level planner). The first experiment tested the ability of each algorithm to solve the 14 test problems.

The 9 training cases, selected because they could all be solved by SPA *plan-from-scratch* procedure, were given as training data to the CBR planners, SPA-cbr, SPA-cbr-cascading, SCBR, and SCBR-cascading. Fourteen test cases (set forth in [18]) were then presented, in order, to each algorithm. Problems that were not be completed in 2 hours were considered unsolved.

Table 3 sets forth the results of this experiment. Cells containing an 'x' represent unsolved problems. As shown in Table 3, the largest number of problems was solved by SCBR-cascading, and the fewest were solved by ALPINE. Unexpectedly, SPA-cbr-cascading performed no better than SPA-cbr. No method was able to solve problem 8.

Table 3. Problems solvable by each algorithm.

	Alpine	SPA	SPA-cbr	SPA-cbr-cascading	SCBR	SCBR-cascading
Prob1	√	√	√	√	√	√
Prob2	×	√	√	√	√	√
Prob3	√	√	√	√	√	√
Prob4	√	√	√	√	√	√
Prob5	√	√	√	√	√	√
Prob6	×	×	×	×	√	√
Prob7	×	×	√	√	√	√
Prob8	×	×	×	×	×	×
Prob9	√	√	√	√	√	√
Prob10	√	√	√	√	√	√
Prob11	√	√	√	√	√	√
Prob12	×	×	×	×	×	√
Prob13	×	×	×	×	×	√
Prob14	×	×	×	×	×	√

Solution Length The mean solution lengths of the six algorithms for the seven problems that all could solve is set forth in Figure 5. The variation among solution lengths was slight, with the shortest solutions produced by Alpine, SCBR, and SCBR-cascading.

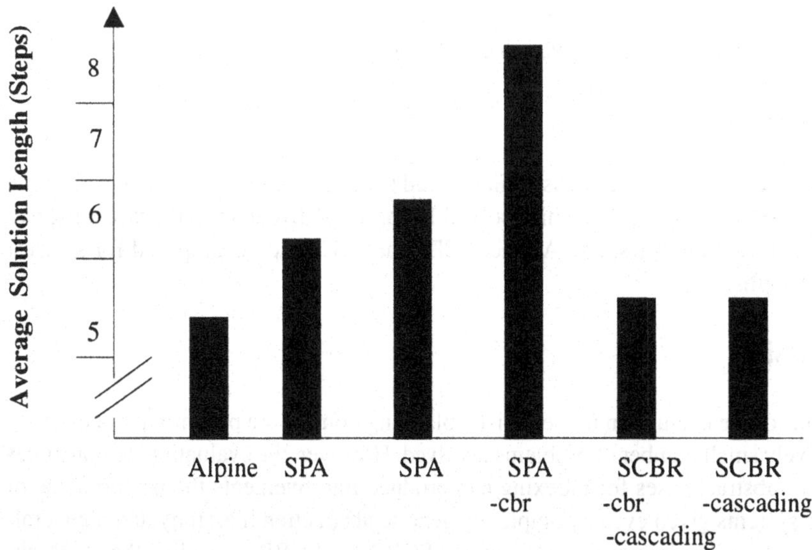

Fig. 5. Average Solution Length for the logistics problems

Execution Time The mean execution times of the six algorithms for the seven problems that all could solve is set forth in Figure 6. Alpine outperforms SPA, SPA-cbr, and SPA-cascading, but the lowest execution times were for SCBR and SCBR-cascading.

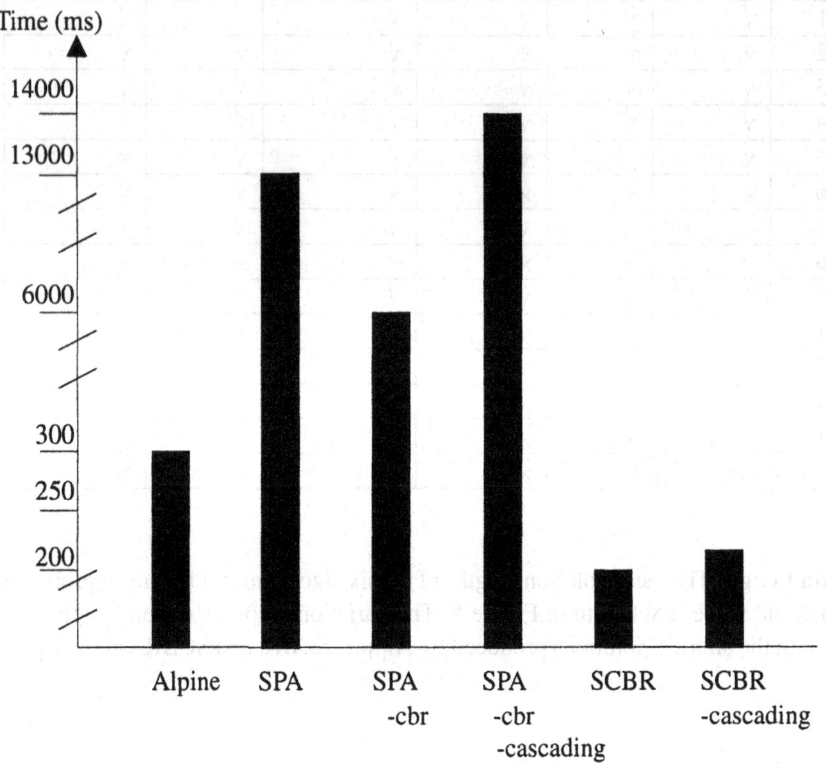

Fig. 6. Mean Execution Time for 7 Planning Problems

3.5 Summary

In the logistics domain, SCBR-cascading solved the largest number of cases—13 of the 14 cases—followed by SCBR, which solved 12 cases. SCBR and SCBR-cascading had the lowest execution times, and Alpine, SCBR, and SCBR-cascading tied for shortest solution lengths.

4 Discussion

The results of the evaluation in the logistic planning domain are preliminary because of the relatively small number of problems involved. However, the evaluation demonstrates that use of abstract cases for indexing can produce improvements the performance of planning systems given even a completely generic abstraction hierarchy and a general-purpose planner. The faster execution time of SCBR and SCBR-cascading than SPA-cbr and SPA-cbr-cascading given identical case libraries and an identical adaptation procedure indicates that SCBR led to retrieval of cases that were less expensive to adapt than the cases retrieved by SPA's ground-level retrieval mechanism.The shorter solution length for SCBR and SCBR-cascading, identical to the solution length for Alpine, also indicates that SCBR retrieved cases that more appropriate for each given problem.

The key distinction between the prefix-reversal task, a domain in which SCBR performed poorly, and the domains in which SCBR performed well, including the route-finding domain [4]and the logistics planning domain, appears to be that the optimal-case utility was high in the latter two problems but low in the prefix-reversal problem. The optimal-case utility was high in the logistics planning domain because the *fit-case* procedure was capable of adapting a case to a high-quality solution even to a very dissimilar problem. This is illustrated by the fact that SCBR-cascading did in fact solve every problem but one using *fit-case* as the adaptation mechanism. SCBR's ability to index the most adaptable case therefore led to greatly improved performance. Similarly, in the route-planning domain [4], the topography of the grids led to a high probability that any two cases would overlap and therefore to a high optimal-case utility. By contrast, cases were very unlikely to overlap in the prefix-reversal problem, and the adaptation mechanism was incapable of adapting arbitrary cases to solutions as good as could be obtained *ab initio*. As a result, the optimal-case utility, and therefore the performance of SCBR as measured by solution quality, was low.

It has been widely recognized that adaptability is a more important criterion for case retrieval than surface similarity to the current problem [17]. Unfortunately, the adaptation costs of a given case cannot, in general, be determined without actually performing the adaptation. However, the cost of adapting an abstraction of a case to an abstraction of the current problem can be a very accurate heuristic for ground-level adaptation costs. The logistics planning experiment demonstrates that SCBR is a general, domain-independent approach to retrieval by adaptation cost. The prefix-reveral experiment indicates, however, that SCBR nevertheless only reduces search cost when the adaptation mechanism and case-library size assures that optimal-case utility is high.

Acknowledgements

This research was supported by NSF Faculty Early Career Development Grant IRI-9502152, a German-American Fulbright Kommission Senior Scholar grant, a Flittie sabbatical grant, and by the University of Kaiserslautern Center for Learning Systems and Applications.

References

1. F. Bacchus and Q. Yang , *Downward Refinement and the Efficiency of Hierarchical Problem Solving*, Artificial Intelligence, 71:43-100, 1996.
2. R. Bergmann and W. Wilke, *On the Role of Abstraction in Case-Based Reasoning,* Advances in Case-Based Reasoning, Third European Workshop, Springer Verlag, 1996.

3. R. Bergmann and W. Wilke, *Building and Refining Abstract Planning Cases by Change of Representation Language,* Journal of Artificial Intelligence Research, 3:53-118, 1996.
4. L. K. Branting & D. W. Aha, *Stratified Case-Based Reasoning: Reusing Hierarchical Problem Solving Episodes,* Proceedings of the Fourteenth International Joint Conference on Artificial Intelligence (IJCAI-95), Montreal, Canada, August, pp. 20 – 25, 1995.
5. L. K. Branting, *Stratified Case-Based Reasoning in Non-Refinable Abstraction Hierarchies,* Proceedings of the Second International Conference on Case-Based Reasoning, Springer, pp. 519-530, July 1997.
6. A. Caprara, *Sorting by Reversals is difficult,* Proceedings of the First Annual International Conference on Computational Molecular Biology, pp. 75-83, January 1997.
7. J. G. Carbonell, C. A. Knoblock, and S. Minton. *Prodigy: An integrated architecture for planning and learning,* In K. Vanlehn, editor, Architectures for Intelligence, Erlbaum, Hillsdale, NJ, 1990.
8. J. Christensen. *A hierarchical planner that generates its own hierarchies.* Proceedings of the Eighth National Conference on Artificial Intelligence, pp.1004-1009, AAAI Press:Boston, MA (1990).
9. W. H. Gates, *Bounds for Sorting by Prefix Reversal,* Discrete Mathematics, 27:47-57 (1979).
10. S. Hanks and D. S. Weld, *A Domain-Independent Algorithm for Plan Adaptation,* Journal of Artificial Intelligence Research 2:319-360, 1995.
11. R. Holte, C. Drummond, M. Perez, R. Zimmer, and A. MacDonald, *Search With Abstractions: A Unifying Framework and New High-Performance Algorithm,* Proceedings of the Tenth Canadian Conference on Artificial Intelligence, Morgan Kaufmann, pp. 263-270 (1994).
12. S. Kambhampti and J. Hendler, *A Validation-Structure-Based Theory of Plan Modification,* Artificial Intelligence 55:193-258, 1992.
13. G.Klein and R. Calderwood, *How do People Use Analogues to Make Decisions?*, Proceedings of the DARPA Workshop on Case-Based Reasoning, Morgan Kaufman Publishers, Inc., 1988.
14. C. A. Knoblock, *Automatically Generating Abstractions for Planning*, Artificial Intelligence 68(2):243-302, 1994.
15. J. Setubal and J. Meidanis, Introduction to Computational Molecular Biology, PWS Publishing Co., 1997.
16. B. Smyth and P. Cunningham, *Deja Vu: A Hierarchical Case-Based Reasoning System for Software Design*, Proceedings of the European Conference on AI, John Wiley, pp. 587-589 (1992)
17. B. Smyth and M. Keane, *Adaptation-Guided Retrieval: Questioning the Similarity Assumption in Reasoning,* Artificial Intelligence (in press) 1999.
18. Y. Tao, *A Multiple-Domain Evaluation of Stratified Case-Based Reasoning*, M.S. Thesis, Department of Computer Science, University of Wyoming, August, 1998.

Bootstrapping Case Base Development with Annotated Case Summaries*

Stefanie Brüninghaus and Kevin D. Ashley

University of Pittsburgh
Learning Research and Development Center, Intelligent Systems Program, and School of Law
3939 O'Hara Street, Pittsburgh, PA 15260
steffi+@pitt.edu, ashley+@pitt.edu

Abstract. Since assigning indicies to textual cases is very time-consuming and can impede the development of CBR systems, methods to automate the task are desirable. In this paper, we present a machine learning approach that helps to bootstrap the development of a larger case base from a small collection of marked-up case summaries. It uses the marked-up sentences as training examples to induce a classifier that labels incoming cases whether an indexing concept applies. We illustrate how domain knowledge and linguistic information can be integrated with a machine learning algorithm to improve performance. The paper presents experimental results which indicate the usefulness of learning from sentences and adding a thesaurus. We also consider the chances and limitations of leveraging the learned classifiers for full-text documents.

1 CBR in Domains where Cases are Texts

Over the last years, a number of CBR systems have been developed for domains where the cases are available as unstructured or semi-structured text documents. Examples of such domains are the law (Ashley & Aleven 1997; Branting 1991; Rissland, Skalak, & Friedman 1993), business problems (Baudin & Waterman 1998) and in particular the fast growing area of helpdesk systems (Lenz 1998; Aha, Maney, & Breslow 1998; Racine & Yang 1997).

Where the task is merely to find the most similar textual cases related to a user's situation, CBR techniques in combination with Information Retrieval (IR) can be used directly to retrieve textual cases. These case-based retrieval models have been applied successfully in systems like FAQ-Finder (Burke et al. 1997) or FaLLQ (Lenz 1998). In many other applications, however, where more advanced CBR is carried out, it is necessary to map the unstructured textual case to a structured, symbolic representation, with which the CBR system can perform its reasoning (Ashley & Brüninghaus 1998).

When the CBR system involves a symbolic comparison of cases or requires the adaptation of cases, the extra effort of indexing the raw cases has to be made. As yet, this has been an almost exclusively manual chore. Having experts manually index texts and represent cases, however, can be prohibitively expensive and time-consuming (Racine &

* This research has been supported by the National Science Foundation, under Grant IRI96-19713. We thank West Group and in particular Peter Jackson for making the WestLaw Thesaurus accessible to us.

Yang 1997; Daniels & Rissland 1997). Such costs may even prevent the development or maintenance of CBR systems. Methods to facilitate indexing or representing cases automatically are desirable.

A promising approach is to start with a small collection of manually indexed cases, and employ these examples to automatically assign indices to new, unseen cases. Previously, we introduced a classification-oriented approach to building a case base from a small set of examples (Brüninghaus & Ashley 1997). Our success, however, was hampered by the fact that most learning algorithms designed for classifying texts are of limited use for small collections.

In this paper, we discuss recent progress toward bootstrapping the development of a larger case base by using a small collection of manually-indexed case summaries. We found that case summaries can be annotated with little extra cost while the initial case base is being constructed. In this way, a collection of short sentences or paragraphs related to the indices in a CBR system can be more easily acquired. These sentences are significantly less complicated than the full documents and can be used as examples for a symbolic tree-learning algorithm. This also allows us to add domain knowledge and linguistic information, and to employ a more powerful representation.

In the remainder of this paper, we first introduce our application, case-based legal argumentation. We show an example of an indexing concept and illustrate why it is difficult to assign it to documents automatically. We then consider problems with widely used text classification methods, and how these problems are addressed by our system SMILE[2]. We discuss its design and demonstrate the learning techniques we use. After reporting a recent experiment, we consider the chances and limitations of further leveraging the learned classifiers. The paper concludes after discussing related work.

2 A Typical CBR Application Involving Cases As Texts: CATO

The law is a domain where CBR has been applied successfully (Ashley & Aleven 1997; Branting 1991; Rissland, Skalak, & Friedman 1993), and where the cases are texts. Our CATO system is an instructional environment for teaching argumentation skills to law students (Aleven 1997), based on a model of case-based argumentation. When trying to convince a court to rule in favor of or against a party's claim, legal advocates compare the problem scenario to previously decided cases. They analogize the problem to favorable cases and distinguish it from unfavorable ones. In doing so, they often compare and contrast cases in terms of prototypical fact patterns, which tend to strengthen or weaken a party's claim. A model of this reasoning has been implemented in CATO. The system deals with claims for trade secret misappropriation, in which a plaintiff complains that the defendant has used its confidential product information to gain an unfair competitive advantage. CATO employs a set of 26 such abstract fact patterns, or *factors*, to compare and contrast cases by means of eight basic argument moves with which it composes arguments how to decide the problem scenario. A hierarchy of legal issues and their interrelations enables CATO to reason with partially matched cases and make arguments about the significance of distinctions (Ashley & Aleven 1997). CATO has a Case Database of 147 cases. For each of these cases, we have (1) a symbolic factor representation, (2) a squib, or short summary of the facts, and (3) the full-text opinion, in

[2] SMart Index LEarner

which the court announces its decision and reasoning.

Each of CATO's factors is an indexing concept and may guide comparisons among cases to which it applies. In trade secret law, for instance, the allegedly misappropriated product information must meet certain criteria to be protectable as a trade secret. If a similar product is available from other manufacturers, the information may be generally available and not be protected against use by competitors. In CATO this fact pattern is represented by a factor favoring plaintiff, F15, Unique-Product, defined as follows:

> *Plaintiff was the only manufacturer making the product. This factor shows that the information apparently was not known or available outside plaintiff's business. Also, it shows that plaintiff's information was valuable for plaintiff's business.*

As an empirical matter, we have found that the evidence for a factor is typically encountered in a few clumps in the case texts, in the form of sentences or short passages. Some examples of sentences from cases in CATO's Case Database which indicate that factor F15 applies are:

- Innovative introduced evidence that Panl Brick was a unique product in the industry. (from *Innovative v. Bowen*)
- It has a unique design in that it has a single pole that a hunter can climb instead of having to climb the tree. (from *Phillips v. Frey*)
- Several features of the process were entirely unique in transistor manufacturing. (from *Sperry Rand v. Rothlein*)
- The information in the diagram was not generally known to the public nor to any of Tri-Tron's competitors. (from *Tri-Tron v. Velto*)
- It appears that one could not order a Lynchburg Lemonade in any establishment other than that of the plaintiff. (from *Mason v. Jack Daniel Distillery*)

As the example sentences suggest, inferring from the text of a case that factor F15 applies is relatively straightforward for a human. As already noted, like other factors, the evidence for factor F15, Unique-Product, is concentrated in a few such sentences. Also, there tend to be only a fairly small number of ways in which courts describe the factual situations related to this factor. In other words, the sentences relevant to F15 follow a small number of patterns, focus on a limited set of issues and use similar wording. (There can be exceptions, however.) Generally, when indexing new cases, experts can identify without much difficulty the passages and sentences that pertain to the factor. In fact, when they read the case, they may simply underline the sentences in the text relevant for the factor.

It can be more difficult to infer from a text that other factors apply, such as F6, Security-Measures. In general, a plaintiff's claim is strengthened to the extent that it takes measures to maintain the security of its secrets. There are, however, many things a plaintiff can do (e.g., lock up the secret, obtain nondisclosure agreements from its employees, prohibit visitors from seeing a process, encode the secret.) The case texts display a much wider variety of different patterns of descriptions from which it may be inferred that F6, Security-Measures, applies.

Even for factors that are easier to infer such as F15, Unique-Product, one still needs some linguistic information. In legal texts, as in texts generally, the negation or restriction of statements is very important. In the sample sentence drawn from the *Mason* case, for example, the negation of "order" is crucial: "It appears that one could not order a Lynchburg Lemonade in any establishment other than that of the plaintiff." If one could order the product somewhere else, it would not be unique, after all! An ability to recognize phrases, like "agreed not to disclose", would also be useful. While the words taken separately are not very predictive for a factor, the combination corresponds to an important concept in trade secret law.

3 Previous Experiments

As noted, at the last ICCBR, we presented a classification-based approach to assigning factors to new cases (Brüninghaus & Ashley 1997). We considered each of CATO's factors as a concept, where the cases in CATO's Case Database were the positive and negative training examples, depending on whether the factor applied or not. In an experiment, we used statistical learning algorithms to induce a classifier for each factor. For most factors, however, the classifiers could not discriminate between positive and negative examples of a factor.

While the statistical text learning methods work very well for simpler concepts, and where the collections are large, assigning indices for CBR is a more difficult problem. As discussed in the previous section, like CBR indices in other applications, CATO's factors are rather complex and abstract concepts. In addition, CATO's database yields a relatively small number of manually-indexed cases for the training set, about 150 documents. Despite the small number of training instances, the vocabulary in the cases is very large. This makes it difficult to apply advanced statistical learning methods which tend to require large numbers of examples to learn text classifiers, usually in the magnitude of thousands of documents.

The complexity of the documents also makes our problem harder than indexing cases in many other domains. Legal opinions are notoriously long and difficult texts. They are usually between two and twenty pages long. The prose style is often dense, and many terms have a specific meaning in a legal context. Frequently, only part of the text deals with the substantive trade secret claim. The court may also discuss jurisdictional and procedural issues or even other claims.

The representations employed in statistical methods for text learning are not powerful enough for indexing such documents. Typically, the statistical methods rely on a bag-of-words model, where a document is represented as a vector of weights over the content words. Stopwords are removed, and all information like word order is discarded. To decide whether a factor is present in a case, however, negation and other linguistic information can be very important. (See Section 2.) Likewise, the bag-of-words representation does not facilitate inclusion of any domain knowledge, for example, to overcome the problems of synonymity.

After analyzing the results in more detail, we decided to take a different approach, which we implemented in SMILE. It takes a set of marked-up sentences from case summaries instead of entire documents as examples, uses a decision tree algorithm to learn rules, and adds domain knowledge in the form of a thesaurus to the induction process.

Since the evidence for a factor can be found within a few sentences in an opinion, it can be better captured by a small set of short rules induced from the relevant portions of the training texts.

3.1 Focus on Smaller Units of Information

Compared to running learning algorithms with full-text documents, employing sentences as examples has three major advantages:

1. It allows focussing on smaller and more relevant examples, namely the marked-up sentences or passages pertaining to a factor. This requires one to tag the sentences referring to a factor manually. The marked-up sentences will, in effect, become the training examples for the learning algorithm. Although it is a manual process, this step adds little work for an expert indexing the cases.
2. The use of marked-up sentences instead of the complete opinions as training examples offers computational advantages. We decided to use a decision tree induction algorithm, which gets hopelessly bogged down by large numbers of attributes. Reducing the complexity of the examples also allows us to add knowledge from performing natural language processing (e.g., parsing which becomes impractical for the full-text opinions.)
3. Learning from marked-up sentences facilitates including domain knowledge, in the form of a domain-specific thesaurus. If the examples are sentences, the knowledge contained in a thesaurus can be better applied at the relevant points.

3.2 Using a Decision Tree Induction Algorithm

As argued above, the evidence for assigning an indexing concept to a case can often be found in a few sentences. Within these sentences, judges tend to use a limited set of phrases and expressions to indicate the presence of a factor. These patterns are best captured by individual rules, like those implicit in the trees learned by a decision tree algorithm. Figure 1 shows how this is reflected in an excerpt from a decision tree learned in the experiments reported in Section 5. The factor F16, Info-Reverse-Engineerable, applies if plaintiff's information could be ascertained by reverse engineering, that is, by inspecting or analyzing the product. The expressions "reverse engineerable", "easily duplicate the information" and "revealed upon inspection" are characteristic for this factor and can be easily found as alternative paths in the tree.

This intuition is supported further if one considers the relation between the instance space in which the examples are represented and nature of the the factors (Aha, Kibler, & Goldstone 1991; Quinlan 1993). The factors comprise a (small number of) different real-world situations. They are not simple, linearly seperable concepts in the instance space. Linear classifiers, which employ a hyperplane to discriminate between positive and negative instances, are ill-suited for the task, as our previous experiments indicate. It is more appropriate to use a learning method (like a decision-tree algorithm) that splits the instance space into multiple class regions, which correspond to the different situations and are defined by the presence/absence of words and phrases in the examples.

3.3 Integrating an Application-Specific Thesaurus

A charateristic of legal texts is the use of different terms that refer to the same concept. A learning algorithm by itself can not cope with this synonymity. For instance, it can-

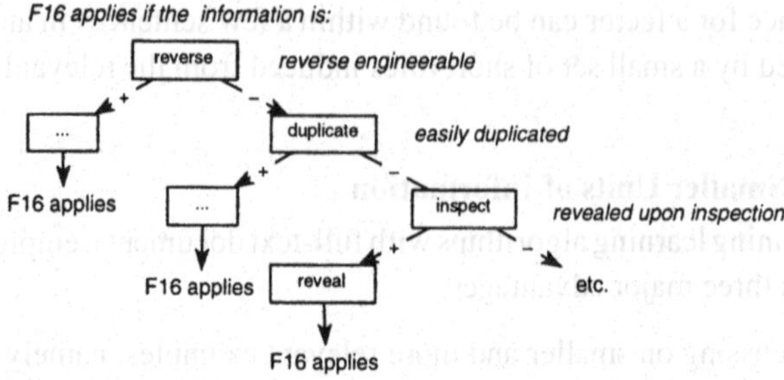

Fig. 1. Rules implicit in a decision tree and the corrspondingtext patterns

not infer that "covenant" is another word for "contract." This is likely to decrease the performance, in particular when the number of training instances is not very large.

Attorneys often use legal thesauri (Statski 1985), which list synonyms and sometimes definitions for terms used in legal documents. (In other domains, similar thesauri and glossaries exist.) Usually, legal thesauri are not available online. For our experiments, we were fortunate to have access to the thesaurus used internally by West Group, one of the largest legal publishers. It comprises about 20,000 sets of synonyms. Each word belongs to between one and six synonym sets. Examples relevant to trade secret law are:

- clandestine concealed disguised hidden secret undisclosed unrevealed
- commodity goods inventory material merchandise product stock supplies
- admission disclosure discovery revelation

4 How SMILE Works

In this section, we show (simplified) examples of how our program works with training instances that are sentences, and illustrate how domain knowledge and linguistic information can be integrated.

4.1 Example Sentences in Case Texts

For the experiments reported here, we marked up the summaries of CATO's cases. An example is the *Forest Laboratories* case[3], which has the factors F1, Disclosure-In-Negotiations, F6, Security-Measures, F15, Unique-Product, and F21, Knew-Info-Confidential. This shows a short section of its squib:

> [f15 Plaintiff's packaging process involved various "tempering steps" that were not used by competitors or described in the literature. f15][f6 Only a handful of plaintiff's employees knew of the packaging operations, and they were all bound by secrecy agreements. f6][f6 There was also testimony that packaging information was closely guarded in the trade. f6]
>
> ... [f1 Plaintiff's president sent a letter to defendant which conveyed plaintiff's manufacturing formula. f1][f21 The letter also stated that the disclosure was made in confidence and that "we agree with you that details on packaging, etc. should be taken up later". f21] ...

[3] *Forest Laboratories, Inc. v. Formulations, Inc.*, 299 F.Supp. 202 (E.D.Wis.1969)

For our classification approach, the bracketed sentences are positive instances for the respective factor; all other sentences are negative instances. A factor can be considered to apply to a case if at least one of the sentences is a positive example for the factor.

For the first experiments, the cases were treated as binary attribute vectors, although we are currently working on improving this representation. We removed all stopwords, and removed the most common endings, like plural-s. The sentence indicating F1 would be internally represented as: (plaintiff president send letter convey manufacture formula).

4.2 Decision Tree Induction

We implemented the basic ID3 algorithm (Mitchell 1997), currently without methods for pruning the trees. We selected this methods because it seems to correspond best to out ideas. However, there is no reason why other learning algorithms could not be used. In particular inductive logic programming may prove useful for the integration of linguistic information.

First, let us consider a simple example. Ideally, judges would describe the facts of a case in simple and straightforward phrases. They would always use the same words or expressions, never use negation, etc. Then the positive (+) and negative (–) instances given to a classifier might look like this[4]:

+ The product was unique.
– His product was identical to plaintiff's.
– The recipe was always locked in a unique safe.
– Plaintiff employed unique security measures.

In inducing the tree, the algorithm recursively selects the attribute that best discriminates between positive and negative examples and splits up the training set, according to whether this attribute applies. The process is repeated until it has a set of only positive or negative examples. Here, ID3 would first split up the examples into those that have the word "product", and those that do not. It would then try to find a way to distinguish between the first and the second example, and select the word "unique". The corresponding decision tree is shown in Figure 2.

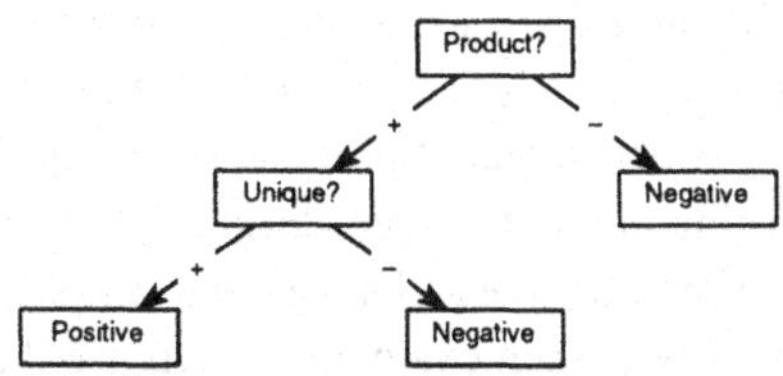

Fig. 2. Decision tree for F15, Unique-Product

Of course, judges do not restrict their factual descriptions in this way. In the next section we discuss how adding knowledge from a legal thesaurus and adding linguistic

[4] To make the examples easier to understand, we show the full text.

knowledge may help, when dealing with the far more complex language found in legal case opinions.

4.3 Adding a Thesaurus

A well-known problem with ID3 is its tendency to overfit the data. In particular with many attributes available, the algorithm learns overly specific trees, which often misclassify new examples. The knowledge in a thesaurus can help to overcome that problem. All words in a synonym group can function like a single attribute, which applies to more cases. This can lead to simpler, less overfitted trees. To illustrate our intuitions about adding a thesaurus, assume that we have the following examples of some concept:

+ He signed the contract.	– He signed the postcard.
+ He signed the covenant.	– He signed the book.

Half of the examples is positive, half negative. No (single) term can discriminate between positive and negative examples. A decision tree algorithm would create a tree as in Figure 3, branching out too much. The knowledge to recognize that covenant and contract are synonyms is missing, and there is no reliable way to make that inference. With the help of a thesaurus, however, it is possible to induce a better tree.

There are two ways to include the information of a thesaurus.

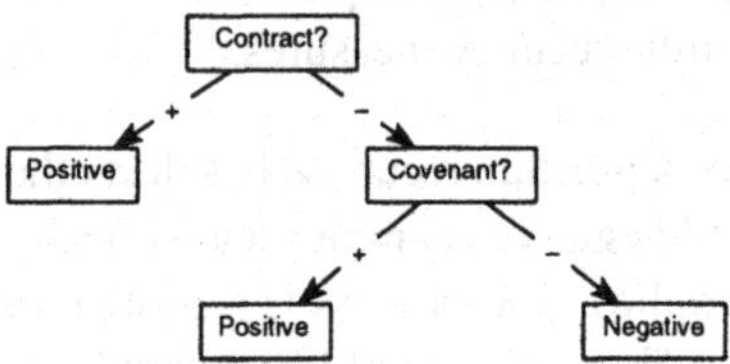

Fig. 3. Decision tree learned without adding a thesaurus

A thesaurus can be used to discover synonyms while inducing a decision tree. Instead of learning a tree where the nodes are words, we can learn a tree where the nodes are categories from the thesaurus. The relevant category in the WestLaw Thesaurus for this example is: · agreement contract covenant promise testament

If we modify the learning algorithm accordingly, ID3 will choose this category to perfectly discriminate between positive and negative examples, shown in Figure 4. This tree will also correctly classify unseen examples which use the term agreement instead of contract or covenant.

Alternatively, one can use a thesaurus to expand examples in advance, by adding all possible synonyms before the learning algorithm is applied. Our positive examples would then appear like:

+ He signed the contract. + agreement covenant promise testament
+ He signed the covenant. + agreement contract promise testament

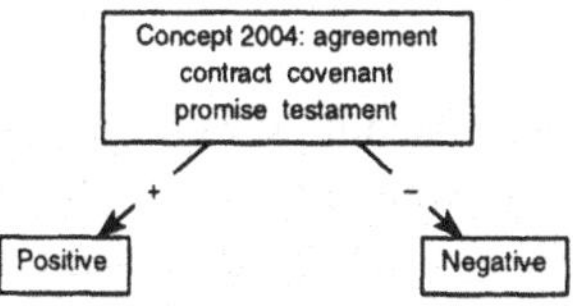

Fig. 4. Decision tree learned with synonym information

A tree can then be learned easily for the example sentences by choosing either the term "covenant" or "contract" to distinguish between positive and negative examples. This also results in a simpler tree, and thereby can help to avoid overfitting.

4.4 Proposed Use of Linguistic Information

The most promising way to include linguistic information about the relation of words in sentences, or about the role of expressions, may be to integrate a parser into the learning system. The version of SMILE evaluated in this paper did not include this linguistic information. Nevertheless, this is a convenient place to dicuss our design for integrating a parser. Assume we have the examples:

+ No other manufacturer made filled chocolate.
– The manufacturer made hunter stands.

The only reliable way to discriminate between the two examples is to include as an attribute the fact that in the positive instance "manufacturer" is modified by "no other". (The terms "filled chocolate" and "hunter stand" are very rare, they would be pruned away from the examples' representation.)

The attribute can be found by parsing the sentence (e.g., using CMU's Link Parser, available from http://www.link.cs.cmu.edu) The output for the positive instance in the example above would be:

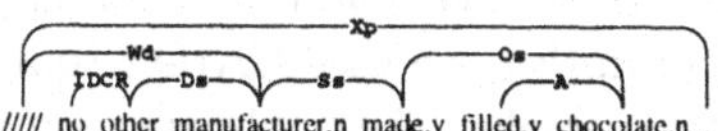

From this parser output, various information can be derived. The subject, object and verb of the sentence are identified, the words' part-of-speech is tagged, and, most interesting for the task at hand, the combination no-other is labeled as determiner of a noun (Ds), and as an idiomatic string stored in the dictionary (IDC).

Similarly, information about phrases, or the role of attributes in the sentence can be derived and used in learning a decision tree. For instance, the phrase "filled chocolate" is indicated by an adjective link (A) between "filled" and "chocolate". As noted above, we have not currently integrated this information in SMILE, but we are in the process of doing so.

5 Experiment

In a simplified environment, we tested how well our approach works with the ID3 algorithm. Our goal was to find out whether using sentences instead of full-text opinions would be useful, and whether there would be any benefit from adding a thesaurus. For the time being, we did not investigate in what ways the representation could be improved, for example, by including linguistic knowledge. That will be the next phase of our experimentation.

The experiments were run as a stratified 5-fold cross validation. We used a separate random partitioning of the positive and negative examples, because the distribution is very skewed. At the same time, we have a rather small number of examples. By keeping the ratio constant, we tried to prevent outliers in the test sets, which can decrease the experiments' validity.

5.1 Experimental Setup and Assumptions

For this experiment, we used a subset of CATO's factors:

- F1, Disclosure-In-Negotiations
- F6, Security-Measures
- F15, Unique-Product
- F16, Info-Reverse-Engineerable
- F18, Identical-Products, and
- F21, Knew-Info-Confidential.

We have selected these factors because we anticipated that they would provide a range of difficulty for the learning algorithm. We expected F15, Unique-Product, to be found much more easily than F6, Security-Measures. Courts employ a small set of patterns and some standard phrasing in discussing a product's uniqueness. By contrast, the squibs identify a very wide variety of different fact situations from which it may be inferred that F6 applies. There are many things a plaintiff can do to maintain the secrecy of its information (e.g., lock up the secret, obtain nondisclosure agreements from its employees, prohibit visitors from seeing a process.)

It is important to note that we have omitted some of CATO's factors which we believe would be even harder to learn from examples than F6. F5, Agreement-Not-Specific, for instance, is often difficult for a human to discover, and asserting its presence requires more abstract inferences. Probably only very advanced natural language understanding would be appropriate. Also, CATO's Case Database contains only five cases in which this factor applies, so it is not a good candidate to show the applicability of a new method.

To simplify the problem further, we used CATO's squibs, rather than the full-text opinions as training and test examples. The squibs are short summaries, about one page of text, whose primary function is to restate the case facts. The drafters of the squibs had CATO's factors squarely in mind in preparing the summaries of the case facts. Thus, finding factors in the squibs is a much easier problem than finding factors in the full-text opinions. We adopted this simplification, however, to get a set of consistently marked-up examples, to avoid having the learning algorithm get bogged down computationally, and to satisfy our curiosity as to whether the method would work with the shorter documents before we undertook to scale up to the more complex opinions. In Section 6, we discuss how this can be leveraged to full-text opinions.

On a practical note, using manually prepared case summaries may appear like a contradiction of the goal of reducing indexing cost. The major problem, however, is that indexing requires an extremely well-trained expert who knows the area of the law as well as the indexing concepts, or factors. On the other hand, it appears to be fairly easy for untrained law students to summarize cases. Even with little knowledge of the specific legal application, they can identify the pertinent facts and at low cost write a squib that's helps an expert to mark up a case.

5.2 Results

We were interested in assessing the effect of two techniques, namely using marked up sentences instead of the full documents to discover the factors, and adding a domain specific thesaurus. The results of the experiments suggest that both are beneficial.

As shown in Table 1, the decision tree algorithm achieved precision and recall of up to 80 % for finding which factor applies to a case.

	f15	f21	f1	f6	f16	f18
Precision	48.78%	32.14%	30.00%	80.55%	44.44%	58.97%
Recall	71.42%	50.00%	60.00%	81.69%	54.54%	63.88%

Table 1. Precision and recall for finding factors in cases

Although these results are positive, there is still room to improve precision and recall. As we pointed out before, the experiments did not include any linguistic knolwedge. In particular, negation was not represented. In Section 2, however, we showed examples why this is necessary for some of the factors.

In order to get a baseline for comparison, we used CATO's factor names, which are intended to capture the meaning of the respective factor. These names were derived from the relevant legal authorities and contain the terms most widely used by judges, attorneys and lawmakers. A human expert will most likely use the factor name as a query, when searching for cases with that factor in an information retrieval system. The results in Table 2 indicate that the factor names are too restrictive, they capture too few real situations, which can be overcome by a machine learning approach.

		F15	F21	F1	F6	F16	F18
ID3 - for sentences	Recall	43.75%	30.30%	5.88%	45.30%	31.03%	34.04%
	Precision	50.00%	50.00%	10.34%	55.03%	45.00%	51.61%
Words from name	Recall	4.17%	6.06%	2.00%	2.79%	20.69%	4.26%
	Precision	100%	40.00%	33.33%	71.43%	60.00%	66.67%

Table 2. Precision and recall for finding whether a sentence indicates a factor

Even more interesting, adding a thesaurus helps when classifying sentences under factors, but the usefulness depends on the factor. In Figure 5, we show the relative improvement of using the thesaurus both during (solid color) and before learning (striped) when compared to the unaided decision tree algorithm. We calculated the difference in precision between the learner that used the thesaurus and the one that did not, and divided by the precision for the plain learning algorithm. The result is the relative change in precision, and allows us to compare the effects across factors. We did the same for accuracy, and for both ways of integrating the thesaurus.

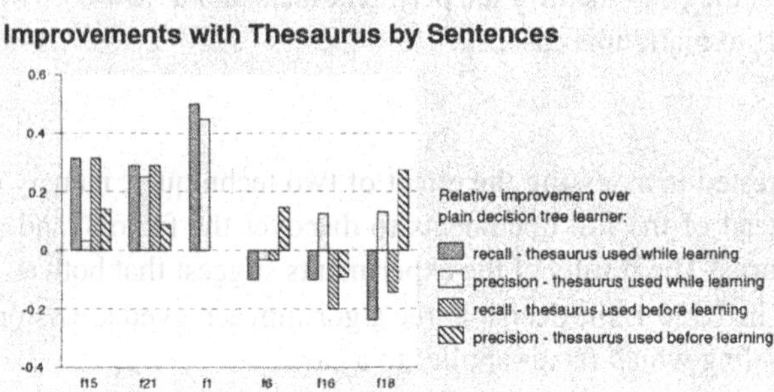

Fig. 5. Relative improvements of precision and recall by adding the thesaurus

The graph indicates, that for factors F15, Unique-Product, and F21, Knew-Info-Confidential, adding the thesaurus clearly improves performance. This confirms our intuitions, see Section 4.3. For F1, Disclosure-In-Negotiations, adding the thesaurus during learning is useful, and adding it before learning is without effect. For F16, Info-Reverse-Engineerable, and F18, Identical-Products, adding the thesaurus increases precision, and decreases recall. It seems that the thesaurus makes the algorithm more "conservative" in discovering positive instances. We will have to study the learned decision trees and misclassifed examples in more detail, before we can really understand the reasons. The thesaurus is also not useful for factor F6, Security-Measures, which could have been expected. In a commercial context, there is a wide variety of measures to keep information secret. They are often very practical matters not related to legal concepts. For those examples, a thesaurus of legal terms is unlikely to show much effect.

In sum, we have found that using a decision tree induction algorithm for marked-up sentences as examples is clearly the right approach to take. It reduces complexity, and yet the individual sentences contain enough information to be useful as examples of the factors. By contrast, in our previous experiments where we attempted to learn factors from full-text opinions, the statistical learning methods could only learn the goal concepts to a much more limited degree. Most of the time the classifiers could not discover the positive instances, which led to low precision and recall.

6 How can this be leveraged?

One of the simplifications in our experiments was the use of CATO's squibs, rather than the full-text opinions. This allowed us to mark up the collection of squibs for the reported experiment, and also greatly reduced the computational complexity of the learning process. The experiments would have been prohibitively time-consuming otherwise - in terms of both human labor and required CPU time. For the cases included in this experiment, we have 2200 sentences in the squibs, with an average length of 7.5 words (after removing stopwords, very infrequent terms and duplicates). The corresponding full-text opinions comprise 28,000 sentences, with an average length of 11.5 words.

However, our ultimate goal is to assign factors to the full-text opinions. We wanted to find out whether the classifiers learned over the squibs would be applicable for this task. Since we do not have the full-text opinions marked up like the squibs, we will focus on an informal discussion of the results for the factors with the best and worst results.

Generally, we found that the usefulness of the decision trees learned from summaries depends very much on the nature of the factor. For factors like F15, Unique-Product, which represent rather well-defined and uniform situations, the classifiers learned from the example sentences in the squibs worked well for opinions. As we expected, the classification rules did not work as well for factors that are more abstract and comprise a wide variety of real-world situations, like factor F6, Security-Measures.

Even though we did not include any linguistic information, the algorithm assigned F15 to the full text-opinions with recall of 75 % and accuracy of 45 %. When we analyzed the cases flagged as false positives, we found many instances like "Defendant's expert stated that the use of this process was indeed known in the industry, although [it] was not specifically discussed in any industry literature," which is an explicit statement that F15 does not apply. Even though this is an incorrectly classified sentence, we think the classifier has worked here as well as we would like. As discussed above, we anticipate that such false positive instances can be filtered out by integrating linguistic knowledge.

The classification rules did not perform as well for factor F6. This factor captures a wide variety of measures, from requiring employees to sign non-disclosure agreements, to locking away recipes. The learned decision trees tend to include the predictive words to cover each of these situations, and hence falsely label many sentences as positive instances of F6.

To our surprise, we also found that the system had spotted instances of F6 in virtually every case opinion. We looked more closely at the sentences classified under F6 and the decision tree's rules. From a few positive examples for F6 that read "... were not allowed to see ...", ID3 had induced a rule to classify sentences with the word "see" as positive instances of F6. In legal opinion texts, however, "see *case-name*" is used very frequently and signals a citation. Conceivably, domain-specific problems like this can be overcome by adding background knowledge to the representation to filter out citations. Another source for false positive classifications were citations of statutes (e.g., " the extent of measures taken by him to guard the secrecy of the information"). This could also be avoided by filtering out these statutory citations.

7 Related work

Overcoming the "knowledge-engineering bottleneck" of indexing textual cases for CBR is an important issue for many applications. There have been a number of approaches for applying CBR in domains where the cases are available as text.

The approach most similar to our work is SPIRE (Daniels & Rissland 1997). Its goal is to facilitate the indexing of legal documents for HYPO-style CBR. For each slot in SPIRE's frame-based case representation, the system has a small library of passages. When a new case text is to be indexed, an IR relevance-feedback module uses these "examples" to retrieve the most promising sections within the new document. Obviously, SPIRE is very similar to our approach. The application is the same, and like SMILE,

SPIRE uses a collection of previously indexed cases (or passages) to facilitate future case indexing. In fact, the results reported in (Daniels & Rissland 1997) encouraged us to pursue our idea to focus on sentences. However, SPIRE harnesses existing tools, and does not harness any additional domain knowledge. While SPIRE's intuitive appeal and simplicity are clearly strengths, it cannot deal, for example, with negation or synonymity. Probably, SPIRE's approach would not work for indexing concepts that are more abstract than the frame-slots it fills, like our factors (especially F6) or where an indexing concept is associated with a number of different fact patterns, like F16 (see Figure 1). SMILE attempts to overcome these problems by integrating domain and linguistic knowledge.

The Indexing Assistant (Baudin & Waterman 1998) helps humans index business reengineering cases. Previous cases are classified under a business taxonomy, so that experience can be reused in similar situations. While the system also takes a text-classification approach, it does not attempt to include any further knowledge, and treats the entire documents as one piece.

The research on conversational CBR further supports our underlying intuition to focus on sentences as instances. In NaCoDAE (Aha, Maney, & Breslow 1998), cases are represented by sets of question/answer pairs and short case summaries, which resemble our marked-up cases. This case structure may be used to assign indices automatically.

FAQ-Finder (Burke et al. 1997) (and its successors) uses an integrated CBR/IR approach to retrieve FAQ-sections related to a user's questions. The system employs additional knowledge in the form of a domain-independent conceptual dictionary, but does not have a deep representation of the user's questions or the documents. Similarly, the FaLLQ system (Lenz 1998) takes a case-based approach to retrieve previous problem solving descriptions. Starting with basic IR techniques, the system integrates different knowledge-levels and uses a case-based approach to define similarity between documents. Unlike our work, neither approach derives a symbolic case representation, and both focus on case-based retrieval of text. Case Advisor (Racine & Yang 1997) uses statistical and IR measures and identifies keywords to index technical problem solving episodes for future retrieval, but it also does not rely on deeper indexing terms, like CATO's factors.

8 Conclusion

We have presented SMILE, an approach to bootstrapping the development and maintenance of case bases in domains where the cases are texts. SMILE uses sentences from a small marked-up collection of case summaries as examples for a machine learning algorithm. Based on our experiments, we think that using case summaries to facilitate the development of case bases in textual domains is a promising approach. The results also indicate that it can be beneficial to apply domain knowledge in the form of a thesaurus. The usefulness of these techniques depends on the nature of indexing concepts. For some of these concepts, the classifiers learned from sentences in case summaries can be leveraged for the full-length documents.

We have also discussed ways to improve the representation from a simple bag-of-words model by adding linguistic information. Together with including further domain knowledge, this will be the focus of our ongoing research.

References

Aha, D., Kibler, D., and Goldstone, R. 1991. Instance-based Learning Algorithms. *Machine Learning* 6:37–66.

Aha, D., Maney, T., and Breslow, L. 1998. Supporting Conversational Case-Based Reasoning in an Integrated Reasoning Framework. In *Proceedings of the AAAI-98 Workshop on Case-Based Reasoning Integrations.*

Aleven, V. 1997. *Teaching Case-Based Argumentation through a Model and Examples.* Ph.D. Dissertation, University of Pittsburgh.

Ashley, K., and Aleven, V. 1997. Reasoning Symbolically about Partially Matched Cases. In *Proceedings of the 15th International Joint Conference on Artificial Intelligence.*

Ashley, K., and Brüninghaus, S. 1998. Developing Mapping and Evaluation Techniques for Textual CBR. In *Proceedings of the AAAI-98 Workshop on Textual Case-Based Reasoning.*

Baudin, C., and Waterman, S. 1998. From Text to Cases: Machine Aided Text Categorization for Capturing Business Reengineering Cases. In *Proceedings of the AAAI-98 Workshop on Textual Case-Based Reasoning.*

Branting, K. 1991. Building Explanations from Rules and Structured Cases. *International Journal on Man-Machine Studies* 34(6).

Brüninghaus, S., and Ashley, K. 1997. Using Machine Learning for Assigning Indices to Textual Cases. In *Proceedings of the 2nd International Conference on Case-Based Reasoning.*

Burke, R., Hammond, K., Kulykin, V., Lytinen, S., Tomuro, N. and Schoenberg, S. 1997. Question-Answering from Frequently-Asked Question Files: Experiences with the FAQ-Finder System. *AI Magazine* 18(1).

Daniels, J., and Rissland, E. 1997. What you saw is what you want: Using cases to seed information retrieval. In *Proceedings of the 2nd International Conference on Case-Based Reasoning.*

Lenz, M. 1998. Defining Knowledge Layers for Textual Case-Based Reasoning. In *Proceedings of the 4th European Workshop on Case-Based Reasoning.*

Mitchell, T. 1997. *Machine Learning.* Mc Graw Hill.

Quinlan, R. 1993. *C4.5: Programs for Machine Learning.* Morgan Kaufman.

Racine, K., and Yang, Q. 1997. Maintaining Unstructured Case Bases. In *Proceedings of the 2nd International Conference on Case-Based Reasoning.*

Rissland, E., Skalak, D., and Friedman, T. 1993. Case Retrieval Through Multiple Indexing and Heuristic Search. In *Proceedings of the 13th International Joint Conference on Artificial Intelligence.*

Statski, W. 1985. *West's Legal Thesaurus and Dictionary.* West Publishing.

Activating CBR Systems through Autonomous Information Gathering

Christina Carrick and Qiang Yang
Simon Fraser University
Burnaby, BC, Canada, V5A 1S6
(ccarrick)(qyang)@cs.sfu.ca

Irene Abi-Zeid and Luc Lamontagne
Defense Research Establishment Valcartier
Decision Support Technology
2459, boul. Pie XI, nord
Val Belair, Quebec, Canada, G3J 1X5
(irene.abi-zeid)(luc.lamontagne)@drev.dnd.ca

Abstract. Most traditional CBR systems are passive in nature, adopting an advisor role in which a user manually consults the system. In this paper, we propose a system architecture and algorithm for transforming a passive interactive CBR system into an active, autonomous CBR system. Our approach is based on the idea that cases in a CBR system can be used to model hypotheses in a situation assessment application, where case attributes can be considered as questions or information tasks to be performed on multiple information sources. Under this model, we can use the CBR system to continually generate tasks that are planned for and executed based on information sources such as databases, the Internet or the user herself. The advantage of the system is that the majority of trivial or repeated questions to information sources can be done autonomously through information gathering techniques, and human users are only asked a small number of necessary questions by the system. We demonstrate the application of our approach to an equipment diagnosis domain. We show that the system integrates CBR retrieval with hierarchical query planning, optimization and execution.

1 Introduction

Case-based reasoning (CBR) has enjoyed tremendous success as a technique for solving problems related to knowledge reuse. Many examples can be found in the CBR literature [17,18,12,11,21]. One of the key factors in ensuring this success is CBR's ability to allow users to easily define their experiences incrementally and to utilize their defined case knowledge when a relatively small core of cases is available in a case base.

Despite the tremendous success, traditional uses of CBR have limited its potential. In previous research, most interactive CBR retrieval systems often involve few users [1] who provide most of the answers to queries in order to retrieve cases. In its most common mode, a CBR system involves just one user, who provides most, if not all, of the necessary information for feature values in order to perform similarity-based retrieval. For example, in a typical help desk operation, a call-center customer service representative (CSR) often enters a conversational mode, in which questions are answered by the customer, and entered by the CSR by hand. This style of interactive problem solving is important, but nevertheless is not the only mode in which to utilize a CBR system.

Our aim is to develop a more autonomous framework in which answers to CBR questions can be gathered automatically from multiple information sources. The motivation for our work derives from the evolution of an industrial-strength CBR system CASEADVISOR, developed by the CBR group at Simon Fraser University [24]. It allows a help desk organization to capture and reuse the experience and knowledge of its most experienced help desk and customer support personnel in a knowledge database that is easy to build, maintain and use. CASEADVISOR represents a typical interactive CBR (or conversational CBR [1]) application. After a user enters a natural language description of a problem, a set of cases that closely match the description is retrieved. These cases are interactively evaluated by a user based on a set of questions associated with them. When a user provides an answer to a question, a nearest neighbor algorithm is used to re-rank all retrieved cases and their associated questions in order to obtain the currently most relevant cases. The process is repeated until the user finds the target case.

Our observation is that much of the interactive question-answering process can in fact be automated. This is because many answers are available at different information sources, such as databases and web sites. In this model, a user is just one of the information sources to be queried. Following this direction, we advocate a novel approach to making such a CBR system "active" in the lifetime of an application.

In this work, the CASEADVISOR system takes up the role of a continual hypothesis evaluator. Each hypothesis is implemented as a case in the CBR system. The answers to the questions of the cases can still be obtained from the user; however, this is just one channel from which to obtain the information. We assume that there is a collection of information sources available to provide answers to the questions, or values to the attributes, in an autonomous way. We also assume that relevant information is distributed, so that no one source contains all of the information necessary to answer a question and information must be autonomously *gathered* and *integrated*. Moreover, an attribute provides only a high-level question which may need to be broken down into sub-questions and tasks by a hierarchical planning process. This task planning is adone autonomously by an information gathering sub-system. In this manner, a passive and purely interactive advisory system is turned into an active, information gathering system by using the questions in the case base as the queries to the information gathering component. We are thus inserting the information gathering component into the *Retrieve* stage of the CBR cycle, where the user may decide to *Reuse* the case at any point where the retrieval is deemed adequate.

This extension to CASEADVISOR has been implemented in JAVA to facilitate access to heterogeneous data sources, and can be applied to many situation assessment domains. Medical diagnosis and scientific theory formation are good examples of the situation assessment process: given some initial information a working hypothesis (a possible diagnosis or theory) is formed. Experimentation and testing then takes place to find further evidence to confirm or refute the working hypothesis, possibly generating alternative working hypotheses in the process. We have so far applied this situation assessment model to a military search and rescue domain and a Cable-TV equipment diagnosis domain. In the former, an initial indication about a missing aircraft will activate a case retrieval and evaluation process, in which various information sources are consulted in a continual manner [23]. In the equipment diagnosis area, again initial indications of an equipment failure will prompt the retrieval of most relevant hypothesis through a CBR retrieval process. A subsequent information gathering process will allow different hypothesis about the equipment fault to be more accurately assessed, and in the assessment process, part of the problem may be fixed. We will highlight the equipment diagnosis area later in our paper.

Our work makes contributions to case based reasoning research in several aspects. First, the model represents a method in which one can turn a passive CBR system into an active CBR system, thus increasing "interactive efficiency" [1]. A second novelty of the system is that a CBR system is used as an *information task generator* to generate information gathering tasks in an autonomous manner. Many well-known CBR systems [4, 5, 13] assume that the values are known for the attributes of retrieved cases. However, in situation assessment tasks, many values are not known. Therefore there is a need for verifying and retrieving these values through sophisticated query planning. Third, since we assume an open system architecture in which many information sources are expected to coexist, the system integrates a CBR component with an information gathering component. The information-gathering component performs global task expansion, planning and optimization.

Well-known CBR systems can be enhanced by our model. Systems such as HYPO [4, 5] and CASEY [13], rely on problem descriptions that are collections of attributes and values to retrieve similar cases. Cases in their case bases are also assumed to have their attribute-values ready for comparison with the incoming problem description. However, these systems do not emphasize on *how* these attributes and values are obtained. Our approach nicely complements these and other CBR systems in that an autonomous model is provided for gathering information in order to execute case based reasoning. In addition, our system complements case based planning (CBP) systems [20] in that, while CBP systems adapt a plan case after a similar plan is identified, in our approach "information plans" are adapted *during the retrieval process* in order to find the most similar case.

The organization of the paper is as follows. We first present a system overview in Section 2. Then we discuss in Section 2.1 the case base representation and the case retrieval process. In Section 2.2 we describe how to use the system to generate questions and how we select one of those questions for execution. We then discuss in Section 2.3 how to use a task planning and execution module to gather the information. Finally, in Section 3, we present a practical example of how our system can reduce the number of questions posed to the customer in a cable TV call centre domain. We conclude the paper with discussions of related works, our future research plans and conclusions.

2 System Overview

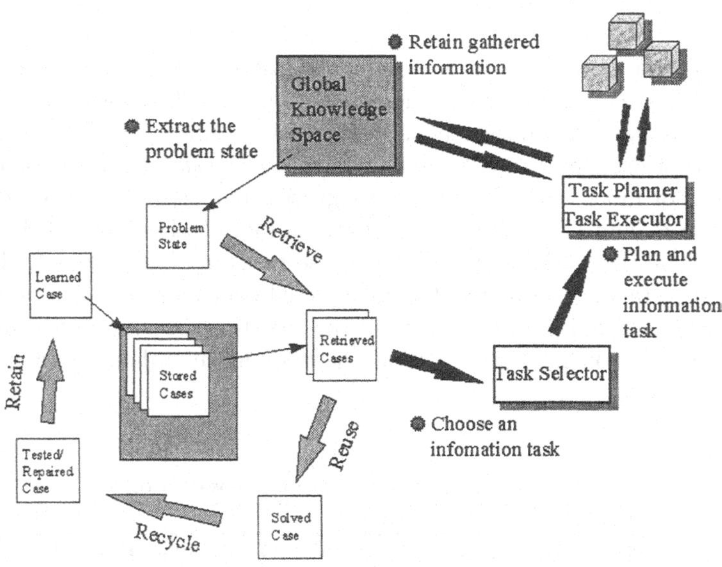

Fig. 1. The situation assessment cycle intersects the CBR cycle in the Retrieve stage.

As shown in Figure 1, our situation assessment system is made up of several complex modules which interact internally in a cyclical fashion as well as externally with a number of data sources, and intersecting the CBR cycle in the Retrieve phase. At the initiation of the cycle, the Global Knowledge Space (GKS) contains all relevant information which is known by the user and has been entered into the GKS. From the GKS is created a problem state, which is used to query the CASEADVISOR case base. This constitutes the situation assessment portion of the system, in which two or more competing hypotheses are produced which best explain the information contained in the GKS. These retrieved hypotheses then form the context for the information gathering task. The Task Selector uses the working hypothesis (that which best explains the data) as well as the competing hypotheses to formulate a set of all questions which may further distinguish the hypotheses. The Task Selector then chooses from that set one question which is to be executed as an information task, and the Task Executor plans and executes that task using the available data sources. (Decomposition of an information task results in **sub-tasks** and possibly **tasks** which may need to be performed in the process of answering the information task.) Should the question be unanswerable, control returns to the Task Selector module which chooses a new question as an information task for the Task Executor. When the Task Executor has obtained an answer to the question, the information is placed in the GKS, an updated problem state is created and used to query the case base, and the set of competing hypotheses is thus re-evaluated.

2.1 Situation Assessment

The situation assessment in our system is provided by a case-based retrieval system. The case base stores previous situations and their associated attributes as cases. A case in our system is defined as a tuple $< H, S, T >$, where H is a textual description of the diagnosis or *hypothesis* of the situation, S is a set of one or more <question,answer,weight> tuples representing a typical *state* leading to H, and T is a conjunction of zero or more *tasks* which may be executed should H be the working hypothesis. These tasks in T are different than those information tasks generated by the unanswered questions from S in that they are not intended to aid in the accuracy of the situation assessment and are merely things which should be done if H is the working hypothesis (such as "Notify supervisor.").

Hypothesis: parental control switch on

Question	Answer	Weight
problem description	poor reception of the cable signal	1.00
channels affected	specific channels	0.70
uses parental control	yes	0.80
has cable box	yes	0.40
outlets concerned	1	0.30

Fig. 2. A sample case from the cable TV call centre domain.

In our cable TV call centre domain, a case consists of a problem cause (the situation) and its associated conditions and effects (the state) as shown in Figure 2. The cable TV case base consists of a number of these cases, and a problem cause can be identified by the given exemplar state. The information contained in the GKS is used to formulate a problem state - the current state represented as a set of existing conditions and/or effects. This is currently accomplished by extracting from the GKS all statements relating to any of the questions in the case base. This problem state is used by the retrieval system to find the cases in the case base which most closely match the problem state using a k-nearest-neighbour algorithm. The problem cause in each case retrieved then becomes a possible hypothesis.

2.2 The Task Selector

Once we have retrieved the most likely hypotheses for a problem state, one question must be chosen to become an information task for execution. This selection involves estimating the costs of performing the information tasks, combining this estimation with the estimated information quality of the questions, and optimizing (possibly trading off) the two.

Information Quality When deciding which high-level information task should be executed to refine the situation assessment, it is useful to take into account how much information can be gained by its execution. It is desirable to maximize information gain so that a working hypothesis can be confirmed or refuted as quickly as possible, with as few questions as possible. As noted in [1], using the information gain formula typically found in decision tree induction (as in [19]) is not feasible when the case space is sparse. For this reason we have used an estimation of information gain which we will denote *information quality* for clarity.

To begin, we consider the information quality for only those questions which are unanswered in the set of retrieved cases. This allows us to eliminate questions which may be unanswered but are irrelevant to the current context (where the context is defined by the set of competing hypotheses). We currently measure information quality by considering three factors which would seem to have some influence on the importance of a question:

- the number of times the question appears in the retrieved cases,
- the weights of the question in the different cases, and
- the ranks of the cases containing the question.

The last two heuristics have previously been used in our CASEADVISOR system. In the current study all of these factors were given equal weighting in calculating the information quality, though we are also studying the effects each of these factors typically has on the information quality of a question. Questions are then ranked according to their estimated information quality, and this ranking can be further utilized in the task selection process.

Estimating Cost of Query Execution The cost of executing an information task far outweighs the cost of planning such a task [10]. It is therefore a worthwhile endeavor to take the time to find a good plan for gathering information. Different data sources may have different monetary costs for accessing them, are able to respond in differing amounts of time, etc. For example, the plan fragment shown in Figure 3 gives four possible locations for finding the answer to the high-level task: the customer profile, the customer accounts database, the

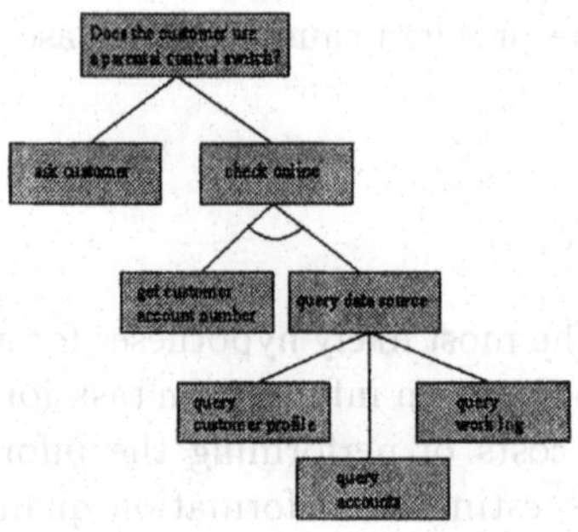

Fig. 3. A partial expansion tree for the query "Does the customer use a parental control switch?"

log of installation and maintenance work, and the customer herself. Checking the work log may incur a high time cost if the data is remotely stored, while local customer profiles may be old or incomplete. Each source has various cost constraints, some of which may be more important than others. The problem is then to find the best execution plan, which minimizes the cost of answering that question.

In order to estimate the cost of answering a question, it is necessary to formulate an execution plan. We accomplish this task by creating a hierarchical task network (HTN) [22, 7] from a library of task schemata[1]. This HTN presents an explicit parent-child relationship on information tasks, where a sub-task can either be directly executed, or can be decomposed into its constituent parts. It also contains any temporal constraints, user-imposed preferences and cost estimates which are important in the estimation of the cost of answering a question. It is also possible to be able to perform a task (or some part of it) in a number of different ways. An execution plan for an information task can then be seen as a constrained AND/OR graph of decompositions (conjunctions) and alternatives (disjunctions). The HTN query plan represented by the AND/OR graph can be different for different situations and information state in the data sources.

Figure 3 shows a partial AND/OR tree for the execution of an information task to find out whether a customer uses a parental control switch. Any path through this tree which covers all children of each encountered AND node and at least one child of each encountered OR node is a possible plan to execute the information task. These schemata contain not only information pertaining to the AND/OR structure of a plan, but

Our system currently estimates execution cost using a mini-max network flow algorithm on its query expansion network. All leaf nodes in AND/OR trees (directly executable queries) have associated with them a cost value which is a function of time cost, dollar cost and reliability cost. For each candidate query, the Task Selector examines all leaf nodes in its AND/OR tree. The cost values

[1] For brevity we do not show the schemata here.

are propagated upward to the root node, taking the sum at AND nodes and the minimum at OR nodes. It then remains to traverse the tree from the root node, taking the minimum at each OR node. The resultant traverse of the tree is a minimum cost solution and the leaf nodes in this traverse form a low-cost query execution plan. The topic of planning and tree traversal will be visited again in Section 2.3.

Combining Information Gain and Execution Cost In choosing an information task (or question) for execution, it is important to pay attention to both the information quality of the question and also the estimated cost of that question. If a question has a very high information content but it is unlikely that we will obtain an answer before final decisions must be made, then perhaps a faster question with slightly less information quality is in order. Thus there can be a trade-off between information quality and execution cost. Currently, our system uses hard-coded parameters in a function of gain and cost, though we are considering the benefits of having user- or domain-specified priorities on the different constraints involved.

2.3 The Task Planner and Executor

The Task Planner and Executor module performs the usual information gathering tasks of planning, optimizing and executing an information task. It receives the information task which has been chosen by the Task Selector module and searches that task's AND/OR tree for the least-cost plan. Since each leaf node specifies how it is to be executed, the leaf nodes in this solution plan are executed by invoking the functions, modules or agents whose calls are contained therein. This AND/OR tree search algorithm returns a low-cost solution plan for answering the question when the AND/OR graph is a tree (i.e. an executable task does not show up twice in the graph). When information sources are shared by different tasks, the optimization problem of finding a lowest-cost solution plan is NP-hard; we are currently experimenting with different heuristic algorithms for solving it.

If all possible solutions to the task fail (i.e. all children of the top-most OR node have been exhausted and no solution has been found), then control returns to the Task Selector module to choose an alternate question for answering. This process continues until a question has successfully been answered or until there are no more question options. In the latter case, processing halts and the working hypothesis is presented as an assessment of the situation. When a question has been successfully executed, the answer to the question is placed in the GKS. This triggers the creation of a new problem state to be formed from the contents of the updated GKS. The problem state is presented to the case-based retrieval system, and hypotheses are retrieved with new matching scores based on the updated input state. This cycle continues until there are no more questions which can aid in the accuracy of the case retrieval, or until halted by the user.

3 Sample Scenario

To demonstrate the utility of our system we show here a sample problem from the cable TV troubleshooting domain. Figure 4 shows three cases retrieved by the customer's problem description of "poor reception", and the six questions which are relevant to those retrieved cases in the order produced by our information quality heuristics.

Case I: signal problems		
problem description	poor reception of the cable signal	1.00
channels affected	specific channels	0.80
local signal	clear	0.95

Case II: customer not subscribed to package		
problem description	poor reception of the cable signal	1.00
channels affected	29 – 58	0.75
channels affected	29 – 43	0.75
channels affected	44 – 58	0.75
subscribed	no	0.50

Case III: parental control switch on		
problem description	poor reception of the cable signal	1.00
channels affected	specific channels	0.70
uses parental control	yes	0.80
has cable box	yes	0.40
outlets concerned	1	0.30

Q1 Which channels are having the problem?
Q2 Is the picture clear on the local set?
Q3 Does the customer use a parental control switch
Q4 Is the customer subscribed to these channels?
Q5 Does the customer have a cable box?
Q6 How many outlets have the problem?

Fig. 4. Cases relevant to the problem description "poor reception", and the questions relevant to those cases.

Figure 5 shows the results of a diagnostic session in which a customer has poor reception on certain cable channels. There were five data sources available in our cable TV domain: a customer profile database, a customer accounts database, a work/installation log, a database of current signal problems, and the customer herself. Figure 5(a) gives the results obtained from the initial problem description, and shows that question Q1 has been chosen for execution. This question is posed to the customer, as we currently have no on-line means of obtaining the information. The response to this question is then added to the problem state and the new retrieval from the case base gives us the results in Figure 5(b). At this point Q2 is chosen for execution. A partial expansion for this information task is shown in Figure 6, and the execution plan chosen is the highlighted path. Note that at node C the first path chosen was to a database of current signal problems, which resulted in failure due to the absence of the requested information at that site. It was then necessary to re-plan and chose an alternate, next-best solution. Once all of the information was obtained and integrated to answer the question, this answer was added to the problem state and again the case base performed a re-assessment.

This process continued through all of the cycles depicted in Figure 5[2]. The four on-line data sources provided answers to all questions but Q1 in a realistic fashion. This shows a tremendous potential for reducing the duration of the question-answer session with the customer. By using information gathering techniques, we also reduce the burden of information search on the call centre employee and speed up retrieval of information, thus diagnosing problems more quickly and servicing more customers in a shorter amount of time.

The sample session just presented shows how our system can be useful with a passive CBR diagnosis mechanism: when a customer recognizes that she has a problem, she can invoke the system with an input problem state and the information gathering component obtains evidence to aid in the diagnosis. But these same mechanisms can also be used in an active manner. Consider the use of active databases and monitoring agents in the information gathering component: instead of waiting for a new question to be posed, these monitors and triggers become activated whenever a relevant change occurs in a data source. We can then use this information to *foresee* a problem. The case base can continually re-rank retrieved cases, based on these changes in the data sources. We then have a system which already has much of the information needed for a diagnosis when a customer calls in with their problem description. This integrated technique can be seen as performing active case-based reasoning in a backward fashion, where the reasoning (AND/OR tree expansion) occurs from the objectives back to the information sources. In [15], we study how to combine active databases and CBR in a *forward* manner. Indeed, an active system such as this could even predict that customers will phone the call centre with a particular problem given changes in the local signal, listed outages, last-minute changes in the TV schedule, etc.

4 Related Work

In the case-based reasoning community, Conversational CBR (CCBR) has attracted substantial research [1]. CCBR, essentially interactive CBR, involves the refinement of diagnoses through interaction or conversation with the user, asking questions which are considered to have high information gain. These questions are based upon the unanswered attributes in the problem case which are relevant to the retrieved cases, and are ranked according to some heuristic such as the number of cases in which the attribute occurs. Popular in help-desk applications, commercial tools such as Inference Corporation's CBR Express exemplify

[2] We had turned off the solution threshold, allowing re-assessment to take place until there were no further questions to be answered.

initial input:	poor cable reception	
retrieved:	signal problems	45
	customer not subscribed to package	27
	parental control switch on	27
chosen question:	Which channels are having the problem?	
sources queried:	customer	

(a)

retrieved:	signal problems	64
	parental control switch on	36
chosen question:	Is the picture clear on the local set?	
sources queried:	GKS, signal problems database, local monitor	

(b)

retrieved:	parental control switch on	56
	signal problems	44
chosen question:	Does the customer use a parental control switch?	
sources queried:	GKS, customer profile database	

(c)

retrieved:	parental control switch on	65
	signal problems	35
chosen question:	Does the customer have a cable box?	
sources queried:	GKS, customer profile database	

(d)

retrieved:	parental control switch on	69
	signal problems	31
chosen question:	How many outlets are having the problem?	
sources queried:	GKS, customer accounts database	

(e)

retrieved:	parental control switch on	71
	signal problems	29

(f)

Fig. 5. Results of a diagnostic session in which a customer has poor reception on certain cable channels. Selected questions are planned and executed among the various data sources, and the increasing amount of known information leads to an increased accuracy in the diagnosis.

CCBR [1]. These systems attempt to find the quickest way to increase the accuracy of diagnosis through estimating information gain. Further research has used model-based inferencing to reduce the number of questions asked of the user by eliminating redundant questions [3]. These systems still remain user-guided however, and therefore need not consider certain problems introduced by IG such as cost estimation and planning information tasks. [2] discusses ongoing research in which state information can be collected from users and also from sensors, leading into research in optimizing cost and gain estimations.

CBR and HTN planning have also been integrated in the NaCoDAE/HTN system [16]. There, however, the CBR is used to interactively generate plans, where these plans are constrained by the HTN. This puts the NaCoDAE/HTN system at the *Revise* stage of the CBR cycle, which is complementary to our

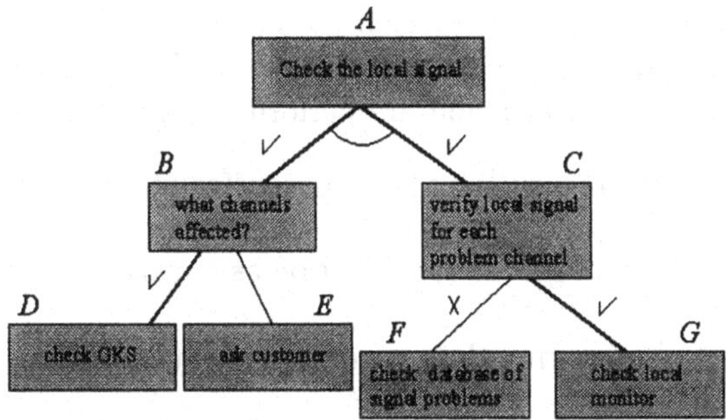

Fig. 6. The task expansion for the information task "Check the local signal."

work. A similar system to NaCoDAE/HTN is our CASEADVISOR system as described in [24], which attaches a case with a decision tree. When a candidate case is identified, the decision tree is evaluated, prompting the user with a series of questions and actions to follow. The decision tree search essentially performs the case adaptation work.

In the area of automated information gathering, many researchers have been investigating methods of reducing the cost of executing a query through query reformulation and optimization [14,9,8,6,10]. This is a query in the database sense, and corresponds to a single question which must be answered through the information gathering component in our work. These generally involve assigning various costs (dollar cost, time cost, accuracy cost, etc.) to data sources and reasoning to minimize those costs. For example, the SIMS system models subsumptive relations which are useful in query formulation, and also facilitates descriptive models of resources for query optimization. The InfoSleuth system is the result of intensive research in ontologies, and also uses a frame-based, three level representation to provide a detailed model of the domain and resources [9]. In more flexible systems such as BIG [14], users are able to specify which costs are more important to them and the cost-minimizing function takes this into account. Thus, the BIG system optimizes IG plans according to user preferences. Given the quality, cost and time features of accessing the various available data sources, BIG attempts to optimize these features with respect to a set of user-specified constraints on the features. This allows for different definitions of "optimal", depending on the user of the system.

5 Future Work

With the support of the preliminary results obtained, we are eager to investigate aspects of our system further. Several variants of the task selection and query planning algorithms are worth investigation, taking into account different constraints and optimizing those constraints. Global optimization of the planning process should take into account various cost, content overlap and information gain information of the information sources. However, this discussion is beyond the scope of this paper. We have several proposals for improving the cost estimation/optimization algorithm and are performing such studies:

- rearranging sub-queries within planning constraints to minimize data source accesses,
- studying the effects of global optimization as opposed to local optimization, and
- learning and/or estimating the cost of a new data source.

Also under investigation are the impacts information quality and execution-time have on the time to converge to an assessment. Perhaps a question with high information content would be worthwhile executing even if the execution time was estimated to be very high, if it would allow convergence to a single situation assessment hypothesis soon afterwards. Discovering a relationship between information quality, execution time and time to convergence would allow us to create a cut-off where we could say that the information quality is not worth the execution time.

Uncertainty in gathered information is another aspect which we consider important in future versions of our assessment system. At present, all information inserted into the GKS is given a weight of 1.0, though there is the option available to weight the information from the GKS with degrees of certainty. Using this option will impact not only the maintenance of the GKS, but also our task selection algorithm as it may be desirable to verify already "known" information which has a low certainty.

We also see as important the problem of displaying to the user all of the useful information about the assessment process, without being obtrusive. Since our program is meant to act as a support to the user, working quietly in the background, we do not wish to overload the user with process information. Indeed, it is information overload which our system attempts to overcome. However, the user should feel in control and this involves giving the user access to the various processes which are taking place within the system. Even if it is not an option for the user to override a system decision, it can make new users more comfortable with the system to simply know the data upon which plans are being made.

6 Conclusions

Using automated information gathering to aid in situation assessment is a novel research topic. We have combined a case-based retrieval system with information gathering techniques which results in a fewer number of questions posed to the user. The advantage of the system is that the majority of trivial or repeated queries to information sources can be done autonomously through an agent-like system, and human users are only asked a small number of necessary questions by the system. Under this model, we can also use the CBR system to continually generate questions that are planned for and executed based on information sources such as databases and the Internet, resulting in an active diagnostic system. In the cable TV call centre domain, this concept shows a tremendous potential for reducing the duration of the question-answer session with the customer. By using information gathering techniques, we also reduce the burden of information search on the call centre employee and speed up retrieval of information, thus diagnosing problems more quickly and servicing more customers in a shorter amount of time. Our system also goes a long way to facilitating self-diagnosis via the internet or an automated phone system, further reducing call centre costs.

Acknowledgments

We thank Canadian Natural Science and Engineering Research Council, Rogers Cablesystems Ltd. and Canadian Cable Labs Fund, Canadian Institute for Robotics and Intelligent Systems (IRIS), Defense Research Establishment Valcartier and Simon Fraser University for their support. We thank Michael Zhang, Geof Glass and Nathan Paziuk for their comments on this work.

References

1. D. Aha and L. Breslow. Refining conversational case libraries. In *Proceedings of the Second International Conference on Case-based Reasoning (ICCBR-97)*, Providence, RI, July 1997.
2. D. W. Aha, L. A. Breslow, and T. Maney. Supporting conversational case-based reasoning in an integrated reasoning framework. Technical Report AIC-98-006, Naval Research Laboratory, Navy Center for Applied Research in Artificial Intelligence, Washington, DC, 1998.
3. D. W. Aha, T. Maney, and L. A. Breslow. Supporting dialogue inferencing in conversational case-based reasoning. Technical Report AIC-98-008, Naval Research Laboratory, Navy Center for Applied Research in Artificial Intelligence, Washington, DC, 1998.
4. K. Ashley. *Modelling legal argument: Reasoning with cases and hypotheticals.* MIT Press, Bradford Books, Cambridge, MA, 1990.
5. K. Ashley and E. Rissland. A case-based approach to modeling legal expertise. *IEEE Expert*, 3(3):70–77, 1988.
6. O. M. Duschka and A. Y. Levy. Recursive plans for information gathering. In *Proceedings of IJCAI-97*, Nagoya, Japan, August 1997.
7. K. Erol, J. Hendler, and D. S. Nau. Htn planning: Complexity and expressivity. In *Proceedings of the 12th National Conference on Artificial Intelligence (AAAI-94)*, pages 1123–1128, Seattle, WA, 1994. AAAI Press/The MIT Press.
8. M. R. Genesereth, A. M. Keller, and O. M. Duschka. Infomaster: An information integration system. In *Proceedings of the ACM SIGMOD Conference*, May 1997.
9. R. J. B. Jr., W. Bohrer, R. Brice, A. Cichocki, J. Fowler, A. Helal, V. Kashyap, T. Ksiezyk, G. Martin, M. Nodine, M. Rashid, M. Rusinkiewicz, R. Shea, C. Unnikrishnan, A. Unruh, and D. Woelk. InfoSleuth: Agent-based semantic integration of information in open and dynamic environments. In *Proceedings of SIGMOD'97*, 1997.

10. C. A. Knoblock, Y. Arens, and C.-N. Hsu. Cooperating agents for information retrieval. In *Proceedings of the 2nd International Conference on Cooperative Information Systems*, Toronto, Canada, 1994. University of Toronto Press.
11. J. Kolodner. *Case-Based Reasoning.* Morgan Kaufmann Publisher, Inc., 1993.
12. J. Kolodner and D. Leake. a tutorial introduction ot case-based reasoning. In D. Leake, editor, *Case-Based Reasoning:Experiences, lessons & Future Directions.* American Association for Artificial Intelligence, 1996.
13. P. Koton. Reasoning about evidence in causal explanation. In *Proceedings of the Seventh National Conference on Artificial Intelligence (AAAI-88)*, Cambridge, MA, 1988. AAAI Press/MIT Press.
14. V. Lesser, B. Horling, F. Klassner, A. Raja, and T. Wagner. Information gathering as a resource bounded interpretation task. Technical Report 97-34, University of Massachusetts Computer Science, March 1997.
15. S. Li and Q. Yang. ActiveCBR: Integrating case-based reasoning and active databases. Technical Report TR 1999-03, School of Computing Science, Simon Fraser University, Burnaby BC Canada, January 1999. http://www.cs.sfu.ca/ qyang/Papers/activecbr.ps.gz.
16. H. Muñoz-Avila, D. C. McFarlane, D. W. Aha, L. Breslow, J. A. Ballas, and D. Nau. Using guidelines to constrain interactive case-based htn planning. Technical Report AIC-99-004, Naval Research Laboratory, Navy Center for Applied Research in Artificial Intelligence, Washington, DC, 1999.
17. T. Nguyen, M. Czerwinski, and D. Lee. Compaq quicksource—providing the consumer with the power of ai. *AI Magazine*, 1993.
18. A. Perini and F. Ricci. An interactive planning architecture: The forest fire fighting case. In M. Ghallab, editor, *Proceedings of the 3rd European Workshop on Planning*, pages 292–302, Assissi, Italy, September 1995. ISO Publishers.
19. J. Quinlan. Induction of decision trees. *Machine Learning*, 1:81–106, 1986.
20. M. Veloso, H. Munoz-Avila, and R. Bergmann. General-purpose case-based planning: Methods and systems. *AI Communications*, 9(3):128–137, 1996.
21. I. Watson. *Applying Case-Based Reasoning: Techniques for Enterprise Systems.* Morgan Kaufmann Publishers, Inc., 1997.
22. Q. Yang. Formalizing planning knowledge for hierarchical planning. *Computational Intelligence*, 6, 1990.
23. Q. Yang, I. Abi-Zeid, and L. Lamontagne. An agent system for intelligent situation assessment. In F. Giunchiglia, editor, *Proceedings of the 1998 International Conference on AI Methodologies, Systems and Applications (AIMSA98)*, volume 1480 of *Lecture Notes in AI*, pages 466–474, Sozopol, Bulgaria, September 1998. Springer Verlag.
24. Q. Yang, E. Kim, and K. Racine. Caseadvisor: Supporting interactive problem solving and case base maintenance for help desk applications. In *Proceedings of the IJCAI 97 Workshop on Practical Applications of CBR*, Nagoya, Japan, August 1997. International Joint Conference on Artificial Intelligence, IJCAI.

Integrating CBR and Heuristic Search for Learning and Reusing Solutions in Real-Time Task Scheduling

Juan Manuel Adán Coello[1], Ronaldo Camilo dos Santos[2]

[1] Instituto de Informática, PUC-Campinas, Cx.P. 317, CEP 13.020-904, Campinas, SP, BRAZIL
juan@zeus.puccamp.br
[2] FEEC/UNICAMP, Campinas, SP, BRAZIL
ronaldo@dca.fee.unicamp.br

Abstract. This paper presents the Case-Based Reasoning Real-Time Scheduling System (CBR-RTS) that integrates into a case-based reasoning framework a heuristic search component. The problem addressed involves scheduling sets of tasks with precedence, ready time and deadline constraints. CBR-RTS reuses the solution of known cases to simplify and solve new problems. When the system does not have applicable cases, it tries to find a solution using heuristic search. A particularly interesting feature of CBR-RTS is its learning ability. New problems solved by the heuristic scheduler can be added to the case base for future reuse. Performed tests have shown that small bases of cases carefully chosen allow to substantially reduce the time needed to solve new complex problems

1 Introduction

According to a widely accepted definition in the real-time systems community, real-time systems are those systems whose correctness depends not only on the logical results of the computations, but also on the time at which the results are produced [1]. To meet that requirement, a real-time software development environment should integrate flexible programming languages that support the specification of real-time constraints with scheduling algorithms that determine when, and where, in the case of a multiprocessor or distributed hardware, the components of a program should execute.

The problem of guaranteeing that the timing constraints of a program are going to be met at run-time is fairly simple when the corresponding task model is also simple. For example, when a program is composed of independent periodic tasks, the rate monotonic or the earliest deadline first scheduling algorithms [2] can be successfully used. As the programming model becomes more complex, as is needed by most real applications, scheduling turns into a computationally intractable problem [3], that is usually solved using heuristic algorithms.

The application of heuristic algorithms requires to map programming model representations to scheduling algorithm representations, usually some kind of directed labeled graph [4].

An inherent characteristic of traditional schedulers based on heuristic search is its lack of ability to learn from experience. New problems identical, or very similar, to other problems already solved in the past have to be solved again, form first-principles, every time they are found. This procedure wastes time and resources usually scarce to deal with problems previously faced, for which it was already found a solution or discovered that the problem can not be solved applying available methods.

According to cognitive scientists, the reuse of known solutions to solve new problems is routinely done by human beings when facing new complex problems. In the artificial intelligence field, this problem solution paradigm is known as Case-Based Reasoning (CBR) [5].

In this work, we study a new scheduling architecture that integrates into a case-based reasoning framework a heuristic search component.

The paper is structured as follows. In section 2 we present the real-time problem being considered. In section 3, we describe the architecture of the Case-Based Reasoning Real-Time Scheduling System (CBR-RTS). In section 4 we discuss some experiments that were conducted to evaluate the system. In section 5 we review some related work. Finally, in section 6, we present some concluding remarks and point out suggestion for future work.

2 The Real-Time Scheduling Problem Addressed

Real-time systems can be classified in two main classes: Soft Real-Time Systems (SRT) and Hard Real-Time Systems (HRT). In SRT systems, the performed tasks should be executed as fast as possible, but it is not vital that they finish before a deadline, however, in HRT systems, if rigid deadlines are not met, severe consequences can take place.

A real-time system consist typically of a control system, the computer and its interfaces, and a controlled system, for example an automated factory, that can be seen as the environment with which the computer interacts. Due to the characteristics of controlled systems, control systems usually are composed of different processes, or tasks, that can be seen as abstractions of sequences of code (computer instructions).

Real-time tasks can be characterized by several constraints, including, timing constraints, periodicity, precedence relations, mutual exclusion relations, resources, preemption and allocation.

Tasks timing constraints can be specified by the parameters arrival time, ready time, computation time and deadline. The arrival time of a tasks, a, is the time when the task is invoked by the system. The ready time, r, is the time when the task becomes ready for execution, and is greater or equal to a. When there are no additional resource restrictions, $r = a$. The computation time, c, is the worst case CPU time needed to execute the task, including associated overhead, for example context switching time. The deadline, d, is the time before which the task must finished its execution, and is relative to the task arrival time. The "absolute" deadline of a task is thus given by $a + d$.

Depending on the arrival pattern of a task it can be classified as periodic or aperiodic. Periodic tasks are executed once each time interval p and all their timing constraints can be determined off-line. In particular, for a given periodic task P, the arrival time of its i-th execution instance, $a[P_i]$, is equal to $a[P_{i-1}] + p$. Aperiodic tasks do not have deterministic arrival times, they can arrive at any time and are related to events whose occurrence is unpredictable, as alarm conditions.

A precedence relation between tasks exists when one task depends on the results produced by the other task execution. If, for example, task A precedes task B, task B can start its execution only after task A finishes.

Mutual exclusion occurs when certain shared resources can not be accessed simultaneously by several tasks, otherwise the resource can go to an inconsistent state. This happens, for example, when several tasks need to read and write concurrently a shared memory position or a record in a file.

Besides the CPU, some task may need additional resources to execute, as I/O units, dedicated processors, etc. In this case, the ready time of the task is usually greater than its arrival time, since it is generally necessary some additional time to allocate the needed resources.

A task can be preemptable or nonpreenptable. A task is preemptable if its execution can be interrupted by higher priority tasks and later resumed at the point where it was interrupted. Nonpreemptable tasks once started execute until they finish or explicitly release the processor.

When there are multiple processor or processing nodes in a system, tasks have to be allocated considering several factors, including, processor load balancing, communication load balance, fault tolerance and resources available in each node.

In hard-real-time systems the scheduling decisions can and must be made off-line. They can be made off-line because the bulk of the computation in those systems is done by periodic tasks, where constraints, particularly timing constraints, are known in advance of their execution. Decisions must be made off-line because in hard-real-time systems it is mandatory that timing constraints are met at run-time. As most scheduling problems are NP-complete, it is not practical to try to find a schedule for a set of tasks dynamically, when they are invoked. If the system includes periodic and aperiodic tasks, there are general techniques that can be used to transform sets of aperiodic tasks into equivalent sets of periodic tasks [6,7].

We will address here the problem of off-line scheduling sets of periodic hard real-time tasks whit timing and precedence relation constraints in monoprocessor computers. This type of scheduling problem is usually represented using acyclic directed labeled graphs, that here we will call scheduling graphs. In a scheduling graph, nodes represent the tasks to be scheduled and arcs their precedence relations. Nodes and arcs labels can be used to specify their timing constrains.

In our system, a node may have attached a computation time, c, a ready time, r , and a deadline, d. The label of an arc can be used to specify the time needed to transfer a message between communicating tasks in a distributed system. But, as we are considering the problem of scheduling in a monoprocessed computer, we will not attach costs to arcs.

Scheduling graph represents all the periodic tasks to be executed, and it is assumed that all the tasks have the same period. If a feasible schedule for this set of tasks is found, the schedule can be indefinitely repeated. When the tasks to be scheduled have

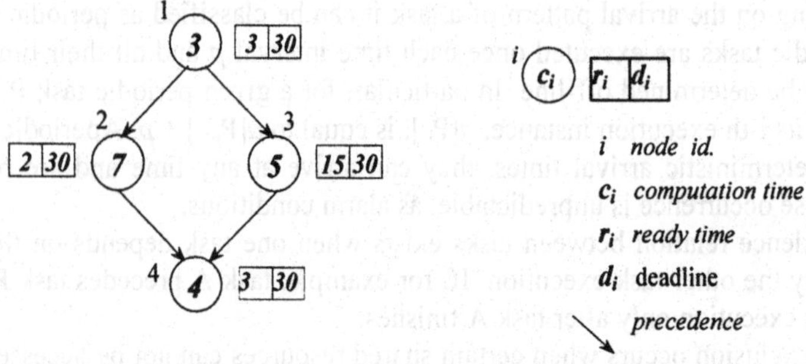

Fig. 1. Representation of a scheduling problem

different periods, we can construct a graph that represents all the occurrences of each task in the cyclic window, defined as the least common multiple (LCM) of the tasks' periods. If that is done, the period of each task instance in the scheduling graph can be defined as being equal to the cyclic window. For example, lets consider that we have two tasks, T_1 and T_2, with periods 50 and 100, respectively, ready times equal to their arrival times and deadlines equal to their periods. In the corresponding scheduling graph, we will have one execution instance of T_2 and two execution instances of task T_1 both will have a period 100 (the LCM of the two tasks periods). The first instance of T_1, T_{11} will have its ready time at time 0 and its deadline at time 50 and the second instance, T_{12} , will have its ready time at 50 and its deadline at 100. Details about the production of scheduling graphs from programs can be found in [4].

Searching for a feasible schedule to a given scheduling graph, constructed as described above, consist in finding the start times of each node in the graph. If we were dealing with a distributed system, we will have also to find an allocation for each node, but this problem will not be considered here.

Figure 1 shows an example of a simple scheduling problem with four tasks, T_1, T_2, T_3 and T_4. Each task is represented by a node, for example, task T_1, represented by node 1, has a computation time, *c*, of 3 time units, ready time, *r*, at 3 time units after its arrival time and deadline at 30 time units after its arrival time. Task T_1 precedes tasks T_2 and T_3, and tasks T_2 and T_3 precede task T_4. The diagram in figure 2 shows a

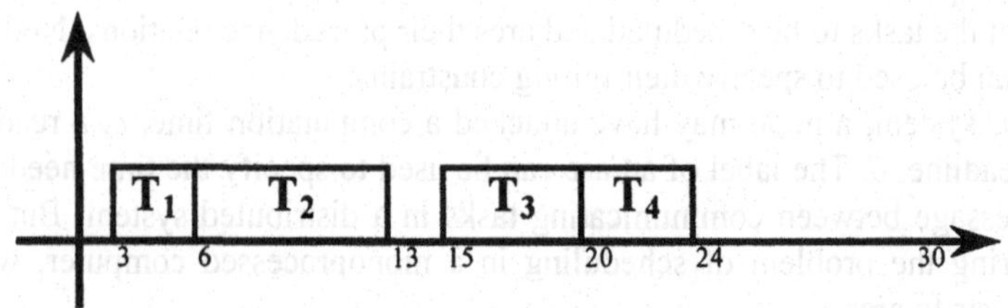

Fig. 2. A schedule to the problem in figure 1

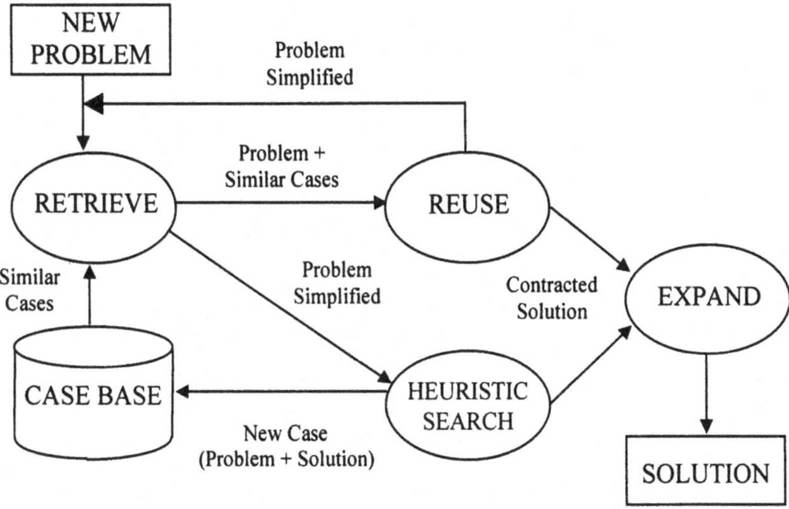

Fig. 3. CBR-RTS System Architecture

feasible schedule for this problem. If this schedule is repeated at each cyclic window, in this case with duration of 30 time units, all tasks will meet their timing constraints.

3 CBR-RTS Architecture

We will begin this section with a brief introduction to the architecture of the system and its functionality and then, on the following subsections, provide additional information together with the presentation of a simple example that illustrates the topics being discussed.

The structure of the CBR-RTS system is presented in figure 3. It consists of a case base (CB), a case retrieval module, a case reuse module, a heuristic search module and a solution expanding module.

The case base stores the description of scheduling problems solved in the past and their respective solutions.

The retrieval module is responsible for finding in the case base old problems similar to the new problem or to parts of it.

The reusing module adapts the retrieved cases to solve the problem. It may happen that with the retrieved cases it is possible to solve the whole problem or only some of its parts. In the latter situation, the parts solved (subgraphs of the original problem graph) are abstracted into a single node in the problem scheduling graph, and we say that the problem was simplified, or contracted. The simplified problem is resubmitted to the retrieval and reusing modules as many times as necessary to find a complete solution to the problem or until there are no more similar cases in the case base. If a

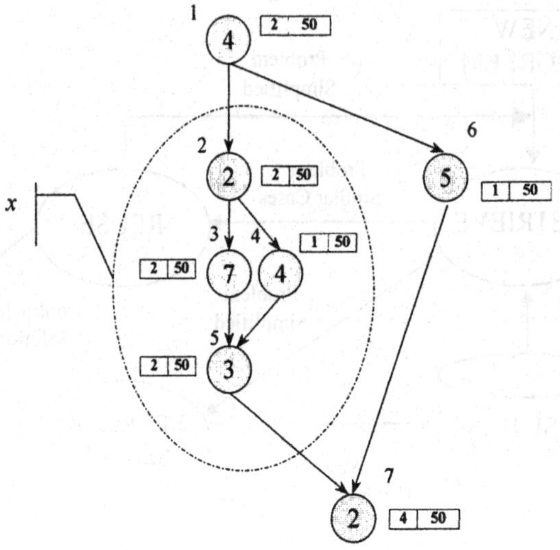

Fig. 4. Graph describing a new problem

solution is found, it is passed to the expander module. If the simplified problem, and consequently, the original problem, could not be solved reusing the stored cases, it is submitted to the heuristic search module.

The heuristic search module implements a dedicated scheduling algorithm that will searches for a feasible solution to the problem. If it finds a solution, it is included, as a new case, in the case base and is submitted to the expander module. If a solution is not found, the original problem, without any simplification, is submitted to the dedicated scheduler that will try to find a solution to the original problem. If one is found, it is outputted and included in the case base.

It is possible to implement a backtracking mechanism that could progressively undo previous simplifications and try new ones, or try to apply the search algorithm to the problem in early stages of simplification, but currently this is not done.

The expander module does the proper unfolding of nodes that abstract parts of the original problem before outputting the problem solution.

In the following subsections we discuss in more detail the architecture and functionality of the system and illustrate it using a simple example, that consists in finding a solution to the problem represented in figure 4.

3.1 Case Representation

A case is stored as a pair (problem,solution). A problem is represented by a labeled acyclic directed graph, as shown in figure 1, where the labels are used to specify its tasks timing constraints. The solution corresponds to a schedule that satisfies the problem timing constraints, as illustrated by the Gantt diagram in figure 2. For a given problem, the corresponding schedule shows the start time of each node (task) in the problem graph.

Figure 5 illustrates a case in the case base. The graph on the left represents the problem, and the Gantt diagram on the right the corresponding solution.

3.2 Case Retrieval

The case retrieval module searches the case base looking for stored cases (old solved problems) similar to the current problem. Since cases are stored as graphs, similarity assessment involves subgraph isomorphism detection. A case is similar to a problem if:

1. The case and the problem are described by isomorphic graphs and the timing constraints of the problem are the same or less strict than those in the case; or
2. The case is part of the problem, i.e., it is described by a graph that is isomorphic to some subgraph of the problem (a subproblem) and the timing constraints of the subproblem are the same or less strict than those in the case.

If r_i, c_i, and d_i are the ready time, computation time and deadline, respectively, of task i in the problem, and r'_i, c'_i, and d'_i the equivalent times for the corresponding tasks in the case, we say that the problem's timing constraints are the same or less strict than those of the case if the following is valid for all corresponding nodes (tasks):

$$r_i \leq r'_i \,;\, c_i \leq c'_i \text{ and } d_i \geq d'_i$$

In the current version of CBR-RTS, subgraph isomorphism detection is done using an implementation made by Messmer [8] of Ullman's algorithm [9].

Figure 4 shows an example of a new problem to be solved and figure 5 a case retrieved from the case base. We can see that that the case is similar to subproblem x in the new problem. Both, the case and the subproblem, are represented by isomorphic graphs and the subproblem's timing constraints are less strict than the case's timing constraints.

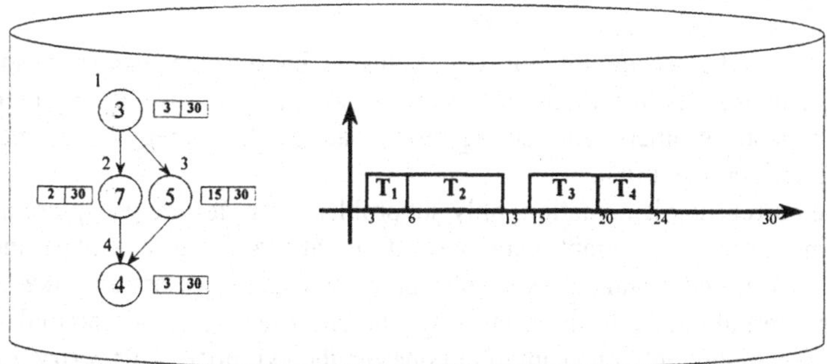

Fig. 5. Old problem in the case base, similar to subproblem x of the new problem

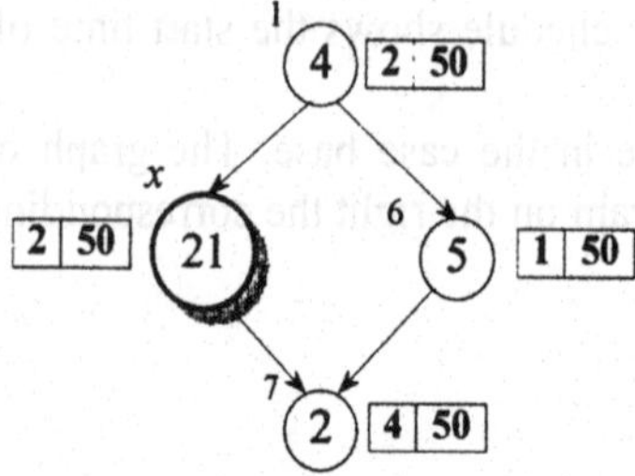

Fig. 6. New problem simplified

3.3 Case Adaptation and Reusing

The retrieval module can find an exact match for a problem in the case base or, more often, one or more partial matches. If an exact match is found, the solution in the case can be used without any adaptation.

When partial matches are found, they can be similar to the complete problem or to some of its subproblems. If there is a case that is similar to the complete problem, the solution to the case can also be applied without any modification, because the tasks in the subproblem have computation times equal or lower than those in the case and, consequently, a schedule that satisfies the case will also satisfy the subproblem.

When a solution is reused as above, it is very likely that the subproblem schedule has some "gaps", because some of its tasks can have lower computation times than that on the case. This is not necessarily a problem since these gaps can be used to schedule aperiodic tasks [10].

When there are retrieved cases similar to subproblems in the new problem, the cases are used to solve the subproblems and the corresponding subgraphs are abstracted to a single node. When this is done we say that the problem was simplified or contracted, because it has now less tasks (nodes) to be scheduled, what usually means that it becomes a simpler scheduling problem, since the complexity of scheduling problems increases with the problem size.

The retrieved cases are not mutually exclusive, because they can share some nodes an arcs. This implies that when the system reuses a certain case, it may be excluding the application of others. The reusing module adopts the strategy of reusing the largest subgraph retrieved first.

In the current implementation, only subproblems that form a group are abstracted. We define a group as a graph composed of an entry node, an exit node and internal nodes. Internal nodes and the exit node can have as predecessors only the entry node or other internal nodes, in the same way, the entry node and the internal nodes can have as successors only other internal nodes or the exit node. This restriction is done to make easier the expansion of the final problem schedule, and in the future can be relaxed.

The node that abstracts a subproblem will receive the ready time, and deadline of

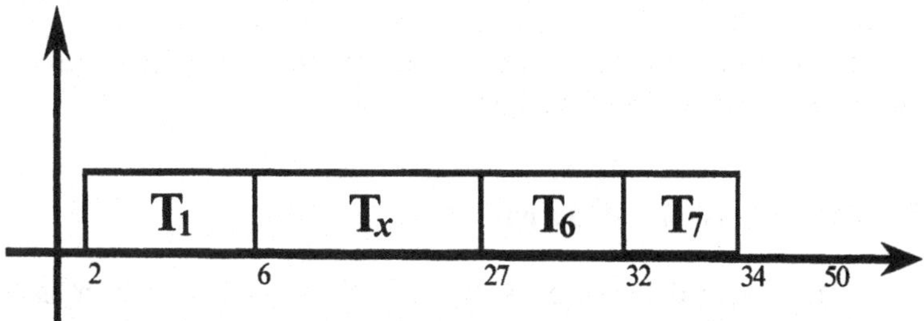

Fig. 7. Schedule produced by PSPS to the new problem simplified

its entry and exit nodes, respectively, and its computation time will correspond to the finish time of the last scheduled task minus the start time of the first schedule task in the case.

The retrieval and reusing cycle continues until the problem is transformed into a single node, in which case the problem is completely solved and the schedule found so for can be expanded, as will be described in section 3.5. If the cycle stops without finding a solution, that is, the problem could not be reduced to a single node and there are no more similar cases in the case base, the simplified problem is submitted to the heuristic search module.

Figure 6 shows the problem in figure 4 simplified using the case shown in figure 5. We can see that subproblem x was replaced by an equivalent node, x. As we can see, node x has the start time of node 2 (the entry node in the subproblem), the deadline of node 5 (the exit node in the subproblem) and the computation time equal to the finish time of last schedule node (node 4) minus the start time of the first scheduled node (node 1) in the case. This simplified problem has no similar cases in the case base, so it will be submitted to the heuristic search module that will try to solve it using a dedicated scheduler.

3.4 Heuristic search

The heuristic search module is used when it is not possible to solve a new problem using solely past experiences stored in the case base. The heuristic search module may find a solution to the problem or discover that the problem is not schedulable. In both situations a new case can be stored in the case base. The problem description (a labeled graph) and the solution (a schedule), or an indication that the problem is not schedulable, are stored in the case base. That is, the system can learn solutions to a new type of problem or learn that this type of problem can not be solved. Both lessons are worth remembering.

In the current version of CBR-RTS, the heuristic search module uses a dedicated scheduler, named PSPS (Periodic and Sporadic Processes Scheduler), based on a branch and bound search algorithm proposed by Xu and Parnas [11].

In our example, the simplified version of the new problem, shown in figure 6, has no similar cases in the case based and is submitted to the heuristic search module, that produces the schedule shown in figure 7.

3.5 Solution Expansion and Output

When a problem is solved, the schedule found for the simplified problem is expanded to restore the subproblems that were abstracted to single nodes during problem simplification.

In our example, figure 8 shows the expansion of the solution produced by the heuristic search module to the problem presented in figure 4. As we can see, in the time interval reserved to node *x* the expander introduced the solution to subproblem *x*. This solution is generated adapting the solution in the case that is similar to subproblem *x*, as shown in figures 5 and 6.

4 CBR-RTS Evaluation

This section discusses the performance of CBR-RTS when applied to solve nine problems of different sizes and complexity. The performance of CBR-RTS in solving these problems is compared to the performance of the PSPS system alone (the dedicated scheduler).

The hypothesis that is being tested is that the reuse of solved old cases can contribute to reduce the time needed to find feasible schedules for new problems. As our retrieval module involves isomorphism graph detection, a NP-hard problems as is our original scheduling problem, several parameters, for example, the size of each case and of the whole case base, will have a major impact on the performance of the system. In the described experiments we decided to evaluate the behavior of CBR-RTS when working with a case base composed of small cases. This case base will rarely allow to solve new problems in one single step, but should permit to simplify large problems that can be solved in multiple retrieve-simplify steps.

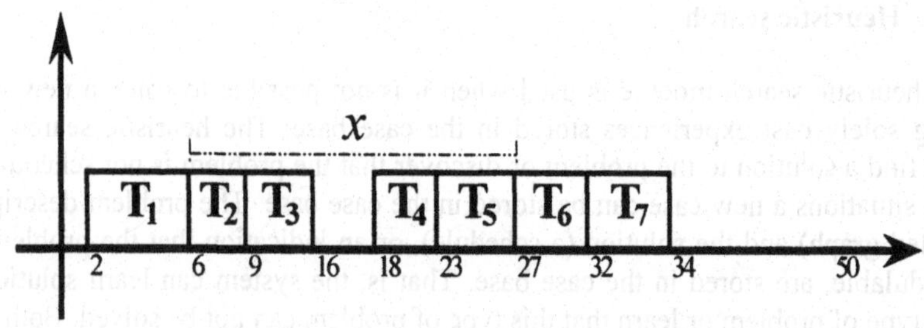

Fig. 8. Final Schedule for the new problem

4.1 The Case Base (CB)

As Miyashita and Sycara [12], we assume that although scheduling is an ill-structured domain, it exhibits some regularities that could be captured in a case. In our context, we assume that scheduling problems tend to present typical structural regularities and attribute values that characterize the main classes of problems handled. Several problems that have identical precedence relations are represented by graphs that share a common structure. These structures can be automatically learned by the system as it faces new problems.

In order to simulate a situation in which CBR-RTS had already passed for a learning period, fourteen small problems, described by graphs from 2 to 6 nodes, were presented to the system. Since the CB is initially empty, and because the presented problems are not similar to each other, they are completely solved by the heuristic search module and stored in the CB. The structure, ready times and execution times of these problems were chosen in a way that they could be highly reusable in the solution of the testing problems described below.

4.2 Testing Problems

After an initial training phase, as described before, nine testing problems, P_1, P_2, ... P_9, were submitted to the system. These problems have different sizes and several combinations of precedence relations and timing constraints. The system was able to find a complete solution to all but the 9th problem reusing the cases stored in the CB. For P_9, after two retrieve-simplify cycles, the system had to use the heuristic search module because there were no similar cases on the CB.

The conducted experiments can give a preliminary idea of the performance of the CBR-RTS system when working with a stable CB, that is, a case base that permits to solve most new problems without having to employ the heuristic search module.

4.3 CBR-RTS Performance

Table 1 shows the total processing times required by CBR-RTS and PSPS for solving problems P_1 to P_9 in a 167 MHz Sun Ultrasparc 1 workstation with 64 MB of RAM. We can see that as problem size and complexity increase there is also a appreciable increase in the relative performance of CBR-RTS compared with PSPS. This means that the cost of reusing stored cases can be sensible lower than that of generating a solution from scratch.

Table 1 also shows CBR-RTS processing times by phase. As expected, we can see that the retrieval phase accounts for most of the processing time of CBR-RTS, indicating that this is an important point to focus in future work.

The solution of problem P_9 is an example of a situation where the system is learning a new case. In this example, CBR-RTS can not find a solution to the problem using only stored cases, but it is able to simplify the problem. The simplified problem is submitted to PSPS (the heuristic search module of the system) that finds a solution in approximately 30% of the time it will require to solve the complete problem.

Table 1. *CBR-RTS and PSPS processing times (seconds)*

		PSPS	CBR-RTS			
Problem #	Problem Size (nodes)	Total Time	Total Time	Retrieval	Reusing	Learning
1	5	0.10	0.25	0.24	0.01	0
2	9	0.07	0.51	0.42	0.09	0
3	9	0.15	0.28	0.26	0.02	0
4	10	0.16	0.40	0.36	0.03	0
5	15	0.29	0.93	0.76	0.17	0
6	16	0.62	0.58	0.51	0.06	0
7	21	1.77	1.03	0.91	0.11	0
8	38	6.99	4.60	3.90	0.69	0
9	25	4.66	2.49	0.94	0.11	1.43

It is clear that the above evaluation is based on a very limited number of examples. The objective was to test the system and have a preliminary idea of its performance. We are working in testing the system to see how it scales up to large problems and case bases.

5 Related Work

In this section we will briefly review some systems that adopt solution strategies similar to ours in the domain of scheduling, and some systems, as Casey [13], that although working in a different domain have in some degree inspired the design of CBR-RTS.

Cunningham and Smyth [14] explore solution reuse in job scheduling. In their work, cases represent highly optimized structures in the problem space, produced using simulated annealing. They address single machine problems where job setup time is sequence dependent (an example of a non Euclidean Traveling Salesman Problem). Their objective is to produce good quality schedules in very quick time. Although we share the same conceptual framework, our work differs in a number of ways. We address distinct types of scheduling problems and we employ different case representations and retrieval and reusing strategies that seem to make our approach amenable for a wider category of scheduling scenarios.

Other systems also combine CBR with some other strategy to solve scheduling problems. CABINS [12], for example, integrates CBR and fine granularity constraint-directed scheduling. CABINS constructs cheap but suboptimal schedules that are incrementally repaired to meet optimization objectives based on the user preferences captured in cases. As in CABINS, we also assume that although scheduling is an ill-structured domain, it exhibits some regularities that can be captured in a case.

Some of the basic ideas of the CBR-RTS system can be found in Casey [13], a well know example of system that integrates CBR and search. Casey is built on top of a model based program implemented using rules that diagnoses heart defects. The case library is constructed using this rule based program. Casey searches the case library to see if it has old cases that can be used to diagnose a new patient, if no similar cases are found, the problem is submitted to the rule based program. When know solutions are reused, Casey can be 2 to 3 orders of magnitude more efficient that the rule based program.

PRODIGY/ANALOGY [15] is also a well know system that combines CBR with search in the solution of planning problems. The case library is seeded by cases solved by a general problem solver, based in a combination of means-ends analysis, backward chaining and state space search. Cases permit to acquire operational knowledge that can be used to guide the generation of solutions for new problems, avoiding a completely new search effort.

Although most CBR systems use flat representations in the form of attribute-value pairs, several authors have addressed the issues raised by structured representations, as the graphs used in CBR-RTS. The interested reader can find more details in [16] and [17].

6 Conclusions

The experiments described in this paper suggest that the CBR-RTS system, based on the integration of CBR with heuristic search, can contribute to reduce the processing time required to schedule complex problems. However, in order to better evaluate the potential and behavior of the system, and the subjacent architecture, it must be submitted to a testing procedure with a wider coverage than that provided by the experiments described in this paper.

CBR-RTS has a modular architecture that easily supports evolution. Each component of the systems constitutes itself an interesting research subject.

The current structure of the case base and the corresponding retrieval algorithm seem adequate for case bases storing a moderate number of small cases, as the ones considered in the experiments described in this paper. New organizations and retrieval strategies might have to be considered when dealing with case bases storing a high number of complex cases.

A particularly important problem in real-time systems is to develop deterministic schedulers that can compute schedules in bounded time. Although in the general case this can not be achieved by the NP-hard nature of scheduling problems, it would be valuable if this could be done in a reasonable amount of situations. Polynomial time subgraph isomorphism algorithms, as the one proposed by Messmer [8], can be used to address this issue.

An interesting extension to the reusing module is to try to employ old cases to solve subproblems even when they do not form a group.

The heuristic search module can also evolve in a number of ways, for example with the creation of a library of methods for solving different types of scheduling problems, besides the one currently considered.

The management of the case base is also an interesting theme. The definition of criteria to be used to decide which new cases to incorporate into the case base is one of the relevant questions to be considered. There are several possibilities here. For example, the case base can be formed only of carefully chosen small cases that permit to simplify a extensive number of large problems, as done in the experiments described in section 4. It could be also interesting to prioritize the memorization of unschedulable problems that require the searching algorithms to spend a lot of time and resources to reach that conclusion.

Currently, the heuristic search module is used only after a problem can not be further simplified. Other integrations between the retrieval and the heuristic search modules are possible and could be interesting to study. For example, instead of trying to find occurrences of stored cases in the problem graph, as done in the current version, the graph could be initially divided into groups and the system could try to see if these groups are present in the case base. After reusing the best retrieved cases to simplify the problem, the groups for which there were no applicable cases could be scheduled by the heuristic search algorithm, before proceeding in the retrieval-simplification process.

Acknowledgments

We thank Fundação de Amparo à Pesquisa no Estado de São Paulo (FAPESP) for partially supporting this research under grant #1996/11200-3. We would also like to thank ICCBR'99 anonymous reviewers for their very useful comments and suggestions. We tried to incorporate their feedback in preparing this version of the paper, naturally, remaining mistakes and omissions are our own.

References

1. Stankovic, J. A. Misconceptions About Real-Time Computing. *IEEE Computer*, October, 1988.
2. Liu, C.L., J. W. Layland. Scheduling Algorithms for Multiprogramming in a Hard-Real-Time Environment. *JACM*, vol. 20. no.1, 1973.
3. Blazewicz, J., J.K. Lenstra and A.H.G.R. Kan. Scheduling Subject to Resource Constraints: Classification and Complexity. *Discrete Applied Mathematics* 5: 11-24, 1983.
4. Adán Coello, J. M., M. F. Magalhães, K. Ramamritham. Developing predictable and flexible real-time systems. *Control Engineering Practice*. 6(1):67-81. 1998.
5. Kolodner, J. Case-Based Reasoning. Morgan Kaufmann, 1993.
6. Mok, A. K. Fundamental Desing Problems of Distributed Systems for the Distributed Hard-Real-Time Environment. PhD Thesis, Dept. of Electrical Engineering and Computer Science. Massachusetts Institute of Technology. 1983.
7. Sprunt, B., L. Sha and J. Lehoczky. Aperiodic Task Scheuling for Hard-Real-Time Systems. *The Journal of Real-Time Systems* 1, 27-60. 1989.
8. Messmer, B. T. Efficient Graph Matching algorithms for Preprocessed Model Graphs. PhD Thesis. Institute of Computer Science and Applied Mathematics, University of Bern, Switzerland, 1996.
9. Ullman, J. R. An algorithm for subgraph isomorphism. *Journal of the ACM*, 23(1):31-42, 1976.

10. Ramamritham, K., G. Fohler, J.M. Adán. Issues in the static allocation and scheduling of complex periodic tasks. In: *Proc. 10th IEEE Workshop on Real-Time Operating Systems and Software*. 1993.
11. Xu, J. and D. L. Parnas. Scheduling processes with release times, deadlines, precedence, and exclusion relations. *IEEE Transactions on Software Engineering*, 16(3):360-369. 1990.
12. Miyashita, K. and K. Sycara. CABINS: A framework of Knowledge Acquisition and Iterative Revision for Schedule Improvement and Reactive Repair. CMU Technical Report CMU-RI-TR-94-34. The Robotics Institute, Carnegie Mellon University, USA, 1995.
13. Koton, P. Reasoning about evidence in causal explanation. In *Proceedings of AAAI-88*. AAAI Press/MIT Press. Cambridge, MA, 1988.
14. Cunningham, P. and B. Smyth. Case-Based Reasoning in Scheduling: Reusing Solution Components. Technical Report TCD-CS-96-12, Department of Computer Science, Trinity College Dublin, Ireland. 1996.
15. Veloso, M. PRODIGY/ANALOGY: Analogical Reasoning in General Problem Solving. In Topics in Case-Based Reasoning, S. Wess, K. Althoff and M. Richter (Eds.) *Lecture Notes in Artificial Intelligence*, Springer-Verlag, 1994.
16. Bunke, H. and B. T. Messmer. Similarity Measures for Structured Representations. In Topics in Case-Based Reasoning, S. Wess, K. Althoff and M. Richter (Eds.) *Lecture Notes in Artificial Intelligence*, Springer-Verlag. 1994.
17. Gebhardt, F. Methods and systems for case retrieval exploiting the case structure. FABEL report no. 39. GMD, Germany. 1995.

Towards a Unified Theory of Adaptation in Case-Based Reasoning

Béatrice Fuchs[1], Jean Lieber[2], Alain Mille[3] and Amedeo Napoli[2]

[1] Université Lyon III, IAE, équipe Modeme
15 Quai Claude Bernard, 69239 LYON cedex 02
[2] LORIA – UMR 7503, BP 239 – 54506 Vandœuvre-lès-Nancy Cedex
[3] LISA-CPE, 43 Bd du 11 Novembre 1918, 69616 Villeurbanne Cedex
Email: fuchs@univ-lyon3.fr, lieber@loria.fr
am@cpe.fr, napoli@loria.fr

Abstract. Case-based reasoning exploits memorized problem solving episodes, called cases, in order to solve a new problem. Adaptation is a complex and crucial step of case-based reasoning which is generally studied in the restricted framework of an application domain. This article proposes a first analysis of case adaptation independently from a specific application domain. It proposes to combine the retrieval and adaptation steps in a unique planning process that builds an ordered sequence of operations starting from an initial state (the stated problem) and leading to a final state (the problem once solved). Thus, the issue of case adaptation can be addressed by studying the issue of plan adaptation. Finally, it is shown how case retrieval and case adaptation can be related thanks to reformulations and similarity paths.

1 Introduction

Case-based reasoning (CBR) associates to a given problem P a solution, which is built by reusing the memorized solution of a problem P' similar to P. The CBR cycle is composed of three main steps: the retrieval in which the similar problem P' is searched in the case base; the adaptation in which the solution of the similar problem P' is adapted; and the possible memorization of the problem P and its solution, in the perspective of a future reuse. The implementation of this reasoning cycle has given birth to the notion of CBR system which takes advantage of a case base, and possibly of other knowledge bases, in order to solve problems of design, interpretation, diagnostic, planning, etc.

Adapting the solution of a known problem in order to solve a new problem is one of the key ideas on which CBR relies. Many researchers of the CBR domain think that adaptation is very difficult to model and depends heavily on the application domain and thus has to be implemented in an ad hoc manner. In this article, a general model of adaptation is proposed, in the same way that plan adaptation is modeled (this approach is also studied in [Hanks and Weld, 1995]). Moreover, the adaptation itself can be considered as a planning process whose initial state is the starting solution (the solution of the known problem P') and final state is the adapted solution (the solution of the problem P). In the following, a plan is considered as a triple (I, G, O) where I is an initial state, G is a goal statement and O is a set of operations allowing to satisfy the goal statement given the data associated with O.

Modeling adaptation in this way enables to theoretically and practically consider the combination of adaptation and retrieval, in order to be sure to retrieve an adaptable case and to guide the adaptation of such a case.

The issue of adaptation in CBR is detailed in section 2 and some of the major contributions about adaptation and its model in CBR are summarized in section 3. Then, our approach is presented in two steps: it is shown that a case can be considered as a kind of plan description (section 4), and it is explained how retrieval and adaptation can be considered in an unified framework (section 5). A complete example of our approach is presented in section 6. A discussion and a conclusion end this paper (sections 7 and 8).

The approach presented in this paper can be the basis of a formalization of CBR and can be reused to design CBR systems possibly in any domain.

2 The issue of adaptation in CBR

The aim of case-based reasoning is to solve a problem called *target problem* (or new problem) and denoted by `target`, by using a *case base* which is a finite set of cases. A case is given by a problem `P` and the solution `Sol(P)` of this problem; it is denoted by the ordered pair (`P`, `Sol(P)`). A case of the case base is called a *source case* and is denoted by (`source`, `Sol(source)`); `source` is called the *source problem*. *Retrieval* consists in choosing in the case base a case (`source`, `Sol(source)`) *similar* to `target`.[1] *Adaptation* consists in taking inspiration from the solution `Sol(source)` in order to solve `target`. It can be symbolized by the figure 1 which can be read this way: "Given `source`, `Sol(source)`, `target` and the relations between these objects, what is `Sol(target)`?" This *adaptation scheme* is inspired from [Carbonell, 1986].

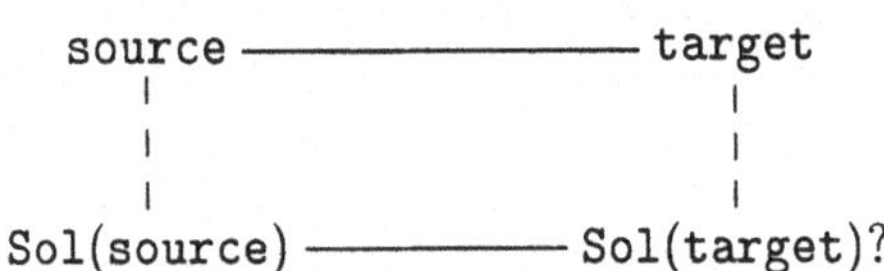

Fig. 1. The adaptation scheme. The vertical dash lines represent the relation between a problem and one of its solutions; the horizontal lines represent the relation between the sources and the targets.

Case-based reasoning relies on the reuse of past experience in order to solve a new problem. By definition, reuse involves that past experience, considered in a new context, has to be adapted to this new context. Thus, the retrieval of a similar case aims at finding

[1] In fact, similarity is generally evaluated between `source` and `target` but `Sol(source)` can play a role in this evaluation. Indeed, the part of `source` which is relevant with respect to its solution `Sol(source)` can be used to assess the similarity (see e.g. [Veloso, 1994]).

an adaptable case. Therefore, it is important that the knowledge used for retrieval is directly linked with the knowledge used for adaptation. In other words, the designer of a CBR system should not dissociate these two knowledge sources in practice. Even if the adaptation task is performed by the user or another problem solving system (then it will be a subproblem of the main problem solving cycle) the retrieval step should be controlled by knowledge directly linked with adaptation. Ideally, the retrieved case is adaptable in order to be reused for solving a new problem.

Let us consider again the adaptation scheme of figure 1. It can be considered along vertical and horizontal dimensions. The vertical dimension corresponds to the relation between the problems and the solutions. This relation is precised in section 4. The horizontal dimension corresponds to the relation between the "targets" (the target problem and its solution that has to be found) and the "sources" (the source problem and its know solution). The two horizontal lines of the adaptation scheme correspond to the retrieval and adaptation processes: the line between problems read from right to left –from `target` to `source`– represents the retrieval process, the line between solutions read from left to right –from `Sol(source)` to `Sol(target)`– represents the adaptation process. Thus retrieval and adaptation can be viewed as two "parallel" processes. This issue is detailed in section 5. Before presenting these two "orthogonal" views of adaptation, some other approaches of adaptation are presented in next section.

3 Some Approaches of Adaptation

Derivational and transformational analogies have been introduced in [Carbonell, 1986] as two different adaptation processes. The former consists in adapting the memorized solution construction process in order to produce a solution to the new problem, whereas the latter consists in copying the memorized solution and substituting some elements by other elements in order to produce the solution of the new problem. In particular, it can be noticed that, when the plan of solution construction is known, then the solution can be immediately computed and thus is also known, and so the *plan of solution construction can be considered to be the real solution* (at least, the solution that should be returned by the retrieval process). By combining retrieval and adaptation and by considering the retrieval/adaptation process as a problem solving in planning, there is no fundamental difference between substituting some elements of solution and substituting some steps, which puts in question the duality between derivational and transformational analogies.

Among the recent works about adaptation, the following ones are the ones which have more inspired our works and which have marked the researches on adaptation (see also [Voß, 1996a]):

- The adaptation-guided retrieval described in [Smyth and Keane, 1996] is an approach of retrieval taking into account some adaptation knowledge. This knowledge is represented by the *adaptation specialists* and the *adaptation strategies*. When a source case is compared to a target problem, the specialists needed to the adaptation of this case are pointed out. The case needing the minimum of adaptation effort is chosen and afterwards adapted by the application of specialists, which is guided by the strategies. The strategies control in particular the order of the application of specialists.

- In [Leake *et al.*, 1997a] is presented an approach to adaptation which relies on a search in memory of the best cases in which some elements of solution will be substituted. This search is based on a contextual similarity (see also [Hammond, 1989], [Leake, 1993], [Leake, 1995], [Leake *et al.*, 1995], [Leake *et al.*, 1996], [Leake *et al.*, 1997b], [Leake *et al.*, 1997c]).
- The adaptation problem can be seen as a constraint satisfaction problem, which involves that a constraint-based model is well-suited for the studied problem (such a model is often well-suited for problems of simulation, design, architecture, etc.). The solution of a new problem is built by satisfying the new constraints and by transforming a memorized solution [Hua *et al.*, 1996] (see also [Hua *et al.*, 1994], [Smith *et al.*, 1995], [Purvis and Pu, 1995], [Smith *et al.*, 1996], [Kumar and Raphael, 1997]).
- In the framework of hierarchical adaptation [Bergmann and Wilke, 1995], abstract cases (i.e., cases that help to consider a problem at different level of abstraction: the more abstract is the context, the "easier" to solve is the problem) are exploited instead of concrete cases and a *refining* of the solutions down the different levels of abstraction enable to build a solution of the new problem (see also [Voß, 1996b], [Voß, 1996c], [Bergmann and Wilke, 1996], [Branting and Aha, 1995], [Smyth, 1996]).
- In [Koehler, 1996], case-based planning is presented in the framework of description logics and is analyzed from a formal viewpoint: cases are plans represented by formulas in a temporal logic and the indexes of these cases are represented by concepts in a description logic. Indexes are organized in a hierarchy which is exploited by a classification process, which is the basic mechanism of retrieval. A problem `source` can be chosen in order to be reused to solve a problem `target` if the indexes associated to the initial and final states of these problems verify the following constraints: $\mathtt{idx}(\mathtt{init}_{\mathtt{target}}) \sqsubseteq \mathtt{idx}(\mathtt{init}_{\mathtt{source}})$ *and/or* $\mathtt{idx}(\mathtt{goal}_{\mathtt{source}}) \sqsubseteq \mathtt{idx}(\mathtt{goal}_{\mathtt{target}})$. The connective *and* corresponds to the *strong* retrieval and the connective *or* to the *weak* retrieval. If the retrieval is strong, then each source case verifying the above conditions can be reused in order to solve `target`. If the retrieval is weak, the best candidate case is the one sharing the more subgoals or preconditions (or both) with the problem `target`. In this circumstances, it is possible to fix a minimum threshold for the adaptation effort and if no candidate satisfy this threshold, the construction of a solution of `target` must be done thanks to a from scratch planner.

Each of these works deals with a specific aspect of adaptation, at a given level of abstraction. However, the adaptation process is always considered to be deconnected to the other operations of the CBR, in particular, of the retrieval process. In order to go further, it is necessary to try to address two challenges: (1) being able to define generally what is a case and to model adaptation independently of any application domain, (2) combining the retrieval and adaptation operations in a single operation. The previous works and some works done with applications have been helpful to Mille, Fuchs and Herbeaux, on the one hand, and to Melis, Lieber and Napoli, on the other hand, to model their viewpoints about adaptation which, together, enable to address the challenges (1) and (2):

- Works like DESIGNER [Chiron and Mille, 1997] in the design domain of supervision systems, like PAD'IM [Fuchs *et al.*, 1995; Mille *et al.*, 1999] in the domain of decision helping, like ACCELERE [Herbeaux and Mille, 1998] or SYSEXPERT (presented at [Mille *et al.*, 1995]) have given a first field of study for an initial attempt to a unified theory of adaptation presented in [Mille *et al.*, 1996]. The adaptation of a case is considered as a plan adaptation which steps are considered at different levels of granularity, which enables to model it with the use of simple operations of adding or removing elements at the same level of granularity.
- The work presented in [Melis, 1995] on the one hand, and the one presented in [Lieber and Napoli, 1996; Lieber and Napoli, 1998], on the other hand, share a common view of adaptation which has involved the notions of reformulation and similarity path [Melis *et al.*, 1998]. A *reformulation* is an ordered pair (r_P, r_S) where r_P is a relation between two problems pb_0 and pb_1 –$\mathrm{pb}_0\ r_P\ \mathrm{pb}_1$– and r_S is a functional relation associating to a known solution $\mathtt{Sol}(\mathrm{pb}_0)$ of pb_0 a solution $\mathtt{Sol}(\mathrm{pb}_1)$ of pb_1 –$\mathtt{Sol}(\mathrm{pb}_0) \xmapsto{r_S} \mathtt{Sol}(\mathrm{pb}_1)$. r_S is called a *specific adaptation function*. Two reformulations (r_P^1, r_S^1) et (r_P^2, r_S^2) can be composed: if $\mathrm{pb}_0\ r_P^1\ \mathrm{pb}_1$ and $\mathrm{pb}_1\ r_P^2\ \mathrm{pb}_2$ then it is possible to adapt a solution $\mathtt{Sol}(\mathrm{pb}_0)$ of pb_0 in a solution $\mathtt{Sol}(\mathrm{pb}_2)$ of pb_2 by applying r_S^1 and r_S^2 in sequence: $\mathtt{Sol}(\mathrm{pb}_0) \xmapsto{r_S^1} \mathtt{Sol}(\mathrm{pb}_1) \xmapsto{r_S^2} \mathtt{Sol}(\mathrm{pb}_2)$. More generally, a sequence $\mathrm{pb}_0\ r_P^1\ \mathrm{pb}_1 \ldots \mathrm{pb}_{q-1}\ r_P^q\ \mathrm{pb}_q$ is called a *similarity path* between pb_0 and pb_q. Retrieval consists in finding a similarity path between a source problem (to be chosen in the case base) and the target problem. Adaptation consists in applying in sequence the specific adaptation functions r_S^i. Thus, retrieval points out not only an adaptable case but also builds a similarity path which will be reused by the adaptation process.

What is presented below is the result of a research work which aims at "unifying" the work described in [Mille *et al.*, 1996] that considers a case as a plan and the work described in [Melis *et al.*, 1998] that combines retrieval and adaptation in a unique process.

4 A case is a kind of plan

A problem to be solved is represented by the description `target` for which a description of a solution `Sol(target)` is required. The problem description contains the goal statement (the descriptors which have to be satisfied by the solution) and the initial context, i.e., the descriptors which are satisfied at the beginning of the problem solving process. For short, a descriptor can be a pair (attribute, value) or a constraint that must be verified. To satisfy a descriptor means either that the value of the corresponding attribute has to be found or that the corresponding constraint must be satisfied. The description of the solution is composed of the descriptors which must be verified *in order to satisfy the goal* given the initial context of the case (remember that the solution is a byproduct of the construction plan of the solution, cf. §3). Recall that a plan is a triple (I, G, O) and according to this view, every case is represented by an initial state I –the initial context–, a final state G –the goal statement– and a sequence of operations O leading from the state I to the state G (for the sake of simplicity, such a sequence is supposed to be a totally ordered list of state-operation pairs). This hypothesis is not too restrictive since the elaboration of the solution can be seen as a plan of problem solving (see [Polya, 1957], [Newell, 1980] and [Laird *et al.*, 1987] for discussions on this viewpoint). This means that an initial state, a goal and a set of operators –enabling to generate a state space– are necessary (such a problem is called a search problem in [Charniak and McDermott, 1985]). The problem solving process for problems such as finding an apartment price or identifying an unknown object relies on a combination of adding, removing and substituting attribute values, and these three operations can be considered as elementary operations associated with a plan. Then, case adaptation can be reduced to plan adaptation, giving a way to take advantage of general and context-less works done on adaptation [Hanks and Weld, 1995].

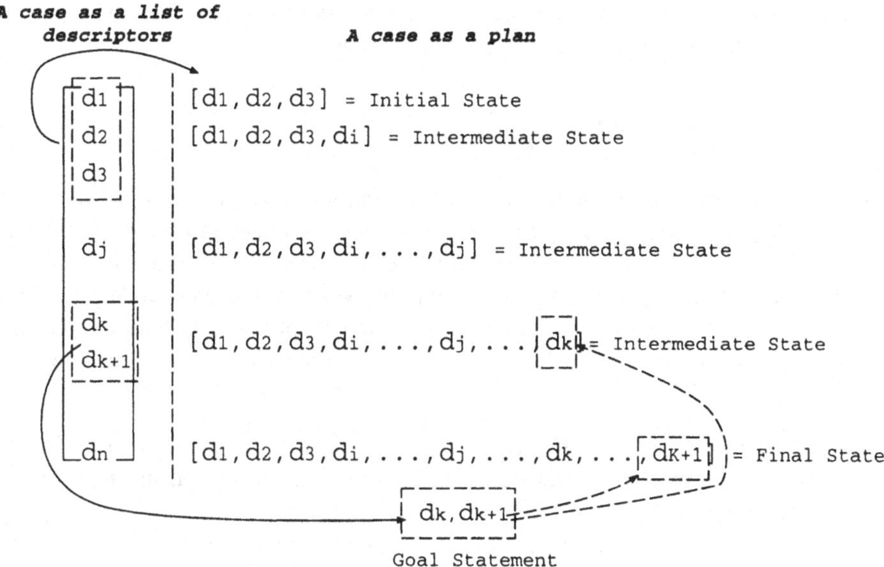

Fig. 2. The descriptors $[d_1, d_2, d_3]$ represent what is true at the beginning of the problem solving process (the initial state), while $[d_k, d_{k+1}]$ represent what has to be true when the problem will be solved (the goal statement). Other descriptors represent different parts of the solution. From the initial state, the problem solving process can be represented by its different intermediate states integrating new solution elements until the goal statement is satisfied.

Plan adaptation has been presented in the literature with two approaches [Hanks and Weld, 1995]: a generative approach in which all the knowledge necessary for generating a solution plan from scratch is available, and a transformational approach in which the previous hypothesis is not necessary and that is based on reuse (to find a solution in the latter case is not warranted). Actually, in both approaches, the knowledge needed to identify the steps to be transformed expresses, in a way or another, the role played by one step (element of the solution) in order to satisfy the goal description and to be conform to the description of the initial state. The differences between the description of the target problem and the description of the retrieved source problem allow to evaluate the variation to be reduced in the description of the source solution in order to elaborate the description of the target problem. For instance, if `source` is the problem "How can I go from Paris to Munich?" and `target` is "How can I go from Lyon to Munich?", the observed difference –the difference between the initial states Paris and Lyon– enables to modify the journey Paris-Munich so that it becomes Lyon-Munich, for example by concatenating the short journey Lyon-Paris and the journey Paris-Munich. In the generative approach, this allows to start from a general plan which is not in contradiction with the problem, and to generate the missing steps, whereas, in the situation of transformational approach, this enables to locate the steps to be substituted or to be modified (either a single modification or a sequence of modifications). In both situations, the adaptation can be decomposed into a generalization of the source case compatible with the target problem, then to a specialization satisfying the descriptors of the target problem. The next section details the generic steps of such an adaptation.

5 Adapting a case like a plan

Solving a problem consists in *building the list (ordered or not) of the solution descriptors leading to the satisfaction of the goal statement.* In planning from first principles (i.e., without the concrete experience represented by a case base) it is a plan generation problem which has been the subject of numerous works. Using a concrete experience, typically in the framework of CBR, involves a different approach, such as the following (illustrated by the figure 3 which is an instantiation of the adaptation scheme presented at the figure 1):

(a) Elaborating an index of the problem `target`, denoted by `idx(target)`. This index is constituted by the relevant descriptors (initial state, goal statement) of the problem to be solved.
(b) Finding an index `idx(source)` of the source case similar to `idx(target)`. Each case from the base must have an associated index to make this comparison possible.
(c) From the index `idx(source)`, the problem `source` can be found easily.
(d) The solution `Sol(source)` of `source` is taken as a starting point for solving the target problem. This item references the correspondence between retrieval in the problem description space and adaptation in the solution description space.
(e) The solution `Sol(source)` is generalized in order to stay consistent with the index `idx(source)`: a solution `Sol(idx(source))` of the index of the source problem is searched.
(f) The solution `Sol(idx(source))` is specialized in order to become a solution `Sol(idx(target))` for the generalization `idx(target)` of the target problem.
(g) Then the solution `Sol(idx(target))` is specialized in order to take into account simplifications made during the generalization of `target` into `idx(target)` (corresponding to elaboration, step (a)).

Note that this approach is a specialization of the more general approach of reformulation (see section 2). Indeed, the steps (a), (b) and (c) can be considered as the

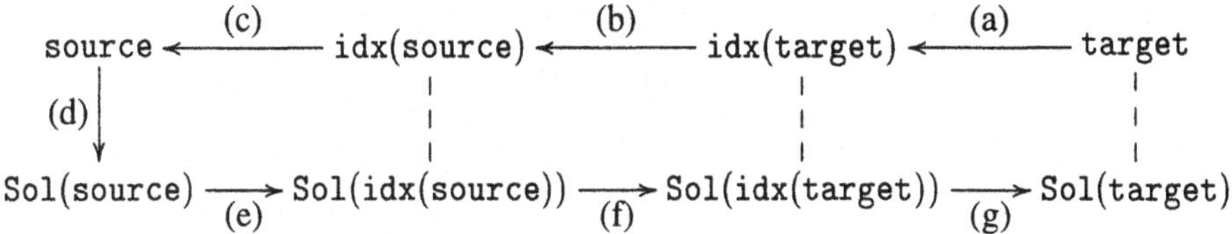

Fig. 3. General scheme of target problem resolution from a source plan.

construction of a similarity path (during retrieval), and the steps (e), (f) and (g) correspond to the application of specific adaptation functions (during adaptation). Note also that step (b) and the corresponding step (f) can be decomposed into several simple steps. In [Lieber and Napoli, 1996], in the framework of *strong classification* step (b) simply consists in searching an index `idx(source)` more general than `idx(target)`; in the framework of *smooth classification*, a whole sequence of relations r_P between an index `idx(source)` to be chosen and the index `idx(target)` is searched.

6 An Example in Route Planning

This example consists in building a route in order to reach an ending town from a starting town by using a network of roads. A case is a route that we denote by (`init`, `goal`, `date`, `vehicle`, `segments`, `duration`) where `init` is the initial town, `goal` is the final town, `date` is the date of the journey, `vehicle` is the vehicle used, `segments` is a sequence of intermediary segments and `duration` is the duration of the journey. A *segment* is denoted by (`start`, `end`) where `start` is the starting town and `end` is the ending town. A target problem is given by an initial town $\texttt{init}_{\texttt{target}}$ and a goal town (to be reached) $\texttt{goal}_{\texttt{target}}$.

The domain theory is given by a set of towns $\{A, B, ..., I\}$, and, for every town T, a set containing some of its direct neighbors T′ ∈ `neighbors`(T): T′ can be reached from T using an elementary route. The known neighbors are represented by the following table:

T	neighbors(T)
A	$\{B,E,G\}$
B	$\{A,C,E\}$
C	$\{B,D,E\}$
D	$\{C,F,I\}$
E	$\{A,C,F,G\}$
F	$\{D,E,H\}$
G	$\{A,E,H\}$
H	$\{F,G\}$
I	$\{D\}$

The distance between two towns T and T′ is defined as follows:

$$d(\mathrm{T},\mathrm{T}') = \begin{cases} 0 & if\ \mathrm{T} = \mathrm{T}' \\ 1 & if\ \mathrm{T} \in \mathtt{neighbors}(\mathrm{T}') \\ +\infty & if\ \mathrm{T} \notin \mathtt{neighbors}(\mathrm{T}') \end{cases}$$

The elaboration step builds an index of the target problem by retaining only the descriptors $\mathtt{init}_{\mathtt{target}}$ and $\mathtt{goal}_{\mathtt{target}}$ that are juged more relevant. The index of the source case is reduced to the pair composed of the initial town and the goal town, other descriptors such as date and vehicle are juged less relevant:

$$\mathtt{idx}(\mathtt{target}) = (\mathtt{init}_{\mathtt{target}}, \mathtt{goal}_{\mathtt{target}})$$
$$\mathtt{idx}(\mathtt{source}) = (\mathtt{init}_{\mathtt{source}}, \mathtt{goal}_{\mathtt{source}})$$

A distance between a source index and a target index is defined as follows:

$$\mathtt{dist}(\mathtt{idx}(\mathtt{source}), \mathtt{idx}(\mathtt{target})) = d(\mathtt{init}_{\mathtt{source}}, \mathtt{init}_{\mathtt{target}}) + d(\mathtt{goal}_{\mathtt{source}}, \mathtt{goal}_{\mathtt{target}})$$

The content of the case base is

case number	idx(source)	Sol(source)
1	(A,C)	$\{((A,B),(B,C)), 2{:}00\}$
2	(C,G)	$\{((C,E),(E,G)), 1{:}30\}$
3	(A,D)	$\{((A,B),(B,C),(C,D)), 3{:}00\}$
4	(D,C)	$\{((D,C)), 1{:}00\}$
5	(H,E)	$\{((H,F),(F,E)), 2{:}00\}$
6	(E,B)	$\{((E,C),(C,B)), 2{:}15\}$
7	(G,D)	$\{((G,E),(E,C),(C,D)), 2{:}45\}$
8	(B,I)	$\{((B,C),(C,D),(D,I)), 3{:}15\}$

A target problem target $=$ $(B, D, \text{February}, \text{2CV Citroën})$ is created. The elaboration of the index of the target gives idx(target) $=$ (B,D). This index is matched with the source case indexes giving the following distance table:

case number	idx(source)	dist(idx(source), idx(target))
1	(A,C)	2
2	(C,G)	$+\infty$
3	(A,D)	1
4	(D,C)	$+\infty$
5	(H,E)	$+\infty$
6	(E,B)	$+\infty$
7	(G,D)	$+\infty$
8	(B,I)	1

The general solving scheme of a target problem presented in figure 3 is the following (illustrated by figure 4):

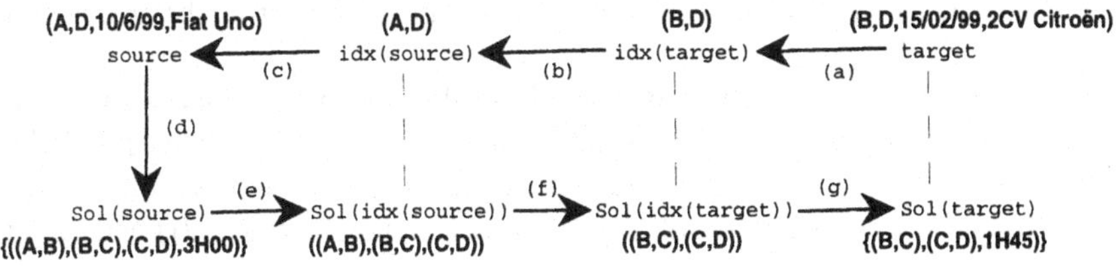

Fig. 4. Solving the target problem by reusing the case 3.

(a) The index of the target problem is built: $\texttt{idx(target)} = (B, D)$.
(b) An index of a source case is searched in the case base. Possible values are (A, D) and (B, I): both minimize $\texttt{dist(idx(source), idx(target))}$. $\texttt{idx(source)} = (A, D)$ is chosen arbitrarily.
(c) From (A, D), the source case $(A, D, \text{June}, \texttt{Fiat Uno})$ is reached.
(d) The solution $\texttt{Sol(source)} = \{((A, B), (B, C), (C, D)), \texttt{3:00}\}$ of the source case is reused for the target problem.
(e) The generalization of $\texttt{Sol(source)}$ in $\texttt{Sol(idx(source))}$ suppresses the descriptor duration: $\texttt{Sol(idx(source))} = ((A, B), (B, C), (C, D))$.
(f) The solution is specialized in $\texttt{Sol(idx(target))} = ((B, C), (C, D))$ by removing the segment (A, B). Such an adaptation operation is described among other ones in [Lieber and Napoli, 1998].
(g) The solution $\texttt{Sol(idx(target))}$ is specialized in $\texttt{Sol(target)} = \{((B, C), (C, D)), \texttt{1:45}\}$ where the descriptor duration has been evaluated and added to the solution.

7 Discussion and Future Work

In this article, a unified model of the retrieval and adaptation steps in CBR is proposed. This model is simple and clear and puts in question the common idea saying that adaptation can be only contextual. Moreover, this proposition could be used for a deep discussion about the two key phases of the CBR cycle. It must be noticed, however, that we have assumed that a problem can be considered as a planning problem, with a general meaning of this notion, i.e., an initial state, a goal statement and a collection of operators which enables to generate a state space are needed (such a problem is called a *search problem* in [Charniak and McDermott, 1985]). Then adaptation can be considered as a sequence of generalizations, specializations and substitutions performed at different levels of abstraction in the process of solution construction. Note that a substitution can be seen as a composition of a removal and an adjunction.

It is necessary to justify more precisely the assumption made on the type of problems and to show that it works correctly on every type of problems: this is one of the first future works. Moreover, we need to make more progress in the formal description of this work in order to formalize the retrieval-adaptation process independently of any context. Then, such a formalization could be used as a guideline during the design of a CBR system.

Some issues of this study must be detailed. First, the links between the vertical and horizontal views of adaptation (sections 4 and 5, respectively) must be studied precisely. Then, the links with the works on plan adaptation have to be pointed out. Finally, the steps (a), (b) and (c) of case retrieval and the corresponding steps (e), (f) and (g) of adaptation must be studied in detail.

To complete this study, the learning step of case-based reasoning must be integrated. In this context, learning is not limited to the storage of a new ordered pair (problem, solution) in the case base, but means also learning new retrieval and adaptation knowledge from retrievals and adaptations already performed and which have led to a stored and analyzed success or failure. Several research directions can be considered, linked with the explanations that can be entailed from a success or a failure of the solving process (such an approach is also studied in [Ihrig and Kambhampati, 1997]). The learning mechanism consists then in exhibiting a sequence of justifications –of success or failure– which will be used as rules during the future adaptations and of "use instruction" during case reuse.

This model work mainly derives from two complementary works –[Mille *et al.*, 1996] and [Melis *et al.*, 1998]– which themselves rely on real-world applications (DESIGNER, PAD'IM, ACCELERE and SYSEXPERT for [Mille *et al.*, 1996] and OMEGA and RESYN/CBR for [Melis *et al.*, 1998]). As future work, we plan to study systematically other applications of CBR in the light of this model. A last future work, which fully justifies this model, is its use for the design of CBR applications. Thus, the usefulness of this formalism and its limitations could be more accurately pointed out.

8 Conclusion

In this paper, elements for a unified theory of adaptation in the case-based reasoning framework are presented. First, the assumption that case adaptation can be considered as a plan adaptation is justified. Under this assumption, the works on adaptation in case-based planning can be reused. Then, case adaptation –seen as a kind of plan adaptation– is defined *in parallel* with case retrieval. Indeed, the steps of the target problem elaboration (or indexing), of the search for an index of the source problem, and of the search for a source problem corresponding to this index are related to three adaptation steps. This point of view is mainly based on the study of real-world applications and can be made operational. More work remains to be done, especially to make more precise and to formalize this study, so that it can be reused for CBR system constrution. Moreover, this study has also to take into account the learning step of CBR to give a complete account of the CBR process.

References

[Bergmann and Wilke, 1995] R. Bergmann and W. Wilke. Building and Refining Abstract Planning Cases by Change of Representation Language. *Journal of Artificial Intelligence Research*, 3:53–118, 1995.

[Bergmann and Wilke, 1996] R. Bergmann and W. Wilke. PARIS : Flexible Plan Adaptation by Abstraction and Refinement. In A. Voß, R. Bergmann, and B. Bartsch-Spörl, editors, *Workshop on Adaptation in Case-Based Reasoning, ECAI-96*, Budapest, Hungary, August 1996.

[Branting and Aha, 1995] L. K. Branting and D. W. Aha. Stratified Case-Based Reasoning: Reusing Hierarchical Problem Solving Episodes. In *Proceedings of the 14th International Joint Conference on Artificial Intelligence (IJCAI'95), Montréal*, volume 1, pages 384–390, August 1995.

[Carbonell, 1986] J. G. Carbonell. Derivational analogy: A Theory of Reconstructive Problem Solving and Expertise Acquisition. In *Machine Learning*, volume 2, chapter 14, pages 371–392. Springer-Verlag, 1986.

[Charniak and McDermott, 1985] E. Charniak and D.V. McDermott. *Introduction to Artificial Intelligence*. Addison Wesley, Reading, Massachusetts, 1985.

[Chiron and Mille, 1997] B. Chiron and A. Mille. Aide à la conception d'environnements de supervision par réutilisation de l'expérience. In *JICAA'97, ROSCOFF, 20-22 Mai 1997*, pages 181–187, 1997.

[Fuchs *et al.*, 1995] B. Fuchs, A. Mille, and B. Chiron. Operator decision aiding by adaptation of supervision strategies. In *Lecture Notes in Artificial Intelligence vol 1010, First International Conference on Case-Based Reasoning, ICCBR'95*, pages 23–32, Sesimbra, Portugal, 1995. Springer-Verlag, Berlin, Germany.

[Hammond, 1989] Kristian Hammond. *Case-based planning: viewing planning as a memory task*. Academic Press, San Diego, 1989.

[Hanks and Weld, 1995] S. Hanks and D.S. Weld. A Domain-Independent Algorithm for Plan Adaptation. *Journal of Artificial Intelligence Research*, 2:3191–360, 1995.

[Herbeaux and Mille, 1998] O. Herbeaux and A. Mille. ACCELERE : un système d'aide à la conception de caoutchouc cellulaire exploitant la réutilisation de l'expérience. *Journal Européen des Systèmes Automatisés*, 1998. Soumis au Journal Européen des Systèmes Automatisés, disponible comme rapport de recherche.

[Hua *et al.*, 1994] K. Hua, I. Smith, and B. Faltings. Integrated Case-Based Building Design. In S. Wess, K.-D. Althoff, and M.M. Richter, editors, *Topics in Case-Based Reasoning – First European Workshop (EWCBR'93), Kaiserslautern*, Lecture Notes in Artificial Intelligence 837, pages 458–469. Springer Verlag, Berlin, 1994.

[Hua *et al.*, 1996] K. Hua, B. Faltings, and I. Smith. CADRE: case-based geometric design. *Artificial Intelligence in Engineering*, 10:171–183, 1996.

[Ihrig and Kambhampati, 1997] L.H. Ihrig and S. Kambhampati. Storing and Indexing Plan Derivation through Explanation-based Analysis of Retrieval Failures. *Journal of Artificial Intelligence Research*, 7:161–198, 1997.

[Koehler, 1996] J. Koehler. Planning from Second Principles. *Artificial Intelligence*, 87:145–186, 1996.

[Kumar and Raphael, 1997] B. Kumar and B. Raphael. Cadrem: A case based system for conceptual structural design. *Engineering with Computers*, 13(3):153–164, 1997.

[Laird *et al.*, 1987] J.E. Laird, A. Newell, and P.S. Rosenbloom. SOAR: An Architecture for General Intelligence. *AI Magazine*, 33(1):1–64, 1987.

[Leake *et al.*, 1995] D. B. Leake, A. Kinley, and D. Wilson. Learning to Improve Case Adaptation by Introspective Reasoning and CBR. In M. Veloso and A. Aamodt, editors, *Case-Based Reasoning Research an Development. Proceedings of the First International Conference on Case-Based Reasoning - ICCBR-95*, pages 229–240, Sesimbra, Portugal, 23–26 octobre 1995. Lecture Notes in Artificial Intelligence, volume 1010, Springer Verlag, Berlin.

[Leake *et al.*, 1996] D. B. Leake, A. Kinley, and D. Wilson. Acquiring case adaptation knowledge: A hybrid approach. In *Proceedings of the 14th National Conference on Artificial Intelligence, Menlo Park, CA*, pages 684–689. AAAI Press, Menlo Park, CA, 1996.

[Leake *et al.*, 1997a] D. B. Leake, A. Kinley, and D. Wilson. A Case Study of Case-Based CBR. In D. B. Leake and E. Plaza, editors, *Case-Based Reasoning Research and Development – Second International Conference, ICCBR'97, Providence, RI, USA*, Lecture Notes in Artificial Intelligence 1266, pages 371–382. Springer Verlag, Berlin, 1997.

[Leake *et al.*, 1997b] D. B. Leake, A. Kinley, and D. Wilson. Case-based similarity assessment: Estimating adaptability from experience. In *Proceedings of the Fourteenth National Conference on Artificial Intelligence*. AAAI Press, Menlo Park, CA, 1997.

[Leake *et al.*, 1997c] D. B. Leake, A. Kinley, and D. Wilson. Learning to integrate multiple knowledge sources for case-based reasoning. In *Proceedings of the 15th International Joint Conference on Artificial Intelligence*. Morgan Kaufmann, 1997.

[Leake, 1993] D. B. Leake. Learning adaptation strategies by introspective reasoning about memory search. In *AAAI93 Workshop on Case-Based Reasoning*, pages 57–63, 1993.

[Leake, 1995] D. B. Leake. Representing self-knowledge for introspection about memory search. In *Proceedings of the AAAI Spring Symposium on Representing Mental States and Mechanisms*, 1995.

[Lieber and Napoli, 1996] J. Lieber and A. Napoli. Using Classification in Case-Based Planning. In W. Wahlster, editor, *Proceedings of the 12th European Conference on Artificial Intelligence (ECAI'96), Budapest, Hungary*, pages 132–136. John Wiley & Sons, Ltd., 1996.

[Lieber and Napoli, 1998] J. Lieber and A. Napoli. Correct and Complete Retrieval for Case-Based Problem-Solving. In H. Prade, editor, *Proceedings of the 13th European Conference on Artificial Intelligence (ECAI-98), Brighton, United Kingdom*, pages 68–72, 1998.

[Melis *et al.*, 1998] E. Melis, J. Lieber, and A. Napoli. Reformulation in Case-Based Reasoning. In B. Smyth and P. Cunningham, editors, *Fourth European Workshop on Case-Based Reasoning, EWCBR-98*, Lecture Notes in Artificial Intelligence 1488, pages 172–183. Springer, 1998.

[Melis, 1995] E. Melis. A model of analogy-driven proof-plan construction. In *Proceedings of the 14th International Joint Conference on Artificial Intelligence (IJCAI'95)*, pages 182–189, Montréal, 1995.

[Mille *et al.*, 1995] A. Mille, J.-L. Di-Martino, and A. Michel. Adaptation : the key-point in Case Based Reasoning. A case study : Digester Programming Helping, 1995. presented at the Workshop on practical developments strategies for industrial strength Case Based Reasoning applications, 16th International Conference on Artificial Intelligence, IJCAI'95, Montreal, Canada.

[Mille *et al.*, 1996] A. Mille, B. Fuchs, and O. Herbeaux. A unifying framework for Adaptation in Case-Based Reasoning. In A. Voß, editor, *Proceedings of the ECAI'96 Workshop: Adaptation in Case-Based Reasoning*, pages 22–28, 1996.

[Mille *et al.*, 1999] A. Mille, B. Fuchs, and B. Chiron. Le raisonnement fondé sur l'expérience : un nouveau paradigme en supervision industrielle ? *à paraître dans la Revue d'Intelligence Artificielle*, 1999.

[Newell, 1980] A. Newell. Reasoning, Problem Solving, and Decision Processes: The Problem Space as a Fundamental Category. In R. Nickerson, editor, *Attention and Performances VIII*, pages 693–718. Lawrence Erlbaum Associates, Hillsdale, NJ, 1980.

[Polya, 1957] G. Polya. *How to Solve it.* Doubleday Anchor Books, New York, NY, 1957.

[Purvis and Pu, 1995] L. Purvis and P. Pu. Adaptation Using Constraint Satisfaction Techniques. In M. Veloso and A. Aamodt, editors, *Case-Based Reasoning Research And Development. Proceedings Of The First International Conference On Case-Based Reasoning - ICCBR-95*, pages 289–300, Sesimbra, Portugal, 23–26 Octobre 1995. Lecture Notes In Artificial Intelligence, Volume 1010, Springer Verlag, Berlin.

[Smith *et al.*, 1995] I. Smith, C. Lottaz, and B. Faltings. Spatial composition using case : Idiom. In Manuela Veloso and Agnar Aamodt, editors, *Case-Based Reasoning Reasearch And Development, Iccbr'95*, pages 88–97, Sesimbra (Portugal), Octobre 1995.

[Smith *et al.*, 1996] I. Smith, R. Stalker, and C. Lottaz. Interactive case-based spatial composition. 1996.

[Smyth and Keane, 1996] B. Smyth and M. T. Keane. Using adaptation knowledge to retrieve and adapt design cases. *Knowledge-Based Systems*, 9(2):127–135, 1996.

[Smyth, 1996] B. Smyth. *Case-Based Design.* PhD thesis, Trinity College, University of Dublin, 1996.

[Veloso, 1994] M. M. Veloso. *Planning and Learning by Analogical Reasoning.* LNAI 886. Springer Verlag, Berlin, 1994.

[Voß, 1996a] A. Voß, editor. *Proceedings of the ECAI'96 Workshop: Adaptation in Case-Based Reasoning*, 1996.

[Voß, 1996b] A. Voß. Structural Adaptation with TOPO. In A. Voß, R. Bergmann, and B. Bartsch-Spörl, editors, *Workshop on Adaptation in Case-Based Reasoning, ECAI-96*, Budapest, Hungary, August 1996.

[Voß, 1996c] Angi Voß. How to solve complex problems with cases. *Engineering applications of artificial intelligence*, 9(4):377–384, 1996.

A Knowledge-Level Task Model of Adaptation in Case-Based Reasoning

Béatrice Fuchs[1], Alain Mille[2]

[1] Université Lyon III, IAE - équipe MODEME, 15 quai Claude Bernard, 69 239 Lyon cedex 02, fuchs@univ-lyon3.fr
[2] CPE-Lyon, LISA, équipe Raisonnement à Partir de Cas, 43 bd du 11 novembre 1918, 69 616 Villeurbanne cedex, am@cpe.fr

Abstract. The adaptation step is central in case-based reasoning (CBR), because it conditions the obtaining of a solution to a problem. This step is difficult from the knowledge acquisition and engineering points of view. We propose a knowledge level analysis of the adaptation step in CBR using the reasoning task concept. Our proposal is based on the study of several CBR systems for complex applications which imply the adaptation task. Three of them are presented to illustrate our analysis. We sketch from this study a generic model of the adaptation process using the task concept. This model is in conformity with other CBR formal models.

1 Introduction

CBR systems reuse the solution of a solved case to build a solution of a new problem. The basic CBR cycle is made of five steps : a request specifying a new problem to solve being given, the system *elaborates*[1] a new problem description named the *target problem*, *retrieves* a case named the *source case* from a *case base*, *reuses* the solution of the source case by adapting it for the target problem, *retains* the new case in order to make it available for further problem solvings.

The adaptation step in CBR is central because it conditions the obtaining of a solution to the problem. This step has been studied in several papers [Hanks and Weld, 1995], [Voß, 1997], [Bergmann and Wilke, 1995], [Voß, 1996], [Leake et al., 1997], [Hua et al., 1993], [Hua et al., 1996], [Koehler, 1996] but it is still difficult to approach and it is rarely implemented in practical applications. Instead of handling adaptation, most systems retrieve a case and simply copy its solution in order to propose it to a user or another kind of reasoning system. So, the needed adaptation step is done outside the CBR cycle. This can be explained by the fact that, from the knowledge engineering point of view, it is difficult to model the reasoning process and the implemented knowledge ; moreover, there is no simple way to warrant the correctness of the solution. Thus, systems where adaptation is taken into account in the CBR cycle are tied to a particular application domain.

[1] This step is generally integrated to the retrieve step in most CBR models.

Very few works are devoted to the formalization of the adaptation process. In particular, few works focus on the following questions : how to decide a modification of a solution element ? Which method is to be used ? What kind of knowledge is used ? How is used domain knowledge ? How can the global consistency of the solution be assessed ? What kinds of reasoning mechanisms are implemented ? How is controled the adaptation process ? etc. In order to give some answers to these questions, we propose in this paper a generic model of adaptation that specifies its reasoning tasks at the knowledge level. The aim of this model is to clarify the existing relations between the retrieval and adaptation tasks by highlighting the pieces of knowledge controling these tasks, the communications between tasks, and implemented inference mechanisms.

In previous works, we proposed a generic model of CBR in order to synthesize functionnalities of these systems [Fuchs, 1997]. This approach provides firstly a description framework of existing systems, and secondly a generic model that constitutes an help for the design of new systems. The adaptation part is presented here. We present in section 2 the task formalisms used for the description. In section 3, we describe the first three steps of CBR, the main focus being on the tasks `retrieve` and `reuse` and their relations. In section 4 presents the general principle of the retrieval - adaptation steps and in section 5 we use the task decomposition formalism to describe the adaptation process in three CBR systems chosen for the importance they give to the adaptation part, and also because they are well documented in the litterature. We end our proposal with a generic model of adaptation using the two task formalisms in section 6.

2 The task formalisms

The problem solving process is classically divided into tasks. A problem can be achieved either in a direct way by an algorithmic method, or by a decomposition into a set of simpler tasks. This representation allows to model which pieces of knowledge control the reasoning process ; moreover, it allows to keep trace of the reasoning process for explanation purpose [Goel, 1996].

We use two task oriented formalisms : a *task specification* formalism close to [Armengol and Plaza, 1994] and a *task decomposition* formalism close to [Aamodt and Plaza, 1994]. The task specification formalism describes the tasks individually (figure 1), by the input pieces of knowledge, a label clarifying the functions performed by the task, the pieces of knowledge produced as output, the knowledge models used as support, and the implemented reasoning mechanisms. This model is similar to the one presented in [Armengol and Plaza, 1994], but its accuracy is superior because every element acting on a task has a precise role (input, output, control, reasoning mechanism).

The second formalism expresses the hierarchical decomposition of tasks into subtasks and a default control associated to the subtasks (figure 2). In this tree representation, the root node is the main task, and the edges are the decomposition relations leading to subtasks.

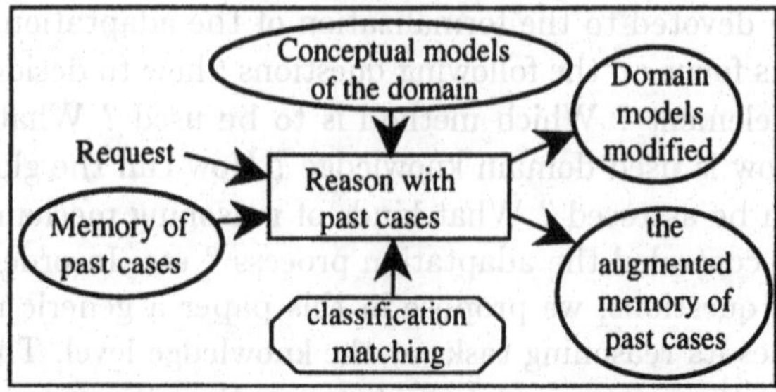

Fig. 1. A partial specification of the main task `Reason with past cases`. The CBR task is activated by a request expressing a problem to be solved, it uses a case base ; its output is the case base augmented with a new solved case. It is supported by knowledge models of the application domain and uses classification and matching mechanisms.

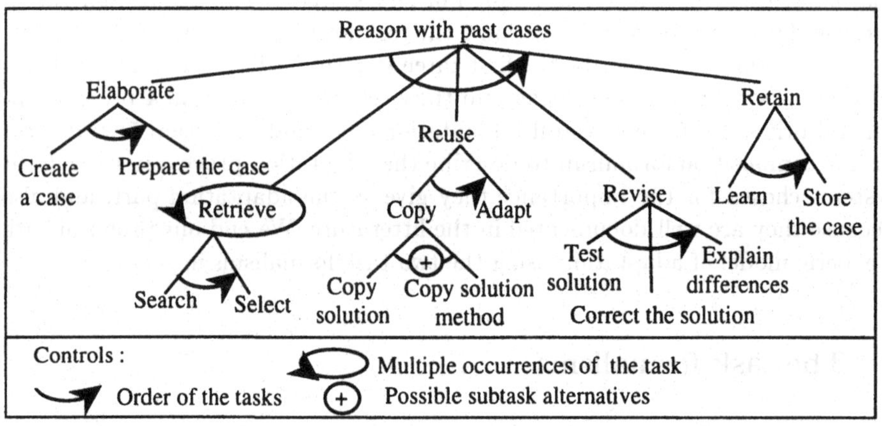

Fig. 2. The partial decomposition (limited to the two first levels) of the main task `Reason with past cases`.

The controls symbols have been added for a better understanding of the model, because links towards subtasks have not always the same meaning. Although controls should be specified in problem solving methods, this model is conform to a task oriented view of knowledge level modeling [Aamodt and Plaza, 1994].

3 The case model

According to this approach, we propose to define the *case model* i.e. a definition of the case that takes into account the problem and solution parts, and also the transformation of a case through reasoning tasks : a case `C` is composed of a problem `Pb`, a solution `S` and a reasoning trace `R` (figure 3) : `C = (Pb, R, S)`.

The problem is described using a set of descriptors[2] D and a request Rq pointing the goal to be reached by the reasoning process. D includes a set of constraints that have to be satisfied by the solution and serves as a partial specification of S : Pb = (D, Rq). The solution S is an object built by the reasoning process R and satisfying the constraints specified in Pb. The reasoning trace R is the set of reasoning steps, intermediate results and decisions that are taken in order to satisfy Rq from the starting state D.

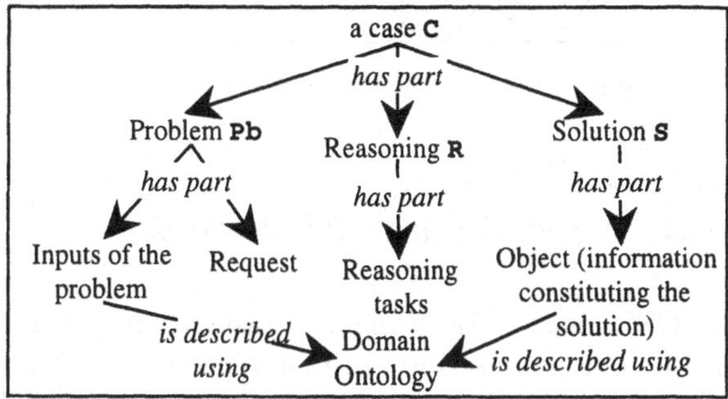

Fig. 3. The case model

A case is created at the beginning of the CBR cycle and contains only the problem part. The reasoning part of the case is the trace of the way the solution has been obtained through the different steps. For example, the matching relations between the source and target problems are included in the reasoning part of the target case. A case takes place as input and output of different reasoning tasks and is modified by an enrichment process all along the CBR cycle. The task specification formal model defines precisely the role played by the different knowledge models, and has the objective to underline the transformation of a case through the different reasoning steps.

Some CBR systems use a case decomposition of a problem in subproblems [Voß, 1997], allowing to guide the reuse of pieces of cases to solve a complete case. Actually, if several authors claim to use multiple cases to solve a new one, from our point of view, it is always possible to see each process of problem solving as a specific CBR cycle using subcases corresponding to the description of the subproblems. Consequently, for a given subproblem to solve, a unique subcase is selected in the CBR concerned subcases base. Figure 4 illustrates this point of view.

According to this point of view, the analysis of CBR tasks does not lack generality when considering the reuse task as involving a single case. When reusing multiple different cases can be expressed as more simple CBR cycles applied to subproblems.

[2] A network of objects, attributes and values.

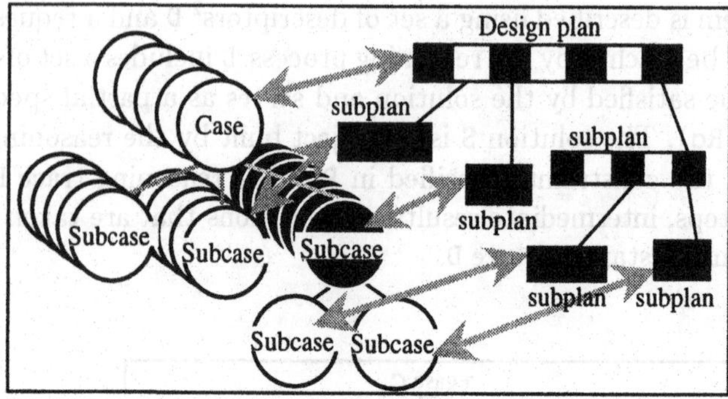

Fig. 4. A point of view on the case decomposition.

4 Principle of the retrieval-adaptation steps

We have modelled the CBR process by using five tasks corresponding to the five main reasoning steps. Let us describe the first three tasks of interest for us (see figure 5). `Elaborate` produces a target problem by collecting the problem descriptors and then prepares the retrieval task : it builds an abstraction of the target problem named *index* by selecting *indices*, i.e. a subset of relevant descriptors. `Retrieve` chooses a source case whose solution will be reused for the target problem. It gradually selects a set of cases from the case-base using the index previously built. Generally, this task is performed by a sequence of cycles, each one being composed of two subtasks : the `search` task extracts a set of source cases, and the `select` task retains only a subset depending on the specific criteria. The `search` task has two subtasks ; the first subtask `match` links the source and target problems in order to underline similarities and differences ; the second subtask `assess` computes a criteria reflecting the similarity or dissimilarity, to be used later by the `select` task. `Reuse` copies the solution of the selected source case and `adapt` modifies it in order to give it consistency with the specific context of the target problem. The matching process is at the basis of the adaptation step.

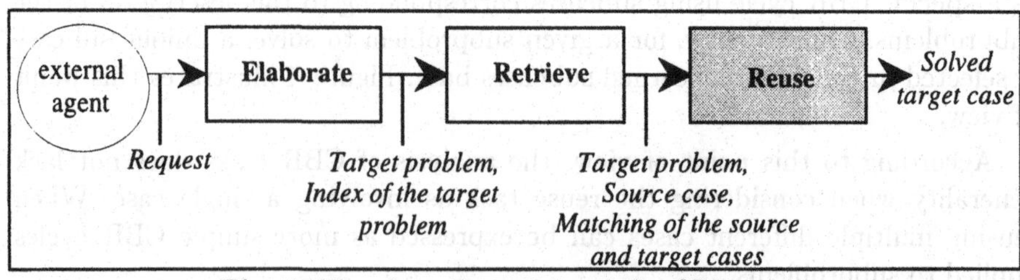

Fig. 5. The three first tasks of the CBR cycle.

We focus now on the adaptation step (grey rectangle on figure 5). The matching task draws a set of relations between source and target cases. These relations express either the identity of some elements, or their dissimilarities although they may have some similarities that have to be underlined by a deeper analysis.

A matching M is a set of relations R_M between descriptors of a source and the target. A matching relation R_M may be expressed as a triple $R_M = (d_s, d_t, R_{st})$, where d_s is a descriptor of the source case, d_t a descriptor of the target, and R_{st} an explanation linking d_s to d_t and made of a sequence of relations of the knowledge network. If d_s and d_t are identical, R_{st} is an identity relation. If not R_{st} expresses for example that descriptors are instances of the same class, or that they play the same role in the context. The matching process is an important step because it summarizes similar elements between source and target problems, and may involve a large amount of knowledge. Every relation between the source and target problems is examined by the adaptation task. An adaptation step is the application of an appropriate adaptation operator depending on the kind of relation considered, taking into account the consequences of the established differences on the solution descriptors. An adaptation operator may remove, add or modify a solution element. When adding or modifying an element, different methods may be used in order to find a new element : abstraction / specialization process, use of explanations, use of causal relations, use of heuristics, etc. Figure 6 summarizes the relationships between matching and adaptation :

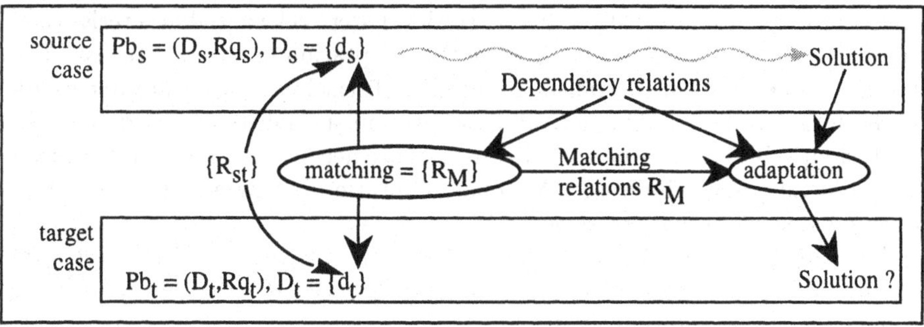

Fig. 6. The matching and adaptation processes and their relationships.

In an approximate way, an adaptation process applies to a solution element a set of relations which are reciprocal of those of the matching process[3]. Thus, differences pointed out by the matching process give a significant indication about the amount of work to be done by the adaptation process in order to modify the solution of the source case, because they are significant of the needed adaptation knowledge.

[3] With the main difference that it must take into account other kinds of relations linking problem elements to solution elements, and that are not necessarily (in general not al all) explicit.

In order to illustrate this principle, we present now three systems to study the adaptation process.

5 A study of three CBR systems

The chosen systems are :

- Déjà Vu, a plant-control software design system [Smyth, 1996]
- PAD'IM, a decision support CBR system in industrial supervision [Mille, 1995], [Fuchs et al., 1995].
- Resyn/CBR, a case-based planner in the domain of organic chemistry synthesis [Lieber, 1997], [Lieber and Napoli, 1996].

5.1 Déjà Vu

Déjà Vu uses an adaptability-guided retrieval method. It assesses a criteria that predicts the adaptability of a case and returns a source case the easiest to adapt, associated to the adaptation rules to apply. The adaptation process uses *adaptation specialists* that perform local modification depending on specification differences of problems, and *adaptation strategies* co-ordinating the application of specialists and treating global consistency problems. An adaptation specialist has a condition part corresponding to the type of specification difference it is able to process, and an action part specifying the adaptation steps of the solution using transformation operators. In the retrieval step, relevant characteristics of the target problem are used to activate the adaptation knowledge to use. The unactivated adaptation specialists are used to discard cases that are not useful for the target problem. The activated adaptation specialists are used to select locally adaptable cases. Adaptation strategies are needed to detect conflict problems in locally adaptable cases. A global adaptation cost is assessed, based on activated specialists and strategies.

Adapting a case uses adaptation knowledge that was activated in the retrieval step, and the matching helps to point out modifications to bring out in order to produce the target solution (figure 7).

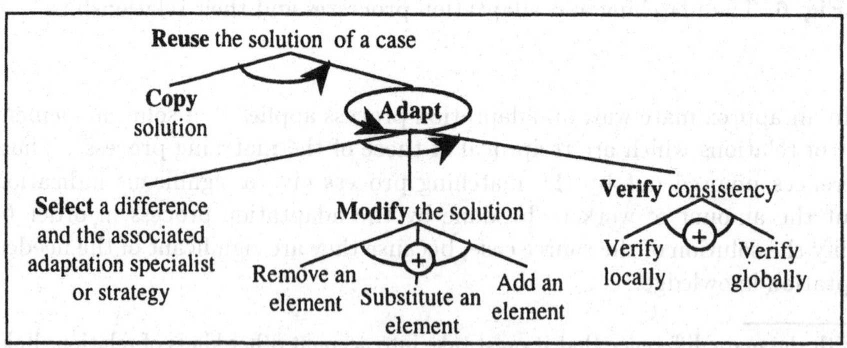

Fig. 7. The decomposition of the reuse task in Déjà Vu.

Adaptation specialists are applied in order to handle specification differences and perform local modifications on solution elements without controlling the modifications performed by other specialists. Adaptation strategies co-ordinate the application of specialists in order to avoid conflicts that may lead to impasses and to check the solution consistency after local modifications.

In Déjà Vu, the retrieve and reuse steps are tightly coupled. Cases are linked to adaptation knowledge activated at the retrieval step. The adaptation process performs modifications already underlined in the retrieval step ; strategies are applied when the consistency checking process points out modification needs after adaptation specialists have been applied.

5.2 PAD'IM

PAD'IM provides an appropriate supervision environment for situations that are similar to known situations. The supervision domain is defined thanks to the *supervision object* concept, specialized in subclasses : the structural object, the function, etc. A supervision environment is composed of a set of dashboards that are viewed by operators on control panels. A dashboard has a set of views representing the evolution of the supervised system and reflects supervision objects. The retrieval of cases (or supervision episodes) begins with a discrimination based on the general context of the supervision episode. A conceptual similarity is assessed by a matching process of the supervision objects and measures the degree of similarity of the objects in the source and target cases. The observed dissimilarities of supervision objects are analyzed in order to produce an explanation of their role in a supervision environment. The matching process summarizes similarities between objects, dissimilarities and their explanation. The search for an explanation tries to find relations between the objects and the different elements describing the situation. Reusing a supervision environment means finding which supervision objects have to be represented in the new supervision environment. The `reuse` task is performed by two subtasks (figure 8). The first subtask `copy` copies the supervision environment of the retrieved episode for the current one and the second subtask `adapt a supervision environment` modifies it.

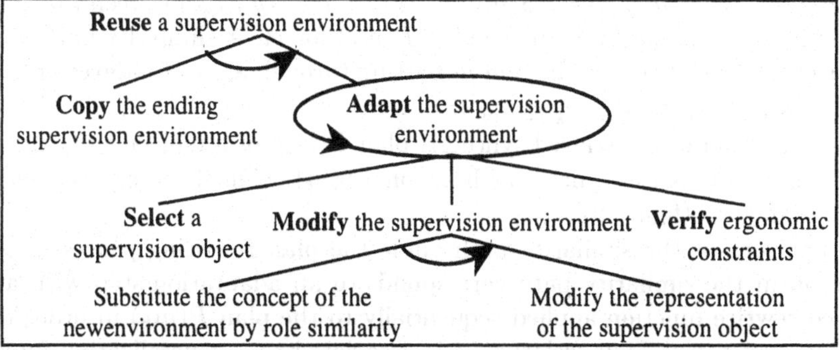

Fig. 8. The decomposition of the `reuse` task in the PAD'IM system.

The starting point for the adaptation of a supervision environment is the matching of supervision objects. It is performed using three subtasks. The first subtask uses the explanations of supervision objects in order to modify those of the newly copied supervision environment in the target case. Explanations guide the adaptation operations : objects are determined by an explanation matching process. A substitution operation is done by the replacement of objects by explanation similarity. A substitution may be for example an abstraction/specialization process.

In the PAD'IM system, the adaptation process is guided by cases matching. The application of an adaptation operation is conditioned by a specification difference. Explanations express dependency relations between a problem and its solution and constitute the adaptation operations to be performed.

5.3 Resyn/CBR

In Resyn/CBR, a case is a synthesis plan that builds a target molecule from basic molecules. Synthesis plans are organized in a co-subsumption hierarchy defining the structural inclusion of networks representing molecules. A synthesis plan is an ordered sequence of transformations that split a target molecule into simpler molecules. A problem is described by a target molecule m to synthesize. A solution is a synthesis plan $C(m)$ of the target molecule. Synthesis plans are indexed by molecules of the co-subsumption hierarchy. The retrieval of a synthesis plan relies on two kinds of classifications : a *strong* one and a *smooth* one. Strong classification classifies the target molecule in the subsumption hierarchy in order to find the most specific subsumers m_k of m and the associated synthesis plan $P(m_k)$. If no subsumers refer to synthesis plans, then smooth classification is tried. Let m_k a source problem, m a target problem, and $M = I(m_k)$ the index associated to a problem m_k, such as $m_k \preceq I(m_k)$. the strong classification sets m_k such as $S(m_k, m) = m_k \preceq M \succeq m$. Smooth classification consists in modifying the molecules M of the hierarchy and the target molecule m in order to obtain a subsumption relation and to try strong classification again. The problem is to find modification functions ϕ and ψ such as : $S(m_k, m) = m_k \preceq M \simeq \phi(M) \succeq \psi(m) \simeq m$. The retrieval task returns a pair $(P(m_k), S(m_k, m))$ where $S(m_k, m)$ is a *similarity path* between m_k and m that ensure the adaptability of the plan $P(m_k)$ for m. A similarity path is a sequence of relations between m_k and m passing through a set of indexes of the hierarchy : $m_k \preceq m_k^1 \preceq ... \preceq m_k^p \succeq m_q \Longleftarrow ... \Longleftarrow m^1 \Longleftarrow m$.

The adaptation of a retrieved synthesis plan $P(m_k)$ of a molecule m_k for a target molecule m creates a new synthesis plan $p(m)$ using the similarity path between m and m_k (figure 9).

The relations of the similarity path guide the plan rewriting process. Every relation in the similarity path corresponds to an adaptation step with an associated rewrite function applied sequentially to the plan $P(m_k)$ in order to obtain the plan $p(m)$. Thus, relation $\preceq$ is associated to a generalization function, relation $\succeq$ is associated to a specialization function, and the relation $\Longleftarrow$

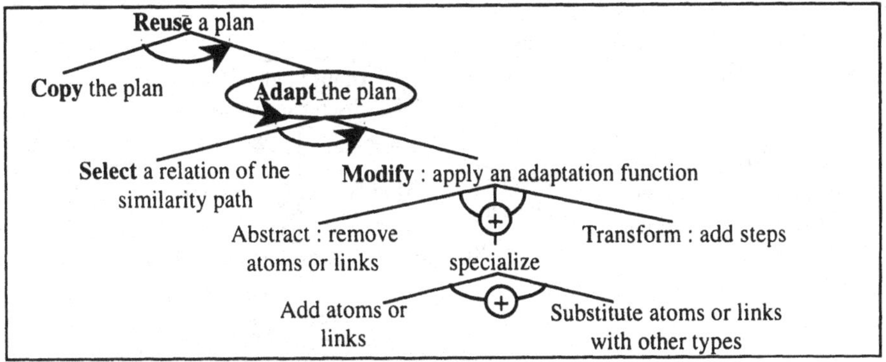

Fig. 9. The task decomposition of the Reuse task in Resyn/CBR.

is associated to a transformation function. The reuse step is easy because the operations that have to be performed are determined during the retrieval step.

In Resyn/CBR, the retrieval and reuse steps are tightly coupled : the adaptation step control relies on the similarity path that underline generalization relations, specialization relations and transformation relations between the source and target cases. The retrieval step warrants the adaptability of the selected case by developping particular relations.

6 A generic model of adaptation

Some invariants can be extracted from the study of these three systems[4], we have summarized them in the hierarchical task model of figure 10 and the specification model of figure 11.

The `reuse` task has two subtasks : the `copy` task copies the solution of the retrieved case for the target problem, and the `adapt` task handles problem differences and discrepancies. The `copy` task copies either the solution or the method that produced the solution of the retrieved case [5], and begins to adapt. This task has been modelled in such a way because most CBR systems represent the reuse step as a copy of the solution followed by modifications of the copied solution.

The `adapt` task focuses first on differences between problems in order to determine the solution elements which have to be modified and the adaptation methods to apply to the solution. The starting point is the matching of the

[4] Other systems, not presented in this paper, have been studied for the analysis.

[5] The distinction between transformational adaptation and derivational adaptation refers to Carbonell's work, but from our point of view, we think that this distinction is not fundamental because it is possible to consider that the solution of the case itself is the reasoning trace. This view has also been modelled in [Aamodt and Plaza, 1994]. Meanwhile, our point of view would need further studies to be fully justified, and our task descriptions are intended to describe transformational adaptation.

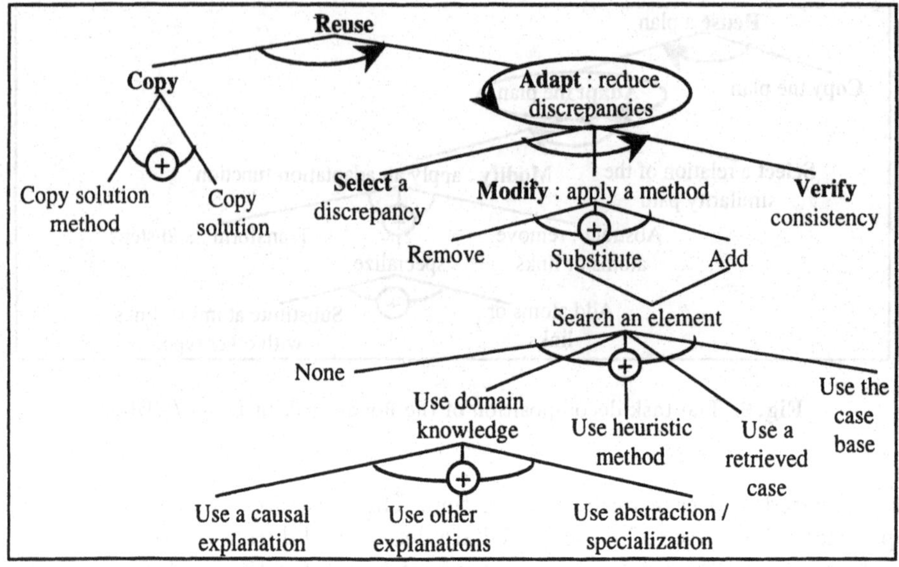

Fig. 10. The decomposition of the reuse task.

cases performed during retrieval ; it determines the differences to be handled by adaptation knowledge. These differences are augmented with new inconsistencies that are detected by the `verify consistency` task after modifications have been performed on solution elements. Discrepancies include problem specification differences as well as inconsistencies (deficiencies, suboptimal results) resulting from solution modification. The adaptation model contains solution transformation operators. Discrepancies are studied in the adaptation task in order to apply specific adaptation operators and to modify solution elements of the target.

Systems performing an adaptability guided retrieval choose cases by highlighting these kinds of relations and the associated adaptation knowledge at the retrieval step, in order to assess firstly the feasibility of the adaptation and secondly an estimated adaptation cost of a source case.

The task `reduce differences` chooses differences, applies consequently the appropriate adaptation knowledge, and controls the consistency of the obtained solution.

When some solution elements are modified, inconsistencies may appear [Maher et al., 1995]. These inconsistencies may be viewed as new differences to handle by the adaptation process and are added to the list for further adaptations. The modification operations may use different methods depending on the kind of relations underlined while handling a difference. Domain knowledge to which are connected cases is used in order to find an element, for example by an abstraction/specialization process.

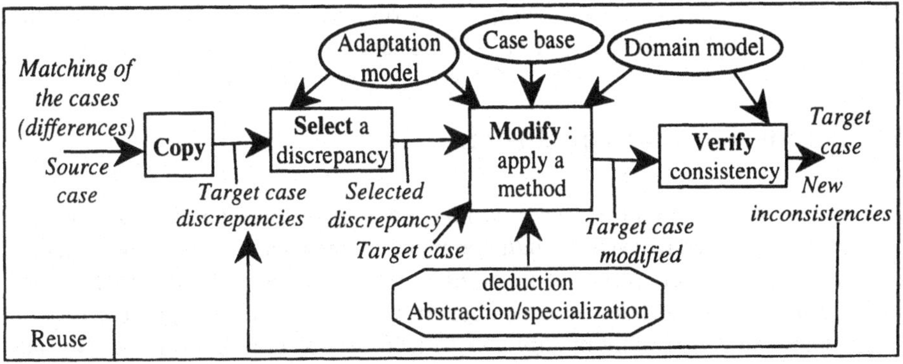

Fig. 11. The specification of the **reuse** task.

Figure 11 underlines knowledge models and knowledge pieces that are implied in the adaptation process. Although we have defined separate knowledge models in our framework (similarity model for retrieval, adaptation model for adaptation, domain model, etc.), each of them have strong relationships with other models. So, we can consider every piece of knowledge of the specification model that acts on a task, and we can compar the above CBR systems according to the knowledge which is implied in the adaptation process.

In Déjà Vu, problem specification differences are matched with premises of adaptation rules in the retrieval step. The adaptation actions to be performed in the adaptation step are already linked to specification differences. The case selected for reuse is chosen if there exists the corresponding adaptation knowledge and if the associated cost is minimal. When adapting the solution, new adaptation needs may appear when modifications are performed, and specific adaptation rules may be triggered consequently. Adaptation action parts of adaptation rules consist in a set of operators to transform graph structures. Basic operators perform substitutions, deletions and insertions.

In the Resyn/CBR system, a similarity path indicates a sequence of relations between the source and target problems passing through indexes of the hierarchy. Every kind of relation is associated to an appropriate adaptation function. So, finding an adaptable case means finding a similarity path whose relations correspond to an adaptation function with a minimal cost. The different kinds of relations are the generalization relation, the specialization relation and the transformation relation. The generalization relation implies the deletion operator, the specialization relation implies the insertion or substitution operator and the transformation relation implies the insertion operator.

In the Pad'im system, problem specification differences are explained by searching a sequence of relations linking a supervision object with an element of the situation. An explanation expresses the role played by a supervision object in a situation and uses the objects and relations of the domain knowledge. The corresponding adaptation action is generic and consists in substituting an object by searching an object having a same role, deleting an object or inserting an object depending on the kind of explanation.

7 Discussion and conclusion

In this paper, we present a way to model the adaptation step of CBR applications at the knowledge level through two kinds of formalisms: a task specification model focusing on the pieces of knowledge involved in a particular task, and a task decomposition model making explicit how the reasoning process can be decomposed in a hierarchy of subtasks to achieve the problem solving. Beyond the simple decomposition framework, the formalism of decomposition allows to express how the different tasks can be brought into operation (iteration, disjunction, conjunction, etc.), while the generic role of each piece of knowledge involved to achieve a task is made explicit in the task specification model. Actually, a relatively complete set of generic models have been developed on the basis of our proper experience of CBR systems development, and we have verified their relevance on several different other systems. We plan to place these generic models at disposal for CBR developers in order to make easier the development of new CBR systems. Researchers and developers can also use our approach to propose domain-dependent generic models. A first corresponding *symbol level* environment has been developed [Fuchs, 1997] for our proper CBR systems, and we are trying to make it available through standard tools.

The adaptation step, although central in the problem solving process, is rarely modelled in the same manner than other steps of CBR. An explicit connexion of this step with the others in order to model uniformly the CBR cycle is justified firstly in order to understand and to study the adaptation process and secondly in order to provide a methodological basis for the engineering of CBR systems. The development of several complex applications and the study of several systems has led us to a generic task model of the adaptation process that caracterizes the knowledge used and the kind of reasoning performed. The task model is decomposed into a small number of subtasks of preparation, modification and control of the adaptation process. The study of the adaptation process may be continued in two complementary directions : a formalization of the adaptation process as a plan modification process strongly coupled to the similarity search process, and the development of adaptation operators explicitely controlled by adaptation knowledge.

References

[Aamodt and Plaza, 1994] Aamodt, A. and Plaza, E. (1994). Case-Based Reasoning : Foundational Issues, Methodological Variations, and System Approaches. *AI Communications*, 7(1):39–58.

[Armengol and Plaza, 1994] Armengol, E. and Plaza, E. (1994). A Knowledge Level Model of Case-Based Reasoning. In Richter, M. M., Wess, S., Althoff, K.-D., and

Maurer, F., editors, *First European Workshop on Case-Based Reasoning - EWCBR-93*, pages 53–64, University of Kayserslautern, Germany. LNAI, vol. 837, Springer Verlag, Berlin.

[Bergmann and Wilke, 1995] Bergmann, R. and Wilke, W. (1995). Building and refining abstract planning cases by change of representation language. *Journal of Artificial Intelligence Research*, 3:53–118.

[Fuchs, 1997] Fuchs, B. (1997). *Représentation des connaissances pour le raisonnement à partir de cas : le système ROCADE.* Thèse d'université, Université Jean Monnet, Saint-Etienne, France.

[Fuchs et al., 1995] Fuchs, B., Mille, A., and Chiron, B. (1995). Operator Decision aiding by Adaptation of Supervision Strategies. In Veloso, M. and Aamodt, A., editors, *First International Conference on Case-Based Reasoning - ICCBR-95*, pages 23–32, Sesimbra, Portugal. LNAI, vol. 1010, Springer Verlag, Berlin.

[Goel, 1996] Goel, A. (1996). Meta cases: Explaining case-based reasoning. In Smith, I. and Faltings, B., editors, *Third European Workshop on Case-Based Reasoning - EWCBR-96*, pages 150–163, Lausanne, Suisse. LNAI, vol. 1168, Springer Verlag, Berlin.

[Hanks and Weld, 1995] Hanks, S. and Weld, D. S. (1995). A domain independant algorithm for plan adaptation. *Journal of Artificial Intelligence Research*, 2:319–360.

[Hua et al., 1996] Hua, K., Faltings, B., and Smith, I. (1996). CADRE : Case Based Geometric Design. *Artificial Intelligence in Engineering*, 10:171–183.

[Hua et al., 1993] Hua, K., Smith, I., and Faltings, B. (1993). Exploring case-based design: CADRE. *Artificial Intelligence for Engineering Design, Analysis and Manufacturing (AI EDAM)*, 7(2):135–144.

[Koehler, 1996] Koehler, J. (1996). Planning from Second Principles. *Artificial Intelligence*, 87:145–186.

[Leake et al., 1997] Leake, D., Kinley, A., and Wilson, D. (1997). Learning to integrate multiple knowledge sources for case-based reasoning. In *Proceedings of the 15th International Joint Conference on Artificial Intelligence*. Morgan Kaufmann.

[Lieber, 1997] Lieber, J. (1997). *Raisonnement à partir de cas et classification hiérarchique. Application à la planification de synthèse en chimie organique.* Thèse d'université, Université Henri Poincaré Nancy 1, Nancy, France.

[Lieber and Napoli, 1996] Lieber, J. and Napoli, A. (1996). Adaptation of Synthesis Plans in Organic Chemistry. In *Workshop on Adaptation in Case-Based Reasoning, ECAI-96*, pages 18–21, Budapest, Hungary.

[Maher et al., 1995] Maher, M. L., Balachandran, M. B., and Zhang, D. M. (1995). *Case-Based Design.* Lawrence Erlbaum Associates, Mahwah, New Jersey.

[Mille, 1995] Mille, A. (1995). *Raisonnement basé sur l'expérience pour coopérer à la prise de décision, un nouveau paradigme en supervision industrielle.* Thèse d'université, Université Jean Monnet, Saint-Etienne.

[Smyth, 1996] Smyth, B. (1996). *Case-Based Design.* Doctoral thesis of the Trinity College, Dublin.

[Voß, 1996] Voß, A., editor (1996). *Proceedings of the ECAI'96 Workshop: Adaptation in Case-Based Reasoning.*

[Voß, 1997] Voß, A. (1997). Case Reusing Systems - Survey, Framework and Guidelines. *Knowledge Engineering Review*, 12(1):59–89.

Development and Utilization of a Case-Based Help-Desk Support System in a Corporate Environment

Mehmet Göker[1] & Thomas Roth-Berghofer[2]

[1] DaimlerChrysler Research and Technology 3, FT3/KL
P.O. Box 2360, D89013 Ulm, Germany
mehmet.goeker@daimlerchrysler.com
Phone: +49 731 5052856 Fax: +49 731 5054210

[2] tec:inno GmbH
Sauerwiesen 2, D67661 Kaiserslautern, Germany
roth@tecinno.com
Phone: +49 6031 606400 Fax: +49 6031 606409

Abstract: Current Case-Based Reasoning (CBR) process models present CBR as a low maintenance AI-technology and do not take the processes that have to be enacted during system development and utilization into account. Since a CBR system can only be useful if it is integrated into an organizational structure and used by more than one user, processes for continuous knowledge acquisition, -utilization and -maintenance have to be put in place. In this paper the short-comings of classical CBR process models are analyzed, and, based on the experiences made during the development of the case-based help-desk support system HOMER, the managerial, organizational and technical processes related to the development and utilization of CBR systems described.

1. Motivation

Case-Based Reasoning (CBR) has long been considered as an AI technology with comparably low maintenance effort. However, with the advent of CBR systems in industrial environments, issues that have to do with the processes involved in putting a knowledge repository into operation in an organization arise. Especially the processes involved in initial and continuous knowledge acquisition, case-base and domain-model maintenance as well as the organizational impact of and impact of the organization on a CBR system have not been analyzed and understood completely. These aspects are currently neither covered in academic CBR models nor supported adequately in commercially available CBR systems.

On the following pages we describe the processes that had to be enacted during the development and utilization of the case-based help-desk support system HOMER [2]. After the processes had been derived from one specific application, they were verified, revised and re-used during several other CBR-projects by means of the INRECA-II[i] methodology [1]. We believe that most of the results can be transferred to other domains and applications

2. Current Case-Based Reasoning Process Models

Several variations of the Case-Based Reasoning process model exist in literature [cf. 3,4,5,6]. The basic idea behind all approaches is to retrieve problem solving experience that has been stored as a case in a case-base, adapt and reuse it to solve new problems and, if not successful, learn from failures.

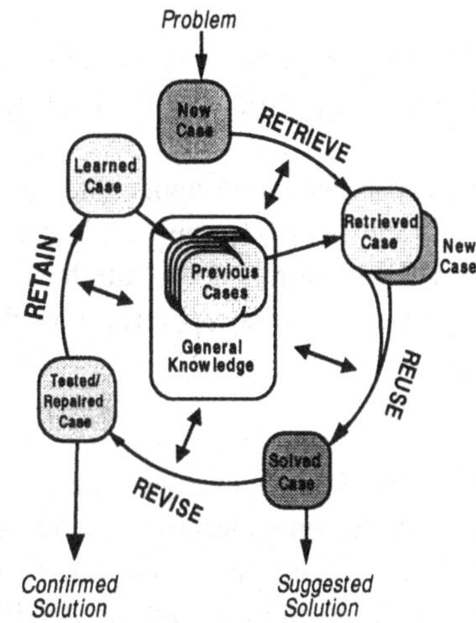

Fig.1: The Case-Based Reasoning Process Model according to Aamodt and Plaza [9]

On the abstract level the CBR process can be described to be comprised of four main tasks (Fig.1): *Retrieve*, *Reuse*, *Revise* and *Retain* [6].

During *Retrieval* the most similar case or cases in the case-base are determined based on the new problem description.

During *Reuse* the information and knowledge in the retrieved case(s) is used to solve the new problem. The new problem description is combined with the information contained in the old case to form a solved case.

During *Revision* the applicability of the proposed solution (solved case) is evaluated. If necessary and possible the proposed case is repaired.

If the case solution generated during the reuse phase is not correct and cannot be repaired, the case-base is updated with a new learned case or by modification of some existing cases in the *Retain* task.

3. Shortcomings of Current Case-Based Reasoning Process Models

3.1. Effects of User Groups

A CBR System is a means to store, share and re-use experience. If the experience stored in a CBR system is only used by the person who enters it, the use of the system will be rather limited. The goal of developing a CBR system, especially in a corporate environment, is to create a means to capture, cumulate and re-use corporate experience with all the benefits that are associated with such a venture [cf. 8].

It has been claimed that "Knowledge Acquisition for a case-based system is natural" [5], and that "CBR offers a significant benefit for knowledge maintenance: a user may be able to add missing cases to the case library without expert intervention" [7]. While this may indeed be true for static domains with a very limited number of users of the system, we would like to be somewhat more cautious to this respect.

If a CBR System is not only used by one user but rather a group of users, the quality (in terms of representation and content) of the new cases that each user creates will vary. This will have a negative effect on the overall quality of the case-base (in terms of correctness, coverage and minimality) and reduce the effectiveness and efficiency of the system in general. Processes that ensure that the overall quality of the case-base does not deteriorate when new cases are entered have to be put in place. Depending on the user group that is going to utilize the system, the content of the case-base and the user interface of the system have to be adapted as well.

3.2. Effects of Time

Current CBR process models base their description on a static view of the domain. While this assumption is acceptable for academic purposes, it does not hold for real world applications.

Every real-world domain changes over time. Solutions that were applicable some time ago will become invalid. Indices that were suitable will become obsolete and similarities will change. Methods to ensure that the CBR system is up-to-date have to be developed and tasks that realize these methods have to be incorporated into the CBR process models.

3.3. Impact on/of the Organization

Both during the development and the utilization of a CBR System, changes in the way knowledge is handled take place within an organization. Personnel has to be dedicated to the task of acquiring and maintaining knowledge, the system has to be integrated into the daily operations and has to become part of the organizational culture. A CBR system can only be successful in the long run, if enough personnel to maintain, use and develop the system are available and set aside by management [cf. 9].

4. Case-Based Help-Desk Support Systems

Help-desks support end-users of complex technical equipment by providing information about the usage of the equipment and keep the systems operational by performing necessary maintenance tasks. Help desk operators are expected to be able to solve problems on very short notice, in a very short time, and to be knowledgeable in all areas that are related to the technical system at hand.

Help-desk operators use their own experiences to solve most of the problems that are relayed to them. However, as systems become more complex, the areas help-desk operators are experts in tend to diverge, i.e., problem solving experience is distributed among experts and the areas of expertise do not necessarily overlap. Nevertheless, when an end-user has a problem, he or she wants it solved as soon as possible. If that expert is not available, the user has to wait, which is annoying and not acceptable in a commercial environment. The problem-solving experience must be available to every help-desk operator at all times [2].

The goal of developing a case-based help-desk support system is to create a knowledge repository that contains problem-solving experiences for a complex technical domain that changes over time. This knowledge repository will be used in an organization, by a group of people with varying levels of expertise, in a time-critical operation. It is obvious that the development and use of such a system does not only involve technical processes, but also raises managerial and organizational issues. In the following sections, we describe the tasks that must be performed to develop a case-based help-desk support system and the processes that have to be put into place to make such a system operational.

5. Processes During Case-Based Help-Desk System Development and Utilization

5.1. Process Types

Table 1 lists the processes that have to be considered and /or performed during the development and utilization of a case-based help-desk system. We distinguish between organizational, technical and managerial processes [1].

Organizational processes cover those parts of the business process that need to be changed in order to make best use of a new software system. *Technical processes* transform and evolve product information from the problem description to the final (software) system. They address the development of the system and the required documentation itself. *Managerial processes* provide an environment and services for enacting the technical and the organizational processes.

		System Development	System Use
Managerial Processes		- Goal Definition - Awareness Creation - CBR-Tool Selection	- Progress Verification and Controlling
Organizational Processes		- Project Team Selection - Initial Domain Selection - Project Team Training - Knowledge Acquisition Process Development - Utilization Process Development	- End-User Training - Continuous Knowledge Acquisition - Utilization Process
Technical Processes	**General IT-System Related**	- System Specification - System Implementation - System Integration - System Verification	- Continuous System Maintenance
Technical Processes	**Knowledge Repository Related**	- Initial Knowledge Acquisition - Core Knowledge Acquisition	- Continuous Knowledge Acquisition and Maintenance

Tab. 1. Processes during case-based help-desk support system development and use.

5.2. Managerial Processes During System Development

Goal Definition. For a case-based help-desk support system project to be successful, precise goals must be determined at the outset. This enables management to fix the direction in which the project should develop and to measure the success of the project upon completion. Hard (quantitative) and soft (qualitative) success criteria should be identified [cf. 9]. Hard criteria are measurable quantities and cover aspects like:

- *problem solution quality* (first-call resolution rate, solution correctness, and consistency, average cost of proposed solution, and so on),
- *process quality* (average time needed to solve a problem, average number of escalations needed, quality of dynamic priority assignment, and so on),
- *organizational quality* (speedup in help-desk operator training, flexibility of staffing, cost per interaction, and so on).

Soft criteria, on the other hand, measure the subjective quality of the help-desk and cover aspects like:

- *end-user satisfaction* (availability of the help-desk, perceived competence, friendliness, and so on),
- *help-desk operator satisfaction* (workload, work atmosphere, repetitiveness of tasks, intellectual stimulation, and so on), and
- *corporate aspects* (preservation of knowledge, publicity, and so on.).

The goals must be communicated to the project team, and the team has to be motivated to achieve them.

When project goals are selected, it is important that these goals be realistic both in terms of their time frame and whether they can be achieved with an acceptable amount of resources.

Awareness Creation and Motivation. The case-based help-desk support system project targets the most precious asset of the employees: their experience. The project's goal is to collect the problem-solving experience of each relevant employee and make it available to whomever needs it in the organization.

Obviously the help-desk operators will have a motivational barrier to giving away their experience. Every employee knows that "knowledge is power." In help-desk environments or domains where experience is being used to solve problems having experience translates into being superior and indispensable, whereas giving away the knowledge can be perceived as becoming obsolete.

However, as soon as help-desk operators become part of a project team and understand that sharing knowledge means that they will get back much more than they invest, most barriers disappear. It has to be made clear that the user and beneficiary of the developed system is not going to be an anonymous "company," but they themselves. They will be able to access the experience of their colleagues and solve problems they could not solve before, as well as end situations in which colleagues constantly pester them for advice. The resulting help-desk system will enable them to work with increased efficiency and effectiveness.

Apart from the help-desk operators, management has to be motivated as well. CBR is perceived to be rather academic by most managers. While to them investing resources into a database project seems to be no problem, investing into CBR is investing into a venture with an uncertain outcome. It has to be clarified that CBR is an established technology and by no means only an academic playground. The case-based help-desk support project must be seen as part of the long-term knowledge management strategy for the company. Since knowledge increases and evolves, the experience in a CBR system must be maintained continuously. System development is only the initial phase in any CBR project.

Without continuous management support and employees who are willing to fill and use the system, any CBR project is bound to fail.

CBR Tool Selection. Based on the project, domain, and user-group specifications, a suitable tool to develop the case-based help-desk support system must be selected. Criteria to be taken into account include:

- the operating environment in which the system is going to be used (hardware and software, network architecture, database type, and so on),
- the complexity of the technical domain (home appliances or networked workstations),
- the level of experience of both the end-users and the help-desk operators,
- the organization of the help-desk (number of levels, physical locations, and so on),
- the project goals that have been defined.

Since the case-based help-desk support system is going to serve as a (long-term) knowledge repository for the organization, this selection should be based not only on technical criteria, but also should take into account economic and organizational considerations, as well as strategic decisions of the company.

5.3. Organizational Processes During System Development

Project Team and Initial Domain Selection. The creation of a project team to serve as the "knowledge engineers" and the selection of a group to serve as initial test users of the system are the first organizational steps that must be taken.

Apart from the person implementing the case-based help-desk support system (*CBR consultant*), the project team should contain help-desk personnel who are very experienced in the relevant subdomain to be modeled and well respected by the help-desk operators outside the project group. Once selected, the members of the group should be kept constant, i.e., fluctuations should be avoided.

The group of initial users should comprise two types of help-desk personnel: One that is on a comparable level of expertise with the project team with respect to the selected subdomain (i.e., expert users) and help-desk personnel who are less familiar with the specific problem area (i.e., novice users). While the expert test-users can communicate to the project group in their language, the novice users will represent the target group for which the system is being implemented. Feedback from both types of users is required for a successful project. After a first "rapid prototype" has been implemented, the expert users can give hints regarding problems with the knowledge modeled in the system. The members of the novice user group, on the other hand, will serve as models of the help-desk operator who will use the system. The vocabulary in which the cases are being represented and the knowledge contained within them has to be adjusted to the novice user group

Which domain one selects for the initial knowledge acquisition is of utmost importance. The domain should be representative of the problems that are being handled at the help-desk, both in terms of complexity and frequency. It should also be a problem area that accounts for a considerable amount of the workload and about which the help-desk operators are interested in sharing (obtaining) knowledge.

Training the Project Team. Training the project team is an organizational process that has a major impact on the success of the help-desk project. At the beginning of the project, the project team is (most of the time) inexperienced with respect to CBR and knowledge acquisition. Since the project group will be responsible for system maintenance and continuous case acquisition after the development has finished, it is very important that they are trained in CBR, as well as in knowledge acquisition and modeling, during the initial knowledge acquisition.

While the project team should also get advanced training to be able to model, fill, and maintain the knowledge in the system, the test users only need to be trained in using the resulting case-based help-desk support system.

Development of the Knowledge Acquisition and Utilization Processes. The introduction and use of a case-based help-desk support system usually causes a re-evaluation and modification of the existing knowledge and information management processes in a help-desk environment. After the development of the case-based help-desk support system is complete, it will serve as the central source of information for the help-desk operators. To ensure a smooth flow of information, the knowledge sources and formats, as well as the qualification of the personnel that requires the knowledge, have to be analyzed, and processes that allow efficient and effective acquisition and use of knowledge have to be developed. One should keep in mind that while the group enacting the initial knowledge acquisition process is the project team and rather experienced, the users who use the system in the end (both in terms of knowledge retrieval and continuous acquisition) may be less qualified.

During the development of HOMER [2], we found it very useful to define three roles for the knowledge acquisition and utilization processes during the use of the help-desk system:

- the help-desk operator,
- the CBR author,
- the CBR administrator.

Help-desk operators are the users from the target group. Their duty is to use the implemented help-desk system in their daily work. If they cannot find an appropriate solution with the system, they will have to solve the problem on their own and generate a new case. Depending on the domain and on managerial decisions, this new case may or may not be made immediately available as an "unconfirmed" case to the other help-desk operators. For maintenance purposes, the operators are also encouraged to comment on the quality and applicability of the cases in the case base.

The unconfirmed, new cases have to be verified in terms of their correctness and suitability for the case base by the CBR author(s). The CBR author is a person with experience both in the domain and in using the CBR system. While the CBR author can decide on the quality and inclusion of a case in the case base, he or she is not allowed to perform modifications on the vocabulary, the similarity, and the adaptation knowledge. These can only be performed by the CBR administrator.

The personnel enacting the roles of the CBR author(s) and the CBR administrator should be included in the project group from the start of the project. It should be noted that both these roles require a considerable amount of resources and should be performed by dedicated personnel. If the organization or the size of the help-desk does not permit dedicating more than one person to these tasks, the duties of the CBR author and CBR administrator should be performed by one person.

5.4. Technical Processes During System Development

General IT-System Development Related Processes. The development of a case-based help-desk support system is similar to any other IT project in most aspects. As usual, the system has to be specified, implemented, integrated, and verified in accordance with standard software engineering techniques. However, the user-interface and the connection to supporting programs (integration) are two features that require additional attention.

The user interface of the case-based help-desk support system has to be developed in accordance with the user group (i.e., second level, first level, or even end-user), the specific domain, and company policies (who is allowed to see what kind of data). It has to present the right data, at the right moment, and on the right level of abstraction.

A case-based help-desk support system cannot operate in isolation. While the CBR system will store experience, it will not contain data regarding device configurations, maintenance contracts, and users. Since this information is needed during problem solving, the system has to have interfaces to the databases containing this information.

Most help-desks use trouble-ticket tools in their daily operations; they record, manage, trace, escalate, and analyze the calls they receive. While these trouble-ticket tools are very useful in handling calls, they do not provide means to capture and reuse problem-solving experience. Depending on the environment, the case-based help-desk support system should also either be integrated into the user interface of the trouble-ticket tool or vice-versa. Data from the trouble-ticket system has to be transferred to the CBR system to initialize the attributes that relate to the data that has already been acquired. Except for very complex second-level applications, it is not feasible to have two points of entry to the problem-solving process.

Initial Knowledge Acquisition for the Case-Based Help-Desk Support System. A CBR system is useless without cases. When the case-based help-desk support system is handed over to the help-desk operators, it has to contain enough cases to cover at least part of the relevant problems at the help-desk. Initial knowledge acquisition serves three major goals:

- training the project team in knowledge acquisition,
- initializing the knowledge in the system,
- collecting enough help-desk cases to bootstrap the system.

During initial knowledge acquisition, the knowledge in the system can be distributed among the *domain model* (vocabulary), *similarity measure*, *adaptation knowledge*, and the *case base*. These *knowledge containers* [10] have to be created and filled. In principle, each container could be used to represent most of the knowledge. However, this is obviously not very feasible, and the CBR consultant should carefully decide on the distribution of knowledge into the containers. After the initial knowledge acquisition is completed, this distribution is more or less fixed and should only be changed with caution.

The processes for the acquisition of knowledge for each container run in parallel and cannot be easily separated during the initial knowledge acquisition. Since the vocabulary lays ground for entering the cases and describing the similarity measures and adaptation knowledge, it has to be available first. However, to be able to create a domain model (i.e., the vocabulary), one has to understand how the domain is structured, and this can only be done by looking at the cases, the similarities, and the adaptation rules.

In our experience, the best way to approach this problem is to create and use standardized forms to acquire an initial amount of cases from the project team. The form should be developed in co-operation with the project team. A sample form that was developed for the initial case acquisition for the HOMER application is shown in Tab. 2.

The first thing that must be done is to ask the project team to fill out as many case acquisition forms as they can. By looking at the elements of the forms, the vocabulary (i.e., the phrases that have to be used and the domain structure) can be derived and a vocabulary that is capable of describing the cases that have been on the forms can be modeled.

By asking the project team what the range of possible values for each attribute on the forms is and inquiring what would have happened if one of the values on a form were different, a broad range of cases can be created and the vocabulary expanded in a short time. Discussions among the project team members raise the level of understanding of both the approach and the problems, and should be encouraged in this early phase. During initial knowledge acquisition, it is also advisable to have more cases on an "everyday" level rather than having a few extremely specific ones.

Homer Case Acquisition	
Problem Nr : 816	**Date:** 26.04.99
Author: S. Itani	**Verified by:** J. Fleisch
Problem Description (Failure)	Printer does print pages full of gibberish
Reason (Fault)	File is Postscript, Printer does not understand PS
Solution	Send File to Postscript Printer, delete file from queue
What did you check to find out what the problem was ?	
Printer Model	HP LJ 6L
File Type	Postscript
Other Notes:	The reverse of this problem did also happen, somebody sent a PCL file to a pure PS printer

Tab. 2. Sample form for initial case acquisition.

While the initial vocabulary is being created and value ranges fixed, questions regarding adaptation rules and similarities should be posed and the results entered into the system.

One of the major challenges one must face when creating a system to capture and represent the experience of domain experts, is determining the level of abstraction with which the domain and the knowledge will be modeled. If the model used is too simplistic, it will cause problems while the experience is being captured and will miss important details. If, however, the domain model is too specific, the user will get lost quickly in useless details, and knowledge acquisition will be very tedious and time consuming. Maintenance is very difficult for both a too-simplistic and a too-complex model.

The decision to use a structured domain model approach as opposed to a textual query-answer-based approach depends on the system's intended users. For inexperienced help-desk operators, a tool with which simple problems can be solved by answering a limited number of questions is of great value [18]. However, for experienced help-desk operators who would not bother to use a system for (subjectively) trivial problems, a structured domain model approach yields better results. The system will be able to present the not-so-obviously similar solutions that the help-desk operators could not find. Since knowledge contained in the domain model is used in similarity calculation, the retrieved solutions will be similar in a semantic and structural manner. The domain model allows the solutions in the case base to be applicable to a broader range of problems.

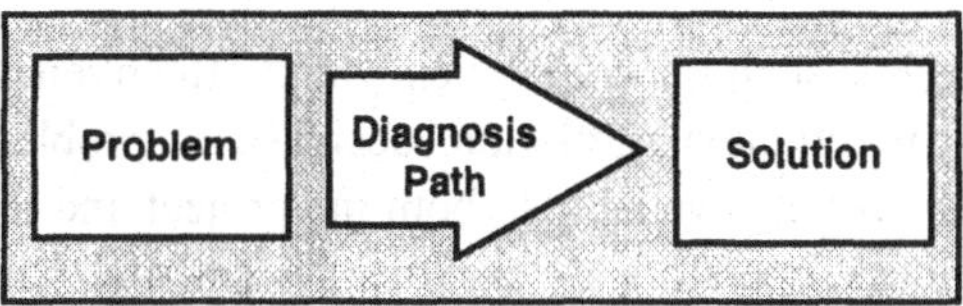

Fig. 2. Basic structure of a help-desk case.

The cases in the help-desk domain should be modeled in accordance with the approach the help-desk operators use in solving problems. We found the approach shown in Fig. 2 very suitable.

The *Problem Description* is the first information the help-desk operator gets from the end-user. This description is what the end-user subjectively perceives as the problem. It may or may not have to do with the actual cause of the failure.

The *Diagnosis Path* consists of the questions the help-desk operator must ask or the information he or she must obtain from various sources to arrive at a diagnosis. The diagnosis path contains the minimal amount of information that is necessary to diagnose the problem.

The *Solution* contains the fault, i.e., what caused the problem, and the remedy, i.e., how to solve the problem. Depending on how the system is implemented and what statistical information is needed for further evaluation, some additional, administrative data may also be added to the case description.

Each complete path from problem description to solution makes up one case.

Once the cases from the initial forms have been entered into the help-desk system, the system should be shown to the project group to verify the results it delivers. Afterwards the initial knowledge acquisition can continue as more cases are entered from additional forms and the knowledge containers are incrementally updated.

Initial knowledge acquisition takes place in two steps. During the first, preliminary knowledge acquisition, the cases for the prototype of the case-based help-desk support system are collected. While the collected cases will help to initialize the knowledge containers and train the project team, the collection of the "core" cases for the system should be done in a second step, the core knowledge acquisition. Nevertheless, the approach that is used in both processes is similar.

6. Using the System

6.1. Managerial Processes During System Use

Project progress with respect to the qualitative and quantitative criteria selected as project goals must be monitored constantly during system development and use [cf. 9]. Regular project reviews should take place. Standard project planning and controlling techniques can and should be applied to case-based help-desk support projects.

Measuring the impact of the help-desk system on the efficiency and effectiveness of the target group (increase in first-call problem resolution, decrease in problem solution time, and so on) and making the results available to both the project and the target groups will motivate the help-desk operators to use the system and help uncover deficiencies.

6.2. Organizational Processes During System Use

Knowledge Utilization and Acquisition Process. The knowledge utilization and acquisition processes that have been defined during system development have to be enacted during system use. The use of the case-based help-desk support system contains the Application Cycle in which the system is used by the help-desk operator and the Maintenance Cycle in which the system is maintained by the CBR author and the CBR administrator (Fig. 3, section 6.3).

During the application cycle, the cases that are stored in the case-based help-desk support system are being used to solve problems. Even if no new cases are being acquired during this cycle, statistical data regarding the quality and usage of the cases (last retrieval time, last application date, success rate and so on) can be collected. This data can be used to determine the quality of the cases and for maintenance purposes.

Whenever a help-desk operator decides that the proposed solution is not appropriate, a new case has to be entered into the case base. However, since the quality of these cases varies according to the user entering them, they cannot be transferred to the case base without being verified by the CBR author. This is done in the maintenance cycle by the CBR author and the CBR administrator.

Training the Help-Desk Operators. Just as the test-users were trained during the project team training, the help-desk operators have to be introduced to the basics of CBR technology and the developed case-based help-desk support system. Since the operators are going to participate in the continuous acquisition of knowledge, standards on how to store cases have to be introduced and taught. Feedback-channels also should be created and introduced during this training.

6.3. Technical Processes During System Use

Continuous Knowledge Acquisition and Maintenance. The knowledge contained in a case-based help-desk support system is an incomplete model of the domain in the real world. Whenever the real world changes, the model in the system has to be updated. The necessity for changes in the model may either arise from real changes in the world or from the learning effect associated with using the case-based help-desk support system. By learning, the system improves the model's coverage of the real world. Since the model is incomplete by definition, with growing knowledge, updates in the knowledge containers will be necessary.

While nobody would consider purchasing a database system with the assumption that it would continue to work without any maintenance at all, there seems to exist a misconception about knowledge-based systems in this respect. All concepts used for maintaining database systems are also applicable to knowledge-based systems. However, because of the semantics associated with the information in knowledge-based systems, additional maintenance operations are necessary. Learning and changes in the real world can make maintenance necessary for each knowledge container.

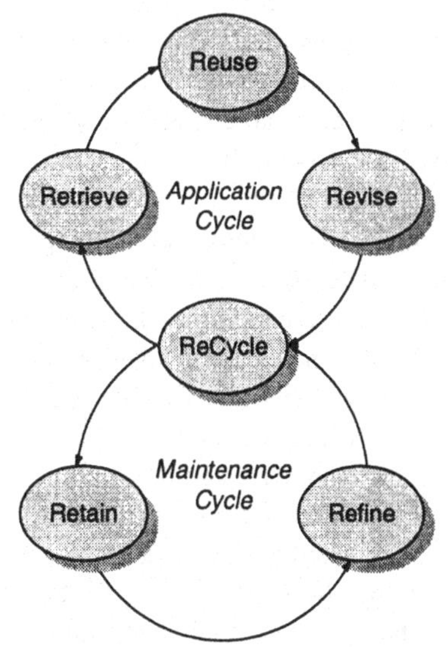

Fig. 3. Processed during the use of a case-based help-desk system

The utilization of a case-based help-desk support system comprises two linked process cycles: the *Application Cycle* and the *Maintenance Cycle* (see Fig. 3).

The *Application Cycle* takes place each time a user solves a problem with the case-based help-desk support system. During the application of the CBR system, the standard tasks *Retrieve*, *Reuse*, and *Revise* must be performed [6]. If the case solution generated during the reuse phase is not correct and cannot be repaired, a new solution has to be generated by the help-desk operator. The solution that has been retrieved by the system or created by the help-desk operator is put to use during the *Recycle* task. The *Application Cycle* is performed by the end-user of the system (help-desk operator).

Whenever a new solution is generated during system use, this case is stored in the case buffer, made available to all help-desk operators as an "unconfirmed case", and sent to the *Maintenance Cycle*. These steps as well as the maintenance cycle itself are not visible to the standard help-desk operator.

The *Maintenance Cycle* consists of the *Retain* and *Refine* tasks. While the *Application Cycle* is executed every time a help-desk operator uses the CBR system, the *Maintenance Cycle* can be executed less frequently, i.e., only when there is a need for maintaining the system or at regular intervals.

During the *Retain* task, the CBR author checks the quality of the new cases that were generated by the helpdesk operators and stored in the case buffer.

The CBR author verifies and approves the representation and content of each case. In terms of representation, the cases should

- contain the information that is necessary and sufficient to solve the problem,
- be described on an appropriate abstraction level.

The content is verified by checking whether the case is

- correct,
- (still) relevant, and
- applicable.

During the *Refine* phase, maintenance steps for the knowledge containers are performed by the CBR administrator. The case base, vocabulary, similarities, and adaptation knowledge have to be refined, and the potentially quality-decreasing effects of external changes in the domain, as well as the inclusion of new cases in the case base, have to be counteracted.

The goal of the *Refine* task with respect to the case base is to keep the case base correct, to have maximal coverage of the problem space, and to have no redundant cases. After each case has been validated in the retain task, their suitability for inclusion in the case base has to be determined.

Before a new case is taken into the case base, it must be checked to see

- whether it is a viable alternative that does not yet exist in the case base,
- whether it subsumes or can be subsumed by an existing case,
- whether it can be combined with another case to form a new one,
- whether the new case would cause an inconsistency, and
- whether there is a newer case already available in the case base.

The operations that have to be performed during case base maintenance vary depending on the application domain and the vocabulary that is used to represent the cases [cf. 12, 13, 14, 15, 16].

Both the inclusion of new cases and changes in the domain may have an effect on the validity and quality of the compiled knowledge containers (vocabulary, similarity, adaptation knowledge) as well. The maintenance of these containers is also performed in the *Refine* step. Since changes in the vocabulary can cause information in the cases to be no longer available or missing (e.g., attributes can be added and deleted, classes can be moved) maintenance of the vocabulary should be performed with utmost caution [cf. 17].

It should be noted that the refinement of the knowledge containers does not necessarily have to be triggered by external events but may also be performed through introspection. By analyzing the content of the knowledge containers, more efficient ways to structure the domain, adaptation rules, and similarities, as well as new cases, can be discovered or derived.

While maintenance operations for the case base can be performed by the CBR author, maintenance of the vocabulary, the similarity, and adaptation knowledge should only be performed by the CBR administrator.

General IT-System-Related Processes. Once the case-based help-desk support system has been put into operation, it has to be debugged, monitored, and updated continuously. The necessity for updates does not necessarily have to come from the help-desk system itself, but may also be initiated by changes in the (IT) environment. Since these processes are not CBR-specific but apply to IT systems in general, we refrain from going into their details here.

7. Summary

Current CBR-process models only cover the technological aspects of CBR system development. While the tasks given in these models suffice to develop systems that are used by a limited number of users in a static environment, problems that arise from larger user groups with differing levels of experience as well as dynamic domains are disregarded. Case-Based Reasoning in real world environments is not necessarily a low maintenance AI-technology and processes related to knowledge acquisition and maintenance play a very important role in the success of CBR projects in corporate environments.

In order to develop case-based help-desk systems that are being used in a dynamic, corporate environment by a large group of users, managerial, organizational and technical processes have to be taken into account. It has to be kept in mind, that once a CBR system is in place, continuous knowledge acquisition and maintenance is necessary. Processes for knowledge acquisition and maintenance have to be developed and put in place, and personnel has to be dedicated to perform these tasks.

8. References

1. Bergmann, R., Breen, S., Göker, M., Manago, M., Wess, S. "Developing Industrial Case Based Reasoning Applications: The INRECA Methodology.", Lecture Notes in Artificial Intelligence, 1612, Berlin, Springer Verlag, 1999
2. Göker M., Roth-Berghofer Th., Bergmann R., Pantleon T., Traphöner R., Wess S., Wilke W., *"The Development of HOMER: A Case-Based CAD/CAM Help-Desk Support Tool"*, Smyth B. & Cunningham P. eds., "Advances in Case-Based Reasoning, Proceedings of the Fourth European Workshop on Case-Based Reasoning EWCBR98 Dublin, September 23-25,1998", LNAI 1488, pp. 346-357, Berlin, Springer Verlag, 1998
3. Riesbeck C., Schank R., *"Inside Case-based Reasoning"*, Lawrence Erlbaum Associates, Publishers, Hillsdale 1989
4. Hammond K., *"Case-Based Planning-Viewing Planning as a Memory Task"*, Academic Press Inc, HBJ Publishers, San Diego, 1989
5. Kolodner J., "Case-based Reasoning", Morgan Kaufmann Publishers Inc, San Mateo, 1993
6. A. Aamodt, E. Plaza., *"Case-Based Reasoning: Foundational Issues, Methodological Variations, and System Approaches"*, AICOM Vol.7 Nr.1, pp.39-59, March 1994
7. Leake D., *"CBR in Context: The Present and the Future"* in Leake D. (ed.), "Case-Based Reasoning – Experiences, Lessons and Future Directions", pp. 3-30, AAAI press / MIT press, Menlo Park California, Cambridge Massachusetts, London, 1996
8. Kitano H., Shimazu H., *"The Experience Sharing Architecture: A Case Study in Corporate-Wide Case-Based Software Quality Control"* in Leake D. (ed.), "Case-Based Reasoning – Experiences, Lessons and Future Directions", pp. 235-268, AAAI press / MIT press, Menlo Park California, Cambridge Massachusetts, London, 1996

9. Stolpmann M. Wess S. *"Optimierung der Kundenbeziehungen mit CBR systemen-Intelligente Systeme für E-Commerce und Support"*, Addison Wesley Longmann (Business & Computing), Bonn, 1999
10. Richter M., *"Introduction"*, in Lenz M., Bartsch-Spörl B., Burkhardt H. D., Wess S. (Eds.), *"Case-Based Reasoning Technology, From Foundations to Applications"*, Lecture Notes in Artificial Intelligence Vol. 1400, pp.1-15, Springer-Verlag, Berlin, Heidelberg 1998. Also: Richter M., "The Knowledge Contained in Similarity Measures", Invited talk at ICCBR95, http://wwwagr.informatik.uni-kl.de/~lsa/CBR/Richtericcbr95remarks.html
11. Wilke W., Vollrath I., Bergmann R., "Using Knowledge Containers to Model a Framework for Learning Adaptation Knowledge", *ECML (European Conference on Machine Learning) Workshop, Prag, 1997*
12. Leake D., Wilson D., *"Categorizing Case-Base Maintenance: Dimensions and Directions"*, Smyth B. & Cunningham P. eds., "Advances in Case-Based Reasoning, Proceedings of the Fourth European Workshop on Case-Based Reasoning EWCBR98 Dublin, September 23-25,1998", LNAI 1488, pp. 196-207, Berlin, Springer Verlag, 1998
13. Smyth B., McKenna E., *"Modeling the Competence of Case-Bases"*, Smyth B. & Cunningham P. eds., "Advances in Case-Based Reasoning, Proceedings of the Fourth European Workshop on Case-Based Reasoning EWCBR98 Dublin, September 23-25,1998", LNAI 1488, pp. 208-220, Berlin, Springer Verlag, 1998
14. Surma J., Tyburcy J., *"A Study on Competence-Preserving Case Replacing Strategies in Case-Based Reasoning"*, Smyth B. & Cunningham P. eds., "Advances in Case-Based Reasoning, Proceedings of the Fourth European Workshop on Case-Based Reasoning EWCBR98 Dublin, September 23-25,1998", LNAI 1488, pp. 233-238, Berlin, Springer Verlag, 1998
15. Racine K., Yang Q., *"Maintaining Unstructured Case-Bases"*, Leake B. & Plaza E. eds., "Case-Based Reasoning Research and Development", Proceedings of the second International Conference on Case-Based Reasoning ICCBR-97 Rhode Island, July 1997, LNAI 1266, pp. 553-564, Berlin, Springer Verlag, 1997
16. Hüttemeister A., "Wartung einer Fallbasis", Diploma Thesis, University of Kaiserslautern, Department of Computer Science, February 1999
17. Heister F., Wilke W., "An Architecture for Maintaining Case-Based Reasoning Systems", Smyth B. & Cunningham P. eds., "Advances in Case-Based Reasoning, Proceedings of the Fourth European Workshop on Case-Based Reasoning EWCBR98 Dublin, September 23-25,1998", LNAI 1488, pp. 221-232, Berlin, Springer Verlag, 1998
18. Thomas, H., Foil R., Dacus, J. : "New Technology Bliss and Pain in a Large Customer Service Center", in: Case-Based Reasoning Research and Development, Proceedings of the ICCBR97, Leake, Plaza (eds.), , pp. 166-177, LNAI1266, Springer Verlag, Berlin, 1997

---

[i] Funding for this work has partly been provided by the Commission of the European Union (INRECA-II: Information and Knowledge Reengineering for Reasoning from Cases; Esprit Contract no. 22196). The partners of INRECA-II are: Acknosoft (prime contractor, France), DaimlerChrysler (Germany), tecInno (Germany), Irish Multimedia Systems (Ireland), and the University of Kaiserslautern (Germany). http://www.inreca.org

Acknowledgements

The authors would like to thank Prof. M. Richter for triggering the ideas that led to this publication during the EWCBR 98 in Dublin.

We would also like to thank the reviewers of this paper for their encouraging and very helpful comments.

Modelling the CBR Life Cycle Using Description Logics *

Mercedes Gómez-Albarrán, Pedro A. González-Calero, Belén Díaz-Agudo and Carlos Fernández-Conde

Dep. Sistemas Informáticos y Programación
Universidad Complutense de Madrid
28040 Madrid, Spain
email:{albarran, pedro, belend, carlosf}@sip.ucm.es

Abstract. In this paper Description Logics are presented as a suitable formalism to model the CBR life cycle. We propose a general model to structure the knowledge needed in a CBR system, where adaptation knowledge is explicitly represented. Next, the CBR processes are described based on this model and the CBR system OoFRA is presented as an example of our approach.

1 Introduction

In the last few years, Description Logics (DLs) have caught a great interest within the CBR community [9, 14, 18]. Their declarative semantics helps in the domain comprehension, the understanding of the case indexes and the formal definition of different powerful inference mechanisms. Their ability to automatically classify concepts and recognise instances is a useful property for the case base management. Their ability to build structured case descriptions provide a flexible and expressive way to represent the cases and their solutions.

In this paper, we propose a domain-independent model for developing CBR systems that takes advantage of DLs, and whose main contributions are:

- the definition of a scheme that structures all the knowledge needed in the CBR processes,
- the structured representation presented for the cases, and
- the use of the DLs inference mechanisms, supplemented with special purpose algorithms, for the retrieval, adaptation and learning CBR tasks. We propose a domain-independent similarity measure for the retrieval of cases that can be complemented with domain-specific similarity knowledge. Our general adaptation scheme is based on substitutions and the search of substitutes is guided by a set of memory instructions. The learning process extends not only to the cases but also to the adaptation knowledge.

* This work is supported by the Spanish Committee of Science & Technology (CICYT TIC98-0733)

The paper is organized as follows. Section 2 describes the basics of DLs. The general scheme for the representation, retrieval, and adaptation and learning processes is defined is Sections 3, 4, and 5, respectively. In Section 6, our approach is applied to OoFRA, a case-based planning system. Limitations of the proposed approach appear in Section 7. Section 8 contains related work and conclusions.

2 Basic Concepts on DLs

The idea of developing knowledge representation systems based on a structured representation of knowledge was first pursued with Semantic Networks and Frame Systems. One problem of these solutions is the need of a formal ground to define the semantics of the knowledge representation. In this way, DLs born trying to provide knowledge representation with this formal ground.

In DLs, there are three types of formal objects [5]:

- *Concepts:* Descriptions with a potentially complex structure, formed by composing a limited set of description-forming operators.
- *Roles:* Simple formal terms for properties.
- *Individuals:* Simple formal constructs intended to directly represent objects in the domain of interest as concept instances.

Concepts can be either primitive or defined. Defined concepts are represented in terms of necessary and sufficient conditions that individuals have to satisfy in order to be recognized as instances of those concepts. Primitive concepts are just represented as necessary conditions, so it is impossible to infer that individuals are instances of primitive concepts. But if it is explicitly asserted that an individual is an instance of a primitive concept, the system will apply all the concept restrictions to the individual. Roles also can be primitive or defined. Primitive roles introduce new necessary conditions in the role, and defined roles introduce both necessary and sufficient conditions.

Concepts, roles and individuals are placed into a taxonomy where more general concepts/roles will be above more specific concepts/roles. Likewise, individuals are placed below the concept(s) that they are instances of. Concepts and individuals inherit properties from more general descriptions as well as combine properties as appropriate. Thus, DL-Systems has two main components: A general schema concerning the classes of individuals to be represented built from primitive concepts and role restrictions, usually referred as *TBox,* and a partial or total instantiation of this schema, containing assertions relating either individuals to concepts or individuals to each other, usually referred as *ABox.*

A key feature of DLs is that the system can reason about concept descriptions, and automatically infer subsumption relations. We say that a concept C subsumes the concept D ($C \succ D$) if all the individuals that satisfy the description of D, also satisfy the description of C. There are several variations of deductive inferences, depending on the particular DL. Some of the most typical are Completion and Classification [3]. In Completion, logical consequences of assertions about individuals are inferred, and in Classification, each new concept is placed under the most specific concepts that subsume it.

The core of DL-Systems is its concept language L, which can be viewed as a set of constructs [2, 5] for denoting concepts and relationships among concepts. An assertion language is also defined which lets express individual features.

3 CBR Knowledge Representation Using DLs

We propose a model where the knowledge needed for the CBR processes is structured in three interrelated but conceptually different portions of a knowledge base $\mathcal{KB}$ represented using DLs (a related categorization of the CBR knowledge in containers was described by Richter [17]): $\mathcal{KB} = \langle \mathcal{B}, \mathcal{DK}, \mathcal{PSK} \rangle$, where

- $\mathcal{B}$ contains the general knowledge used to structure and represent the cases.
- $\mathcal{DK}$ contains the domain knowledge used for case representation, query formulation and case adaptation.
- $\mathcal{PSK}$ contains the CBR process support knowledge, i.e. the knowledge, apart from the one in $\mathcal{DK}$, that is used in case retrieval and adaptation.

$\mathcal{B}$ is domain independent but the knowledge included in $\mathcal{DK}$ and $\mathcal{PSK}$ depends on the specific application domain where this representation model is applied. We will describe the $\mathcal{PSK}$ contents in Sections 4 and 5. The $\mathcal{DK}$ portion models the specific domain being considered: the basic domain entities are formalized as DLs individuals described by the concepts of which they are instances, and the relations they have with other individuals. In this section, we mainly deal with the $\mathcal{B}$ portion, where case structure is detailed.

The $\mathcal{B}$ portion It contains a distinguished concept CASE to represent the general case structure. The stored cases are represented as individuals that are automatically classified as instances of CASE. Moreover, each case is linked by DLs relations –*desc* and *sol*– to its descriptive components, the *description* of a problem –or situation– and a *solution* to this problem, respectively.

The description of a CASE instance c_i is a $\mathcal{DK}$ individual d_i that represents the characteristics of the problem –or situation– described by case c_i. Instance d_i is also used as the case index in the organization and retrieval tasks.

The solution of a CASE instance c_i is a $\mathcal{B}$ individual s_i that represents the solution of the problem d_i described by case c_i. The solution s_i is connected –through the *r-has-item* relation– with a set (possibly ordered) of instances each representing a solution component or *item*. Each one of these items is in its turn described by its relations with other individuals. The relation *contents* links each solution item with a $\mathcal{DK}$ individual that formalizes this part of the solution. Optionally, the *item-number* relation is used to identify an item when the representation of some kind of order among the items is required. The dependency relations –*depends-on-description* and *depends-on-item*– are used to include adaptation knowledge in a solution item $item_j$, relating it with the description component(s) and/or the solution item(s) that have an influence on it, i.e. with the components where a change will cause $item_j$ adaptation. The use of this adaptation knowledge will be broadly explained in Section 5.

4 Retrieval

Retrieval is implemented as a two step process: first, a number of individuals are retrieved and, second, they are ranked by applying a similarity function.

There are two different methods to implement retrieval using the reasoning mechanisms available in DLs:

- Retrieval based on *concept classification*, where a concept description c_q is built using the restrictions specified in the query. This concept is then classified, and finally all its instances are retrieved.
- Retrieval based on *instance recognition*, where an individual is built and a number of assertions are made about it based on the features specified in the query. Instance recognition is applied to retrieve the most specific concepts of which this individual is an instance, and then all the instances of these concepts are retrieved.

There are two main differences between these two methods:

- The type of restrictions that can be included, since concept description language and assertion language are different. Concept description language is richer because restrictions about role type and cardinality can be included.
- Instance completion. There are a number of inferences that are only applied to individuals. DLs systems do not enrich concept descriptions with inferred constraints, but just take the concept definition as it is, and classify it accordingly. On the other hand, when an individual is recognized as instance of a given concept, based on the sufficient conditions for belonging to that concept, then necessary conditions on the concept definition are automatically asserted on the individual.

So, both approaches have its pros and cons, namely expressiveness vs. completion. We have decided to implement retrieval as an instance recognition process mainly for one reason: instance completion accomplishes a kind of query completion where additional constraints can be automatically inferred from those explicitly asserted by the user. In this way, we have a straightforward method to let the domain knowledge assist in the crucial process of query formulation.

Although it is not likely to happen, the most specific concepts of which the individual representing the query is recognized as an instance may have no more instances. In that situation the most specific concepts subsuming those concepts would be selected, and their instances retrieved. This process should be repeated until a non empty set of instances is retrieved.

Once the system has retrieved a number of instances representing the candidate case descriptions, these are ranked by their similarity with respect to the individual representing the query. For this purpose we apply a domain-independent similarity function along with a number of domain-specific heuristics, as described in the following subsection.

This model also allows for the definition of a *minimum similarity threshold* such that new individuals are retrieved until one is found whose similarity with the query is above the given threshold. The number of retrieved individuals is increased by accessing to the instances of more and more abstract concepts. This way, we cope with the fact that it is not guaranteed that the most similar individuals can be found among those that are instances of the most specific concepts of which the query is an instance.

4.1 Similarity Measure

Similarity is computed for a given pair of individuals, where an individual can represent a case description or, in general, the value of a given feature. As described in Section 3 an individual is defined in terms of the concepts of which that individual is an instance and the slots asserted for it, which are represented as relations connecting the individual to other individuals or primitive values. Therefore, a similarity measure should take into account both types of features.

Concept-based similarity To define a similarity measure on concepts we use an idea taken from the *vector space model* used in Information Retrieval [19]. In this model, every indexable item is represented by an attribute vector, and the similarity between two items is obtained by some kind of algebraic manipulation of the vectors associated with them. We consider as attributes the concepts defined in the knowledge base, $C = \{c_1, \ldots, c_N\}$, and say that individual i has attribute c_j if i is an instance of c_j. This way, an attribute vector is associated with every individual, and the *conceptual similarity* between two individuals is computed as the cosine of the angle formed by the vectors which represent them, a similarity function usually applied in the vector space model.

Slot-based similarity A slot is defined by a relation (*role*) and a set of individuals (*fillers*). We consider comparable only those slots with the same relation, and obtain the similarity between two slots as the similarity between their sets of fillers. When comparing sets of individuals we recursively apply the function of similarity between individuals, accumulating for every individual of one set the maximum of the results obtained by comparing that individual with every individual of the other set. This recursion ends when comparing individuals without slots, which similarity is given by the concept-based similarity term.

The similarity between two individuals is computed as the sum of their concept-based similarity and the similarity among their slots. A more detailed description of the similarity function can be found in [6].

This domain-independent function can accurately take into account the structure of the knowledge base. Nevertheless, our framework also allows for the integration of domain-specific similarity knowledge in one of the following ways:

Concept-specific similarity knowledge This kind of restriction lets specify that instances of a given concept should be compared by a subset of their slots. This way, descriptive slots can be distinguished from those others that provide additional information, but should not be considered when determining the similarity between two individuals.

Relation-specific similarity knowledge This kind of restriction lets specify that an alternative function should be applied when computing the similarity between the fillers of a given role (i.e., the values of a given attribute). For example, this mechanism could be used to specify the similarity between values of primitive types by specifying the function to be applied on those relations that are to be filled by primitive values.

According to the knowledge base division presented in Section 3, domain-specific similarity knowledge is explicitly represented in $\mathcal{PSK}$. A high level mechanism is in charge of combining the different similarity measures, trying first to obtain domain-specific measures and if none apply, computing the domain-independent function.

5 Adaptation

Built upon the model for structuring the knowledge needed in CBR tasks described in Section 3, we propose a substitution-based adaptation mechanism. Adaptation is guided by the explicit representation of dependency relations – *depends-on-description, depends-on-item*, generalized as *dependsOn*– stored in case solutions, as a process that propagates changes from description to solution items, as follows:

1. The list L of items in the solution that need to be adapted are obtained. These items are those that depend on a feature of the case description which has been substituted by a new value in the query, or those others that depend on a solution item that needs to be adapted.
2. Every item in L is substituted by a proper new item. First, those that only depend on values from the case description, then, those that depend on other items of the solution that have already been adapted. Of course, circularity is not allowed in the dependency relation.

The search for substitutes is accomplished as a kind of *specialized search* which takes advantage of the knowledge base organization. This process can take one of two forms: a general purpose search algorithm, or the replay of previously learnt search knowledge represented as *search heuristics*.

5.1 Specialized Search

Specialized search, as described in [11], is a way of finding appropriate substitutes for a case solution element, where instructions are given about how to find the needed item. In our model, memory instructions correspond to a relation path that connects one case item with another case element. We assume that, whenever an item of the case is said to depend on a case element, a path of relations exists connecting both individuals. Formally:

$$dependsOn(i_1, i_2) \Leftrightarrow_{def} \exists r_1, \ldots, r_n : ((compose\; r_1 \ldots r_n)\; i_2\; i_1)$$

The path of relations leads to the place of the knowledge base where substitutes have to be found. For example, if *dependsOn*(i_1, i_2) stands and i_2 has already been substituted for another value i'_2, then a substitute i'_1 for i_1 has to be found, such that: first, there is a connection between i'_2 and i'_1 *similar* to that between i_2 and i_1; and second, i'_1 is similar to i_1.

In other words, we are searching for a substitute in the surroundings of i_1 that is connected to i'_2. In order to implement this process we need to find the shortest path between i_2 and i_1 and, then, use that path and i_1 to find the appropriate i'_1. The first problem is reduced to that of searching for the shortest path in the directed acyclic graph defined by the individuals in the knowledge base. The second process is the goal of the search operator which is described in the next subsection.

5.2 Search Operator

The search operator takes as arguments: the individual o which has substituted an element that previously appeared in the case; an ordered list of relations – relation path– $[r_1, \ldots, r_k]$ that connects the $\mathcal{DK}$ individual that o has substituted with the $\mathcal{DK}$ individual i that has to be substituted due to its dependency on the already substituted individual; and the individual i. The operator searches for those individuals connected to o through $[r_1, \ldots, r_k]$ which are instances of the most specific concept of which i is an instance. If none is found, or a minimum similarity threshold has been specified such that none of the retrieved individuals is above that threshold, then search restrictions are generalized. Two kinds of generalizations are applied:

1. Rising the abstraction level of the concepts whose instances are being considered.
2. Rising the abstraction level of the relations that connect o to the instances being considered.

This way, we take advantage of the two terminological abstraction hierarchies that can be defined in DLs, namely, the concept hierarchy and the relation hierarchy. Generalizations are applied on both, concepts and relations, level by level, until proper substitutes are found.

As an example, let's consider the situation depicted in Figure 1. Here, the search operator would find substitutes in two steps:

1. First, it searches for individuals connected to o through $[r_1, \ldots, r_k]$ which are instances of C_1. And none is found.
2. Second, the concept and the relation path are generalized. Supposing that only r_{k-1} among $[r_1, \ldots, r_k]$ can be generalized, individuals connected to o through $[r_1, \ldots, r^G_{k-1}, r_k]$ which are instances of C are retrieved: a, b and c. These individuals will be ranked by the similarity function, and the most similar will be returned.

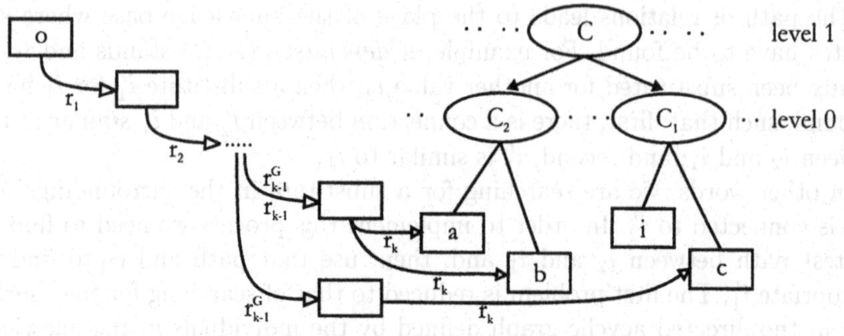

Fig. 1. Search (o, $[r_1, \ldots, r_k]$, i)

5.3 Search Knowledge Learning

The search as described in the two previous sections is implemented as an algorithm that finds a relation path and retrieves individuals that satisfy the given restrictions, generalizing them if needed. The cost of this process depends on the size of the knowledge base and it may become quite expensive when applied to knowledge bases of realistic size. To alleviate this problem, the system includes a learning component that records every successful search as a *search heuristic.*

Search heuristics are represented as individuals in the $\mathcal{PSK}$ portion of the knowledge base including the following slots:

`origin`	< *concept* >
`destination`	< *concept* >
`path`	< *relation – list* >
`concept-level`	< *integer* >
`relation-level`	< *integer* >
`weight`	< *integer* >

which indicates that instances of *origin* and *destination* are connected through the relations in *path*, and that the recorded search was successful when the relation path was generalized to *relation – level* and the individuals were instances of *destination* rised to *concept – level*. Since more than one heuristic may exists connecting the same pair of concepts, the *weight* slot is included in order to record the number of times that an heuristic has been successfully applied.

When searching for substitutes, search heuristics are first considered if applicable. An heuristic is applicable when the dependency being processed, *depends-On*(i_1, i_2), involves an instance of *destination* and *origin*, respectively. Of course, applicable heuristics are tried in weight order. And, only when none of the applicable heuristics retrieves substitutes, the general algorithm is applied.

6 OoFRA: a CBR System for Framework Reuse

Object-oriented frameworks are collections of interdependent classes that define reusable and extensible architectural designs for specific domains. When developing software based on framework reuse, the generic architecture defined by the framework must be customized and/or extended. Extensible systems tend to be very sophisticated and complex, so that users do not often know the concepts, commitments and decisions involved in the solutions provided. In the case of frameworks, this results in implementations which do not *map* the domain organization. A domain entity does not correspond to a specific framework class, but to a group of classes that collaborate. The actions a domain entity can make correspond to methods that are not defined in a specific class, but they are dispersed among the group of classes corresponding to the entity.

Due to their potentially large size and complexity, the ability to quickly understand and extend frameworks is a critical issue. One way to simplify framework reuse is to profit from prototypical examples about usual mechanisms for extending and customizing them. So, we have developed OoFRA (Object-oriented Framework Reuse Assistant), a CBR system whose case base is populated with these prototypical usage examples, and deals with the retrieval and adaptation tasks. Our system uses LOOM, a knowledge representation system descendant of the KL-ONE system [13]. We have applied the approach described in the previous sections to support the reuse of the framework, included in the VisualWorks environment, for developing applications with Graphical User Interface (GUI). A previous prototype of this system can be found in [7].

6.1 The Knowledge Base of the System

Following the representation model described in Section 3, OoFRA knowledge base consists of three portions $\mathcal{KB} = \langle \mathcal{B}, \mathcal{DK}, \mathcal{PSK} \rangle$. Next, we describe them.

The $\mathcal{DK}$ portion It contains general purpose GUI concepts and concepts specific to the framework, together with the instances of these concepts representing the GUI entities, and the framework classes, methods and collaborations.

The general purpose GUI concepts are the types of the GUI entities and of the operations that can be made on/by these entities. Some concepts specific to the framework are: those corresponding to the object-oriented concepts class and method; and the concept *contract* that represents the collaborations among classes relating the target of the collaboration to the classes that collaborate.

The instances of the general purpose GUI concepts represent the GUI entities and actions. They define the domain terminology which acts as a description language that will be used in the case indexing and in the user query formulation. The individuals representing the classes, methods and collaborations of the framework are used in the solution description and in the adaptation process.

The $\mathcal{B}$ portion Let's see the case structure and the information stored in each case component by means of an example: the case that shows how to obtain the selected text in an input field, whose representation is depicted in Figure 2 (shady boxes correspond to $\mathcal{DK}$ individuals).

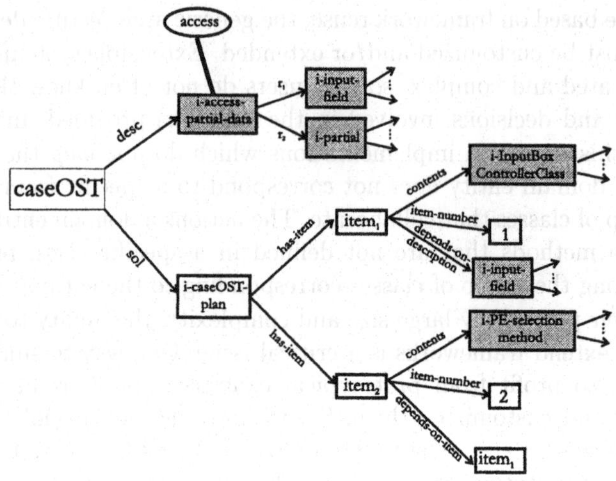

Fig. 2. Example case: Obtain selected text in an input field

The case description is *i-access-partial-data*, a $\mathcal{DK}$ individual representing the framework extension/customization problem that the case is intended to help solve: the GUI action "access part of the text shown in an input field".

The solutions in OoFRA cases consist of an ordered sequence of steps. So, the cases can be seen as plans. In the sample case the solution consists of two steps. The first step records the controller class accessed in this part of the solution, represented by the $\mathcal{DK}$ individual *i-InputFieldControllerClass*, and the class dependency on an element of the description, represented by *i-input-field*, the $\mathcal{DK}$ individual corresponding to the widget that appears in the problem description. The second step shows the method of the previous step class used in this part of the solution, represented by the $\mathcal{DK}$ individual *i-PE-selection-method*, and the method dependency on the class from the first step.

The $\mathcal{PSK}$ portion It comprises a set of search heuristics and the comparison criteria showing the descriptive slots for the $\mathcal{DK}$ individuals. An example of search heuristic is "to find the controller class that collaborates for a widget, first, look for the contract target related to the widget, second, look for the contract corresponding to this contract target and, third, look for the class that acts as the controller component". An example of comparison criterion is the one that establishes the aspect considered when comparing two methods: two methods are similar if their operation specifications are similar.

6.2 Case Retrieval in OoFra

Let's illustrate the case retrieval with a simple situation. Let's suppose the user tries to find a usage case that explains how to obtain the selected element in a list-box. The user builds the description of her action selecting a verb that corresponds to a domain action, for instance *access*, and the appropriate values for some/all the verb modifiers, for instance, *list-box* for the widget, *data* for the accessed widget part and *single selection* for the number of selections.

From this information, and applying the retrieval mechanism described in Section 4, the closest case found by the system is the one that shows how to obtain the selected text in an input field. However, this case needs to be adapted in order to be useful: the class and the method used are related to an input field, not to a list-box.

6.3 Adapting a Case in OoFRA

First, let's see why does our system adapt the case retrieved in the previous section. Both solution steps need to be adapted. In the first step, the class accessed depends on the GUI widget appearing in the problem description solved, and the widget in the user problem description is different from the widget in the retrieved case problem. So, it should be substituted by another class. The method used in the second step depends on the class accessed in the first one. Therefore, a change in the class involves a change in the method.

Now, let's see how does our system adapt the case. When applying the search operator to the first step, the origin is the individual of the $\mathcal{DK}$ base representing the widget *list-box*, the heuristic selected is the one that helps to find the controller of a widget and the comparison criterion is the one that can be applied to classes. The search operator returns *i-SequenceControllerClass*, the $\mathcal{DK}$ individual representing the class that acts as the controller of a list-box, as the substitute for the original class. When applying the search operator to the second step, the origin is the class returned by the adaptation of the first step, the heuristic is the one that helps to find the methods of a class and the comparison criterion is the one that can be applied to methods. The system tries unsuccessfully to find methods of this class similar to the one is going to be substituted. So, the system relaxes the adaptation process generalizing the relation paths and the level used to look for similar individuals.

Let's see, for instance, what happens when generalizing the relation path in the adaptation of the first step (Figure 3). The relation path resulting from the heuristic chosen in the first adaptation attempt starts in the $\mathcal{DK}$ individual representing a list-box, and, through the relations *inverse-contract-target*, *inverse-contract* and *controller-comp*, ends in the $\mathcal{DK}$ individual *i-SequenceControllerClass* that represents the list-box controller. On generalizing the relation path, only the last relation can be substituted by the more abstract relation *contract-comp*. The generalized path leads, then, to the four classes that collaborate when the widget is a list-box.

On generalizing the level used when searching similar individuals, these four classes, together with the class *i-ActiveWindowClass*, can be considered as possible substitutes for the class *i-InputBoxControllerClass*. However, before computing the similarity, the class *i-ActiveWindowClass* is excluded because it is not connected with the origin given to the search operator.

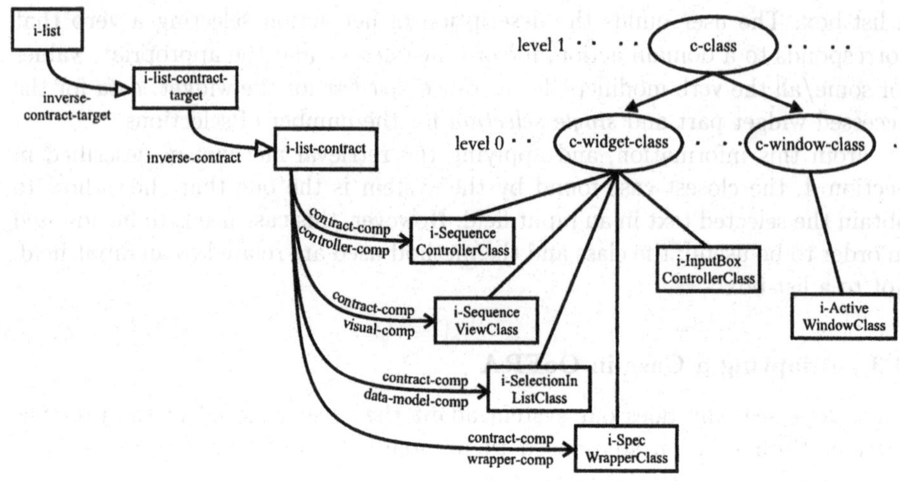

Fig. 3. Use of generalized relation paths in the OoFRA adaptation process

The similarity function is applied to the rest of the classes. According to the comparison criterion for classes, the four classes can act as substitutes. The application of the relaxed adaptation process to the second step is similar to this of the first one. The result of the case adaptation consists of four pairs (class, method), each one corresponding to one of the classes, that are shown ordered by similarity value to the user as appropriate substitutes for the class and the method in the retrieved case.

7 Limitations of the proposed approach

In order to point out the main limitations of the approach here described, we separately consider the two main proposals it comprises: to use DLs as the formalism to represent the knowledge needed by a CBR system; and to take advantage of the DLs reasoning mechanisms to implement the CBR processes. As a representation mechanism, DLs surpasses the average in expressiveness, with the plus of a formal grounded semantics. On the other hand, efficiency is the minus, since DLs can not compete with standard data base technology in terms of retrieval speed. With regard to the implementation of the CBR processes, as we have shown through this paper, special purpose algorithms must supplement DLs reasoning mechanisms. Nevertheless, this combination suffers from some limitations:

– The concept hierarchy should be balanced in depth. The similarity function takes into account not only shared features but also the total number of features an individual has. So, those individuals which are deep in the hierarchy –i.e., have more features– will never be chosen if individuals, with a similar –or even smaller– number of shared features with the query, exist higher in the hierarchy. This situation should be avoided when it is the result of an unbalanced knowledge representation, where a portion of the domain has been described in more detail -with more levels of abstraction- than others, and individuals from different parts of the $\mathcal{KB}$ are to be compared.

- The adaptation process has the general limitation of substitution based methods, which can not change the structure of the solution being adapted. More specific is the need for an explicit representation of dependencies between description and solution items, restricting the possible adaptations, which, in a sense, has to be foreseen, since only recorded dependencies are explored in case adaptation.
  Finally, a limitation is imposed by the basic assumption of the adaptation process: a dependency can only be stated if a relation path exists between the dependent individuals. This restriction may be taken into account when developing the $\mathcal{KB}$, or more probably, may lead to changes in the $\mathcal{KB}$ as the case base gets populated.

The application of the proposed model to the OoFRA system has offered a satisfactory runtime performance although, there has not been an exhaustive, formal and precise study about its scaling-up. As future work we are studying the efficiency issues based on the empirical studies (e.g. [8]) that evaluate how certain DLs implementations behave with respect to typical and random knowledge bases, instead of the analytical studies to determine the worst case performance. The more expressive a DLs is, the higher the computational cost of the reasoning tasks than can be performed in it. That makes necessary to consider the particular CBR application expressiveness and performance requirements to choose an adequate DLs.

The real knowledge bases used in [8] range from 138 to 435 concepts and from 10 to 52 roles. Moreover, the randomly generated knowledge bases range from 0 to 150 concepts (small), to 2000 concepts (large) and to 5000 concepts (very large). These previous performance results and our feedback from OoFRA make us feel optimistic with respect to the behaviour results of our model.

8 Related Work and Conclusions

During the last few years, many researches have suggested the use of DLs to organize, represent and retrieve cases in CBR systems like MRL [9,10], CATO [1], RESYN/CBR [14,15], ORA [6] and a diagnosis system for the French telephone network [4,18]. The common ground is to take advantage of the DLs reasoning mechanisms for some tasks in the CBR life cycle.

The approach presented in this paper proposes the use of DLs as a suitable formalism to represent all the knowledge used by the CBR processes and to model the tasks involved in the CBR life cycle. A particularity of our approach is the formalization of a domain independent scheme to represent cases where solutions include explicitly represented adaptation knowledge.

As in [1,4,18], we use DLs instances to represent the cases, but instead of considering a simplified representation approach, we take advantage of DLs as a formalism to represent complex and structured cases –and indexes– in the line of [16]. In [16] cases are represented as structured concepts composed of features classified in a subsumption hierarchy. We represent cases with two main components –its description and its solution– that are automatically organised by the subsumption relation. The use of the subsumption relation to automatically organise cases or indexes is also shared by [1, 4, 9, 15, 18].

We have defined a retrieval process where a DLs instance is created with the user requirements, and is automatically completed by the DLs instance completion mechanism. A domain independent numerical similarity measure for cases has been described, where case structure and knowledge base organization is accurately taken into account. Also, we have shown how the domain-independent similarity measure can be integrated with domain-specific similarity knowledge. Previous works also select the best cases by using a numerical approach [9, 21] or a declarative approach [16, 14].

A main contribution in using classification for case adaptation is done in [14, 15]. Although the authors consider a frame-based case representation, the ideas are also applicable to DLs. In [14] the adaptation process takes advantage of the hierarchy to generalise certain case's components –using the least common subsummer operation– according to the query case. In [15], the concept hierarchy is used to qualitatively measure case distances. The *similarity path* that separates on the hierarchy the query case description from other case's descriptions, is used as a sequence of *generalization* and *specialization* steps to be applied to the case *solutions*. Case adaptation proposed in [14, 15] allows only the generalization and/or specialization of case components. We present a general adaptation scheme based on substitutions that uses DLs to represent the case we want to adapt, to identify the item that should be substituted in the solution, and to guide the search towards the most suitable replacement.

When using DLs instances/concepts to represent cases/indexes, there is a simple way to learn new cases or indexes: adding additional instances or concepts to the hierarchy, that are automatically positioned at the correct place by the DLs reasoning mechanisms. Apart from this simple approximation to case learning, we have included adaptation knowledge learning that also takes advantage of the DLs reasoning mechanisms: search knowledge is learnt by memorizing and weighting the search heuristic succesfully used to find a substitute for a non apropriate solution component. In [12] a related approach –not using DLs– for acquiring adaptation knowledge is presented.

With regard to the application of CBR to software reuse, in [21] a CBR approach to code reuse is presented. In [20] CBR is presented as a candidate technology for the reuse of software knowledge due to the big number of commonalities existing between the CBR cycle and the reuse tasks.

As a final conclusion, we have shown the practical applicability of the proposed model in the implementation of the CBR processes, by developing OoFRA, an effective assistant in object-oriented framework reuse.

References

1. Ashley, K. & Aleven, V., 1993: "A logical representation for relevance criteria", in *Topics in CBR* (Wess S., Althoff K. & Richter M., eds.), Springer-Verlag.
2. Borgida, A., 1996: "On the Relative Expressiveness of Description Logics and Predicate Logics", *Artificial Intelligence Journal*, vol. 82, no. 1-2, pp. 353-367.
3. Brachman, R.J., McGuinness, D.L., Patel-Schneider, P.F., Resnick, L. & Borgida, A., 1991: "Living with CLASSIC: When and How to Use a KL-ONE-Like language", in *Principles of Semantic Networks*, Morgan Kaufmann.
4. Coupey, P., Fouquere, C. & Salotti, S., 1998: "Formalizing Partial Matching and Similarity in CBR with a Description Logic", *Applied Artificial Intelligence*, vol. 12, no. 1, pp. 71-112.
5. Donini, F.M., Lenzerini, M., Nardi, D., & Schaerf, A., 1996: "Reasoning in Description Logics", in *Foundation of Knowledge Representation*, CSLI-Publications.
6. Fernández-Chamizo, C., González-Calero, P., Gómez-Albarrán, M. & Hernández-Yáñez, L., 1996: "Supporting Object Reuse through Case-Based Reasoning", *Procs. EWCBR '96.*
7. Gómez-Albarrán, M., González-Calero, P. & Fernández-Chamizo, C., 1998: "Framework Understanding through Explicit Knowledge Representation", *Procs. IBERAMIA '98.*
8. Heinsohn, J., Kudenko, D., Nebel, B., and Profitlich, H., 1994: "An empirical analysis of terminological representation systems". *Artificial Intelligence*, vol. 68, pp. 367-398
9. Koehler, J., 1994: "An Application of Terminological Logics to Case-based Reasoning", *Procs. KR '94.*
10. Koehler, J., 1996: "Planning from Second Principles", *Artificial Intelligence*, vol. 87, pp. 145-186.
11. Kolodner, J., 1993: *Case-Based Reasoning*, Morgan Kaufmann.
12. Leake, D. B., Kinley, A., & Wilson, D., 1996: "Acquiring Case Adaptation Knowledge: A Hybrid Approach", *Procs. AAAI '96.*
13. Mac Gregor, R., 1991: "The evolving technology of classification-based knowledge representation systems", in *Principles of Semantic Networks: Explorations in the Representation of Knowledge* (J. Sowa, ed.), Morgan Kaufmann.
14. Napoli, A., Lieber, J., & Courien, R., 1996: "Classification-Based Problem Solving in Case-Based Reasoning", *Procs. EWCBR '96.*
15. Napoli, A., Lieber, J. & Simon, A., 1997: "A Classification-Based Approach to Case-Based Reasoning", *Procs. DL '97.*
16. Plaza, E., 1995: "Cases as Terms: A feature term approach to the structured representation of cases", *Procs. ICCBR '95.*
17. Richter, M., 1995: "The knowledge contained in Similarity Measures". Invited talk given at ICCBR'95. October, 25. http://wwwagr.informatik.uni-kl.de/ lsa/CBR/Richtericcbr95remarks.html
18. Salotti, S. & Ventos, V., 1998: "Study and Formalization of a Case-Based Reasoning System using a Description Logic", in *Procs. EWCBR '98.*
19. Salton, G. & McGill, M. J., 1983: *Introduction to Modern Information Retrieval*, McGraw-Hill.
20. Tautz, C., & Althoff, K., 1997: "Using Case-Based Reasoning for Reusing Software Knowledge", *Procs. ICCBR '97.*
21. Yen, J., Teh, H.,& Liu X., 1994: "Using Description Logics for Software Reuse and Case-Based Reasoning", *Procs. DL '94.*

An Evolutionary Approach to Case Adaptation

Andrés Gómez de Silva Garza and Mary Lou Maher

Key Centre of Design Computing
Department of Architectural and Design Science
University of Sydney NSW 2006
Australia

FAX: (+61-2) 9351-3031
Phone: (+61-2) 9351-2053
E-mail: {andres,mary}@arch.usyd.edu.au

Abstract. We present a case adaptation method that employs ideas from the field of genetic algorithms. Two types of adaptations, case combination and case mutation, are used to evolve variations on the contents of retrieved cases until a satisfactory solution is found for a new specified problem. A solution is satisfactory if it matches the specified requirements and does not violate any constraints imposed by the domain of applicability. We have implemented our ideas in a computational system called GENCAD, applied to the layout design of residences such that they conform to the principles of feng shui, the Chinese art of placement. This implementation allows us to evaluate the use of GA's for case adaptation in CBR. Experimental results show the role of representation and constraints.

1 Introduction

Many different methods have been proposed for performing the task of case adaptation in CBR. They have been surveyed in several publications, including [1], [2], and [3]. Different approaches may be better for different domains, different knowledge representation schemes, different reasoning tasks, or other reasons. Approaches may differ on the types of adaptation they support, the amount of change in a case they permit an adaptation to make, the number of cases they can rely on to generate solutions to new problems, and other factors. The adaptation method we present here is flexible, in that it allows for a wide variety of options along all of these dimensions. In our approach, several types of adaptation are available, cases may end up being completely transformed or just slightly tweaked, and final solutions may contain features from one or many cases.

In this paper we present a case adaptation method based on genetic algorithms. In this method, cases are adapted incrementally and in parallel, until a satisfactory solution is found for a given problem. We have employed this approach for design, though it can be used for other reasoning tasks. Within design, we have tried it out on several domains, though in this paper we focus on just one, introduced below. The main concern of this paper is to describe our process model for case adaptation, not to discuss the quality of the designs produced by the application.

Our case adaptation method supports two broad types of adaptation: parametric and structural. Parametric adaptation of cases is achieved through mutation. Structural adaptation of cases is achieved through crossover. Depending on the specifics of a given domain and the richness of the representation chosen for it, several mutation and crossover operators, with different nuances in the effects they produce, can potentially be made available.

The method assumes that the requirements of a new problem will partially match, and therefore result in retrieving, more than one case in memory. These retrieved cases are used to seed an evolutionary process, i.e., they form its initial population. The adaptations produced by the crossover and mutation operators of the evolutionary process are evaluated, and the best ones selected to participate in the next round of genetic adaptations, until a satisfactory solution is found. Evaluation requires domain knowledge in order to recognise whether proposed solutions are acceptable for a given domain or not; crossover, mutation, and selection can operate independently of the domain.

Depending on which randomly evolved variations on the originally retrieved cases are selected to remain in the population after being evaluated, final solutions may have evolved from just one of the cases, or from all of them. They may differ greatly in structure and/or in parameter values from all of the originally retrieved cases, or may be similar to one or several of them. Thus, the method is useful in a wide variety of problem situations and domains requiring different types and degrees of adaptation.

In the following sections we discuss our evolutionary case adaptation method in more detail, we present an implementation for a specific domain and the knowledge representations we have adopted for this domain, and we give some experimental results.

2 Case Adaptation Method

We have developed a process model of design that combines the precedent-centered reasoning capabilities of case-based reasoning (CBR) (see for example [1]) with the incremental evolution of multiple potential solutions, an idea taken from the paradigm of genetic algorithms (GA's) (see for example [4]). The process model involves the use of CBR as the overall reasoning strategy and the use of a GA to perform the case adaptation subtask. Because a general-purpose, knowledge-independent GA is used, case adaptation is knowledge-lean. It is only in the evaluation module of the GA that domain knowledge is required so that proper decisions are made about which potential solutions generated by the GA are useful to keep in future GA cycles.

Our process model is shown in Fig. 1. In this model we assume the existence of a case memory in which descriptions of previously existing solutions are stored. Each case is represented as a set of attribute-value pairs. The cases that are retrieved from memory given a new problem specification are adapted by repeatedly combining and modifying their descriptive features. After each cycle of combination and modification, solutions are evaluated and the best are selected, to be adapted in the next cycle. Through this incremental, evolutionary process, the case adaptation method converges to a satisfactory solution to the new problem. The solution will contain features and/or modifications of features from several of the cases that were initially retrieved from memory. Thus, our process model adapts past solutions by evolving different combinations of their features in parallel and continuously, until a satisfactory combination is found.

The main emphasis of our process model is on proposing new solutions based on the knowledge contained in previously known solutions, i.e., it is a precedent-based approach. But a major component is the evolutionary approach to adapting the known solutions in order to generate solutions to new problems. The two strategies of CBR and GA's complement each other. The cases retrieved from memory serve as the initial population for a genetic algorithm, while the genetic algorithm adapts the cases until it finds an acceptable solution.

The combination subtask of case adaptation performs several cut-and-paste crossover operations. Each crossover is done on two randomly-chosen "parents" from the population of potential solutions, at randomly-chosen crossover points, and produces two "offspring" suggested solutions. The modification subtask performs several mutation operations. Each mutation produces a new "offspring" suggested solution by:

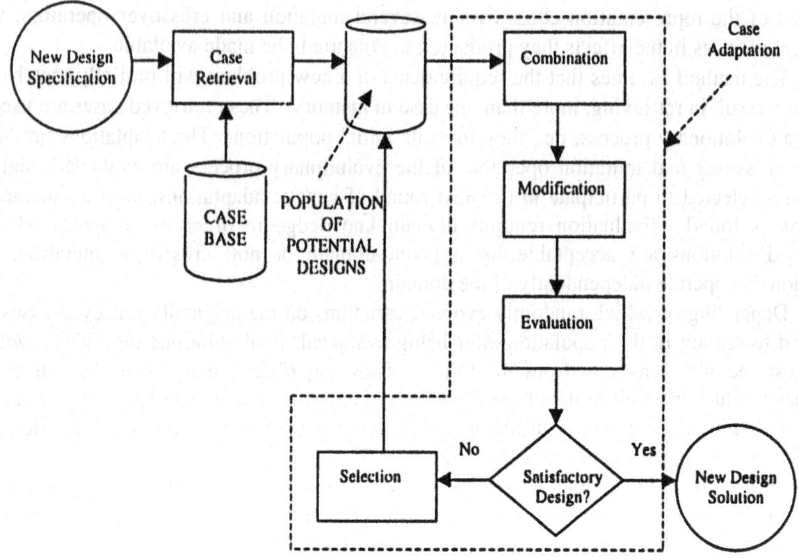

Fig. 1. Evolutionary case adaptation method.

- randomly choosing a "parent" from the population of potential solutions,
- randomly selecting an element to mutate in the description of the parent,
- randomly choosing an attribute of that element to mutate, and
- randomly selecting a new value for that attribute.

Knowledge of which values are valid for which attributes can be used so that mutation does not suggest completely nonsensical solutions. If the process model were to be used to design buildings, for instance, it would be a waste of time for mutation to change the value of the *number-of-stories* attribute from 25 to 834 or –15, for instance.

The evaluation subtask of case adaptation analyses a suggested solution according to domain constraints. Depending on the domain, different constraints may have to be satisfied in order for a solution to be considered acceptable or satisfactory. A fitness value is assigned during evaluation to each suggested solution. The total fitness F of a given solution, given N constraints (C_1 through C_N) and M problem requirements (R_1 through R_M), is calculated with the following equation:

$$F = \sum_{i=1}^{N} C_i + \sum_{j=1}^{M} R_j$$

where C_i = 0 if constraint C_i is not violated by the solution or
C_i = 1 if constraint C_i is violated by the solution, and
R_j = 0 if requirement R_j is met by the solution or
R_j = 1 if requirement R_j is not met by the solution.

Convergence to an acceptable solution occurs if an individual in the population has a total fitness of 0, meaning that none of the constraints has been violated and all of the problem requirements have been met.

The selection subtask of case adaptation takes all of the evaluated individuals in a population of suggested solutions, including those inherited from previous adaptive cycles and those generated in the current one, and keeps the k best ones to serve as the initial population of the next cycle. The value of k, as well as the number of offspring produced at each cycle by crossover and mutation, is chosen so that the size of the population does not change from one cycle to the next. Thus, the value of k depends on the number of cases initially retrieved from memory.

In this method of case adaptation, the synthesis of potential solutions is done in a task- and domain-independent fashion. The power of mutation can be enhanced by providing access to some simple domain knowledge, namely the values that are valid for the attributes that describe objects in the domain, as mentioned above. But on the whole, domain knowledge is needed only for evaluating the generated solutions to determine their quality. In other words, recognition (analytical) knowledge, rather than generative knowledge, is needed to apply our method to a given domain.

3 Implementation and Domain

We have implemented our ideas in a computational system named GENCAD written in Common LISP. Our method of case adaptation has been applied to the structural engineering design of high-rise buildings [5] and to the layout design of residences such that they conform to the principles of feng shui (pronounced "fong sway"), the Chinese art of placement. Here we describe the feng shui application.

Feng shui, also known as Chinese geomancy, is an ancient technique that, among other things, determines the quality of proposed or existing layouts of residences according to several rules of thumb. Some of these heuristics seem to have a basis in common sense, or in a psychological or sociological appreciation of the human beings that inhabit (or intend to inhabit) the residence. Other heuristics seem to be of a more superstitious nature.

There are several different feng shui sects that may contradict each other or place different priorities on different aspects of residential layouts. Despite this variety, of prime importance to performing any feng shui analysis is information on the relative positions of objects. In addition, other attributes of objects are usually also taken into account, such as their orientations, shapes, and relative sizes. In our work we have used the knowledge of feng shui presented in [6], which corresponds to the Tibetan black-hat sect of feng shui.

Feng shui analyses different aspects of a residential layout to determine its auspiciousness or lack thereof. Some classes of inauspicious layouts can be "cured" by the proper placement of an acceptable curing object. Thus, feng shui knowledge is complex, in that some potentially bad layouts can actually be acceptable if the proper cure is present. It is not just a matter of determining whether a layout is "good" or "bad," but even if it would normally be considered bad, one has to determine whether it has been cured or not before rejecting it outright.

The feng shui knowledge contained in [6] applies to three different levels of description of a residence:

- The landscape level (the location of a residence with respect to other objects in its environment such as mountains, rivers, roads, etc.),
- The house level (the relative placement of the rooms and functional spaces within a residence, such as bedrooms and bathrooms, as well as the connections between them, such as doors and windows), and
- The room level (the location of furniture, decorations, and other objects within each room or functional space in a residence).

GENCAD applies its case adaptation GA to one of the three levels of description of a residence at a time. This is because there are very few feng shui constraints that relate objects belonging to different levels of description; the constraints involve relations between objects within the same level. Thus, potential solutions to the new problem at the landscape level can be evolved (and evaluated) independently from potential solutions to the same new problem at the house level, etc. For other domains, GENCAD's GA might have to operate on and evolve hierarchical solutions containing several levels of description at once. This will have implications for the speed of convergence as well as the complexity of the implementation of the crossover and mutation operators.

4 Knowledge Representation

Feng shui analysis assumes knowledge of spatial relationships among the objects at the different levels. Absolute locations and exact measures of distances and other geometric quantities are not as important. Because of this, a qualitative spatial representation has been chosen to describe the locations of objects within each of the three levels. We locate objects on each level in a 3x3 spatial grid, with each sector within the grid assigned a unique number between 1 and 9 to identify it. The grid is shown as follows, with north assumed to be at the top of the page:

1	2	3
4	5	6
7	8	9

Objects can occupy more than one grid sector, and grid sectors can contain more than one object, making the representation flexible. The resolution of this representation is not high, but considering the qualitative nature of a typical feng shui analysis and the number of objects that typically need to be represented at each of the three levels, it is adequate in most cases.

4.1 Case Representation

GENCAD's case library currently contains 12 cases, each of which describes one of Frank Lloyd Wright's prairie houses, obtained from [7]. Note that the designs of these houses do not necessarily conform to the principles of feng shui. However, designs that are acceptable to feng shui practitioners can still be generated by evolving combinations and mutations of the features of the design cases. If the original cases did conform to feng shui practice, given a new problem, convergence to a solution acceptable to feng shui practitioners might be faster, but this is not a requirement of our case adaptation method.

Each of GENCAD's design cases is a residence described at the landscape, house, and room levels. Within each level, objects are represented using attribute-value pairs to describe features that are relevant to feng shui analysis. Some attributes such as locations and types of objects are required for all objects, whereas others such as shapes and steepness are optional, and don't even make sense for some objects. A diagrammatic example of a residence at the landscape level is shown in Fig. 2. This is followed by an abbreviated version of the symbolic case representation of the same residence.

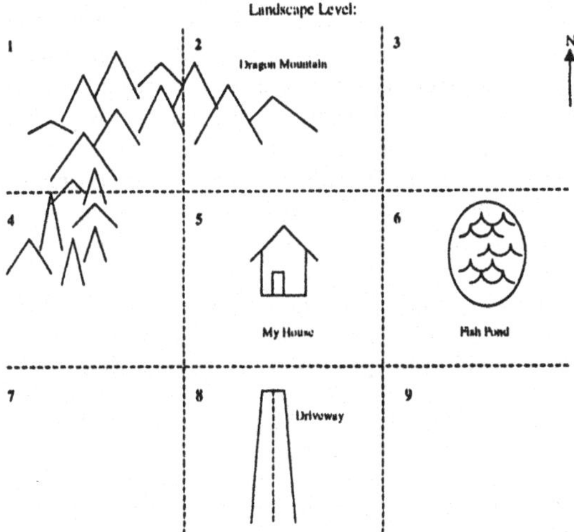

Figure 2. A residence and its place in the landscape.

```
(((level landscape)
  (elements (((type mountain) (name dragon-mountain)
              (location (1 2 4)) (steepness high) ...)
             ((type pond) (name fish-pond) (location (6))
              (clarity murky) ...)
             ((type house) (name my-house) (location (5)))
             ...)))
  ...)
```

When running GENCAD at the landscape level, this is the fragment of a case that would form part of the population of the GA. The fragments describing the house and room levels would be dealt with separately. The list of attribute-value pairs is modified through mutation and combined with that of other cases through crossover as the GA proceeds.

4.2 Representation of Feng Shui Analysis Knowledge

Feng shui analysis knowledge is used in the evaluation function of the GA. We have taken the text description of the analysis knowledge and converted it to a set of constraints; each constraint is implemented as a procedure. There are several constraints at each of the three levels of feng shui description.

An example of a feng shui constraint at the landscape level, quoted directly from [6], is:

```
A house facing a hill will be bad...CURE: If a house faces
a mountain and the backyard is a garden, place a spotlight
in the back of the garden and shine it toward the top of
the house, or install a flagpole at the rear of the garden
to balance ch'i.  [Page 35]
```

This constraint is implemented by first finding the description of all the houses and mountains/hills at the landscape level, particularly their locations and the orientations of the houses (if known). A predicate *facing* has been written that, given the location and orientation of an object, and the location of a second object (within the 3x3 grid), determines whether or not the first object faces the second (even partially). If any of the houses is located and oriented such that it faces any of the mountains/hills in the landscape, then the constraint has been violated. However, first we must check whether or not a cure is present for the constraint violation, i.e., if there is a garden behind the violating house, and if so whether there is a flagpole in it, or a spotlight oriented towards the house. A predicate *behind* has been written that, given the location of an object, and the location and orientation of a second object, determines whether or not the first object is behind the second. The pseudocode that performs this analysis, i.e., the procedural representation of the constraint, given a proposed solution at the landscape level S, is shown as follows:

```
Get the list H of all houses in S;
Get the list M of all mountains/hills in S;
Get the list C of all potential cures for this constraint
   in S;
For each house h in H or until a bad omen has been found:
   Get the location lh of h;
   Get the orientation oh of h;
   For each mountain/hill m in M or until a bad omen has
   been found:
      Get the location lm of m;
      If facing(lh,oh,lm) Then:
         Get the list G of all gardens in S;
         Set flag g-behind? to False;
         Repeat
            Get the next unprocessed garden g in G;
            Get the location lg of g;
            If behind(lg,lh,oh) Then
               Set flag g-behind? to True;
         Until g-behind?=True or all gardens in G have
            Been processed;
         If g-behind?=True Then
            For each potential cure c in C or until a bad
            omen has been found:
               Get the location lc of c;
               Get the type tc of c;
               If tc=spotlight Then:
                  Get the orientation oc of c;
                  If facing(lc,oc,lh) and subset(lc,lg)
                     Then signal a bad omen situation;
               Else
                  If subset(lc,lg)
                     Then signal a bad omen situation;
```

5 Evaluation and Experimental Results

In this section we evaluate our evolutionary case adaptation method according to three issues: the coverage of the method, its efficiency, and the quality of the solutions it produces.

5.1 Coverage

Often, CBR is criticised because even large case bases are not guaranteed to cover the entire search space, thus making some problems unsolvable using "pure" CBR. In our framework, even small case bases can provide sufficient information on typical structures and contents of solutions to problems in the domain for the method to eventually converge to a solution. Of course, the larger the case base, the more cases are likely to be retrieved given a new set of problem requirements, and the faster the GA is likely to find a satisfactory adaptation of their features and converge.

If N cases are initially contained in the population of the GA, then after 1 cycle of the GA the proposed solutions in its population will combine features from at most 2 cases (due to crossover). Thus, after N-1 cycles some of the proposed solutions in the population can combine features from all of the N retrieved cases. The selection operator in the GA ensures that only those combinations that seem to be leading towards an acceptable solution are kept for future GA cycles, i.e., it helps to prune the search.

But even an exhaustive search of all the possible combinations of the features of all retrieved cases is not guaranteed to find satisfactory solutions to the new problem. The inclusion of a mutation operator in the GA, in addition to combination, ensures that all points in the search space can potentially be reached. Of course, whether a certain point will be reached or not depends on the particular sequence of mutations and combinations followed during a given application of the GA to the retrieved cases. The mutation operator introduces into the proposed solutions features that weren't present in any of the originally retrieved cases, or different values for those features that were present. Thus, our method can potentially cover the entire search space, even if a large case base is not available.

5.2 Efficiency

We have explored the efficiency of combining GA's with CBR by comparing our method with a GA that is exactly the same except for the lack of cases. In the alternative method, instead of initiating the GA search with a population consisting of cases retrieved from memory, we initiated it with randomly generated "cases" (i.e., random starting points in the search space). In this way, any differences in efficiency will be attributable to the use of CBR as the guiding framework, and we can evaluate our decision to combine the two AI paradigms of CBR and GA's.

In order to perform this efficiency experiment, GENCAD was run 20 times using 12 cases retrieved from a case base of floor plans of Frank Lloyd Wright prairie houses, and 20 times using 12 randomly-generated cases, on the same problem. The problem specification for this test problem (at the landscape level) is:

```
(((level landscape)
  (requirements ((house 1) (river 1) (trees 2)))))
```

This problem specification can be interpreted as "we want to build a house on a property in which there is a river, and we're thinking of planting two clumps of trees around the house." The problem is now to use GENCAD to generate a configuration containing these four elements, specifying their relative positions within the landscape, such that the configuration is auspicious according to the principles of feng shui.

GENCAD was given a limit of 500 GA cycles in which to find an acceptable solution, i.e., if convergence did not occur by cycle 500, the search was ended without a solution being given. Some of the cases in the randomly generated case base, as well as the Frank Lloyd Wright cases, do contain two clumps of trees, and/or a house, and/or a river in the landscape. In addition, there are configurations of these four types of element that are valid according to feng shui practice. Therefore, achieving a solution through the cyclical combination and/or mutation of the cases retrieved from either case base is theoretically possible.

In the experiment, 5 of the 20 trials using the random starting points converged. Similarly, 5 of the 20 trials using the Frank Lloyd Wright cases converged. Thus, whether cases or random starting points are used to initiate the search doesn't seem to make a difference as far as the frequency of convergence. However, a clear difference can be seen when we analyse the number of GA cycles required before convergence occurred (in those trials in which it did occur), as seen in Table 1.

Table 1. GA cycles required before convergence:

Trial #	Random	Trial #	FLW cases
1	114	25	54
9	333	31	34
11	357	36	32
14	274	37	406
17	160	39	90
Avg.:	241.6	**Avg.:**	123.2

As can be seen from the results, when cases are used to guide (i.e., provide starting points for) the search, convergence occurs on average twice as fast as when the search is initiated from random starting points. This demonstrates the efficiency of combining the ideas of CBR with those from GA's. Convergence does not always occur, as can also be seen (or does not occur within a reasonable number of iterations). Whether it will converge or not, or how rapidly it will converge, can vary greatly due to the random nature of the genetic operators of crossover and mutation. However, the process can be applied again and again to the same problem, using the same initial set of retrieved cases, and it is possible that it will converge in future attempts.

5.3 Quality

The use of CBR as the overall framework helps ensure that the solutions proposed by our method are of high quality. For example, a typical problem specification for a floor plan layout at the house level is that the house should have 3 bedrooms and 2 bathrooms. A residence of this size typically also has, as a minimum, a kitchen, a living room, and a dining room. These are not normally given as requirements, but it is an implicit assumption that any solution will have these additional rooms.

Now let us assume that we used the problem specification mentioned in the last paragraph to perform a GA search using randomly generated initial solutions, or to perform an exhaustive search of the solution space, for instance. Such searches would most probably eventually find a solution that has 3 bedrooms and 2 bathrooms, and that satisfies any domain constraints (such as relationships among the rooms acceptable to feng shui practitioners). But it would be likely that these would be the only components that would be present in the solution. Unless further knowledge and heuristics were used to guide the search, solutions would be minimalistic.

Instead, by using cases that include kitchens, living rooms, and dining rooms (and perhaps additional rooms that might be considered to be useful *post facto* such as pantries) to initiate the search, the solutions to which our method will converge will most likely also include these important but unspecified rooms. Thus, the quality of solutions proposed by our method is equal or greater than if CBR were not used as the guiding framework. Cases provide complete scenarios that serve to guide both the structure and contents of proposed solutions.

6 Discussion

We have presented a case adaptation method that is based on ideas from genetic algorithms. Variations on retrieved cases are evolved incrementally, and at each cycle their quality is verified and the best variants from amongst the initial population plus the new variants generated at the current cycle are kept. This evolutionary method of case adaptation combines the benefits of case-based reasoning and other knowledge-based approaches with those of general-purpose problem solvers such as genetic algorithms.

For instance, being able to use starting points for problem solving search based on similar past experiences, and being able to apply the process model to highly-specialised problem solving domains are two advantages of CBR. On the other hand, having a large number of operators with greatly differing effects available, and being able to apply the process model to a wide variety of problem solving domains are two advantages of GA's. Our evolutionary method of case adaptation benefits from having all of these characteristics.

Domain knowledge is required and represented in the form of constraints used for the evaluation of proposed solutions; this is recognition knowledge, not generative knowledge. This difference with other approaches is especially important in applying our method to tasks such as design. In design it is relatively easy to recognise whether a proposed design is an acceptable solution for a given problem or not, whereas it is quite difficult to come up with a set of reasoning steps or heuristics to follow that will lead to the generation of acceptable designs. The knowledge engineer's task of knowledge elicitation and knowledge acquisition is thus simplified when using our evolutionary approach to case adaptation.

This use of constraints for evaluation rather than generation is one of the differences between our work and that of others that have used constraint-satisfation techniques in the context of CBR, for instance [8], [9], [10], or [11]. In these projects, constraints with potentially complex interactions guide the generation of solutions to new problems by adapting past cases. This generation of solutions uses domain knowledge or heuristics to make what is generally an NP-complete problem tractable. In our method, the constraints are independent of each other, and they help in a cumulative fashion to eliminate bad solutions, rather than in a mutually interacting way to generate good ones.

There has been other work in the past that has combined concepts from GA's with CBR. [12] presents a GA that is initialised based on the information held in cases. However, in [12] cases contain descriptions of past executions of a GA (e.g., the values of the GA parameters, the task environment in which those parameter values were used successfully, etc.), irrespective of the type of problem being solved with the GA. Thus, cases help the GA dynamically adapt to changing problem situations; the authors use concepts from CBR in aid of GA's. In our work, on the other hand, cases contain descriptions of known solutions for the type of problem being solved, and these cases provide guidance for the search that our case adaptation GA will perform; thus, we use concepts from GA's in aid of CBR.

The research presented in [13] is more similar to ours, in that cases contain descriptions of solutions to the type of problem being solved, and a GA is used to adapt the cases to solve the problem. However, [13] is not a pure CBR approach, as only a small fraction (10%-15%) of the initial population in the GA comes from cases in memory; most of the initial population is generated at random, as in a classical GA. The authors do this for valid reasons of balancing exploration and exploitation in their GA search, but it provides a different flavour to their research. Again, their work places more of an emphasis on the GA, and on making it efficient and effective, than on contributing to CBR research. In contrast, we have examined the possibilities of using a GA for case adaptation from the perspective of CBR.

References

1. Kolodner, J.L.: *Case-Based Reasoning*, Morgan Kaufmann Publishers (1993)
2. Leake, D.B.: *Case-Based Reasoning: Experiences, Lessons, & Future Directions*, AAAI Press/The MIT Press, Boston (1996)
3. Maher, M.L. and Pu, P. (eds.): *Issues and Applications of Case-Based Reasoning in Design*, Lawrence Erlbaum Associates, Mahwah, New Jersey (1997)
4. Mitchell, M.: *An Introduction to Genetic Algorithms (Complex Adaptive Systems Series)*, MIT Press, Boston (1998)

5. Gómez de Silva Garza, A. and Maher, M.L.: A Knowledge-Lean Structural Engineering Design Expert System, *Proceedings of the Fourth World Congress on Expert Systems*, Mexico City, Mexico (1998)
6. Rossbach, S.: *Interior Design with Feng Shui*, Rider Books, London (1987)
7. Hildebrand, G.: *The Wright Space: Pattern & Meaning in Frank Lloyd Wright's Houses*, University of Washington Press, Seattle (1991)
8. Zhang, D.M.: *A Hybrid Design Process Model Using Case-Based Reasoning*, Ph.D. dissertation, Department of Architectural and Design Science, University of Sydney, Australia (1994)
9. Hinrichs, T.R.: Plausible Design Advice Through Case-Based Reasoning, in Maher, M.L. and Pu, P. (eds.), *Issues and Applications of Case-Based Reasoning in Design*, 133-159, Lawrence Erlbaum Associates, Mahwah, New Jersey (1997)
10. Faltings, B.: Case Reuse by Model-Based Interpretation, in Maher, M.L. and Pu, P. (eds.), *Issues and Applications of Case-Based Reasoning in Design*, 39-60, Lawrence Erlbaum Associates, Mahwah, New Jersey (1997)
11. Pu, P. and Purvis, L.: Formalizing tne Adaptation Process for Case-Based Design, in Maher, M.L. and Pu, P. (eds.), *Issues and Applications of Case-Based Reasoning in Design*, 221-240, Lawrence Erlbaum Associates, Mahwah, New Jersey (1997)
12. Ramsey, C.L. and Grefenstette, J.J.: Case-Based Initialization of Genetic Algorithms, *Proceedings of the Fifth International Conference on Genetic Algorithms*, 84-91, Morgan Kaufmann Publishers (1993)
13. Louis, S.J. and Johnson, J.: Robustness of Case-Initialized Genetic Algorithms, *Proceedings of FLAIRS (Florida Artificial Intelligence Conference) '99*. To appear (1999)

REMEX - A Case-Based Approach for Reusing Software Measurement Experienceware

Christiane Gresse von Wangenheim

Federal University of Santa Catarina - Production Engineering
Florianópolis, Brazil
gresse@eps.ufsc.br

Abstract. For the improvement of software quality and productivity, organizations need to systematically build up and reuse software engineering know-how, promoting organizational learning in software development. Therefore, an integrated support platform has to be developed for capturing, storing and retrieving software engineering knowledge. Technical support is complicated through specific characteristics of the software engineering domain, such as the lack of explicit domain models in practice and the diversity of environments. Applying Case-Based Reasoning, we propose an approach for the representation of relevant software engineering experiences, the goal-oriented and similarity-based retrieval tailorable to organization-specific characteristics and the continuous acquisition of new experiences. The approach is applied and validated in the context of the Goal/Question/Metric (GQM) approach, an innovative technology for software measurement.

Keywords. reuse, experience factory, case-based reasoning, software engineering, software measurement, GQM

1 Introduction

Today almost any business involves the development or use of software. However, state-of-the-practice is that software systems often lack quality and many software projects are behind schedule and out of budget [17]. In order to successfully plan, control and improve software projects, organizations need to continuously evolve software engineering (SE) know-how tailored to their specific characteristics and needs [8,10]. Experiences from their software projects have to systematically captured and reused across the organization. This enables the consolidation of organization wide SE know-how into competencies that empower the company to achieve considerable improvements and benefits [32]. Currently, reuse of SE knowledge is done in an ad-hoc, informal manner, usually limited to personal experiences. For the systematic acquisition and organization-wide communication of these experiences, corporate memories [2,8,18,20] have to be built (see Figure 1). In the software domain, the *Experience Factory* (EF) approach [8] proposes an organizational infrastructure for the analysis and synthesis of all kinds of software life cycle experiences or products. It acts as a repository for those and supplies these experiences to various software projects. However, for the operationalization of an EF in practice, we need a clever assistant that supplies the right experiences from the *Experience Base* (EB) to the user on demand.

In order to comprehensively support the software development process, various types of *experienceware* (EW) [18], including expertise and lessons learned (e.g., how to apply design inspections), quality models (e.g., distribution of rework effort per fault type), and deliverables (e.g., software measurement plans, requirement documents) related to several processes (e.g., design inspection, measurement) in different environments have to be retrieved addressing various purposes: facilitation of the planning or execution of software projects, prevention of past failures by anticipating problems, and guidance for the solution of occurring problems. And, since each software project is different, it is very unlikely to find an artifact fulfilling the needs of the actual project completely. Thus, experiences have to be retrieved from projects with "similar" characteristics, assuming that similar situations (or problems) require similar solutions. In the SE domain, for example, we assume, that measurement programs with similar goals use similar quality models or that similar problems occurring during design inspections have corresponding solutions. Due to the lack of general SE models in practice, organizational software know-how has to evolve in an incremental manner by learning from each new software project. Thus, the EF has to support continuous learning by capturing and integrating new experiences when software projects are planned and executed. In this context, *Case-Based Reasoning* (CBR) [5] plays a key role [10,18,20,27], as it provides a broad support for similarity-based retrieval for all kinds of EW and continuous incremental learning. However, the operationalization of the EF is not trivial, as relevant SE knowledge has to be identified, modeled and represented in the EB. Methods for goal-oriented retrieval providing support for different processes, objectives, and environments in the SE domain and for the continuous acquisition and integration of new experiences have to be developed. In this paper, we propose a case-based approach for an integrated support platform enabling organizational learning from SE experiences tailorable to organization specific characteristics. The approach is based on our experiences on reusing GQM-based measurement know-how (e.g., in the context of the industrial transfer and research projects [11,26]).

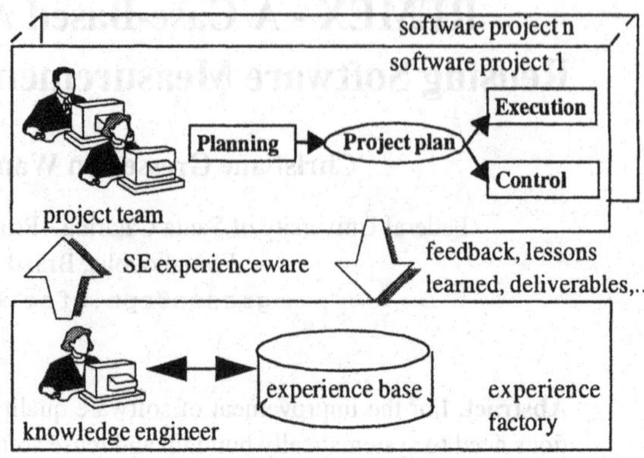

Fig. 1. Experience factory organization

2 Reuse of GQM Measurement Plans

In this section, we give a short overview on software measurement, the application domain of our approach, and provide scenarios illustrating the reuse of measurement EW. Software measurement is an essential infrastructure technology for the planning, control and improvement of software projects. Organizations have to collect quantitative and qualitative data concerning their software products and processes, to build an empirical justified body of knowledge. A specific technology for goal-oriented measurement is the *Goal/Question/Metric* approach (GQM) [9], which supports the definition and implementation of operationalizable software improvement goals. Based on a precisely specified measurement goal, relevant measures are derived in a top-down fashion via a set of questions and models. This refinement is documented in a GQM plan, providing a rationale for the selection of the underlying measures. Data is collected wrt. the measures and interpreted in a bottom-up fashion in the context of the models, question and goals, considering the limitations and assumptions underlying each measure. The establishment of measurement programs, which in practice requires a significant planning effort, can be substantially facilitated by reusing measurement EW [16], as illustrated in the following scenario.

Measurement Program at ABS/IntelliCar
GQM Goal
Analyze the software development process in order to improve the reliability from the viewpoint of the software developer at ABS/IntelliCar
GQM Questions
Q1. What is the total number of defects detected before delivery? Q2. What is the distribution of defects? Q3. Does the type of inspections have an impact on their effectiveness? Q4. Does the experience of developers have an impact on number of faults introduced in the system? ...
Quality Models
Effectiveness of inspections *Context*: company IntelliCar, automobile domain *Assumptions*: The defect density is comparable across documents. *Computation*: effectiveness = (number of defects detected in inspection)/(size of document * training duration) *Attributes*: number of defects detected in inspections; size of document; duration of training

Fig. 2. Excerpt of simplified example of GQM plan

Suppose a company, IntelliCar, which produces embedded software for automobiles has two main departments: FI which develops software for fuel injection devices and ABS which develops software for ABS brake control devices. As the company produces embedded software, one of its most important goals is to produce zero-defect software. Therefore, department FI established successfully a quality improvement program based on measurement two years ago. Now, also department ABS wants to start measurement-based improvement. As the contexts of both departments are similar and the improvement goal is the same, experiences available in department FI can be reused at ABS in order to reduce the planning effort and to improve the quality of the measurement program. Based on the measurement goal «*Analyze the software development process in order to improve the reliability from the viewpoint of the software developer at ABS/IntelliCar*», relevant quality aspects and influence factors have been acquired during interviews with the developers of department ABS. These are represented as a set of questions in the GQM plan, as shown in Figure 2. Now, in order to operationalize the questions of the GQM plan, quality models have to be developed. Assume, for example, that the question «*Q3. Does the type of inspection have an impact on the effec-*

tiveness of inspections?», has also been evaluated in a similar measurement program in department FI. Then, the respective model can be reused, assessing its applicability based on its underlying assumptions. If necessary, the model is adapted to the specific characteristics of ABS. For example, assuming that inspector capabilities vary extensively between departments, the effectiveness of inspections is expected to depend not only on the size of the inspected document (as stated in the reused model), but also on the training of inspectors, then the new factor is included in the model.

While defining a model for question Q2, it turned out that an operational refinement of the question is impossible due to missing information concerning defect classification. The solution of this problem can be guided by experiences describing how a similar problem has been successfully solved at department FI (see Figure 3) by suggesting follow-up interviews in order to acquire the required information completely. In addition, reusing organizational glossaries can support the consistent usage of terms (e.g. *defect*) and reusing taxonomies representing generalization relations can help the refinement of abstract concepts (e.g. *«distribution of defects»* in Q2). Other phases of the measurement planning process can be supported accordingly through the reuse of measurement EW [16].

Context	company IntelliCar; department FI
Problem	Question of the GQM plan cannot be refined into an operational quality model due to missing information.
Cause of Problem	During the interviews the necessary knowledge has not been acquired completely from the project personnel.
Solution	A follow-up interview was performed with the person(s) who mentioned the respective quality aspects during the first interviews in order to clarify the formulation of the GQM question.
Outcome	The required knowledge was acquired completely and the respective quality model was defined.

Fig. 3. Example of problem experience

3 Representation of GQM Experienceware

In order to facilitate and improve the planning of GQM-based measurement programs through reuse of EW, an Experience Base is developed, modeling and representing relevant measurement EW.

3.1 GQM Experienceware Cases

As today wrt. most SE technologies no formal knowledge exists, the principal source are individual project experiences. Thus, SE EW is primarily captured in form of cases in the *GQM-Experience Base* (GQM-EB)[1], representing context-specific experiences gained in a particular software project in a specific organization. In order to provide comprehensive support, different types of EW cases are modeled by using a flexible, object-oriented frame-like representation formalism based on [24,28] and are stored in the GQM-EB [15,19]:

- *GQM Product Experienceware Case (GQM-PEC).* These cases include GQM products developed during the planning of a GQM-based measurement program. GQM-PECs are reused in similar software projects as a basis for the development of respec-

1. Here, we consider a specific instantiation of the experience base focusing on EW on the planning of GQM-based measurement programs.

tive products, resulting in a reduction of planning effort and improved quality of the GQM products.

- *GQM Problem-Solution Experienceware Case (GQM-PSEC).* GQM-PSECs explicitly capture problem solution strategies that have been adopted in past measurement programs (see Figure 3). Reusing GQM-PSECs can warn for potential failures in advance and guide a solution fitting the application context. Due to the specific nature of experiential knowledge, GQM-PSECs are represented as cases describing a specific problem, its cause, the solution applied and the outcome achieved.

Experienceware Cases are represented by a set of relevant attributes and interdependencies based on domain models (see Section 3.2) [29]. To enable the retrieval of EW cases from similar software projects, the environment from which the case has been obtained is characterized. This is done through a minimal set of characteristics (e.g., business sector, improvement goals, development process used), which allows to identify similar cases and to discriminate different ones. In order to assess the reuse potential of the case, cases are enhanced by basic information (e.g., viewpoint, representativeness). Information about past reuses of a case, such as preconditions for reuse, required adaptations, cost and frequency of reuse, are explicitly captured [19] in order to facilitate the reuse of experiences and their adaptation to specific project characteristics.

3.2 General Domain Knowledge

In order to model relevant EW and facilitate the consistent representation and acquisition of new experiences across software projects, general domain knowledge on GQM EW is represented in the GQM-EB [16,19].

GQM EW Models. Entities related to GQM EW are explicitly modeled in a hierarchy of classes [16,28] (see Figure 4). Each class is structured by a set of attributes represent-

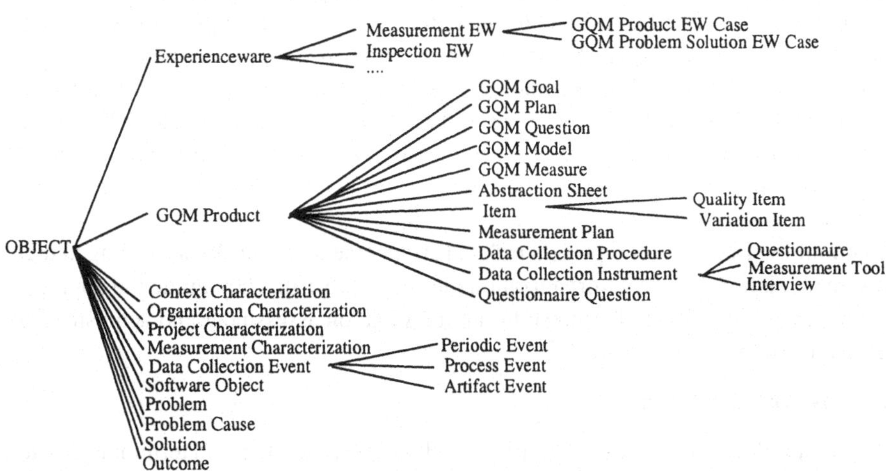

Fig. 4. GQM EW Classes (is_a relation)

ing basic values or relationships to other entities. Attributes are defined through an identifier, description, cardinality, its type or kind of relationship, a default value and explicitly stating if the attribute has to be specified (mandatory) when a new instance of this class is acquired [15].

Class	GQM Measure					
Description	defines data to be collected					
Attributes	Identifier	Description	Cardinality	Type or Kind	Default	Mandatory
	id	identifies the GQM measure	1	Identifier	-	yes
	assumptions	about the applicability of the measure	0..1	Text	none	no
	description	describes data to be collected	0..1	Text	-	yes
	scale	defines scale of the measure	0..1	Scale	-	yes
	unit	declares unit of the measure	0..1	Unit	-	no
	range	declares range of the values of the measures	0..1	Text	-	no
	model	references the corresponding model	0..*	defined-by [GQM-Model])	-	yes
	...					

A GQM measure defines which data has to be collected. It includes the explicit definition of assumptions concerning the application of the measure. Regarding the expected values, scale, unit (only in case of numerical values) and range have to be defined.As GQM measures are derived from models which determine the attributes to be measured, this is represented as a defined-by relation. Based on the GQM measure the collection procedure defining when, how, and by whom the data has to be collected is defined.

Fig. 5. Simplified example of the class GQM Measure

Type Definitions. Type definitions model qualities of SE entities, such as, developer experience, or categorize concepts, e.g., programming languages as Unordered Symbol with the possible values «Delphi, C++, etc.». Type definitions are used to type class attributes. They facilitate the situation assessment and support the manual adaptation of retrieved EW cases by explicitly indicating alternatives, as well, as the consistent acquisition of experiences across projects. For each type, its related supertype, range and the local similarity measure are specified. For example, the experience level of developers might be classified through the Ordered Symbols: none, low, medium, high, using the standard local similarity measure for ordered symbols. For symbol types, the meaning of each value is explicitly defined through range definitions, e.g., «high» experience may be defined as worked for more than 2 years in the application domain. In addition, for numerical types, the unit is explicitly stated, e.g., person-hours.

Glossaries. Glossaries define terminology and basic concepts related to software measurement [16,19]. For example, «Failure: is the inability of the software to perform a required function wrt. its specifications». A glossary supports the adequate use of terms, their consistency across an organization, and ensures that the reuse of GQM products is based on sound assumptions.

Taxonomies. Taxonomies represent ordered arrangements of entities according to their presumed relationships, e.g., organization hierarchy [16,19]. They guide the appropriate refinement of objects of interest during the situation assessment and acquisition of new experiences.

3.3 Knowledge Levels

Software products, processes, resources as well as characteristics and terminology vary between different organizations. Therefore, the domain model has to be tailored to the specific environment. Generally, we can identify different levels of knowledge valid in different scopes of domains:

- **Software measurement domain.** Here, general knowledge on GQM-based measurement is represented, which is transferrable between organizations. This level includes

GQM EW models, general valid types and range definitions (e.g., on measurement scale), and general valid terms in the glossary (e.g., software process).

- **Organization domain.** Here, organization specific knowledge related to software measurement is represented. If the GQM technology is modified in a particular organization, the respective knowledge from the upper level is adapted accordingly. Type and range definitions are enhanced by organization specific definitions. For example, one organization could classify *«experience of the developers»* into the categories *(expert-participated in system development; medium-participated in training; none)*, whereas another organization might classify experience into (*high-working for more than 2 years, medium-worked once, low-never worked in application domain*). The glossary and taxonomies are completed by organization specific terms.
- **Project domain.** At this level, instantiations of GQM EW cases are represented gathered from particular software projects. For example, a GQM-PEC including a GQM plan from a measurement program of the project HYPER at the department ABS/IntelliCar.

4 Experience-Based Support of GQM Planning

4.1 Determination of Retrieval Goals

During the planning of GQM measurement programs the GQM-EB can be inquired to find useful EW to guide, support and improve various SE tasks in a specific environment. In order to provide comprehensive support for several SE tasks, various types of experiences have to be retrieved, from different viewpoints in different environments addressing various purposes: support of software projects by reusing similar products developed in the past, prevention of failures by anticipating problems, guidance for the solution of problems by reusing solution strategies adopted in past similar problems, and the identification of patterns of experiences for the maintenance and evolution of the EB. Thus, a goal-oriented retrieval method [14] is developed that retrieves a set of relevant experiences wrt. a specific reuse goal. Based on reuse scenarios, retrieval goals are determined explicitly specifying the following dimensions:

Retrieve <object>
to <purpose>
concerning <process>
from the <viewpoint>
in the context of <environment>

For example, *«retrieve lessons learned to guide problem solution concerning software measurement from the viewpoint of quality assurance personnel at IntelliCar»*.

Based on the retrieval goals, reusability factors are determined. This includes the specification of relevant indexes[1] and their importance and the parametrization of the similarity measure. For example, for the retrieval of a solution strategy, relevant indexes might be the problem description and the task when the problem occurred, whereas potential problems wrt. a specific task might be identified based on the task only.

1. As index we denote attributes of the case, which predict the usefulness of the case concerning the given situation description, and which are used for retrieval and determination of the similarity value.

4.2 Retrieval Process

Considering different retrieval goals, a goal-oriented method for similarity based retrieval is defined, including the following steps [14]:

Step 1. Situation assessment. The current situation is described by the user specifying the retrieval goal and a set of indexes related to the specific retrieval goal based on a predefined indexing scheme. The importance of each index wrt. the specific retrieval goal is stated through a *relevance factor* assigned to each index. Relevance factors are stored in the EB and can be manually adapted by the user. To facilitate the assignment, relevance factors are classified into «essential, important, less important, irrelevant». Indexes marked as essential are perfectly matched to the ones in the situation assessment, the ones marked as important or less important are partially matched and the ones marked as irrelevant are not further considered. Unknown indexes are explicitly marked. Table 1 illustrates a situation assessment with an exemplary set of indexes. The situation assessment is further supported by general domain knowledge [19]: glossaries can be used for a consistent usage of terminology across projects and taxonomies guide and direct the appropriate definition of indexes. Type and range definitions facilitate the identification of the present values and guarantee a consistent description across projects.

Reuse goal			**GQM Experience Base (excerpt)**		
object	lesson learned (PSEC)		**CASE PSEC_003**	**CASE PSEC_007**	**CASE PSEC_011**
purpose	guide problem solution				
process	sw measurement				
viewpoint	quality assurance personnel				
environment	IntelliCar				
Indexes					
department	irrelevant	ABS	Fuel Injection	Fuel Injection	Fuel Injection
staff size	less important	10	15	100	50
application domain	essential	automobile	automobile	automobile	automobile
improvement goal	important	improvement of sw system reliability	improvement of sw system reliability	improvement of sw system reliability	cost reduction in sw development
programming language	irrelevant	Ada	Fortran	Ada	C
dev. experience	less important	high	medium	low	low
sw system size	less important	*unknown*	15 KLOC	80 KLOC	60 KLOC
measurement maturity	important	initial	--	--	--
task	essential	measurement goal definition	measurement goal definition	development of measurement plan	measurement goal definition

Table 1. Simplified retrieval example

Step 2. Exact matching of indexes marked as essential. In a first step, the cases of the EB are perfectly matched with the situation assessment wrt. the indexes marked as essential, determining a set of potential reuse candidates. Table 1 shows a simplified example: while comparing the cases of the EB with the situation assessment, case PSEC_03 and PSEC_11 are considered as potential reuse candidates, because the values of the indexes marked as essential («application domain» and «task») are equal to the present ones. PSEC_07, which describes an experience regarding the development of the measurement plan, is not further considered, as the value of the index «task» is different to the one of interest.

Step 3. Partial matching of similar cases. For all potential reuse candidates a similarity value is computed by partially matching the indexes (except the ones marked as *essential)* using a specific similarity measure wrt. the retrieval goal (see Section 4.3). Cases with a higher similarity value than a given threshold are considered as sufficiently similar and proposed to the user as reuse candidates ranked by their similarity values. Continuing the example shown in Table 1, case PSEC_03 is considered more similar to the given situation than PSEC_11, because the values of the indexes of PSEC_03 marked as important or less important are more similar to the current ones (especially regarding «staff size», «improvement goal»).

Step 4. Selection of reuse candidate(s). Based on the proposed reuse candidates the user can select the most appropriate case(s) and, if necessary, manually adapt them to fit the current needs. Informed decisions are further supported by experiences explicitly captured in the EB about the reuses of a particular case in the past [19] (see Section 3.1). If the system fails to propose reuse candidates, general domain knowledge, e.g., GQM product models, is available to support the SE tasks.

4.3 Similarity Measure for the Retrieval of Experienceware

For the identification of «similar» EW cases concerning various retrieval goals (see step 3/Section 4.2), we define a generic similarity measure sim(Sit´,E_k´) [14] that can be parameterized for a specific goal. Taking into account specific characteristics of the SE domain, such as the lack of explicit domain models in practice, diversity of environments, incompleteness of data, and the consideration of «similarity» of experiences, the similarity measure is based on the following assumptions (see [14] for details):

- Depending on the retrieval goal, a particular set of indexes is defined for situation assessment and matching. A set of indexes C is represented as a list of features $C_g=\{C_{g1}, C_{g2},...\}$ wrt. the particular retrieval goal g. The range of the value c_i of the feature C_{gi} is defined by the respective range definition W_i (see Figure 6).

	Example Index Set	Type/Range	Relevance Vector R_g		Present Situation Sit´={(C_{gi}, s_i)	Case E_k	FS
C_1	staff size	Interval of numbers [0,50]	less important (0.15)	s_1	10	15	W
C_2	improvement goal	String	important (0.35)	s_2	"improvement of system reliability"	"improvement of system reliability"	E
C_3	measurement maturity	Ordered Symbol: {initial, low, routine}	important (0.35)	s_3	initial	*unknown*	U
C_4	sw system size	Number [0,100]	less important (0.15)	s_4	*unknown*	15KLOC	R

Fig. 6. Example

- The present situation is assessed based on the set of indexes wrt. the retrieval goal, represented as a list of feature-value pairs Sit´={(C_{gi}, s_i) ∈ Sit | relevance factor (S_i) ≠ essential} including the features $C_{gi} \in C_g$ and their values $s_i \in W_i$.
- In the EB, an EW $\text{case}_k = (E_k, \varepsilon_k)$ represents an experience by feature-value[1] pairs (experience $E_k=\{(E_{k1}, e_{k1}), (E_{k2}, e_{k2}),...\}$ with the features E_{ki} and their values $e_{ki} \in W_i$

1.Here, values represent atomic values or relations to other entities.

(and with $E_k' \subseteq E_k$ and $\forall\ E_{ki}' \in C_g$ and their respective values e_{ki}'), describing the know-how gathered in a software project, the context from which its originates, and its relationships (see Figure 6). In addition, a threshold $\varepsilon_k \in [0,1]$ is stated for each case that determines, if the case is sufficiently similar to the situation assessment to be proposed as a reuse candidate.

- In the SE domain, many cases may have a low similarity value, due to few identical values, although they might be quite similar (e.g. programming languages C and C++). Thus, local similarity measures are introduced. Generic local similarity measures $\upsilon'(s_i,e_{ki}') \in [0,1]$ for basic value types W(v) are defined in [19,28]. Local similarity thresholds $\theta_i \in [0,1]$ are introduced for each index C_{gi} determining if the values are considered as (sufficiently) similar.
- *Relevance factors* are defined, which reflect the importance of a feature concerning the similarity of cases wrt. a specific retrieval goal (see Figure 6). Here, for each retrieval goal *g* a specific index set C_g is used. Thus, for each index $C_{gi} \in$ index set C_g, a relevance factor $\omega_{gi} \in [0,1]$ is defined in dependence on the specific retrieval goal g. For each retrieval goal, those relevance factors are represented by a *relevance vector* $Rg = \{\omega g_1, \omega g_2, \ldots\}$ with $\sum \omega g_i = 1$ normalized in the EB.
- In order to explicitly deal with incomplete knowledge, the similarity of two objects is expressed through a linear contrast of weighted differences between their common and different features [6,30]. The following *Feature Sets* (FS) are distinguished:
  - E: Set of corresponding features of the given situation and the stored case ($E = \{Cg_i \mid (Cg_i \in Sit' \cap E_{ki}')$ and $(\upsilon'(s_i,e_{ki}') \geq \theta_i)\}$). For example, if both, the situation assessment and the stored case state the feature «experience of developer» as high.
  - W: Set of contradicting features of the given situation and the stored case ($W = \{Cg_i \mid (Cg_i \in Sit' \cap E_{ki}')$ and $(\upsilon'(s_i,e_{ki}') < \theta_i)\}$). For example, if in the past no effort reporting tools were available, but now in the given situation the feature «effort reporting tools» is stated as available.
  - U: Set of unknown features in the actual situation description ($U = \{Cg_i \mid (Cg_i \in E_{ki}' - Sit')\}$). For example, when initiating a software project certain information, such as «software system size» may be stated as unknown in the situation description.
  - R: Set of redundant features not contained in the stored case ($R = \{Cg_i \mid (Cg_i \in Sit' - E_{ki}')\}$). For example, the feature «developer experience» may not have been considered initially, but later become important for the identification of relevant cases.

  For each set, a specific weight $\alpha, \beta, \gamma, \delta \in [0,1]$ is defined.

The global similarity measure is defined as:

$$sim(Sit',E_k') = (\alpha \textstyle\sum_{si\in E} \omega_{ik}\upsilon'(s_i,e_{ki}')) / ((\alpha \sum_{si\in E} \omega_{ik}\upsilon'(s_i,e_{ki}')) + (\beta \sum_{si\in W} \omega_{ik}(1-\upsilon'(s_i,e_{ki}'))) + (\gamma \sum_{si\in U} \omega_{ik}(1-\upsilon'(s_i,e_{ki}'))) + (\delta \sum_{si\in R} \omega_{ik}(1-\upsilon'(s_i,e_{ki}'))))$$

Based on the similarity value calculated, a $case_k$ is considered as reuse candidate, if all features marked as essential in the given situation exactly match the respective features of the case, and if $sim(Sit',Ek') \geq$ global similarity threshold ε_k of $case_k$.

5 Continuous Acquisition and Integration of Experienceware

The incremental evolution based on feedback from industrial applications is essential for continuously building and improving SE know-how. Consequently, the knowledge in the GQM-EB has to be enhanced and updated each time a new measurement program is run in the organization. This means that we have to continuously capture new experiences from the quality assurance personnel. In order to keep the effort related to the knowledge acquisition minimal, this process is intertwined in the retrieval/reuse process (see Figure 7): Information provided by the user as input to the retrieval process, such as a context characterization, and reused experienceware from the GQM-EB are in parallel used for the creation of new EW cases.

For example, while reusing EW in order to support the solution of a problem encountered (see Section 2) concerning the definition of a quality model, the user provides the following situation assessment: «*organization:* IntelliCar; *application domain:* automobile; *problem:* Question of GQM plan cannot be refined into model». This information is used for the retrieval process, and in parallel for the description of a new case documenting experiences regarding the present situation. Information contained in a similar case retrieved and reused in order to solve the current problem, is used to supplement the new case description (see Figure 8). The generated new case is reviewed by the user before storage in the EB. Additional information (e.g. basic information) is added, and if necessary, deviations from the reused case are adjusted, e.g., if a solution different to the one stated in the reused case was applied. The acquisition of new experiences is further guided through GQM EW models, which explicitly address relevant dimensions to be captured. Glossaries and taxonomies facilitate the consistent description of experiences across software projects. The new acquired experiences are integrated into the existing EB to be available for future reuse. This implies that EW cases have to be stored, domain models enhanced and, if necessary, generic patterns of cases have to be created or modified.

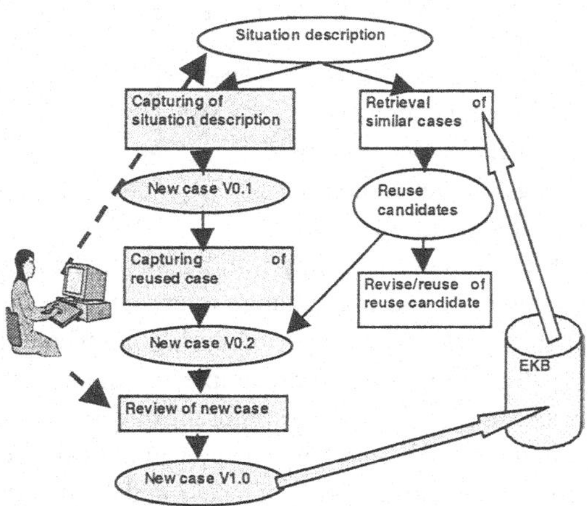

Fig. 7. Integration of acquisition process

Project-specific cases (GQM-PECs or GQM-PSECs) acquired in parallel to the retrieval process are stored as instances of GQM EW cases in the GQM-EB. Based on protocols on the retrieval/reuse process and comparisons of the reused and new case, reuse information is added to the reused case. For example, the date of reuse is added, the frequency of reuse is increased, and attributes which have been adapted to fit the new situation are explicitly listed.

In addition, project-specific cases are evaluated wrt. their similarity to other cases of the GQM-EB. If the new case differs only in small details from a case reused, an abstract case subsuming the project-specific cases is created through case generalization. The development of generic patterns through the knowledge engineer can be guided by taxonomies which provide a basis for the derivation of abstractions.

Based on an evaluation of new terms defined in the specific GQM EW case through the knowledge engineer, the organizational glossary and taxonomies are enhanced.

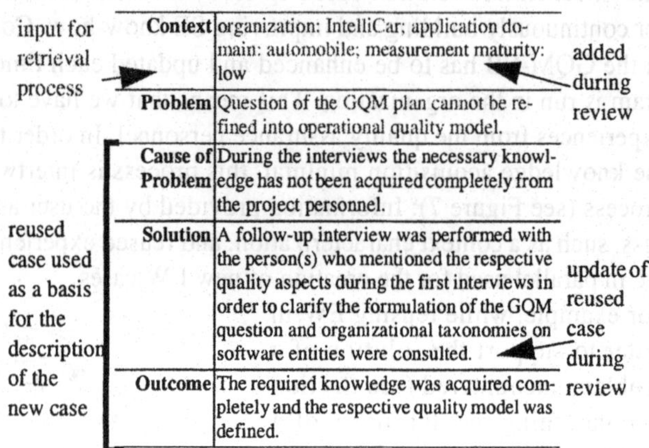

Fig. 8. Simplified example of acquisition

The continuous evolution and customizing of the EF to a specific environment may also require the modification of the representation of EW cases, the indexing scheme and similarity measure based on user feedback from the application. Due to the fact, that indexes depend on the specific environment and may change over time, the continuous tailoring of the indexing scheme needs to be supported during the whole life cycle of a GQM-EB through the knowledge engineer. For example, supplemental context characteristics of software projects may become relevant for the discrimination of cases. As shown in Figure 8, the attribute «*measurement maturity*» had not been considered as a relevant characteristic for the context description of a case in the past, because all experiences were related to projects without variations concerning the maturity. Since a new measurement program is established in a project with a different level of maturity, this attribute has become relevant for the distinction of cases and is added to the context characterization.

Continuous learning has also to take place wrt. the similarity measure and its parametrization for specific retrieval goals in order to improve and optimize its performance. Therefore, the retrieval and reuse process is supervised and, based on the feedback, appropriately tailored to the specific environment through the knowledge engineer. Here, protocols documenting the user´s (re-)actions and user-provided critics and suggestions can serve as a basis for the maintenance through the knowledge engineer (see Table 2).

Feedback	Implication for update
Index manually added for retrieval	•Addition of index to the indexing scheme
Relevance factor manually modified	•Modification of weight assigned to the index •Index frequently marked as irrelevant might be removed from the index scheme
Increasing number of retrieved reuse candidates	•Changing optimistic strategy for similarity measure into a more pessimistic •Increase of tresholds
Frequent rejection of cases suggested as reuse candidates	•If a specific case is affected: increase of global treshold of the case •If different cases are affected: review of indexing scheme and similarity measure under consideration of additional critics and suggestions of the user

Table 2. Examples of retrieval feedback and its implications

Based on a careful analysis of the causes, the selection of indexes and/or the similarity measure have to be adapted accordingly in order to improve retrieval results in the future.

6 Discussion

In the software domain, various approaches exist for reuse primarily focusing on software code, e.g, based on library and information science, knowledge-based systems, or database management technologies [12]. However, the majority of those approaches fails to recognize the complexity of SE experience in general, often requires a thorough classification of the domain, or does not provide any means for similarity-based retrieval.

Recently, CBR has been recognized as a promising approach for the operationalization of learning organizations in the SE domain [2,3,18,22,27]. Applications are developed in different SE areas, like capturing and formalizing best practices (e.g., [20]), effort prediction (e.g., [13]), change management [23], and requirements acquisition (e.g., [25]). However, so far there does not exist an approach on reusing software measurement EW. Only few approaches offer flexible similarity-based retrieval methods, for example, through a context concept as a "similarity environment for the retrieval" [1,31], dynamic ranking of importance ratings of indexes [21], or partitioning the case base through the use of *prototypes* [7]. However, if multiple retrieval goals have to be supported by a case base, this is not sufficient. The creation of distinct case bases for test selection and diagnosis in PATDEX [6,31], can be seen in analogy to different retrieval goals, although inefficient due to administration and maintenance reasons. In contrast, our approach, systematizes the concept of goal-oriented retrieval through a flexible and tailorable retrieval method and similarity measure based on the advanced similarity model of PATDEX which explicitly deals with unknown information, filter attributes, and local similarity measures.

Besides integrating experiential knowledge (in form of cases) and general domain knowledge as in several CBR systems, our approach explicitly models different levels of knowledge focusing on different scopes.

Concerning the tailoring and continuous evolution of the EF to organization specific characteristics, only a few systems offer mechanisms for the systematic and integrated acquisition of user feedback and learning possibilities regarding the similarity measure as, e.g., the tailoring of relevance factors (see [4] for an overview), which represent the basis for the continuous evolution of our approach.

7 Conclusion

For the successful planning and improvement of software measurement, EW has to be captured in corporate memories and reused across the organization. Based on our experiences on the application of the GQM approach in practice, we develop a case-based approach for the operationalization of organizational learning in software measurement focusing on the technical aspects. Relevant measurement EW is modeled, a goal-oriented method for similarity-based retrieval tailorable to specific environments is developed, and an acquisition process intertwined into the retrieval/reuse process described.

Currently, we are implementing the approach. Further empirical research will have to be carried out in experiments and industrial transfer projects to assess strengths and weaknesses of the approach.

References

1. Althoff, K.-D., et al.: Case-Based Reasoning for Decision Support and Diagnostic Problem Solving: The INRECA Approach. Proc. 3rd German Workshop on Case-Based Reasoning, Germany (1995)
2. Althoff, K.-D., Bomarius, F., Tautz, C.: Using Case-Based Reasoning Technology to Build Learning Software Organizations. Proc. of Workshop on Building, Maintaining, and Using Organizational Memories at the 13th European Conference on AI (1998)
3. Althoff, K.-D., et al.: CBR for Experimental Software Engineering. In M. Lenz et al. (eds.), Case-Based Reasoning Technology - From Foundations to Applications, LNAI 1400, Springer Verlag (1998)
4. Althoff, K.-D.: Evaluating Case-Based Reasoning Systems: The Inreca Case Study. Postdoctoral Thesis, University of Kaiserslautern, Germany (1997)
5. Aamodt, A., Plaza, E.: Case-Based Reasoning: Foundational Issues, Methodological Variations, and System Approaches. AI Communications, 17(1) (1994)
6. Althoff, K.-D., Wess, S.: Case-based Knowledge Acquisition, Learning and Problem Solving in Diagnostic Real World Tasks. Proc. of the 5th European Knowledge Acquisition for Knowledge-Based Systems Workshop, Scotland/UK (1991)
7. Barletta, R.: A Hybrid Indexing and Retrieval Strategy for Advisory CBR Systems Built with ReMind. Proc. of the 2nd European Workshop on Case-Based Reasoning (1994)
8. Basili, V. R., Caldiera, G., Rombach, H. D.: Experience Factory. In J. J. Marciniak (ed.), Encyclopedia of Software Engineering, John Wiley & Sons (1994)
9. Basili, V. R., Caldiera, G., Rombach, H. D.: Goal Question Metric Paradigm. In J. J. Marciniak (ed.), Encyclopedia of Software Engineering, John Wiley & Sons (1994)
10. Barr, J.M., Magaldi, R.V.: Corporate Knowledge Management for the Millennium. In I. Smith, B. Faltings (eds.), Advances in Case-Based Reasoning, Springer Verlag (1996)
11. CEMP Consortium. Customized Establishment of Measurement Programs. Final Report, ESSI Project Nr.10358 (1996)
12. Frakes, W. B., Gandel, P. B.: Representing Reusable Software. Information and Software Technology, 32(10) (1990)
13. Finnie, G. R., Wittig, G. W., Desharnais, J.-M.: Estimating Software Development Effort with Case-Based Reasoning. Proc. of the 2nd Int. Conf. on Case-Based Reasoning, RI (1997)
14. Gresse von Wangenheim, C., Althoff, K.-D., Barcia, R.M.: Intelligent Retrieval of Software Engineering Experienceware. Proc. of the 11th Int. Conf. on Software Engineering and Knowledge Engineering, Germany (1999)
15. Gresse von Wangenheim, C.: REMEX - A Case-Based Approach for Reuse of Software Measurement Experienceware. Technical Report PPGEP-C3002.99E, Graduate Program in Production Engineering, Federal University of Santa Catarina, Brazil (1999)

16.Gresse, C., Briand, L. C.: Requirements for the Knowledge-Based Support of Software Engineering Measurement Plans. Journal of Knowledge-Based Systems, 11 (1998)

17.Gibbs, W.W.: Software´s Chronic Crisis. Scientific American (1994)

18.Gresse von Wangenheim, C.: Knowledge Management in Experimental Software Engineering - Create, Renew, Build and Organize Knowledge Assets. Proc. of the 10th Int. Conf. on Software Engineering and Knowledge Engineering, San Francisco, California (1998)

19.Gresse von Wangenheim, C., von Wangenheim, A., Barcia, R. M.: Case-Based Reuse of Software Engineering Measurement Plans. Proc. of the 10th Int. Conf. on Software Engineering and Knowledge Engineering, San Francisco, California (1998)

20.Henninger, S.: Capturing and Formalizing Best Practices in a Software Development Organization. Proc. of the 9th Int. Conf. on Software Engineering and Knowledge Engineering, Spain (1997)

21.Kolodner, J. L.: Case-Based Reasoning. Morgan Kaufmann, San Francisco, California (1993)

22.Kitano, H., Shimazu, H.: The Experience-Sharing Architecture. In D. Leake (ed.), Case-Based Reasoning Experiences: Lessons Learned & Future Directions (1996)

23.Lam, W., Shankararaman, V.: Managing Change During Software Development: An Incremental, Knowledge-Based Approach. Proc. of the 10th Int. Conf. on Software Engineering and Knowledge Engineering, San Francisco, California (1998)

24.Manago, M. et al.: Casuel: A Common Case Representation Language. Technical Report Deliverable D1, Esprit Project Inreca P6322 (1994)

25.Maiden, N.A., Sutcliffe, A. G.: Exploiting Reusable Specifications Through Analogy. Communications of the ACM, 35(4) (1992)

26.Kempter, H., Leippert, F.: Systematische Software-Qualitätsverbesserung durch zielorientiertes Messen und Bewerten sowie explizite Wiederverwendung des Software-Entwicklungs-Know-how. Proc. of the BMBF-Seminar Software Technology, Germany (1996)

27.Tautz, C., Althoff, K.-D.: Using Case-based Reasoning for Reusing Software Knowledge. Proc. of the 2nd Int. Conference on Case-Based Reasoning, Springer Verlag (1997)

28.Tautz, C., Gresse von Wangenheim, C.: REFSENO: A Representation Formalism for Software Engineering Ontologies. Proc. 5th German Conf. on Knowledge-Based Systems, Germany (1999).

29.Tautz, C., Gresse von Wangenheim, C.: REFSENO: A Representation Formalism for Software Engineering Ontologies. Technical IESE-Report 015.98/E, Fraunhofer Institute for Experimental Software Engineering, Kaiserslautern, Germany (1998).

30. Tversky, A.: Features of Similarity. Psychological Review, 84 (1977)

31. Wess, S.: Fallbasiertes Problemlösen in wissensbasierten Systemen zur Entscheidungsunterstützung und Diagnostik. Ph.D. Thesis, University of Kaiserslautern, Germany, infix Verlag (1995)

32. Zand, M., Samadzadeh, M.: Software Reuse: Current Status and Trends. Journal of Systems and Software, 30 (3) (1995)

A Unified Long-Term Memory System*

James H. Lawton

Air Force Research Laboratory
Rome Research Site
Rome, NY 13441
lawton@ai.rl.af.mil

Roy M. Turner & Elise H. Turner

Department of Computer Science
University of Maine
Orono, ME 04469
{rmt,eht}@umcs.maine.edu

Abstract. Memory-based reasoning systems are a class of reasoners that derive solutions to new problems based on past experiences. Such reasoners use a *long-term memory* (LTM) to act as a knowledge base of these past experiences, which may be represented by such things as specific events (i.e. *cases*), plans, scripts, etc. This paper describes a Unified Long-Term Memory (ULTM) system, which is a dynamic, conceptual memory that was designed to be a general LTM capable of simultaneously supporting multiple intentional reasoning systems. Through a unique mixture of content-independent and domain-specific mechanisms, the ULTM is able to flexibly provide reasoners accurate and timely storage and recall of episodic memory structures. In addition, the ULTM provides support for recognizing opportunities to satisfy *suspended goals*, allowing reasoning systems to better cope with the unpredictability of dynamic real-world domains by helping them take advantage of unexpected events.

1.0 Introduction

Memory-based reasoning systems are a class of reasoners that derive solutions to new problems based on past experiences. Included in this class are case-based [7,2] and schema-based [15] reasoners. The purpose of a *long-term memory* (LTM) in a memory-based reasoning system is to act as a knowledge base of the past experiences, which may be represented by such things as specific events (i.e. *cases*), plans, scripts, etc. The key functions of an LTM are the storage and retrieval of such representational structures. The proper performance of both of these functions is based directly on how the structures are organized in the LTM's knowledge base, and to what extent the LTM can match new experiences to existing structures.

The Unified Long-Term Memory (ULTM) system is a dynamic, conceptual memory [9,5,7] that was designed to be a general LTM capable of simultaneously supporting multiple intentional reasoning systems. Through a unique mixture of content-independent and domain-specific mechanisms, the ULTM is able to flexibly provide reasoners accurate and timely storage and recall of episodic memory structures. In addition, the ULTM provides support for recognizing opportunities to

* This material is based upon work supported by the National Science Foundateion under Grant No. BES—9696004.

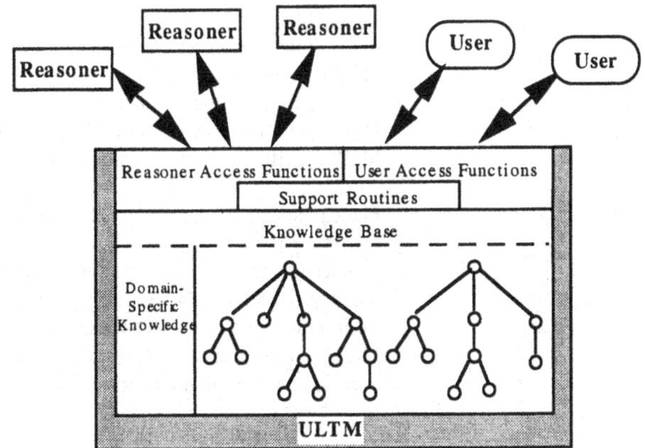

Fig. 1 – ULTM Overview

satisfy *suspended goals*, allowing reasoning systems to better cope with the unpredictability of dynamic real-world domains by helping them take advantage of unexpected events.

As shown in Fig. 1 both reasoning systems and the people who develop them (i.e. "users") access the ULTM's knowledge base through its interface functions. The knowledge base is divided into two parts: the domain-specific knowledge, which the ULTM uses to control its behavior and interaction with the reasoning system(s) using it, and the memory items themselves. The memory items stored in the ULTM's knowledge base represent the various reasoners' experiences. As with many such memory systems, the basic structure for storing and organizing items in the memory is a Memory Organization Packet (MOP) [9]. Unlike most conceptual memories, the MOPs in the ULTM are generic in nature, meant to be the building blocks that reasoning systems will use to create their own structures to be stored in and retrieved from memory. These are the structures the reasoners actually work with, and, although they will be called different names in the various reasoning systems, we generically refer to these representations as either a case, if it represents a specific experience, or a MOP, if it represents a generalization of several cases or other MOPs. These MOPs and cases are organized into a hierarchy, with more general MOPs pointing to (loosely speaking), or *indexing*, more specialized MOPs or cases.

The ULTM has been tested with two particular memory-based reasoners: *Orca*[1] [16,17] and *CoCo* (a generalization of JUDIS [13]). Orca is a schema-based reasoning (SBR) system currently being developed as an intelligent control system for autonomous underwater vehicles (AUVs). SBR systems represent most or all problem-solving knowledge explicitly as MOP-like declarative knowledge structures called *schemas*, which are used to guide all facets of behavior. CoCo is a conversational controller that is to be part of a natural language interface to a system of multiple AUVs. CoCo uses knowledge about intentions and conventions in discourse, represented as *Conversation MOPs* (or C-MOPs) [4], to organize the conversation goals of a distributed system.

---

[1] In fact, much of the core functionality of the ULTM is based on Orca's schema memory.

Slot	Description
`predictive`	A list of those features expected (by the user) to uniquely identify items in memory.
`elaboration-heuristics`	MOP-specific heuristic functions for index elaboration.
`preference-heuristics`	MOP-specific preference heuristics for MOP selection.
`index-generation-heuristics`	MOP-specific heuristic functions for generating indices.
`suspended-goals`	Place to attach goals in the hope they will be recalled opportunistically.
`bookkeeping`	A placeholder for bookkeeping information, such as recency and frequency statistics, generalization information, and predictive feature tracking.
`exemplars`	Place to store cases and MOPs that, while they fit the current MOP, could not be immediately indexed.

Fig. 2 - MOP Slots

This paper describes the unique capabilities of the ULTM. These include the ability to support multiple reasoning systems simultaneously, the various mechanisms for providing domain-specific knowledge to the ULTM that is used to "fine-tune" the retrieval and storage processes for each reasoner, and the support for recognizing potential opportunities to satisfy suspended goals. It is assumed that the reader is familiar with conceptual memory and memory-based reasoning. Background information on these topics can be found in [9,5,7].

2.0 Memory Structures

A key contribution of the ULTM is that it is capable of supporting multiple memory-based reasoning systems simultaneously. The foundation for this capability lies in the core memory structures used: the MOPs. The ULTM's MOPs are an extension of traditional MOPs. They are generic in nature, providing basic support for knowledge representation, along with extensive support for memory functions. It is expected that the reasoning systems using the ULTM will base their memory structures (i.e. their plans, scripts, etc.) on the ULTM structure MOP[2], inheriting these core capabilities.

As with other conceptual memories, the memory items in the ULTM's knowledge-base are organized as a network in which each node is either a MOP or a specific experience (i.e. a case). Each MOP contains generalized information characterizing the episodes it indexes, called its *norms* or *content frame*, and a set of indices for those episodes based on their differences. Indices point from an *indexing MOP* to either an individual case or another, more specialized MOP (the *indexed MOP*), thus forming a MOP/sub-MOP hierarchy [5].

In addition to the actual memory items, the ULTM's knowledge base contains the domain-specific knowledge needed for correct memory operation. Much of this knowledge is in the form of reasoner-specific *heuristic functions*, which are used to tailor the ULTM's retrieval and storage mechanisms to fit the particular domain. This knowledge is associated with the corresponding memory items through slots in the

---

[2] The knowledge representation system used by the ULTM is the frame system FrameWork [14], which is itself implemented using the Common Lisp Object System (CLOS) [11].

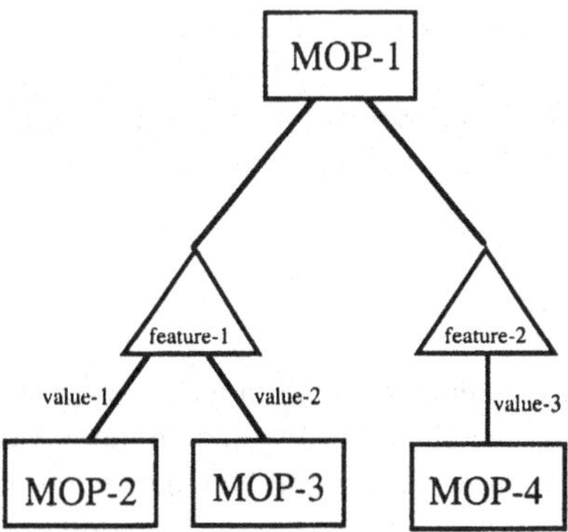

Fig. 3 – Index Structure

MOP structure, which are listed in Fig. 2. The meaning of each of these slots is explained throughout the remainder of this paper.

An index (see Fig. 3) in a conceptual memory is a two-tiered structure of features and values, which are taken from an *indexing vocabulary* [7]. An indexing vocabulary is a set of feature names and associated values that are used to construct the indices in the MOPs. The ULTM's indexing vocabulary (shown in the example in Section 4.3) requires the feature names to be slots in the MOPs being used by the reasoning system. The implementer of the reasoning system (i.e. the "user") must specify which slots of the system's frames should be considered *predictive features*, those that will be used to search and generate indices, by listing those slots in each MOP's `predictive` slot. The ULTM's indexing vocabulary also requires that the index values be described as properly formatted predicated functions, as used in [16,17].[3]

3.0 Memory Retrieval

Memory retrieval occurs when a reasoning system requests the LTM to recall any memory items matching a given *probe*, which is a description of a situation made up of features and associated values. The LTM searches its collection of stored experiences, recalling those that most closely resemble the probe.

The ULTM uses the standard retrieval process for MOP-based conceptual memories: directed search [5,7]. Memory retrieval is initiated by a reasoning system by calling the `retrieve` function. This function performs a search starting from the appropriate starting points, or *contexts*, looking for items in memory that most closely match the given probe, guided by the predictive features.

Determining which (if any) of the MOPs or cases indexed from a given MOP match a probe proceeds as follows: for each feature listed in `predictive`, one or more values are found either in the probe, working memory (if appropriate), or

[3] Using a more principled approach to indexing vocabularies, such as the Universal Index Frame (UIF) for intentional systems [10], is being considered for future work. But, since the UIF is too general to be used directly, customizing it was beyond the scope of this project.

through *index transformation*. These values are then matched against the MOP's indices, by determining if they can make index value's predicate functions true. If there is a match, the MOP or case pointed to by the matching index is added to a set to be searched further or (possibly) returned.

3.1 Index Transformation

When a value for a feature cannot be found in the given probe or in working memory, or when the value does not match any of the known index values, it may be necessary to infer a value for that feature. Sycara and Navinchandra [12] identify three general methods to perform this process of *index transformation*: elaboration, mutation and abstraction.

Both index elaboration and mutation use heuristics to infer values for features when none can be found in the given probe or in working memory. Elaboration heuristics provide more detail, while mutation heuristics make key changes to known values (e.g. changing sizes, substituting ingredients, etc.) [12]. In the ULTM, we lump both of these transformation methods together and refer to them simply as transformation heuristics.

Since index transformation relies heavily on domain-specific knowledge, it is impossible for any LTM to infer values for every feature. Instead, the ULTM provides a mechanism for the user to provide this domain-specific knowledge in the form of heuristic functions associated with MOPs. While the ULTM does provide a few generic index transformation functions, it is expected that the user will provide the majority of these heuristics.

Because specifying transformation heuristics may be complicated, the ULTM actually provides two mechanisms to add them: as rules of a rule-based system or as regular functions. The rule-based system provides a simple, expressive mechanism for adding elaboration knowledge that may be generally applicable, especially in cross-domain applications. However, there may be times when expressing the desired heuristic information is too difficult using the somewhat restrictive rule syntax, or when the heuristic knowledge may only be applicable to a given set of MOPs or cases (those used by a particular reasoner). In these situation the user would use the more general heuristic function mechanism.

Adding a new transformation rule requires first defining the new rule and then adding the rule to the ULTM's index rule-based system (`index-RBS`). For example, in the SMART simulator [17] where Orca is tested, it is possible to get values for the depth and altitude of an AUV directly from working memory. Suppose, however, one needed to determine how deep the water is at the AUV's current location, which we will call the bottom-depth. This value, the sum of the AUV's depth and altitude, is not directly available, and thus must be computed. The rule that computes this is[4]:

```
Rule index-bottom-depth-rule
    If feature is bottom-depth
       and ?d = current depth from WM
       and ?a = current altitude from WM
```

[4] For the sake of readability, this rule is not given in the actual index-RBS rule syntax.

```
Then
   Conclude bottom-depth = (?d + ?a)
```

Similarly, this heuristic could be described in a function, (e.g. `index-bottom-depth-fcn`). Once this function is defined, the ULTM would be told when to apply it by associating the function (through the `elaboration-heuristics` slot) with the MOP (or MOPs) for which elaborating the bottom-depth feature may be needed. What is important is that in either case (rule or function), if the ULTM cannot find a value for a given predictive feature in the probe or working memory, it will employ any relevant elaboration heuristics to infer a value. In this way a user can tailor and augment the ULTM's general directed search mechanism to insure correct behavior.

Index abstraction is another, somewhat more general, form of index transformation. Instead of using heuristic rules or functions, index abstraction exploits the structure of knowledge represented in a hierarchical frame system. If a direct match for a feature value cannot be found, abstraction attempts to find a match on a similar value (where similar refers to how closely connected the two values are in the knowledge hierarchy) by traversing up generalization and down specialization links.

The ULTM does not do retrieval-time index abstraction, however. Rather, when indices are created, their values are abstracted as much as possible (with respect to the indexing MOP). This method is more efficient, since abstraction need only be done once, and it uses the execution context in effect at storage time, which more accurately describes the situation under which the MOP or case is being stored. This storage-time index abstraction is discussed in more detail in Section 4.1.

3.2 Preference Heuristics

The search of memory described above will produce a set of MOPs and/or cases (which we will collectively refer to as MOPs) that have matched the various features in the given probe. However, the retrieval should only return a limited number of MOPs: those that match "best." The problem of choosing the best matching MOPs, known as the *selection problem* [6], is handled by the ULTM through the use of *preference heuristics* [6]. These heuristics are functions that rank the set of MOPs according to various criteria.

The ULTM provides several of the more common heuristic functions, which are based on those used in PARADYME [6]. These functions rank the retrieved cases based upon the following criteria: how well they (i.e. the retrieved cases) relate to the reasoner's current goals, how salient and specific the features of the retrieved cases are with respect to the given probe, and how frequently and recently the retrieved cases were previously recalled. Each of the common heuristic functions provided by the ULTM is given a particular case and a list of other cases to rank it against. It returns a numeric score -- either a bonus (value > 0), penalty (value < 0), or neutral (0) value -- which is added to the cases' composite score. The cases are ranked by highest composite score after applying all of the relevant preference heuristics.

While the set of preference heuristic functions provided in the ULTM should be generally applicable to many intentional reasoning systems, it is likely that the reasoners using the ULTM will also need to apply some domain-specific knowledge to the ranking of retrieved cases. To support this, a mechanism is provided to allow the user to specify their own MOP-specific heuristics, by associating new preference heuristic functions with relevant MOPs through their `preference-heuristics` slot. The ULTM automatically applies these additional functions whenever it retrieves MOPs or cases that have such functions associated with them, adding their returned values to the composite score.

3.3 Predictive Feature Tracking

The ULTM provides limited support for predictive feature tracking, which refers to the recording of how often each predictive feature leads to a reminding. This is done by keeping a record of *feature references*, which are how often each of a MOP's predictive features is used, as well as *MOP references*, which are how often a MOP has been searched. This information is automatically associated with the MOPs (through their `bookkeeping` slot), and is retrieved with a set of accessor functions.

One should note that this form of feature tracking is very limited. It does not keep track of which features actually *contributed* to determining which MOPs were actually returned by a memory search. Rather, it merely tracks which features led to possible choices, at the individual MOP level. To truly track the predictiveness of a given feature, the ULTM's mechanism would need to be extended with more sophisticated machine learning techniques.

Also, the ULTM does not currently do anything with this tracking information. Rather, it is provided for use by reasoning systems in such things as preference heuristics and perhaps feature "forgetting." For example, one could create a preference heuristic that gives a bonus to MOPs or cases that were arrived at through features with a high feature-reference to mop-reference ratio. Similarly, one could remove (forget) features from a MOP's `predictive` list if that ratio drops below a certain threshold.

4.0 Memory Storage

As new events are experienced, the reasoning process may want to store them in memory so that they may be later retrieved. The same search process is used to find a place to store a new MOP or case in memory as would be used to retrieve it. That is, using the case as a probe, its features are used to first select an initial context, and then to traverse indices matching those features. At each MOP encountered during the search, there are four possibilities that may occur for each of the MOP's predictive features that the probe has a value for (modified from [5]):

1) Nothing else is indexed in the MOP by that feature.
2) One or more other MOPs are indexed in the MOP by that feature,
but with values that differ from the probe's.
3) One or more other MOPs are indexed by that feature/value pair.
4) The feature/value pair is one of the MOP's norms.

For the first of these possibilities, we know that the probe (the MOP or case being stored) contains a value for a predictive feature that is not currently being used in an index. As such, we could just generate an index using that feature/value pair. But in the ULTM, to be consistent with the retrieval process, as well as to keep the number of indices from growing out of control, we do not. Instead, we collect all of these "leaf" MOPs found during the search of the knowledge base and, after the search has completed, pass them through the preference heuristics. For each MOP selected by the preference heuristics, a set of indices is generated by determining the differences between it and the probe. MOP differences are determined by comparing the values for each predictive feature in the indexing MOP against values for those features in the probe (the indexed MOP). Values that differ are used to generate indices. The index generation process is discussed in Section 4.1. It may also be necessary to update the norms of any MOP we add indices to, which is done through the process of *MOP generalization*, described in Section 4.2.

For the second possibility, we could treat the MOP currently being searched similarly to how it is treated in the first possibility: as a leaf node. But, since it is actually an internal node, we know that it would be unlikely to be selected by the preference heuristics (because of the specificity preference). Thus, in the ULTM we have decided to directly index the probe under the current MOP when this situation occurs. We know the probe has a value for a predictive feature that is not currently being used in an index, so we can simply generate an index using this feature/value pair (using the index generation process described in Section 4.1). As before, it may be necessary to update the indexing MOP's norm (Section 4.2). It should be noted that for this possibility indices are generated during the search process.

In the third possibility, there are two situations we need to contend with. First, if the probe is more specialized than the sub-MOP that was found indexed under the current MOP, then the search simply continues from the indexed sub-MOP. Otherwise, the probe is indexed under the current MOP, using the same difference method described for possibility 1 above. Unlike possibility 1, however, these indices are generated during the search.

Finally, for the fourth possibility, no indices are generated for the given feature/value pair. So that it won't be lost, however, if the probe cannot be indexed by any predictive feature, it is added to the MOP's `exemplars` list. The MOPs in this list, along with any indexed MOPs, are used to update a MOP's norms through the generalization process (Section 4.2).

4.1 Index Generation

Once a location for the MOP or case being stored is found, one or more indices must be generated for it. The ULTM uses the same mechanism for generating new indices, regardless of which possibility from Section 4.0 applies. The index generation process, shown in
Fig. 4, is given a feature and a value, which we will call the *probe filler*, that was found for that feature either in the probe, in working memory, or through transformation. The job of the index generation mechanism is to first abstract the probe filler as much as possible (with respect to the corresponding filler in the

indexing MOP, called the *MOP filler*) and then convert it into a properly formatted index value (predicate function). In keeping with its overall philosophy, the ULTM provides a set of general mechanisms which can be augmented with domain-specific knowledge to accomplish this task.

The probe filler is first *minimally abstracted*, which converts certain "raw" values (e.g. numbers and instance objects) into more standard values used by the ULTM. Next, any *slot-specific abstraction heuristics* are applied to the probe filler. These functions allow the user to abstract any value in non-standard (i.e. domain-specific) ways, thus extending the abstraction mechanism. By using such functions, indices can be generated that match less specific probes. The ULTM first looks for slot-specific abstraction heuristics associated with the probe, and then with the indexing MOP.

For example, suppose we are indexing `new-MOP` under `old-MOP`, the feature we are indexing on is `depth`, and we are given a probe filler of 50. Minimal abstraction would convert 50 into the range: `(range (low 50) (high 50))`. Suppose further that the `depth` slot of `new-MOP` has a slot-specific abstraction heuristic function associated with it that abstracts a range representing a depth by subtracting 10 from the low value and adding 10 to the high value, thus "widening" the range. The new value for depth would thus be the range: `(range (low 40) (high 60))`.

After applying any slot-specific abstraction heuristics, the highest abstraction of the probe filler (with respect to the corresponding MOP filler) is found. This primarily applies to values for which an abstraction hierarchy can be used (e.g. frames). If the probe filler is a descendent of the MOP filler, it is abstracted as far as possible up the hierarchy such that it is still a descendent of the MOP filler. If the probe filler is not a descendent of the MOP filler, but they do have a common ancestor, then the probe filler is abstracted up to the common ancestor. The MOP filler will be updated later during MOP generalization (Section 4.2). If the fillers are unrelated, no further abstraction is performed.

After the probe filler has been abstracted as much as possible, it is used to generate index values (i.e. properly formed predicate functions). While a default predicate form is provided by the ULTM (a general pattern matching predicate), the ULTM provides a mechanism to apply MOP-specific heuristic functions to the abstracted

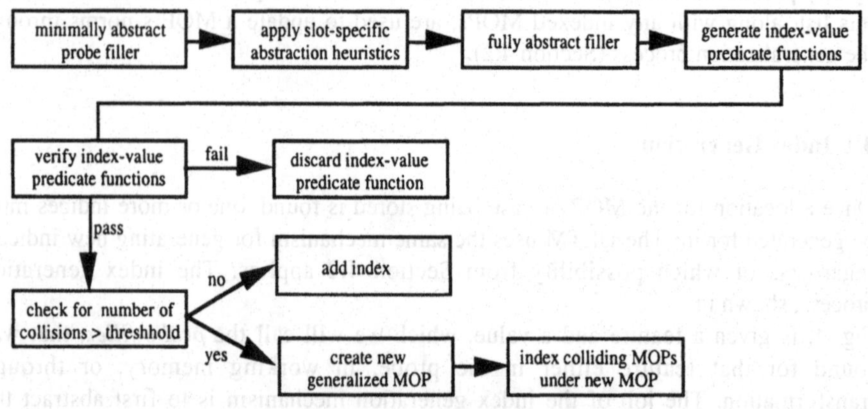

Fig. 4 - Index Generation Process

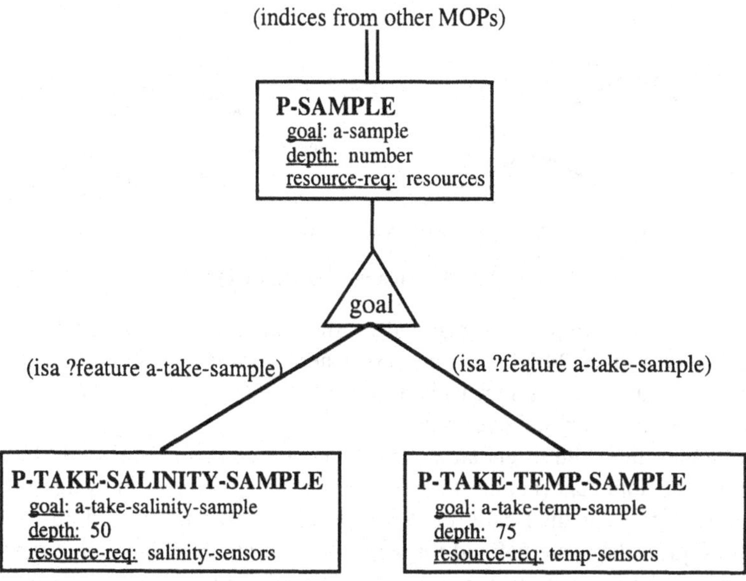

Fig. 5 - Initial Memory Contents

filler to produce index values. These heuristics are associated with MOPs through the `index-generation-functions` slot.

It is possible to generate an index that is too abstract, especially using the default mechanisms. To detect this, we verify the generated index functions by seeing if they match the indexing MOP. If they do, the index function is discarded. If not, the index function next must be tested to see if it causes a *collision* with any of the indexing MOP's existing indices. Two indices collide if their index values match and they point to different sub-MOPs. An index is simply added to the indexing MOP if it does not cause a collision.

If the index does cause a collision, but the number of colliding indices is below a certain threshold value, the index is also just added to the indexing MOP as usual. When, however, the number of colliding indices exceeds the threshold, a new MOP is created as a generalization of the colliding MOPs. The newly created MOP is indexed under the current indexing MOP, while the colliding MOPs are indexed under the new MOP by their differences.

4.2 MOP generalization

Generalization [5,7] is the process by which the memory system updates the content frames of MOPs. *Initial generalization* occurs when a new MOP is formed because of a collision. In this situation, the generalization mechanism is given a new MOP and several sub-MOPs. It must fill the content frame of the new MOP with the features common to the sub-MOPs. That is, for each feature the sub-MOPs have in common, it must find the *central tendency* of the fillers for that feature in all of the sub-MOPs. The central tendency is a sort of "average" value of the fillers taken together, and may be defined differently for each type of filler.

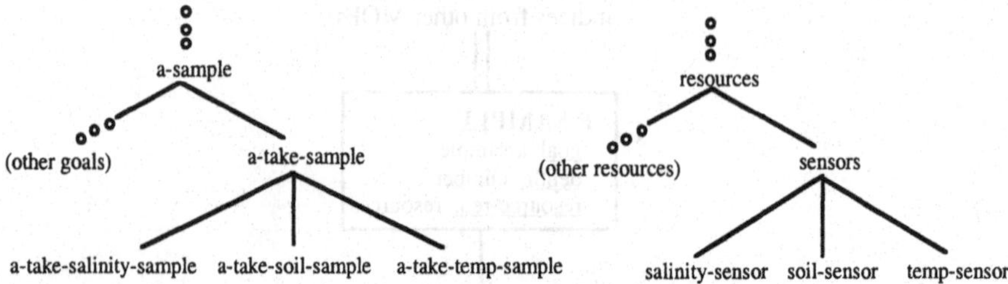

Fig. 6 - Abstraction Hierarchy

Generalization updates are made after the number of new sub-MOPs (those indexed under a given MOP since the last generalization) exceeds a threshold value. The same central tendency mechanism is used to update a MOP's feature values as was used when it was initially generalized.

To compute the central tendency of a collection of input values, the ULTM first determines the dominant (i.e. most commonly occurring) type of the values. Based on the dominant type, it then calls the appropriate specialized procedure. Currently, specialized procedures are defined for symbols, sets, numbers (including ranges), lists and frames. Users may create other specialized central tendency procedures to support domain-specific filler types.

4.3 Storage Example

This section presents an example of the storage process in detail. To start, suppose our memory contains, among other things, plans for different ocean sampling missions (see Fig. 5)[5]. We wish to add P-TAKE-SOIL-SAMPLE, a plan that describes how to perform a soil sampling mission. For the sake of this example, we will assume that P-SAMPLE's only predictive feature is GOAL, that our knowledge base contains the abstraction hierarchy (fragments) of goals and resources as shown in Fig. 6, and that the ULTM's index collision threshold is set to 3.

We will assume the search arrives at P-SAMPLE. Since the probe (P-TAKE-SOIL-SAMPLE) is not a specialization of the MOPs already indexed under P-SAMPLE (P-TAKE-SALINITY-SAMPLE and P-TAKE-TEMP-SAMPLE), it is determined that possibility 1 from Section 4.0 applies. P-TAKE-SOIL-SAMPLE is thus indexed under P-SAMPLE using the difference procedure from Section 4.0, which determines that the two plans do differ on the predictive feature GOAL.

The probe has a filler of A-TAKE-SALINITY-SAMPLE for the feature GOAL. Minimal abstraction does not change this value, and we will assume that there are no slot-specific heuristics associated with the GOAL slots of either P-TAKE-SALINITY-SAMPLE or P-SAMPLE. We next abstract A-TAKE-SALINITY-SAMPLE up the abstraction hierarchy (Fig. 6) to A-TAKE-SAMPLE. The ULTM's default index-generation heuristic is used to generate the index value function `(isa ?feature A-TAKE-SAMPLE)`. While this function will verify, it causes collisions with the existing indices for both P-TAKE-SALINITY-SAMPLE and P-TAKE-TEMP-SAMPLE. Since the collision threshold (3) has

5 We omit many of the details of the various MOPs, focusing on only those features and values that are relevant to indexing in this specific example.

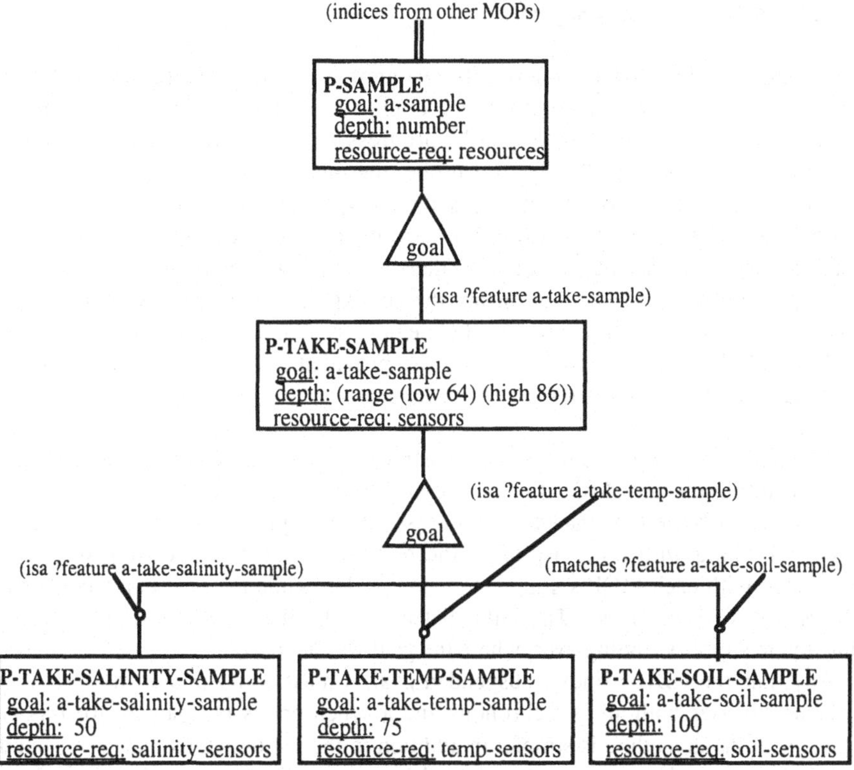

Fig. 7 - Final Memory Contents

been met, we must use our collision handling procedure, which causes a new MOP (which we'll call `P-TAKE-SAMPLE`) to be generated and initially generalized. Initial generalization fills `P-TAKE-SAMPLE`'s `GOAL` slot with `A-TAKE-SAMPLE`, its `DEPTH` slot with `(range (low 64) (high 86))`[6], and its `RESOURCE-REQ` slot with `sensors`. The final structure of memory is shown in Fig. 7.

5.0 Support for Opportunism

When using reasoning systems that utilize a conceptual memory, goals that cannot be immediately satisfied can be suspended and stored in memory, indexed by the blocked goals along with the features that are blocking their progress, but which are not currently available. This process is referred to as *predictive encoding* [8]. These suspended goals can then presumably be found by the regular search mechanism the memory system uses whenever a reasoning system requests a retrieval with an appropriate probe. This approach is referred to as *opportunistic memory* [3], and is supported by the ULTM.

[6] Computed as the mean of 50, 75, and 100 ± (0.5 * standard deviation), which is 75 ± 11.

5.1 ULTM Opportunism Support

There are two sides to the opportunity recognition problem: the reasoning system's and the memory system's. First, the reasoning system must be able to identify what circumstances are blocking a goal's progress. Then, using the goal and the circumstances impeding it to form a probe, the memory system can use its regular search mechanisms to find places to attach the suspended goal. Any time in the future the memory system retrieves a MOP or case with a suspended goal attached to it, it needs to notify the reasoner, which must then determine what to do with that goal.

To provide support for opportunism, the ULTM's `MOP` structures have a slot called `suspended-goals`, which is used by the memory system to associate suspended goals with the MOPs. Further, two functions are provided to allow reasoning systems to suspend and remove goals in memory: `suspend-goal-in-ltm` and `unsuspend-goal-in-ltm`.

The function `suspend-goal-in-ltm` searches *all* memory contexts (i.e. all starting points), retrieving any MOP the goal could be associated with. All contexts are searched to increase the chances that a cross-domain opportunity will be recognized. The goal, along with a descriptor of the reasoning system suspending the goal, is associated with each MOP's `suspended-goals` slot, while the goal maintains a list of MOPs it is suspended on. The latter list is used by the `unsuspend-goal-in-ltm` function to simplify finding everywhere the goal was attached.

Any time the ULTM finds a suspended goal, it must notify one or more reasoning systems. It uses both an asynchronous and a synchronous mechanism for this task. The synchronous method is simple: in addition to the list of MOPs that were found to match the probe, the `retrieve` function also returns a list of suspended goals that are attached to those MOPs.

The synchronous mechanism allows the reasoning system making a retrieval request to detect when a suspended goal has been found. However, that reasoning system may not be the one that originally suspended the goal. The asynchronous notification mechanism is able to notify the reasoner that suspended the goal by calling a *handler function* registered by the reasoner. These handlers are user-defined, and are expected to send a message to the registered reasoner, allowing it to deal with the suspended goal asynchronously.

5.2 Beyond Suspended Goals

We, along with almost all other researchers working in the field of opportunistic reasoning, have focused almost exclusively on the recognition of opportunities to satisfy suspended goals. This is for a good reason: goals are fundamental to intentional reasoning systems. In fact, Francis [1] claims that opportunities *must be* relevant to some goal held by the reasoning system. In spite of this contention, in this section we consider predictively encoding in memory things other than goals that would lead to opportunity recognition.

Stepping back for a moment, we note that the key functionality of the predictive encoding mechanism is not that it can support the recall of suspended goals, but rather that it allows the reasoning system to be *reminded* of something, anything, that has been previously considered (reasoned about). Thus we can conceivably store anything in memory that will cause the reasoner to interrupt its current activity and reconsider whatever it was reasoning about when the item was stored.

For example, in the near future we will be undertaking a study into utilizing opportunistic memory to recognize when a group of AUVs should restructure their organization (the *re-organization problem*). Using such an approach, a reasoner would select an initial organization for a group of AUVs based upon the given mission and the currently available resources (e.g. the number of AUVs and the equipment they carry). Suppose, however, that during the process of deciding on the initial organization, another organization (represented by some structure which we will call `Org-1`) is considered that would be superior, but cannot be selected because some resources are missing. `Org-1` could be predictively encoded in memory, using the missing resources as recall cues. Should those resources later become available, `Org-1` would presumably be recalled by the memory system, which would notify the reasoner.

The problem is that the reasoner must then determine what to do with this reminding. When the item suspended in memory was a goal, this was fairly easy: just recheck the conditions that caused the goal to be suspended, and reactivate it if they are now met. We can do this because our reasoning systems already have the infrastructure for dealing with goals. Reasoners would have to be modified to handle remindings of other types. At this point, the extent of those modifications is a research issue to be dealt with in the near future. It should be noted, though, that there is nothing in the ULTM's support for opportunism, as described in Section 5.1, that precludes using it for suspending things other than goals.

6.0 Summary

The ULTM is a dynamic conceptual memory system that is capable of supporting multiple reasoning systems simultaneously. It uses established structures and procedures for all primary memory functions. Through a unique mixture of content independent and domain specific mechanisms, it is able to provide reasoners accurate and timely storage and recall of episodic memory structures in a flexible and robust manner. Additionally, the ULTM provides support for recognizing opportunities to satisfy suspended goals, allowing reasoning systems to better cope with the unpredictability of dynamic real-world domains by helping them take advantage of unexpected events.

References

1. Francis, A.G. Jr. (1997). "Memory-Based Opportunistic Reasoning", Ph.D. Thesis proposal, Georgia Institute of Technology.
2. Hammond, K. (1990). "Case-Based Planning: A Framework for Planning from Experience", *The Journal of Cognitive Science*, 14(3).

3. Hammond, K. (1993). "Opportunistic Memory", *The Journal of Machine Learning*, 10(3).
4. Kellermann, K., Broetzmann, S., Lim, T.-S., and Kitao, K. (1989). "The conversation mop: Scenes in the steam of discourse", *Discourse Processes*, 12(1):27-61.
5. Kolodner, J. (1981). "Organization and Retrieval in a Conceptual Memory for Events", *Proceedings of the Seventh International Joint Conference on Artificial Intelligence.*
6. Kolodner, J. (1989). "Selecting the Best Case for a Case-Based Reasoner", *Proceedings of the Eleventh Conference of the Cognitive Science Society.*
7. Kolodner, J. (1993). *Case-Based Reasoning*, Morgan Kaufman, San Mateo.
8. Patalano, A., Seifert, C., and Hammond, K. (1991). "Predictive Encodings: Planning for Opportunities", *Proceedings of the Fifteenth Conference of the Cognitive Science Society.*
9. Schank, R. (1982). *Dynamic Memory*, Cambridge University Press, New York.
10. Schank, R. and Osgood, R. (1990). "A content theory of memory indexing", Northwestern University, Institute for Learning Sciences Technical Report no. 2.
11. Steele, G. (1990). *Common Lisp: The Language (Second Edition)*, Digital Press, Bedford, MA.
12. Sycara, K. and Navinchandra, D. (1991). "Index Transformation and Generation for Case Retrieval", In *Proceedings of the 1991 Case-Based Reasoning Workshop (DARPA)*, Bareiss, E. (ed.), Morgan Kaufman, San Mateo, CA.
13. Turner, E. (1990). "Integrating Intention and Convention To Organize Problem Solving Dialogues", Ph.D. Dissertation, Georgia Institute of Technology technical report GIT-ICS-90/02.
14. Turner, R. (1987). "Issues in the design of advisory systems: The consumer-advisor system", in *Proceedings of the Eleventh Annual Conference of the Cognitive Science Society*, Detroit, MI.
15. Turner, R. (1994). *Adaptive Reasoning for Real-World Problems: A Schema-Based Approach*, Lawrence Erlbaum Associates, Hillsdale, NJ.
16. Turner, R. (1995a). "Context-Sensitive, Adaptive Reasoning for Intelligent AUV Control: Orca Project Update", In *Proceedings of the 9th International Symposium on Unmanned Untethered Submersible Technology (AUV'95)*, Durham, New Hampshire.
17. Turner, R. (1995b). "Intelligent Control of Autonomous Underwater Vehicles: The Orca Project", Roy M. Turner. In *Proceedings of the 1995 IEEE Conference on Systems, Man, and Cybernetics*, Vancouver, BC, Canada.
18. Turner, R. (1997). "Orca Documentation (for Version 2.1)", CDPS Research Group in-house report, University of Maine. http://cdps.umcs.maine.edu/Docs/orca-2.0/

Combining CBR with Interactive Knowledge Acquisition, Manipulation and Reuse*

David B. Leake and David C. Wilson

Computer Science Department
Indiana University, Lindley Hall
150 S. Woodlawn Ave
Bloomington, IN 47405, U.S.A.
{leake,davwils}@cs.indiana.edu

Abstract. Because of the complexity of aerospace design, intelligent systems to support and amplify the abilities of aerospace designers have the potential for profound impact on the speed and reliability of design generation. This article describes a framework for supporting the interactive capture of design cases and their application to new problems, illustrating the approach with a discussion of its use in a support system for aircraft design. The project integrates case-based reasoning with interactive tools for capturing expert design knowledge through "concept mapping." Concept mapping tools provide crucial functions for interactively generating and examining design cases and navigating their hierarchical structure, while CBR techniques provide capabilities to facilitate retrieval and to aid interactive adaptation of designs. The project aims simultaneously to develop a useful design aid and more generally to develop practical interactive approaches to fundamental issues of case acquisition and representation, context-sensitive retrieval, and case adaptation.

1 Overview

Aerospace design is a complex process that requires designers to address complicated issues involving numerous specialized areas of expertise. No single designer can be an expert in every relevant area, and becoming proficient may require years of experience. Consequently, intelligent systems to support and amplify the abilities of human designers have the potential for profound impact on the speed and reliability of design generation. An appealing approach, which has been applied in systems such as (Domeshek *et al.*, 1994), is to augment the designers' own design experiences with relevant information from prior designs: to provide support with case-based reasoning.

Ideally, case-based design support tools will include three related capabilities to aid design reuse: capture of and access to specific design experiences, support

* This research is supported in part by NASA under award No NCC 2-1035. The authors gratefully acknowledge support from Northwestern University while on leave and many contributions by Alberto Cañas, Mary Livingston, and James Newkirk.

for new designers as they try to understand the lessons of those prior experiences; and support for adapting prior designs to fit new design goals. For practical application, the tools must not depend on extensive domain knowledge; for designer acceptance, they must leave the designer in control. This article describes principles for addressing these goals and their application in the case-based design aid DRAMA (Design Retrieval and Adaptation Mechanisms for Aerospace).

The DRAMA project integrates case-based reasoning with interactive tools for capturing expert design knowledge through *concept mapping* (Novak and Gowin, 1984), with the goal of leveraging off the strengths of both approaches. We are applying concept mapping tools from the Concept Mapping group at the University of West Florida, led by Dr. Alberto Cañas, to provide an interactive interface and crucial functions for generating and examining design cases, as well as navigating their hierarchical structure. CBR techniques provide the capabilities to facilitate retrieval and to aid interactive adaptation of designs. The implemented DRAMA system supports browsing of prior design knowledge and proactively provides designers with concrete examples of designs and design adaptations from similar prior problems. At the same time, it unobtrusively acquires new examples from the user's interactive design process.

The project develops "knowledge-light" (Wilke *et al.*, 1997) interactive approaches to addressing fundamental CBR issues of case acquisition, case adaptation, and context-sensitive retrieval. The system demonstrates that fully integrating a CBR system into the design environment enables the system to dynamically adjust the relevance criteria used to retrieve prior experiences, exploiting task-based information without requiring the user to provide it explicitly. In addition, the system illustrates the benefits of interactively capturing and manipulating cases at a "middle level" between traditional highly structured cases with fixed representations, and unstructured textual cases.

The system differs from previous approaches in allowing multiple case representations that users themselves can develop and revise. In interactive CBR systems, a user's ability to understand and apply a prior case may depend not only on its content, but on how its representation matches the user's conceptualization of the domain: A seemingly more distant case may be more useful to the user if it is more understandable. This raises interesting research questions about supporting user-defined representations and reconciling the divergent benefits of flexibility, customization, and case standardization as the case library grows.

2 The Task Domain

A significant concern at NASA is "knowledge loss:" that critical aerospace design expertise is the domain of a few experts and will be lost when they retire. This has given rise to knowledge preservation efforts, a number of which have employed CBR. For example, the RECALL tool at the NASA Goddard Space Flight Center was developed to store and access textual reports of important lessons (Bagg, 1997). However, different experts may conceptualize designs very differently, making it hard for others to interpret descriptions of prior designs.

To make records more comprehensible, new projects have investigated the use of concept mapping. The goal of concept mapping for design is to capture not only important features of the designs themselves, but also the designers' conceptualizations of those designs—the relationships and rationale underlying their components. This raises the question of how to organize and access the knowledge that concept maps capture, and how to facilitate its reuse. Our framework uses interactive CBR techniques to support retrieval and reuse of designs represented as concept maps.

3 Tenets of the Approach

Our tenets shaping the DRAMA framework are:

- **The system should leverage a designer's knowledge, rather than attempting to replace it.**
  This requires interactivity and support rather than autonomous design generation. All parts of the process must accept user control.
- **The system should support multiple conceptualizations of the design space.**
  The system must both allow multiple (potentially idiosyncratic) representations and support standardization when that does not impose a burden.
- **Support information should automatically be focused on the current task.**
  This requires that the system monitor the task context in order to anticipate information needs and to determine how to fulfill them.
- **Learning must play a central role, both at the design level and at the level of design manipulation.**
  This requires the capability to capture and reuse cases both for designs and design processes.

All the examples in this paper focus on cases containing designs, but the framework could be applied to representations of processes as well. Core system methods provide a domain-independent framework for interactive capture, graphical manipulation, and experience-supported reuse of design knowledge.

4 Background

Case-based Design Support: Case-based reasoning is widely used in design-aiding systems. The Clavier system (Hinkle and Toomey, 1995), for example, is a case-based advisory system put into production use to suggest and critique designs of autoclave layouts at Lockheed. Research systems address support for tasks such as architectural design (Goel *et al.*, 1991; Hua and Faltings, 1993; Gebhardt *et al.*, 1997; de Silva Garza and Maher, 1996; Smith *et al.*, 1995), circuit design (Vollrath, 1998), and conceptual design of aircraft subsystems (Domeshek *et al.*, 1994). Many of these systems display impressive capabilities, but at the expense of considerable development effort to tailor them to domain-specific needs. We instead provide a framework for building up case knowledge and indexing criteria. Specific case representations, rather than being predefined, are developed incrementally through interactions with users as the system is applied. Users can easily augment and adjust the case representation as needed, with simple analogical mapping processes allowing disparate types of cases to be retrieved.

Concept Mapping: Concept mapping is a process to reveal an individual's internal cognitive structures by developing external representations of concepts and propositions. A concept map (CMap) is a two-dimensional representation of a set of concepts constructed so that the interrelationships among them are evident. Individual concepts are linked to related concepts through one or two-way links, each link associated with a label/proposition describing the relationship. The vertical axis generally expresses a hierarchical framework for the concepts; for example, a concept map of design problems might represent a hierarchy of abstract and more specific problems. However, we stress that there is no requirement that they represent particular relationships; they are compatible with *any* structured representation.

Semantic networks are a form of concept map, but concept maps are not constrained by syntactic rules and have no associated semantics; they are normally seen as a medium for informally "sketching out" conceptual structures. The visual presentation of information in concept maps provides a natural starting point for organizing and accessing information in multiple forms (e.g., images or video clips), which also are contained in the CMap. For example, Figure 1 shows a sample CMap describing the basic structure of the Boeing 777 aircraft, annotated with an associated image and diagram. This CMap is displayed by the CMap tools described in a later section.

Concept mapping has been used in educational contexts to help students clarify and compare their understanding. A recent effort integrated concept mapping into a set of knowledge construction and sharing tools linking over a thousand schools in Latin America (Cañas *et al.*, 1995). It is currently being used to capture a NASA Mars expert's knowledge in CMaps organizing multimedia resources, to be made available to the public on the World Wide Web, and for knowledge construction and sharing among astrobiologists. The application of concept mapping to design is intended both to help an expert clarify his or her own conceptualizations and to make those conceptualizations available for examination by the expert or others (e.g., members of a design team seeking to understand the expert's design to evaluate or modify it, or novices seeking to increase their own understanding). Through differences in maps that different designers generate for the same concepts (whether in the features and relationships they include, or in the level of granularity they use), concept mapping can illuminate their different perspectives. For example, a designer specializing in airflow might include features such as wing or surface shapes and operational constraints that dictate them (e.g., the need for short-field landings), while an avionics designer would focus on aspects such as aircraft control systems.

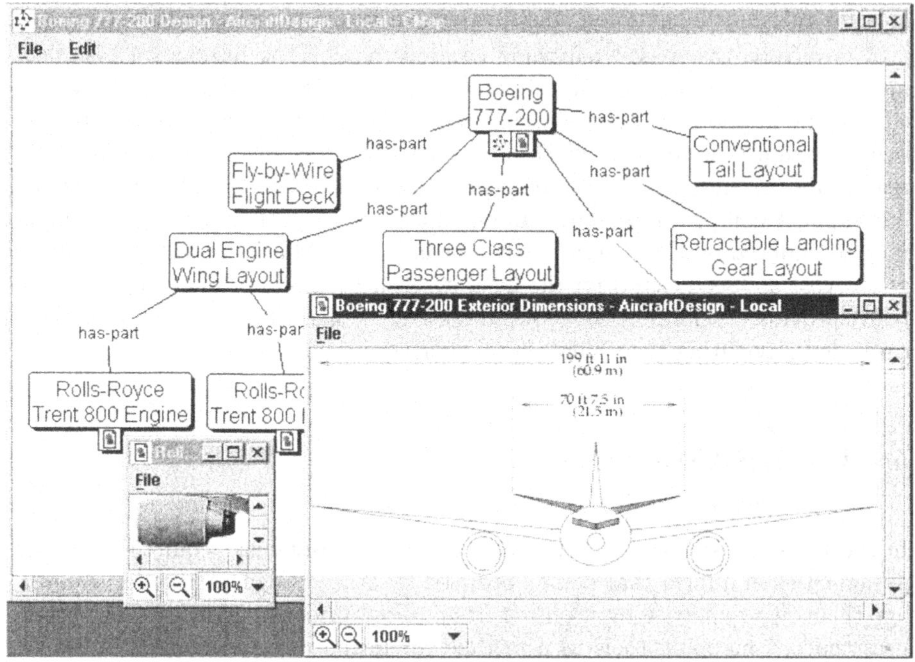

Fig. 1. Sample screen images from the CMap Editor.

Manual procedures have been developed to aid the initial generation of CMaps (e.g., Jonassen *et al.*, 1993, pp. 138–139; Novak and Gowin, 1984, pp. 24–36), and computerized tools have been developed to facilitate this process and to capture its results. The CMap tools, developed at the Institute for Human and Machine Cognition of the University of West Florida, support interactive definition and arrangement of initial maps, and manual browsing through concept map-based multimedia environments and case libraries.[1] The system also allows concept maps to be defined hierarchically, so that the nodes of any map can be associated with complete maps describing them at a finer-grained level.

Motivations for Integrating CMaps and CBR: The integration of CBR methods with interactive CMap tools provides benefits for both. Existing CMap tools provide an interactive medium for representing and examining designs, but their framework does not provide facilities for retrieval of relevant CMaps. Likewise, although the tools provide capabilities for interactively defining new

[1] The CMap tools are publicly available from http://cmap.coginst.uwf.edu/.

CMaps and manipulating their structure by adding, deleting, or substituting components, they provide no support for the decision-making required by that adaptation process. Consequently, their usefulness can be extended by the addition of automatic aids for retrieving relevant CMaps, for navigating CMaps and locating relevant information, and for reusing prior CMaps.

Conversely, case-based reasoning can leverage off the interactive case definition and revision capabilities of the CMap tools. The CMap tools provide a convenient method for entering case information in an intermediate form between textual descriptions (which are easy to generate but hard for systems to reason about) and rich structured representations (which are hard to generate but support complex reasoning). In our domain, the push to use concept mapping to understand the design process means that CMap cases will be available at low cost as "seed cases" for the CBR system. In addition, the CMap tools already provide crucial functions for interactively generating and examining these cases and navigating their hierarchical structure.

5 The DRAMA System

In the DRAMA system, concept maps are used to organize acquired aerospace design cases in a form that can be browsed by other designers in order to leverage their own expertise by profiting from stored prior experiences. The system uses concept mapping tools as a method for initial capture, manual browsing, and manual modification of design cases represented as concept maps. It uses interactive CBR techniques to retrieve relevant prior cases and to retrieve alternatives to support adaptation. In addition, it uses CBR to manage and present cases that record the rationale for particular decisions and cases that suggest adaptations of designs. The following sections discuss the main features of the system.

5.1 Using CMaps to organize and represent design information

In DRAMA, CMaps represent two types of information. First, they represent user-definable/modifiable hierarchies of aircraft and part types. This information is used to organize specific design cases and to guide similarity assessment during case retrieval. Such organization provides the designer with browsable hierarchies of aircraft (e.g. dividing military and commercial aircraft), aircraft components (e.g. specific wings, engines, fuel tanks), and component configurations (e.g. fuel tanks inside or outside the aircraft) for reference during the design process.

Second, CMaps represent specific information about particular designs such as their components and component relationships. Each component is represented as a CMap, enabling interactive viewing and manipulation of hierarchical designs at different levels of granularity.

5.2 How the system supports design

To illustrate the design process, the following sections present a simple example involving the coarse-grained configuration of an airliner after an initial set of "seed case" designs has been provided to the system, along with hierarchies of aircraft types organizing those designs. The steps described include retrieval of a similar prior design as a starting point, retrieval support for adaptation and refinement of system suggestions, and the capture of a new adaptation for future use. The concept maps used in the following figures are simple examples; those used by expert designers would include finer-grained technical details at lower levels of the hierarchy. NASA domain experts are currently developing richer concept maps to explore the framework as applied to a design initiative for reusable spacecraft.

Retrieving a relevant prior design: The case-based design process begins by selecting a similar example as a starting point. In addition, or if no sufficiently similar prior example exists, the designer is free at any point to develop designs from scratch and add them to the CMap library for future use.

The designer may choose either of two interfaces for the initial search process, one non-interactive and the other interactive. The first (non-interactive) option, the "Design Finder," is a simple and traditional CBR retrieval interface. The interface presents selection boxes for choosing the desired features of a design from a pre-defined set of standard attribute types (e.g., aircraft type, manufacturer, model number, etc.). Currently the system uses a standard predefined feature set, but features could also be derived automatically from the set of designs. Given the list of features, the system performs nearest-neighbor retrieval, according to a predefined feature weighting scheme, to retrieve references to potentially-relevant CMaps. These are presented to the designer along with a match score. The designer can browse and select from the alternatives to bring up the CMap for a particular design.

The second interface allows the designer to interactively navigate the hierarchy of concept maps, exploring alternative "views" of aircraft and aircraft component types. In our sample scenario, the designer is considering alternatives for increasing the fuel efficiency of a large airliner. The first step is to establish a context for the design by locating the CMap node for an aircraft similar to the one envisioned; the designer then chooses to consider possible engine types. The designer could also simply navigate to and browse specific engines, but in that case less contextual information would be available to aid in adaptations.

The designer first navigates through the types of aircraft to select an aircraft, and pulls up the top-level concept map for its design. The designer then selects (by clicking on the concept map) the particular part to adapt. In this example, the selection is the engine. If no CMap is already present for the component selected (e.g., the designer wishes to fill in a sketchy design by specifying its engine), the designer can use the interactive CMap tools to create a new CMap from scratch, or can browse the CMaps for designs, import a design, and then adapt as desired. If a CMap is already present for the part and it has been defined at a sufficient level of detail, the designer may also decompose the part representation into its component CMaps and make the revisions in the sub-components (with CBR support). Alternatively, the designer may define new component substructures, making the representation more detailed.

When the previous case has been retrieved, the designer has four choices, as shown in Figure 2: to *adapt* it (changing the representation in memory, e.g., when continuing work on a design begun in a previous session); to *derive* a new design, by having the system make a copy to adapt; to ask the system to use its hierarchy of aircraft parts to form an abstraction of the current design's structure as a template to fill in; or to ignore the proposed design and begin a new design from scratch.

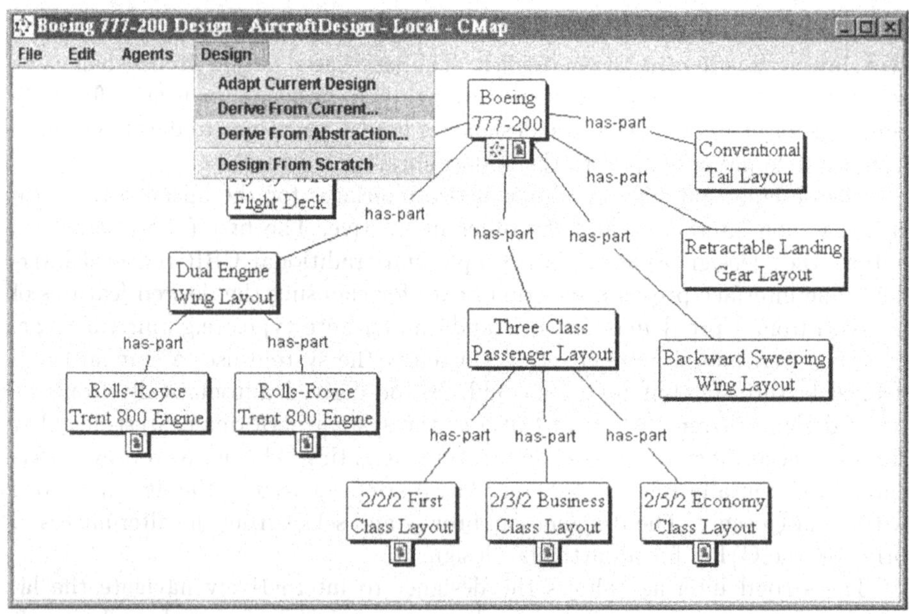

Fig. 2. Beginning derivation of a new design from a prior case.

Adapting designs: Once the designer has navigated, for example, to the engine of a particular aircraft, the system supports three ways of examining why the engine was used and the alternatives that may exist. First, the designer may simply interactively browse stored information, following links in the CMap to examine associated information such as finer-grained concept maps, video clips of explanations from previous designers, photographs, or specifications for the engine. Second, the designer may request information about similar designs. The designer may request to have this retrieval targeted to either:

- Focus on designs with components similar to the one that is currently of interest (e.g., CMaps that show aircraft using similar engines)
- Focus on designs that provide similar contexts for the current type of component (e.g., CMaps that show the engines of similar aircraft)

The algorithms underlying this retrieval are described in Section 6.3.

Retrieved alternatives are listed in order of goodness of match according to the chosen focus. The designer may also enter additional criteria to be matched against any textual annotations of rationale recorded by previous designers. For example, the designer may request that fuel-efficient engines be weighted more heavily. This prompts a re-sorting of options, using simple text matching techniques from information retrieval to decide which prior rationale to consider most relevant.

Suggesting prior adaptations: When the designer selects a component of an aircraft to adapt, the system has access to the following information: the component affected, any designer input of additional retrieval criteria, and the design itself. This information is used to index into stored records of prior adaptations to suggest adaptations that have been previously performed in similar contexts to address similar issues. Note that this adaptation process does not assume knowledge of complex constraints. DRAMA's method reduces the amount of knowledge that must be encoded, requiring the designer to evaluate the possibilities suggested.

Performing adaptations: The designer may select any of the suggested engines to browse further or to substitute for the engine in the design. The designer may also simply delete or add a component to the representation using the CMap tools. Adaptations of concept maps can be thought of as falling into three general categories corresponding to the support that they require: additions, deletions, and substitutions. DRAMA's framework supports the designer's performance of these operations as follows:

- Additions: The designer may use the hierarchical browser or plain-text retrieval capability to retrieve potentially-relevant components to be linked into the design.
- Deletions: The system can warn of potential deletion issues by proactively retrieving similar deletions, checking them for problems, and presenting those problems to the designer.
- Substitutions: The system can support substitution by retrieving and suggesting candidate substitutions, using both the explicitly-stated criteria and contextual information from the current map to guide the retrieval. It retrieves these from two sources: From stored adaptation cases encapsulating prior substitutions, and from analogous nodes in similar designs.

When the designer states a goal and finds a suitable substitution, the system learns adaptation cases, following research on case-based adaptation learning (Leake *et al.*, 1997; Sycara, 1988). These package the query, information about the CMap that was used as context for the search, and the selected result.

Storing rationale and design cases: After the designer performs a substitution, the designer is prompted to enter an optional textual annotation of why the new alternative is preferable to the old. This question focuses rationale capture: The designer does not record a rationale for the component as a whole (which could involve countless factors), but simply for why it is the *better* component in the current context. Focusing the explanation process in this way is related to the common idea in CBR of aiming explanations at expectation failures (Hammond, 1989; Leake, 1992; Schank, 1982). During future adaptations, this rationale will be provided with other information about the component, and it can also be used as an additional index when retrieving possible substitutions. Adapted cases are placed into the system's hierarchies of cases at the point where the designer found the most similar previous case.

This approach to rationale capture differs strongly from traditional rule-based or model-based approaches. The information in CMaps and additional learned features corresponds to the "weak explanations" advocated by Gruber and Russell (1992), providing just enough information to guide a designer's own reasoning process towards inferring important aspects of the design.

6 Perspective on issues and methods

DRAMA's approach is relevant to a number of fundamental issues for developing practical case-based applications. This section highlights its contributions on addressing these issues.

6.1 Interactive case acquisition

Experience deploying CBR has shown that CBR may require significant "case engineering" effort (Aha and Breslow, 1997; Kitano and Shimazu, 1996; Mark *et al.*, 1996; Voß, 1994). Research CBR systems often use carefully-structured case representations, which enable powerful reasoning at a high knowledge acquisition cost (Kolodner, 1993). At the other end of the spectrum, current projects in *textual case-based reasoning* (Lenz and Ashley, 1998) address how to exploit case information already stored in textual form. For such systems, case acquisition cost is negligible, but exploiting case context is much more difficult.

CMaps provide a middle ground. CMap representations include structural information and are intended to concisely represent key concept properties, facilitating their use by AI systems. However, concept maps do not necessarily use any standard syntax or standard set of attributes. This places them at a middle point between classic structured case representations and purely textual cases. It makes them more difficult to manipulate autonomously within an AI system, but also makes them more flexible if experts use distinctions that were not anticipated, and "forgiving" when non-experts in AI are called upon to encode their knowledge. Domain experts who use the CMap tools seem to have few problems adapting to the concept mapping process.

6.2 Guiding the user towards useful representations

Although users of DRAMA are free to change existing representations or devise new representations if needed, the system uses two methods to help standardize representations. First, when a user draws a CMap and is about to fill in a new link or node, it presents the user with menu of alternatives from previous maps. If one of these is suitable, the user may select it. This builds up a set of standard link types and concept types over time. The second is that the baseline process for generating new design CMaps is modification of previous designs. The system is intended to begin with a set of CMaps that reflect the conceptualizations of a particular expert designer, reflecting that designer's coherent view of the factors important in a design. When new designs are generated by adaptation, significant portions of old representations are reused for new tasks, resulting in representations with similar structure and content. The two approaches facilitate the case engineering task while guiding accumulated design knowledge towards a coherent representation scheme that includes structural information. We intend to perform empirical tests to determine the additional value of the CMap structure, compared to, for example, applying pure information retrieval techniques on the concept map's textual content alone.

6.3 Similarity assessment for semi-structured information

Retrieving candidate design components for making suggestions requires comparing the current concept map to those in memory. Concept maps afford both structural and content information. Link structures can be viewed with or without consideration of their labels (because not all corresponding labels are guaranteed to have been assigned the same names, requiring all names to match may be too strong a constraint). Their structural properties may be compared by, e.g., applying structure-mapping approaches from analogical reasoning (e.g., (Falkenhainer *et al.*, 1989)). The DRAMA system is beginning to address these issues by considering a simple model of structure and content in retrieval.

The current system retrieves candidate design components in a two-stage process: retrieving relevant designs (e.g., designs for similar aircraft) and choosing relevant concepts (e.g., the engines) from those designs. The second step is required because the corresponding roles of concept map designs may not provide direct indications of how the components should be mapped (e.g., whether a link designated "tail engine" in one concept map should correspond with one designated simply "engine" in another).

Given a user-selected component (e.g. a particular engine) to be adapted and the goal of finding other engines from similar designs, DRAMA first retrieves similar designs, using a matching procedure that compares map structure and content (based on the distance of corresponding concepts in hierarchical concept memory), when they are included in the set of concepts. Second, DRAMA chooses the closest matching concept from each of the retrieved maps. Because concept maps lack a rigid semantic structure, the concept is selected both by matching available role structure (an abstraction of the component in question, if available, represents a type of slot to be filled) and by distance in concept memory (where the closest-matching concepts are successively paired). The results are ranked by the inverse of each map's summed distance. This gives an indication of the relative goodness of each design suggestion within the overall pool of suggestions.

Once candidate concepts have been retrieved and displayed, the user can adjust the relative ranking by entering textual descriptions of desired properties. The system compares these with the properties annotating the candidates using simple IR methods. Suggestions for candidates that are supported by similar textual rationale are given added weight in the ranking.

6.4 Interactive indexing and retrieval

Ideally, the CBR retrieval process takes into account both high-level goals and concrete design features. Applied CBR systems tend to rely on the user to explicitly provide this information (whether all at once or incrementally). Conversational case-based reasoning (CCBR) systems guide the retrieval process through an interactive dialogue of questions (Aha and Breslow, 1997). However, because poor questions or question organization may prevent retrieval or slow identification of the right cases, a substantial case engineering effort may be required to craft the set of questions.

DRAMA's alternative approach is to attempt to integrate the CBR process tightly enough into the user's task process that it can infer a substantial part of the needed contextual features directly from monitoring the user's task. The system has access not only to the user's retrieval request (e.g., to find a substitute engine), but also to a significant part of the context surrounding the request that will determine the relevance of the retrieval (e.g., the aircraft for which the engine is needed). The designer may also augment this context with additional information (e.g., that the goal is to find a more fuel-efficient engine that could substitute), but is not required to do so. When the designer does provide information, the system learns new rationale-based indices, by storing the information that the selected substitution is believed to satisfy the designer's constraint. We note that in itself, a feature such as "high fuel efficiency" is not enough to fully specify a retrieval—an airliner designer seeking a high efficiency engine would not consider the high-efficiency engine from a Cessna. In DRAMA, the features stored from designer queries are used only to filter candidates that are already believed to fit the task context.

DRAMA also differs from existing CCBR systems in what it retrieves. Initially, both DRAMA and CCBR systems are aimed at retrieving the most appropriate complete solution from previous cases. However, in its retrieval to support adaptation, DRAMA provides the ability to perform retrievals focused on subparts of the problem for the user to compose. As the user adapts part of the design, the retrieval context changes automatically, loosely corresponding to CCBR systems' adjusted rankings as more information becomes available.

7 Future Directions

The DRAMA system is an ongoing project. The CMap tools are already in use for concept mapping at NASA, and the goal of the project is to test the system in the context of a design project for the next generation of reusable spacecraft. The concrete experience from this test will provide feedback and data to adjust details of the interface, functionality, and indexing algorithms. It will also provide data for conducting controlled tests of the quality of recommendations provided by the system. Because the system lacks the knowledge to evaluate the quality of the designs produced, the designer using the system bears the responsibility of assuring that adaptations are reasonable; the key question is how well the system aids designers in their work. However, knowledge-based tools could be developed to provide some verification, and this would be highly desirable.

Because the CMap tools provide the capability to share CMaps across the World Wide Web, designs from multiple designers and sites can be imported into the system's design process. Work is under way at the University of West Florida to develop CMap facilities for managing concurrent CMap generation and modification. Ideally, the design context for a particular engine, for example, could be updated as other designers make other changes in the specifications.

The system's capability to deal with non-uniform representations is being enhanced by the use of IR methods such as thesaurii to aid matching. In addition to refining the system as an aid to recording and reusing design information, we see a long-term opportunity to apply it to reuse of information about *design processes*. A CMap-style interface could be used to capture traces of the steps used in generating a design (e.g., conceptual design, specification, numerical simulations, etc.), to capture how a design was formulated and to guide reasoning throughout the design process.

8 Conclusions

Our experience with the DRAMA system provides a case study of some central issues for interactive CBR systems. Our integration of CBR with CMaps was motivated by the complexity of aerospace design, for which autonomous intelligent design tools are currently infeasible. However, the framework applies to other design tasks as well. It provides a general "knowledge-light" model for flexible graphically-based case acquisition, manipulation, and reuse.

The DRAMA project has identified a number of principles that we expect to have broad implications for integrations between CBR components and interactive systems:

- Representations should be easily comprehensible and interactively adaptable by end users; visually-based representations may be especially useful.
- Support for representation generation should help assure consistent representations, but must not prevent the users of interactive systems from developing new representations or representational elements when needed.

- CBR's "retrieve and adapt" process to build new cases can facilitate standardization by reusing prior representational components. This can naturally build up the case library and the representational vocabulary in parallel.
- The same types of similarity considerations used to guide retrieval can be used to suggest representational vocabulary as cases are built.
- Retrieval should tolerate representational discrepancies.
- Interactive support systems should be sufficiently integrated into the processes they support to be able to unobtrusively monitor and exploit information about the task context.

The overall conclusion is that interaction must be across all parts of the CBR system—initial knowledge capture, representation, retrieval, and adaptation—and across the larger task. Frameworks that allow the user and system to support each other in a shared task context, building up and using shared knowledge, have the potential to leverage off the strengths and alleviate the weaknesses of both system and user.

References

[Aha and Breslow, 1997] D. Aha and L. Breslow. Refining conversational case libraries. In *Proceedings of the Second International Conference on Case-Based Reasoning*, pages 267–278, Berlin, 1997. Springer Verlag.

[Bagg, 1997] T. Bagg. RECALL: Reusable experience with case-based reasoning for automating lessons learned. http://hope.gsfc.nasa.gov/RECALL/homepg/recall.htm, 1997.

[Cañas *et al.*, 1995] A Cañas, K. Ford, J. Brennan, T. Reichherzer, and P. Hayes. Knowledge construction and sharing in quorum. In *World Conference on Artificial Intelligence in Education*, 1995.

[de Silva Garza and Maher, 1996] A. Gómez de Silva Garza and M. Maher. Design by interactive exploration using memory-based techniques. *Knowledge-Based Systems*, 9(1), 1996.

[Domeshek *et al.*, 1994] E. Domeshek, M. Herndon, A. Bennett, and J. Kolodner. A case-based design aid for conceptual design of aircraft subsystems. In *Proceedings of the Tenth IEEE Conference on Artificial Intelligence for Applications*, pages 63–69, Washington, 1994. IEEE Computer Society Press.

[Falkenhainer *et al.*, 1989] B. Falkenhainer, K. Forbus, and D. Gentner. The structure-mapping engine: Algorithm and examples. *Artificial Intelligence*, 41:1–63, 1989.

[Gebhardt *et al.*, 1997] Friedrich Gebhardt, Angi Voß, Wolfgang Gräther, and Barbara Schmidt-Belz. *Reasoning with complex cases.* Kluwer, Boston, 1997.

[Goel *et al.*, 1991] A. Goel, J. Kolodner, M. Pearce, and R. Billington. Towards a case-based tool for aiding conceptual design problem solving. In R. Bareiss, editor, *Proceedings of the DARPA Case-Based Reasoning Workshop*, pages 109–120, San Mateo, 1991. DARPA, Morgan Kaufmann.

[Gruber and Russell, 1992] Thomas Gruber and Daniel Russell. Generative design rationale: Beyond the record and replay paradigm. Knowledge Systems Laboratory KSL 92-59, Computer Science Department, Stanford University, 1992.

[Hammond, 1989] K. Hammond. *Case-Based Planning: Viewing Planning as a Memory Task.* Academic Press, San Diego, 1989.

[Hinkle and Toomey, 1995] D. Hinkle and C. Toomey. Applying case-based reasoning to manufacturing. *AI Magazine*, 16(1):65–73, Spring 1995.

[Hua and Faltings, 1993] K. Hua and B. Faltings. Exploring case-based design - CADRE. *Artificial Intelligence in Engineering Design, Analysis and Manufacturing*, 7(2):135–144, 1993.

[Jonassen *et al.*, 1993] David Jonassen, Katherine Beissner, and Michael Yacci. *Explicit methods for conveying structural knowledge through concept maps*, chapter 15, page 155. Erlbaum, Hillsdale, NJ, 1993.

[Kitano and Shimazu, 1996] H. Kitano and H. Shimazu. The experience sharing architecture: A case study in corporate-wide case-based software quality control. In D. Leake, editor, *Case-Based Reasoning: Experiences, Lessons, and Future Directions*, pages 235–268. AAAI Press, Menlo Park, CA, 1996.

[Kolodner, 1993] J. Kolodner. *Case-Based Reasoning.* Morgan Kaufmann, San Mateo, CA, 1993.

[Leake *et al.*, 1997] David Leake, Andrew Kinley, and David Wilson. A case study of case-based CBR. In *Proceedings of the Second International Conference on Case-Based Reasoning*, pages 371–382, Berlin, 1997. Springer Verlag.

[Leake, 1992] D. Leake. *Evaluating Explanations: A Content Theory.* Lawrence Erlbaum, Hillsdale, NJ, 1992.

[Lenz and Ashley, 1998] M. Lenz and K. Ashley, editors. *Proceedings of the AAAI-98 workshop on textual case-based reasoning.* AAAI Press, Menlo Park, CA, 1998.

[Mark *et al.*, 1996] William Mark, Evangelos Simoudis, and David Hinkle. Case-based reasoning: Expectations and results. In D. Leake, editor, *Case-Based Reasoning: Experiences, Lessons, and Future Directions*, pages 269–294. AAAI Press, Menlo Park, CA, 1996.

[Novak and Gowin, 1984] J.D. Novak and D.B. Gowin. *Learning How to Learn.* Cambridge University Press, New York, 1984.

[Schank, 1982] R.C. Schank. *Dynamic Memory: A Theory of Learning in Computers and People.* Cambridge University Press, Cambridge, England, 1982.

[Smith *et al.*, 1995] I. Smith, C. Lottaz, and B. Faltings. Spatial composition using cases: IDIOM. In *Proceedings of First International Conference on Case-Based Reasoning*, pages 88–97, Berlin, October 1995. Springer Verlag.

[Sycara, 1988] K. Sycara. Using case-based reasoning for plan adaptation and repair. In J. Kolodner, editor, *Proceedings of the DARPA Case-Based Reasoning Workshop*, pages 425–434, San Mateo, CA, 1988. Morgan Kaufmann.

[Vollrath, 1998] I. Vollrath. Reuse of complex electronic designs: Requirements analysis for a CBR application. In P. Cunningham, B. Smyth, and M. Keane, editors, *Proceedings of the Fourth European Workshop on Case-Based Reasoning*, pages 136–147, Berlin, 1998. Springer Verlag.

[Voß, 1994] A. Voß. The need for knowledge acquisition in case-based reasoning – some experiences from an architectural domain. In *Proceedings of the Eleventh European Conference on Artificial Intelligence*, pages 463–467. John Wiley, 1994.

[Wilke *et al.*, 1997] W. Wilke, I. Vollrath, K.-D. Althoff, and R. Bergmann. A framework for learning adaptation knowedge based on knowledge light approaches. In *Proceedings of the Fifth German Workshop on Case-Based Reasoning*, 1997.

When Experience Is Wrong: Examining CBR for Changing Tasks and Environments*

David B. Leake and David C. Wilson

Computer Science Department
Indiana University, Lindley Hall
150 S. Woodlawn Ave
Bloomington, IN 47405, U.S.A.
{leake,davwils}@cs.indiana.edu

Abstract. Case-based problem-solving systems reason and learn from experiences, building up case libraries of problems and solutions to guide future reasoning. The expected benefits of this learning process depend on two types of regularity: (1) *problem-solution regularity,* the relationship between problem-to-problem and solution-to-solution similarity measures that assures that solutions to similar prior problems are a useful starting point for solving similar current problems, and (2) *problem-distribution regularity,* the relationship between old and new problems that assures that the case library will contain cases similar to the new problems it encounters. Unfortunately, these types of regularity are not assured. Even in contexts for which initial regularity is sufficient, problems may arise if a system's users, tasks, or external environment change over time. This paper defines criteria for assessing the two types of regularity, discusses how the definitions may be used to assess the need for case-base maintenance, and suggests maintenance approaches for responding to those needs. In particular, it discusses the role of analysis of performance over time in responding to environmental changes.

1 Introduction

Case-based reasoning (CBR) solves new problems by retrieving stored cases encapsulating records of similar problems, and adapting their lessons to fit the new circumstances. Case-based problem-solving is based on two central premises about the regularity of the problem-solver's world (e.g., Kolodner, p. 8). The first, which we call *problem-solution regularity,* describes the relationship between problem descriptions and solutions that assures that similar problems have similar solutions. This regularity is needed to guarantee that cases for

* The authors' research is supported in part by NASA under award No NCC 2-1035. The authors are currently on leave at the Computer Science Department of Northwestern University and gratefully acknowledge its support. The authors also thank the anonymous reviewers for their helpful comments.

similar prior problems are likely to be useful starting points for new reasoning. The second, which we call *problem-distribution regularity,* describes the relationship between new problems and those previously encountered. This regularity is needed to assure that the system will have the cases it needs for the problems it is called upon to solve.

The successes of numerous CBR systems bear out that for many tasks and domains, appropriate similarity metrics can be devised to provide sufficient problem-solution regularity, and that problem-distribution regularity is often sufficient to enable effective CBR. Unfortunately, no matter how good initial similarity metrics might be for a given task and domain, and no matter how complete a case library a system may build up, changes in task and domain characteristics may render obsolete prior similarity criteria or cases. Developers have cited the problem of dealing with changing task characteristics as the reason for rejecting CBR for some tasks (Talebzadeh *et al.*, 1995), and the long-term use of CBR systems makes such changes increasingly likely during a system's lifetime. In order to perform as well as possible despite changing circumstances, a CBR system must be able to evaluate how well the regularity assumptions apply and to signal the need for maintenance or to invoke its own maintenance strategies as needed.

This paper presents initial steps towards understanding and responding to deviations from desired regularities. First, it defines measures that can be used to calculate the amount of problem-solution regularity and problem-distribution regularity that exist for the problem sequences that a system encounters. Second, the paper discusses methods that may be used to respond to, and (ideally) to exploit changing characteristics of the problems the CBR system solves and of the environment in which its solutions must be applied.

In particular, the paper describes opportunities for maintenance strategies that perform their changes based on analysis of problem-solving and case-base characteristics over time—*diachronic case-base maintenance strategies* as described in (Leake and Wilson, 1998). In general, determining the right response to shifting context requires knowledge that is unlikely to be available from a single snapshot of the CBR system's state. However, by examining *trends* in retrieval performance, system errors, and presented problems, the system may be able to respond more effectively.

2 Defining Regularities for Case-Based Reasoning

It is well-known in the CBR community that case-based reasoning depends on two relationships: the relationship between *similarity of problems* and *similarity of solutions*, and the relationship between *prior problems* (solved by the system or provided as seed cases) and *new problems.* However, to our knowledge, there are not yet precise definitions of what these relationships mean. Such definitions would be useful to quantify and compare the relationships in order to understand the effects of different similarity metrics, case bases, and problem sequences on the performance of different CBR systems. Equally important, such definitions give criteria for monitoring the appropriateness of a system's similarity criteria and case library for dealing with current problems, in order to identify the need for system maintenance. This section proposes working definitions as a basis for future discussion and study.

2.1 Basic assumptions and definitions

Throughout our definitions, we will make some standard assumptions. First, we assume that there is a fixed CBR system that processes problems in a problem space P and that the solutions for these problems are elements of a solution space S. Cases are pairs $(p, s) \in C = P \times S$, the set of all possible cases. The system begins with a finite "seed" case base $B_1 \subseteq C$. As the system is used, it processes a sequence of problems Q $= p_i, p_{i+1}, \ldots, p_j$, where each $p_k \in P$ for $k = i, \ldots, j$. We define the sequence to start with an arbitrary index because, as we discuss in section 8.2, it is sometimes useful to consider the subsequence that starts after some initial set of problems has been processed.

Adding to the case base: We assume that after each problem is processed and the resulting solution has been evaluated, a new case with the problem and its correct solution are added to the case base. This means that each problem p_k is processed using an updated case base B_k that includes the results of previous processing. Note that this does not imply that the system can solve all problems presented to it: The correct stored solution may be based on external feedback if the system generates an incorrect solution or fails to generate a solution.

How problem distance guides retrieval: The CBR system uses a "problem distance" function $PDist : P \times C \rightarrow [0, \infty)$ to measure the distance between a new problem and the problem description of a stored case. $PDist(p, c)$ is zero if p is the same problem solved by c. Given a new problem, the CBR system retrieves the case closest to that problem according to $PDist$. However, there is no guarantee that the case considered closest by this function will actually be "close" to the problem in any useful way. This function simply reflects the similarity metric built into the system, whether or not it is useful.

How usefulness of retrievals is judged: The evaluator of the system uses a "real distance" function $RDist : P \times C \rightarrow [0, \infty)$ to measure how far the solution in a case is from the solution for a given problem. This function measures the usefulness of retrieved solutions according to the evaluator's goals for the retrieval process, which may not be classic "similarity." For example, if the evaluator's primary goal is to minimize the adaptation time required to generate a new solution, "real distance" could be measured in adaptation time: $RDist(p, c)$ could be the time to adapt the solution from case c to solve problem p, with some upper limit on the amount of time allowed. $RDist$ could also be defined to reflect other retrieval goals. For example, if reliability of adaptation is an issue, it could consider cases "closer" to a problem if they can be adapted to solve the problem using more reliable adaptations (regardless of adaptation time).

We stress that *RDist* does not necessarily correspond to any function within the CBR system; it is an external criterion. For example, *RDist* might be calculated off-line to determine the retrievals the CBR system *should have* made. Thus efficiency of calculating the *RDist* function is comparatively unimportant. It might be possible, for example, to calculate *RDist* for adaptability by simply adapting all stored cases to the new problem and seeing which adaptation was fastest.

In an ideal CBR system, the cases with the closest *problems* (according to *PDist*) would also have the closest *solutions* (according to *RDist*). In practice, of course, the actual similarity metric is likely to differ from the ideal (see Smyth and Keane, 1996, for an empirical demonstration). In some situations the deviations may be substantial enough to impair system performance.

2.2 Defining problem-solution regularity

The goal of our definition of problem-solution regularity is to capture how well *PDist* approximates *RDist* in practice. Because this depends on the specific context in which the CBR system is solving problems, our definition explicitly depends on:

- the goals for retrieval (as captured by *RDist*),
- the set of seed cases available to the system, and
- the problem sequence that the system is called upon to solve.

As background for our definition, for any input problem, we can calculate two sets of cases according to the formulas below. The first set of cases, which we designate by CCP for *Closest Cases to Problem*, contains all the cases within a case base B whose problem descriptions are closest to the input problem. The second, which we designate by RCC for *Real Closest Cases*, contains the cases whose solutions are within a user-specified neighborhood of the optimal solution. The size of the neighborhood is determined by a user-specified non-negative parameter ϵ.

$$CCP(PDist, p, B) = \{c \in B | PDist(p, c) = min_{c' \in B} PDist(p, c')\} \quad (1)$$

$$RCC(RDist, p, B, \epsilon) = \{c \in B | RDist(p, c) \leq min_{c' \in B} RDist(p, c') + \epsilon\} \quad (2)$$

If $\epsilon = 0$, RCC returns the optimal cases for solving the problem according to the "real" distance metric.

We let B_k designate the case library used when processing problem p_k. This case library contains the initial seed cases and all the new cases added to the case base processing problems before p_k. Following the notion of *precision* in information retrieval, we then define:

$$SimPrecision(PDist, RDist, p_k, B_k, \epsilon) = \frac{CCP(PDist, p_k, B_k) \cap RCC(RDist, p_k, B_k, \epsilon)}{CCP(PDist, p_k, B_k)} \quad (3)$$

This function measures the probability that a case returned as optimal by the similarity function will actually be within ϵ of an optimal case.[1]

Given these definitions, we define the problem-solution regularity as the average *SimPrecision* over the problem sequence Q, starting with case base B_i, as follows:

$$ProbSolnReg(PDist, RDist, Q, B_i, \epsilon) = \qquad (4)$$
$$\frac{\Sigma_{k=i,\ldots,j} SimPrecision(PDist, RDist, p_k, B_k, \epsilon)}{j-i+1}$$

When ϵ is set to 0, this function calculates the average probability that a case for a maximally-similar problem will actually be optimal. With non-zero values for ϵ, this function provides information about the average probability that a maximally-similar problem (according to the system's similarity metric) will be acceptably close to a maximally useful case, which determines the quality of the similarity metric.

We note that when *ProbSolnReg* is used to compare the problem-solution regularity of different systems, *RDist* must be same for both systems. If different systems have different "real" costs (e.g., because of differences in adaptation capabilities), differences in the values of *ProbSolnReg* for the two systems may not predict their relative performances.

2.3 Defining problem-distribution regularity

The second regularity assumption of CBR is that new problems will tend to resemble the problems addressed in previous cases (either in the seed case base, or in cases learned during prior processing). We call this ***problem-distribution regularity***. It determines the likelihood that, as new problems are processed (and new cases with their solutions are added to the seed case base), the case base will contain cases for similar problems. When the case base does contain similar problems, and when (in addition) there is sufficient problem-solution regularity, this will result in retrieval of cases whose solutions are close to the actual solutions according to *RDist*.

ProbDistReg calculates the percentage of cases in a problem sequence $Q = p_i, ..., p_j$ for which there are sufficiently close cases in the current case bases B_k built up from the seed case base B_i, according to a user-specified distance limit $\epsilon \geq 0$.

$$ProbDistReg(Q, B_i, \epsilon) = \qquad (5)$$
$$\frac{1}{j-i+1} * \Sigma_{k=i,\ldots,j} \begin{cases} 1, \text{If } min_{c \in B_k} PDist(p_k, c) < \epsilon \\ 0, \text{Otherwise} \end{cases}$$

[1] Because we assume that the system will reason from a single most similar case, the IR notion of *recall* is not relevant here. It would be relevant if, e.g., the system attempted to increase reliability by generating and comparing solutions starting from multiple cases.

Together, *ProbSolnReg* and *ProbDistReg* provide measures that describe the performance of a CBR system. Individually, each one identifies problems that can be addressed by either refining the similarity metric or the solutions stored in cases (for *ProbSolnReg*) or by adding to the case library (for *ProbDistReg*).

3 Perspective on Regularity-Related Research

In this section we consider the importance of the regularities and compare our perspective to related research; in the following sections we look at its practical application.

Work on Problem-Solution Regularity: The importance of problem-solution regularity underlies the considerable attention to similarity criteria in CBR research. Faltings (1997) uses probability theory to prove that for prediction tasks, the assumption that a problem with similar features to an earlier one is likely to have a similar solution is guaranteed to be true on average. The issue of how to define practical similarity metrics for particular tasks remains a central research focus of the field, making it useful to have criteria for comparing different similarity metrics.

Recent CBR work has developed methods for making retrieval criteria explicitly reflect the underlying "true" retrieval criterion that we have called *RDist*. A primary example is adaptation-guided retrieval (Smyth and Keane, 1996), which replaces the traditional similarity criterion with estimated cost of adaptation, in order to retrieve cases that satisfy the goal of easy adaptation.

Work on Problem-Distribution Regularity: The key question of problem-distribution regularity is whether the case library will contain the cases a system needs to solve the problems it encounters. The importance of problem-distribution regularity is recognized by developers of CBR applications, who attempt to gather representative and well-distributed sets of cases for their systems (e.g., (Kriegsman and Barletta, 1993; Watson, 1997)).

Recent work on case-base competence (Smyth and McKenna, 1998; Zhu and Yang, 1998) has developed methods for estimating the range of problems that can be solved by a system with a given case-base. The purpose of this work is to assure that problem-solution regularity is sufficient, to give an indication of the likely system success rate, and to help identify regions of the case base in which additional cases may be needed.

Problem-distribution regularity is closely related to case-base competence, but our work differs from that work in two ways. The first difference concerns the role of problem distribution. Analysis of case-base competence assumes a uniform distribution of problems in order to make analysis more tractable. Likewise, it is customary for empirical evaluations of CBR systems to use a randomly-generated set of problems uniformly distributed in the problem space (e.g., (Veloso, 1994)). However, our definition explicitly references the particular problem sequence on which the behavior is measured. While we agree with Smyth and McKenna (1998) that assuming a uniform distribution can provide a very useful overall view, considering specific details of problem presentation order and distribution can be useful as well. For example, the quality of a CBR system's performance can depend strongly on the order of case presentation (Fox, 1995; Redmond, 1992), making it desirable for the formulas to be usable for exploring the effects of different orderings. Likewise, as we discuss later in this paper, if the system can identify "hot spots" in case-base accesses, examining problem distribution regularity may make it possible to reorganize the case base to speed likely retrievals, or to delete (or deactivate, e.g., by placing in secondary storage) cases that are not being used.

Second, our definition of problem-distribution regularity depends on a user-defined threshold for what constitute sufficiently similar stored cases, rather than considering only whether the problem can or cannot be solved. Using a user-defined criterion for whether a stored case is "close enough," rather than simply whether *some* solution can be generated, is important when the quality of solutions depends on the amount of adaptation performed, or when there are changeable limits on the amount of effort that can be expended on adaptations. For example, in some domains, available domain theories are strong enough for local adaptations but are not sufficiently reliable for more substantial changes (e.g., Cheetham and Graf, 1997).

Work on Case-Base Maintenance: Many researchers are examining issues in *case-base maintenance* (CBM) for improving the performance of CBR systems (for an overview, see Leake and Wilson, 1998). CBM research addresses issues such as assuring that the cases in the case base cover the space of possible problems (Smyth and McKenna, 1998; Zhu and Yang, 1998) and deleting superfluous cases to improve space efficiency or utility of retrieval (Smyth and Keane, 1995). These do not address, however, how to maintain the case-base in response to specific task needs—for example, to build coverage in precisely those areas that tend to arise in current problems—or how to predict the need for future maintenance from current problems, in order to proactively revise the case base before problems occur. Salganicoff (1997) has studied the problem of learning time-varying functions in instance-based learning, and proposes a method based on de-activating old instances when similar new ones are available, and selectively re-activating those that are consistent with new data. Ideally, augmenting CBR systems with the ability to detect regularity problems and respond to problem trends will improve their ability to avoid future failures and organize their case bases for efficient access.

4 Calculating the Regularity Values

In order to apply the formulas to trigger maintenance, practical means are needed to calculate their values. Because *ProbDistReg* depends only on the levels of similarity between new problems and the cases retrieved to deal with them (which are available as a byproduct of normal processing), *ProbDistReg* can be calculated easily.

On the other hand, calculating *ProbSolnReg* is problematic, because calculating *RDist* requires complete information about the "right" retrievals. (If this information could be calculated inexpensively at retrieval time, the system could always make perfect retrievals.) Nevertheless, it is sometimes possible to take advantage of information available after a problem is solved to estimate whether the right case was retrieved. The ROBBIE system (Fox and Leake, 1995), for example, detects problems in its similarity criteria by first solving the current problem, and then using the solution as the index for another retrieval, to determine if the solution from another case is more similar to the final result. If so, perfect similarity criteria would have favored that case, so the failure to retrieve it shows a flaw in problem-solution regularity.[2]

Alternatively, ProbSolnReg calculations could be done off-line at times when high processing cost is acceptable, to trigger off-line maintenance to improve future on-line performance.

5 Using the Formulas as Maintenance Triggers

The previous definitions provide a basis for judging the levels of regularity for particular systems, case bases, and problem sequences. By monitoring the levels of regularity and their changes, it is possible to identify needs for maintenance. For example,

- When problem-solution similarity falls below acceptable levels, it may signal:
  - Failure of the similarity metric to capture features that have become important in predicting *RDist* for current problems (e.g, if a route planner does not consider the direction of old paths when doing retrieval, and is called upon to plan paths in a new area with many one-way streets).
  - Changes in the problem-solving environment that require adjusting the solutions that would have applied to the same problems in the past, so that *RDist* itself has changed and *PDist* must be adjusted to be consistent (e.g, if roads have been closed, blocking paths that would previously have been successful).
- When problem-distribution regularity falls below acceptable levels, it may signal:
  - Insufficient case coverage of the current problems (additional cases would increase the chance of having one available within the acceptable neighborhood).

[2] This approach does not apply to all domains, however. For example, if solutions are a single numeric value, the fact that a case in memory happens to have the correct value may be coincidental. If a CBR system estimates the price of a bunch of carrots based on the price of a bunch bought the week before, even if its estimate is wrong it is probably not appropriate to adjust its similarity to consider the carrots more similar to a light bulb that happens to cost precisely the correct amount.

  • Flawed or insufficient adaptation knowledge (improving adaptation knowledge would increase the size of the neighborhood of cases that is usable).
- When problem-distribution regularity is high for a subset of the case base, it may signal:
  • A "hot spot" in the case base (which enables reorganizing the case base to facilitate access to active regions, or deactivating cases from less frequently used regions.)

6 Determining How to Respond: The Role of Diachronic Analysis

Once a regularity problem has been found, it is necessary to select strategies for responding. Normally, CBR systems consider only the current problem and state of the case base when responding to processing failures (e.g., by revising the indices for a case or storing a new case with the correct solution). However, considering trends in problems may enable better response strategies. For example, knowing that problem-solution regularity has dropped from acceptable levels to a current unacceptable level is more informative than simply knowing that the level is unacceptable, because a change in performance must be caused by changes in either the problem distribution or the environment. For example, if a system for estimating building costs consistently generates estimates that are too low, that trend suggests that a general change is needed to prevent that class of failures in the future.

One response strategy is to simply update the cases in the case base (e.g., increasing the recorded prices), but this may lose useful historical information. It may also require monitoring the update history and ages of cases, in order to make sure that all cases are updated properly. Another alternative is to keep the values of cases unchanged, but to add a "lazy" maintenance rule to adjust case solutions after they have been retrieved (Leake and Wilson, 1998)).

Leake and Wilson (1998) describe a class of maintenance strategies that collect data over time, over a sequence of snapshots of system processing, in order to identify trends in how case-base contents and usage are changing. They call policies based on analyzing the performance of the case-base over time *diachronic maintenance policies.* Diachronic analysis is useful, for example, for determining whether coverage problems—shown by low problem-distribution regularity—should prompt the search for additional cases. If problem-distribution regularity shows an *increasing trend*, showing that the cases being processed are filling the important regions of the case base, it may suffice to simply let the normal case learning process fill the case base. However, if the level of problem-distribution regularity is low and stable, or even decreasing, steps must be taken to increase the coverage of the case library.

Diachronic analysis is also useful to find and exploit trends in problems presented to the case base. If the problems that the system must solve consistently fall within a small neighborhood, it may suggest that the system should exploit the locality of the "hot spot" by reorganizing the case base to make cases in that region easier to access. In a distributed case base, cases in the hot spot are candidates for pre-fetching. If space limitations require that some cases be deleted, for efficiency reasons the system should also focus competence-preserving deletion (Smyth and Keane, 1995) on regions other than the hot spot, in order to minimize adaptation cost on likely problems by keeping the active regions more densely populated with nearby cases.

Finally, diachronic analysis is useful for monitoring and guiding the maintenance process itself: The history of maintenance operations applied will affect choices of which operations *should* be applied. For example, if maintenance has just added a large set of cases to the case base to improve problem-distribution regularity, the choice of whether to search for still more cases should be determined by observing the effects of the new cases over some period of time, rather than simply based on the value of $ProbDistReg$ as soon as the next input problem is processed.

7 Tools for Trend Detection

Performing diachronic maintenance requires methods for detecting underlying trends in sequences of values over time. Trend detection for numeric values can be done by a number of statistical techniques. These include simple methods such as linear regression models that attempt to find the equation of the line that best fits the data as well as time series analysis techniques such as autoregressive moving averages (ARMA) and autoregressive integrated moving averages (ARIMA). Research in machine learning has studied "concept drift," in which hidden changes in context over time cause learned experiences to become inaccurate (e.g., Salganicoff, 1997). A number of techniques have been applied to concept drift problems in time ordered domains for learning hidden context (Harries *et al.*, 1998; Lane and Brodley, 1998), and could be applied to adjusting similarity criteria when problem-solution regularity becomes insufficient due to concept drift.

8 Two Examples: Error Trends and Hot Spots

In this section we illustrate the usefulness of trend-based reasoning for responding to drops in problem-solution regularity and to patterns in problem distribution.

8.1 Addressing Solution Error Trends:

As a simple example of the use of trend detection, we show how regression techniques can augment a case-based price estimating system, in order to make its predictions more robust despite inflation. Trend-based corrections are triggered by drops in problem-solution regularity: When the solutions predicted based on similar prior problems are no longer close to the real solutions determined by feedback to the program, maintenance is performed. The method we describe is still primarily case-based, rather than regression-based: Detected trends influence case adaptation, but the primary information source is still cases.

As our case data changing over time, we selected a college summary from the magazine *U.S. News and World Report.*[3] The data we used included information on 1302 colleges, with 28 features for each one (e.g., enrollment, student test scores, etc.). The task was to predict tuition costs. Because multi-year data was not available, we simulated the increase as a normal distribution of increases around an annual inflation rate.

We used the following simple strategy for detecting and responding to error trends. The system records and monitors the percent errors between retrieved cases and evaluations. A cumulative error level is maintained by summing successive error percentages, with the expectation that accumulated percent errors due to random fluctuations (both positive and negative) will remain below a reasonable threshold magnitude. If the activation level persists above the threshold value for a specified amount of time, the system triggers a statistical analysis for possible underlying error trends. In the current system, the percentage error trend is approximated by performing a simple linear regression analysis on the sequence of error data. A maintenance rule is then installed that uses the computed regression line to forecast the percentage error for the current year and modifies cases according to the predicted error value as they are retrieved.

Experiments used query samples of 5 to 20 probes from the case set for each year over a 10 to 20 year span, selecting queries by two methods. The first method constructed a random problem distribution by selecting query cases at random. The second method constructed a highly regular problem distribution by restricting the query population to a set of similar instances, according to the system's similarity metric. The samples were used as probes in their respective years, over the varying year spans. The underlying annual inflation rate was varied in separate experiments between 2 and 5 percent for each year, which fluctuated according to a random normal distribution to represent yearly variations. Average error rates were measured for the baseline (no learning), case learning alone, maintenance alone, and combined case learning/maintenance. Each experiment was repeated 10 times, each time re-selecting the query sample, to obtain results on average.

While the results did not give a clear picture of how adjustments in individual parameters affected the outcomes, a general picture did emerge. With a random problem distribution, case learning performed better than the baseline, trend-based maintenance performed better than case learning, and the combination gave equivalent or better results. With the regularized problem distribution, the combination performed best, followed by case learning, then maintenance, and finally the baseline. A representative trial with an inflation rate of 2 percent over 15 years and sample size of 5 queries/year gave the following results. The randomized distribution showed average errors of 18 percent in the baseline, 17 percent in case learning, and 14 percent in both maintenance and combined trials. The regularized distribution showed average errors of 18 percent in the

[3] Available from http://lib.stat.cmu.edu/datasets/.

baseline, 14 percent with maintenance, 13 percent with case learning, and 12 percent in the combined trials.

The experiments point to some interesting observations. First, they suggest that maintaining existing cases can be as effective as learning new cases, and that augmenting case learning with diachronic maintenance can be beneficial. Second, it is worth noting that the individual trials of maintenance alone produced highly consistent results, while the individual trials involving case learning fluctuated a great deal in producing the average. This may indicate that detecting general trends is a more stable method of dealing with change over time than case learning. Third, we note that typical problem distributions will likely fall somewhere between the extremes of uniform sampling (where maintenance strategies alone were better than case learning) and highly focused sampling (where case learning worked better). Consequently, more experiments will be required to determine the interplay of the two along varying levels of problem-distribution regularity.

8.2 Addressing Hot Spots

A second potential use of trend detection is to respond to "hot spots" in the case base. In practice, case accesses are often non-uniform. For example, a primary motivation for the development of the GizmoTapper CBR support system for Broderbund computer games was to aid the Broderbund help desk in handling the increased queries it received soon after Christmas (Watson, 1997). The problem patterns for any domain are likely to be strongly domain-specific, but if those patterns can be detected automatically the system may be able to optimize access to information that is likely to be in demand.

To observe query distribution patterns in a real-world information source, we gathered data on accesses to Indiana University web pages for various online information repositories. These pages provide academic information (e.g., requirements for the BA degree) as well as homework assignments, etc. A sampling of access results for a year of logs are shown in Figure 1, with each band reflecting the total accesses to files within the directory. (Numbers of accesses are normalized to show the percent of maximum accesses per month from January 1998 to February, 1999. Patterns that might not have been expected (but that are easily explainable) emerge. For example, department academics pages are heavily accessed in the Fall (presumably by new students), but less frequently accessed in the Spring, as students become familiar with policies, and seldom in the summer. Pages for classes offered in Spring and Fall reflect that in their accesses. Temporal patterns are not always present—no pattern is apparent in the "Types Forum" accesses at the front of the graph—but there appears to be considerable regularity.

Various methods could be used to detect or predict hot spots, such as clustering on the problems processed, predicting problem distributions from a model of the task the CBR system serves (if available), or collecting user profiles that associate users with particular access patterns. Once a hot spot has been hypothesized, the problem-distribution regularity formula can be applied to measure the adequacy of its coverage. Insufficient coverage is a sign to examine the current

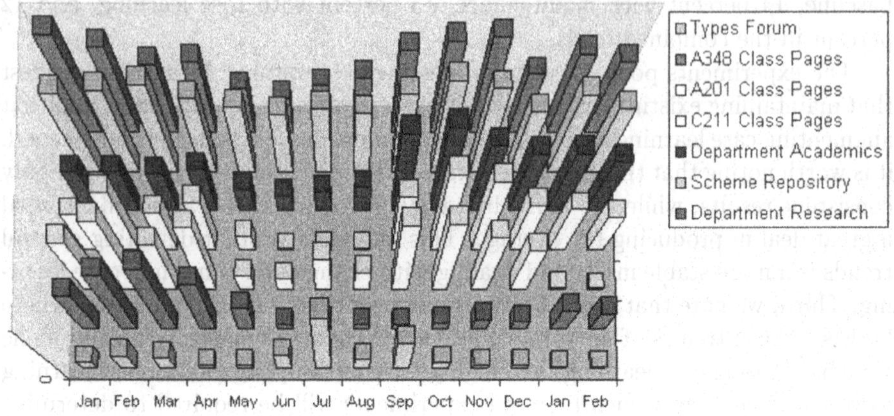

Fig. 1. Web page accesses by month.

problem sequence for new hot spots. We are preparing an experiment to compare different hot spot detection strategies for different input problem sequences.

9 Considerations for costs and benefits

The processes described here depend on processing steps that increase the overhead of the CBR system, such as processes for trend detection and for reorganizing the case base in response to hot spots. More study must be done on the costs involved, but there may be important mitigating factors. First, trend analysis can be done off-line, when the system is otherwise idle. Second, in interactive CBR systems, cost and benefit analysis must weigh not only the costs incurred by the system, but also those avoided by the user. If trend analysis can, for example, warn the user of environmental changes that render prior cases obsolete, the real-world benefits may be substantial (e.g., for a realtor setting the price of a house). This may counterbalance increased computation costs.

10 Conclusions

The definitions presented here are useful for three reasons. First, they delineate the factors that affect regularity assumptions for CBR and their relationships—that regularity is not a property of the system or world individually but of the relationship between task, system, and the external world. Second, they provide a quantitative criterion for comparing the performance of particular CBR systems. Third, and most important for this paper, is that by giving standards for measuring regularity, they also give standards for detecting changes that require maintenance.

As CBR systems are more widely fielded for long-term use, it will become necessary to monitor both problem-solution regularity and problem-distribution regularity assumptions and to respond intelligently when they fail. This paper provides a practical starting point for how to detect and respond to situations in which the reuse of experiences goes wrong.

References

[Cheetham and Graf, 1997] W. Cheetham and J. Graf. Case-based reasoning in color matching. In *Proceedings of the Second International Conference on Case-Based Reasoning*, pages 1–12, Berlin, 1997. Springer Verlag.

[Faltings, 1997] Boi Faltings. Probabilistic indexing for case-based prediction. In *Proceedings of the Second International Conference on Case-Based Reasoning*, pages 611–622, Berlin, 1997. Springer Verlag.

[Fox and Leake, 1995] S. Fox and D. Leake. Using introspective reasoning to refine indexing. In *Proceedings of the Thirteenth International Joint Conference on Artificial Intelligence*, pages 391–397, San Francisco, CA, August 1995. Morgan Kaufmann.

[Fox, 1995] S. Fox. *Introspective Reasoning for Case-based Planning.* PhD thesis, Indiana University, 1995. Computer Science Department.

[Harries *et al.*, 1998] M. Harries, K. Horn, and C. Sammut. Learning in time ordered domains with hidden changes in context. In *Papers from the AAAI 1998 Workshop on Predicting the Future: AI Approaches to Time-Series Problems*, pages 29–33. AAAI, 1998.

[Kolodner, 1993] J. Kolodner. *Case-Based Reasoning.* Morgan Kaufmann, San Mateo, CA, 1993.

[Kriegsman and Barletta, 1993] M. Kriegsman and R. Barletta. Building a case-based help desk application. *IEEE Expert*, 8(6):18–26, December 1993.

[Lane and Brodley, 1998] T. Lane and C. Brodley. Approaches to online learning and concept drift for user identification in computer security. In *Papers from the AAAI 1998 Workshop on Predicting the Future: AI Approaches to Time-Series Problems*, pages 64–70. AAAI, 1998.

[Leake and Wilson, 1998] D. Leake and D. Wilson. Case-base maintenance: Dimensions and directions. In P. Cunningham, B. Smyth, and M. Keane, editors, *Proceedings of the Fourth European Workshop on Case-Based Reasoning*, pages 196–207, Berlin, 1998. Springer Verlag.

[Redmond, 1992] M. Redmond. *Learning by Observing and Understanding Expert Problem Solving.* PhD thesis, College of Computing, Georgia Institute of Technology, 1992. Technical report GIT-CC-92/43.

[Salganicoff, 1997] M. Salganicoff. Tolerating concept and sampling shift in lazy learning using prediction error context switching. *Artificial Intelligence Review*, 11(1-5):133–155, 1997.

[Smyth and Keane, 1995] B. Smyth and M. Keane. Remembering to forget: A competence-preserving case deletion policy for case-based reasoning systems. In *Proceedings of the Thirteenth International Joint Conference on Artificial Intelligence*, pages 377–382, Montreal, August 1995. IJCAI.

[Smyth and Keane, 1996] B. Smyth and M. Keane. Design à la Déjà Vu: Reducing the adaptation overhead. In D. Leake, editor, *Case-Based Reasoning: Experiences, Lessons, and Future Directions.* AAAI Press, Menlo Park, CA, 1996.

[Smyth and McKenna, 1998] B. Smyth and E. McKenna. Modelling the competence of case-bases. In P. Cunningham, B. Smyth, and M. Keane, editors, *Proceedings of the Fourth European Workshop on Case-Based Reasoning*, pages 208–220, Berlin, 1998. Springer Verlag.

[Talebzadeh *et al.*, 1995] Houman Talebzadeh, Sanda Mandutianu, and Christian Winner. Countrywide loan-underwriting expert system. *AI Magazine*, 16(1):51–64, 1995.

[Veloso, 1994] M. Veloso. *Planning and Learning by Analogical Reasoning.* Springer Verlag, Berlin, 1994.

[Watson, 1997] Ian Watson. *Applying Case-Based Reasoning: Techniques for Enterprise Systems.* Morgan Kaufmann, San Francisco, 1997.

[Zhu and Yang, 1998] J. Zhu and Q. Yang. Remembering to add: Competence-preserving case-addition policies for case based reasoning. 1998.

Case Library Reduction Applied to Pile Foundations

Celestino Lei[1], Otakar Babka[1], and Laurinda A. G. Garanito[2]

[1] Faculty of Science and Technology, University of Macau
P.O. Box 3001, Macau (via Hong Kong)
Ph.: +853 3974 471, Fax: +853 838 314
babka@umac.mo, m986218@sftw.umac.mo

[2] Laboratório de Engenharia Civil de Macau
Rua da Sé, 30, Macau
Ph.: +853 343 372
laurin48@macau.ctm.net

Abstract. The case-based reasoning paradigm is applied in support of decision making processes related to pile foundations. Based on this paradigm, the system accumulates experience from previously realized pile foundations. This experience can be drawn when new situations with similar attributes of geotechnical situation of the site and geometric characteristics of the piles are encountered. Two case libraries were created based on previously realized sites. The representativeness of the case libraries and the efficiency of the search process are facilitated by the use of a genetic algorithm reduction.

1 Introduction

The Case-Based Reasoning (CBR) paradigm facilitates the effective reuse of previously accepted results [1], [2], [3], [4].

In the presented research, this paradigm is applied to support any decision concerning the structure of pile foundations of construction sites. Objectives of case library representativeness are discussed in the next paragraph, followed by discussion about weight-setting and reduction methods. The reduction method chosen for the application is based on *Genetic Algorithms* (GA) [5], [6], [7], [8], briefly discussed in a subsequent part of the paper. The application of this paradigm to *pile foundations* is studied afterwards, together with the results of the reduction.

2 Representativeness of Case Libraries

Case-based reasoning relies on past case history. For a new problem, case-based reasoning strives to locate a similar previous solution.

When solving a new problem, the most similar old case is retrieved from the case library. Retrieval methods are based mainly on some modification of the nearest neighbor algorithm [9], [10], [11], [12], [13]; or induction [14], [15], [16]. As the case library gets larger in size, the retrieval process becomes more time-consuming, especially for nearest neighbor methods, where time complexity is generally linear.

A case-based reasoning system can only be as good as its case library [9], and the quality of case libraries can be judged in two aspects:

- *Representativeness of the library* – The quality of the decision, and especially its accuracy, can be improved by employing a more appropriate representation of the case and with a cautious selection of cases.
- *Effectiveness of the retrieval* – Effectiveness is mainly based on (i) the complexity of retrieval algorithms, and (ii) the size and organization of the library.

There is a mutual relationship between these two aspects: the case library size and organization are strongly related with its representativeness. Therefore, the majority of the approaches striving to improve case libraries affects both aspects.

2.1 Case authoring

With the progress of case-based reasoning, more complex case libraries have been constructed. Researches have begun addressing more practical problems assisting case authors [17], [18]. The former claims that case-based reasoning can eliminate the need for knowledge engineering, required for expert systems, have been questioned. *Case authoring,* sometimes referred as *case engineering* [19], has emerged, developing principles and guidelines for case library design. Authoring cases is a difficult process. It can be expensive in time (e.g. long learning curves) or money (e.g. for training fees, consulting fees, or for purchasing case libraries). Novice case authors tend to build rather poorly designed case libraries, causing problems and dissatisfaction to users, with possible commercial consequences for the case-based reasoning product market. Therefore, case-based reasoning product vendors provide library design guidelines for their products.

Supporting the case authoring process, such guidelines are usually essential for library design. However, working with an extensive list of rules – in a written form – can be tedious and not very effective. Aha [19] suggests a software tool revising the library according to the guidelines. He focuses on Conversational Case-based Reasoning engines conducting an interactive end-user conversation to incrementally extract a query. The CLIRE (Case LIbrary REvisor) system, described in [17], is a realization of the software revising tool. The system assists case authors by revising case libraries, improving the conformance with the design guidelines.

2.2 Competence Model

McKenna and Smyth have proposed a Competence Model [20] to judge the coverage of a case-base. This model is based on the concepts of *retrieval space* and *adaptation space* of some target problem. The retrieval space for a certain target problem is the set of cases which is retrieved for solving that problem. The adaptation space is the set of cases in the library which can be adapted to solve a certain target problem.

With these sets, the *coverage* of a case can be calculated as the set of target problems which that case can solve. This concept of *coverage*, combined with the calculation of similarity between cases and case density, is further extended to a group of cases and to the whole case-base.

The coverage of a case-base can then be used to judge the competence of that case-base, as shown in [20].

3 Feature reduction

The retrieval method used in the presented research was based mainly on nearest neighbor. This approach has many advantages compared with other methods [21], [11]. It supports incremental learning from new cases. Another advantage is the relatively easy implementation of the method. However, there are some negative points that limit its applicability. Besides poor generalization performance of the classical nearest neighbor method, this method suffers from noisy features.

The similarity function plays a crucial role in nearest neighbor retrieval. This function is sensitive to imperfect features, some of them being *noisy*, *irrelevant*, *redundant*, or *interacting* [13]. A cautious selection of features can reduce dimensionality, improving efficiency and accuracy.

This general problem has been studied by researchers for long time ([22], [23], [24], [25], and others). Feature selection algorithms usually consist of three parts [25]: (i) Search algorithm, (ii) Evaluation function, and (iii) Performance function itself. Search algorithms can be grouped into three categories [23]: exponential, randomized, and sequential. The first one is rather problematic because of its exponential time complexity in number of features. Genetic and simulated annealing search method is used in the randomize algorithm, achieving high accuracies [23], [24]. Sequential algorithms can add and subtract features using a hill climbing method, with a quadratic complexity [25].

A group of *weight-setting methods* faces this problem by parameterizing the similarity function with feature weights [13]. One of the weight-setting approaches adopts the *hill climbing method*. Weights are changed iteratively in an effort (i) to increase the similarity function for adjacent cases of the same class, and (ii) to decrease the function for adjacent cases of the other classes. This method was applied by Salzberg [26] to EACH (Exemplar-Aided Constructor of Hyperectangles).

Feature weights can alternatively be assigned using *mutual information* [27] between the class of the training cases and the value of the feature. The mutual information can positively influence accuracy. Wettschereck and Dietrich [12] describe an improvement of accuracy of EACH.

Feature weights were also modified iteratively with the help of genetic algorithm [28]. The fitness function worked with recency and training accuracy.

Selected weight-setting methods are analyzed from the perspective of *k*-nearest neighbor similarity function in [13]. A five-dimensional framework was introduced, categorizing and comparing the selected methods.

Binary weights of features were used in the presented research. This means that either a feature is used in the similarity function with a weight of 1 or it is ignored completely (i.e. with a weight of 0). The problem with possible imperfect features was solved by the reduction of the features. Motivated by Skalak [8], [24], we decided to use *genetic algorithms* as a core of our reduction method. This method is flexible, not too complex for realization, and no domain-specific knowledge is needed. It is true that the search for the acceptable reduction can be long. However, this reduction is done basically only once. Guarded by the fitness function, the process does not require much human operator intervention. In addition, the reduction can have a substantial impact on analysis of features and their representativeness. Besides that, we had a positive experience with a similar reduction used for the handwritten digit recognition system (HWDR) [29], [30].

For this system, a handwritten digits database with 6116 bitmaps was obtained from the Elsevier Science FTP site. Within these bitmaps, 2030 were selected as the unseen test cases and the remaining 4086 were considered to be the case library. Several feature extraction methods were used, so that each digit bitmap is converted into a case with numerical features.

Several recognition engines were devised in that system, in which one of them uses the case-based reasoning approach. This recognizer uses the nearest neighbor method to retrieve the case in the case library which has the smallest Euclidean distance with respect to the test case.

Due to the size of the case library, the recognition process was time consuming. Therefore, the case library was reduced using genetic algorithms and the original case library with 4086 cases was reduced to 300 cases. After this reduction, the recognition accuracy of the system was changed from 95.96% to 94.63%. Although with a slight decrease in recognition accuracy, the time required for case retrieval was reduced dramatically, to less than 1% of the original time required.

Similar experiments were done for reducing the number of features of the case library, with very positive results. The number of features was reduced from 342 to 50, with a slight decrease in recognition accuracy from 95.96% to 95.47%.

Features were selected using several alternative ways [29], [30]. This selection uses no domain-specific knowledge, selecting numerous features. The method, based on genetic algorithms, showed capability to select representative features from that wide range of features, still maintaining accuracy after this massive reduction for both features and cases. Motivated by this good result, we decided to test the ability of this methodology also on the pile foundation application.

The presented research is focusing on features reduction, since the particular case libraries used for testing possibly contain redundant or irrelevant features. On the other hand, the number of cases is rather limited in this stage of the research. The reduction of cases will be reconsidered after extension of the case libraries.

4 Genetic Algorithms

Genetic algorithms [5], [6], [7], [8] share many concepts and rules of the living world, working with *individuals* in a *population*. Each individual contains some genetic information encoded in the form of *genes* — numeric values that are characteristic to each individual. Another characteristic of each individual is its *quality* measure. The way how this quality is calculated depends on the particular scenario in which the genetic algorithm is applied. A *generation* is a particular state of the population. Fig. 1 illustrates the relationships between all these entities and concepts:

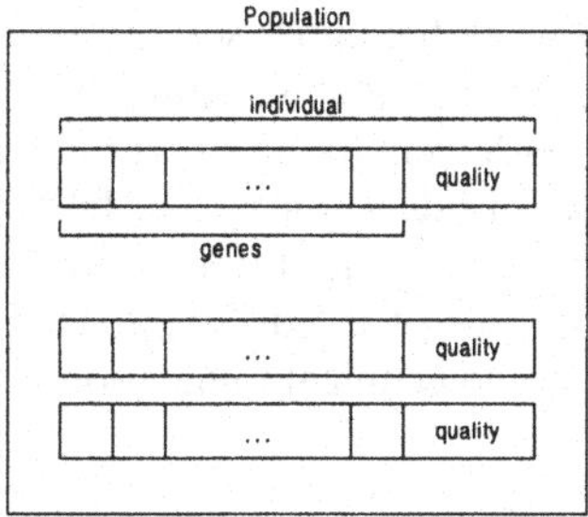

Fig. 1. The structure of a population

For the first generation, the population is filled with individuals created by assigning random values to their genes. For the subsequent generations, new individuals are generated and their genes are obtained through the *crossover* process. At the end of each generation, the two individuals with the highest quality values are selected for crossover. When a new individual is generated, the individual in the population with the least quality will be excluded from the population, so that the population size is kept constant.

During the crossover process used in our experiments, the first half of the genes of the descendant are randomly selected among the genes of the ancestor with the higher quality value. If a repeated value is selected, this is rejected and that gene will be re-selected. Each of the remaining genes of the descendant is randomly selected from those of the other ancestor. If the selected gene is already present among the previously selected ones, this gene will be randomly selected from all the possible gene values, until there are no repeated genes.

In the approach presented in this research, each gene corresponds to a feature number (i.e. 1 for the first feature, 2 for the second, etc.). Each individual then corresponds to a candidate set of reduced features. The quality of each individual is calculated according to whether this candidate of the reduced library could produce good results for the particular application considered.

For the majority of the reduction experiments, there is no significant decrease of the quality of results. On the other hand, the speed is increased substantially.

Despite of the practical use of the genetic algorithm for case library reduction, it has the drawback of being dependent on random events. This implies that the test results can hardly be regenerated exactly as it was done before and that a large number of tests should be done to obtain an average of the results. The difference between the best-case and worst-case behavior can be very significant.

5 Brief Description about Pile Foundations

Different types of foundations are used for civil engineering construction purposes, depending on the geological composition of the site and the type of construction.

Pile foundations are used when the upper soil layers cannot sustain the load of the structure. Piles transfer the load of that structure to the lower and more resistant layers, avoiding detrimental settlement to the structure that they support.

The system here referred considers purely pre-fabricated concrete piles (PHC – pile, high-strength concrete), driven at different locations under the action of a hammer. Fig. 2 shows an example of the different steps gone through during a civil construction work, in terms of geotechnical foundations.

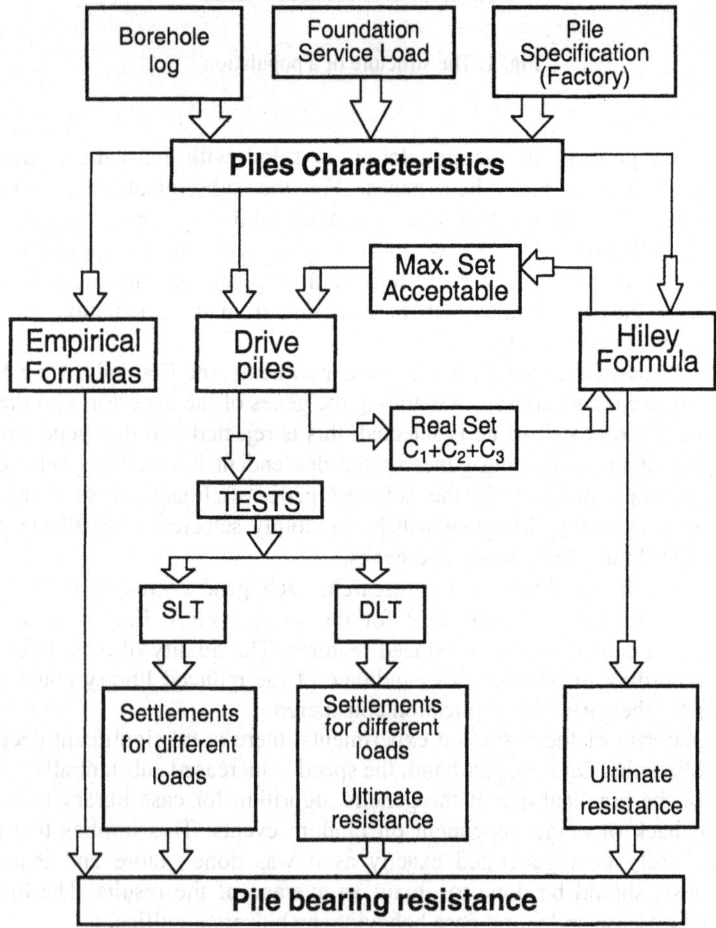

Fig. 2. Workflow during pile foundation decisions

The site investigation allows the collection of the necessary soil information, thus giving an idea of the appropriate foundation type to be chosen. Normally, site investigation includes drilling boreholes in the construction area, from the ground surface to the bedrock or strong soil layer, and performing standard penetration tests (SPT) at 1.5m to 2m intervals.

Basically, the standard penetration test consists of driving a standard sampler by dropping a 63.5kg hammer onto a drive head from a height of 76cm. The number of blows required for a penetration of 300mm after an initial setting drive of 150mm is called standard penetration test value (N-value). The SPT values yield information on engineering characteristics of the soil, and on the nature and sequence of soil layers.

Considering the type of construction, pile service load, and site investigation results, the designer chooses appropriate geotechnical structures. If piles are chosen as the structure, related calculations need to be performed to define pile characteristics, its bearing resistance, the total number of piles needed and their distribution on the site.

The design of a pile foundation depends on the pile working load and on the depth of the strong layer given by the standard penetration test. The diameter of a pre-cast driven pile should be chosen in accordance with the structural design of the pile, which is recommended by the manufacturer.

The construction phase generally starts with pile driving. After this phase, some piles are statically or dynamically tested in order to estimate the piles' behavior.

The Hiley formula [31], [32] has been widely used for the design of driven piles. The formula defines the maximum pile penetration (average penetration under the last few blows) accepted during pile driving operations. The calculation is based on the designed pile load, the geometry of the pile, hammer's characteristics, and the soil parameters that can be obtained by the pile load test results.

After this description of some of the steps performed while developing decisions related to pile foundations, the next paragraph focuses on the issues involved when applying the case-based reasoning paradigm in this application area.

6 Application of CBR to Pile Foundations

Several case-based reasoning systems have been developed in the field of civil engineering by other researchers (e.g. CASECAD, CASESYN, etc.) [33], [34]. In the presented research, the case-based reasoning paradigm was applied to support the decisions in pile foundations [32], [35]. Cases are organized to define a particular scenario consisting of soil information, pile geometric characteristics, and pile test results. The case library consists of pieces of information related to piles driven and tested in different construction sites and their corresponding geotechnical data.

The knowledge contained in the case library is used as a reference for a new construction site, whenever the new situation can be compared to an existing one in the library. Using the system here described, it is possible to evaluate the bearing resistance of a pile, from a similar stored case where piles were tested statically or dynamically and the soil information is known. Moreover, the parameters used in the Hiley formula [31], [32] previously calibrated by pile load tests, can be reused in a similar situation.

The features related to soil information are considered as the input features. Another set of features that describe the pile characteristics and the pile test results are the output features. These output features are only present in the cases which were successfully solved.

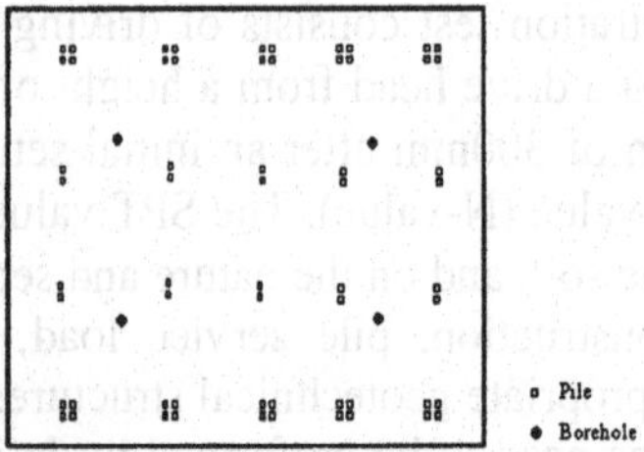

Fig. 3. Distribution of boreholes and piles in one site

In general, the number of boreholes is less than the number of piles (Fig. 3). There is a one-to-many relation between boreholes and piles. This was the reason why it was decided to maintain two case libraries for the application: one for the boreholes' data (the *borehole library*) and another for the piles' data (the *pile library*).

During the operation of the system, when a new site is encountered, the borehole's characteristics are structured in the form of a new borehole case. The system will then look through the borehole library for the most similar case. After that, the pile library is browsed for the associated piles related to the borehole case just retrieved. Then a solution is proposed for the new case and the new solution is retained in the case libraries. The workflow of the system is presented in Fig. 4:

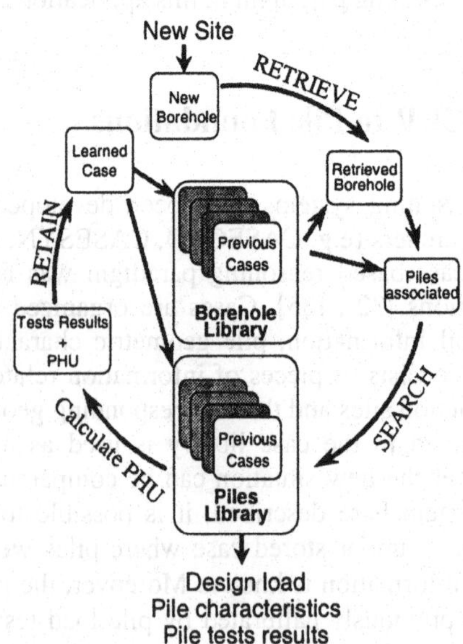

Fig. 4. Case-based reasoning scheme applied to pile foundation decisions

In the above figure, PHU refers to the ultimate load given by Hiley Formula [31], [32].

Each point in a construction site could be considered as a new case to the case-based reasoning system. When considering this new case, the library case which is most similar to the new case is retrieved from the case library. After retrieving the most similar case, in order to fit it closer to the new situation, the retrieved case can be adapted according to the new case's features. Tasks and systems are analyzed from the viewpoint of adaptation in [36], concluding that identification tasks can be achieved also without adaptation. On the other hand, rather wider adaptation is expected for design tasks. In consonance with this conclusion, only limited role of adaptation was found in the present scope of our CBR application. However, it should grow with more design oriented development of the application.

In order to model the scheme shown in Fig. 4, the ReMind case-based reasoning tool by Cognitive Systems was used. This tool provides case input, retrieval, adaptation and retention capabilities suitable for this application. However, since ReMind does not provide any case library reduction capability, another system has been developed to perform the task of case library reduction using genetic algorithms. The experiments described in section 8 and the associated results refer to this, our system for case library reduction.

7 Case Library Structure

In order to support the test application, two case libraries are used: the *borehole library* and the *pile library*.

Primary attention was paid to the *borehole library* in the presented stage of the research. The borehole library stores information about each borehole, including the following the following features:

- Identification of the borehole
- Depth of the borehole
- 2 features corresponding to the geographical coordinates of the borehole
- 8 features corresponding to calculations related to N-values
- 8 features which are 4 pairs of fields describing the material and depth of each soil layer

This gives a total of 20 features for the borehole library.

Regarding the pile library, the geometric characteristics, the load test results, as well as the parameters used in the Hiley Formula are defined for each pile. The details for each feature [32] are related to civil engineering and fall outside the scope of the presented research.

8 Reduction Procedure

In order to test the efficiency of the process of reduction of the number of features in the boreholes case library, 10 cases were randomly selected from the total of 61 cases to form the test library. The remaining 51 cases constitute the case library.

Initially, the case library contains 20 features and all features are used in the nearest neighbor search. Each case in the test library is applied to the nearest neighbor search to look for the most similar case in the case library. This result is stored as a reference result for the subsequent searches using a reduced number of features.

The genetic algorithm is then applied to the features, reducing them to a specified number. During the experiments, the features were reduced to 15, 13, 10, 9, 7, 6, 5, and 3. The quality of each reduction is calculated in terms of the number of test cases that had the same nearest case as that obtained from the initial results when all the features were used. In this way, a quality of 10 means that all 10 test cases had the same results as using all features and a quality of 0 means that none of the test cases were classified as if all features were used.

At the beginning of each experiment, 5 individuals are created in the population using the random generation method. After this first generation, the subsequent generations are created using the half and half crossover method. As the generations evolve, there might be a case when all 5 individuals in the population have the same quality. When this situation occurs, only the best individual is kept and the remaining ones are replaced by new randomly generated individuals, regardless of their quality. This method is used to avoid the possibility of entering a deadlock in which the individuals no longer evolve, since all of them have the same quality.

The next paragraph describes the results obtained during the experiments conducted for the presented research.

9 Reduction Results

As stated previously, the experiments were conducted in order to reduce the original borehole library to a different number of features. Due to space constraints, the graphical results are only shown for the situations of reducing to 10, 8 and 7 features. The graph below (Fig. 5) shows the evolution of generations when reducing the original borehole library with 20 features to 10 features.

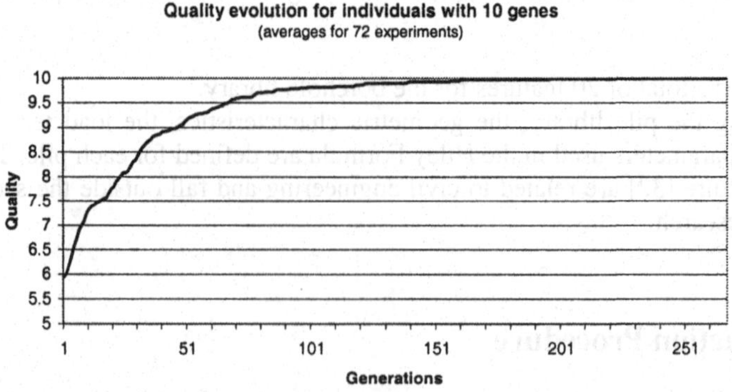

Fig. 5. Graph showing the evolution of the individuals' quality when reducing to 10 features

The values shown on the graph are averages for 72 experiments. In the worst case of the experiments, 267 generations were needed in order to find a subset of features that gives the same level of classification as using all features. On average, 59.75 generations are needed to achieve that level of accuracy.

The following graph (Fig. 6) shows the results for the reduction to 8 features:

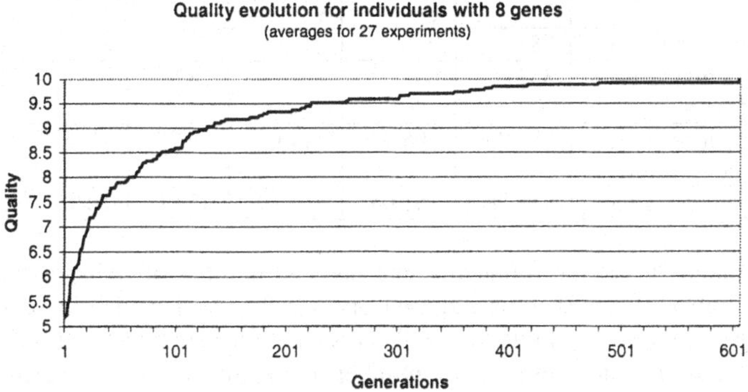

Fig. 6. Graph showing the evolution of individuals' quality when reducing to 8 features

As one might expect, when reducing to 8 features, the number of generations required for producing a reduced library which could have the same accuracy as the original library is greater than that for reducing to 10 features. In the worst case, 606 generations were needed and 205.37 generations are needed on average.

The next graph (Fig. 7) shows the results for the reduction to 7 features:

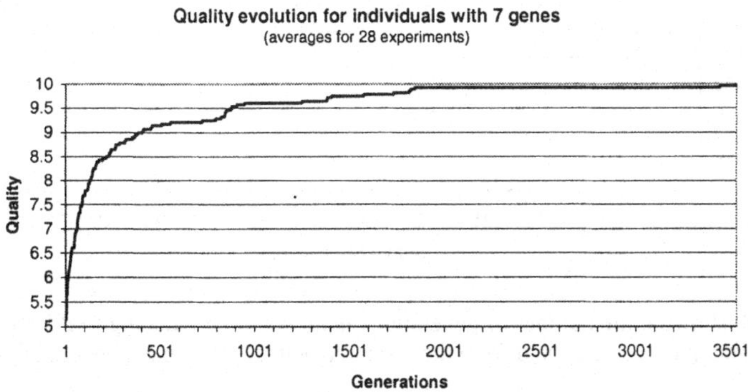

Fig. 7. Graph showing the evolution of individuals' quality when reducing to 7 features

There is a significant difference between the results for reduction from to 8 and 7 features. For the case of reducing to 7 features, in the worst case, 3527 generations were needed to obtain the same level of classification as using all the 20 features. On average 951.25 generations are needed for that level of accuracy.

The following table (Table 1) summarizes the experimental results for successful experiments.

Table 1. Statistical information regarding each set of experiments

	Number of reduced features					
	7	8	9	10	13	15
No. of experiments	28	27	21	72	85	13
Generations in the worst situation	3527	606	802	267	37	3
Generations in the average situation	951.25	205.37	114.05	59.75	10.96	1.31
Standard deviation	933.28	151.05	163.89	45.81	10.15	0.75

From Table 1, it can be found that the less the number of reduced features, the more the number of generations required and the standard deviation related to the number of generations gets higher as well. This table further shows that the number of generations required to reduce the number of features varies greatly between experiments.

The next graph (Fig. 8) shows the exponential growth of the number of generations required to obtain a reduced library which is at least as accurate as the full library.

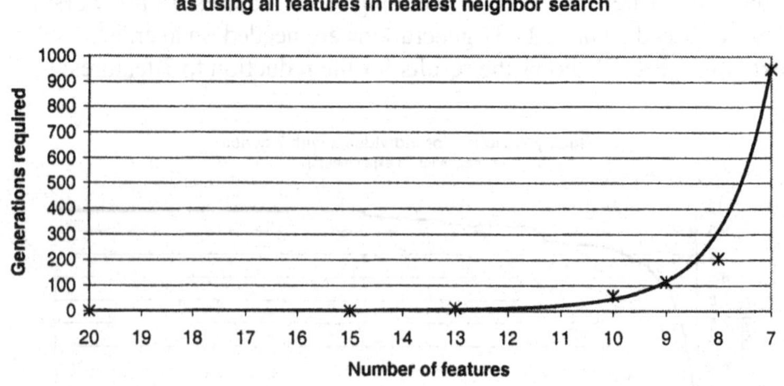

Fig. 8. Graph showing the number of generations required when reducing to different numbers of features. The line was generated from the 7 sample points using an exponential interpolation.

From these experiments, one can notice that there is a trade-off between the degree of reduction of the case library and the time required for that reduction.

After conducting the many tests of reducing the number of features to different values, it was found that the features that are finally discovered by the system do not differ very much. This shows that, although the initial situation of each experiment is different (since the initial population is randomly generated), the final collection do converge to some similar subset of features. This is one of the very positive results found.

Trying to find limits, experiments were also conducted for reducing to 6, 5, and 3 features. However, as expected, this is obviously an excessive reduction. For instance, when reducing to 3 features, after 5461 generations, only 60% of the test cases were classified according to the reference classification done with all features considered.

From the experiments, it was found that features could be substantially reduced in this application. On the other hand, with the help of this method, limits of the reduction for the given date are recognizable. For the presented library, the number of features should not be less then eight (see Fig. 6, 7, 8).

10 Conclusion

The presented application was developed on a research level. Generally, borehole and pile library were provided with limited number of cases in present time. Data is not complete for all sites. However, despite this limited source of data, the general results are promising. CBR facilitates incremental learning. The environment can be deployed with a limited set of "seed cases" to be augmented progressively. According to experts in the geotechnical area, this application can be very useful for future foundation designs, helping them predict the behavior of piles without the need of so many piles tests.

Selection of representative features of the borehole library was studied in this research. Imperfect features were reduced with the help of genetic algorithms. Adopting this methodology, that we have originally developed for pattern recognition application, feature reduction of the borehole library was also positive, although the nature of the application, and the source, characteristics and size of data differ significantly. Although a possible generalization of this conclusion is limited by two experiments, results suggest a positive evaluation for the presented approach.

The feature reduction of the pile library is logically the next step of the research. After these libraries are supplied with more cases, we will again employ case reduction, using the same approach.

As another direction for further research, during the application of the genetic algorithm for case library reduction, the method itself could decide for the appropriate number of features. This might be accomplished by giving higher quality values to those individuals with a lesser number of features. In this way, the genetic algorithm might be influenced towards generating individuals with less number of features.

Furthermore, the genetic algorithm could also decide on the suitable population size according to needs.

References

1. A. Aamodt, E. Plaza, *Case-Based Reasoning: Foundational Issues, Methodological, and System Approaches*, IOS Press, 1994.
2. B. W. Davis, *Global Similarity Visualization and Searches in Case-Based Reasoning*, http://cimic.rutgers.edu/~badavis/research/cbr_vis.html

3. B. Smyth, Case Adaptation & Reuse in Déjà Vu, in *Proceedings of ECAI-96 Workshop on Adaptation in Case-Based Reasoning*, 1996, ftp://ftpagr.informatik.uni-kl.de/pub/ECAI96-ADAPT-WS/smyth.ps
4. W. Wilke, R. Bergmann, Adaptation with the INRECA - System, in *Proceedings of ECAI-96 Workshop on Adaptation in Case-Based Reasoning*, 1996, ftp://ftpagr.informatik.uni-kl.de/pub/ECAI96-ADAPT-WS/wilke.ps
5. H. Chen, J. Kim, *GANNET: Information Retrieval using Genetic Algorithms and Neural Nets*, 1994, http://ai.bpa.arizona.edu/papers/gannet93.html
6. H. Chen, L. She, A. Iyer, G. Shankaranarayanan, *A Machine Learning Approach to Inductive Query by Examples: An Experiment using Relevance Feedback, ID3, Genetic Algorithms, and Simulated Annealing*, 1995, http://ai.bpa.arizona.edu/papers/expert94.html
7. D. A. Muresan, *Genetic Algorithms for Nearest Neighbor: Final Report*, 1997, http://www.cs.caltech.edu/~muresan/GANN/report.html
8. D. B. Skalak, Using a genetic algorithm to learn prototypes for case retrieval and classification, in *Proceedings of the AAAI-93 Case-based Reasoning Workshop*, 1993.
9. J. Kolodner, *Case-based Reasoning*, Morgan Kaufmann Publ., U.S.A., 1993.
10. S. Berchtold, B. Ertl, D. A. Keim, H.-P. Kriegel, T. Seidl, *Fast Nearest Neighbor Search in High-dimensional Space*, in ICDE'98, 1998.
11. B. V. Dasarathy, *Nearest neighbor (NN) norms: NN patterns classification techniques.* IEEE Computer Society Press, Los Alamitos, CA, USA, 1991.
12. D. Wettschereck, T. G. Dietrich, An experimental comparison of the nearest neighbor and nearest hyperectangle algorithms, in *Machine Learning*, 19, 5-28, 1995.
13. D. Wettschereck, D. W. Aha, Weighting features, in *Proceedings of the First International Conference on Case-Based Reasoning*, Lisbon, Portugal, Springer-Verlag, 1995.
14. G. P. Ingargiola, *Building Classification Models: ID3 and C4.5*, Temple University, 1994, http://yoda.cis.temple.edu:8080/UGAIWWW/lectures/C45
15. H. Chen, Machine Learning for Information Retrieval: Neural Networks, Symbolic Learning, and Genetic Algorithms, in *Journal of the American Society for Information Science*, 1994, http://ai.bpa.arizona.edu/papers/PS/mlir93.ps.Z
16. H. G. Solheim, *Building Classification Models*, http://yoda.cis.temple.edu:8080/UGAIWWW/C45
17. D. W. Aha, L. A. Breslow, Refining conversational case libraries, in *Proceedings of the Second International Conference on Case-Based Reasoning*, pp. 267-278, Providence, RI, Springer-Verlag, 1997.
18. R. Heider, E. Auriol, E. Tartarin, M. Manago, Improving quality of case bases for building of better decision support system. in R. Bergmann and W. Wilke (Eds.) *Fifth German Workshop on CBR: Foundation, Systems, and Application (Technical Report LSA-97-01E)*, University of Kaiserlautern, Department of Computer Science, 1997.
19. D. W. Aha, A proposal for refining case libraries, in R. Bergmann & W. Wilke (Eds.), *Fifth German Workshop on Case-Based Reasoning: Foundations, Systems, and Applications (Technical Report LSA-97-01E)*, University of Kaiserslautern, Department of Computer Science, 1997.
20. E. McKenna, B. Smyth, A Competence Model for Case-Based Reasoning, in *9th Irish Conference on Artificial Intelligence and Cognitive Science*, Ireland, 1998, http://ww.cs.ucd.ie/staff/bsmyth/papers/Cascade%20Submit.doc
21. P. Ricci, P. Avesani, Learning a local similarity metric for case-based reasoning, in Case-based reasoning research and development, M. Veloso and A. Aamondt, (Eds.), *Proceedings of the First International on Case-based Reasoning*, ICCBR-95, Sesimbra, Portugal, October 23-26, 1995, Springer, pp. 301-312.
22. K. S. Fu, Sequential methods in pattern recognition and machine learning, New York, Academic Press, 1968.
23. J. Doak, *An evaluation of feature selection methods and their application to computer security,* Technical Report CSE-92-18. University of California, Department of Computer Science, Davis, CA, USA, 1992.

24. D. Skalak, Prototype of feature selection by sampling and random mutation hill algorithms, in *Proceedings of the Eleventh International Machine Learning Conference*, Morgan Kaufmann Publ., U.S.A., pp. 293-301, 1994.
25. D. W. Aha, R. L. Bankert, A comparative evaluation of sequential feature selection algorithms, in *Proceedings of the Fifth International Workshop on Artificial Intelligence and Statistics* (pp 1-7). Ft. Lauderdale, FL: Unpublished. (NCARAI TR: AIC-94-026), 1995.
26. S. L. Salzberg, A nearest hyperrectangle learning method, in *Machine Learning*, 6, 251-276, 1991.
27. C. E. Shannon, A mathematical theory of communication, in *Bell System Technology Journal*, 27, 379-423, 1948.
28. J. D. Kelly Jr., L. Davis, A hybrid genetic algorithm for classification, in *Proceedings of the Twelve International Conference on Artificial Intelligence*, Sydney, Australia, Morgan Kaufmann, pp. 249-256, 1991.
29. O. Babka, S. I. Leong, C. Lei, M. W. Pang, Reusing Data Mining Methods for Handwritten Digit Recognition, in *Proceedings of World Multiconference on Systems, Cybernetics and Informatics (SCI'98)*, 1998.
30. S. I. Leong, C. Lei, M. W. Pang, *HWDR – Handwritten Digit Recognition – Final Report*, Bachelor degree graduation project report, University of Macau, 1998.
31. H. N. Ferreira, L. N. Lamas, L. Hong Sai, S. Qiang, *Guia de Fundações LECM*, Macau, 1997.
32. L. A. G. Garanito, *Case-based Reasoning and Piles Foundations*, Master's Thesis, University of Macau, 1997.
33. M. L. Maher, A. G. de S. Garza, Developing Case-Based Reasoning for Structural Design, in *IEEE Expert*, Volume 11, Number 3, 1996, http://www.arch.su.edu.au/%7Eandres/ieee-expert96.ps
34. M. L. Maher, A. G. de S. Garza, The Adaptation of Structural System Designs Using Genetic Algorithms, in *Proceedings of the International Conference on Information Technology in Civil and Structural Engineering Design – Taking Stock and Future Directions*, Scotland, 1996, http://www.arch.su.edu.au/%7Eandres/glasgow96.ps
35. O. Babka, L. A. G. Garanito, Case-based Reasoning for Pile Foundation, in *Proceedings of Symposium on Science & Technology and Development of Macau*, Dec. 1-4, 1998, Macau, pp. 295-300.
36. K. Hanney, M. Keane, B. Smyth, P.Cunningham, Systems, tasks, and adaptation knowledge: revealing some revealing dependencies, in Case-based reasoning research and development, M. Veloso and A. Aamondt (Eds.), *Proceedings of the First International on Case-based Reasoning*, ICCBR-95, Sesimbra, Portugal, October 23-26, 1995, Springer, pp. 461-470.

Case Representation, Acquisition, and Retrieval in SIROCCO

Bruce McLaren and Kevin Ashley

University of Pittsburgh
Intelligent Systems Program
3939 O'Hara Street
Pittsburgh, PA 15260
bmclaren+@pitt.edu, ashley+@pitt.edu

Abstract. As part of our investigation of how abstract principles are operationalized to facilitate their application to specific fact situations, we have begun to develop and experiment with SIROCCO (System for Intelligent Retrieval of Operationalized Cases and COdes), a CBR retrieval and analysis system applied to the domain of engineering ethics. SIROCCO is intended to retrieve decided engineering ethics cases and previously applied ethics codes to assist engineers and students in analyzing new cases. Here we describe a limited but expressive language designed to represent a wide range of ethics cases in SIROCCO, a world-wide web tool developed to perform case acquisition and support a measure of consistency in representation, and an experiment to validate the initial phase of SIROCCO's retrieval algorithm and test its sensitivity to small variations in case description.

Introduction

Developing methods for representing cases and problems is still a serious challenge for CBR. On the one hand, a case representation must be expressive enough for users to accurately describe a problem or case. On the other hand, CBR systems must reason with cases in a computationally tractable fashion. We have been directly confronted with this problem in our attempts to represent cases in engineering ethics.

Professional engineers face a wide range of factual scenarios that raise ethical issues. The National Society of Professional Engineer's Board of Ethical Review (NSPE BER) has analyzed and published over 400 ethics cases. A review of the titles of just some of the 64 cases we have already represented suggests the enormous scope of the scenarios: Gifts, Responsibility for Public Safety, Political Contributions, Supplanting Another Engineer, Plagiarism, Criticism of Another Engineer, Engineer's Disclosure of Potential Conflict Of Interest, Declining Employment After Acceptance, and Misrepresentation of Firm's Staff.

In addition, the ethics code provisions that the NSPE BER employ to analyze the cases and rationalize its recommendations are very abstract. The NSPE code of ethics comprises 74 provisions involving issues such as public safety, conflicts of interest, confidentiality, and more. Most of these provide only very general guidance. Often, code provisions provide guidance which conflicts with that of other provisions.

Given the wide range of specific scenarios and code provisions, it is interesting to observe how principles, typically too abstract to apply deductively, are nevertheless applied systematically to the scenarios. Our study of the NSPE BER cases revealed that the Board employed a variety of *operationalization techniques* to bridge the gap between abstract principles and specific fact situations (McLaren and Ashley, 1998). (Mostow, 1983) first introduced the notion of operationalization in the comparatively well-defined domain of card playing. However, the NSPE BER's operationalization techniques are applied in a far less structured and more complex problem domain.

Our goal is to make these operationalization techniques explicit in a computational model and leverage them for the retrieval of past cases and analysis of new ethical problems. We have been developing SIROCCO (System for Intelligent Retrieval of Operationalized Cases and COdes), a computational model intended to retrieve decided cases and previously applied principles in order to frame analyses of new engineering ethics cases. SIROCCO is not intended to reach conclusions for the new cases but, rather, to identify relevant information for the analysis of the cases. Ultimately, our goal is to deliver SIROCCO to engineers and engineering students as a tool for improving access to an on-line resource of ethics experience. We also intend to incorporate SIROCCO into an intelligent tutoring environment for engineering students.

We are not the first to address how cases can be used to enrich the meaning of abstract rules. To some extent, researchers in case-based legal reasoning all must address this issue. (Branting, 1994), for instance, sketches a computational model to bridge the gap between legal theories (similar in some respects to principles) and specific case facts focusing on how to determine a precedent's controlling effect. CATO (Aleven, 1997) employs a Factor Hierarchy that relates specific factors to more abstract factors and ultimately to legal issues. BankXX (Rissland et al, 1996) searches a legal network including legal theories for information benefiting a side in a dispute.

In our own earlier work on ethics, we attempted to model components of case-based or casuistic ethical argument (Ashley and McLaren, 1995). Casuistry is a form of ethical reasoning in which decisions are made by comparing a problem to paradigmatic case examples of high level principles (Jonsen and Toulmin, 1988). As compared to legal reasoning, the domain of engineering ethics appears to involve a less well-defined and explicit model of argumentation. In addition, ethical problems are not constrained to only two solutions (e.g., plaintiff won or lost).

A limitation of our earlier work, however, was its impoverished scheme for representing cases. We represented cases at a more abstract, or issue, level. In the current work, we wanted to let case enterers describe, in a somewhat specific manner, what actually occurred in a problem scenario and when. None of the case representations in the above work supported the representation of a range of cases as wide as those presented in our domain nor dealt with as wide a range of abstract rules. None enables users to specify event time ordering, information which often appears to be important in analyzing moral obligations. Nor has the AI & Law research focused on operationalization of abstract rules, as we have.

Although natural language is the ideal medium for describing a scenario, especially in domains like ethics and law where cases typically are communicated textually, CBR systems cannot yet process complex textual case descriptions. Recent work in textual CBR approaches the problem through improved methods of processing case texts. To the extent that the work has focused on interpreting or adapting complex case texts, it is promising but still limited (Daniels and Rissland, 1997; Bruninghaus and Ashley, 1997). As a result, there is still a need for developing alternative means of representing cases. Indeed, even textual CBR methods often assume that an underlying representation has been developed and will ultimately support case-based reasoning.

Like others before us (e.g., Branting 1990), we have opted for defining a limited, yet expressive, language for representing a case. As with any limited language, there are trade-offs: Do the limitations constrain case enterer's descriptions enough so that a program can identify similarity between cases? On the other hand, do the limitations constrain users so much that they can no longer adequately describe what happened? For instance, while GREBE's relational representation allowed users to describe scenarios flexibly, variations in the way users described similar scenarios threatened to foil its structure mapping algorithm. Our use of a case acquisition tool supports representational consistency (by, for instance, presenting case examples, guidance, and definitions), and our language allows us to address a wider range of cases than, for example, GREBE's workman's compensation domain.

Here we report on our development of a language for representing ethics case scenarios. The language supports users in describing case events and their time ordering. The web-based case acquisition tool has various features to help ensure that different users describe similar cases and problems consistently enough for SIROCCO to match similar cases. In addition, SIROCCO employs a two-stage retrieval algorithm intended to match similar cases flexibly enough despite inevitable small variations in the way cases are described. While our two-stage approach is based on that of several researchers in analogy (e.g., Thagard et al, 1990; Forbus et al, 1994), we focus more specifically on coverage of time-dependent scenarios and leveraging of goal-specific knowledge. To date, we have implemented the first stage and report the results of an experiment designed to evaluate it.

Case Acquisition and Representation in SIROCCO

As noted above, in some ethics cases multiple principles apply with conflicting results. In these cases, the BER needs to determine not only whether and what code principles apply and what conclusions follow from the applicable principles, but also which principles are paramount in the given circumstances. For instance, Case 92-6, figure 1, pits an obligation to one's client against an obligation to public safety.

As previously discussed, the NSPE board employs operationalization techniques to resolve such ethical dilemmas. For instance, in Case 92-6 the board employed a technique we call "Define Code Superiority" to determine that codes related to

Engineer B's obligation to the public override codes related to his obligation to the client. In this circumstance, the board decided that Engineer B should have been more forthright and reported the potential hazard of the drums to the client or appropriate authorities.

> Technician A is a field technician employed by a consulting environmental engineering firm. At the direction of his supervisor Engineer B, Technician A samples the contents of drums located on the property of a client. Based on Technician A's past experience, it is his opinion that analysis of the sample would most likely determine that the drum contents would be classified as hazardous waste. If the material is hazardous waste, Technician A knows that certain steps would legally have to be taken to transport and properly dispose of the drum including notifying the proper federal and state authorities.
>
> Technician A asks his supervisor Engineer B what to do with the samples. Engineer B tells Technician A only to document the existence of the samples. Technician A is then told by Engineer B that since the client does other business with the firm, Engineer B will tell the client where the drums are located but do nothing else. Thereafter, Engineer B informs the client of the presence of drums containing "questionable material" and suggests that they be removed. The client contacts another firm and has the material removed. (NSPE, 1958-1997)

Fig. 1. Facts of Case 92-6

We have devised a web site (www.pitt.edu/~bmclaren/ethics) to facilitate users in transcribing cases like this into the Ethics Transcription Language (ETL), a standard format that SIROCCO can process. The web site contains a Participant's Guide with instructions on how to transcribe ethics cases into ETL. It has a Reference Shelf including a standard vocabulary and an example set of 47 transcribed cases.

ETL's standard vocabulary comprises: (1) *Actor & Object Types*, a list of the types of actors and objects which may appear in the engineering ethics scenarios, (2) *Fact Primitives*, a list of the actions and events in which the actors and objects may participate, and (3) *Time Qualifiers*, a list of temporal relations which specify how the actions and events relate to each other in time. Currently, ETL has 70 Actor & Object Types, 190 Fact Primitives, and 11 Time Qualifiers.

In ETL a case is described as an ordered list (i.e., the Fact Chronology) of short sentences. Each is a Fact and satisfies the grammar of a <Fact> as shown in figure 2.

In essence, each Fact Phrase's Fact Primitive is a verb phrase that indicates a specific action or event involving actors, objects, or similarly constituted Fact-Phrases. It is treated, in effect, like a function with up to three arguments (Fact-Primitive arg1 [arg2] [arg3]), where arg1 is the Actor-Or-Object serving as the subject of the verb phrase. In the Fact Chronologies, human case enterers put arg1 before the Fact Primitive as they would the subject of a verb. Each Fact is listed in a table in approximate chronological order as indicated by its Fact-#. Time Qualifiers specify more specific information about the chronological ordering.

While it is by no means easy or quick to transcribe a new case into ETL, the web site offers some amenities to ease the task. First, the Participant's Guide offers a step-by-step tutorial. It instructs the case enterer on how to (1) identify the actors (e.g. engineers, client firms) and objects (e.g., test samples) involved in each scenario, (2) transcribe the scenario into a set of chronological facts, and (3) identify the questioned facts, and the actor or actors whose ethical behavior is questioned. Second, the Reference Shelf makes it easy to browse through and select from the lists of possible Actor & Object Types, Fact Primitives and Time Qualifiers. To make the former two lists easier to search, they are organized hierarchically by categories. Third, each term in the above lists comes complete with helpful information (e.g., a description of usage, cross references to other related terms, standard variations in form such as inverse, plural, negative) and hyper-linked examples of its use in representing other cases. Fourth, when the transcribed case is submitted, a computer program scans the ETL transcript, identifying any errors in structure and syntax and translating the transcript into the internal representation used by SIROCCO.

<Fact> := <Fact-#> <Fact-Phrase> [(Questioned Fact <X>)]
<Time-Qualifier> [,<Time-Qualifier>, ...]
<Fact-Phrase> := <Fact-Primitive> [<Fact-Modifier>] <Actor-Or-Object>
[<Actor-Or-Object> | (<Fact-Phrase>)]
[<Actor-Or-Object> | (<Fact-Phrase>)]
<Fact-#> := <Positive-Integer>
<Fact-Primitive> := *An instance of a Fact-Primitive*
<Actor-Or-Object> := *An instance of an Actor or an Object*
<Fact-Modifier> := partially | substantially | limited | extensive
<Time-Qualifier> := Pre-existing fact |
After the start of <Fact-#> [, <Fact-#>, ...] |
Starts at the same time as <Fact-#> [, <Fact-#>, ...] |
<Time-Period> after the start of <Fact-#> [, <Fact-#>, ...] |
After the conclusion of <Fact-#> [, <Fact-#>, ...] |
Immediately after the conclusion of <Fact-#> [, <Fact-#>, ...] |
<Time-Period> after the conclusion of <Fact-#> [, <Fact-#>, ...] |
Ends <Fact-#> [, <Fact-#>, ...] |
Occurs during <Fact-#> [, <Fact-#>, ...] |
Occurs as part of <Fact-#> [, <Fact-#>, ...] |
Occurs concurrently with <Fact-#> [, <Fact-#>, ...] |
<Time -Period> := <Y> Days | <Y> Weeks | <Y> Months | <Y> Years
<X> := Empty | <Positive-Integer>
<Y> := Many | Several | <Positive-Integer>
<Positive-Integer> := 1 ... N

Key: | = Alternative; [ ] = Optional; < > = Grammar element
Regular font indicates literal placement of language (e.g., "Pre-existing fact ")
Italicized font indicates a general description (i.e., "*An instance of a Fact-Primitive* ")

Fig. 2. The Grammar for the Ethics Transcription Language (ETL)

Submitting a new problem situation to SIROCCO involves the steps described above. Submitting a case to the case base, complete with outcome and analysis, requires an additional step. As led by the Participant's Guide, the case enterer notes the board's conclusions as well as the codes and cases the board cites to justify their conclusions. While the web site supports this task, we will not further describe it here. Figure 3 shows a Fact Chronology for Case 92-6. The table of actors and objects is shown in figure 4. The case enterer has designated Facts 11 and 12 as the Questioned Facts; these facts correspond most closely to the questions stated by the board.

The Fact Primitives are categorized into three types to ensure that Time Qualifiers are used consistently: Events, States, and Terminating Events. Events have relatively short duration, States have relatively long duration, and Terminating Events are special events that typically end a State. In selecting Fact Primitives, Case Enterers are instructed to take the primitive's type into consideration. For example, <is employed by> in Fact 3 in figure 3 is a State primitive. It represents a relatively long time period during which some of the other events of this case occur. If the case facts had focused on the events of being offered and accepting employment, then certain Event Fact primitives would have been more appropriate (e.g., <is offered employment by>, <accepts an offer of employment from>).

1. Client Y **<owns facility>** Client Y Site.	Pre-existing fact
2. Client Y **<hires the services of>** Consulting Environmental Firm X.	After the start of 1
3. Technician A **<is employed by>** Consulting Environmental Firm X.	Pre-existing fact
4. Technician A **<has supervisor>** Engineer B.	Occurs during 3
5. Technician A **<collects test samples>** Collected Samples X **<from>** Client Y Site.	Occurs during 2, 4
6. Technician A **<believes>** (Collected Samples X **<may be hazardous material>**).	After the conclusion of 5
7. Technician A **<knows>** (Client Y Site **<may be hazardous to safety>**).	After the conclusion of 5, Occurs concurrently with 6
8. Technician A **<knows>** (Government Authority **<should be informed about the hazard or potential hazard>**).	Occurs concurrently with 7
9. Technician A **<informs>** Engineer B **<that>** (Technician A **<believes>** (Collected Samples X **<may be hazardous material>**)).	After the conclusion of 6
10. Engineer B **<instructs>** Technician A **<to>** (Technician A **<records the existence of>** Collected Samples X.)	After the conclusion of 9
11. Engineer B **<provides limited information to>** Client Y **<regarding>** Client Y Site. *[Questioned Fact 1]*	After the conclusion of 10
12. Engineer B **<does not inform>** Client Y **<that>** (Technician A **<believes>** Collected Samples **<may be hazardous material>**). *[Questioned Fact 2]*	Occurs as part of 11
13. Client Y **<hires the services of>** Engineering Firm Y.	After the conclusion of 11
14. Engineering Firm Y **<removes material from>** Client Y Site.	Occurs during 13

Fig. 3. Fact Chronology of Case 92-6

1. Technician A --> **Engineering Technician.**
2. Consulting Environmental Firm X --> **Engineering Firm.**
3. Engineer B --> **Engineering Manager.**
4. Client Y --> **Client Firm.**
5. Client Y Site --> **Facility or Site.**
6. Collected Samples --> **Test Samples.**
7. Government Authority --> **Government Authority.**
8. Engineering Firm Y --> **Engineering Firm.**

Fig. 4. Actors and Objects in Case 92-6

After the case enterer has identified the Facts and marked the Questioned Facts, he or she (she henceforth) assigns Time Qualifiers to clarify the chronological relationships among Facts. Each Time Qualifier has information to guide the choice (e.g., its intended use, what one needs to know to apply it, links to other possible Qualifiers and to examples from other cases.) Each fact in the chronology must have at least one Time Qualifier. The Fact Chronology of Case 92-6, figure 3, shows a number of examples of Time Qualifiers. The most critical temporal relationships are that Facts 11 and 12, in which Engineer B fails to fully inform Client Y of the hazardous materials, occur after Fact 9, in which Technician A informs Engineer B of the existence of the materials. The Time Qualifiers "After the conclusion of" and "Occurs as part of" in Facts 11 and 12 capture this temporal information.

The goal is for the case enterer to represent the important events in the case as accurately as possible, given the limited set of Fact Primitives, Actors, and Objects. The case enterer is asked to do her best despite the limitations. Occasionally, case enterers identify important missing Fact Primitives or Actor or Object Types. They apprise us and we add the new terms into the vocabulary as appropriate. However, at this stage, the size of the vocabulary seems to have leveled off.

The Fact Chronology of figure 3 is only one interpretation of the facts of Case 92-6. For a variety of reasons, different case enterers may produce different interpretations. Despite the guidance provided in the Participant's Guide, a case enterer must still make judgments such as: (1) Deciding which facts are relevant. For instance, Facts 13 and 14 in figure 3 could have been considered irrelevant and deleted from the Fact Chronology. (2) Adding facts implied but not explicitly stated in the text. (3) Deciding whether a sentence should be multiple facts. The optional arguments of a Fact Primitive may be filled by other <Fact-Phrase>s as in Facts 6-10 and 12 in figure 3. This flexibility may lead to alternative formulations. (4) Selecting terms. The Fact Primitives contain a number of synonyms and related terms.

It is an empirical question whether ETL is expressive enough, and the similarity metrics flexible enough, to support SIROCCO in effective case retrieval despite the limitations discussed above. We provide empirical evidence in this paper that at least Stage 1 of SIROCCO's retrieval algorithm works reasonably well[1].

SIROCCO situates all primitives within an abstraction hierarchy known as the *Fact Hierarchy*. For instance, the primitives <hires the services of> (steps 2 and 13 of figure 3) and <employs> (step 3 of figure 3) are both sub-types of the more abstract fact <Work as an Employed or Contract Professional Engineer>. The Fact Hierarchy, developed through an analysis of the NSPE corpus of cases, is a characterization and abstraction of the most important actions and events that typically occur in engineering ethics scenarios. The Fact Hierarchy is an important component of SIROCCO's retrieval algorithm. Cases potentially may be retrieved and matched based on similarity at higher levels of the hierarchy. This will help with the problem of multiple interpretations of the facts, discussed above.

The provisions of the NSPE code of ethics are also cast in an abstraction hierarchy, the *Code Hierarchy*. For instance, Code I.1. ("Engineers ... shall: Hold paramount the safety, health, and welfare of the public in the performance of their professional duties."), highly relevant to Case 92-6, is one of 8 codes in the code abstraction group "Duty to the Public." The Code Hierarchy is adapted from a subject reference list

---

[1] By the way, we do not consider the current web site the last word in supporting case entry. With some additional Java or Java Script programming, the web site could automate more of the case entry processes. But the current web site does make case entry feasible via the WWW and at least six case enterers across the U.S. have used it to add 35 cases to the case base.

found in (NSPE, 1958-1997) and is an important component of the benchmark function used in the experiment discussed in this paper.

SIROCCO's Retrieval Algorithm

Given its case base of engineering ethics dilemmas transcribed into ETL, SIROCCO:

1. Accepts a new fact situation, also transcribed into ETL;
2. Retrieves and matches existing cases using a two-stage algorithm; and
3. Frames an analysis of the new fact situation using operationalizations of past cases and codes.

We have fully implemented a version of ETL and SIROCCO's Stage 1 retrieval algorithm. Stage 1 is a fast and efficient, but somewhat coarse, retrieval based on matching Fact Primitives. Stage 2 is a more expensive structural mapping that focuses on the most critical facts, on the chronology of facts, and on the types of actors and objects in the scenario. We have begun implementing Stage 2 and have designed, but not yet implemented, the analysis portion of the program. In this paper we report on an evaluation of SIROCCO's Stage 1 algorithm and, thus, focus our description on that aspect of the program. For a more complete description of the phases and ultimate output of SIROCCO see (McLaren and Ashley, 1998).

Stage 1 retrieves a preliminary set of matching cases using *content vectors* (Forbus, et al. 1994), data structures associated with each case that summarize the Fact Chronologies. A content vector represents a count of each Fact Primitive that appears in a chronology. For instance, the content vector of Case 92-6, the example discussed in the previous section, associates the value 2 with Hires-the-Services-Of because the primitive <hires the services of> appears twice in the Fact Chronology (see steps 2 and 13 in figure 3). Figure 5 depicts the content vector of 92-6, as well as the content vector of Case 89-7, a case that is relevant to 92-6[2].

To perform retrieval, SIROCCO takes the content vector of the input case and computes the dot product of that vector against all of the other cases' content vectors. Since all content vectors are pre-computed and stored in a hash table, computation is fast. Figure 5 shows the dot product between Cases 92-6 and 89-7. 89-7 is highly relevant to 92-6, and the dot product calculation bears this out. With a dot product of 10, 89-7 is ranked as the 4th highest case in our corpus of 63 cases (excluding 92-6).

From an architectural viewpoint, given the two-stage retrieval, it is more important for Stage 1 to retrieve as many relevant cases as possible than it is to avoid retrieving irrelevant cases. Stage 2 will not be able to seek additional relevant cases beyond those Stage 1 finds. Stage 2, on the other hand, will be capable of making finer distinctions between cases, such as comparing the temporal relations between steps. Of course, too many irrelevant cases retrieved by Stage 1 would flood the computationally more expensive Stage 2. The right number of cases to retrieve in Stage 1 and pass to Stage 2 is an empirical question; we currently estimate 10.

---

[2] Note that content vectors are also defined for higher level facts in the fact hierarchy for each case. This facilitates computation of similarity at more abstract fact levels.

Content Vector of Case 92-6:

((Owns-Facility . 1) (Hires-the-Services-Of . 2) (Employs . 1) (Supervises . 1) (Collects-Test-Samples-From . 1) (Believes . 1) (Knows . 2) (Informs-That . 2) (Instructs-To . 1) (Provides-Limited-Information-To-Regarding . 1) (Removes-Materials-From . 1)))

Content Vector of Case 89-7:

((Hires-the-Services-Of. 1) (May-Be-Hazardous-To-Safety . 1) (Instructs-To . 1) (Inspects . 1) (Discovers-That . 1) (Knows . 1) (Informs-That . 2) (Writes Paper/Article 1) (Provides-Limited-Information-To-Regarding . 1)))

Dot Product of Cases 92-6 and 89-7:

```
+ 2    [ 2 (92-6) * 1 (89-7)]      Hires-the-Services-Of
+ 2    [ 2 (92-6) * 1 (89-7)]      Knows
+ 4    [ 2 (92-6) * 2 (89-7)]      Informs-That
+ 1    [ 1 (92-6) * 1 (89-7)]      Instructs-To
+ 1    [ 1 (92-6) * 1 (89-7)]      Provides-Limited-Information-To-Regarding
----
10
```

Fig. 5. Content Vectors of Cases 92-6 and 89-7 and the Resulting Dot Product

We also expect *Code Instantiations* to enhance the effectiveness of both retrieval stages, but we have not evaluated their contribution here. A Code Instantiation relates a questioned fact, certain critical facts, and the order of those facts to a code; the case enterers identify them as they transcribe cases. Code Instantiations will help Stage 1 by offsetting the current default assumption, implemented in the dot product computation, that all Fact Primitives are equal. Code Instantiations will increase the dot product of those cases matching the most critical facts. In Stage 2, they will focus the structural mapping routine on a smaller number of critical facts.

An Evaluation of SIROCCO's Stage 1 Retrieval Algorithm

We undertook a formative evaluation to assess how well SIROCCO's Stage 1 retrieval algorithm works. Because of the architectural assumption above, the experiment focused on Stage 1's capability to retrieve relevant cases, as opposed to its capability of avoiding the retrieval of irrelevant cases. In addition, we compared SIROCCO's exact match retrieval algorithm with versions that match at higher levels of the Fact Hierarchy. Intuitively we expect that relevant cases might be missed if only exact fact matches were attempted.

The Benchmark Function: Citation Overlap

To evaluate SIROCCO we first needed a benchmark to objectively compute the similarity between cases. Because to our knowledge no such function exists, either in a comparable CBR system or within the domain of engineering ethics, it was necessary to define our own. From an analysis of our corpus, it was clear that the most objective and feasible similarity measure is *citation overlap*. When two cases cite the same code, or codes from the same category (i.e., *code citation overlap*), there is a strong indication that the cases are relevant to one another. Likewise, when one case directly cites another, or when two cases share a citation to a third case (i.e., *case citation overlap*), there is strong indication of relevance. Citation overlap has also been used as a metric in other work (Cheng, Holsapple, and Lee, 1996).

Our benchmark function had to account for overlaps of both code and case citations and their relative contributions to relevance. For code citation overlap, we used the information retrieval metrics *recall* and *precision*, combined by the weighted F-measure function (Lewis et al, 1996; van Rijsbergen, 1979, pp. 173-176) (See figure 6).

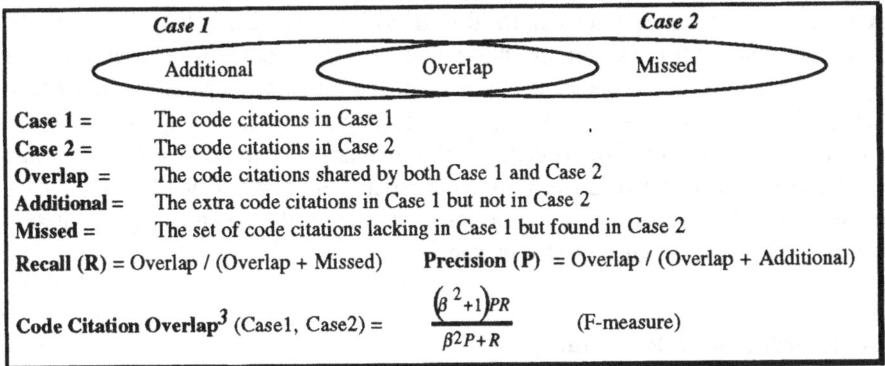

Fig. 6. Quantitative Measurement of Code Citation Overlap

Two codes can "overlap" abstractly by sharing a common ancestor in the Code Hierarchy (below the root node). Overlap is calculated by taking 1 divided by the number of levels between the codes and the level at which they share an ancestor.

Intuitively, the F-measure is a good choice for the code citation overlap because it measures the degree with which "issues" are shared between cases. Shared codes represent, roughly speaking, common issues between cases, while unshared codes represent issues relevant to one case but not the other. The more issues two cases share, proportionally speaking, the more likely they are to be relevant to one another. The F-measure computes this through a form of intersection, also imposing a penalty for lack of intersection (i.e., missing relevant codes, including irrelevant codes).

With respect to case citation overlap, we applied a shortest path algorithm between the cases. Viewing the case base as a network, with cases as nodes and case citations as edges, the shortest path between Case 1 and Case 2 is defined as the minimum number of edges between Case 1 to Case 2. Case citation overlap is computed as:

$$\textbf{Case Citation Overlap}\ (\text{Case1}, \text{Case2}) = \frac{1}{\mathit{ShortestPath}(\mathit{Case1}, \mathit{Case2})} \text{ or 0, if there is no path}$$

Thus, for instance, a direct citation between two cases results in case citation overlap = 1.0 (1/1) and a case citation shared by two cases (i.e., a case node exists between the two cases) results in case citation overlap = 0.5 (1/2).[4]

[3] ß < 1.0 gives greater weight to precision; ß = 1.0 gives equal weight to recall and precision; ß > 1.0 gives greater weight to recall. The code citation overlap ranges from 0.0 to 1.0.

The final step in computing citation overlap is combining the code citation overlap and the case citation overlap into a single measure. We implemented citation overlap as the weighted sum of the constituent overlap functions:

$$\textbf{Citation Overlap}\ (Case1, Case2) = \frac{(\alpha - 1)CodeCitationOverlap(Case1, Case2) + CaseCitationOverlap(Case1, Case2)}{\alpha}$$

To establish the benchmark it was necessary to fix the α and ß values of the citation overlap. We set ß = 2.0 to favor the recall component of the F-measure. Informal analysis of the corpus indicated that overlapping code citations are much stronger indicators of relevance than non-overlapping codes are of irrelevance. Although we have no rigorous empirical evidence, we calculated that 77.2% of the direct case citations in our corpus, those with the most obvious relevance to one another, also share at least one code citation. For the measures depicted in figure 6, ß = 2.0 establishes that Overlaps > Missed >> Additional in terms of importance.

We fixed $\alpha = 3.0$, favoring the code citation overlap over the case citation overlap by a 2-1 ratio in our weighted function. This reflects the fact that while the presence of case citation overlap is a strong indicator of relevance, the absence of case citation overlap is not a strong indicator of irrelevance.

The Experimental Procedure

Our experimental procedure is summarized in figure 7. For each Case X in our corpus of 64 cases we first calculated the citation overlap against all other cases (excluding the case itself). We then sorted the resultant list of citation overlap values, keeping only the top N cases or those above a specified threshold, whichever resulted in a shorter list. We then applied SIROCCO's Stage 1 retrieval algorithm to Case X, retrieving the top N cases according to the dot product calculation. Next, we compared SIROCCO's list of retrieved cases with the citation overlap list by computing recall between the two lists. After performing these calculations for all cases in the corpus, we calculated the mean recall value across all cases.

For the experiments reported in this paper, N was set to 10. This value strikes a balance between retrieving too few and too many cases. Because of the relative crudeness of the dot product calculation, we believed that setting N too low would allow too many relevant cases to go unretrieved. On the other hand, setting N too high would result in SIROCCO's Stage 2 algorithm being flooded with too many cases to process.

We ran the experiment varying threshold values from 0.0 to 1.0. Lower threshold values allow lower rated cases, according to the citation overlap metric, to be

---

[4] The F-measure is not appropriate for case citation overlap because direct case citations, while rare, are "overriding" indicators of relevance. That is, if Case X cites Case Y, either directly or indirectly, we can conclude that Cases X and Y are relevant to one another. Whether Cases X and Y share additional case citations is far less important to the relevance assessment. The shortest path algorithm models this overriding importance of the citation path. (Note, however, that the shortest path algorithm completely ignores additional shared citations. On the other hand, this has negligible effect on the overlap calculation, since case citations are relatively sparse in the corpus.)

compared to SIROCCO's retrieval. Higher threshold values, on the other hand, filter out the lower rated cases, comparing SIROCCO's retrieval only to the *best* possible cases. We hypothesize (and hope) that SIROCCO would perform better at higher threshold levels, since in this condition we are more likely to be comparing SIROCCO to the most relevant cases in the case base.

```
Run-SIROCCO-Experiment (N, Citation-Overlap-Threshold)
For Case X of All-Cases
    For Case Y of All-Cases (Excluding Case-X)
        Citation-Overlap-Results = Apply Citation-Overlap (Case X, Case Y)
        Add Citation-Overlap-Results to Citation-Overlap-List
    End For
    Citation-Overlap-List = Sort (Citation-Overlap-List, N, Citation-Overlap-Threshold)
    SIROCCO-Retrieval-List = Apply SIROCCO-Stage1-Retrieval (Case X, N)
    If (Citation-Overlap-List is not empty) then
        Comparison-Value [X] = Recall (SIROCCO-Retrieval-List, Citation-Overlap-List)
End For
Mean-Recall = Calculate-Mean (Comparison-Value [1 ... Length (All-Cases)])
```

Fig. 7. Pseudo-code Description of SIROCCO's Experimental Procedure

We experimented with four different versions of SIROCCO's Stage 1 retrieval algorithm. The versions varied by level of abstraction at which facts were matched. The different versions were:

- *Primitive:* Exact matches between Fact Primitives.
- *Immediate Group:* Matches between Fact Primitives 1 level up the Fact Hierarchy.
- *Sibling Group:* Matches between Fact Primitives 2 levels up the Fact Hierarchy.
- *Root Group:* Matches between Fact Primitives at the "root group" level, i.e., one level beneath the root of the Fact Hierarchy.

As a baseline, we also compared a randomly selected set of cases against the citation overlap at each threshold value.

We chose recall as the metric to compare SIROCCO's retrieval with the citation overlap because of the architectural assumption discussed earlier. It is more important that Stage 1 retrieve a high percentage of relevant cases than filter out irrelevant cases.

Experimental Results and Analysis

Figure 8 depicts the results of our experiment, comparing SIROCCO's Stage 1 retrieval algorithm (4 different versions) against the citation overlap at threshold levels ranging from 0.0 to 1.0.

Notice, first of all, that Primitive, the exact matching algorithm, performed as well as or better than the other 3 versions of the algorithm, and much better than the random comparison, at every threshold level. In fact, in a paired difference t-test, comparing Primitive's recall to the random recall, we found that Primitive performed significantly better than random at every threshold level using a significance level of

0.001. Further, Primitive performed consistently, if marginally, better than the other versions of the algorithm at higher threshold levels. Notice also that SIROCCO's retrieval gradually, but consistently, improved up to approximately the 0.8 threshold level.

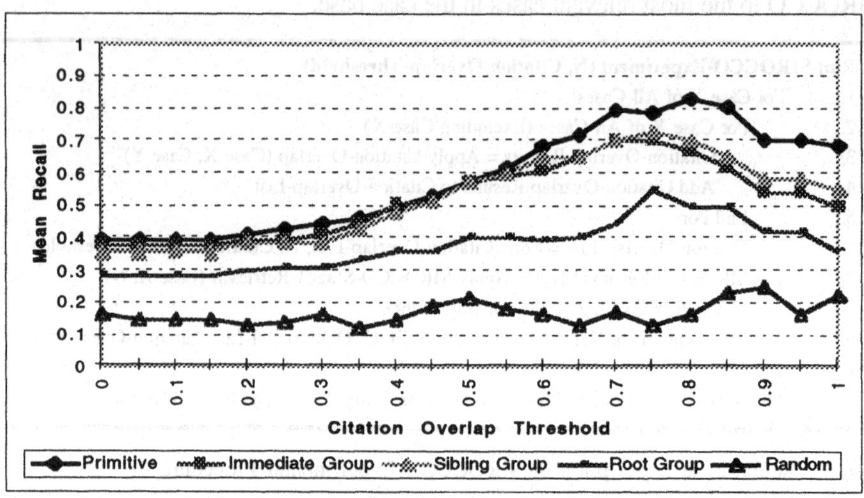

Fig. 8. Results of Comparing SIROCCO's Stage 1 retrieval against the Citation Overlap Benchmark

The results and differences between the various approaches were less impressive at the lower threshold levels. Here, however, SIROCCO's retrieval was compared to less selective sets of citation overlap cases, since the threshold was so low. Many of the cases rated in the top N by the citation overlap in this region are marginally relevant cases. Thus, we did not expect SIROCCO to perform particularly well against the benchmark under this condition. Still, as compared to random selection, the algorithm arguably performed reasonably well even in this region.

How does one assess the relative merits of the different versions of SIROCCO's retrieval algorithm? Clearly, the methods Primitive, Immediate Group, and Sibling Group performed almost identically up to the 0.55 threshold level, at which point the Primitive method performed only slightly better than the other two approaches at the remaining threshold levels. This was not altogether surprising. There are clearly situations in which an exact match is preferred, such as the matching of the most critical facts of two scenarios. On the other hand, there are also situations in which an abstract match may ultimately yield a more relevant case, for instance, in matching highly similar primitives such as <is employed by> and <is hired to provide services for> between cases which exhibit other similarities.

To study this issue in more detail, we examined how several cases fared using the different retrieval algorithms at the 0.6 threshold level. In particular, we were interested in why certain cases yielded low recall (<= 0.5) using the exact match retrieval method (i.e., Primitive), but then improved to 1.0 using one of the more abstract retrieval methods. Two cases, 70-4 and 89-2, led to a clearer understanding of this behavior. In Case 70-4, the fact chronology is moderately short (7 steps) but, more telling, the 2 most critical facts of the scenario were not matched exactly in *any* other cases. However, moving up the Fact Hierarchy led to matches with abstractly similar, yet specifically different, cases, and recall improved from 0.0 for the Primitive method to 1.0 for the Sibling Group method. Case 89-2 is a similar situation: a chronology of only 7 steps in which 5 key steps were unmatched at the Fact Primitive level. Again, moving up the Fact Hierarchy led to improved matching, this time at the Immediate Group level.

These anecdotal findings suggest that it may be fruitful to heuristically combine the different retrieval methods. For instance, cases yielding low dot product matches at the Fact Primitive level (such as 70-4 and 89-2 did) may be improved by combining the retrieval scores from the Fact Primitive and the Immediate Group levels (and so on). We will experiment with such heuristics as we further develop SIROCCO.

We noted that retrieval may fail when Fact Chronologies were excessively long. For instance, SIROCCO did not retrieve a single overlapping case at threshold = 0.6 for Case 77-11, an unusually long 17-step chronology. Upon examining the detailed matching data, it was clear that 77-11's long chronology led to dot product "swamping" with many cases, undervaluing the few highly critical steps of the chronology. Our plan to extend Stage 1 through the use of Code Instantiations will be advantageous in these situations. Code Instantiations will focus more attention (and value) on the critical steps of a fact situation, rather than treating all steps equally.

Finally, it should be noted that in the experiment cases were dropped from consideration when there were no other cases with citation overlap >= threshold (See step 8 in figure 7). While this was reasonable as part of the experimental procedure, it begs the question: How would SIROCCO perform when there are no reasonably relevant cases to retrieve? Given our intent to represent a wide range of cases, such a situation is not unlikely. We believe, again, that the Code Instantiations will assist the program in performing sufficiently well when retrieval matches are weak. The Code Instantiations will allow the program to find other cases that, while not relevant at the overall case-level, may share relevance at the level of key facts

Conclusions

In this paper, we have described SIROCCO, a case-based retrieval system designed and developed as part of our exploration into how abstract principles are applied to specific fact situations. We have devised a limited but expressive case representation language that models the actors, objects, facts, and chronology of facts in a wide range of engineering ethics scenarios. A web site acts as the case acquisition tool for the system and supports a measure of consistency in the representation. Finally, we described an experiment in which we tested an initial stage of SIROCCO's retrieval algorithm. Our results indicate that SIROCCO retrieves cases at an acceptable performance level and is not overly sensitive to small variations in case description. We also uncovered ways in which we could extend and improve SIROCCO's retrieval algorithm.

References

Aleven, V. (1997). *Teaching Case-Based Argumentation Through a Model and Examples.* Ph.D. Dissertation, University of Pittsburgh.

Ashley, K. D. and McLaren, B. M. (1995). Reasoning with Reasons in Case-Based Comparisons. In the *Proceedings of the First International Conference on Case-Based Reasoning* (ICCBR-95). Pp, 133-144. Lecture Notes in Artificial Intelligence 1010. Springer Verlag. Heidelberg, Germany.

Branting, L. K. (1990) *Integrating Rules and Precedents for Classification and Explanation: Automating Legal Analysis.* Ph.D. Dissertation. U. Texas at Austin AI Lab. AI 90-146.

Branting, L. K. (1994). A Computational Model of Ratio Decidendi. *Artificial Intelligence and Law* 2: 1-31. Kluwer Academic Publishers. Printed in the Netherlands.

Bruninghaus, S., and Ashley, K. D. (1997) Using Machine Learning to Assign Indices to Legal Cases. In the *Proceedings of the Second International Conference on Case-Based Reasoning* (ICCBR-97). Pp. 303-314. Lecture Notes in Artificial Intelligence 1266. Springer Verlag. Heidelberg, Germany.

Cheng, C. H., Holsapple, C. W. and Lee, A. (1996). Citation-Based Journal Rankings for AI Research: A Business Perspective.. *AI Magazine,* Vol. 17, No. 2.

Daniels, J. and E. Rissland. (1997) Finding Legally Relevant Passages in Case Opinions. In the *Proceedings of the Sixth International Conference on AI and Law* (ICAIL-97). Pp. 39-46. ACM Press: New York.

Forbus, K. D., Gentner, D. and Law, K. (1994). MAC/FAC: A Model of Similarity-based Retrieval. *Cognitive Science* 19, Pp. 141-205.

Jonsen A. R. and Toulmin S. (1988). *The Abuse of Casuistry: A History of Moral Reasoning*. University of CA Press, Berkeley.

Lewis, D. D., Schapire, R. E., Callan, J. P., and Papka, R. (1996). Training Algorithms for Linear Text Classifiers. In the *Proceedings of the 19th Annual International ACM-SIGIR Conference on Research and Development in Information Retrieval.* Zurich.

McLaren, B. M. and Ashley, K. D. (1998). Exploring the Dialectic Between Abstract Rules and Concrete Facts: Operationalizing Principles and Cases in Engineering Ethics. In the *Proceedings From the Fourth European Workshop on Case-Based Reasoning.* Pp, 37-51. Lecture Notes in Artificial Intelligence 1488. Springer Verlag. Heidelberg, Germany.

Mostow, J. (1983). Machine transformation of advice into a heuristic search procedure. In *Machine Learning*, vol. 1.

NSPE (1958-1997). *Opinions of the Board of Ethical Review,* Vol. I - VII and *NSPE Ethics Reference Guide.* Published by National Society of Professional Engineers, Alexandria, Virginia.

Rissland, E. L., Skalak, D. B., and Friedman, M. T. (1996). BankXX: Supporting Legal Arguments through Heuristic Retrieval. *AI and Law* 4: 1-71. Kluwer, Dordrecht.

Thagard, P., Holyoak, K., Nelson, G., and Gochfeld, (1990). Analog Retrieval by Constraint Satisfaction, *Artificial Intelligence* 46, Pp. 259-310.

van Rijsbergen, C. J. (1979). *Information Retrieval.* Butterworths, London, second edition

Flexibly Interleaving Processes

Erica Melis* Carsten Ullrich

Universität des Saarlandes, FB Informatik
D-66041 Saarbrücken, Germany
melis@cs.uni-sb.de

Abstract. We discuss several problems of analogy-driven proof plan construction which prevent a solution for more difficult target problems or make a solution very expensive. Some of these problems are due to the previously assumed fixed order of matching, reformulation, and replay in case-based reasoning and from a too restricted combination of planning from first principles with the analogy process. In order to overcome these problems we suggest to interleave matching and replay as well as case-based planning with planning from first principles.
Secondly, the restricted mixture of case-based planning and planning from first principles in previous systems is generalised to intelligently employing different planning strategies with the objective to solve more problems at all and to solve problems more efficiently.

1 Introduction

The common CBR cycle [1] consists of a sequence of the subprocesses matching + reformulation/ retrieval, replay, adaptation, and storage. However, empirical psychological results, e.g. in [6], question this fixed sequence of subprocesses of analogical reasoning.

Secondly, previous CBR systems focus on a single problem solving strategy only. This might be justified if no domain knowledge is available that could be used to solve a problem from first principles. In case-based planning (CBP), however, knowledge such as planning operators is available while control knowledge may not. In several computational case-based planning systems (including analogy-driven proof plan construction) one kind of combining case-based planning with planning from first principles is realized in which planning from first principles is employed to close open subgoals remaining after the derivational replay of a source plan or to close subgoals remaining after the transfer of abstract steps, see [3]. That is, these systems use planning from first principles for the adaptation of retrieved and replayed source plans.

Empirical evidence shows, however, that analogical reasoning can more generally be combined with standard problem solving. Psychologically this fact has been experimentally verified, e.g., in physics problem solving [18]. In physics problem solving VanLehn and Jones found that poor problem human solvers

* This work was supported by the Deutsche Forschungsgemeinschaft, SFB 378

use analogy instead of problem solving from first principles even when this is not most effective, whereas good problem solvers use analogy to learn control knowledge that is missing and to fill other knowledge gaps. Nelson, Thagard, and Hardy [16] discuss the need for a unified theory of analogy, rule-based reasoning, and explanation.

For computational case-based planning we shall question both, the previous fixed sequence of subprocesses of case-based reasoning and the restricted combination of case-based planning with planning from first principles. In particular, we demonstrate how some problems that prevent analogy-driven proof plan construction from replaying proofs that are considered analogous by mathematicians or from being efficient can be solved by interleaving several subprocesses of analogy. Furthermore, we shall show that we need more flexibility in choosing between case-based planning and planning from first principles than that resulting from closing remaining subgoals by sourceplanning from first principles.

In the remainder, we first briefly review the original analogy-driven proof plan construction. Then we discuss the problems of this and similar approaches to case-based planning and then describe solutions to these problems. Finally, we discuss a generalization to multi-strategy planning.

2 Analogy-Driven Proof Plan Construction

Analogy-driven proof plan construction was first introduced in [11] and realized in the proof planner *CLAM*[14]. Compared with previous approaches to theorem proving by analogy, its main novelties are the analogical transfer at the abstract level of proof *plans* and the need for *reformulations* of proof plans that go beyond symbol mapping. Often, these reformulations are a prerequisite for successfully second-order[1] matching a source with a target theorem that do not match in the first place. The original analogy-driven proof plan construction, as realized on top of the proof planner *CLAM* and in the ΩMEGA system [2], is outlined in Table 1.

To start with, repair-matching tries to second-order match and when no proper match is found, an appropriate reformulation is applied to the problem and then matching is tried again. When a repair-match of the problems is obtained, the found reformulations are realized.

That is, the reformulations do not only change the theorem and proof assumptions but also the proof plan. For instance, Add-Argument may duplicate whole subplans[2] or adding an antecedent may introduce an additional subgoal into the plan.

Some of the frequently needed reformulations are

- symbol-to-symbol and symbol-to-term mapping,

[1] As opposed to first-order matching, second-order matching may match function and relation variables.

[2] Actually, the routine of the original Add-Argument reformulation that checks and changes operators and subgoals of the source plan is quite complicated, since it has to traverse and analyse the whole plan and to predict local changes.

input: source plan, source theorem and assumptions, target theorem and assumptions
output: (partial) target plan

Repair-match: Attempt to second-order match source and target problems triggers reformulations of the source plan.
Reformulation: source plan ← reformulated source plan.

Replay: until source plan exhausted **do**
  Get next operator M from source plan.
  Check M's justifications.
  if justifications hold, **then** transfer M to target,
  else choose suitable action.
Plan: Plan from first principles for remaining open goals.

Table 1. Outline of analogy-driven proof plan construction

- swapping function arguments,
- duplicating arguments of functions,
- adding an antecedent to a formula,
- freezing function arguments to constants,
- abstractions, and more complex reformulations such as
- adding/removing final or initial plan segments.

The first five reformulations have been realized in the implementations described in [14] and [12]. For instance, in ABALONE [14] the reformulation Condt is applied when a source theorem Th_s is repair-matched with a target theorem $C \rightarrow Th_t$, where Th_s and Th_t match. Condt introduces C as a subgoal and closes a certain plan branch, if C is disproved.

The last kind of reformulations correspond to Carbonell's T(ransformation)-operators final-segment concatenation and initial-segment concatenation [5], where a final plan segment reduces the theorem to a (set of) subgoals and an initial segment transforms assumptions to other proof assumptions. Consider, for instance, the source theorem $Th_s : \ldots \forall x.x \in setA \rightarrow x \in setB$ and the target theorem $Th_t : \ldots \rightarrow setA' \subseteq setB'$. Initially, Th_s does not match with Th_t. Only when the operator `ApplyDefinition` applies the definition of $\subseteq$ to Th_t, then the resulting subgoal matches Th_s. Of course, the additional segments can be longer than one step and more diverse than just the operator `ApplyDefinition`.

2.1 Problems with this Analogy

When experimenting with analogy-driven proof plan construction on increasingly difficult problems a mathematician would consider analogous, we discovered several problems some of which are discussed below. Essentially, the discussed problems fall into four classes: (1) How to recognize the transfer of a source *sub*plan, (2) how to realize segment concatenations efficiently, (3) when to execute plan reformulations, and (4) on which goals to replay which operators?

1. The first class includes the following problems
   (a) **Subplans.** More often than not, a whole source plan cannot be transferred analogically but a *sub*plan is transferable. For example, if the source plan proves the theorem $A \wedge B$ and the target theorem B' matches with B, then only the subplan satisfying B should be transferred. Therefore, it is desirable to replay a subplan only. How do we know which subplan?
   (b) **Irrelevant matches.** Matching proof assumptions that do not belong to the replayed part of the source proof causes an unnecessary overhead.
2. **Final- and initial segment concatenation.** The search space for a sequence of reformulations that yields final- or initial-segment concatenation is potentially infinite, because potentially any sequence of plan operators has to be considered (such as `ApplyDefinition`, `Normalize`, etc). An efficient choice of a sequence of reformulations would require a severe restriction of the operators that can possibly be added and a restriction to short segments. This is comparable with Kolbe and Walther's 'matching modulo evaluation' in [10] that allows to add one application of a definition in case a symbol mapping reformulation does not yield a match between source and target theorem. In domains with a limited choice of operators as equality proofs, this approach may be adequate as the search space is small. In more complex proofs as planned with the ΩMEGA system, this restriction is too strict.
   An alternative way to realize certain segment concatenations is to prove the implication $(Th_s \rightarrow Th_t)$ – as Koehler proposed in [8] – and, if successful, add the resulting proof as an initial segment of the target plan (and similarly for the proof assumptions, add a subplan as a final segment). This alternative, however, excludes a combination with other reformulations, even with symbol or term mapping because the implication to be proved is fixed and therefore, a transfer of the plan is only possible when the source and target problem share the same predicates.
3. The third class of problems concerns the decision as to when and how reformulations should be applied.
   (a) **Reformulating before the replay?**
   When a reformulation is applied *before* the replay as realized previously, it may become pretty difficult to reformulate the source plan appropriately, because many local situations have to be distinguished. For instance, an additional conjunct C in a definition causes different changes depending on whether the definition is applied in forward planning or in backward planning. In forward planning, an `AndE` operator is introduced and the assumption C is added, whereas in backward planning the operator `AndI` is introduced and the goal C is added. Moreover the changes depend on the position at which C occurs in the target formula. For instance, if C is an additional conjunct hidden in a subformula of a definition as, e.g., in $(F \equiv A \wedge C \rightarrow B)$, the reformulation should affect those parts of the source plan that deal with establishing A.
   (b) **Inserting an operator or reformulating.** It is difficult to decide in advance whether the same (source) operator should be applied in

the target again or whether the plan has to be reformulated first. For instance, an operator might be applicable to a conjunctive goal as well as to a goal that is not a conjunction and in this case we do not need to apply the reformulation AddConjunct.

(c) **Origins of symbols.** In case a symbol- or term mapping is needed to repair-match the source and the target theorem, the mapping cannot generally be applied to subgoals and operators. For instance, the operator `ComplexEstimate` that is used for planning proofs of limit theorems applies, among others, the Triangle Inequality $|A+B| \leq |A|+|B|$ that contains the symbol $+$. Now if the source theorem is LIM+: $\lim_{x \to a}(f(x)+g(x)) = L_1 + L_2$ and the target theorem LIM* is $\lim_{x \to a}(f(x)*g(x)) = L_1 * L_2$, a mapping $+ \mapsto *$ would be triggered. How does this mapping affect the occurrence, change, or replacement of $+$ in a proof plan that contains `ComplexEstimate`?

As a partial solution, function- and relation symbols could be indexed. Running the source plan (again) with these indices would indicate, where which occurrence of a symbol in subgoals originates from. This indexing is realized in [9] and [14]. It may be reasonable for small proofs but produces a considerable overhead which often is unnecessary. Moreover, such a discrimination of symbols does not tell anything about the symbols occurring in operators.

(d) **Plan reformulation.** A reformulation that changes the content of operators does not fit our general philosophy, *not* to act at the low level of a logical calculus but at the plan-level in case-based proof planning. Hence, in [14] reformulations of a proof plan introduce, delete, or replace operators and subgoals (as opposed to the reformulations originally experimented with in the ΩMEGA system).

4. **Corresponding goals.** Since an operator specifies a program that produces a – not necessarily fixed – sequence of inference steps, more often than not the target subgoals/assumptions to which the next operator should be applied, are not known in advance but only after the actual application of the preceding operator. Even the number of subgoals that an operator produces may depend on the planning context. Hence, one cannot decide in advance (before any operator is replayed), on which goal to replay an operator. Suppose, in the source the operator O_1 is applied to the goal g_{s1} and O_1 was replayed on a target goal g_{t1} and produced the subgoals $g_{t11} \ldots g_{t1n}$. If the next operator O_2 was applied to one of the source subgoals produced by O_1, then – because of the goal-dependency justification – it has to be replayed on one of the g_{t1i}. Hence, we have to find the corresponding subgoals. To see that this really might be a problem, consider the following example. The operator `ModusPonensBackward` is applicable to any goal. Hence, choosing the wrong goal will most likely create a false analogical transfer.

3 Solving the Problems

In this section we describe our solutions to the above mentioned problems. Table 2 gives an outline of the revised analogy-driven proof plan construction.

---

input: source plan, source theorem and assumptions, target theorem and assumptions
output: (partial) target plan

Repair-match or plan:
  until
    a cheap second-order repair-match between target theorem and a source (sub)goal g_s down to depth d is found

  do plan from first principles for target goal.

$M :=$ operator satisfying g_s
Interleaved match/replay:
until source plan exhausted **do**

  Repair-Match:
  Find target goal g_t corresponding to g_s by extending the repair-match.
  ReplayRef:
  if M applicable **then** apply M to g_t and
  advance source plan ($M :=$ next operator, $g_s :=$ goal satisfied by M)
  else apply reformulation triggered by repair-match or by the failed application conditions.

Plan: Plan from first principles for remaining open goals.

Table 2. Outline of the revised analogy-driven proof plan construction

In the **repair-match or plan** cycle, we establish a connection between the target theorem and a source (sub)goal. First, we try to repair-match the target theorem with the source theorem. In case no collection of *simple* reformulations[3] of the source goal matches the target theorem, we try to match with subgoals down to depth d (parameter) in the source plan until a simple repair-match with a subgoal can be established. If no cheap repair-match is found, we plan one step from first principles and restart the **repair-match or plan** cycle. The planning step yields a step in a final plan segment.

In the **match/replay** cycle, we try to replay an operator M from the source plan. In order to apply M in a correct way (problem 4), we first find the target goal corresponding to the currently treated g_s by repair-matching the g_s against

[3] Simple reformulations are: symbol mapping, term mapping, permutation of arguments, freezing arguments, duplication of arguments, adding conjuncts, adding antecedents.

those target goals that satisfy the same goal dependencies as g_s. If M is applicable, M is replayed in the target. Otherwise, a reformulation triggered by the repair-match or by the failed application conditions of the operator to be replayed is applied in a way corresponding to the local situation. For instance, the reformulation AddConjunct triggered by repair-matching source and target goals may result in additionally applying the operator `AndIntro` and in introducing a new subgoal.

Eventually, when the source plan is exhausted, the remaining open goals are tackled by planning from first principles.

More often than not – but depending on the generality of the operators – the application conditions of an operator still hold when the repair-match consists of swapping arguments, symbol mapping, or term mapping. Then, no proper plan change is necessary at all and the repair-match is used only to specify the goal correspondences.

Reformulations represent heuristics on how to resolve critical differences between goals or assumptionsof source and target and on how to change plans when a replay is not possible in the first place. Since reformulations change a plan by adding, removing, and replacing operators rather than by changing the (code of the) operators directly (see problem 3d), an interesting conclusion is that domain-dependent knowledge has to be used in order to determine by which operator to replace a source operator in order to be applicable to the reformulated goal. For instance, in proving theorems for real numbers that involve estimations, the correspondence between a source goal $a < b$ and a target goal $a > b$ requires to replace a $\texttt{Solve}_<$ operator by a $\texttt{Solve}_>$ operator.

3.1 What do the Solutions look like?

How does this new analogy-procedure solve the above mentioned problems?

Problem 1a. Going down the source plan for repair-matching means to restrict the potential replay to *sub*plans. For example, let $Th_t : A \wedge B \rightarrow C$ be the target theorem, $Th_s : F$ the source theorem and $g_{s_1} : A' \wedge B' \rightarrow C'$ a source subgoal of depth one which results from applying the operator `ApplyDefinition` on Th_s. To find the (sub)plan to be transfered, we start by repair-matching Th_t and Th_s. As no cheap repair-match is found, we continue by stepwise going down the source plan to match the subgoal g_{s_1} with Th_t. Here, a cheap repair-match is possible. As a result the subplan whose root node is g_{s_1} is replayed analogically as illustrated in Figure 1.

Problem 1b is solved by matching assumptions when needed only. It does not make much sense to try to match every source assumption with a target assumption *before* the replay of the proof plan because not every source assumption belongs to the partial plan that is actually replayed. Therefore, this matching takes place within the **interleaved match/replay** routine.

Problem 2 is solved by the planning part in the **repair-match or plan** cycle which produces a plan segment as shown in Figure 2. Consider the following example: let be $Th_s : A \wedge B \rightarrow C$ be the source theorem and $Th_t : F$ the target

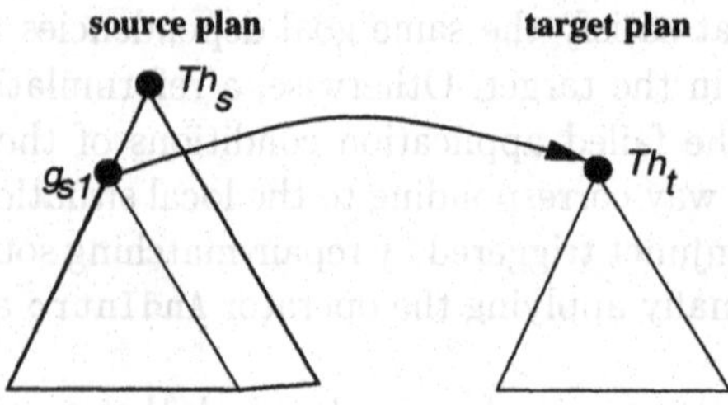

Fig. 1. Finding a subplan for the replay

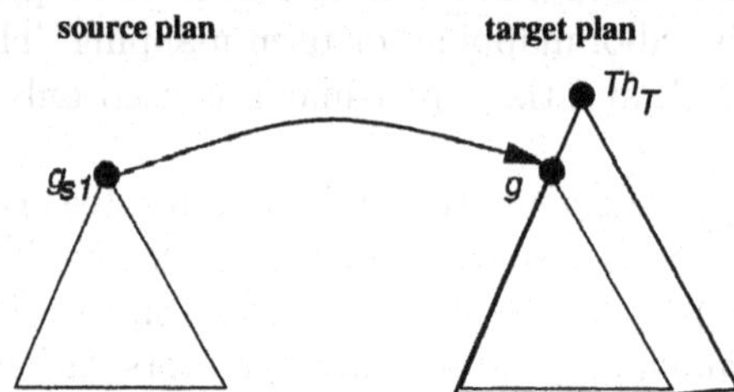

Fig. 2. Planning produces segment concatenation

theorem. No cheap repair-match is found (even when looking at the subgoals), so we plan from first principles in the target. This suggests the application of the operator ApplyDefinition which has the subgoal $g_{t_1} : A' \wedge B' \to C'$. Now, repeating the cycle, we find a cheap repair-match between Th_s and the newly created g_{t_1}. This yields a final-segment concatenation. An initial-segment concatenation is naturally produced by planning for remaining goals including those suggested as new target lemmata by certain reformulations.

Problem 3. By delaying the application of a reformulation, we have exact information about the locally needed reformulations (e.g., is an operator applicable without any reformulation of the plan as asked in problem 3b) including the (local) effects of a reformulation that are clearly understood (thus solving problem 3a). For instance, let's assume that the last operator we replayed produced the target subgoals $g_{t_1} : A' \wedge B'$ and $g_{t_2} : C' \vee D'$. The next operator to be replayed is ApplyDefinition, which was applied in the source plan on $g_{s_1} : A$. Repair-matching g_{s_1} with g_{t_1} and g_{t_2} returns the cheapest match $m : g_{s_1} \mapsto g_{t_1}$ even though g_{t_1} contains an additional conjunct. Now the application of the operator ApplyDefinition is tried. If it is not applicable due to failing application conditions, then the failure is analyzed. The failure analysis might find that the cause is the additional conjunct B'. This would trigger a reformulation that locally introduces the additional planning step AndIntro with the subgoals $g_{t_3} : A'$ and $g_{t_4} : B'$. On $g_{t_3} : A'$ the replay of ApplyDefinition is finally possible.

Problem 4 is solved by the **interleave match/replay** cycle because at that point in the analogy procedure the set of target subgoals is known that contains the goal that corresponds to a given source subgoal.
To summarize, interleaving matching and analogical replay with planning from first principles can help to reduce prohibitively large search spaces when searching for reformulations and their possible effects on a proof plan. Interleaving processes in analogy-driven prof plan construction allows for simpler reformulations at the plan-level and for a more tractable matching. The interleaving results in a more flexible analogy that is easier to implement and more powerful.

An example for a proof plan produced by our case-based planning is a partial plan for LIM*, i.e., the goal
$\lim_{x \to a} f(x) = L_1 \wedge \lim_{x \to a} g(x) = L_2 \to \lim_{x \to a} f(x) * g(x) = L_1 * L_2$, shown in Figure 3, where light circles represent nodes in the proof plan with closed subgoals and operators, darker circles represent open goals, the triangles represent hypotheses and proof assumptions and squares are coreferences). The source plan is one of

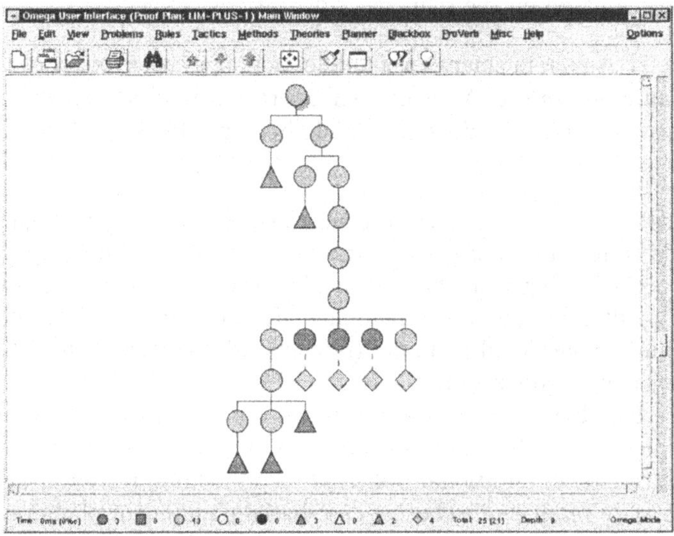

Fig. 3. Screenshot from planning LIM* by analogy to LIM+ in OMEGA (open goals are darker)

LIM+ defined by the assumptions $\lim_{x \to a} f(x) = L_1$, $\lim_{x \to a} g(x) = L_2$ and the goal $\lim_{x \to a} f(x) + g(x) = L_1 + L_2$. For LIM*, first some planning from first principles introduces `Normalize` operators and then case-based planning replays operators of the plan of LIM+ as long as possible. Then planning from first principles satisfies the remaining open goals.

4 Flexibly Planning with Multiple Strategies

In the above procedure, the subprocesses of analogy, planning, match, reformulation, and replay are interleaved when needed. Similarly, we may ask: Why should we solve a planning problem *only* by analogy in the first place rather than calling the analogy by need only? In particular, it is conceivable that different planning operations can be interleaved when necessary or when efficient. For instance, instead of encoding a fixed sequence of planning from first principle, expansion of operators, and instantiation of meta-variables, an intelligent interleaving of these planning operations is useful.

From a case-based reasoning perspective, we propose a flexible mixture of case-based planning with planning from first principles. This is in accordance with the psychological results cited in the introduction. Further psychological evidence suggests that the unreflected analogical transfer of *all* steps of a plan, independent on how simple the subproblem is, is a rather novice-like behaviour [18].

In order to describe our multi-strategy approach, first we define what a planning strategy is based on the refinement operations defined in [7].

Definition 1. Any refinement or modification operation on partial plans is called a *planning strategy.* A refinement operation refines a partial plan π by adding steps and or constraints to π and thereby reduces the set of potential solutions.

In fact, case-based planning can be considered a particular refinement operation. It adds steps and order constraints to a partial plan. Similarly, plan-space or state-space planning from first principles, the expansion of a complex operators [17], difference-reduction planning [4], and the instantiation of meta-variables can be considered planning (refinement) strategies; they go, however, beyond the scope of this paper.

The case-based planning strategy suggests the next planning operator rather than searching for it. Thereby this strategy may reduce the search in planning. However, it causes an additional overhead for matching, retrieval, and adaptation. Hence, only *intelligently* chosing case-based planning or planning from first principles can reduce the overall effort in planning.

Hence, if only one operator is applicable in a plan node after the control-rules have been evaluated (i.e., no branching occurs), then it does not make sense to choose case-based planning because it causes more overhead than planning from first principles. Therefore, case-based planning pays and is chosen in particular, when control knowledge is absent or rare.

We designed a meta-planner that has several strategies at its disposal [13] in order to employ different planning strategies in a flexible way. In the ΩMEGA system [2], we just implemented a first prototype of the multi-strategy planner that has an analogy strategy as one of several planning strategies. The meta-planner decides which of several strategies to use in a particular situation. The meta-planner does not cause much overhead other than evaluating control heuristics.

For instance, for planning LIM*, first some default planning from first principles is performed. That is, the applications of operators such as `Quantifier-Elimination` and `Normalization` are planned essentially without any search. A branching of the search space occurs for the first time when the `Focus` operator is to be applied. The reason is that `Focus` can be applied to any existing subformula of the assumption. If no control knowledge supports the choice of the subformula, the number of subformulae is the branching factor. Therefore, the case-based planning strategy is called and it replays the `Focus` operator with a similar instantiation of the subformula to be focused on in LIM+ and then `Unwraphyp` and `ComplexEstimate` operators are replayed, etc. Certain subgoals cannot be closed by analogical replay but are satisfied by the strategy planning from first principles. After completing the top-level plan of LIM*, the instantiation strategy is applied for particular meta-variables. Then the (complex) operators, indicated by the light circles in Figure 3, can be expanded to subplans by the expansion strategy such that eventually the fully expanded plan has about 420 steps. The remaining meta-variables are instantiated only when certain operators are expanded.

Qualitatively, a flexible choice of strategies allows more problems to be solved without changing the code of the planner or of strategies such as case-based planning. Moreover, new strategies can be integrated more easily into planning.

Quantitatively, i.e., in order to yield a more efficient planning process, the decision which strategy to choose in a particular planning situation needs to address the well known utility problem discussed, e.g., in [15]. So, the meta-planner should decide to call case-based planning only when the analogy-drivenproof plan construction is superior to planning from first principles in terms of estimated costs. Currently, the meta-planner aims at reducing the costs only because other measures such as the quality of proof plans are even more difficult to evaluate. In particular, the estimation $cost_{fp} > cost_{cbp}$, where fp means planning from first principles and cbp means case-based planning, may be computed based on

$$cost_{fp} \approx n \cdot (mc + ac) \cdot b^{(l-1)}, \quad cost_{cbp} \approx (rmc + rc + ac) \cdot l, \tag{1}$$

where n is the number of alternatives in the current planning situation *after* the evaluation of control knowledge, mc is the average match costs of a single operator, ac is the average cost of an operator application, b is the average branching factor, l is the expected length of the remaining plan, rmc is the average cost of repair matching, and rc is the average cost of a reformulation.

If $cost_{fp} > cost_{cbp}$ then case-based planning is preferred, oherwise planning from first principles. This means that if the saved search overweights the overhead of the case-based planning strategy caused by the matching and reformulation, then choosing case-baed planning is superior to planning from first principles.

The estimation of $cost_{fp}$ is related to the number n of alternative operators remaining *after* the evaluation of control-rules. That is, the available control knowledge decreases the estimated costs for planning from first principles considerably. Therefore, the better the control knowledge, the more likely will the choice of standard planning be as opposed to case-based planning.

A lesson for case-based reasoning in general is its controlled use, i.e. case-based reasoning should be chosen only when it is superior to other problem solving strategies, i.e., when other strategies cannot find a solution or when analogy has lower estimated costs than other working strategies. Of course, control heuristics are necessary, e.g. heuristics that evaluate the complexity of the plan reformulations and compare this with the branching of the search space.

5 Conclusion and Future Work

We presented a more flexible analogy procedure that can interleave planning from first principles with repair-matching and that interleaves repair-matching with replay in case-based proof planning. The greater flexibility leads to a better performance and allows to solve more problems with our analogy-driven proof plan construction.

The comparison with our previous procedure is explained in detail above. Compared with Veloso's case-based planning [19] our procedure has reformulations and the repair-match rather than a simple symbol match, Veloso's match does not allow to match one symbol of the source to several symbols in the target, and our analogy can plan from first principles not just for initial-segment but also for final-segment concatenations. Furthermore, the proof planning domain is more complicated than the typical planing domains.

We have just implemented an even more radical interplay of case-based planning with other planning strategies that allows to invoke case-based planning or planning from first principles dependent on the planning situation. A meta-planner chooses the strategies according to strategic control knowledge. Although some strategic knowledge is encoded into the estimation (1), we expect it to be a crude estimation. Therefore, we plan to rather learn the strategic control decisions.

References

1. A. Aamodt and E. Plaza. Case-based reasoning: Foundational issues, methodological variations, and system approaches. *AI Communications*, 7:39–59, 1994.
2. C. Benzmueller, L. Cheikhrouhou, D. Fehrer, A. Fiedler, X. Huang, M. Kerber, M. Kohlhase, K. Konrad, A. Meier, E. Melis, W. Schaarschmidt, J. Siekmann, and V. Sorge. OMEGA: Towards a mathematical assistant. In W. McCune, editor, *Proceedings 14th International Conference on Automated Deduction (CADE-14)*, pages 252–255, Townsville, 1997. Springer.
3. R. Bergmann, H. Munoz-Avila, M.M. Veloso, and E. Melis. Case-based reasoning applied to planning. In M. Lenz, B. Bartsch-Spörl, H.-D. Burkhard, and S. Wess, editors, *Case-Based Reasoning Technology from Foundations to Applications*, volume 1400 of *Lecture Notes on Artificial Intelligence (LNAI)*, pages 169–200. Springer, 1998.
4. A. Bundy, Stevens A, F. Van Harmelen, A. Ireland, and A. Smaill. A heuristic for guiding inductive proofs. *Artificial Intelligence*, 63:185–253, 1993.

5. J.G. Carbonell. Learning by analogy: Formulating and generalizing plans from past experience. In R.S. Michalsky, J.G. Carbonell, and T.M. Mitchell, editors, *Machine Learning: An Artificial Intelligence Approach*, pages 137–162. Tioga, Palo Alto, 1983.
6. K.J. Holyoak, L.R. Novick, and E.R. Melz. Component processes in analogical transfer: Mapping, pattern completion, and adaptation. In K.J. Holyoak and J.A. Barnden, editors, *Advances in Connectionist and Neural Computation Theory*, volume 2, pages 113–180. Ablex Publishing, 1994.
7. S. Kambhampati and B. Srivastava. Universal classical planner: An algorithm for unifying state-space and plan-space planning. In M. Ghallab and A. Milani, editors, *New Directions in AI Planning*, pages 61–78. IOS Press, Amsterdam, Oxford, 1996.
8. J. Koehler. Planning from second principles. *Artificial Intelligence*, 87, 1996.
9. Th. Kolbe and Ch. Walther. Reusing proofs. In *Proceedings of 11th European Conference on Artificial Intelligence (ECAI-94)*, Amsterdam, 1994.
10. Th. Kolbe and Ch. Walther. Second-order matching modulo evaluation – a technique for reusing proofs. In *Proceedings of the 14th International Joint Conference on Artificial Intelligence*, Montreal, 1995. Morgan Kaufmann.
11. E. Melis. A model of analogy-driven proof-plan construction. In *Proceedings of the 14th International Joint Conference on Artificial Intelligence*, pages 182–189, Montreal, 1995.
12. E. Melis. The Heine-Borel challenge problem: In honor of Woody Bledsoe. *Journal of Automated Reasoning*, 20(3):255–282, 1998.
13. E. Melis. Proof planning with multiple strategies. In *CADE-15 workshop: Strategies in Automated Deduction*, 1998.
14. E. Melis and J. Whittle. Analogy in inductive theorem proving. *Journal of Automated Reasoning*, 22:2 117–147, 1999.
15. S. Minton. Quantitative results concerning the utility of explanation-based learning. *Artificial Intelligence*, 42:363–391, 1990.
16. G. Nelson, P. Thagard, and S. Hardy. Integrating analogy with rules and explanations. In *Advances in Connectionist and Neural Computation, Analogical Connections*, volume 2, pages 181–206. Ablex, 1994.
17. A. Tate. Generating project networks. In *Proceedings of the Fifth International Joint Conference on Artificial Intelligence*, pages 888–893. Morgan Kaufmann, 1977.
18. K. VanLehn and R.M. Jones. Better learners use analogical problem solving sparingly. In *Proceedings of the Tenth International Conference on Machine Learning*, pages 338–345, Amherst, MA, 1993. Morgan Kaufmann.
19. M.M. Veloso. Planning and Learning by Analogical Reasoning. Springer Verlag, Berlin, New York,x 1994.

A Case Retention Policy Based on Detrimental Retrieval

Héctor Muñoz-Avila

Department of Computer Science
University of Maryland
College Park, MD 20742-3255
munoz@cs.umd.edu
(301) 405-2684 | FAX: 405-6707

Abstract. This paper presents a policy to retain new cases based on retrieval benefits for case-based planning (CBP). After each case-based problem solving episode, an analysis of the adaptation effort is made to evaluate the guidance provided by the retrieved cases. If the guidance is determined to be detrimental, the obtained solution is retain as a new case in the case base. Otherwise, if the retrieval is beneficial, the case base remains unchanged. We will observe that the notion of adaptable cases is not adequate to address the competence of a case base in the context of CBP. Instead, we claim that the notion of detrimental retrieval is more adequate. We compare our retain policy against two policies in the CBP literature and claim that our policy to retain cases based on the benefits is more effective. Our claim is supported by empirical validation.

1 Introduction

With the increasing use of CBR technology in real-world applications, case bases have become larger and the question of how to maintain them has become a necessary issue to address (Leake & Wilson, 1998; Watson, 1997, Chapter 8). In recent years researchers have turned their attention towards case base maintenance. Policies have been studied for reducing the size of the case base without sacrificing competence (Racine & Yang, 1997; Kitano & Shimazu, 1996; Smyth & Keane, 1998).

A complementary issue to overall policies to maintain a case base, is the policy to retain new solutions obtained from case-based planning episodes. An ideal case retention policy should add new cases in the case base only if the competence of the case base is improved. However, establishing adequate case retention policies can be very difficult; if the case retention policy is too restrictive, opportunities to increase the competence of the case base will be lost. If the case retention policy is too permissive, the case base will grow too much making overall case maintenance costly and may even loose competence. Increasing the benefits over the costs of retaining knowledge is a common problem for learning systems (Markovich & Scott, 1993). In the context of case-based planning (CBP), two case retention policies have been proposed:

- *Eager Case Retention Policy.* This is a "default policy"; every new solution is retain as a new case in the case base. It is directly inherited from the CBR problem solving cycle (Lenz et. al. 1998; Aamodt & Plaza, 1994).
- *Case Retention Policy based on Retrieval Failures.* This is a more elaborate policy (Ihrig & Kambhampati, 1996). During the adaptation process, the retrieved cases can be either extended to a solution of the new problem or parts of the cases must be revised to obtain the solution. In the first situation, the retrieval is said to fail and the adapted solution is retain as a new case in the case base.

Intuition suggest that the Eager Case Retention Policy is too permissive and yield large case bases. The Case Retention Policy based on Retrieval Failures requires a more careful analysis. The first problem we faced to make this analysis is that no appropriate conceptual tools have been developed to analyze the competence in the context of CBR. Smyth and Keane (1998) observed that competence is reduced if adaptable cases fail to be retrieved or if non-adaptable cases are retrieved. We state that the notion of adaptable cases is not appropriate for CBP. Instead we proposed measure competence based the notions of beneficial and detrimental retrieval.

Based on the notions of beneficial and detrimental retrieval, we will observe that the Case Retention Policy based on Retrieval Failures may decrease the competence of the case bases and propose a new policy, *Case Retention Policy based on Detrimental Retrieval*, to address this flaw. We claim that our policy will result in more competent case bases. Our claim will be supported by empirical evaluation.

The next sections introduce the adaptation method used for this study, analize the Case Retention Policy based on Retrieval Failures, introduce the Case Retention Policy based on Detrimental Retrieval, present empirical studies, discuss related work, and make some final remarks.

2 Adaptation by Derivational Replay

The adaptation method that we use is Derivational Replay (Veloso & Carbonell, 1993). In this method, instead of storing the solution plan *Sol* in the case, the derivational trace followed to obtain *Sol* is stored. The derivational trace is the sequence of planning decisions that were taken to obtain *Sol*.

The notion of derivational trace can be illustrated with an example in the logistics transportation domain (Veloso, 1994). A typical problem in the logistics transportation domain is to place the objects at different locations starting from a configuration from objects, locations and transportation means. There are differents sorts of locations and means of transportation. The means of transportation have certain operational restrictions. For example, a truck can only be moved between two places located within the same city. Figure 1 illustrates a typical situation in the logistics transportation domain. In this situation there are three post offices A, B and C. In A there is a package p_1 and a truck. In B

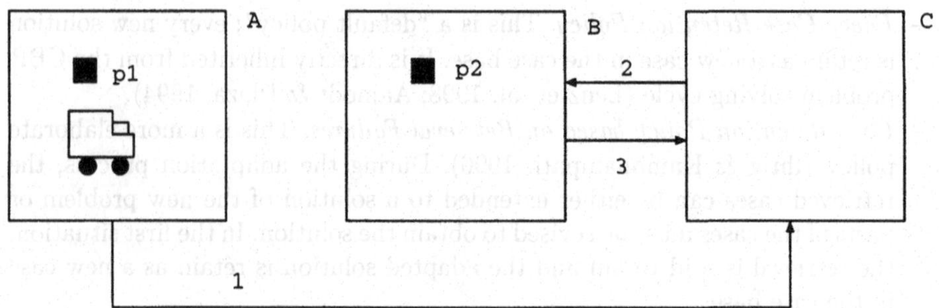

Fig. 1. A situation in the logistics transportation domain.

there is a package p_2. Suppose that two goals g_1 and g_2 are stated consisting of relocating p_1 and p_2, respectively, in C. The arrows in Figure 1 depict a plan followed by the truck. In this plan, p_1 is loaded in the truck, the truck is moved from A to C (arc 1), where p_1 is dropped. Then, the truck is moved from C to B (arc 2), where p_2 is loaded. Finally, the truck is moved from B to C (arc 3), where p_2 is dropped. The derivational trace generating this plan has the form "1: apply the action *load* to load p_1 in the truck", "2: apply the action *move* to drive the truck from A to C", and so on.

When adapting a case with derivational replay, the derivational trace is followed by applying the planning decisions to the new problem. A planning decision in the derivational trace is only replayed if no inconsistency will occur as a result of replaying it. For example if the decision says "order the action resulting from applying decision X before the action resulting from applying decision Y" and in the current plan these actions are already in the opposite order, the decision is not replayed because a cycle would be introduced in the plan.

Adaptation with derivational replay presupposes an interaction with the a first-principles planner (Bergmann et. al., 1998). That is, part of the planning process is performed by replaying decisions of one or more cases and the rest of the planning is done by the first-principles planner. In the particular approach we will follow replay is done first and, then, the partial solution obtained by replay is completed by the first-principles planner. This strategy is particularly suitable for partial-order planners such as the one that we use in this study, CAPLAN (Weberskirch, 1995), because of their capability to interleave actions in the plan (Ihrig & Kambhampati, 1994).

Other aspects of derivational replay involve the construction and application of justifications (Veloso, 1994; Muñoz-Avila, 1998), however, we omit further discussion of this issue for the sake of simplicity.

3 Case Retention based on Retrieval Failures

This policy states that the adapted solution is retained as a new case if a retrieval failure occurs (Ihrig & Kambhampati, 1996):

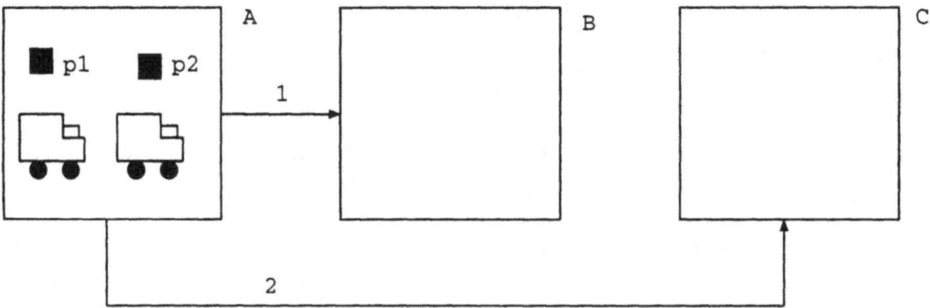

Fig. 2. Distributing 2 packages with 2 trucks.

Definition 1 (Retrieval Failure, Adequate Retrieval). *Given a solution plan Sol of a problem P obtained by adapting a case C, the retrieval of C is a* **failure** *with respect to P and Sol if at least one decision replayed from C was revised by the first-principles planner to obtain Sol. Otherwise the retrieval of C is said to be* **adequate**. *The partial solution obtained after replay is called the* **skeletal plan**.

This definition says that the retrieval of a case is considered adequate if the partial solution obtained after replay (i.e., the skeletal plan) can be extended to a complete solution without having to revise any of the decisions that were replayed from the case. Decisions replayed from the cases are only revised if no extension of the skeletal plan is possible.

Example of a Retrieval Failure. Suppose that a case is stored in which the following problem is solved: two packages are located in a post office A, one of them must be relocated to a post office B and the other one to a location C. Suppose that two trucks are available at A and the solution plan stored in the case consists of two subplans: one uses one truck to relocate one package in B and the other subplan uses the other truck to relocate the other package in C (see Figure 2). If the problem is modified such that only a single truck is available, using the case results in a retrieval failure: initially, the skeletal plan obtained after replay will replicate the two subplans in the case by using two trucks. A condition of the form "different trucks t_1 and t_2" will remain unsolved in the skeletal plan (see Figure 3). When the first-principles planner tries to complete the skeletal plan, it will find that the condition cannot be satisfied. As a result part of the skeletal plan will be removed. Specifically, one of the two subplans will be removed by the first principles planner. The other subplan will remain, and will be completed by driving back the truck to A, picking the other package and moving it to the remaining post office to drop it (see Figure 4).

This case retention policy was proposed as part of a framework for case-based planning (Ihrig & Kambhampati, 1996). We avoid discussing the framework as it is beyond the purpose of this paper and concentrate solely on the policy.

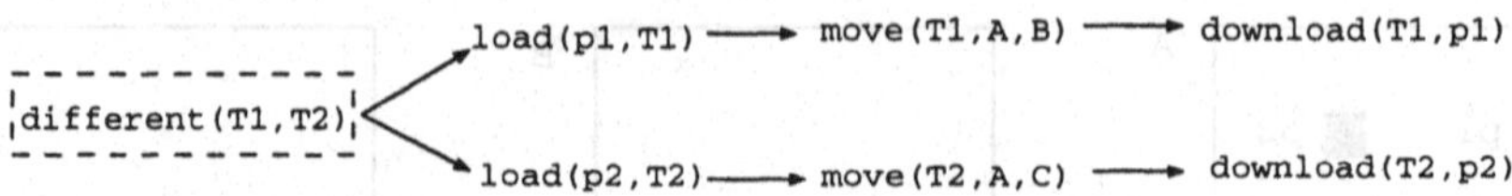

Fig. 3. Skeletal plan obtained after replay. The dashed box represents an unsolved condition to be achieved by the first-principles planner.

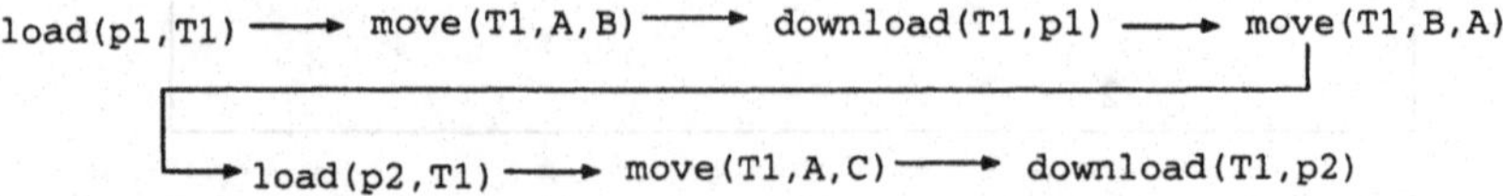

Fig. 4. Plan obtained after revising parts of the skeletal plan.

4 Case Retention based on Detrimental Retrieval

Loosely speaking a case is adaptable with respect to a new problem if it can be modified to obtain a solution of the new problem. In the context of CBP, this notion is frequently not useful. For example, partial-order planners have been shown to be complete (McAllester & Rosenblitt 1991). That is, all possible solutions of any solvable problem can be generated. As a direct consequence of this, derivational replay based on a partial-order planner is also complete (Muñoz-Avila, 1998). This means that any case is adaptable with respect to any solvable problem. Thus, establishing the competence of a case base based on the notion of adaptability is not useful.

An alternative is to use the notion of Retrieval Failure. According to this notion, the retrieval of a case is adequate if the partial solution obtained after replay can be extended to a complete solution without having to revise any of the decisions that were replayed from the case (i.e., without revising any part of the skeletal plan). However, we identified the following problems:

1. **Increase in Redundancy.** There are situations where, even if the retrieval is a failure, the effort to complete the solution might not be large. In this situation retaining a new case is clearly unnecessary. An example of such a situation is the following: Suppose that the case described at the end of the previous section is actually a small part of a case involving the distribution of several packages between and within several cities. Suppose that a new problem is presented that is almost the same as this case except that only one truck is available for one of the cities (i.e., the same mismatch as in the example in the previous section). Clearly, the retrieval will be a failure, however, the extent of the revision is so small compared to the size of the complete solution that retaining the new solution does not increase the competence to the case base.
2. **Decrease in Competence.** There are situations in which the retrieval of the case is adequate but the completion effort of the skeletal plan is large. As an example, suppose that the case base contains a single case consisting of

a single action moving a truck from one location to another. If a problem is given, requiring several packages to be distributed within the city, this case would be retrieved several times and the retrieval will always be successful. However, this particular case is not helpful to solve the problem and, even worse, the adapted solution is not retained into the case base because no retrieval failure occurs.

These problems relate to the *benefit* of retrieving the case.

The fact that the retrieval of the case is not a failure does not necessarily imply that retrieving it results in a benefit to the case-based problem solving process. One difficulty in assessing the benefit is that there is no domain-independent procedure for measuring it. To precisely measure the benefit of solving the problem with the case-based planner it would be necessary to know the effort required by the first-principles planner to solve the problem alone. This is, of course, not feasible. Instead, we introduce a heuristic measure to determine the benefit of the retrieval:

Definition 2 (Detrimental Retrieval). *Given a solution plan Sol of a problem P obtained by adapting a case C, then the retrieval of C is* **detrimental** *with respect to P and C if:*

$$searchSpace(Sol)/searchSpace(Sk_C) > thr_{det}$$

where Sk_C indicates the skeletal plan obtained from replaying C, thr_{det} is a predefined threshold and searchSpace(Sol) *returns the size of the search space explored to obtain the plan Sol. The threshold thr_{det} is called the detrimental threshold. Nondetrimental retrievals are said to be* **beneficial**.

The function *searchSpace(Psol)* counts the number of decisions made to compute the skeletal plan Sk_C. Thus, *searchSpace(Sol)* $\geq$ searchSpace(Sk_C) always holds. The detrimental threshold thr_{det} determines how eagerly cases will be learned. If, for example, $thr_{det} = 1$, then any change made to find *Sol* causes the retrieval to be considered detrimental. That is, the retrieval will only be consider beneficial if Sk_C is a solution of P. If the value of thr_{det} is set to 2, the retrieval is detrimental if the size of the search space explored to complete the case is at least as big as the number of replayed decisions.

We will now show that the concept of retrieval failure (resp. adequate retrieval) is independent of the concept of detrimental retrieval (resp. beneficial retrieval). That is, There are situations in which the retrieval fails but it is beneficial or the retrieval is adequate but detrimental. In the first situation, some replayed decisions were revised to obtain a solution but the effort to complete the solution was within acceptable limits. In the second situation, no replayed decisions were revised but the effort to complete the solution was too large. The examples discussed at the beginning of this section serve to illustrate these situations. We can now introduce the Case Retention Policy based on detrimental Retrieval:

The Case Retention Policy based on Detrimental Retrieval retains an adapted solution as a new case if and only if the retrieval of the cases is detrimental with respect to the problem and the solution.

5 Empirical Validation

The goal of the experiments is to compare the three policies for retaining cases by examining the competence of the resulting case bases.

5.1 Problem Domains

We performed experiments in the domain of process planning and in an extension of the logistics transportation domain. The domain of process planning is characterized by the high number of interactions between subplans (Muñoz-Avila & Weberskirch, 1996a).[1] The source of the interactions are ordering restrictions on the use of manufacturing resources; namely, the cutting tools and the clamping machine. For example, to machine two different areas of a piece of raw material, mounting different cutting tools may be required. Thus, the machining subplans of these areas interact, which means than one has to be executed before the other one.

The logistics transportation domain was originally specified in (Veloso, 1994). In this domain, there are also resources; namely, trucks and airplanes. However, in contrast to the domain of process planning, the more resources are made available, the less likely it is that subplans will interact. For example, if two packages must be relocated within the same city and two trucks are available, each truck can be used to relocate one package. The extension of the logistics transportation domain adds the following restrictions: trucks must not be moved into the same post office more than once and problem-specific restrictions such as not allowing the truck to move from a certain post office to another post office (Ihrig and Kambhampati, 1996). This restriction is added to create more efficient plans.

5.2 The CBP System

The case-based planner used for the experiments is CAPLAN/CBC (Muñoz-Avila & Weberskirch, 1996b). CAPLAN/CBC has an static and a dynamic mode to compute similarity. In the static mode, similarity between a problem and a case remains the same independent of previous case-based planning episodes. In the dynamic mode, similarity is computed based on feature weighting, in which the weights of the features are recomputed depending on whether the retrieval was a failure or adequate (Muñoz-Avila & Hüllen, 1996). In this way, we will observe the effects of the three policies for static similarity metrics and for dynamic similarity metrics, which are likely to improve the accuracy of the retrieval over a period of several CBP episodes.

[1] The domain specification can be downloaded from wwwagr.informatik.uni-kl.de/~caplan.

5.3 Experimental Setup

The experiment consisted of 5 runs. In each run, a problem, called the pivot problem, was first introduced. A solution for the pivot problem was found; the solution together with the problem were used to form a case, C. All feature weights of C were set to 1. Then, some features of the pivot problem were randomly selected. A new goal and new features that do not occur in the pivot problem were also introduced. Taking as basis the pivot problem, new problems were formed by changing the selected features, or/and by retaining the new goal and the new features. Changing a selected feature means changing the relations between the objects mentioned in the feature. For example, if a feature states that a truck is in a certain location, the changed feature will state that the truck is in another location. The problem collection met the following conditions:

1. For every problem in the collection, at least 75% of its features match features in the new problem. Thus if the static similarity metric is used and the retrieval threshold is less or equal then 75%, C is always retrieved.
2. The number of times that selected features were changed in the collection is the same. For example, if a selected feature indicates the location of a truck and another selected feature indicates that a post office is in a certain city, the number of problems in which the truck is changed of location is the same as the number of problems in which the post office is changed of city.
3. If n denotes the number of selected features, then problems were ordered in a way that within a sequence of n problems, $Problem_{mn+1}, ..., Problem_{mn+n}$, the number of changes of a selected feature is the same ($m = 0, 1, ...$). For this reason, the number of problems in the collection is a multiple of the number of selected features.

In the experiments the multiple factor was 5. In addition, in the logistics transportation domain 5 features were selected and in the domain of process planning 6. Thus, the collections consisted of 25 problems in the first domain and 30 in the second one. The total number of problems involved were 125 in the logistics transportation domain and 150 in the domain of process planning.

Discussion about the Experimental Setup. The ideal experiment to show the increase of reliability with feature weighting is to form all possible combinations of collections of problems and show that the increase occurs in average. Because such a process implies a combinatorial explosion, we stated conditions (2) and (3) to equally distributing the effect of every change in the fixed features and of capturing the average situation.

5.4 The Results

The detrimental threshold was set to 2 and the following items were measured:

1. *Percentage of cases retrieved.* This is a measure of how many cases are retained with the Eager Case Retention policy. Because of Condition (1), 100%

of the cases are retrieved with the static mode. However, with the dynamic mode this percentage will be reduced.
2. *Percentage of retrieval failures.* This is a measure of how many cases are retained with the Case Retention Policy based on Retrieval Failures.
3. *Percentage of detrimental retrievals.* This is a measure of how many cases are retained with the Case Retention Policy based on detrimental retrieval.
4. *Percentage of case-based, problem-solving episodes in which the retrieval is a failure but beneficial.* This is a measure of how many cases are retained with the Case Retention Policy based on retrieval failure but that shouldn't have been because of the low adaptation effort. Thus, it measures the redundancy resulting from this policy.
5. *Percentage of case-based, problem-solving episodes in which the retrieval is adequate but detrimental.* This is a measure of how many cases are not retained with the Case Retention Policy based on retrieval failure but that should have been because of the significant adaptation effort. Thus, it measures lost opportunities to gain competence with this policy.

	Dynamic					**Static**
Items	**1**	**2**	**3**	**4**	**5**	
% Cases Retr.	82	71	63	51	49	100
% Retr. Failures	41	26	19	7	4	47
% Detrim. Retr.	15	12	17	11	15	24
% Fail. & Ben.	8	6	3	2	1	11
% Adeq. & Detrim.	5	3	8	2	7	16

Table 1. Comparison of policies to create cases in the domain of process planning.

	Dynamic					**Static**
Items	**1**	**2**	**3**	**4**	**5**	
% Cases Retr.	94	84	73	65	57	100
% Retr. Failures	37	27	15	9	6	41
% Detrim. Retr.	33	24	20	21	19	37
% Fail. & Ben.	18	10	5	2	1	24
% Adeq. & Detrim..	20	12	9	11	10	23

Table 2. Comparison of policies to create cases in the logistics transportation domain.

The results are summarized in tables 1 and 2. Each row shows each of the five items in the order listed before. Each column i averages the results for the i-th sequence of each run with the dynamic retrieval mode. The sixth column shows the results for the whole collection with the static retrieval mode.

5.5 Discussion of the Experiment Results

These results confirm the independence between the concepts of retrieval failure and detrimental retrieval. First, consider the results with the dynamic retrieval mode (i.e., first 5 columns). Even in the last sequences, when the percentage of retrieval failures decreases (for example, 4% in the 5th sequence of the first domain), detrimental retrieval episodes are still likely to occur (i.e., 15%). Thus, the adaptation effort is significant independent of the fact that the retrieval tends to be adequate. Second, in the results of the static retrieval mode (i.e., the 6th column), we observe that a significant percentage of both retrieval failures (47% and 41% for the two domains) and detrimental retrievals (24% and 24%) occur.

A second observation is that, as expected, the Eager Case Retention Policy increases the redundancy of the case base dramatically. For example, with the dynamic retrieval mode, at the 5th sequence, 49% and 57% of the cases for the two domains are retained even though only 15% and 19% of the retrievals were detrimental. In the static mode the situation is worst, with 100% of the cases retained but only 24% and 37% being detrimental.

The Case Retention Policy based on Retrieval Failures reduces the redundancy in a significant way. In particular, in the 5th sequence with the dynamic retrieval mode, only 1% of the retained cases for both domains is redundant (row 4th, column 5th). However, 7% and 10% of the cases for both domains should have been retained but they were not because no retrieval failure occurs (row 5th, column 5th). With the static mode (column 6th), both redundancy and lost opportunities to increase competence are significant.

In summary, the Eager Case Retention Policy will result in increasing redundant case bases. Case Retention Policy based on Retrieval Failures reduces redundancy in a significant way, particularly in the dynamic mode, but the price to pay is a significant lost in opportunities to gain competence.

6 Related Research

The Detrimental Retrieval Policy is complementary to overall case maintenance as proposed in (Smyth & Keane, 1995). In our approach, new solutions are not retained in the case base if they are covered by existing cases. Some of those cases must be pivotal and as such the new solution would have been deleted anyway. Thus, maintaining the case base must be less costly if cases are retained by the Detrimental Retrieval Policy.

Another question is whether the Retention of cases by the Detrimental Retrieval Policy makes overall case maintenance unnecessary. The answer is *no* because redundancy may still occur. For example, (Muñoz-Avila, 1998) reports a negative effect of feature weighting in CBP identified as *specialization* of the cases. This situation occurs when an existing case would have been retrieved to solve the current problem if (1) the case feature weights would had not been updated and (2) the retrieval of that case would had been beneficial. However, because of the updated feature weights, the case is not retrieved. Although in the experiments performed in (Muñoz-Avila, 1998), the percentage of specialized cases was small, it is possible that specialization occurs at a larger scale in some domains. In such situations, overall case base maintenance is necessary.

7 Conclusion

We studied previous policies for case Retention in the context of CBP and concluded that Eager Case Retention Policy is flawed because its too permissive resulting in large case bases. More interestingly, we observed that the Case Retention Policy based on Retrieval Failures may result in decreased competence and increased redundancy. We proposed an alternative policy, Case Retention Policy based on Detrimental Retrieval, and showed through experimental validation that it is more effective.

Acknowledgements

This research was supported in part by grants from the Naval Research Laboratory, the Office of Naval Research, and the Deutscher Akademischer Austauschdienst (DAAD). We will also like to thank Len Breslow for reviewing early versions of this paper and the ICCBR-99 reviewers for their thoughful suggestions.

References

Aamodt, A. & Plaza, E. (1994). Case-based reasoning: Foundation issues, methodological variations and system approaches. *AI-Communications*, 7(1):pp 39–59.

Bergmann, R., Muñoz-Avila, H., Veloso, M., Melis, E. (1998). Case-based reasoning applied to planning tasks. In M. Lenz, B. Bartsch-Spoerl, H.-D. Burkhard, & S. Wess (Eds.) *Case-Based Reasoning Technology: From Foundations to Applications.* Berlin: Springer.

Ihrig, L. & Kambhampati, S. (1996). Design and implementation of a replay framework based on a partial order planner. In Weld, D., editor, *Proceedings of AAAI-96.* IOS Press.

Ihrig, L., & Kambhampati, S. (1994). Derivational replay for partial-order planning. *Proceedings of AAAI-94*, AAAI Press.

Kitano, H. & Shimazu, H. (1996). The experience-sharing architecture: a case study on corporate-wide case-based software quality control. In *Case-Based Reasoning: Experience, Lessons, & Future Directions*, Leake, D. B. (Editor). MA: AAAI Press / MIT Press.

Leake, D.B., & Wilson, D.C. (1998). Categorizing case-base maintenance: dimensions and directions. preprint.

M. Lenz, B., Bartsch-Spoerl, H.-D. Burkhard, & S. Wess (Eds.). (1998). *Case-Based Reasoning Technology: From Foundations to Applications.* Berlin: Springer.

Markovitch, S., & Scott, P.D. (1993). Information Filtering: selection Mechanisms in learning systems. *Machine Learning*, 10.

McAllester, D. & Rosenblitt, D. (1991). Systematic nonlinear planning. *Proceedings of AAAI-91*, AAAI Press.

Muñoz-Avila, H. (1998). *Integrating Twofold Case Retrieval and Complete Decision Replay in CAPlan/CbC.* PhD Thesis. University of Kaiserslautern, Germany.

Muñoz-Avila, H. & Hüllen, J. (1995). Feature weighting by explaining case-based planning episodes. In *Third European Workshop (EWCBR-96)*, number 1168 in LNAI. Springer.

Muñoz-Avila, H. & Weberskirch, F. (1996a). A specification of the domain of process planning: Properties, problems and solutions. Technical Report LSA-96-10E, Center for Learning Systems and Applications, University of Kaiserslautern, Germany.

Muñoz-Avila, H. & Weberskirch, F. (1996b). Planning for manufacturing workpieces by storing, indexing and replaying planning decisions. In *Proc. of the 3nd International Conference on AI Planning Systems (AIPS-96).* AAAI-Press.

Kirsti, R., & Qiang, Y., (1997). Maintaining Unstructured Case Bases, in Case-Based Reasoning Research and Development, In Leake D., B., and Plaza E., (Eds). *Proceedings of the International Conference on Case Based Reasoning*, Springer.

Smyth, B., & Keane, M.T., (1995). Remembering to forget: A competence-preserving case deletion policy for case-based reasoning systems. In: *Proceedings of the International Joint Conference on Artificial Intelligence.*

Smyth, B., & Keane, M.T., (1998). Adaptation-guided retrieval: Questioning the similarity assumption in Reasoning. *Artificial Intelligence*, 102.

Veloso, M. (1994). *Planning and learning by analogical reasoning.* Number 886 in Lecture Notes in Artificial Intelligence. Springer.

Veloso, M. & Carbonell, J. (1993). Derivational analogy in prodigy: Automating case acquisition, storage, and utilization. *Machine Learning*, 10.

Watson, I., (1997). *Applying Case-Based Reasoning: Techniques for Enterprise Systems.* Morgan Kaufmann Publishers.

Weberskirch, F. (1995). Combining SNLP-like planning and dependency-maintenance. Technical Report LSA-95-10E, Centre for Learning Systems and Applications, University of Kaiserslautern, Germany.

Using Guidelines to Constrain Interactive Case-Based HTN Planning

Héctor Muñoz-Avila[†‡], Daniel C. McFarlane[‡], David W. Aha[‡], Len Breslow[‡], James A. Ballas[‡], & Dana S. Nau[†]

† Department of Computer Science
University of Maryland
College Park, MD 20742-3255
lastname@cs.umd.edu
(301) 405-2684 | FAX: 405-6707

‡ Navy Center for Applied Research in AI
Naval Research Laboratory
Washington, DC 20375
lastname@aic.nrl.navy.mil
(202) 404-4940 | FAX: 767-3172

Abstract. This paper describes *HICAP*, a general-purpose, interactive case-based plan authoring architecture that can be applied to decision support tasks to yield a hierarchical course of action. It integrates a hierarchical task editor with a conversational case-based planner. HICAP maintains both a task hierarchy representing guidelines that constrain the final plan and the hierarchical social organization responsible for these tasks. It also supports bookkeeping, which is crucial for real-world large-scale planning tasks. By selecting tasks corresponding to the hierarchy's leaf nodes, users can activate the conversational case-based planner to interactively refine guideline tasks into a concrete plan. Thus, HICAP can be used to generate context sensitive plans and should be useful for assisting with planning complex tasks such as noncombatant evacuation operations. We describe an experiment with a highly detailed military simulator to investigate this claim. The results show that plans generated by HICAP were superior to those generated by alternative approaches.

1 Introduction

Planning a course of action is difficult, especially for large hierarchical organizations (e.g., the U.S. Navy) that assign tasks to elements (i.e., groups or individuals) and constrain plans with guidelines (e.g., doctrine). In this context, a concrete plan must adhere to guidelines but should also exploit organizational knowledge where appropriate (e.g., standard procedures for solving tasks, previous experiences when reacting to unanticipated situations). Case-based reasoning (CBR) can be used to capture and share this knowledge.

In large planning environments, automatic plan generation is neither feasible nor desirable because users must observe and control plan generation. We argue that, rather than relying on an automatic plan generator, users prefer and can greatly benefit from the assistance of an intelligent plan formulation tool with the following characteristics:

- *Guidelines-driven*: Uses guidelines to constrain plan generation.
- *Interactive*: Allows users to edit any detail of the plan.
- *Provide Case Access*: Indexes plan segments from previous problem-solving experiences, and retrieves them for users if warranted by the current planning scenario.
- *Perform Bookkeeping*: Maintains information on the status of and relations between task responsibilities and individuals in the organizational hierarchy.

This paper describes HICAP, a general-purpose plan formulation tool that we designed to embody these characteristics.[1] HICAP (Hierarchical Interactive Case-Based Architecture for Planning) integrates a task decomposition editor, HTE (Hierarchical Task Editor) (Muñoz-Avila et al., 1998), with a conversational case-based planner, NaCoDAE/HTN. The former allows users to edit and select guidelines for refinement, while the latter allows users to interactively refine plans encoded as hierarchical task networks (HTNs) (Erol et al., 1994). Refinements use knowledge of previous operations, represented as cases, to augment or replace standard procedures.

The following sections describe the application task, HICAP's knowledge representation, its architecture, its empirical evaluation, and a discussion of related work.

2 Planning Noncombatant Evacuation Operations

Noncombatant evacuation operations (NEOs) are conducted to assist the U.S.A. Department of State (DoS) with evacuating noncombatants, nonessential military personnel, selected host-nation citizens, and third country nationals whose lives are in danger from locations in a host foreign nation to an appropriate safe haven. They usually involve the swift insertion of a force, temporary occupation of an objective (e.g., an embassy), and a planned withdrawal after mission completion. NEOs are often planned and executed by a Joint Task Force (JTF), a hierarchical multi-service military organization, and conducted under an American Ambassador's authority. Force sizes can range into the hundreds and involve all branches of the armed services, while the evacuees can number into the thousands. More than ten NEOs were conducted within the past decade. Publications describe NEO doctrine (DoD, 1994), case studies (Siegel, 1991; 1995), and more general analyses (e.g., Lambert, 1992).[2]

The decision making process for a NEO is conducted at three increasingly-specific levels: strategic, operational and tactical. The strategic level involves

[1] Implemented in Java 2, the HICAP applet can be run from www.aic.nrl.navy.mil/hicap. HICAP was introduced in (Muñoz-Avila et al., 1999), which did not include the evaluation described here.

[2] See www.aic.nrl.navy.mil/~aha/neos for more information on NEOs.

global and political considerations such as whether to perform the NEO. The operational level involves considerations such as determining the size and composition of its execution force. The tactical level is the concrete level, which assigns specific resources to specific tasks.

JTF commanders plan NEOs in the context of doctrine (DoD, 1994), which defines *general* guidelines (e.g., chain of command, task agenda) for designing strategic and operational plans; tactical considerations are only partly addressed. Doctrine is abstract; it cannot account for the detailed characteristics of specific NEOs. Thus, JTF commanders must always adapt doctrine to a NEO's specific needs, and do so in two ways. First, they dynamically modify doctrinal guidance by eliminating irrelevant planning tasks and adding others, depending on the operation's needs, resource availabilities, and relevant past experiences. For example, although NEO doctrine states that a forward command element must be inserted into the evacuation area with enough time to plan the insertion of the JTF's main body, this is not always feasible (e.g., in *Operation Eastern Exit*, combined elements of the JTF were inserted simultaneously due to the clear and imminent danger posed to the targeted evacuees (Siegel, 1991)). Second, they employ experiences from previous NEOs, which complement doctrine by suggesting tactical refinements suitable for the current NEO. For example, they could draw upon their previous experiences to identify whether it is appropriate to concentrate the evacuees in the embassy or to plan for multiple evacuation sites.

3 Knowledge Representation

Because HTNs are expressive representations for plans, we used a variant of them in HICAP. A HTN is a set of tasks and their ordering relations, denoted as $N = \langle\{T_1, \ldots, T_m\}, \prec\rangle$ $(m \geq 0)$. The relation $\prec$ has the form $T_i \prec T_j (i \neq j)$, and expresses temporal restrictions between tasks.

Problem solving with HTNs occurs by applying *methods* to decompose or reduce tasks into subtasks. Each method has the form $M = \langle l, T, N, P\rangle$, where l is a label, T is a task, N is a HTN, and $P = \langle p_1, \ldots, p_k\rangle$ is a set of preconditions for applying M. When P is satisfied, M can be applied to a task T to yield N.

HICAP's HTN consists of three task types. First, *non-decomposable* tasks are concrete actions and can occur only at a network's leaves. Next, *uniquely decomposable* tasks correspond to guideline tasks (e.g., doctrine), and are solved by unconditional methods ($k = 0$). Finally, *multi-decomposable* tasks must be solved in a specific problem-solving context.

There are two sources of knowledge for decomposing multi-decomposable tasks: standard operating procedures (SOPs) and recorded episodes. SOPs describe how to reduce a task in a typical situation. Recorded episodes describe how tasks were reduced in situations that are not covered by SOPs. In our representation, SOPs and recorded episodes are both represented as methods and we loosely refer to both as *cases*. However, there is an important difference in the way SOPs and recorded episodes are applied. To apply a SOP to reduce a task, all its preconditions must be matched because they are typically rigid in their use. In contrast, recorded episodes can be applied to reduce a task even if some of its preconditions are not satisfied.

When reducing a task T, HICAP retrieves all cases (i.e., standard procedures and recorded episodes) that can decompose T. If all the preconditions of a SOP are met, then it should be used to decompose T. Otherwise, a case corresponding to the most similar episode should be used. For example, standard NEO procedures state that the evacuees must be concentrated in the embassy prior to troop deployment, but this is not always possible: in Operation Eastern Exit, only some of the evacuees were concentrated in the embassy after the Joint Task Force was deployed. This occurred because escorted transports were not available to gather these evacuees, who were unable to reach the embassy due to the dangerous conditions in the surrounding areas (Siegel, 1991). Likewise, the evacuees of *Operation Sharp Edge* (Sachtleben, 1991) were concentrated in several places, forcing multiple separate evacuations.

4 HICAP: An Interactive Case-Based Planner

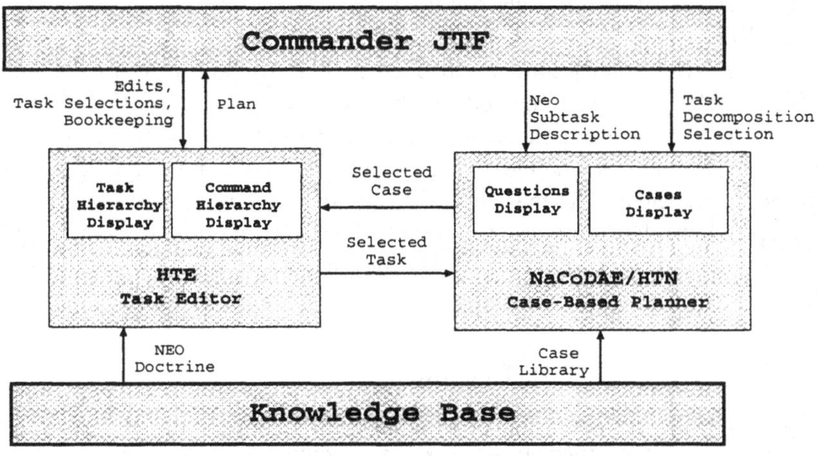

Fig. 1. The HICAP architecture.

HICAP (Figure 1), which integrates HTE with NaCoDAE/HTN, inputs a HTN describing the guidelines for an application along with a set of cases for each multi-decomposable subtask. It displays all uniquely decomposable tasks as expanded. Under user control, HICAP outputs an elaborated HTN whose leaves are concrete actions as specified by case applications and manual edits. In this way, HICAP satisfies the requirements stated in Section 1. First, all plans formulated using HICAP are in accordance with the guidelines or user modifications of them. Second, HICAP supports interactive task editing and triggers conversations for tasks that can be decomposed by case application. Third, it incorporates knowledge from previous problem solving episodes as cases, which serve as task decomposition alternatives. Finally, it allows users to visually check that all tasks are assigned to JTF elements, and to record/update their completion status.

4.1 Hierarchical Task Editor

In complex environments where dozens of tasks must be performed by many people, tracking the completion status for each task can be challenging. For example, during the NEO Operation Eastern Exit, the task to inspect evacuees prior to embarkation was not assigned (Siegel, 1991). One of the evacuees produced a weapon during a helicopter evacuation flight. Although it was immediately confiscated, this oversight could have resulted in tragedy and illustrates the difficulties with planning NEOs manually.

The Hierarchical Task Editor (HTE) (Muñoz-Avila et al., 1998) serves HICAP as a bookkeeping tool to track the status of each task. HTE inputs a knowledge base consisting of a HTN task agenda, its ordering relations, the organization's command hierarchy, and an assignment of tasks to command elements. It allows users to edit the knowledge base and select tasks to refine by invoking NaCoDAE/HTN, thus tailoring the plan to the particular circumstances of the current NEO.

For our NEO application, we encoded a HTN to capture critical planning doctrine (DoD, 1994), yielding 200+ tasks and their ordering relations. Next, we used this doctrine to elicit the JTF command hierarchy commonly used in NEO operations. Finally, we elicited relations between tasks and the JTF elements responsible for them. The mapping of tasks to command elements is many-to-one. Figure 2 displays (left) the top level tasks that, according to doctrine, must be performed during a NEO and (right) the elements in the JTF responsible for them.

4.2 Conversational Task Decomposer

NaCoDAE/HTN, an extension of the NaCoDAE conversational case retrieval tool (Aha & Breslow, 1997; Breslow & Aha, 1997), supports HTN planning by allowing users to refine selected tasks into concrete actions. When given a task T to refine by HTE, NaCoDAE/HTN uses T as an index for initial case retrieval and conducts an interactive *conversation*, which ends when the user selects a case $C = \langle l, T, N, P \rangle$. Network N is then used to decompose T (i.e., into a set of subtasks represented as T's child nodes). Subtasks of N might themselves be decomposable, but non-decomposable tasks corresponding to concrete actions will eventually be reached. Task expansions are displayed by HTE.

During conversations, NaCoDAE/HTN displays the labels of the top-ranked cases that can decompose the selected node and the top-ranked questions from these cases whose answers are not yet known for the current situation. The user can select and answer any displayed question; question-answer pairs are used

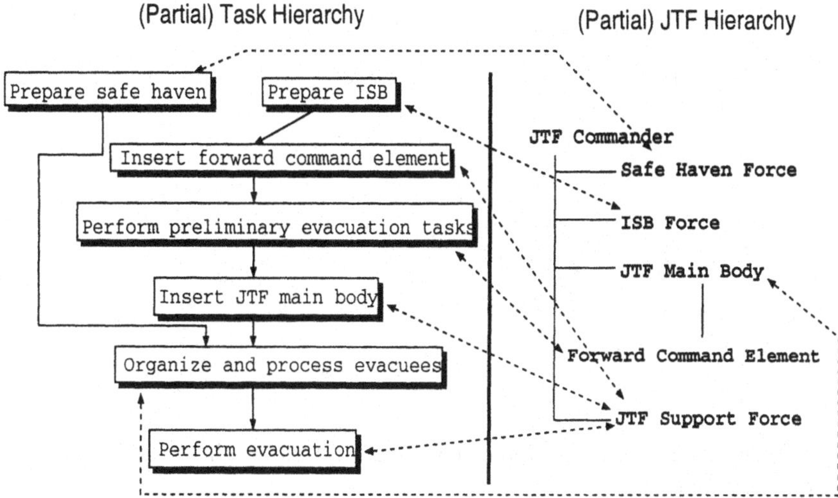

Fig. 2. Top level NEO tasks and their assignment to JTF command elements (double arrows denote assignments; arrows denote task orderings; ISB = intermediate stage base).

to compute the similarity of the current task to its potential decomposition methods (cases). Cases are ranked according to their similarity to the current situation (Aha & Breslow, 1997), while questions are ranked according to their frequency among the top-ranked cases. Answering a question modifies the case and question rankings. A conversation ends when the user selects a case for decomposing the current task.

Some of the displayed cases are standard procedures; they can only be selected to decompose a task after all of their questions have been answered and match the current planning scenario. That is, preconditions of the standard procedures must match before they can be applied. In contrast, cases based on previous experiences can be selected even if some of their questions have not been answered, or if the user's answers differ. Thus, they support partial matching between their preconditions and the current planning scenario.

5 Example: NEO Planning

During NEO planning, users are first shown the tasks corresponding to doctrine, and revise them as needed. They can expand any task and view its decomposition. In Figure 3, the user has selected the *Select assembly areas for evacuation & Evacuation Control Center sites* task, which is highlighted together with the command element responsible for it.

Standard procedure dictates that the embassy is the ideal assembly area. However, it is not always possible to concentrate the evacuees in the embassy. Alternative methods can be considered for decomposing this task. When the

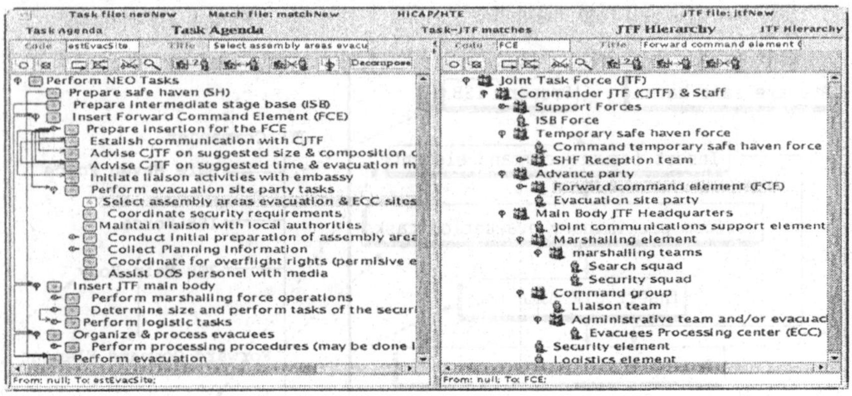

Fig. 3. HTE: Task agenda (left) and command hierarchy (right) displays (arrows denote ordering constraints).

military planner selects this task, HICAP displays the alternatives and initiates a NaCoDAE/HTN conversation (see Figure 4 (top)).

If the user answers *Are there any hostiles between the embassy and the evacuees?* with *uncertain*, a perfect match occurs with the case labeled "Handle situation in which it is unknown whether hostiles are present," which now becomes the top-ranked case (Figure 4 (bottom)). Figure 5 (left) shows the decomposition when selecting this case to decompose this task in HTE; two new subtasks are displayed, corresponding to this case's decomposition network. *Send unmanned air vehicle to* ... is a non-decomposable concrete action. If the user tells HICAP to decompose *Determine if hostiles are present*, HICAP will initiate a new NaCoDAE/HTN dialogue (Figure 5, right).

The user can again prompt a dialogue by selecting the *The UAV detects hostiles* alternative and decomposing its subtasks. This cycle, in which HICAP displays alternatives and the user answers questions and selects an alternative, continues until non-decomposable tasks (i.e., concrete actions) are reached, which form part of the final plan.

6 The Case-Based Planning Cycle in HICAP

The case-based planning component of HICAP, Nacodae/HTN, typically performs three steps: retrieval, revise, and retain. As illustrated in Section 5, the adaptation process can be viewed as embedded in the conversational retrieval process.

6.1 Case Retrieval

We previously explained that, during a conversation, cases are ranked according to the proportion of their question-answer pairs that match the current scenario.

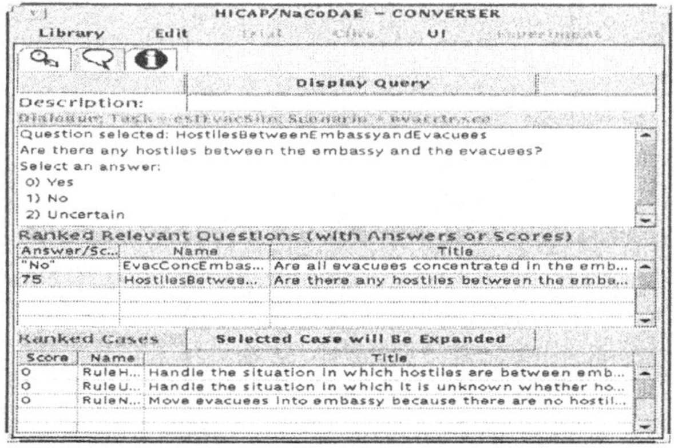

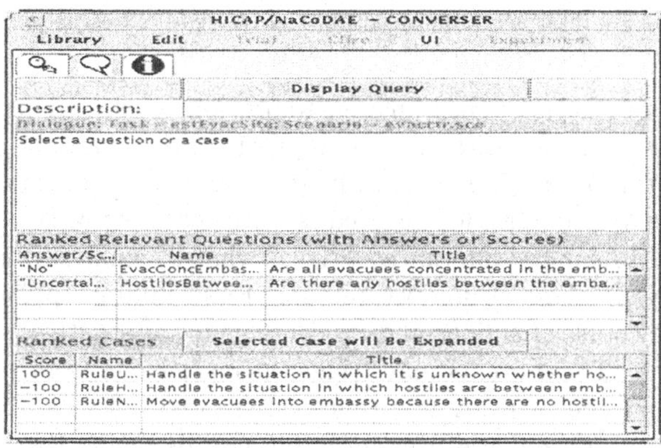

Fig. 4. NaCoDAE/HTN: Before (top) and after (bottom) answering a question. The top window lists possible answers to selected questions, while the lower windows display the ranked questions and cases.

More specifically, a case c's similarity score is computed with a query q using

$$\text{case\_score}(q, c) = \frac{\text{num\_matches}(q, c) - \text{num\_mismatches}(q, c)}{\text{size}(c)} \tag{1}$$

where $\text{num\_matches}(q, c)$ ($\text{num\_mismatches}(q, c)$) is the number of matches (mismatches) between the states (i.e., $\langle q, a \rangle$ pairs) of q and c, and $\text{size}(c)$ yields the number of $\langle$q,a$\rangle$ pairs in c's state.[3]

6.2 Case Revision

The user can revise the current solution by editing the task hierarchy (in HTE) and by selecting alternative cases during a NaCoDAE/HTN conversation. In

[3] Matching for numeric-valued questions is implemented using a suitable partial matching routine, but we focus on symbolic and boolean questions here.

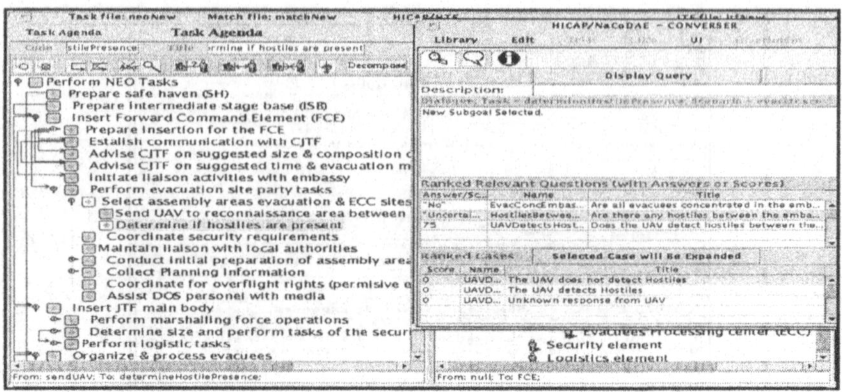

Fig. 5. HICAP's interface after selecting the *Determine hostile presence* task.

addition, the user can revise their answers to previously selected questions, which can modify case rankings. Although, revising an answer does not alter the plan automatically, the new ranks may prompt the user to change their case selection, which in turn may prompt additional edits to the task hierarchy.

This ability to explore alternatives (i.e., "what-if" analyses) is particularly important in NEO planning for two reasons. First, military planners typically plan for a main course of actions and for contingency alternatives should certain key events occur. These events may trigger changes to answers and case rankings, thus helping the user formulate these alternatives. Second, NEO planning is dynamic in nature and the user must be able to replan due to unforeseen contingencies.

6.3 Case Retention

NaCoDAE incorporates an approach introduced by Racine and Yang (1997) for maintaining case libraries. It evaluates whether any case "subsumes" another case (i.e., whether its question-answer pairs are a proper subset of the question-answer pairs of another case). If so, the subsuming case will block the subsumed case from being retrieved. A case library evaluation function alerts the user to all such pairs of cases in the case library. The user can then decide which of the two cases to revise and/or delete.

7 Empirical Validation

An experiment was run to test HICAP's effectiveness in choosing successful plans for an example NEO subtask. In particular, we showed the importance of considering episodic records over standard procedures. A larger experiment, demonstrating the capability of HICAP to generate a complete NEO plan, is currently under development.

Two researchers performed the experiment: one operated a military simulator while the other operated HICAP. A strict blind was imposed to ensure that the HICAP user had no advance knowledge concerning the simulated hostile forces, and had to take appropriate, realistic ations to acquire this knowledge. This tests HICAP's utility for planning under realistic situations where decision makers have uncertain information about the state of the world. We hypothesized that HICAP would allow users to choose a relatively successful plan from among known tactical options. HICAP's strategy was evaluated versus three other planning strategies: *random choice*, *heuristic choice*, the *most frequently used plan* used in previous NEOs. Because their definitions require explaining the scenario, we define them in Section 7.3.

7.1 The ModSAF Simulation System

We used Marine Corps SAF (MCSF), a variant of ModSAF (Modular Semi-Automated Forces), to evaluate the quality of NEO plans elicited using HICAP. ModSAF, developed by the U.S.A. Army to inject simulated auxiliary forces into training exercises, has been deployed to simulate real-world military scenarios (Ceranowicz, 1994). It is a finite state simulation with modular components that represent individual entities and parts of entities. For example, a simulated tank would have physical components such as a turret. It would also have behavioral components that represent its nominal tasks such as move, attack, target, and react to fire. Certain 3D aspects are also represented (e.g., terrain elevation, trees and vegetation, rivers, oceans, atmospheric conditions) that can affect sensory and movement behavior. The realism of ModSAF/MCSF simulations is sufficient for training exercises.

Figure 6's MCSF snapshot displays a simulated American embassy, a host country government compound, and some simulated objects. For example, a simulated transport helicopter is positioned at the heliport within the embassy site.

MCSF is a non-deterministic simulator that models several sources of stochastic variation. Some events are determined by a random number generator; others are highly sensitive to the initial startup conditions. MCSF simulates the behavior of military units in context as they follow given tactical orders. Therefore, MCSF can simulate simplified NEO subtasks in which a single planning decision determines tactical orders.

7.2 Experimental Setup

We created a NEO subtask scenario for this evaluation concerning how to move 64 evacuees from a meeting site to an embassy. The meeting site was at a crossroads in an uninhabited area outside but nearby the embassy's city. Evacuees had to be transported (8 per vehicle) through this undeveloped area, which had heavy tree cover, and out through the city to the embassy. Evacuees had to pass near a local government complex to enter the embassy grounds. This NEO context requires only a single tactical plan decision with four distinct choices:

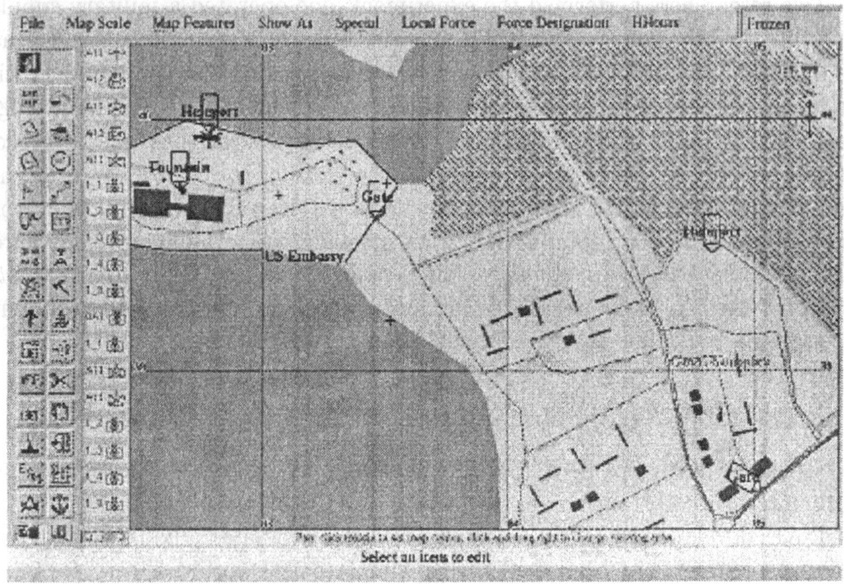

Fig. 6. A MCSF snapshot.

1. Land evacuation using 8 armored trucks
2. Land evacuation using 8 armored trucks with an escort of 8 tanks
3. Air evacuation using 8 transport helicopters
4. Air evacuation using 8 transport helicopters with an escort of 8 attack helicopters

The kind of military units used in the simulation are typical of those available to the Marine Expeditionary Units that frequently perform NEO's. A detailed terrain database of the Camp Lejeune (North Carolina, U.S.A.) area was chosen to simulate the environment. We chose this location because Marine Expeditionary Units train there for NEOs.

Two scenarios were defined that were identical except for the type of hostile forces. All hostiles were two-person dismounted infantry teams. Hostile teams in both scenarios were armed with two automatic rifles and a portable missile launcher. Each scenario included only one type of missile for hostile teams (i.e., either anti-tank missiles or anti-air missiles, but not both). These types of infantry teams, positioned in an urban environment, are typical of the kinds of hostile forces encountered in real NEO's. The positions of the hostile teams were the same for both scenarios and selected to ensure that the opposing forces will meet.

All four plan options were simulated ten times for each of the two scenarios. This resulted in 80 (2 scenarios × 4 plan choices × 10 simulations) total MCSF runs. Each of the eight plan-and-scenario combinations was repeated ten times because MCSF is non-deterministic. For example, slight differences produced

Table 1. Summaries of casualties, to individual evacuees and military teams (mean & standard deviation), averaged over 80 MCSF simulations.

	Scenario 1 (anti-tank)			Scenario 2 (anti-air)		
Tactical Plans	**Evacuees**	**Friends**	**Hostiles**	**Evacuees**	**Friends**	**Hostiles**
Land	6.4 5.1	0.8 0.6	5.5 1.3	0	0	4.2 0.8
Land/Escort	3.2 10.1	7.4 1.5	6.5 1.8	0	0	7.6 0.6
Air	56.0 9.2	7.0 1.2	0	64.0 0.0	8.0 0.0	0
Air/Escort	0	0.8 1.5	8.0 0.0	20.0 18.6	6.3 4.4	5.7 2.9

by MCSF's stochastic movement models yield strikingly different formations of friendly units when they first encountered the hostile teams. These differences can often yield drastically different simulated battle outcomes.

The HICAP user had no knowledge of the scenarios being tested; scenario information was gradually extracted through the questions prompted by NaCoDAE/HTN. That is, case-based planning was done with incomplete information about the world. Furthermore, the effects of actions were uncertain; the only way to learn the effects of an action was to actually execute it. This contrasts with traditional planning approaches that assume an action's effects are known a priori (Fikes and Nilsson, 1971).

7.3 Alternative Planning Strategies

HICAP's decision-making performance was compared with three baseline strategies. First, *random choice* simply averaged the results of all four planning choices. Second, *heuristic choice* always sent an escort, and its results were the average of the choices that include escorts. Finally, the *most frequently used* plan strategy for this subtask in recent NEOs (i.e., conducted during the past decade) was to move evacuees using escorted land vehicles.

7.4 Results

Table 7.4 summarizes the casualty results for the 80 total simulations, which each required approximately 15 minutes to run. The success measures were taken from the U.S.A. Navy's Measures of Effectiveness (MOE's) published in the Universal Naval Task List. Recommended MOEs are specified for evaluating each kind of military operation. There are several MOE's for the tactical aspects of NEO's, but only three were chosen as most important for evaluating the results of this experiment: (1) the number of evacuees safely moved, (2) the number of casualties to friendly forces, and (3) the number of casualties to hostile forces.

HICAP did not choose the same tactical plan for both scenarios. For the first (anti-tank) scenario, it chose to move the evacuees by helicopter with an attack helicopter escort. For the second (anti-air) scenario, it chose to move evacuees by armored truck with a tank escort.

HICAP's conversational case-based planning method was evaluated by comparing the success of its chosen plans to plans chosen by the other three plan

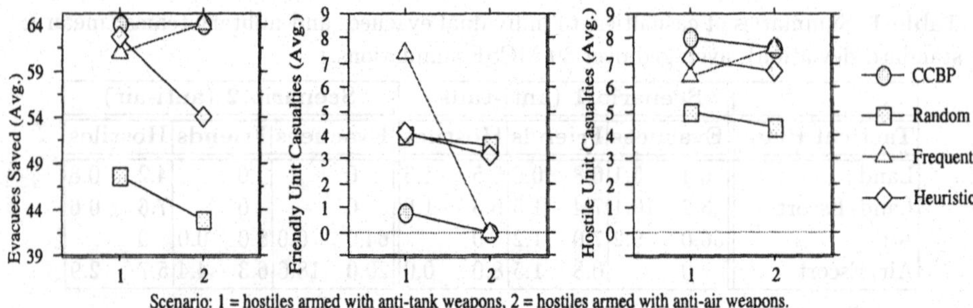

Fig. 7. Comparison of plan selection strategies using Navy MOEs for NEOs.

selection strategies. Figure 7 compares the effectiveness of these four strategies. Overall, HICAP selected plans of higher quality than the other strategies because its plan selection decisions are tailored to the characteristics of each scenario.

8 Related Research

Case-based planning (CBP) has been extensively researched (Bergmann et al., 1998). Our research is closely related to studies on hierarchical CBP (e.g., Kambhampati, 1993; Bergmann & Wilke, 1995; Branting & Aha, 1995). HICAP differs from these other approaches in that it includes the user in its problem solving loop. This is particularly important for applications like NEO planning, where completely automated tools are unacceptable. MI-CBP (Veloso et al., 1997) uses rationale-directed CBP to suggest plan modifications in a mixed-initiative setting, but does not perform doctrine-driven task decomposition.

Some researchers have used CBP with HTNs for military tasks. For example, Mitchell (1997) used integrated CBP to select tasks for a tactical response planner. NEO planning requires that each task be addressed - no choice is involved - and we use CBP to instead choose *how* to perform a task. HICAP's interactions instead focus on retrieval rather than plan adaptation and learning.

9 Conclusion and Future Work

The HICAP case-based planner helps users to formulate a course of action for hierarchical tasks. It is the first tool to combine a task guideline decomposition process with CBR to support interactive plan formulation. It yields plans that benefit from previous experiences and conform to predefined guidelines. HICAP also supports experience sharing, thus allowing planners to exploit knowledge from other planning experts. These design characteristics enhance HICAP's acceptance by military planning personnel.

We are currently integrating HICAP with a generative HTN planner that can evaluate numeric expressions (Nau et. al., 1999), which is particularly important for NEOs because decisions often depend on resource capability and availability (i.e., determining whether a helicopter requires in-flight refueling for a given mission). HICAP will serve as the plan formulation component for the Space and Naval Warfare Systems Command's Interactive Decision Support (IDS) system. When completed, IDS will perform distributed NEO plan formulation, execution, monitoring, and replanning.

Our collaborative research with IDS partners will focus on associating temporal durations with tasks, developing a resource tracking module (i.e., to solve resource conflicts), implementing a strategy for justifying case rankings, integrating HICAP with a powerful dynamic planner (i.e., SIPE-2 (Wilkins, 1998)), and integrating existing GUIs for plan authoring. We will also investigate methods for performing information gathering in HICAP using a planning approach (e.g., Carrick et al., 1999).

Acknowledgements

Thanks to ONR Program Managers Michael Shneier and Paul Quinn, and Program Officer Lt. Cdr. Dave Jakubek, for their encouragement throughout this project. This research was supported by grants from the Office of Naval Research, the Naval Research Laboratory, and the Army Research Laboratory. Many thanks to members of the Center for Naval Analyses and ONR's Naval Science Assistance Program for their guidance and support. And thanks to our ICCBR-99 reviewers for their thoughtful suggestions, which improved this paper.

References

Aha, D. W., & Breslow, L. A. (1997). Refining conversational case libraries. *Proceedings of the Second International Conference on CBR* (pp. 267–278). Providence, RI: Springer.

Bergmann, R., Muñoz-Avila, H., Veloso, M., Melis, E. (1998). Case-based reasoning applied to planning tasks. In M. Lenz, B. Bartsch-Spoerl, H.-D. Burkhard, & S. Wess (Eds.) *CBR Technology: From Foundations to Applications*. Berlin: Springer.

Bergmann, R. & Wilke, W. (1995). Building and refining abstract planning cases by change of representation language. *Journal of AI Research, 3*, 53–118.

Branting, L. K., & Aha, D. W. (1995). Stratified case-based reasoning: Reusing hierarchical problem solving episodes. *Proceedings of the Fourteenth International Joint Conference on AI* (pp. 384–390). Montreal, Canada: Morgan Kaufmann.

Breslow, L., & Aha, D. W. (1997). *NaCoDAE: Navy Conversational Decision Aids Environment* (TR AIC-97-018). Washington, DC: Naval Research Laboratory, Navy Center for Applied Research in Artificial Intelligence.

Carrick, C., Yang, Q., Abi-Zeid, I., & Lamontagne, L. (1999). Activating CBR systems through autonomous information gathering. To appear in *Proceedings of the Third International Conference on Case-Based Reasoning.* Munich, Germany: Springer.

Ceranowicz, A. (1994). *Modular Semi-Automated Forces. Proceedings of the Winter Simulation Conference of the ACM* (pp. 755–761). New York, NY: IEEE.

DoD (1994). *Joint tactics, techniques and procedures for noncombat evacuation operations* (Joint Report 3-07.51, Second Draft). Washington, DC: Department of Defense.

Erol, K., Nau, D., & Hendler, J. (1994). HTN planning: Complexity and expressivity. *Proceedings of the Twelfth National Conference on Artificial Intelligence* (pp. 1123–1128). Seattle, WA: AAAI Press.

Fikes, R.E., & Nilsson, N.J. (1971). Strips: A new approach to the application of theorem proving in problem solving. *Artificial Intelligence, 2*, 189–208.

Kambhampati, S. (1994). Exploiting causal structure to control retrieval and refitting during plan reuse. *Computational Intelligence, 10*, 213–244.

Lambert, Kirk S. (1992). *Noncombatant evacuation operations: Plan now or pay later* (Technical Report). Newport, RI: Naval War College.

Mitchell, S.W. (1997). A hybrid architecture for real-time mixed-initiative planning and control. *Proceedings of the Ninth Conference on Innovative Applications of AI* (pp. 1032–1037). Providence, RI: AAAI Press.

Muñoz-Avila, H., Breslow, L.A., Aha, D.W., & Nau, D. (1998). *Description and functionality of HTE* (TR AIC-98-022). Washington, DC: NRL, NCARAI.

Muñoz-Avila, H., Aha, D.W., Breslow, L. & Nau, D. (1999). HICAP: An interactive case-based planning architecture and its application to noncombatant evacuation operations. To appear in *Proceedings of the Ninth National Conference on Innovative Applications of Artificial Intelligence.* Orlando, FL: AAAI Press.

Nau, D. S., Cao, Y., Lotem, A., & Muñoz-Avila, H. (1999). SHOP: Simple Hierarchical Ordered Planner. To appear in *Proceedings of the Sixteenth National Conference on Artificial Intelligence.* Stockholm, Sweden: Morgan Kaufmann.

Racine, K., & Yang, Q. (1997). Maintaining unstructured case bases. *Proceedings of the Second International Conference on CBR* (pp. 553–564). Providence, RI: Springer.

Sachtleben, G.R. (1991). Operation Sharp Edge: The Corps MEU (SOC) program in action. *Marine Corps Gazette, 11*, 76–86.

Siegel, A.B. (1991). *Eastern Exit: The noncombatant evacuation operation (NEO) from Mogadishu, Somalia, in January 1991* (TR CRM 91-221). Arlington, VA: Center for Naval Analyses.

Siegel, A.B. (1995). *Requirements for humanitarian assistance and peace operations: Insights from seven case studies* (TR CRM 94-74). Arlington, VA: CNA.

Veloso, M., Mulvehill, A.M., & Cox, M.T. (1997). Rationale-supported mixed-initiative case-based planning. *Proceedings of the Ninth Conference on Innovative Applications of Artificial Intelligence* (pp. 1072–1077). Providence, RI: AAAI Press.

Wilkins, D.E. (1998). *Using the SIPE-2 planning system: A manual for Version 5.0* (Working Document). Menlo Park, CA: Stanford Research International, Artificial Intelligence Center.

Speed-Up, Quality and Competence in Multi-modal Case-Based Reasoning

Luigi Portinale[1], Pietro Torasso[2], Paolo Tavano[2]

[1] Dipartimento di Scienze e Tecnologie Avanzate
Universita' del Piemonte Orientale "A. Avogadro" - Alessandria (ITALY)
[2] Dipartimento di Informatica
Universita' di Torino - Torino (ITALY)

Abstract. The paper discusses the different aspects concerning performance arising in multi-modal systems combining Case-Based Reasoning and Model-Based Reasoning for diagnostic problem solving. In particular, we examine the relation among speed-up of problems solving, competence of the system and quality of produced solutions. Because of the well-know utility problem, there is no general strategy for improving all these parameters at the same time, so the trade-off among such parameters must be carefully analyzed. We have developed a case memory management strategy which allows the interleaving of learning of new cases with forgetting phases, where useless and potentially dangerous cases are identified and removed. This strategy, combined with a suitable tuning on the precision required for the retrieval of cases (in terms of estimated adaptation cost), provides an effective mechanism for taking under control the utility problem. Experimental analysis performed on a real-world domain shows in fact that improvements over both speed-up and competence can be obtained, without compromising in a significant way the quality of solutions.

1 Introduction

Multi-modal reasoning systems are problem solving architectures relying on the integration of different forms of reasoning to solve a given task. Case-Based Reasoning (CBR) is often considered a fundamental "modality" of such systems (see [1,4]). The reason is twofold: on the one hand, CBR can be profitably adopted in a variety of different problem solving tasks like diagnosis, planning or design; on the other hand, the integration of CBR with other forms of reasoning may alleviate some basic problems of any CBR system like the competence on a given problem space or the quality of the obtained solutions. One of the main reasons for adopting such kinds of hybrid architectures is then related to the possibility of improving the "performance" of a problem solver based on first-principles (i.e. a problem solver which solves problems from scratch without exploiting past experience or heuristics). The term performance is very general and different specific issues related to this aspect can be identified: usually the integration is pursued in order to *speed-up* problem solving, so performance is identified with the resolution time; in other cases, different modalities may exhibit different *competence* in the problem space, so performance is measured as the percentage of problems that can be solved with respect to the whole problem space; finally, in some situations different methods may provide solutions of different *quality*, because for instance, different approximations or heuristics are used, so in this case performance is measured as a suitable metric with respect to optimal solutions.

Unfortunately, it is well-known that an improvement obtained with respect to a given parameter can be paid as a worsening with respect to a different parameter: this is the *utility problem*. First identified in the context of Explanation-Based Learning [6], the utility problem has a strong impact on CBR [5, 12] and on multi-modal architectures involving CBR [9, 15].

In the present paper, we will present a formal and experimental analysis of the different aspects involved in the utility problem for a multi-modal diagnostic architecture combining CBR and Model-Based Reasoning (MBR): the system ADAPtER [7]. We will discuss inter-relationships among speed-up of problem solving, competence of the problem solver and quality of produced solutions. As expected, the presence of the utility problem makes quite problematic to devise a suitable treatment of the above issues, having the goal of keeping the global performance of the system to an acceptable level. Even if there is no general solution that may guarantee an improvement over all the parameters, we will show that a good policy of management of the case library can produce profitable results in this direction. We will discuss a learning strategy called *Learning by Failure with Forgetting* (**LFF**) and its impact on the overall performance of the system, measured over both speed-up and competence as well as quality. The term learning has to be intended in a very general meaning, as such a strategy involves not only addition of cases to the case memory(learning), but also case deletion (forgetting).

We will show the impact of **LFF** on performance by means of an experimental comparative analysis performed on a real-world problem concerning the diagnosis of failures in an industrial plant. Even if such analysis is relative to the ADAPtER architecture, we argue that several results generalize to multi-modal CBR systems.

2 Multi-Modal Diagnostic Reasoning: An Overview

The system ADAPtER [7] is a diagnostic problem solving architecture combining CBR and MBR. In particular, the MBR component makes use of behavioral models which represent the faulty behavior of the system to be diagnosed and adopts a formal notion of diagnosis [3]. The architecture of ADAPtER was motivated by two main reasons:

- to improve the performance, in terms of computation time of a pure model-based reasoning system, by providing it with capabilities of learning by experience;

– to define a formal approach to the problem of adapting retrieved solutions, by exploiting model-based reasoning focussed on the relevant part of the model.

Previous works [8, 9] have shown that such goals can be actually obtained, even if theoretical results on worst-case complexity seem to challenge the first point: in fact, adapting a retrieved solution of an already solved problem to be a solution of a new problem is in general of the same order of complexity than solving the problem from scratch (see [8]). Fortunately, in practice the worst case results are too pessimistic and experimental data show that considerable speed-up may be obtained by resorting to adaptation with respect to resolution from scratch.

Because of these considerations, the control strategy of ADAPtER is based on viewing CBR as the the problem solving method most frequently used, relying on MBR just in case of CBR failure. This means that the MBR component should only be invoked to deal with situations that are not suitably covered by the case base[1]. At a very high level of abstraction, the problem solving strategy of ADAPtER can then be summarized as follows:

```
IF CBR(new-case) succeeds
                    THEN return(cbr-solution)
                    ELSE BEGIN
                         MBR(new-case);
                         LEARN(new-case);
                         return(mbr-solution)
                         END
```

However, considering only improvements on computational time may have some drawbacks, because of a negative impact on other performance aspects, resulting in a utility problem. In the next sections we will analyze in details such issues.

3 Performance Issues

Despite the fact that, in the adaptation step, CBR uses essentially the same reasoning mechanisms of MBR, the CBR component has sometimes to sacrifice some aspects, in order to obtain speed-up. In particular, the MBR component is able to produce all the "minimal diagnoses" for the input problem, i.e. all the solutions involving the minimal (with respect to set inclusion) number of faults. If we restrict our attention to fault models (i.e. to models describing the faulty behavior of the system to be diagnosed), minimal diagnoses are the most concise representation for the whole set of diagnoses; for this reason a minimal diagnosis is in this case preferred over a non minimal one.

[1] Notice that the integration between the two components is tighter than it may appear, since the adaptation step of the CBR component makes use of the same reasoning mechanisms involved during MBR; the main difference concerns the fact that the adaptation step uses these mechanisms in a focussed way, driven by the retrieved solution.

On the other hand, the CBR component in not always able to get this result, since it adopts a "local" strategy for searching a solution starting from the ones that have been retrieved. Part of the problem is intrinsic to the CBR approach, since the input problem is solved by first retrieving and then adapting a solution of another problem. If the input problem has a large number of possible alternative solutions, it is clear that just adapting a single solution of a similar problem has limited chances of getting all the solutions to the input problem[2]. For this reason the set of diagnoses obtained by the CBR component on a given problem may not cover all the possible solutions. A second problem concerns the "minimality" issue: because of the local search strategy adopted in adaptation, the CBR component may obtain non-minimal diagnoses. In other words, in ADAPtER, while the MBR component is correct and complete, the CBR one is only correct; moreover, if we measure the optimality of a solution in terms of minimality, while MBR is always producing optimal solutions, CBR may not. So, improving the speed-up may negatively impact on the *quality* of the produced solutions.

To actually measure the impact of the multi-modal architecture on the quality parameter, we should compare the two set of solutions produced by the whole integrated system and the MBR component respectively. The assumption is of course that MBR is producing optimal solutions. A possibility is then to consider the percentage of cases for which ADAPtER produces exactly the set of solutions produced by the MBR module. The above requirement is very restrictive, since no comparison on the actual difference between a solution produced by the integrated system and the minimal ones is considered[3]. Even if the quality metric can be relaxed in a more favorable way for ADAPtER, we have adopted the above criterion in the experiments we have performed; this has allowed us to consider results in the most pessimistic hypothesis.

Apart from speed-up and quality, there is another parameter which is worth considering: *competence*. The CBR module has a reduced competence with respect to MBR: while the MBR component is in principle able to solve any diagnostic problem in the modeled domain, this is not true for the CBR component whose competence strictly depend on the content of the case base. The control strategy of ADAPtER addresses this problem by invoking MBR every time there is a lack of competence in the CBR component. As we will see in detail in the next sections, this also triggers the learning of the solution(s) of the input case provided by the MBR component, in order to fill the competence gap.

However, in practice the evaluation of competence can be trickier: in real-word applications, diagnostic problem solving has to be performed under limited

[2] Some CBR systems may address this problem by combining multiple cases (and multiple solutions) to solve the input problem, however if the given task or domain is not modular, very complex adaptation strategies will be needed to get all possible solutions.

[3] For example, in ADAPtER, diagnostic solutions may contain logical symbols, called *assumptions*, that are used to model incompleteness in the model (see [2] for details); since assumptions are not informative about faults, it could be reasonable to consider as equivalent solutions differing only for assumption symbols.

resources and computation time is a critical resource (especially when considering diagnosis of real-time systems). In case the diagnostic system is asked to provide a solution within a predefined time constraint, the *practical competence* may be different from *theoretical competence*. In such situations, the practical competence of the MBR module may be quite far from the theoretical one, as there may be diagnostic problems that are not solvable within the specified time limit. This problem is unavoidable, since there are diagnostic problems whose actual complexity coincides with the prediction of theoretical complexity (NP-complete problem [8]). It turns out that a principled integration between CBR and MBR could also produce benefits in terms of practical competence.

Next section will discuss how speed-up, quality and competence should be traded-off for tackling the utility problem.

4 Trading-off Speed-up, Quality and Competence

Since performance can be measured over different parameters, and since an improvement on performance on a given parameter may degrade the performance over another parameter, we also need to determine to what extent we have to improve a single parameter, in order to obtain a globally efficient system. The aim of this section is to analyze in detail speed-up, quality and competence, by identifying their relationship to the utility problem. In particular, in the following we make the following assumptions: we can tune retrieval strategies, by being more or less demanding on the "goodness" of retrieved cases[4]; we assume adaptation is a fixed strategy that cannot be tuned; finally, we assume a dynamic case library, where cases may be added or deleted depending on the circumstances. This mean that we may act on two different parameters:

- the precision of retrieval;
- the content and dimension of the case library.

The term precision refers in this context to the "goodness" of retrieved cases: more precise is the retrieval, higher has to be the match between retrieved cases and the current one. Actually ADAPtER does not use surface similarity for retrieving cases from the case memory, since it adopts an adaptation-guided retrieval strategy [10]. For this reason, an increase in the precision level has the effect that the retrieved cases have a lower estimated adaptation cost. More precisely, the retrieval module of ADAPtER returns the most promising cases according to the estimated adaptation cost, just in case this cost is below a given threshold. An increase in the precision level can be obtained simply by decreasing the threshold used. This means that with a more demanding precision level, retrieval may fail, because it is unable to find a case with a estimated adaptation cost below the more restrictive threshold.

The goal is then to identify a level of retrieval precision and a suitable case library, such that the overall performance of the system, measured in terms of

[4] We measure the goodness of a case as the expected cost of adapting its solutions to the current problem (see [10] for more details).

computation time, quality and competence, could justify the multi-modal choice. Let us consider two different scenarios characterized by two extreme strategies with respect to the above parameters (i.e. level of precision and case memory size): S_1, characterized by a *low precision of retrieval* and a *small size case memory* and S_2 involving a *high precision of retrieval* and a *large case memory size.* Let us now consider how such scenarios could influence the system performance and, in particular, how they impact on the single performance parameters (i.e. speed-up, competence and quality). Such a kind of a-priori analysis could be useful to identify situations where the effect of a given strategy is not obvious and experimental analysis has to be carried on, in order to determine the actual performance of the system.

In order to speed-up computation, the ADAPtER choice is to avoid as much as possible the use of MBR because of its computational cost[5]. However, to pursue this goal, the CBR component should have a quite high probability of solving the input diagnostic problem; this implies that it has a significant amount of work to perform (searching for an adaptable case in a quite large case memory and using complex reasoning mechanisms during adaptation) with the consequence of increasing computation time.

Scenario S_1. By considering the scenario $S1$, its effect is a potential increase of the speed-up, since given a fixed adaptation strategy, retrieval and matching (in our case the estimation of the adaptation cost) can be reasonably fast, because of the limited size of the case memory. However, by adopting $S1$ the quality of solution is in general not very high, because low precision in retrieval and few cases in memory imply in general fair adaptation results. Moreover, we cannot rely too much on MBR for quality, since if the strategy works with respect to its goal, the number of calls to MBR has to be kept limited. With respect to competence, it is not obvious what influence $S1$ may have. Indeed, competence may be fair because retrieval has a larg probability of failure (a small case library) and adaptation is also more prone to failure (the retrieved cased are not very good for adaptation). This is certainly a reduction of competence for a pure CBR system, but in a multi-modal architecture like ADAPtER, such failures trigger the MBR component that may be able to solve the problem. However, because of possible time constraint, even in this case there may be a failure in solving the problem, producing a reduction of competence. On the other hand, the influence on competence of a low retrieval precision may also be positive; indeed, in this situation $S1$ may be able to retrieve and adapt cases that, if a higher precision was required, would not have been considered for adaptation (i.e. they would not have been retrieved). This aspect points out the importance of performing an experimental evaluation (see section 6).

Scenario S_2. By considering now quality and competence, a natural way for improving both is to adopt scenario $S2$. Naturally, $S2$ will in general have a negative impact on speed-up, by augmenting the overall computation time. While in general the quality of solutions seems to benefit from a more precise retrieval

[5] This is in agreement both with the experimental data (see [9, 15]) and with computational complexity results [8].

and from a larger number of stored cases, the influence on competence is also in this case trickier. In fact, it may happen that by requiring a high precision in retrieval, some problems will not be solved, because no suitable case is retrieved at that precision level. This is in fact the dual aspect of the issue discussed above (i.e. competence improvement with lower precision retrieval).

As the above discussion suggests, there seems to be no way of improving all the parameters at the same time. A real possibility that may be pursued is to exploit multi-modal reasoning to speed-up computation and to improve competence; this has to be done by keeping under control the unavoidable degradation of the quality of solutions.

5 Learning by Failure with Forgetting

Essential to the case memory management task is the possibility of devising a strategy able to keep stored only useful cases. Some approaches to case memory management in pure CBR systems address this point by trying to estimate the "coverage" of each case in memory and by using this estimate to guide the case memory revision process [13]. This may also have the advantage of providing the basis for interactive tools of *case base visualization* [14]. We have experienced such a kind of approach in the context of ADAPtER, by defining automatic case replacement strategies using information about adaptability among cases [11]. The general idea is that, when a case represents a candidate for learning (i.e. when a case is going to be added in memory), stored cases that cover the same portion of the problem space are considered for replacement (see [11] for a strategy involving the replacement of a single stored case against the new learned case).

Even if this kind of approach may be quite effective in controlling the growth of the case library, the results obtained have not been completely satisfactory; some analysis we have performed showed in fact that a significant number of cases stored in the library were never been used to solve a new problem. They were stored in memory when presented to the system for resolution, because of a failure of the CBR component; after that, no other case presented to the system was able to replace them, but no input problem was solved by using them. This kind of "useless cases" has the only effect of augmenting the retrieval time, without providing any actual advantage in terms of competence or quality. For this reason we have decided to investigate an alternative strategy based on an idea similar to the garbage collection process adopted by some programming languages; we called this strategy *Learning by Failure with Forgetting* (**LFF**).

From the conceptual point of view, the approach is based on an *on-line learning* process where cases are learnt in case of failure of the CBR component; this may occur either during retrieval (no case with the desired level of matching is retrieved) or during adaptation (the adaptation heuristics fail in constructing a solution from the retrieved one). In this situation, the case is solved by MBR and stored into the library. However, since uncontrolled case addition may produce an over-sized case memory [11], this process is interleaved with periodical *forgetting*, where stored cases are tested for their utility and possibly eliminated.

Given this kind of strategy, it becomes fundamental to suitably define the usefulness of a stored case and the triggering process of the forgetting. Informally a case is useless when it has either never been retrieved or never been adapted with success, despite the fact it has been in memory for a significant period of time. In particular, the fact that a case has been retrieved by exhibiting a subsequent failure in adaptation is more important and critical than the situation in which a case has never been retrieved. The former situation represents a potentially dangerous situation: the presence of *false positives* in the library (i.e. the presence of cases that may appear useful for solving a problem but that are actually not) . This may "fool" the multi-modal system, with a possibly significant slow-down during problem solving and with potential problems also for competence. While for never retrieved cases the memory permanence time is obviously important (less time the case has spent in memory, less probable is in general its retrieval), for cases generating adaptation failure it should be important to detect them as soon as possible, without considering how much time they have spent in memory. We propose then to classify stored cases into two categories informally defined as follows: a stored case is *useless* when it is an "old" case and it has never been retrieved; a stored case is a *false positive* when both the following conditions hold:

- it has been retrieved at least once with adaptation failure;
- the number of adaptation failures involving such a case is greater than the number of adaptation successes.

To make operative the above definition we need to formalize the notion of "old case". We define a *time window* with respect to which we evaluate the utility of a case. In particular, given a time window of width τ, we consider as "old cases" those cases that have been stored before $t_i + \frac{\tau}{2}$, being t_i the last time point considered for case memory revision.

To summarize, the system starts at time t_0 with an empty case memory and learn a new case every time a failure in the CBR component occurs. A *time stamp* is incremented when a new case is presented to the system for resolution[6]. Every τ time instants (i.e. at time $t_{i+1} = t_i + \tau$), a forgetting process is triggered and all cases stored at time $t' < (t_i + \frac{\tau}{2})$ are considered as "old cases". By considering suitable statistics, useless and false positive cases are identified and eliminated from memory.

More formally, the following parameters are stored together with a case C:

$\langle entered, C, t_E \rangle$
$\langle adaptation\_success, C, n_S \rangle$
$\langle adaptation\_failure, C, n_F \rangle$

where t_E is either the time of storage of case C or the last time point where a forgetting has occurred; n_S is the number of adaptation successes for case C and n_F the number of adaptation failures of C.

[6] In the **LFF** strategy time is assumed to be discrete, with time points identified by the sequence of cases submitted to the system.

When C is stored in memory at time t', we set $t_E = t'$ and $n_S = n_F = 0$. If C is retrieved and the adaptation of one of its solutions is successful, parameter n_S is incremented; on the contrary, if a failure in adaptation occurs when using C, parameter n_F is incremented. If the case C is not deleted at forgetting time t, then we set $t_E = t$; in fact, at time t only useful cases will remain in memory and they will now be considered as they would have been learnt all at time t.

Given these parameters, we can define more formally the classification of stored cases.

Definition 1. *A stored case C is* useless *at forgetting time t if there exist items $\langle entered, C, t_E\rangle$ with $t_E < t + \frac{\tau}{2}$ and $\langle adaptation\_success, C, 0\rangle$.*
A stored case C is a false positive *if there exist items $\langle adaptation\_failure, C, n_F\rangle$ with $n_F > 0$ and $\langle adaptation\_success, C, n_S\rangle$ with $n_F > n_S$.*

Notice that the above classification is not mutually exclusive, since an "old case" that has been retrieved at least once with failure and never with success is both useless and false positive.
Another point that deserves discussion concerns the determination of the time window; in fact, to consider a fixed dimension τ for the time window might not be suitable, since the need for forgetting does not depend only from time. In particular, a parameter that has to be taken into account for forgetting is the size of the case memory. The aim of our approach is to take under control the growth of the case memory, in order to tune performance parameters like computation time, quality and competence; for this reason it appears reasonable to link the occurrence of the forgetting process to the size of the case memory. In particular, it seems reasonable to restructure the library only when the system exhibits a stable behavior. This means that a minimum number of cases has to be examined from the last forgetting and that the *failure rate*, defined as the percentage of cases that have not been solved by the CBR component in a given time window, must not be too high. ADAPtER obtains this goal by triggering forgetting when the current time stamp TS satisfies the following condition:

$$TS > \max(\delta, k|CM|)$$

where δ and k are positive constants and $|CM|$ is the size (cardinality) of the case memory. The parameter δ is used to assure that, even if the case memory has a rapid growth (as is the case in the initial phase of the life of the system, in particular if an empty initial memory is assumed), forgetting does not take place for a suitable time interval (i.e. at least δ cases have to be examined from the last forgetting). Every time a forgetting occurs, the time-stamp TS is reset.

Since the **LFF** strategy learns a new case when the MBR component is invoked, the width τ of the current time window resulting from the above criterion is related to the *failure rate* exhibited in such a window by the CBR component. Given a period of observation of N cases, if the CBR component exhibits M failures in such a period, we define the *failure rate* as $f_r = \frac{M}{N}$.

The relationship between f_r and τ can be formally stated by means of the following theorem.

Theorem 1. *Given an observation period of N cases with M failures (i.e.* $f_r = \frac{M}{N}$*), then* $N > k|CM_N|$ *if and only if* $f_r < \frac{1}{k} - \alpha$*, where* $|CM_N|$ *is the size of the case memory at time N and* α *is a positive constant depending on the size of the initial case memory.*

Proof. Since after N cases, M failures have occurred we have that $|CM_N| = M + |CM_0|$ being $|CM_0|$ the size of the initial (possibly empty) case memory. By substitution in the relation $N > k|CM_N|$ we get

$N > k|CM_0| + kM$; by considering $M = f_r N$ we get

$N > k|CM_0| + kf_r N$ and then

$f_r < \frac{1}{k} - \alpha$ with $\alpha = \frac{|CM_0|}{N}$

The above theorem states that a forgetting will occur in a given time window if and only if the failure rate is less than a quantity that is less of the inverse of k. It formally proves that the constant k is inversely related to the failure rate; this means that if a low failure rate is expected, we can set a large value for k, by letting the system working without forgetting for a significant amount of time and with a limited growth of the case memory size. Of course, if we set a value of k that is too large for the exhibited failure rate, the above theorem implies that an overgrowing of the case memory will occur, since the satisfaction of the condition for triggering the forgetting will tend to be postponed. On the contrary, setting a value of k too small with respect to the actual fault rate will have the effect of an excessive occurrence of forgetting, by producing the equivalent of *thrashing* in paged operating systems.

In the experiments we will describe in the next section, we have considered a value of $k = 3$ and of $\delta = 300$.

6 Experimental Results and Discussion

In this section we will report on the experimental results we have performed by implementing the **LFF** case management strategy in ADAPtER. We have considered a real-world domain concerning the diagnosis of faults in an industrial plant and we have generated a batch of 2500 cases[7]. The batch of cases has been automatically generated by means of a simulator we have developed, working on the faulty model of the domain at hand (see [11] for more details about the parameters of the simulator.). We are then guaranteed to deal with cases that are significant for the given domain. We have considered cases with multiple faults and in particular, the number of faulty components was at most 3. We have performed several experiments for evaluating the impact of the **LFF** strategy on performance aspects of ADAPtER; in particular, we have evaluated how the growth of the case memory is kept under control by **LFF**, depending on different thresholds on retrieval precision, and its relationship with computation time, competence and quality of produced solutions. We performed these experiments

[7] We have also performed a slightly reduced analysis on a batch of 5000 cases, with comparable results.

by starting the system with an empty case memory and by setting a time out of 100 seconds of CPU-time on resolution time (both for MBR and ADAPtER).

Table 1 compares the average computation time (given in msec. on a Pentium II). for solving a problem with pure MBR with the average computation time of ADAPtER using different thresholds on retrieval: $\sigma_1 = 12, \sigma_2 = 24$ and $\sigma_3 = 30$. Retrieval and adaptation times are also shown. For each mean value, we also show (in brackets) the width of a 95% confidence interval on that value. Given a

	MBR	$\sigma_1 = 12$	$\sigma_2 = 24$	$\sigma_3 = 30$
AVG Resol. Time	6014.86 (823.70)	4613.13 (733.12)	2962.60 (595.43)	2090.44 (483.03)
AVG Retr. Time		194.67 (3.79)	163.72 (2.99)	151.82 (2.64)
AVG Adapt. Time		48.32 (1.32)	77.25 (3.60)	88.85 (6.02)
Unsolved cases	107	84	55	35

Table 1. Computation Time Results

threshold σ_i, retrieval is successful if and only if the estimated adaptation cost of the retrieved solution is less than σ_i; smaller is the threshold, higher is the required precision for retrieval. In particular, for the given domain, σ_1 is a very restrictive threshold (i.e. it corresponds to a very high precision). We can notice from table 1 that a significant speed-up is obtained by reducing precision of retrieval. This produces a slight decrease of retrieval time and a slight increase of adaptation time. However, as one can expect, augmenting precision has the effect of increasing the number of cases where CBR fails in providing a solution and therefore the expensive step of MBR has to be performed (unsolved cases in table 1). This can also be observed by considering the number of failures of the CBR component with respect to the number of examined cases and with respect to the given threshold (figure 1). More precise is the retrieval, higher is the number of failures, since higher is the probability of not retrieving a suitable case: data seem to suggest that the increase in probability of adapting the retrieved solution does not compensate the larger failure rate of retrieval.

Figure 2 reports the temporal evolution of the size of the case memory, depending on the number of cases examined by ADAPtER. We can notice the particular pattern produced by **LFF**, with a drastic lowering of case memory size in correspondence of each forgetting. Again, more demanding in term of precision is the retrieval strategy, larger is the case memory, even if the number of stored cases is actually kept under control (370 cases after 2500 resolutions for σ_1, 115 for σ_2 and 99 for σ_3). Notice also, that higher is the precision, lower is the number of activations of the forgetting phase; this is due to the higher failure rate that causes the system to take more time to reach a stable phase.

The second parameter we have measured has been competence. In figure 3 we have plotted the number of cases which ADAPtER as a multi-modal system (CBR+MBR) was unable to solve within the time-out of 100 seconds of CPU-time, with respect to the number of cases examined by the system. We can

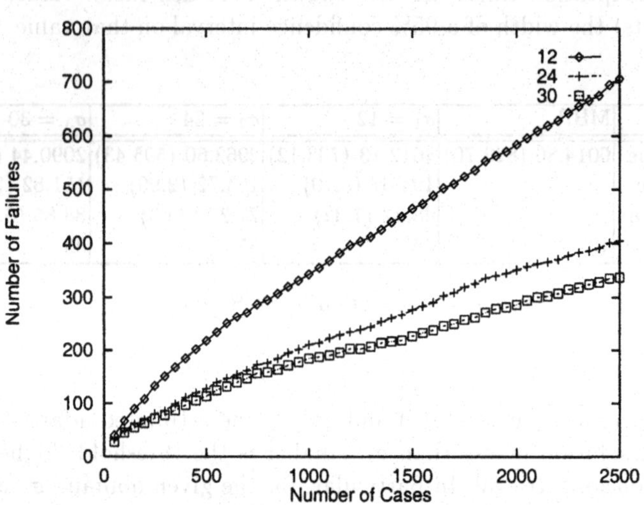

Fig. 1. Number of Failures of CBR Component

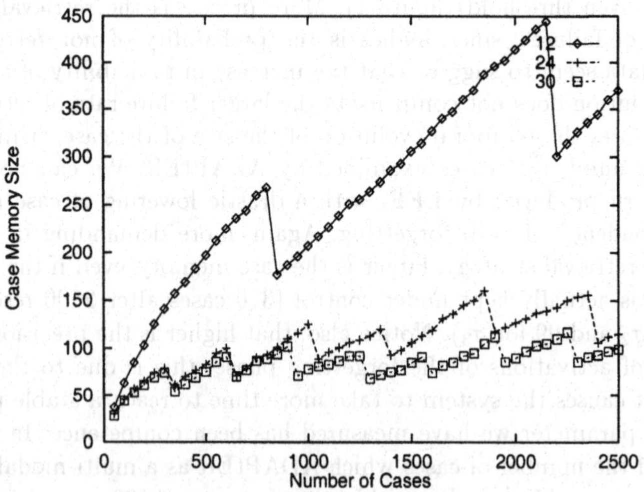

Fig. 2. Case Memory Size

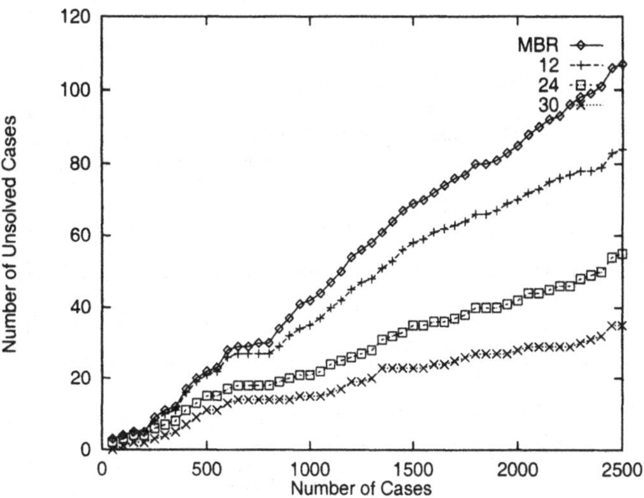

Fig. 3. Competence: Number of Unsolved Cases

notice that a less precise retrieval strategy may improve global competence, while being able to store less cases in memory and to reduce average resolution time. Moreover, with the considered thresholds, ADAPtER is always better in practical competence that pure MBR. For instance, on the considered batch, the 4.28% of the cases (i.e. 107 cases) are not solved by MBR within the given time limit, while with σ_3, ADAPtER fails in just the 1.4% of the cases (i.e. 35 cases).

Finally, we have investigated the quality of solution. As we mentioned in section 3, we have adopted a very restrictive criterion for estimating the quality of a solution provided by ADAPtER: the percentage of cases for which it returns the minimal solutions. The quality metric is then a number in $[0, 1]$ with 1 corresponding to optimum (100%). Quality values are plotted in figure 4 with respect to the number of considered cases. Higher is the precision of retrieval strategy, higher is the average quality, so the trade-off due to the utility problem occurs. The important aspect to point out is the quite high quality obtained, even by considering the very restrictive criterion we mentioned before: after 2500 case, we got an average quality of 71% for σ_1, 66% for σ_2 and 65% for σ_3.

However, just considering the quality in terms of minimality of the set of solutions is not enough; indeed, also the intrinsic quality of the problem should be taken into account. In fact, a diagnostic problem could be considered completely solved if the number of (minimal) diagnoses is limited (it should be just one in order to single out the faulty components). There is a number of reasons why the set of (minimal) diagnoses is larger than one. In a model-based approach to diagnosis there may be parts of the model that do not fully account for the possible diagnostic problems that may be encountered. This does not mean that the model-based system is not able to solve some problem, but that the model is not sufficiently detailed in order to discriminate among competing diagnoses (for example, the model makes use of qualitative abstractions that do not allow

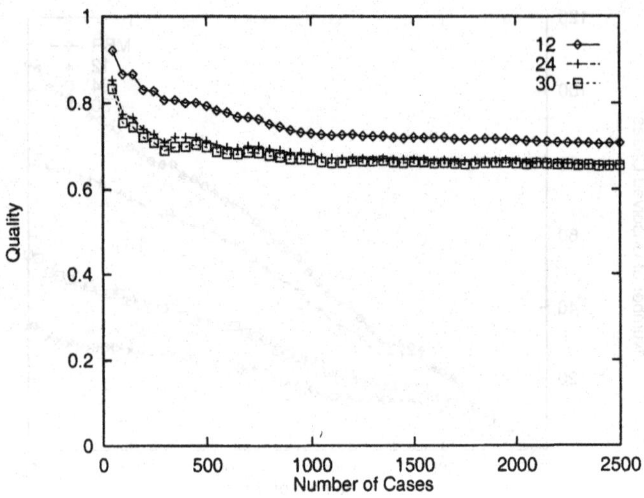

Fig. 4. Quality of Solutions

the diagnostic systems to distinguish among similar behaviors). Sometimes the problem does not concern the model, but the system to be diagnosed: the absence of sensors or measurable parameters in the artifact to be diagnosed prevents the diagnostic system to have sufficient information for discrimination. More often, the reason of a large number of diagnoses depends on the under-specification of the description of the diagnostic problem (typically just some of the relevant observable parameters are known in the specific case). Table 2 specifies the quality of solutions produced by ADAPtER with respect to different classes of problems. Problems in class 1 and 2 correspond to problems having 1 and 2 minimal solutions respectively. For each class, the corresponding number of cases in the batch of 2500 cases is reported (in brackets the corresponding percentage over all the batch). The average quality for the given class is shown, together with the average cumulative quality (the average quality by considering all cases in a class less or equal than the current one) that is shown in brackets. If we take

Class	Number of cases	$\sigma_1 = 12$	$\sigma_2 = 24$	$\sigma_3 = 30$
1	734 (29%)	99% (99%)	95% (95%)	95% (95%)
2	602 (24%)	66% (82%)	65% (80%)	64% (79%)

Table 2. Quality of Solutions wrt Classes of Problems

into consideration the set of problems for which pure MBR provides just a single solution (i.e. problems with a complete specification in terms of observables), we can see that the quality is very high and therefore for well-defined problems, the multi-modal system provides in almost all the cases exactly the minimal diagnosis. Data reported in table 2 confirm the hypothesis that precision in retrieval is directly related to quality, but that the differences are not very relevant. On the other hand, a plausible explanation of the significant difference in quality between problems with one minimal solution with problems with two solutions concerns the difficulty of the CBR component to cover the whole set of solutions provided by MBR, by adapting a single retrieved solution.

References

1. D. Aha and J. Daniels (eds.). *Proc. AAAI Workshop on CBR Integrations*. AAAI Press, 1998.
2. L. Console, L. Portinale, D. Theseider Dupré, and P. Torasso. Combining heuristic and causal reasoning in diagnostic problem solving. In J.M. David, J.P. Krivine, and R. Simmons, editors, *Second Generation Expert Systems*, pages 46,68. Springer Verlag, 1993.
3. L. Console and P. Torasso. A spectrum of logical definitions of model-based diagnosis. *Computational Intelligence*, 7(3):133–141, 1991.
4. E. Freuder (ed.). *AAAI Spring Symposium on Multi-modal Reasoning*. AAAI Press, 1998.
5. A.G. Francis and A. Ram. The utility problem in case-based reasoning. Technical Report ER-93-08, Georgia Tech, 1993.
6. S. Minton. Learning effective search control knowledge: an EBL approach. Technical Report CMU-CS-88-133, Dept. of Computer Science, Carnagie-Mellon Univ., 1988.
7. L. Portinale and P. Torasso. ADAPtER: an integrated diagnostic system combining case-based and abductive reasoning. In *Proc. 1st ICCBR, LNAI 1010*, pages 277–288. Springer Verlag, 1995.
8. L. Portinale and P. Torasso. On the usefulness of re-using diagnostic solutions. In *Proc. 12th European Conf. on AI - ECAI 96*, pages 137–141, Budapest, 1996.
9. L. Portinale and P. Torasso. Performance issues in ADAPtER a combined CBR-MBR diagnostic architecture. In *Proc. AAAI Spring Sympos. on Multi-Modal Reasoning*, pages 47–52, AAAI Press, Stanford, 1998.
10. L. Portinale, P. Torasso, and D. Magro. Selecting most adaptable diagnostic solutions through Pivoting-Based Retrieval. In *Proc. 2nd ICCBR, LNAI 1266*, pages 393–402. Springer Verlag, 1997.
11. L. Portinale, P. Torasso, and P. Tavano. Dynamic case memory management. In *Proc. ECAI 98*, pages 73–78, Brighton, 1998.
12. B. Smyth and P. Cunningham. The utility problem analysed: a case-based reasoning perspective. In *LNAI 1168*, pages 392–399. Springer Verlag, 1996.
13. B. Smyth and M.T. Keane. Remembering to forget. In *Proc. 14th IJCAI*, pages 377–382, Montreal, 1995.
14. B. Smyth and E. McKenna. Modeling the competence of case-bases. In *Proc. 4th EWCBR, LNAI 1488*, pages 208–220. Springer Verlag, 1998.
15. M. van Someren, J. Surma, and P. Torasso. A utility-based approach to learning in a mixed case-based and model-based reasoning architecture. In *Proc. 2nd ICCBR, LNAI 1266*, pages 477–488. Springer Verlag, 1997.

A Case-Based Methodology for Planning Individualized Case Oriented Tutoring

Alexander Seitz

Dept. of Artificial Intelligence
University of Ulm
D-89069 Ulm, Germany
seitz@ki.informatik.uni-ulm.de

Case oriented tutoring gives students the possibility to practice their acquired theoretical knowledge in the context of concrete cases. Accordingly, tutoring systems for individualized learning have to take the skills of students at applying their knowledge to problem solving into account. This paper describes a case-based methodology for planning tutoring processes depending on the skills of individual users. We develop methods for retrieving tutoring plans of users with similar skills and present adaptation techniques for improving these plans based on the student's behavior during the corresponding tutoring process. The developed methodology is based on the notion that a student has to perform threads of associations in the process of problem solving.

Introduction

A steadily increasing number of case oriented tutoring systems [1,7,11,12] reflects the experience that education should be viewed as a two-stage process: after systematic knowledge has been internalized from literature, lectures, courses etc, it has to be consolidated by practically applying it to concrete tutoring cases. This is especially true for domains where diagnostic problem solving constitutes an essential element [10].

A salient feature of case oriented tutoring systems is that a student is trained in applying his knowledge instead of learning it from scratch. In several domains, as for example medicine, a huge amount of cases would be necessary to impart all relevant knowledge. On the contrary, those systems should improve the students' skill in applying learned knowledge in the context of concrete cases.

Great effort has been made in the past decades to adapt tutoring systems to the demands and knowledge of individual users. They are based on facts like the user's goal, knowledge of the domain, background, experience or preferences [2]. One common technique for representing the knowledge of users is the 'overlay model' [3]. It identifies the knowledge entities of a learning domain and represents which entities are already learned by the student. User models are often used for offering explanations for students' problem solutions regarding their individual problem-solving behavior [13] or planning tutoring processes based on the users knowledge and preferences [9]. Unfortunately, in domains with a large knowledge background it is difficult and expensive to build an explicit model of all domain knowledge that might be known by the student and is used for problem solving [8]. For example, this applies to many fields of medicine. Case oriented tutoring systems emphasize the training of students' skills to apply their learned knowledge, which causes additional problems to create an explicit user model.

In the following sections a methodology is described that allows the representation of student's skills by representing the methods by which the student is tested on these skills. A case base of test scenarios is built to plan further tutoring processes for new students.

Association threads as a basis for modeling tutoring processes

One major purpose of case oriented learning is the consolidation of learned knowledge by applying it within the context of concrete cases. The application of knowledge may be identified as a process of performing a thread of associations to solve a problem. This can be illustrated by examining the mental work done by medical students when they have to suggest a therapy for a patient in a tutoring case. An expert in this domain is able to perform direct associations between medical findings like pain at certain anatomic regions, and diagnoses or therapy prescriptions that result from them. With a decreasing level of skill, the student has to encounter a more detailed thread of associations. For example, he does an explicit abstraction from concrete patient descriptions, like "I have got pain in my belly" to the concept "pain at the lower right abdomen" and explicitly thinks of differential diagnoses for this finding. Then he tries to recall findings necessary to confirm or rule out certain diagnoses and to recognize them in the patient descriptions. After having found a diagnosis he thinks of treatments that are recommended for it. Figure 1 illustrates this chain of reasoning.

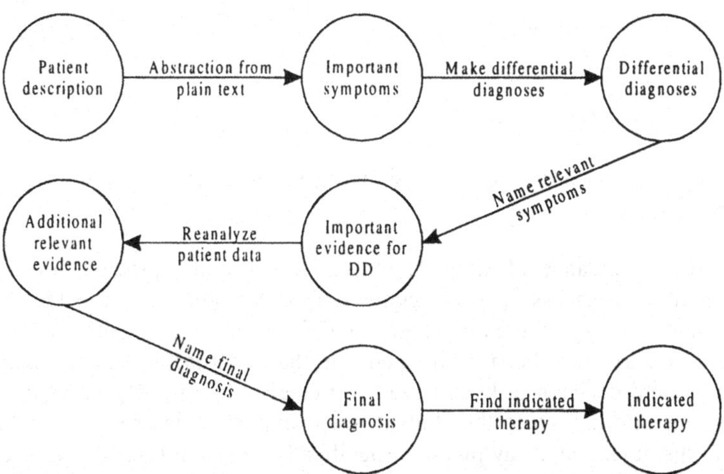

Fig. 1. Association thread in a medical problem solving procedure

As mentioned above, it can be rather difficult to explicitly represent the background knowledge that is necessary to perform certain tasks in a tutoring case.

This hampers especially an explicit modeling of user knowledge. But still it is possible to model a student's skill on applying his background knowledge to perform those tasks by representing the way he is tested on them. The more he is guided in his association threads made for solving a problem, the more it is assumed that it is difficult for him to perform those associations. The other way round, students with lower skills in certain tasks should be more guided in performing those tasks. This method conforms to the idea of case oriented tutoring, where students should learn to apply the knowledge they have acquired in lectures, seminars, or from textbooks. On the other hand, it should be contrasted to problem based learning [14], where students develop and extend their knowledge by means of tutoring cases. But nevertheless a case oriented tutoring system could be equipped with corrections and comments to student actions, tips, or links to information pages in order to improve the student's knowledge.

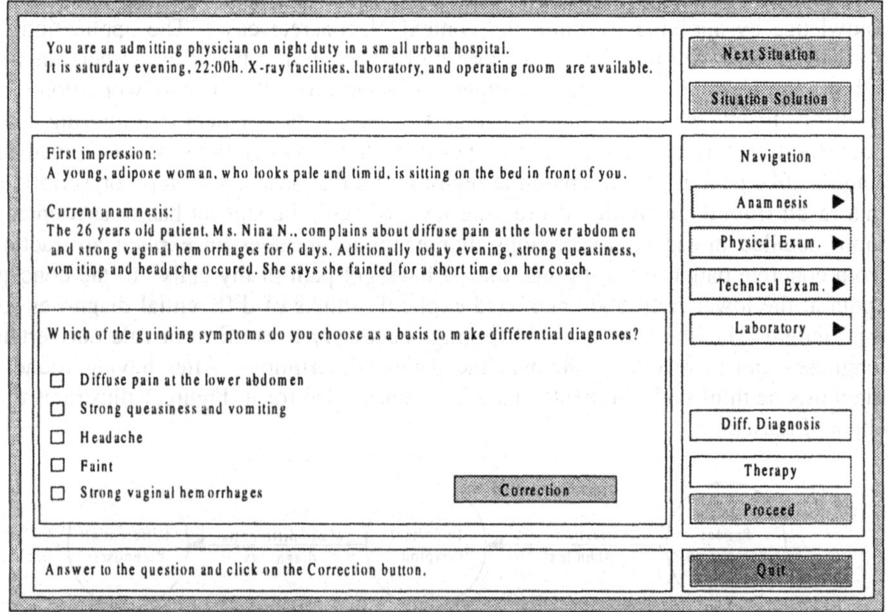

Fig. 2. Realization of a decision task for finding important guiding symptoms in a patient description.

To allow a guidance of students through the tutoring process, an appropriate execution model is necessary. In the context of the collaborative project Docs'n Drugs [4], a discrete event simulation approach [6] for the implementation of dynamic tutoring processes has been developed. In that approach, variable networks of information and decision tasks are used to model tutoring processes. Both kinds of tasks present information to the student, for example by describing a dialog with a patient or displaying an x-ray picture. Specifically, decision tasks demand interaction from the user, for example making a diagnosis. This structure lends itself to a translation of association threads into sequences of information and decision tasks. For example, the association step 'abstract from patient information' could be transformed into a task where patient information is presented followed by a decision task of selecting or stating the important guiding symptoms. An example how this could be realized is depicted in Figure 2.

Tutoring processes that are modeled according to those ideas can be adapted to students through making association steps explicit by inserting appropriate information and decision tasks. Other adaptation techniques could be pruning the number of possible answers in a decision task or raising the difficulty of questions in it. For example if a student who has difficulties in making reasonable diagnoses, the system should support him by reducing the number of choices for possible diagnoses. Or he could be guided to explicitly think of preliminary tasks like deciding whether necessary evidence for a diagnosis can be found in the patient description.

Thread Configurations

One case in case oriented learning can comprise several learning objectives. In medical cases, for example, the student has to perform several tasks:

- Request for examinations to gather sufficient patient information for a final diagnosis.
- Initiating urgent accompanying measures while taking care of a patient.
- Deciding which therapy is necessary.
- Judging if the patient has to be informed about surgical treatments.

Thus the learning objectives of a case can be described by a set of association threads that the student has to perform in order to follow the given tasks. These threads are sequences of association steps necessary for solving the tasks. Thereby, the last association step within a thread is always obligatory as it produces the result of a thread.

To realize different levels of guidance within a tutoring process, it must be possible to vary the method of how a student is tested on certain association steps. Different configurations of information and decision tasks that vary in difficulty can implement those association tests. It is the task of the author to define an appropriate set of possible test procedures for each association step and to order its elements according to their difficulty. Formally, an association test class A for each association step is extensionally defined by a set of association test categories, which represent the different methods of testing a student on the association step:

$$A = \{c_1, \ldots, c_n\}. \tag{1}$$

The test categories of an association test class A are ordered by a bijective function f on the elements of A. Increasing ordinals correspond to test scenarios with increasing difficulty.

$$f : A \to \{0, \ldots, |A| - 1\}. \tag{2}$$

The author of a tutoring process may define that the highest category of a certain association test class corresponds to omitting the association test. If that category is used in the tutoring process, it is assumed a priori that the student performs the association step correctly.

By the presented formalism we can define a thread as a sequence *th* of association test classes for each association step that has to be tested within the thread:

$$th = \langle A_1, A_2, \ldots, A_n \rangle. \tag{3}$$

Finally we can obtain instances of a thread by instantiating its association test classes with concrete test categories. The instantiation of all threads of a tutoring case is called a thread configuration for that case. Figure 3 shows an abstract view of transforming association threads into a thread configuration.

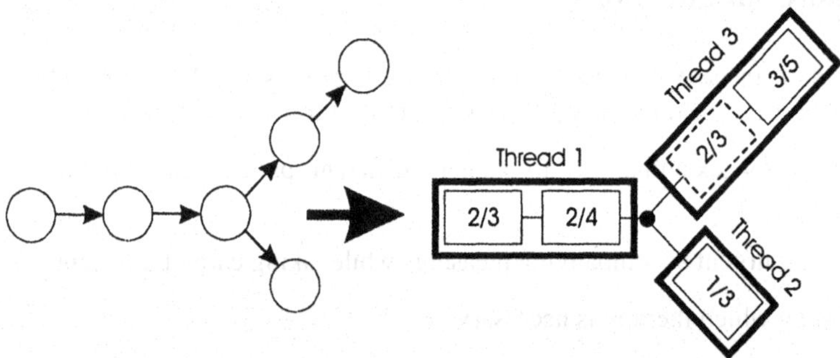

Fig. 3. Transformation of association steps into a thread configuration. The first number in a number pair denotes the association test category used for testing an association step while the second one is the number of possible test categories for this association step. Notice that both thread 2 and 3 have to be passed. Dashed association steps are optional to the student

As an example, we will take a closer look at a thread containing the following association steps:

- Find important guiding symptoms in a patient description.
- Which groups of tentative diagnoses should be considered?
- Which differential diagnoses are candidates for being the final diagnosis?
- Choose examinations that help to exclude or confirm tentative diagnoses.
- Decide on a final diagnosis.
- Think of an appropriate therapy for the final diagnosis.

Figure 2 shows how the first task could be implemented. After the student has selected some items and pressed the "Correction" button, the tutoring system comments his choice by showing the correct answers. Then he is able to enter the next task by pressing the "Proceed" button. For this task, we substitute a new multiple choice question for the previous one, which is depicted in Figure 4 and repeat the procedure described.

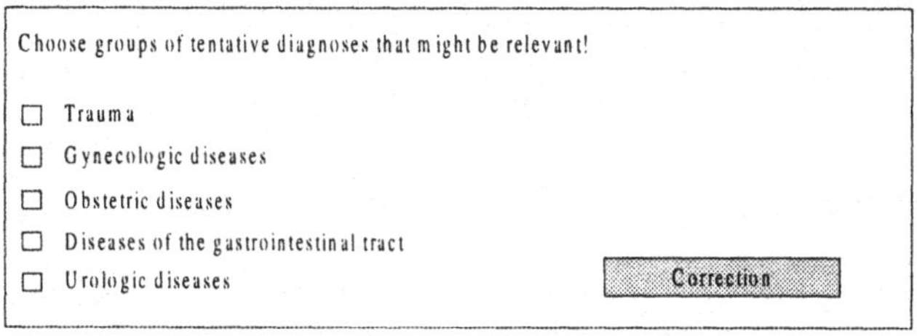

Choose groups of tentative diagnoses that might be relevant!

☐ Trauma
☐ Gynecologic diseases
☐ Obstetric diseases
☐ Diseases of the gastrointestinal tract
☐ Urologic diseases

Correction

Fig. 4. Decision task for selecting tentative diagnosis groups

In a case with high difficulty, these questions may be omitted if we assume that the student performs those tasks correctly. Thus we just display the information about the first impression and the current anamnesis and allow the student to enter the differential diagnosis task by making the corresponding "Differential Diagnosis" button active. Otherwise, this button becomes active after the student has passed the multiple choice task for tentative diagnosis groups. Tests on correct differential diagnoses can be realized by offering the selection of items in a diagnosis list, as shown in Figure 5.

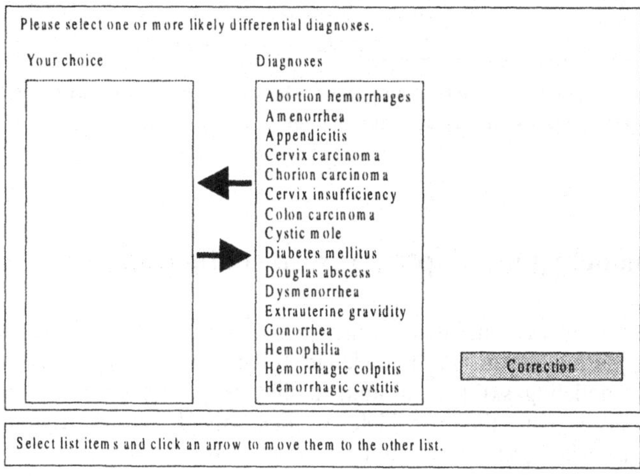

Fig. 5. Decision task for selecting tentative diagnoses. The right list shows possible selections, while the left one displays the student's actual tentative diagnosis list

. Again, the student is able to let the system correct his choice. The difficulty of this task may be reduced by narrowing down the list of choices in the diagnosis selection list. We could also substitute a multiple choice question with few answers for the selection list or omit the entire differential diagnosis task. To realize the task of selecting examinations in order to collect information to make a final diagnosis, we may offer a set of navigation buttons instead of explicitly asking questions. Figure 6 shows active buttons for the relevant groups of examinations. Clicking one of these buttons pops up a menu of possible examinations in this group. The student is able to select one or more examinations from the menus. He finishes this task by clicking the "Proceed" button again. We can vary the difficulty of this task by reducing the number of menu items or make one or more examination group buttons inactive. Finally, the final diagnosis and therapy tasks may be implemented in the same way as for the tentative diagnosis groups tasks.

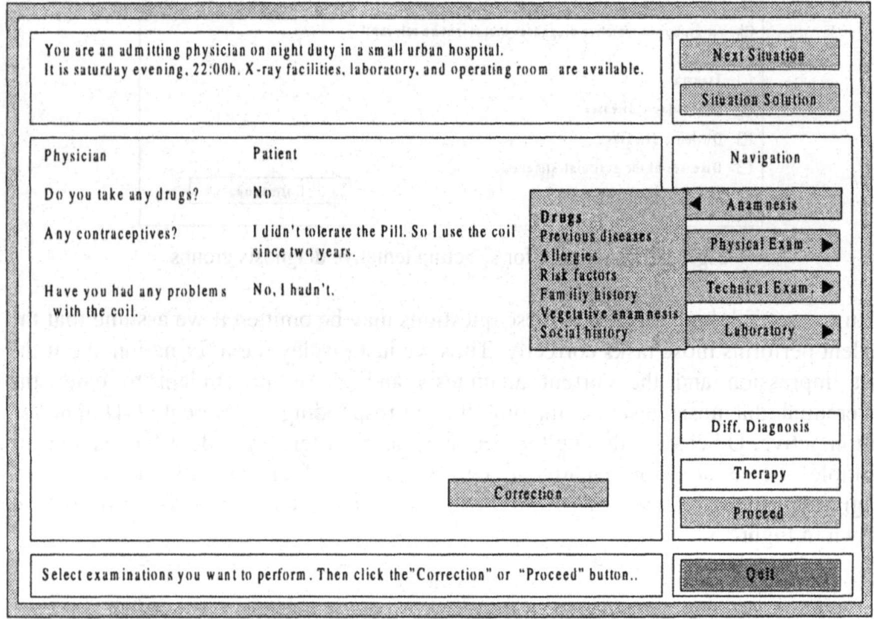

Fig. 6. Task for selecting relevant examinations. The student can get information about the patient by selecting items in the examination menus

Student modeling by adapting thread configurations

As stated above, in case oriented learning it is important to focus on the skills of a student to apply his background knowledge in the context of concrete cases. Instead of explicitly modeling skills of a student, they may be represented as the way a student is tested on them, which is determined by corresponding thread configurations. Appropriate configurations for a certain student can be obtained by adapting model thread configurations of a tutoring case to the problems that arise when the student works at that case.

Adaptation of thread configurations

If a thread of association steps solves a problem, and intermediate steps within this sequence are performed perfectly by the student, an adaptation to rise the difficulty of the thread appears to be reasonable. In this case the sequence is adapted by increasing the difficulty for the well performed steps. As mentioned above, the maximum difficulty for an association step may be modeled by making the performing of this step optional to the student, assuming he is able to perform it correctly.

On the other hand if single association steps are performed badly by the student, as he shows bad test results or makes wrong decisions, a decrease in the difficulty level of the association step should be performed. This can be done for example by reducing the set of possible choices for the critical step or extending the given thread by making the association step just before the critical one obligatory. A reduction of choices makes it easier for the student to solve a given problem. Extending the thread with explicit milestones helps the student to form association steps in his mind.

Case-Based planning of the tutoring process

The difficulty of tutoring cases for individual students should be demanding the student's skills on solving those cases. Thus the overall goal of planning tutoring processes for case oriented learning is to optimally adapt those processes to the skills of a student in the sense of optimizing their difficulty. For that, both skills of the student on cases he previously worked on and the improvement of his skills with every case must be taken into account. These aspects can be modeled by the sequence of adapted thread configurations of the tutoring cases he had been working on. For example, the history of how a student solved a set of tutoring patient cases provides not only facts about the problems a student had when working at those cases, but also how fast he improved his problem solving skills from case to case.

A tutoring process has to test the student on a number of association steps that are necessary to solve the underlying tutoring case. The difficulty of those test procedures cannot be considered separately, but must be seen in the context of the whole case. For example, the difficulty of a differential diagnosis task strongly depends on how much the student has been guided and helped to collect and understand patient information in previous abstraction or information tasks. Thus the subgoal of optimizing the test procedure for a single association step may interact with other subgoals. Apart from that, if explicitly created tutoring plans for a couple of student stereotypes are not sufficient, the author of tutoring cases is faced with the difficult problem of formulating planning knowledge based rules for individualized tutoring processes. Summing up, there are two major problems we have to deal with.

1. Acquisition of planning rules for individualized tutoring.
2. Pursuing a set of interacting subgoals.

Case-based planning is especially suitable for both of these problems [5]. Instead of creating new plans from scratch, it supports the reuse of old plans, which pursue a set of subgoals and may be adapted by modification rules. The repaired plans can be stored and used for an optimized planning in new situations.

We express tutoring plans by thread configurations. For the planning of optimal configurations, cases are defined by a sequence of thread configurations that correspond to the performance of a student on a series of tutoring cases. It is assumed that a number of students are confronted with the same sets of tutoring cases within a tutoring phase. A tutoring phase may be a practical training or a seminar about a certain subject.

The case base is initially filled with one or more model configuration sequences built by authors of the tutoring system. This corresponds to building 'rule of thumb' plans for some student stereotypes. Generally these sequences have to be adapted as mentioned in the previous section when a student goes through tutoring processes based on them. Finally, the adapted sequence will be stored as a new case for further reuse. Given a set of initial or adapted configuration sequences, tutoring plans for further students can be based on them. Assume that a student has passed the tutoring process for a tutoring case based on a model configuration for this case that has been adapted to the students' skills. Now the system searches for sequences of thread configurations in the case base with a thread configuration for the actual tutoring case that is similar to the one that has been constructed by the adaptation process. By adopting the corresponding configuration of the found sequence, the system can plan the tutoring process for the next tutoring case the user has to solve, by using the associated thread configuration in the found sequence. Eventually, the adopted configuration has to be adapted to the student. For the tutoring process planning of the third tutoring case, adapted configurations for the passed two cases can be used for searching similar tutoring processes and so on. If thread configurations had to be adapted within this process, the users' history is stored in the case base as a new exemplar for a tutoring process.

By this methodology, not only the process of finding students with similar skills is realized, but also profiles of students with a similar improvement of skills are tracked down and used as a basis for further tutoring process planning. Case authors do not have to explicitly formulate tutoring process planning rules but to formulate some model plans for further refinement. Furthermore, the subgoals of tutoring association steps are planned as a coherent set, with regard to the student's behavior in previous tutoring cases.

Similarity between thread configurations

The similarity of different thread configurations for a series of tutoring cases is reduced to separately comparing configurations for each thread within those cases.
For single thread configurations, instances of each association step in both configurations within a thread are compared. To realize that granularity of similarity assessment, we define a method *dist* that returns the distance between two elements of a association test class A:

$$dist : A \times A \rightarrow [0,1] \tag{4}$$

A simple definition of *dist* may be based on the ordering function f:

$$dist_A(c_i, c_j) = \begin{cases} \dfrac{|f_A(c_i) - f_A(c_j)|}{|A| - 1}, \text{if } |A| > 1 \\ 0 \quad , \text{if } |A| = 1 \end{cases} \tag{5}$$

Two thread configurations for the same tutoring case consist of the same set of threads. Also the class of association tests at the same position in a thread in the two cases is the same. Threads only vary in the association test categories at the same position in a thread and thus can be viewed as two instances of a sequence of association test classes:

Let th_1 and th_2 be the two instances, namely

$$th_1 = \langle c_{11}, c_{12}, \ldots, c_{1n} \rangle \text{ and } th_2 = \langle c_{21}, c_{22}, \ldots, c_{2n} \rangle . \tag{6}$$

Then the similarity between the two threads represented by th_1 and th_2 can be computed by the summation

$$sim(th_1, th_2) = \frac{\sum_{i=1}^{n} dist_{A_i}(c_{1i}, c_{2i})}{n} \tag{7}$$

The summation is performed over the association test classes A_i in the thread for which we want to compare the two instances. The range of values for *sim* is the interval [0,1], according to the definition of *dist.*

The thread configuration for a tutoring case consists of instantiations for each thread in it. Thus the similarity between two thread configurations of a tutoring case may be computed as the mean value of the similarities between corresponding thread instances. In the same way the similarity of two thread configurations of a series of tutoring cases can be defined as a mean value of similarities between corresponding case thread configurations.

Conclusion

The presented methods allow the modeling of student skills by a history of how well a student has performed on a series of tutoring cases. By this means, the explicit representation of a student's knowledge, which is especially difficult for case oriented systems, can be avoided. Moreover, case histories make it possible to model the improvement of student's skills and thus can be used for retrieving and adapting appropriate tutoring plans for further tutoring cases.

On the other hand, the acquisition of tutoring cases is made easier by the methods described. The author of a tutoring case builds a set of test configurations for each association step that has to be performed within the tutoring case. The elements of the obtained sets just have to be ordered according to their difficulty. An explicit assignment of user stereotypes or difficulty levels to association tests is not necessary. Only a small set of model configurations for given student stereotypes must be defined.

Further cooperative work within the scope of the project Docs'n Drugs will be dedicated to the implementation of thread configurations as corresponding networks of information and decision for testing and evaluating the proposed methods.

Additionally, research will focus on more sophisticated similarity measures between thread configurations and explicit weightings of threads that take their different importance for the tutoring process into account.

References

1. Baehring T., Weichelt U., Schmidt H., Adler M., Bruckmoser S., Fischer M.: ProMediWeb: Problem based case training in medicine via the World Wide Web. Proceedings ED-MEDIA II, Freiburg (1998).
2. Brusilovski, P.: Methods and techniques of adaptive hypermedia. User Modeling and User-Adapted Interaction 6 (1996) 87-129.
3. Carr B., Goldstein I.P.: Overlays: A Theory of Modeling for Computer-Aided Instruction. MIT Press, Cambridge, MA/London (1977).
4. Docs'N Drugs – Die virtuelle Poliklinik. http://www.docs-n-drugs.de
5. Hammond K.: Case-Based Planning. Academic Press, INC., Boston (1989).
6. Martens, A., Uhrmacher, A.M.: Modeling Tutoring as a Dynamic Process - A Discrete Event Simulation Approach. In: Proc. European Simulation Multiconference ESM'99 Vol.1, Warsaw 1.-4.6.1999, SCS, Gent, to appear.
7. Nuthalapathy F., Oh J., Elsner Ch., Altman M.: Interactive Electronic Problem Based Learning (iePBL): An Internet based Application for Clinical Medical Education in the PBL Case Format, Proceedings of the ED-MEDIA World-Conference, Freiburg (1998).
8. Ohlson, S.: Impact of Cognitive Theory on the Practice of Courseware Authoring. In: Journal of Computer Assisted Learning 4 (1993) 194-221.
9. Papagni M., Cirillo V., Micarelli A.: Ocram-CBR: A Shell for Case-Based Educational Systems. In: Leake D., Plaza E.: Case-Based Reasoning Research and Development. Springer, Heidelberg (1997) 104-113.
10. Patel V.L., Kaufman D.R., Arocha J.F.: Steering through the murky waters of scientific conflict: situated and symbolic models of clinical cognition. Artificial Intelligence in Medicine 7 (1995) 413-428.
11. Scheuerer C. et al.: NephroCases. Proceedings of ED-MEDIA/ED-TELECOM 98 (1998) 2075-2076.
12. Schewe S., Reinhardt T., Betz C.: Experiences with a Knowledge Based Tutoring System for Student Education in Rheumatology. In Proc. 5. Deutsche Tagung XPS'99 – Wissensbasierte Systeme – Bilanz und Perspektiven, Wuerzburg, 1999.
13. Weber G.: Episodic Learnier Modeling. Cognitive Science 20 (1996) 195-236.
14. Wetzel, M.: Problem Based Learning: An Update on Problem Based Learning at Harvard Medical School. Annals of Community-Oriented Education, 7 (1994) 237-247.

Building Compact Competent Case-Bases

Barry Smyth & Elizabeth McKenna

Department of Computer Science, University College Dublin,
Belfield, Dublin 4, IRELAND
{Barry.Smyth, Elizabeth.McKenna@ucd.ie}

Abstract. Case-based reasoning systems solve problems by reusing a corpus of previous problem solving experience stored as a case-base of individual problem solving cases. In this paper we describe a new technique for constructing compact competent case-bases. The technique is novel in its use of an explicit model of case competence. This allows cases to be selected on the basis of their individual competence contributions. An experimental study shows how this technique compares favorably to more traditional strategies across a range of standard data-sets.

1 Introduction

Case-based reasoning (CBR) solves problems by reusing the solutions to similar problems stored as cases in a case-base [9]. Two important factors contribute to the performance of a CBR system. First there is *competence,* that is the range of target problems that can be successfully solved. Second, there is *efficiency*, the computational cost of solving a set of target problems.

Competence and efficiency both depend critically on the cases stored in the case-base. Small case-bases offer potential efficiency benefits, but suffer from reduced coverage of the target problem space, and therefore from limited competence. Conversely, large case-bases are more competent, but also more susceptible to the utility problem and its efficiency issues [see eg., 6, 11, 12, 14]. Very briefly, the utility problem occurs when new cases degrade rather than improve efficiency. For example, many CBR systems use retrieval methods whose efficiency is related to the case-base size, and under these conditions the addition of redundant cases serves only to degrade efficiency by increasing retrieval time.

A key performance goal for any CBR system has to be the maintenance of a case-base that is optimal with respect to competence and efficiency, which in turn means maximising coverage while minimising case-base size. There are two basic ways of working towards this goal. The most common approach is to employ a case deletion strategy, as part of the run-time learning process, in order to ensure that all cases learned increase competence and efficiency. Recent research has suggested a number of successful deletion policies for machine learning systems [see eg., 11, 12], and more recently, a set of novel policies designed specifically for CBR systems [16].

Deletion works well by drawing on valuable statistical run-time performance data, but its starting point is an initial case-base that may be far from optimal. A second (complimentary) approach is to tackle the construction of the initial case-base itself. Instead of building a case-base from all available training instances we select only those that are likely to contribute to performance. This ensures that the initial case-base is near-optimal from the start. This process is referred to as *editing* the training data, and in this paper we present a new editing technique designed specifically for CBR systems.

Section 2 focuses on related editing work from the machine learning and pattern recognition literature that can be adapted for CBR. These techniques lack an explicit model of case competence, which, we argue, limits their effectiveness in a CBR setting. Section 3 addresses this issue by describing a competence model that can be used during case-base editing. Finally, Section 4 describes a comprehensive evaluation of the new approach.

2 Related Work

Related work on pruning a set of training examples to produce a compact competent edited set comes from the pattern recognition and machine learning community through studies of nearest-neighbour (NN) and instance-based learning (IBL) methods. In general, nearest neighbour methods are used in classification problems, regression tasks, and for case retrieval. Training examples are represented as points in an n-dimensional feature space and are associated with a known solution class (classification problems) or continuous solution value (regression tasks) or even a structured solution representation (case-based reasoning). New target instances (with unknown solutions) are solved by locating their nearest-neighbour (or k nearest neighbours) within the feature space [see eg., 1, 5, 7, 8, 18].

Since the 1960's researchers have proposed a variety of *editing* strategies to reduce the need to store all of the training examples. For instance many strategies selectively add training examples to an edited training set until such time as consistency over the original training set is reached; that is, until the edited set can be used to correctly solve all of the examples in the original training set [5, 7, 8, 18, 20, 21, 22].

Cases used in CBR systems are similar to the training examples used in classification systems and hence many of the same ideas about editing training data can be transferred to a CBR setting. The central message in this paper is that the successful editing of training data benefits from an explicit competence model in order to guide the editing process. Previous NN and IBL research reflects this, but the available models were designed for classification domains and not for case-based reasoning. We argue the need for a new competence model designed for the specific requirements of a case-based reasoner.

2.1 Condensed Nearest Neighbour Methods

A common approach for editing training data in NN and IBL methods is the condensed nearest neighbour method (CNN) shown in Algorithm 1. CNN produces an edited set of examples (the e-set) that is consistent with the original unedited training data (the o-set) [5, 8].

```
O-SET ← Original training examples
E-SET ← {}
CHANGES ← true

While CHANGES Do
          CHANGES ← false
          For each case C∈O-Set Do
            If E-SET cannot solve C Then
              CHANGES ← true
              Add C to E-SET
              Remove C from O-Set
            EndIf
          EndFor
EndWhile
```

Algorithm 1. Condensed Nearest-Neighbour Algorithm

CNN makes multiple passes through the training data in order to satisfy the consistency criterion. In classification problems a single pass is not sufficient as the addition of a new example to the e-set may prevent an example from being solved, even though it was previously solved by the smaller e-set. IB2, a common instance-based learning approach to editing, employs a version of CNN that just makes one pass through the training data and hence does not guarantee consistency [1].

The CNN has inspired a range of variations on its editing theme [1, 4, 5, 7, 18] but this represents just one half of the editing story. A second strategy was inspired by the work of Wilson [22]. While CNN filters correctly classified cases, so-called "Wilson editing" filters incorrectly classified cases. As with the seminal work of Hart [8], Wilson editing has inspired many follow-up studies [see 3, 10, 13, 19]. A full review of this large body of editing work is beyond the scope of this paper and the interested reader is referred to the references provided.

2.2 Competence Models

The CNN method suffers from two important shortcomings. First, the quality of the edited set depends on the order in which training examples are considered. Different orderings can result in different size edited sets with different competence characteristics.

A second problem is that the CNN approach adopts a naïve competence model to guide the selection of training examples. Its strategy is to add an example, e, only if it cannot be solved by the edited set built so far – by definition such an example will make a positive competence contribution. However, this is only true in the context of the edited set that has been built so far. In reality after more examples are added, it may turn out that the example, e, does not make any significant competence contribution because it is covered by later examples. In classification problems one approach is to select boundary examples for the edited set as these provide necessary and sufficient class descriptions. CNN as it stands tends to select such boundary examples but also contaminates the edited set with redundant interior examples [5, 7, 18] – it should be noted that alternative approaches, which focus on the selection of non-boundary (interior) cases or the generation of classification prototypes, do also exist (eg, [4, 21, 22]).

To address these issues the reduced NN (RNN) algorithm processes the final CNN edited set to delete such redundant examples. Briefly, if the removal of an example has no effect on consistency it is permanently deleted [7].

An alternative strategy is to order examples before CNN processing. One successful ordering policy for classification problems is to use the distance between an example and its nearest unlike neighbour (NUN). The NUN concept is based on the idea that training examples with different classes lie close to each other only if they reside at or near the boundaries of their respective classes; such examples have small NUN distances. By sorting examples in ascending order of NUN distance we can ensure that boundary examples are presented to CNN before interior examples and in this way increase the chances that interior examples will not be added to the final edited set [5, 18].

The NUN concept is a competence model for classification problems. It predicts that the competence of an individual example is inversely proportional to its NUN distance and as such provides a means of ordering training examples by their competence contributions.

2.3 Editing Case-Bases

The question we are interested in is how can CNN type techniques be best used in a CBR setting? In a more general sense however we are interested in how existing editing approaches from the classification community can be married with case-based deletion policies to produce a CBR-centric hybrid editing strategy.

Clearly the CNN concept is appropriate for CBR systems, but of course on its own it will produce sub-optimal case-bases that are order dependent and that include redundant cases. In the previous section we described how the NUN concept provided insight into the competence of training examples within classification problems. An analogous competence model is needed for case-based reasoning.

While conventional nearest-neighbour methods (or more correctly nearest-neighbour classifier rules) are often used in CBR systems, there are often a number of distinctions worth noting [9]. Firstly, cases are often represented using rich symbolic descriptions, and the methods used to retrieve similar cases are correspondingly more elaborate. Secondly, and most importantly, the concept of a correct solution can be very different from the atomic solution classes found in classification systems, where there are a small number of possible solution classes and correctness is a simple equality test. For example, in case-based planning or design problems, solutions are composite objects and the concept of correctness usually refers to a proposed target solution that is functionally or behaviourally equivalent to the true target solution (eg., [9, 15]).

As a result, CBR competence is different from competence in classification problems where boundary training examples can offer complete class coverage. Cases do tend to be clustered according to gross solution classes. However, the ability of a boundary case to solve an interior case is entirely dependent on the potential for solution adaptation and the availability of limited adaptation knowledge. Thus, the distinction between boundary and interior cases is no longer well-defined.

An implication of this argument is that the NUN distance metric may not be an appropriate competence model for CBR applications. A new competence model, designed specifically for CBR, is needed.

3 Modelling Case Competence

The idea that one can accurately model the competence of a case-base is a powerful one. In fact it has lead to a number of important developments in CBR in recent times, most notably in case deletion [16] and case-base visualisation and authoring support [17]. In this section we will argue that similar competence models can also be used to guide the construction of a case-base. This model differs from the model introduced by Smyth & Keane [16] in that it provides the sort of fine-grained competence measures that are appropriate for a CNN-type editing approach. In contrast the work of Smyth & Keane focused on a coarse-grained competence model capable of highlighting broad competence distinctions between cases, but incapable of making the find-graining distinctions that are important here. We will describe a new metric for measuring the relative competence of an individual case, and present this as a mechanism for ordering cases prior to case-base construction (editing).

3.1 A Review of Case Competence

When we talk about the competence of a case we are referring to its ability to solve certain target problems. Consider a set of cases, C, and a space of target problems, T. A case, $c \in C$, can be used to solve a target, $t \in T$, if and only if two conditions hold. First, the case must be retrieved for the target, and second it must be possible to adapt its solution so that it solves the target problem. Competence is therefore reduced if adaptable cases fail to be retrieved or if non-adaptable cases are retrieved [15]. We can model these relationships according to the definitions shown in Def. 1 – 3.

Def 1: RetrievalSpace($t \in T$)={$c \in C$: c is retrieved for t}

Def 2: AdaptationSpace($t \in T$)={$c \in C$:c can be adapted for t}

Def 3: Solves(c,t)
iff $c \in$ [RetrievalSpace(t)$\cap$AdaptationSpace(t)]

Two important competence properties are the *coverage set* and the *reachability set*. The coverage set of a *case* is the set of all *target problems* that this case can be used to solve. Conversely, the reachability set of a *target problem* is the set of all *cases* that can be used to solve it.

Def 4: CoverageSet($c \in C$)=$\{t \in T$:Solves(c,t)$\}$

Def 5: ReachabilitySet($t \in T$)=$\{c \in C$:Solves(c,t)$\}$

If we could specify these two sets for every case in the case-base, and all possible target problems, then we would have a complete picture of the competence of a CBR system. Unfortunately, this is not feasible. First, due to the sheer size of the target problem space, computing these sets for every case and target problem is intractable. Second, even if we could enumerate every possible problem that the system might be used to solve, it is next to impossible to identify the subset of problems the system would actually encounter. Clearly, the best we can do is to find some approximation to these sets by making some reasonable, simplifying assumption.

So, to characterise the competence of a case-base in a tractable fashion we make the following **Representativeness Assumption**:

The case-base is a representative sample of the target problem space.

To put it another way, this assumption proposes that we use the cases in the case-base as proxies for the target problems the system is expected to solve. This assumption may seem like a large step, as it proposes that the case-base is representative of all future problems encountered by the system. It could be argued that we are assuming that all the problems faced by the system are already solved and in the case-base. We think that this greatly overstates the reality of the situation and underestimates the contribution that adaptation knowledge can play in modifying cases to meet target problems. Furthermore, we would argue that the representativeness assumption is one currently made, albeit implicitly, by CBR researchers; for if a case-base were not representative of the target problems to be solved then the system could not be forwarded as a valid solution to the task requirements. In short, if CBR system builders are not making these assumptions then they are constructing case-bases designed *not* to solve problems in the task domain. Of course implicitly this assumption is made by all inductive learners, which rely on a representative set of example instances to guide their particular problem solving task.

Armed with the representativeness assumption, we can now provide tractable definitions for coverage (Def. 6) and reachability (Def. 7):

Def 6: CoverageSet($c \in C$)=$\{c' \in C$:Solves(c,c')$\}$

Def 7: ReachabilitySet($c \in C$)=$\{c' \in C$:Solves(c',c)$\}$

Intuitively, the relative sizes of these sets seem to capture the relative competence of different cases. For example, cases with large coverage sets seem important because they can solve many other problems and therefore should solve many of the future target problems. Conversely, cases with small reachability sets seem important because they must represent regions of the target problem space that are difficult to solve (regions with a rich solution topology that require more cases for sufficient coverage). Unfortunately an accurate measure of true case competence is more complex than this. Overlapping sets between different cases can reduce or exaggerate the relative competence of an individual case (see also [16, 17]).

3.2 Relative Coverage

Previous work on the competence of cases has ignored ways of measuring the *precise* competence contributions of *individual* cases. For example, Smyth & Keane [15] present a number of competence categories to permit a coarse-grained competence assessment. Alternatively Smyth & McKenna [17] focus on the competence of groups of cases. We are interested in developing a more fine-grained measure that is similar in spirit to efficiency models such as the utility metric [11, 12].

To measure the competence of an individual case one must take into account the local coverage of the case as well as the degree to which this coverage is duplicated by nearby cases. To do this we define a measure called *relative coverage* (RC), which estimates the unique competence contribution of an individual case, c, as a function of the size of the case's coverage set (see Def. 8).

$$\mathrm{RelativeCoverage}(c) = \sum_{c' \in \mathrm{CoverageSet}(c)} \frac{1}{|\mathrm{ReachabilitySet}(c')|}$$

Def 8:

Some of the cases covered by c will also be covered by other cases, thereby reducing c's unique competence. For this reason, the relative coverage measure weights the contribution of each covered case by the degree to which these cases are themselves covered. It is based on the idea that if a case c' is covered by n other cases then each of the n cases will receive a contribution of 1/n from c' to their relative coverage measures.

Figure 1 displays a number of cases and their relative coverage values. Case A makes an isolated competence contribution that is not duplicated by any other cases. Its coverage and reachability sets contain just a single case (case A itself) and so its relative coverage value is 1; case A is a pivotal case according to the competence categories of Smyth & Keane [16]. Case B makes the largest local competence contribution (its coverage set contains 3 cases, B, C and D) but this contribution is diluted because other cases also cover C and D. The relative coverage of B is 11/6 (that is 1+1/2+1/3). B is also a pivotal case but using relative coverage we can see that it makes a larger competence contribution than A; previously such fine-grained competence distinctions were not possible. Cases C and D make no unique competence contribution as they only duplicate part of the existing coverage offered by B. Consequently, C and D have relative coverage values of 5/6 and 1/3 respectively; they are both auxiliary cases according to the competence categories of Smyth & Keane [16].

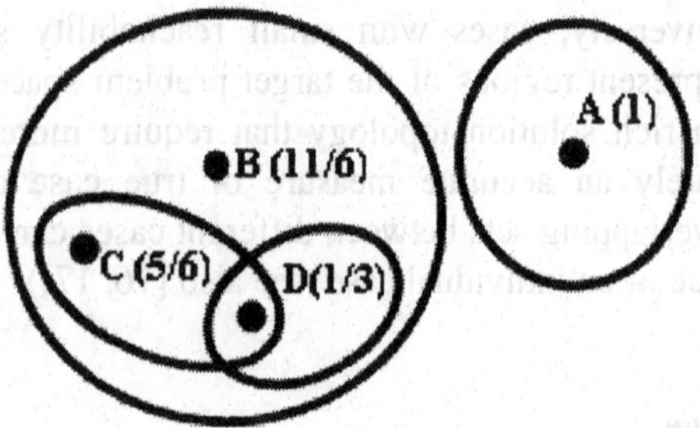

Fig. 1. Relative coverage values for cases. Each ellipse denotes the coverage set of its corresponding case and each RC value is shown in brackets.

3.3 Relative Coverage & CNN

In Section 2 we suggested that the CNN editing procedure could be used to construct compact competent cases-bases once a suitable measure could be found to sort cases by their likely competence contributions. Relative coverage is this measure. Our proposed technique for building case-bases is to use CNN on cases that have first been arranged in descending order of their relative coverage contributions. This will allow competence-rich cases to be selected before less competent cases and thereby maximise the rate at which competence increases during the case-base construction process.

4 Experiments

Our new editing technique is based on a specific model of competence for case-based reasoning. We argue that it has the potential for guiding the construction of smaller case-bases than some existing editing methods without compromising competence, specifically CNN on its own or CNN with NUN distance ordering. In turn we believe that, as an ordering strategy, relative coverage will continue to perform well in traditional classification problems. In this section we validate these claims by comparing the consistency, size, and competence of the case-bases produced using the different editing techniques on a range of standard data-sets.

4.1 Experimental Setup

Three different editing techniques are compared for this experimental study (1) CNN – the standard CNN approach; (2) NUN – CNN with cases ordered according to their NUN distances; (3) RC – CNN with cases ordered according to their relative coverage values.

Four different data-sets are used. Two, Credit (690 cases) and Ionosphere (351 cases), represent classification problems and are available from the UCI Machine Learning Repository (www.ics.uci.edu/~mlearn/MLRepository.html) [2]. The other 2 are more traditional CBR data-sets. Property (506 cases) is also from the UCI repository and Travel (700 cases) is available from the AI-CBR Case-Base Archive (www.ai-cbr.org). The important point to note is that Property and Travel are not used as classification data-sets. Instead they are used to build a case-based recommendation system where the objective is to locate a case that is sufficiently similar to a given target problem across a range of solution features. Consequently, the concept of a single solution class is no longer valid in keeping with many CBR applications and domains.

4.2 Consistency Growth

This first experiment is designed to investigate how the consistency of a case-base (that is, competence with respect to the initial training data) varies as more cases are added. We are interested in comparing the rate of increase of consistency for the various editing strategies across the different data-sets.

Method: For each data-set, 3 case-bases (edited sets) are constructed by using each of the editing strategies on the available training cases. As each case is added to a case-base, the consistency of that case-base is measured with respect to the initial training cases; that is, we measure the percentage of training cases that can be solved by the case-base built so far.

Results: This experiment generates 4 consistency graphs (one for each data-set), each containing 3 plots (one per editing strategy). The results are shown in Figures 2(a)-(d) as graphs of percentage consistency versus case-base size as a percentage of overall training set size.

Discussion: In this experiment 100% consistency is achieved by RC with fewer cases (albeit marginally fewer) than with any other editing strategy. Unfortunately, as we shall see in the next experiment, this result does not hold in general. However, aside from the size of the final edited case-bases, we do notice that the graphs indicate that the RC method is selecting more competent cases more quickly that the other strategies. For example, in the Travel domain the consistency of the case-base produced by the RC strategy at the 10% size level is approximately 65% (that is 65% of the training set can be solved by a 10% subset). In contrast, the CNN policy produces a case-base with only 40% consistency, and NUN produces a case-base with only 45% consistency at this 10% size level. Similar results are found in the Property domain. The results on the classification data-sets are not as positive, but still bode well for RC. The RC policy generally out-performs CNN and keeps pace with NUN particularly for small case-base sizes. This leads us to conclude that the relative coverage measure is also a valid measure of competence in traditional classification domains.

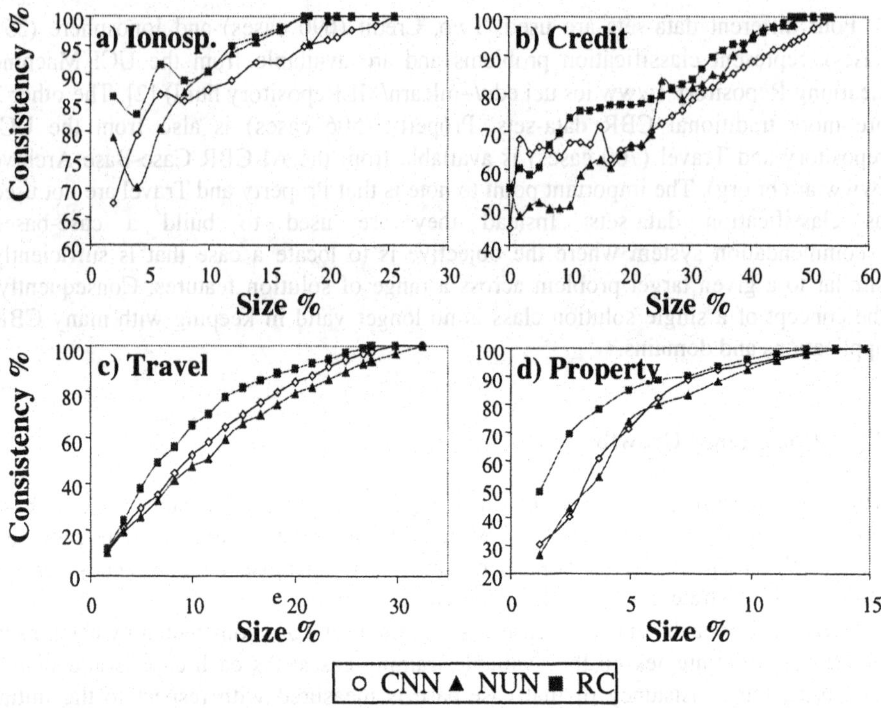

Fig. 2(a)-(d). Case-Base Consistency versus Size.

4.3 Size vs Competence

While consistency is a measure of performance relative to the training set, the true test of editing quality is the competence of the edited set on unseen test data. In this experiment, we compare the sizes of the case-bases to their competence on unseen target problems.

Method: Each editing strategy is used to generate case-bases for the 4 data-sets. However, this time 100 random test problems are removed from the training set before case-base construction. The final size of the case-bases (at the 100% consistency mark) and their competence over the 100 test problems is noted. This process is repeated 100 times, each time with a different set of 100 random test problems, to generate 1200 case-bases.

Results: For each data-set and editing strategy we compute the mean case-base size and competence over the 100 test runs. The results are shown in Table 1. Each cell in the table holds two values: the mean size (top value) and competence (bottom value) of the case-bases produced by a given editing strategy on a given data-set.

Discussion: RC and NUN produce smaller case-bases than the standard CNN approach for the classification data-sets (Ionosphere & Credit) – NUN case-bases are marginally smaller than the RC case-bases, but to compensate the competence of the

RC case-bases is higher. In fact, with the Credit data-set the RC method produces a case-base with a competence value that is higher than the CNN case-base which is, on average, nearly 50 cases larger.

RC produces significantly smaller case-bases than both of the other editing strategies for the CBR data-sets (Travel & Property). This is because relative coverage is an explicit competence model for CBR while NUN is designed for classification problems. In fact, we notice that in these data-sets the NUN method is performing even worse than CNN – further evidence that the NUN distance concept is not appropriate in a CBR setting.

Dataset/Editing	CNN	NUN	RC
Ionosphere	61.93 85.78	46.39 84.44	49.47 85.3
Credit	344.84 58.85	297.43 58.95	299.19 60.44
Travel	184.28 89.25	196.98 88.72	165.42 86.4
Property	55.19 95.92	57.81 95.53	45.44 94.62

Table 1. A comparison of different editing strategies over the test data-sets in terms of mean case-base size and competence. The upper value in each cell is the average size of the case-bases produces and the lower value is the average competence value.

One of the problems with this experiment is that it is impossible to compare case-bases with different sizes and competence values. For example we've already noted that the RC method produces slightly larger case-bases than NUN in the classification problems, but that these case-bases have better competence values. Conversely, in the CBR data-sets, RC is producing much smaller case-bases, but these case-bases have slightly lower competence values. What do these competence differences mean? Are the competence drops found in the CBR data-sets because the RC method is selecting cases that generalise poorly over the target problems, or are they a natural implication of the smaller case-bases? If we remove cases from the CNN and NUN case-bases (or conversely add cases to the RC case-bases) so that all case-bases are normalised to the same size, how would this change their competence values? These questions are answered in the next experiment.

4.4 Normalising Competence

This experiment compares the competence of the case-bases produced by the different strategies after normalising each with respect to the size of the RC case-bases. The argument could be made that this size-limiting experiment is artificial and that is serves only to hamper the performance of the other algorithms. However we disagree. We are not just interested in the ultimate size and competence of the edited case-base that is produced by a particular editing policy. We are interested in how competence grows as more cases are added. If, for example, the RC policy is seen to more aggressively increase competence than the competing policies then this is an important advantage, particularly if our editing strategies must work within a resource-bounded setting where, for example the maximum size of the edited set is limited.

Method: Each of the CNN and NUN case-bases from the previous experiment are normalised with respect to their corresponding RC case-base by adding or removing cases as appropriate. To ensure fairness cases are added or removed using the appropriate strategy. For example, if a case is removed from a NUN case-base then it will be the last case that was added.

Results: The results are shown in Table 2. Each value is the mean competence of the case-bases produced by each of the editing strategies once they have been normalised to the appropriate RC case-base size.

Discussion: The results are positive. The competence of the RC case-bases is higher than the corresponding case-bases produced by the other strategies after normalisation. This demonstrates that the RC method is selecting cases that are more competent than those selected by any other method, backing up the results found in section 4.2 when consistency was measured. Moreover, the relative coverage measure performs well in both classification and CBR settings, while the NUN method performs relatively poorly in the CBR data-sets. In fact, in Table 2 we see that the normalised competence values for the NUN case-bases are smaller than the competence values for the CNN case-bases, for the CBR data-sets.

Dataset/Editing	CNN	NUN	RC
Ionosphere	84.26	85.23	85.3
Credit	58.36	59.3	60.44
Travel	85.03	83.23	86.4
Property	92.65	91.9	94.62

Table 2. The competence values of all case-bases normalised to the RC case-base size.

5 Conclusions

The ability to edit training data prior to learning has been an important research goal for the machine learning community for many years. We have adapted a traditional editing procedure, CNN, for use with case-based reasoning systems. The central idea behind the adaptation is that effective editing must be based on an accurate model of case competence, so that the competence of a case-base can be optimised with respect to its size. A new editing technique was introduced, based on a novel measure of case competence called relative coverage. This new technique was evaluated with respect to a number of more conventional editing strategies and on a variety of classification and CBR data-sets. The results were positive but tentative. The new method performed well on all data-sets and out-performed all rivals on the CBR data-sets. In general we saw that the relative coverage measure allowed our editing technique to select cases with higher competence contributions than those cases selected by any competing editing strategy.

However, before closing we would like to emphasise that this research represents the tip of the iceberg of case-base editing. Obviously our current experiments need to be extended to include a broader range of traditional editing techniques such as the Wilson-editing approaches [3, 10, 13, 19, 22]. We have described a competence model for CBR that appears to benefit the editing process, and we have integrated this into one particular editing approach. Future work will consider the more general properties of this model with respect to other editing strategies. We believe that, ultimately, the optimal approach to editing case-bases will incorporate a range of ideas from a variety of editing approaches.

References

1. Aha, D. W., Kibler, D., and Albert, M.K.: Instance-Based Learning Algorithms. Machine Learning, **6** (1991) 37-66
2. Blake, C., Keogh, E. & Merz, C.J: UCI Repository of machine learning databases [http://www.ics.uci.edu/~mlearn/MLRepository.html]. Irvine, CA: University of California, Department of Information and Computer Science (1998)
3. Broder, A.Z., Bruckstein, A.M., and Koplowitz, J.: On the Performance of Edited Nearest neighbor Rules in High Dimensions. IEEE Transactions on Systems, Man, and Cybernetics, SMC-**15**(1), (1985) 136-139
4. Chang, C.L.: Finding Prototypes for Nearest Neighbor Classifiers. IEEE Transactions on Computers, **2-3**(11), (1974) 1179-1184
5. Dasarathy, B.V.: Nearest Neighbor Norms: NN Pattern Classification Techniques. IEEE Press, Los Alamitos, California (1991)
6. Francis, A.G. and Ram, A.: A Comparitive Utility Analysis of Case-Based Reasoning and Control Rule Problem Solving. In: Proceedings of the 8th European Conference on Machine Learning (1995)
7. Gates, G.W.: The Reduced Nearest Neighbor Rule. IEEE Transactions on Information Theory, **18**(3) (1972) 431-433
8. Hart, P.E.: The Condensed Nearest Neighbor Rule. IEEE Transactions on Information Theory, **14** (1967) 515-516
9. Kolodner, J. Case-Based Reasoning. Morgan-Kaufmann, San Mateo, California (1993)
10. Koplowitz, J. & Browm, T.A.: On the Relation of Performance to Editing in Nearest-Neighbor Rules. Proceedings of the 4th International Joint Conference on Pattern Recognition, IEEE Computer Society Press (1978) 214-216
11. Marckovitch, S. & Scott, P.D.: Information Filtering: Selection Mechanisms in Learning Systems. Machine Learning, **10** (1993) 113-151
12. Minton, S.: Qualitative results concerning the utility of explanation based learning. Artificial Intelligence, **42**(2-3) (1991) 393-391
13. Penrod, C.S & Wagner, T.J.: Another Look at the Edited Nearest Neighbor Rule. IEEE Transactions on Systems, Man, and Cybernetics, **SMC-7**(2) (1977) 92-94
14. Smyth, B. & Cunningham, P.: The Utility Problem Analysed: A Case-Based Reasoning Perspective. In: Smith, I. & Faltings, B. (eds.): Advances in Case-Based Reasoning. Lecture Notes in Artificial Intelligence, Vol. 1168. Springer-Verlag, Berlin Heidelberg New York (1996) 392-399
15. Smyth, B. & Keane, M.T.: Adaptation-Guided Retrieval: Questioning the Similarity Assumption in Reasoning. Artificial Intelligence, **102** . (1998) 249-293

16. Smyth, B. & Keane, M.T.: Remembering to Forget: A Competence Preserving Deletion Policy for Case-Based Reasoning Systems. In: Proceedings of the 14th International Joint Conference on Artificial Intelligence. Morgan-Kaufmann. (1995) 377-382
17. Smyth, B. & McKenna, E. Modelling the Competence of Case-Bases. In: Smyth, B. & Cunningham, P. (eds.): .): Advances in Case-Based Reasoning. Lecture Notes in Artificial Intelligence, Vol. 1488. Springer-Verlag, Berlin Heidelberg New York (1998). 208-220
18. Tomek, I.: Two Modifications of CNN. IEEE Transactions on Systems, Man, and Cybernetics, 7(2) (1976) 679-772
19. Wagner, T.J.: Convergence of the Edited Nearest Neighbor. IEEE Transactions on Information Theory, **IT-19**(5) (1973) 696-697
20. Wilson, D. R. & Martinez, T.R.: Instance Pruning Techniques. In: Proceedings of the 14th International Conference on Machine Learning (1997) 404-441
21. Wilson, D. R. & Martinez, T.R.: Reduction Techniques for Exemplar-Based Learning Algorithms. Machine Learning (1998)
22. Wilson, D. L Asymptotic Properties of Nearest Neighbor Rules Using Edited Data. IEEE Transactions on Systems, Man, and Cybernetics, **2-3** (1972) 408-421
23. Zhang, J.: Selecting Typical Instances in Instance Based Learning. In: Proceedings of the 9th International Conference on Machine Learning (1992)

Footprint-Based Retrieval

Barry Smyth & Elizabeth McKenna

Department of Computer Science
University College Dublin
Belfield, Dublin 4, IRELAND

Barry.Smyth@ucd.ie
Elizabeth.McKenna@ucd.ie

Abstract. The success of a case-based reasoning system depends critically on the performance of the retrieval algorithm used and, specifically, on its efficiency, competence, and quality characteristics. In this paper we describe a novel retrieval technique that is guided by a model of case competence and that, as a result, benefits from superior efficiency, competence and quality features.

1 Introduction

Case-based reasoning (CBR) systems solve new problems by retrieving and adapting the solutions to previously solved problems that have been stored in a case-base. The performance of a case-based reasoner can be measured according to three criteria: 1) Efficiency – the average problem solving time; 2) Competence – the range of target problems that can be successfully solved; 3) Quality – the average quality of a proposed solution. Recently, researchers have begun to investigate methods for explicitly modelling these criteria in real systems. Their aim is twofold. On the one hand, it is important to develop predictive performance models to facilitate evaluation and comparative studies (see for eg., [7,12]). However, in addition, the models can also be used to drive the development of new techniques and algorithms within the CBR problem solving cycle. For example, a variety of different efficiency and competence models have been used recently to guide the growth of case-bases during learning and case-base maintenance [8, 11, 12].

In this paper we return to the classic problem of case retrieval and propose a novel retrieval method, *footprint-based retrieval*, which is guided by a model of case competence. The next section surveys related work on retrieval. Section 3 describes the model of case competence that forms the basis of our new retrieval method, which is discussed in Section 4. Finally, before concluding, Section 5 describes a comprehensive set of experiments to evaluate the performance of the new algorithm.

2 Related Work

The retrieval process has always received the lion's share of interest from the CBR community. All CBR systems have at least a retrieval component, and the success of a given system depends critically on the efficient retrieval of the right case at the right time. Every retrieval method is the combination of two procedures; a similarity assessment procedure to determine the similarity between a given case and target problem, and a procedure for searching the case memory in order to locate the most similar case. Research on the former topic has focussed on developing efficient and accurate similarity assessment procedures capable of evaluating not just the similarity of a case but also other criteria such as its adaptability (see for eg., [5, 10]).

In this paper we focus on the search procedure. Research in this area has been concerned with reducing the search needed to locate the best case without degrading competence or quality [2, 3, 4, 6, 9, 1, 15]. The simplest approach to retrieval is an exhaustive search of the case-base, but this is rarely viable for large case-bases. Thus the basic research goal is to develop a strategy that avoids the need to examine every case. Most approaches achieve this by processing the raw case data in order to produce an optimised memory structure that facilitates a directed search procedure.

One approach is to build a decision-tree over the case data (see for eg., [14]). Each node and branch of the tree represents a particular attribute-value combination, and cases with a given set of attribute-values are stored at the leaf nodes. Case retrieval is implemented as a directed search through the decision tree. These approaches are efficient but may not be appropriate for case-bases with incomplete case descriptions, or where the relative importance of individual case features can change.

Spreading activation methods (eg., [2]) represent case memory as an interconnected network of nodes capturing case attribute-value combinations. Activation spreads from target attribute-value nodes across the network to cause the activation of case nodes representing similar cases to the target. The approaches are efficient and flexible enough to handle incomplete case descriptions, however there can be a significant knowledge-engineering cost associated with constructing the activation network. Furthermore the spreading-activation algorithm requires specific knowledge to guide the spread of activation throughout the network. Related network-based retrieval methods are proposed by Lenz [6] and Wolverton & Hayes-Roth [15].

Perhaps the simplest approach to controlling retrieval cost is to employ an exhaustive search on a *reduced* case-base. This strategy is common in the pattern-recognition community to improve the performance of nearest-neighbour techniques by editing training data to remove unnecessary examples (eg., [1, 4]). Many editing strategies have been successfully developed, often maintaining retrieval competence with an edited case-base that is significantly smaller than the full case-base.

With all of the above methods there is an inherent risk in not examining every case during retrieval. The optimal case may be missed, which at best can mean sub-optimal problem solving, but at worst can result in a problem solving failure. In this paper we propose a novel retrieval method based on the idea of searching an edited subset of the entire case-base. The key innovation is that retrieval is based on two searches of two separate edited subsets. The first search identifies a reference case that is similar to the target problem. This case acts as an index into the complete case-base, and the second search locates the best available case in the region of the reference case. In this sense our method is related to the "Fish-and-Shrink" strategy [9] where cases are linked according to specific *aspect* similarities. However, our method is unique in its use of an explicit competence model to guide the selection of a non-arbitrary case.

3 A Model of Case Competence

Competence is all about the number and type of target problems that a given system can solve. This will depend on a number of factors including statistical properties of the case-base and problem-space, and the proficiency of the retrieval, adaptation and solution evaluation components of the CBR system in question. The competence model described in this section is based on a similar model first introduced by Smyth & McKenna [12]. The present model introduces a number of important modifications to increase the effectiveness and general applicability of the model.

In this paper, the crucial feature of our competence model is that it constructs a subset of the case-base called the *footprint set*, which provides the same coverage as the case-base as a whole. This footprint set, and its relationship to the complete case-base, is central to our new retrieval algorithm.

3.1 Coverage & Reachability

Consider a set of cases, C, and a space of target problems, T. A case, $c \in C$, can be used to solve a target, $t \in T$, if and only if two conditions hold. First, the case must be retrieved for the target, and second it must be possible to adapt its solution so that it solves the target problem. Competence is therefore reduced if adaptable cases fail to be retrieved or if non-adaptable cases are retrieved. We can model these relationships according to the definitions shown in Def. 1 – 3.

Def 1: RetrievalSpace(t)={$c \in C$: c is retrieved for t}

Def 2: AdaptationSpace(t)={$c \in C$: c can be adapted for t}

Def 3: Solves(c,t) iff $c \in$ [RetrievalSpace(t) $\cap$ AdaptationSpace(t)]

Two important competence properties are the *coverage set* and the *reachability set*. The coverage set of a *case* is the set of all *target problems* that this case can solve. Conversely, the reachability set of a *target problem* is the set of all *cases* that can be used to solve it. By using the case-base as a representative of the target problem space it is possible to estimate these sets as shown in Def. 4 & 5 (see also [11]).

Def 4: CoverageSet(c)={$c' \in C$:Solves(c,c')}

Def 5: ReachabilitySet(c)={$c' \in C$:Solves(c',c)}

Furthermore, we use the term *related set* to refer to the set produced from the union of a case's coverage and reachability sets.

Def 6: RelatedSet(c)= CoverageSet(c) ∪ ReachabilitySet(c)

3.2 Relative Coverage

The size of the coverage set of a case is only a measure of its local competence. For instance, case coverage sets can overlap to limit the competence contributions of individual cases, or they may be isolated and exaggerate individual contributions [11, 12]. It is actually possible to have a case with a large coverage set that makes little or no contribution to global competence simply because its contribution is subsumed by the local competences of other cases. At the other extreme, there may be cases with relatively small contributions to make, but these contributions may nonetheless be crucial if there are no competing cases.

Def 7:
$$\mathrm{RelativeCoverage}(c) = \sum_{c' \in \mathrm{CoverageSet}(c)} \frac{1}{|\mathrm{ReachabilitySet}(c')|}$$

For a true picture of competence, a measure of the coverage of a case, relative to other nearby cases, is needed. For this reason we define a measure called *relative coverage* (RC), which estimates the unique competence contribution of an individual case, c, as a function of the size of the case's coverage set (see Definition 7). Essentially, relative coverage weights the contribution of each covered case by the degree to which these cases are themselves covered. It is based on the idea that if a case c' is covered by n other cases then each of the n cases will receive a contribution of 1/n from c' to their relative coverage measures.

The importance of relative coverage is that it provides a mechanism for ordering cases according to their individual, global, competence contributions. In section 3.4 we will see how this allows us to represent the competence of a complete case-base in terms of a subset of cases called the *footprint set*.

3.3 Competence Groups

As a case-base grows clusters of cases tend to form distinct regions of competence. We can model these regions as *competence groups* (see Figure 1). A competence group is a collection of related cases, which together make a collectively independent contribution to overall case-base competence.

Def 8: For c1, c2 ∈ C, SharedCoverage(c1, c2)
iff [RelatedSet(c1) ∩ RelatedSet(c2)]

The key idea underlying the definition of a competence group is that of *shared coverage* (see Definition 8). Two cases exhibit shared coverage if their related sets overlap. This is seen as an indication that the cases in question make a shared competence contribution, and as such belong to a given competence group.

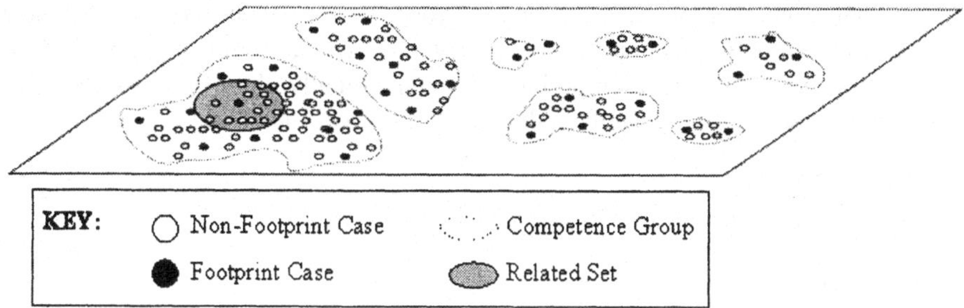

Figure 1. The formation of competence groups and the footprint set in a case-base.

Shared coverage provides a way of linking related cases together. Formally, a competence group is a maximal collection of cases exhibiting shared coverage (see Definition 9). Thus, each case in a competence group must share coverage with some other case in the group (this is the first half of the equation). In addition, the group must be maximal in the sense that there are no other cases in the case-base that share coverage with any group member (this is the second half of the equation).

Def 9: For $G = \{c1,\ldots,cn\} \subseteq C$,

$$\text{CompetenceGroup}(G) \text{ iff } \forall ci \in G, \exists cj \in G-\{ci\}: \text{SharedCoverage}(ci,cj) \wedge \forall cj \in C-G, \neg\exists cl \in G: \text{SharedCoverage}(cj,cl)$$

3.4 The Footprint Set

The footprint set of a case-base is a subset of the case-base that covers all of the cases in the case-base[1] – it is related to the concept of a minimal consistent subset in classification research (see for eg., [3]). By definition, each competence group makes a unique contribution to the competence of the case-base. Therefore, each competence group must be represented in the footprint set. However, not all of the cases in a given competence group are included in this subset (see Figure 1). For example auxiliary cases make no competence contributions [11] – an auxiliary case is a case whose coverage set is completely subsumed by the coverage set of another case.

The construction of the footprint set is carried out at the group level. For each group we compute its *group footprint*, that is, the subset of group cases that collectively cover the entire group. The algorithm in Figure 2 is used for identifying the group footprint cases; it is a simple modification of the CNN/IB2 algorithms (see for eg., [1, 4]). The first step is to sort the cases in descending order of the relative coverage values; this means that cases with large competence contributions are added before cases with smaller contributions, and thus helps to keep the footprint size to a

[1] The footprint concept used here should not to be confused with Veloso's concept of footprint similarity (see [13]). Our present notion is based on the footprint concept introduced in [11].

minimum. The group footprint is then constructed by considering each case in turn, and adding it to the group footprint only if the current footprint does not already cover it. Note that a number of passes over the group cases may be necessary if new additions to the footprint can prevent previously covered cases from being solved, as does occur in many classification problem domains. Finally, the overall footprint set is the union of all of the cases in the individual group footprints.

```
Group ← Original group cases sorted according to their RC value.
FP    ← {}
CHANGES ← true

While CHANGES Do
     CHANGES ← false
     For each case C∈Group Do
               If FP cannot solve C Then
                         CHANGES ← true
                         Add C to FP
                         Remove C from Group
               EndIf
     EndFor
EndWhile
```

Figure 2. The Group Footprint Algorithm.

Note that the relationship between the footprint set and the complete case-base is preserved. By using the related set of a footprint case we can associate it with a set of similar cases from the complete case-base. This critical link between the footprint set and the case-base is a key element in our new retrieval algorithm.

```
Target ← Current target problem
CB ← Original case-base
FP ← Footprint Set

Stage 1
     ReferenceCase ← a case in FP that is closest to the Target.

Stage 2
     RelatedSet ← RelatedSet(ReferenceCase)
     BaseCase ← a case in RelatedSet that is closest to Target
```

Figure 3. The Competence-Guided Retrieval Procedure.

4 Footprint-Based Retrieval

The objective in this paper is to present footprint-based retrieval, a simple but novel approach to case retrieval that is comprised of two separate stages. Stage one is designed to focus the search in the local region of the case-base that contains the target problem. Stage two then locates the nearest case to the target in this region. The key innovation of the approach stems from its direct use of a model of case competence to guide the retrieval process. The basic algorithm is shown in Figure 3 and the retrieval process is illustrated in Figure 4.

4.1 Stage 1: Retrieving from the Footprint Set

The footprint set is typically much smaller than the full case-base, and this means that the process of searching the footprint set is much less expensive than searching the entire case-base. During the first stage of retrieval the target problem is compared to each case in the footprint, in order to locate the case that best matches the target. This case is termed the *reference case*.

The reference case provides important clues concerning the ultimate solvability of the target problem, even at this early stage of problem solving. For example, the reference case may be able to solve the target problem as it stands, and further retrieval work may not be needed, especially if an optimal case is not required. However, the real importance of the reference case is that it provides an index into the full case-base for the next stage of retrieval.

4.2 Stage 2: Retrieving from the Related Set

The reference case may, or may not, be able to solve the current target problem, it may even be the closest case to the target in the entire case-base – however, this cannot be guaranteed. The objective of the next stage of retrieval is to compare the target problem to other (non-footprint) cases in the case-base in order to locate the most similar case in the entire case-base. The footprint case selected in stage one acts as a reference point for this next stage of retrieval. Only the cases nearby to the reference case need to be compared to the target.

During the construction of our competence model the related set of each case, c, is computed. The cases in this set are precisely those cases that are nearby to c. Therefore, during the second stage of retrieval each of the cases in the reference case's related set is compared to the target problem. Again, as in stage one, this is an inexpensive procedure, compared to searching the entire case-base, since each related set contains only a very small subset of the entire case-base.

4.3 Discussion

One way to think about the proposed retrieval method is as a single search through one subset of the entire case-base. In this sense the new technique looks very similar to other methods such as CNN retrieval. However, there is one important difference. The subset used by a technique such as CNN is computed once, at training time, without reference to a specific target problem – essentially an eager learning technique. However, the new method combines cases from a similar once-off subset of the entire case-base with additional cases that have been chosen with respect to a particular target problem – the additional cases are chosen according to a lazy learning policy.

This turns out to be an essential feature. It allows the proposed retrieval approach to adapt its search space to the characteristics of an individual target problem. This in turn greatly improves the competence and quality of the retrieved cases.

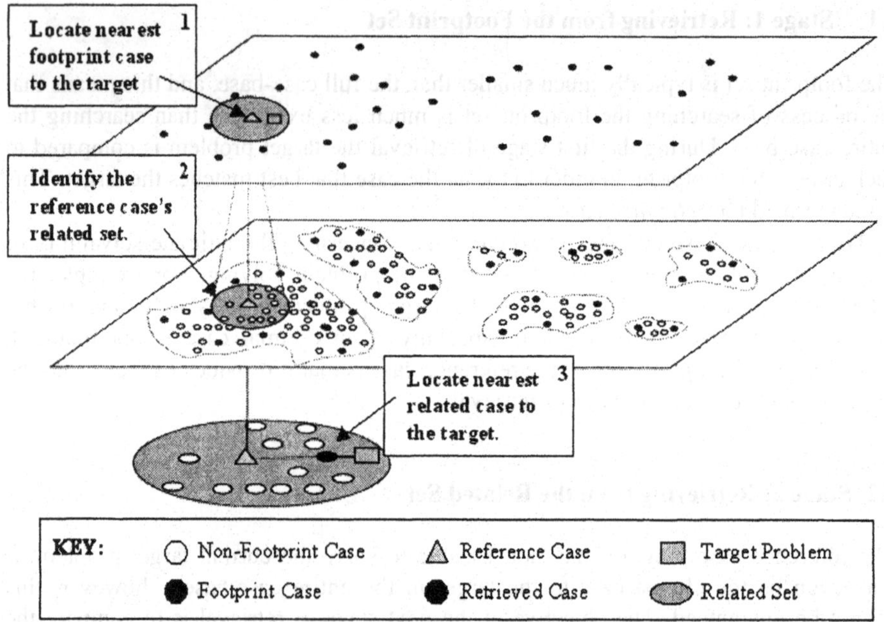

Figure 4. Footprint-based retrieval is a two-stage retrieval process. First, the footprint case that is nearest to the target problem is identified. Second, the case from its related set that is nearest to the target is identified and returned as the base case.

5 Experimental Studies

The footprint-based retrieval technique has been described, which, we claim, benefits from improved efficiency, competence, and quality characteristics. In this section we validate these claims with a comprehensive experimental study.

5.1 Experimental Setup

Altogether four different retrieval methods are evaluated; all use a standard weighted-sum similarity metric. The first (Standard) is the brute force, nearest-neighbour method where the target case is compared to every case in the case-base and the most similar case is retrieved. The second method (CNN) is a standard way to reduce retrieval time by producing an edited set of cases using the standard CNN approach. The third method (FP) is analogous to the CNN method, except that the footprint set of cases is used as the edited set – this is equivalent to running stage one of footprint-based retrieval only. Finally, the fourth technique (FPRS) is the full footprint-based approach. Note that by comparing the FP and FPRS results in the following sections we can evaluate the contributions of each retrieval stage separately.

Two standard data-sets are used in the study. The first is a case-base of 1400 cases from the Travel domain. Each case describes a vacation package using a range of continuous and discrete features such as: type of vacation; number of people; length of stay; type of accommodation, etc. The case-base is publicly available from the AI-CBR case-base archive (see http://www.ai-cbr.org). The second data-set contains 500 cases from the Property domain, each describing the residential property conditions in a particular region of Boston. This data-set is publicly available from the UCI repository (see http://www.ics.uci.edu/~mlearn/MLRepository.html)

These data-sets are processed to produce a range of different case-base sizes and target problem sets. In the Travel domain we produce 10 case-base sizes, ranging from 100 cases to 1000 cases, with accompanying target problem sets of 400 cases. For the Property domain we produce 6 case-base sizes from 50 to 300 cases, and 200 target problems. In each domain, for each case-base size n, we produce 100 different random case-bases and target problem sets to give 1000 test case-bases for the Travel domain and 600 test case-bases for the Property domain. There is never any direct overlap between a case-base and its associated target problem set.

5.2 Efficiency

The first experiment is concerned with evaluating the efficiency of the retrieval algorithms over a range of case-base sizes. Efficiency is measured as the inverse of the number of cases examined during retrieval. This is a fair measure as all four algorithms perform a simple search through a set of cases using the same similarity operator.

Method: Each case-base of size n is tested with respect to its target problem set and the average retrieval cost for the set of targets is computed. This cost is then averaged over the 100 case-bases of size n. This produces an average retrieval cost per target problem for each case-base size.

Results: These retrieval efficiency results are shown in Figure 5(a) - (d) as plots of efficiency (inverse number of cases examined during each retrieval) versus case-base size, for the Travel domain and the Property domain, respectively. Figures 4 (a) and (b) show the mean retrieval cost for each of the four retrieval algorithms as case-base size increases, however since the CNN, FP, and FPRS curves are difficult to distinguish, Figures 5(c) and (d) show additional detail over a restricted efficiency range. As expected, the Standard retrieval method performs poorly, while the three edited retrieval methods perform much better. Note that the FP curves also show how small the footprint set is with respect to overall case-base size.

Discussion: For small and medium case-base sizes both of the footprint-based methods (FP and FPRS) out-perform the CNN approach. However, eventually the FPRS method may become marginally less efficient than the CNN and FP methods;

this is seen after the 600 case mark in the Travel domain (see Figure 5(c)), but is not evident in the Property domain.. The reason for this is the second stage of retrieval in the FPRS method. CNN and FP do not incur this extra cost. For small and medium sized case-bases the related sets of cases are small and so this extra cost does not register as significant. However, as the case-base grows, so too does the average size of a related set, and therefore, so too does the cost of this second phase of retrieval. This second stage cost remains low however, and, we argue, is comfortably offset by the significant benefits for FPRS when it comes to competence and quality, as we shall see in the following sections.

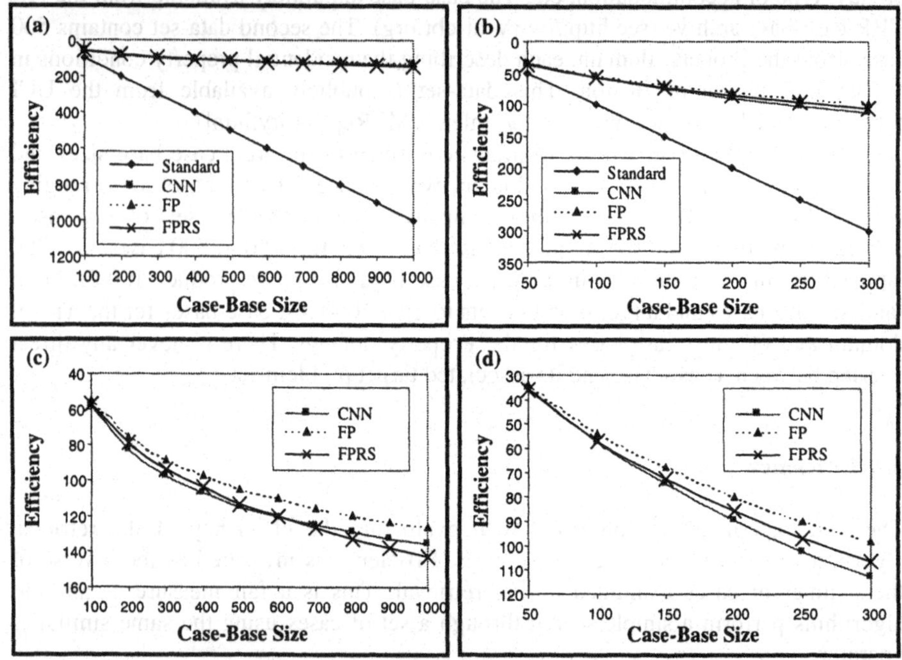

Figure 5. Efficiency vs. Case-Base Size for the Travel (a & c) and Property (b & d) domains respectively. Graphs (c & d) show additional detail for the CNN, FP, and FPRS results.

5.3 Competence

There is typically a tradeoff between the efficiency and competence of a retrieval technique. In particular, since the footprint and CNN methods do not examine every case in the case-base, it is possible that important cases are missed during retrieval thereby limiting the overall problem solving competence. In this experiment we look at how each retrieval method performs in terms of competence, where competence is defined to be the percentage of target problems that can be successfully solved by a given retrieval algorithm.

Method: Each case-base of size n is tested with respect to its associated set of target problems, and the competence of each retrieval method over these target problems is computed (that is, the percentage of target problems that can be correctly solved using each retrieval method). This cost is averaged for each of the 100 case-bases of size n to compute a mean competence for each case-base size and retrieval method.

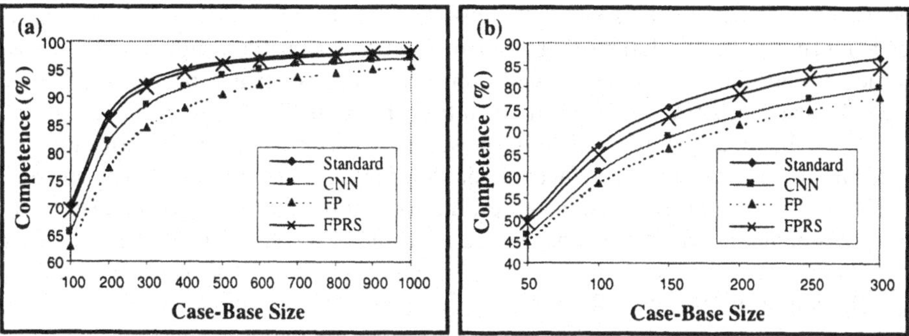

Figure 6. Competence *vs.* Case-Base Size for (a) the Travel, and (b) the Property domains.

Results: The results are displayed as graphs of competence versus case-base size for each domain in Figure 6(a) and (b). Each graph shows the results for the four different retrieval methods. The trade-off between retrieval efficiency and retrieval competence now becomes clearer. By definition, the Standard retrieval method defines the optimal competence for each case-base size in the sense that it guarantees the retrieval of the nearest case to a given target problem, which for our purposes is assumed to be the correct case. This assumption is typical in most traditional CBR systems but it may not hold in other domains such as classification problems – future work will focus on this issue further. In this experiment the important thing to note is the difference between each of the edited retrieval methods and the Standard method. It is clear that in both domains, and for every case-base size, the FPRS method outperforms the CNN and FP methods. In fact the FPRS method exhibits competence characteristics that are nearly identical to the optimal Standard method results. For example, Figure 6(b) shows that for the Property domain the competence of the Standard method, at the 300 case mark, is 86%. Compare this to competence of 84.5% for the FPRS method but only 77% and 79% for the FP and CNN methods respectively.

Discussion: The reason for the improved competence of the FPRS method is its second, target-specific retrieval stage. During this stage the FPRS method searches a small but dense set of cases from the original case-base in the region of the target problem, and thus benefits from the additional detail of the full case-base in the vicinity of the target problem. The CNN and FP methods derive no such benefit from their single stage search since their edited sets lack the detail of the original case-base in the region of the target problem.

5.4 Quality

In many problem solving settings (for example classification problems) the notion of solution quality is not meaningful – the concept of quality is implemented as the accuracy of class prediction, and a solution class is either correct or it is not. However, in other domains and tasks quality is vitally important. There may be a wide range of correct solutions to a problem that lie on a quality continuum. Different retrieval algorithms can have similar competence characteristics but very different quality characteristics – they may facilitate the solution of the same range of problems, but the quality of their proposed solutions may differ significantly. In general, solution quality is a function of the distance between the target and the retrieved case. As this distance increases, the amount of adaptation needed also tends to increase, and as adaptation work increases, solution quality tends to degrade. This correlation between similarity distance, adaptation effort, and ultimate solution quality is typical in many CBR systems. Of course pairing similarity and quality in this way does simplify the quality issue, but we believe that it is nonetheless a valid and useful pairing, one that allows us to at least begin to understand the implications that footprint-based retrieval may have for solution quality. The question to be answered in this experiment then is exactly how close do the CNN, FP, and FPRS methods get to the optimal quality level of the Standard approach?

Method: As in the earlier experiments, each case-base of size n is tested with respect to its target problem set. This time the average distance between target and retrieved case is computed. This distance is then averaged over the 100 case-bases of size n to produce a mean distance per target problem for each case-base size. The inverse of this average distance is used as a quality measure.

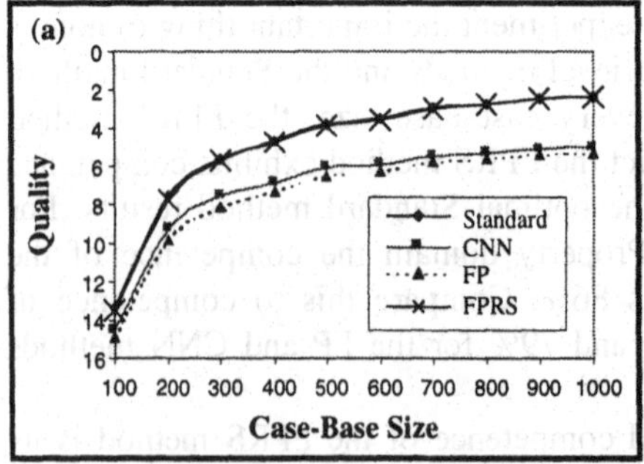

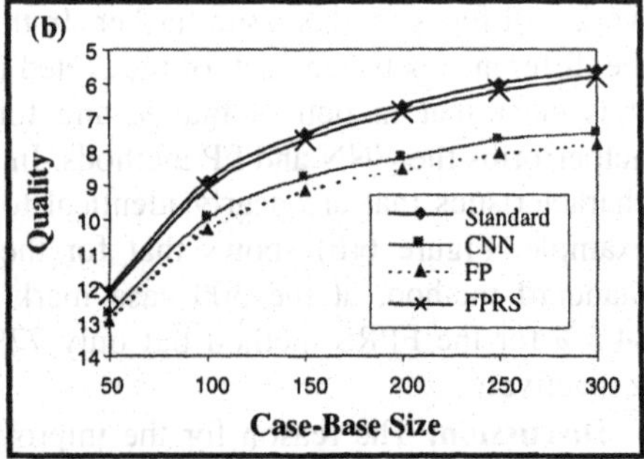

Figure 7. Quality *vs.* Case-Base size for (a) the Travel, and (b) the Property domains.

Results: The results are displayed in Figure 7(a) and (b) as graphs of quality (decreasing average distance) versus case-base size for the Travel and Property domains, respectively. The results show a clear separation of the four algorithms into two groups. The Standard and FPRS methods perform significantly better than the FP and CNN methods. In fact, the FPRS method displays a retrieval quality that is virtually identical to that of the Standard method. For example, Figure 7(a) shows that for the Travel domain the average distance of retrieved case from a target problem, at the 1000 case mark for the Standard and FPRS methods, is 2.33 and 2.37, respectively. This is compared to values of 5.1 and 5.3 for the CNN and FP methods respectively. Thus, the quality of FPRS is more than twice that of a CNN or FP.

Discussion: Clearly, from a quality viewpoint, the FPRS method benefits greatly from its second retrieval stage, a benefit that can be seen directly in the graphs as the difference between the FPRS and FP quality curves. In fact, it is interesting to note that for both domains, the difference in quality between the FPRS method and the CNN and FP methods is itself increasing with case-base size.

5.5 Optimality

So far we have seen that the FPRS method benefits from superior efficiency, competence and quality characteristic. We have shown that the method approaches the optimal competence and quality characteristics of an exhaustive case-base search, while at the same time benefiting from the efficiency characteristics of edited case-base methods such as CNN. This last experiment is a refinement of the above competence and quality experiments. It is concerned with investigating retrieval optimality, that is, the ability of a retrieval algorithm to select the closest case to a target problem. Obviously, the Standard method will always retrieve this optimal case. The same is not true of CNN since it may not have access to these optimal cases – they may have been dropped during the editing process. The question that remains to be answered is: how often does the FPRS method retrieve the optimal case?

Method: As in the earlier experiments, each case-base of size n is tested with respect to its target problem set. This time we are interested in how often each of FPRS, FP, and CNN select the same case for a target problem as the Standard method.

Results: The results are displayed in Figure 8(a) and (b) as graphs of optimality versus case-base size for the Travel and Property domains, respectively. The results show clearly that the FPRS method is far superior to the CNN and FP methods. In fact in both domains, and for all case-base sizes, FPRS optimality is at least 90%. In contrast, the optimality of the CNN and FP methods decreases with case-base size and fall to as low as 15% for the Travel domain (at 1000 cases) and 35% for the Property domain (at the 300 case mark).

Discussion: Of course the reason for the poor performance of the CNN and FP methods is that they do not have access to an entire case-base, and therefore, they do not always have access to the optimal case. For example, in the Travel domain, the CNN case-base at the 1000 case mark contains an average of 135 cases, that is, 13.5% of the total cases. Therefore, all other things being equal, we can expect the optimality of CNN, at the 1000 case mark, to be as low as 13.5%, a prediction that conforms well to the observed value of 15% optimality (see Figure 8(a)). While the FPRS method does not explicitly eliminate any cases from the case-base, during any given retrieval it is limited to a search of a small subset of these cases; namely, the FP set plus the related set of the reference case. Like the CNN subset, the FPRS subset is small relative to the entire case-base. For example, at the 1000 case mark in the Travel domain, the FPRS subset is about 14% of the case-base, and so one might expect FPRS optimality to be comparably low. However, the results show that the FPRS method has a retrieval optimality of 96% for the 1000 case mark in the Travel domain (see Figure 8(a)). The critical factor is that part of the FPRS subset is target specific. The related set has been chosen with reference to a specific target problem and, therefore, it is likely to contain the optimal case for a given target. This makes all of the difference, and ensures near perfect retrieval optimality for the FPRS method.

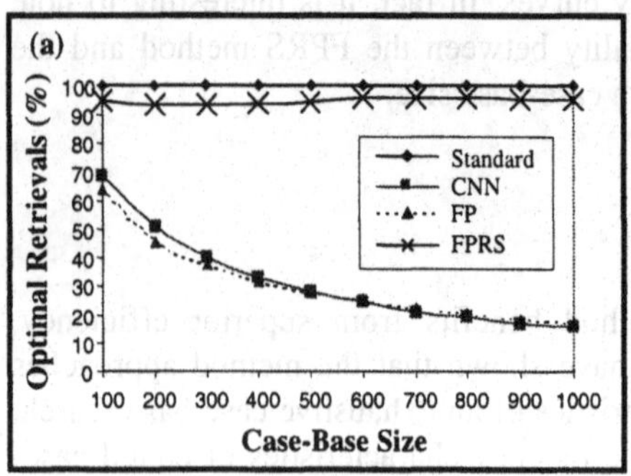

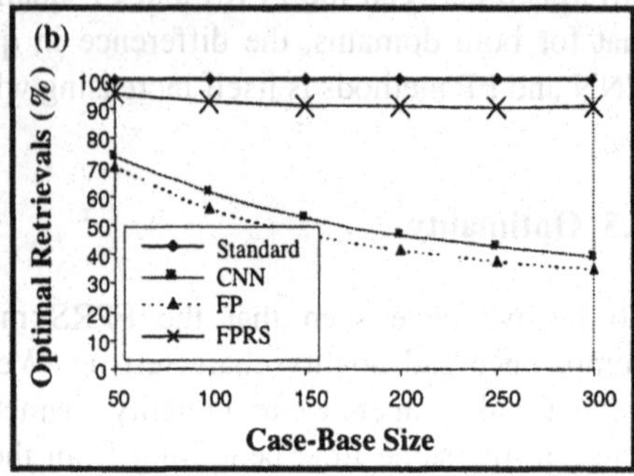

Figure 8. Percentage of Optimal Retrievals *vs.* Case-Base size for (a) the Travel, and (b) the Property domains.

6 Conclusions

In this paper we describe footprint-based retrieval, a novel retrieval approach that uses an explicit model of case competence to guide search. The approach consists of two distinct stages. During stage one, a compact competent subset of the case-base is searched to retrieve a case that is similar to the current target problem. This case acts as a reference point for the full case-base. During stage two the cases nearby to this reference case are searched and the closest one to the target is retrieved. A comprehensive evaluation of the retrieval technique shows that the approach benefits from superior efficiency, competence, and quality characteristics when compared to more traditional retrieval techniques.

The new method relies heavily on the availability of a comprehensive model of case competence and, of course, there is a cost associated with the construction of this model. In fact we can show that the model construction is $O(n^2)$ in the size of the case-base. However, for an existing case-base this can be thought of as an additional once-off setup cost and as such does not contribute an additional runtime expense.

Obviously the success of footprint-based retrieval will depend very much on the properties of the footprint set constructed for a given case-base. In this paper we have described one particular footprint construction algorithm based on CNN. However, other variations are possible and our future research will focus on a complete investigation of alternative approaches to footprint construction.

Our current work continues to investigate the issue of performance modelling in CBR, and we believe that predictive models hold the key to a wide range of open problems. We are currently building a range of applications to demonstrate a variety of different uses for performance models such as our model of competence. For example, we have already applied competence models to the problems of case-base maintenance, case deletion, case-base construction, and authoring support.

References

1. Aha, D.W., Kibler, D., and Albert, M.K.: Instance-Based Learning Algorithms. Machine Learning **6** (1991) 37-66.
2. Brown, M.G.: An Underlying Memory Model to Support Case Retrieval. In: Topics in Case-Based Reasoning. Lecture Notes in Artificial Intelligence, Vol. 837. Springer-Verlag, Berlin Heidelberg New York (1994) 132-143.
3. Dasarathy, B.V.: Nearest Neighbor Norms: NN Pattern Classification Techniques. IEEE Press, Los Alamitos, California (1991)
4. Hart, P.E.: The Condensed Nearest Neighbor Rule. IEEE Transactions on Information Theory, **14** (1967) 515-516.
5. Leake, D.B., Kinley, A., and Wilson, D.: Case-Based Similarity Asessment: Estimating Adaptability from Experience. In: Proceedings of the 14th National Conference on Artificial Intelligence. AAAI Press (1997)
6. Lenz, M.: Applying Case Retrieval Nets to Diagnostic Tasks in Technical Domains. In: Smith, I. & Faltings, B. (eds.): Advances in Case-Based Reasoning. Lecture Notes in Artificial Intelligence, Vol. 1168. Springer-Verlag, Berlin Heidelberg New York (1996) 219-233
7. Lieber, J.: A Criterion of Comparison between two Case-Bases. In: Haton, J-P., Keane, M., and Manago, M. (eds.): Advances in Case-Based Reasoning. Lecture Notes in Artificial Intelligence, Vol. 984. Springer-Verlag, Berlin Heidelberg New York (1994) 87-100
8. Minton, S.: Qualitative Results Concerning the Utility of Explanation-Based Learning, Artificial Intelligence, **42**(2,3) (1990) 363-391
9. Schaaf, J. W.: Fish and Shrink: A Next Step Towards Efficient Case Retrieval in Large-Scale Case-Bases. In: Smith, I. & Faltings, B. (eds.): Advances in Case-Based Reasoning. Lecture Notes in Artificial Intelligence, Vol. 1168. Springer-Verlag, Berlin Heidelberg New York (1996) 362-376
10. Smyth, B. and Keane. M. T.: Adaptation-Guided Retrieval: Questioning the Similarity Assumption in Reasoning. Artificial Intelligence **102** (1998) 249-293
11. Smyth, B. & Keane, M.T.: Remembering to Forget: A Competence Preserving Deletion Policy for Case-Based Reasoning Systems. In: Proceedings of the 14th International Joint Conference on Artificial Intelligence. Morgan-Kaufmann. (1995) 377-382
12. Smyth, B. & McKenna, E.: Modelling the Competence of Case-Bases. In: Smyth, B. & Cunningham, P. (eds.): .): Advances in Case-Based Reasoning. Lecture Notes in Artificial Intelligence, Vol. 1488. Springer-Verlag, Berlin Heidelberg New York (1998). 208-220
13. Veloso, M. Flexible Strategy Learning: Analogical Replay of Problem Solving Episodes. Proceedings of the 12th National Conference on Artificial Intelligence (1994) 595-600.
14. Wess, S., Althoff, K-D., Derwand, G.: Using k-d Trees to Improve the Retrieval Step in Case-Based Reasoning. In: Topics in Case-Based Reasoning. Lecture Notes in Artificial Intelligence, Vol. 837. Springer-Verlag, Berlin Heidelberg New York (1994) 167 – 181
15. Wolverton, M., and Hayes-Roth, B.: Retrieving Semantically Distant Analogies with Knowledge-Directed Spreading Activation. In: Proceedings of the 12th National Conference on Artificial Intelligence, (1994) 56-61.

Is CBR Applicable to the Coordination of Search and Rescue Operations? A Feasibility Study

Irène Abi-Zeid[1], Qiang Yang[2], and Luc Lamontagne[1]

[1]Defence Research Establishment Valcartier, 2459 boul. Pie-XI,
Val Belair, Quebec, G3J 1X5, Canada
{irene.abi-zeid, luc.lamontagne}@drev.dnd.ca
[2]Simon Fraser University, School of Computing Science
Burnaby, British Columbia, V5A 1S6. Canada
qyang@cs.sfu.ca

Abstract. In response to the occurrence of an air incident, controllers at one of the three Canadian Rescue Coordination Centers (RCC) must make a series of critical decisions on the appropriate procedures to follow. These procedures (called incident prosecution) include hypotheses formulation and information gathering, development of a plan for the search and rescue (SAR) missions and in the end, the generation of reports. We present in this paper the results of a project aimed at evaluating the applicability of CBR to help support incident prosecution in the RCC. We have identified three possible applications of CBR: Online help, real time support for situation assessment, and report generation. We present a brief description of the situation assessment agent system that we are implementing as a result of this study.

1 Introduction

In response to the occurrence of an air incident, controllers at one of the three Canadian Rescue Coordination Centers (RCC) must make a series of critical decisions on the appropriate procedures to follow in order to deal with the incident. These decisions and procedures (called incident[1] prosecution) include an assessment of the degree of emergency, a formulation of the hypotheses on what might have happened and where, the development of a plan for the search and rescue (SAR) missions and in the end, the generation of reports. The workflow of a controller may be roughly described as follows:

1. Receive alert;
2. Classify the situation through an interactive Q/A process;
3. Iteratively narrow down the range of hypotheses by gaining new information through the information gathering process (communications search);

[1] The term usually used in a RCC is case prosecution. However, to avoid confusion with a case in CBR we will use the term incident prosecution.

4. Initiate search planning;
5. Further narrow down the hypotheses using the new information gained;
6. Initiate SAR missions, task resources and monitor progress. At the same time, record important events;
7. Generate report.

It is important to note that not all air incidents lead to search planning. Incident prosecution is often limited to receiving the alert, classifying the situation, narrowing down the range of hypotheses (steps 1 to 3) and generating a report (7).

Prosecuting a SAR incident is knowledge intensive and exhibits strong real time characteristics. A typical controller handles two to three incidents at the same time. Furthermore, the Canadian RCCs receive well over 5,000 incidents per year. It would therefore be beneficial to develop a decision support system for automating as much of the process as possible, and for capturing and reusing the knowledge. Cottam *et al.* [2], [3] describe work done in the UK on a generic knowledge acquisition approach for search and rescue planning and scheduling operations. The authors found that the SAR problem solving is structured enough to allow a decision support system to advise the human controller.

Having such a system would enable RCC controllers to better support and coordinate their incident prosecution in real time, to streamline the incident reporting procedures, and to help train junior operators using realistic SAR scenarios. As part of an effort to design decision aid tools for the RCC controller, we decided to investigate and evaluate the applicability of CBR to help support incident prosecution in the RCC.

We begin in section 2 by describing the incident prosecution process. Section 3 presents our approach for evaluating the applicability of CBR to the RCC environment. This includes a brief description of the interviews conducted with the controllers as well as a summary of the related documents and databases surveyed. Section 4 presents our findings and recommendations on how CBR could be used, and section 5 presents the agent system that we are developing as a result of this study. We conclude in section 6.

2 Incident Prosecution in the RCC

In general, SAR incident prosecution can be broken down into three phases where each phase can somewhat overlap the adjacent ones. For example, when a telephone call is received (first notice), the operation enters an *uncertainty* phase. In this phase the controller will collect information about the details of the flight plan and people involved. If not enough information has been obtained, the operation will progress into the *alert* phase whereby the controller will expand the information gathering activities and alert SAR agencies. If a certain amount of time has passed after the uncertainty phase without obtaining more information about the plane, the operation enters the *distress* phase. In this phase the controller initiates the tasks that consist of planning, coordinating, and monitoring search missions. Once the cause of the incident and the location of the aircraft are determined, he may be required to mobilize and monitor the rescue process. Tasks in this phase involve notifying various agencies involved, including hospitals and police, notifying the relatives and dispatching planes or helicopters to the crash site. An incident report will be filed in the end, and news dispatches will be sent out to various media agencies before the incident is closed.

The tasks conducted in the uncertainty and alert phases are called situation assessment (SA), a process similar to diagnosing a patient by a doctor. SA refers to the tasks of finding out the true nature of the incident by formulating and verifying hypotheses through an information gathering process. It is much like detective work. Over 90% of the incidents are false alarms, caused by faulty equipment, power lines or even Electronic Locator Transmitters (ELT) that the pilots forgot to turn off. Furthermore, the receipt of reports on an overdue (late) aircraft does not necessarily imply that the aircraft itself has crashed somewhere. Rather, there are many possibilities why the craft has gone missing, ranging from the fact that the pilot may have landed halfway to refuel, to the possibility that the pilot never took off in the first place. To summarize, the decision process in incident prosecution consists of situation assessment and mission planning and monitoring. Figure 1 presents a schematic description of the controller's tasks.

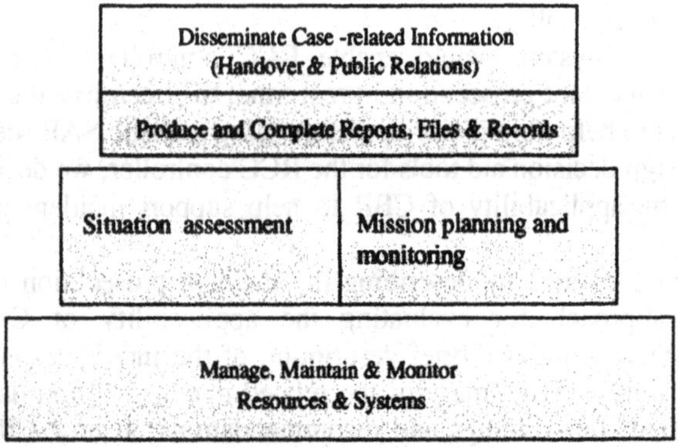

Fig. 1. Schematic description of a controller's tasks

2.1 Why CBR?

In the past, CBR has been applied to areas similar to our problem. These include classification, diagnosis and planning. The PROTOS system is used for classifying hearing disorders [12]. Based on the knowledge on a given patient, PROTOS finds a similar case and uses that case's class to determine the patient's disorder type. The CASEY system is designed to obtain a causal explanation regarding a patient's disorder given his signs and symptoms [8]. The CHEF system was designed to suggest recipes for cooking [5]. Given the goals of the meal, including style and ingredients, CHEF produces a sequence of actions by modifying a previously used recipe. It indexes the failures it has encountered in the past and uses domain specific knowledge to address these failures. MI-CBP is a Mixed-Initiative Case-Based planning system that is the integration of two systems: ForMAT, a case-based system for supporting military force deployment planning within the military transportation domain and Prodigy/Analogy for automating plan construction or adaptation [17].

From our initial knowledge of the SAR domain, we felt that there was at least one possibly worthwhile application for CBR: Situation assessment. When the first notice is received, a controller could retrieve from a case base cases with similar initial information. He then could adapt the past problem solving strategies regarding hypotheses formulation and information gathering. We have therefore concentrated in this study on situation assessment and excluded the mission planning and monitoring part of the controller's tasks.

3 Our Approach

The initial questions that we asked are:

- What is a case? Can a RCC incident be considered a CBR case?
- Do controllers make use of past incidents in their operations (implicitly or explicitly)?
- Can the incidents be compared, generalized?
- Is there sufficient historical information? And can the information be exploited by CBR techniques?
- Is it possible to quantify similarity and dissimilarity?
- Is the knowledge of a controller more rule-based or case-based?

In order to try to answer these questions, we went through a series of interviews as well as through the documents and the databases that consigned the historical RCC incident information. We summarize our observations below.

3.1 Interviews

Our first task was to get familiar with the RCC operations and the accumulated data. This was accomplished through visits to the RCCs and interviews with controllers: Six visits to RCC Victoria over a six months period, a review of four days of taped interviews with RCC Trenton, individual discussions with experienced controllers on other occasions, and participation in a one-week training course provided to controllers. This allowed us to gain first hand experience in actual operations of the RCC, and to assess the dataflow and workflow of the organization.

During the first visit, an overview of the operations of the RCC was given by a senior controller. This was followed by an overview of CBR given by us. We had prepared a set of questions for the interviews. These were mostly related to the activities of a controller. We then asked about the training required and some important factors that make a successful controller. We learnt that incidents are currently being recorded on paper in real time, using a checklist and tables. In the future, a database front-end system (CaseMaster) will be used to record all incident information, including the major actions taken by the RCC controllers and the time and circumstances of the action. This system has been tested and will be used in the near future.

During our various meetings, the controllers expressed the following concerns: First, it is very time consuming to brief or communicate with another controller in the RCC or at another RCC about the current incident information. Second, it is time consuming to file reports at the end. Third, it is sometimes possible to forget factors that should be evaluated while narrowing down potential hypotheses especially in the presence of incomplete information. They felt that recorded incidents could help address these problems. They rejected a rule-based system as a potential decision aid because they felt it was too "rigid". Furthermore, they confirmed that they retrieved similar incidents and solved new problems by making use of past incidents, especially for device related analogies. For example, if an incident involves a Beaver plane, then past knowledge about the most breakable devices on that plane can serve as a hint for the possibilities for the current incident.

3.2 Procedures Manual

In order to complement our knowledge acquisition process, we studied the national SAR manual [11] and RCC Victoria Standard Operations Procedures [14] for carrying out SAR operations in Canada. One of the most interesting aspects of the manuals is a collection of possible scenarios and their corresponding solutions. It is interesting to note that this method of presenting scenario-solution pairs is consistent with the problem-solving model of CBR.

3.3 Historical Data

We examined the RCC Victoria Statistical Summary [15]. This 8-page document reports on the annual operational figures. It begins with a national comparison of the incidents that occurred in 1996. It then separately reports on the use of assets and resources for marine, air and land SAR incidents in 1996. The summary is very useful in providing a big picture of the SAR incidents handled at RCC Victoria and the corresponding statistical figures, however it is not of any practical use for CBR.

3.4 Incident Logs

As incidents are prosecuted, information is recorded in incident logs containing incident descriptions, unit assisted descriptions, type of incident, difficulty level, action taken, weather report, resources used, critical factors and anomalies, etc. This information will be recorded in electronic form in the near future. The most interesting aspect of these forms is the manual logging of pertinent chronological descriptions of the actions taken by the controllers.

3.5 Statistical Database Model SISAR

When the operations are completed, information is logged into SISAR, a statistical database which keeps information similar to the one contained in the incident logs. However, SISAR only provides categorical summaries of an incident, recording information such as the number of persons on board and the type of aircraft involved. It does not record all the relevant causal factors and the process followed by a controller to narrow down the hypotheses. Our study concluded that not enough detail is provided in the SISAR database logs about the events that occur and the reasoning that goes on.

4 Results

In studying the SAR domain and investigating the application of CBR, we focused on the following issues [7], [9]:

1. What is a case?
2. What are the indexes?
3. How are the cases acquired?
4. Is there any adaptation?
5. What are some recommendations?

Our results are summarized in the form of answers to each of the above questions. In defining what is a case, we kept in mind that a case normally consists of the following elements:

- Name and id;
- Keywords for retrieval;
- Facts denoting problem solving context;
- Solution used in the past;
- Outcomes denoting success or failure;
- Solution context;
- Interpretations and annotations of the case;
- Links to other cases

4.1 CBR for Online Help

The first envisaged application of CBR was to provide online help with procedures during real time incident prosecution. This is similar to using CBR for help desks in technical troubleshooting. The main purpose of such a system would be to remind the controller of the appropriate procedures when the controller is aware of the stage in which the SAR operation is. For example, when a controller is aware that he is in the uncertainty phase and would like to consult the operational procedures as outlined in the National SAR Manual.

Description of a Case. In this application, a case would consist of a pair, where the first element of the pair is a problem resolution context or phase (for example, air-case-uncertainty-phase), and the second element is a procedure itself that may be presented in textual format on the computer screen. As an example, consider the procedure for a distress phase operation taken from [11].

Case name: Distress phase of Air SAR

Case content: RCC action during DISTRESS phase of an aircraft emergency:

- Initiate action with appropriate SAR units and services;
- ...
- When the incident involves an aircraft of foreign registry, RCC shall inform National Defense Operations Center to advise appropriate embassy if required;
- Develop rescue plan if casualties require assistance, notify medical facilities, police/coroner, establish the most expeditious means and method of rescue.

Description of the Indexes. The indexes for these cases are all the relevant information that one can use to classify the current situation in terms of phase information. In the air SAR phase identification example, the indexes can be the following questions:

- Aircraft didn't land on time and lost communication? (yes/no);
- ...
- Following the uncertainty phase, communications search received no new information? (yes/no);

Acquiring the Cases and Using Adaptation. Major sources of the case information are the SAR manuals and the training manuals. There are probably simple forms of adaptation that can be performed on these procedures, although in the current practice, these adaptations are mostly done by the controllers.

Recommendations. Our observations are that the experienced controllers have already mastered all the basic procedures indicated in the SAR manuals. This assertion is based on the fact that they are actually doing their job in the operational environment. We suspect that this method of using CBR where cases are recorded as operational procedures would be limited to training and to providing assistance to junior air SAR controllers.

4.2 CBR for Situation Assessment

We present here the most promising application of CBR to incident prosecution: Situation assessment. Recall that the first part of incident prosecution involves finding out which of the hypotheses holds for the current situation. A hypothesis is a plausible cause and outcome for the incident. An example of a hypothesis on a cause of incident is "mechanical failure" for the outcome "crash". A lot of information must be gathered by the RCC controller in order to narrow down the hypotheses space. For example, the controller may check the weather condition to see whether the likelihood of a crash is large given an overdue report. At the same time, a request will be sent out to get the flight plan of the pilot in order to find all airports where the pilot might have landed, and so on. CBR can be used to rank and eliminate various hypotheses and to determine the associated information gathering tasks.

Description of a Case. A case may consist of each possible hypothesis (cause, outcome). It consists of both the problem attributes and the associated methods to operate on them. In particular, a case here would consist of the following elements:

- A hypothesis for the possible cause and possible outcome of the incident;
- A hierarchical task network (HTN) [4], [16] for the information gathering process to confirm the hypothesis (Fig. 2);
- A record of executed information gathering tasks for the current hypothesis object, and the information gathering steps yet to be executed for further confirming the hypothesis;
- An evaluation function of priorities for not-yet executed information gathering tasks;
- Indices with weights attached to the expected values of the answers to the queries.

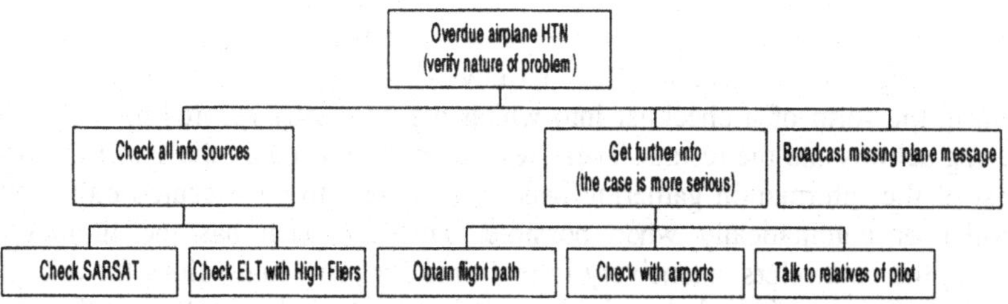

Fig. 2. An information gathering HTN example for an overdue airplane

Description of the Indexes. For the controller to assess the current situation, rank the remaining hypotheses, and weigh the next steps, a channel must exist between the known facts and knowledge and the system stored HTNs and hypotheses. This channel is provided by a layer of indexes. The cases may be indexed by different problem features:

- Overdue planes;
- ELT signals;
- Flare sightings;
- Crash reports;
- Mayday calls;
- Problem context;
- Weather reports;
- Vehicle involved;
- People involved;
- Fight path and location information.

Acquiring the Cases and Using Adaptation. Cases can be acquired through three sources. First, the National SAR Manual and other written documents provide a detailed outline of procedures and possibilities for the air SAR causes. Second, additional causes and hypotheses can be obtained from the RCC controllers and pilots themselves. The controllers we have met all have vast amount of experience on a potential range of hypotheses. Third and most importantly, causes can be obtained from a systematic scanning of the incident logs. The adaptation is in the form of selecting a task in an HTN to expand, and in adding and deleting new tasks in the HTN of a retrieved case. To expand a task, one has to determine which subtasks to execute and which information sources to access given several alternatives. Choosing an appropriate alternative will have an important impact on the effectiveness of the SAR operation.

Recommendations. There are two ways to use CBR in the context of a case as defined throughout this section. The first envisaged way was to have an interactive system in the form of a checklist into which the controller records his information gathering actions and the results. These results are then used by the system to update the list of the information gathering tasks that remain to be executed either by the controller or automatically when possible. This approach has the limitation of involving the controllers extensively in real time for providing values for indexes. It would therefore be difficult to win over the support of the controllers for such a system.

The second envisaged way, (and the one currently under development) is to use case-based HTN retrieval as a reminder list in the background and as means to acquire automatically the information that is available electronically. Information gathering is seen here as a planning task [6], [13]. The resulting system would be in the form of a background intelligent agent with minimum interaction with the controller. A limitation with this approach is that a fairly sophisticated monitoring and filtering system that reports on relevant incoming information must be assumed for telephone sources.

4.3 CBR for Report Generation

We present here the third possibility for using CBR: Raw CBR cases for report generation.

Description of a Case. A case in this approach would be a full recording of the history of events unfolding along a time line. An example is shown below:

Begin case:

Case 009:

Indexes:

Weather condition: clear

Caller: Airport staff

....

Table 1. An example of a chronological list of actions and events.

Events Time	Events
10:23am	Call received about an overdue plane: Information: small plane; expected landing time 9 am; Person On Board unknown;
10:25am	Called to obtain flight path plan information
10:30	Called to talk to wife of pilot
10:30am	Electronic Locator Transmitter (ELT) signal received along flight path

Forgotten Tasks:

A call to RCMP should have been initiated at 10:25am.

A request for more information should have been sent out to airports at source and destination.

Pitfalls to be avoided

Wait for more information before phoning the wife.

Outcome

Plane landed to refuel in an airport along the flight path.

End Case.

Description of the Indexes. The indexes for this case base would be a combination of the initial triggers for the case, and the contextual information such as the weather report and the type of airplane. As such, the set of indexes is not very different from those outlined in subsection 4.2.

Acquiring the Cases and Using Adaptation. One of the most promising methods would be to use an enhanced version of the CaseMaster system. In this situation, we are not looking at adapting the solutions to the incident but rather to adapt old reports based on the contents of the new incident. Here, CBR is used more as means for organizing, storing and retrieving incident logs.

Recommendations. In addition to generating reports, cases may be used as means of communication between controllers. Furthermore, they could serve as a basis for generating useful indexes for the application described in subsection 4.2. In this manner, we ensure that the case base index is always current and up to date.

5 A Brief Description of ASISA: Agent System for Intelligent Situation Assessment

We present in this section a brief description of an initial prototype to assist the controller in situation assessment. This is the result of the second recommendation. This tool, ASISA: Agent System for Intelligent Situation Assessment, is a combination of CBR and Hierarchical Task Network (HTN) planning techniques. In this initial prototype, cases are used to describe hypotheses and to encapsulate information-gathering queries for identifying the correct hypothesis. Figure 3 presents a schematic description of ASISA.

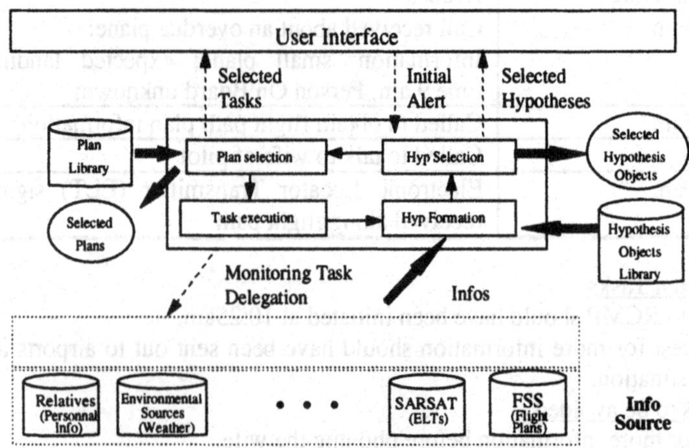

Fig. 3. A diagram illustrating the main components of ASISA

First, upon receiving an initial indication of a problem, the available relevant information is input into the system. The system retrieves a collection of similar cases from the case base. They consist of the hypotheses H_1, H_2, ... H_n that can be used to characterize the current situation, where each of the H_i's provides a plausible cause for the current case such as "plane crashed due to mechanical failure". Subsequently, the system enters a cycle in which it identifies (from the case base) the information gathering tasks described by the HTN associated with each hypothesis object. These HTNs are refined by the plan selection module and used by the task execution module to determine the information gathering actions to be executed next. The process continues until a final conclusion about the nature of the incident is reached by the ASISA system. The overall workflow for this iterative process is depicted in Figure 4.

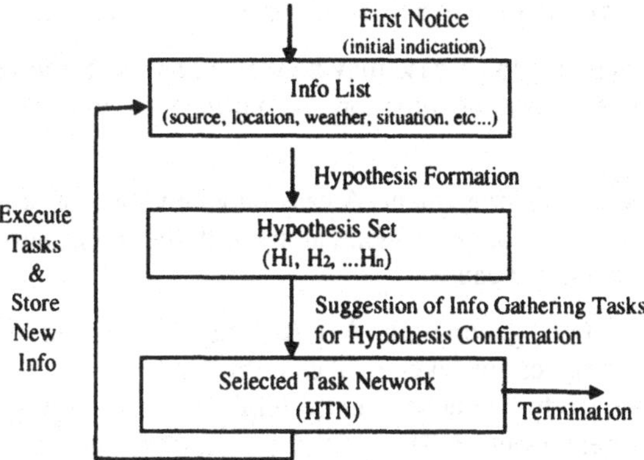

Fig. 4. Information flow in ASISA

The agent-based ASISA system will benefit the SAR controller in several ways. First, because the agent is constantly monitoring a variety of information sources, it can help filter out a large quantity of irrelevant information, and help the controller concentrate on the critical information only. Second, given the overwhelming workload during the high seasons for air incidents, the agent system can help improve the accuracy and shorten the time required for assessing a case. This effect translates directly into one of saving more lives. Third, for junior air SAR controllers, the agent-based system can become a handy decision support system and a tutoring system. We expect that the learning speed of the new controllers will be improved with the help of our agent system.

5.1 Related Work

HICAP (Hierarchical Interactive Case-based Architecture for Planning) [9] is a planning architecture developed to support planning of Noncombatant Evacuation Operations by assisting military commanders in interactively refining plans. It is similar to what is proposed in ASISA in the sense that it uses HTN to represent tasks and subtasks. However, a major difference with ASISA is that while HICAP is meant to be highly interactive, ASISA is meant to be very little intrusive and with minimum interaction with the controller. The reason is that incident prosecution is a real-time operation where the controller has no time to interact with a computer. Since most of the controller's activities are conducted over the phone, one of our ongoing research projects is to monitor telephone conversations and try to extract the information necessary to feed the ASISA system. However at this point, we assume that such information is readily available for ASISA.

Another application domain for ASISA has been identified as the cable TV troubleshooting domain that bears resemblance with the search and rescue problem domain [1].

6 Conclusions

Our study has revealed three possible ways to use a CBR system for incident prosecution, each corresponding to a different usage of the case information:

1. CBR for online help: A case may be viewed as a specific procedure on how to deal with a certain situation as outlined in the standard operational procedures;
2. CBR for situation assessment: A case may be viewed as a hypothesis on the cause and outcome of an incident, along with the information gathering tasks for ascertaining that cause;
3. CBR for report generation: A case may be viewed as a step-by-step recording of all actions taken by the controller.

As a result of this study, we are currently implementing ASISA, an agent system for situation assessment where CBR is used for storing, and retrieving hypothesis along with their associated information gathering tasks represented as HTNs.

Many issues still need to be explored with regards to CBR and SAR, mainly the applicability of CBR to support the second phase of incident prosecution: Mission planning and monitoring.

References

1. Carrick C., Qiang Y., Abi-Zeid, I., Lamontagne L.: Activating CBR Systems through Autonomous Information Gathering. ICCBR'99 (1999)
2. Cottam, H., Shadbolt, N., Kingston, J., Beck, H., Tate, A.: Knowledge Level Planning in the Search and Rescue Domain. In Bramer, M.A., Nealon, R. (eds.): Research and Development in Expert Systems XII. SGES Publications (1995) 309-326
3. Cottam, H., Shadbolt, N.: Knowledge Acquisition for Search and Rescue. Proceedings of the 10th Knowledge Acquisition for Knowledge Based Systems Workshop, KAW 96 (1996)
4. Erol, K. Hierarchical Task Network Planning: Formalization, Analysis and Implementation. Ph.D. Thesis, University of Maryland (1994)
5. Hammond, K. Case Based Planning: A Framework for Planning from Experience. Journal of Cognitive Science, 14 (3) (1990)
6. Knoblock, C. and Ambite, J.-L.: Agents for Information Gathering. In Bradshaw, J. M. (ed.): Software Agents. (1997) 347-374
7. Kolodner, J.: Case Based Reasoning. Morgan Kaufmann Publishers, Inc. (1993)
8. Koton, P.: Reasoning about Evidence in Causal Explanation. In Proceedings of the 1998 AAAI Conference. AAAI Press/MIT Press (1988)
9. Leake, D.: Case Based Reasoning: Experiences, Lessons and Future Directions. AAAI Press (1996)
10. Munoz-Avila, H., Aha D. W., Breslow L., Nau D.: HICAP: An Interactive Case-Based Planning Architecture and its Application to Noncombatant Evacuation Operations. NCARAI Technical Note AIC-99-002 (1999)
11. National SAR Manual. December (1995)

12. Porter, B., Bareiss, R., and Holte, R.: Concept Learning and Heuristic Classification in Weak Theory Domains. Artificial Intelligence (45) (1990) 229-263
13. Pryor, L. and Collins G.: Planning to perceive: A utilitarian approach. In Working notes of the AAAI Spring Symposium on the Control of Selective Perception. March (1992)
14. RCC Victoria Standard Operating Procedures (1997)
15. RCC Victoria 1996 Statistical Summary (1996)
16. Sacerdoti, E. D.: Planning in a hierarchy of abstraction spaces. In Allen, J., Hendler J., and Tate A. (eds.): Readings in Planning. Morgan Kaufman (1990) 98-108
17. Veloso, M. M., Mulvehill A. M., Cox M. T.: Rationale-Supported Mixed-Initiative Case-Based Planning. In Proceedings of the Ninth Conference on Innovative Applications of Artificial Intelligence. AAAI Press (1997) 1072-1085

Integrating Case-Based Reasoning and Hypermedia Documentation: An Application for the Diagnosis of a Welding Robot at Odense Steel Shipyard

Eric Auriol[1], Richard M. Crowder[2], Rob MacKendrick[3], Roger Rowe[4] and Thomas Knudsen[5]

[1] AcknoSoft, 15 rue Soufflot, 75 005 Paris, France, auriol@ibpc.fr

[2] Department of Electrical Engineering, University of Southampton, Southampton, UK, SO17 1BJ, rmc1@soton.ac.uk

[3] Parallel Applications Centre, Chilworth, Southampton, SO167NS, UK, rmk@pac.soton.ac.uk

[4] MultiCosm Ltd, Chilworth, Southampton, SO167NS, UK, R.Rowe@multicosm.com

[5] Odense Steel Shipyard Ltd, PO Box 176, DK 5100 Odense C, Denmark, tdk@oss.dk

Abstract. Reliable and effective maintenance support is a vital consideration for the management within today's manufacturing environment. This paper discusses the development a maintenance system for the world largest robot welding facility. The developed system combines a case-based reasoning approach for diagnosis with context information, as electronic on-line manuals, linked using open hypermedia technology. The work discussed in this paper delivers not only a maintenance system for the robot stations under consideration, but also a design framework for developing maintenance systems for other similar applications.

1 Introduction

Odense Steel Shipyards (OSS) builds container ships of a quality and size that cannot be matched by their competitors. OSS achieves this advantage by using a high level of automation in their design and production processes. This is typified by the company's wide spread introduction of robotic welding systems, in particular the B4 robot station.

The use of high technology production facilities requires the introduction of effective maintenance systems. The main purpose of these systems is to minimise production costs by ensuring the reliability, and production quality of the manufacturing systems. In addition the maintenance cost should be minimised by effective use of resources.

Any form of maintenance requires the application of knowledge held by people familiar with the system. At OSS these are the operators and the system specialists. The operators are responsible for operating and undertaking maintenance of the robot.

At OSS the operators are concerned with the entire system, and will have engineering expertise to solve many problems. Robot specialists will have in depth knowledge of the robotic systems, and therefore will be called upon when an operator is unable to rapidly solve a problem. It is the case (both at OSS and generally) that there are more operators than robot specialists available for the maintenance of the system, as specialists are shared amongst a number of robot installations. One approach to minimising maintenance costs is to develop a system that enables the operator to undertake more of the maintenance tasks. This will minimise the time currently wasted in waiting for robot specialists.

To undertake a maintenance task reference has to be made to the information stored in documentation. In the case of the robot being considered in the paper, this information consists of a considerable number of loose leave documents, drawings ranging from A4 to A0, and proprietary information. This by its very nature can be easily damaged, or lost when taken on to the factory floor. The solution is the computer-based integration of a diagnostic system with a document storage and retrieval system.

This paper discusses aspects of the HELPMATE* project that is developing a computer-based system capable of supporting the operator to diagnose and repair faults within the B4 welding station. The developed application, *Freya*, required the integration of a Case Based Reasoning (CBR) system (*Kate* developed by AcknoSoft) with an open hypermedia system (*MicroCosm Pro* developed by MultiCosm).

1.1 The Target System: the B4 Robot Station

OSS's B4 robot station is the world's largest robot station for arc welding. The robot station is designed to weld ship hull sections up to 32 × 22 × 6 meters, and 400 tonnes in weight. The robot station consists of 12 individual robot gantries, each with 8 degrees of freedom, suspended 17m above the shop floor, and is capable of welding up to 3 kilometres of steel per day. As OSS only has once such installation, any failure will impact on the material flow through the yard.

The B4 robot station is designed by OSS, including a cell control system called Rob-Ex (Robot Execution system). Rob-Ex is capable of handling the planning and scheduling of the robot's welding jobs, followed by downloaded the post-processed robot program to the local robot controller for execution. Rob-Ex also includes subsystems that schedule and plan preventative maintenance activities.

While the Rob-Ex system has a fault detection capability, where the detected fault is communicated to the operator as a code, Rob-Ex does not provide any diagnostic information. The resolution of the fault is down to the operators and specialists. While some faults (e.g. replacement of welding wire) can be resolved with ease, more difficult faults (e.g. a drive or servo failure) will require information from system documentation, or in extreme cases discussion with the B4's system specialist.

---

* **H**ypermedia with **E**nhanced **L**inking **P**roviding **M**aintenance and **A**nalysis **T**ools for **E**ngineering

1.2 Benefits to OSS

The B4 robot station is a key installation on the Yard, and because there are no replacement or backup installations, the work performed on the B4 robot station directly influences the output of the Yard. For the B4 robot station, and other installations with the same crucial role, a diagnosis hypermedia maintenance tool, which the HelpMate technology provides, is essential for the following reasons:

- The reliability of the installation is improved;
- The quality of the work performed by the installation is improved;
- As reliability improves, planning on the entire production line is easier;
- Time wasted waiting on maintenance experts is minimised;
- Experts can be released from existing installations, and be used for development of new technology;
- The maintenance costs are minimised.

2 Case-Based Reasoning and Inductive Learning

2.1 Principles

Case-Based Reasoning (CBR) and inductive learning are different but complementary methods for utilising past information in solving problems. Case-Based Reasoning [1] stores past examples, and assigns decisions to new data by relating it to past cases. A case is defined as the description of a problem that has been successfully solved in the past, along with its solution. When a new problem is encountered, CBR recalls similar cases and adapts the solutions that worked in the past for the current problem. Inductive learning [2] creates a general description of past examples, and then applies this description to new data. Inductive learning extracts a decision tree from the whole case history and then uses this general knowledge for problem solving.

In all its various meanings, inductive learning or "induction" has to do with reaching conclusions about a whole class of facts based on evidence on part of that class. Recorded cases of equipment failure and repair, legal cases and their adjudication, or the credit records of debtors all are a small part of the potential events in each of these areas. The original idea of what we call induction is to generalise the lessons of past cases into rules, in order to remain consistent with the way human experts think while providing the input to expert systems that knowledge engineers failed to [3, 4].

The inductive method is based on a decision tree created from case history. The diagnosis system then uses this tree for problem solving. Inductive learning requires that the data be structured, for example by using classes of objets with slots. A standard relational database schema can easily be mapped onto this object model. It allows defining the vocabulary used to describe the cases. For example, an error code on a control panel or the weld quality.

Instead of building a generalisation of a database as the inductive learning approach does, CBR directly looks for similar cases in the database, with respect to the requirements of the user. CBR offers flexible indexing and retrieval based on similarity. For applications where safety is important, the conclusions can be further confirmed, or refuted, by entering additional parameters that may modify the similarity values. CBR appeals to those professionals who solve problems by recalling what they did in similar situations. It works well even in domains that are poorly understood or where rules have many exceptions.

2.2 Application in HelpMate

We used the Kate suite of CBR tools to capture the experience in the form of a case base. We followed the INRECA2 methodology [5] so that we could apply a classical CBR development:

1. Defining an initial data model
2. Creating a questionnaire and acquiring the cases
3. Defining the fault tree and the similarity measures
4. Updating the previous points when additional knowledge / cases are available

We worked in close co-operation with the B4 robot cell specialist at each step of the development. However, it appeared quickly that this approach did not match completely with the specialist's one, since he expressed his knowledge directly in terms of rules. Therefore we developed an additional tool to capture his knowledge in a theoretical failure tree, in order to extract automatically analytical cases from this tree. We then moved from the normal development scheme presented above, to a more integrated one where cases can be described both in an analytical way by the specialist, and in a standard way by using the system and logging its results. We finally chose to apply an inductive learning approach in order to create a common decision tree from both the analytical and the real cases. Additionally, we kept track of statistics of the cases reached when the system is running so that the measure of similarity between the problem and the different solutions evolves over time in order to favour the most probable solutions. Therefore, the different steps are:

1. Defining / updating the data model
2. Creating / updating analytical cases through the theoretical failure tree
3. Creating / updating real cases through analysing the log reports
4. Merging the analytical and the real cases
5. Creating / updating the decision tree
6. Updating the statistical records of cases to assess the similarity

At the time when the system was put into operation (15th of February 1999), the case base contained more than 250 cases. The application covered an estimated 95 % of the known faults which generate an error code on Rob-Ex (in excess of 40 error and sub-error codes), giving access to approximately 80 repair procedures.

3 Hypermedia Documentation

3.1 Principles

Whilst the CBR technology provides the diagnosis, CBR does not provide any of the information required to undertake a repair. In most cases extra information is needed, including the location of the fault, together with the relevant repair and recommissioning procedures. In the case of a large industrial plant this information is currently supplied in paper or electronic format from a large number of suppliers. Hence even if the fault is known, the operator still has to locate the correct procedure, from what in many robotic systems can be a small library of information.

Hypermedia is particularly suited to engineering applications, as information is conventionally organised into a large number of relatively small documents, with a considerable amount of cross-referencing. In addition at any one time the user will only require assess to a small fraction of the available information resource.

The concept of industrial strength hypermedia as a solution to information management in manufacturing was initially proposed by [6]. Malcolm argued for hypermedia systems that had evolved beyond a stand-alone status to become a technology that integrates resource over the complete engineering enterprise. In a previous industrial hypermedia application, Crowder *et al.* [7] demonstrated that by using an open hypermedia system, a common knowledge base can be used for a range of tasks.

In any hypermedia application two sets of data are required, the resource documents and the linking information. It should be noted that a number of industrial information systems have the link information embedded within the resources, resulting in a closed application [8]. The use of embedded information will restrict the application of hypermedia systems to industrial applications, as any document change, however minor, could lead to a significant re-authoring exercise. An open hypermedia system permits the development of industrial strength hypermedia, which incorporates an easily maintained system which can be integrated with existing networks, databases, and as discussed in this paper knowledge based system technologies.

3.2 Application in HelpMate

The B4 robot station information consists of a considerable number of loose leave documents, drawings ranging from A4 to A0, and proprietary information, including engineering drawings, location drawings, test schedules. To speed the processing of text based material, use is made of optical character recognition software capable of processing documents in Danish. During the development of this application, at times it was considered quicker to redraw, or re-enter the information in the correct format, than convert the documents to electronic format, particular if the quality was poor.

However some concern has been expressed with the maintenance of the audit trail in this situation.

In all over one hundred documents were converted to populate the resource base of the pilot system. Following the construction of the resource base, the link base can be constructed. MicroCosm is supplied with a set of tools that ensure authoring is an efficient process. Three different types of approach to linking are required:

- Structural linking of the documents, for example indexes to sections of manuals. This is a routine process that can easily by automated. The hierarchical structure of many technical documents comes to the aid of the industrial author as most chapters, sections, and subsections, etc. are formatted using heading styles or at least have a different format to the rest of the text
- The robot specialist who is experienced in the subject area makes manual links. This turns the information into a cognitive and pedagogical structure that is easy to navigate.
- The robot specialist makes the links between the solutions provided by the KATE system and the information resources provided.

The development of the application is by necessity an iterative process. The robot specialist was asked which documents were linked, and then the developers implemented this and confirmed with by the robot specialist. In this way the operators can capture the organisational memory for use in the cell.

The number of incorporated documents in the delivered system was more than 500 and the number of links was more than 2000.

4 Integration Between CBR and Hypermedia

The Freya system required the technology partners to extend their basic software, Kate [9] and MicroCosm Pro [10], to function in an integrated manner as a hypermedia diagnostic system interfacing to the Rob-Ex cell control system. The generic integrated part has been called KateCosm, and is designed to be reused for other similar applications. The KateCosm architecture is based onto three reusable objects:

- The Kate filter
- The MicroCosm filter interface for creating indirect links (set of functions)
- The Kate system book

These different parts are detailed below.

4.1 The KateCosm Architecture

MicroCosm Pro integrates the various required functions into a single application system. MicroCosm systems contain "filters" that carry out actions (e.g. Compute Links) requested by the User or requested by other filters: MicroCosm "viewers" present resources such as documents or video clips to the User and capture the actions the User wishes to apply to the resource. The communication is via an internal message protocol that can be extended to other system components via the Windows

DDE system. A new *Kate filter* is added to MicroCosm to integrate Rob-Ex and Kate into the MicroCosm system. Being a filter it can receive messages from other parts of MicroCosm and it can send messages to be handled by other components. The filter accepts messages from the Rob-Ex filter, to pass control codes from the Rob-Ex system into Kate. The filter embodies a new set of common functions (a Windows' DLL) that serves as the MicroCosm side of the code interface to Kate. The filter receives MicroCosm messages from Kate indicating the links to be made available and generates the MicroCosm messages that cause MicroCosm to present the links (typically by a MicroCosm Results box).

MicroCosm Pro is an environment that supports reading and authoring from the same configuration and via the same User interfaces (though it is always possible to install MicroCosm so that authoring of hypermedia links is unavailable for particular users). MicroCosm supplies "linkbase filters" to create and edit the links. The request to add a link is made via a Viewer's "Action" menu item while the documents are in the viewer: the request is passed to the linkbase filter which in turn communicates with the user to capture further details about the intended new link (a link title, for instance).

MicroCosm's link creation process supports Button Links - the standard hypertext concept in the WWW or Windows Help, and "Generic Links". The latter are associations between a phrase, the source selection, and a destination that may be in any document. But rather than applying just to a single occurrence of the phrase in a given document, a generic link applies to any occurrence of the phrase anywhere in the document set. Consequently the link has to be authored once only - but is effective from any number of documents.

The generic link idea is taken further in KateCosm to tailor links to the CBR environment - the "Indirect Link", or *Linking by Reference*. These indirect links have Source Selections that refer to a Kate data model, expressed by the Classes, Slots and Values used in the Case. This offers a number of benefits - thus Natural Language can be switched just by substituting a new table, and Diagnostic cases can be rearranged without having to re-author the associated hypermedia links. KateCosm has a *MicroCosm Filter User Interface* for authoring indirect links.

The MicroCosm Pro message model ties the KateCosm software components together. Events from Rob-Ex are presented to other MicroCosm filters as MicroCosm messages. MicroCosm messages are communicated from Kate to MicroCosm to indicate the hypermedia links to be offered to the user at each stage during the consultation. In the latter case the messages indicate the Table indexes of the hypertext links needed at a given stage in the consultation.

A Kate CBR application can be written in one of two ways – using a scripting language (e.g., ToolBook) to develop all the CBR case screens, or by programming these screens directly using the C interfaces to Kate. KateCosm takes advantage of the ToolBook approach to minimise application development effort and complexity. Kate offers a ToolBook System script, the *System Book*, to integrate Kate with other software; the KateCosm integration exploits this script which has been extended to cope with the new functionality required.

4.2 Freya Architecture

Freya is the application based onto the KateCosm architecture, specifically designed to diagnose the B4 robot station. Therefore we retrieve the main components of KateCosm, applied to the welding robot specific data model, case base and hypermedia documentation. Figure 1 presents the architecture.

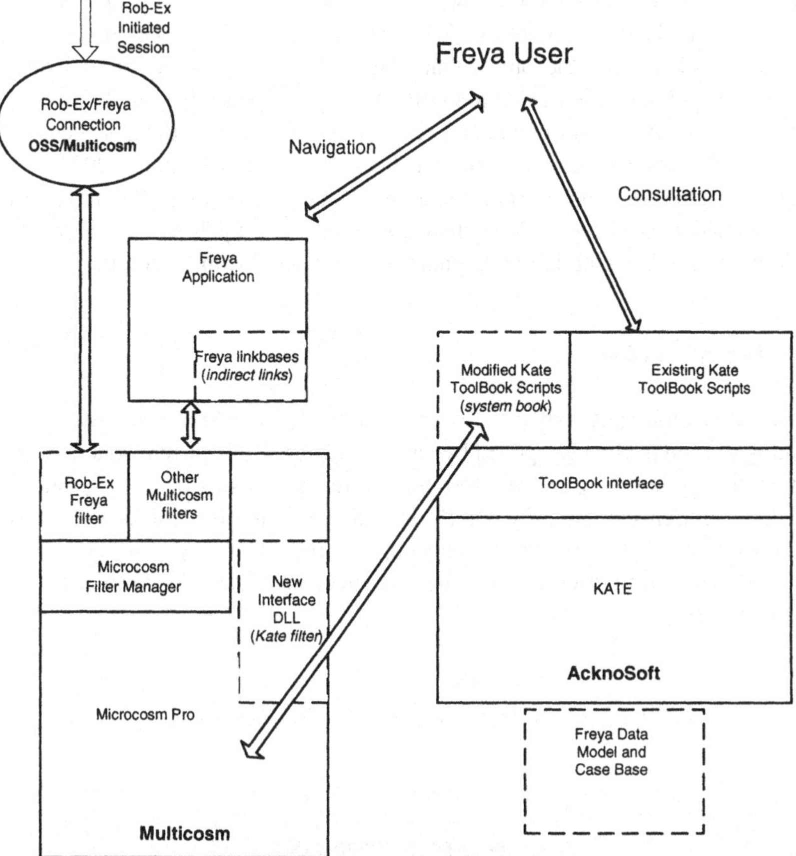

Fig. 1. Freya Architecture. The Freya user starts the navigation in the MicroCosm environment and can follow the links found in the Freya linkbases. From there he can start a consultation and launch the Freya system book. When browsing the fault tree, the indirect links between the Freya data model and the Freya linkbases are displayed automatically and the user can follow them thank to the Kate filter.

5 Current State of the Application

A small-scale pilot system has been used at OSS since the summer 1998, to obtain initial users feedback, and to let the operators gain confidence in the technology. The feedback has been highly positive with the users taking a degree of ownership of the project. This can be achieved by actively encouraging the users to voice their concerns and criticism, and feeding this back into the design process. As will be appreciated the factory floor is a hostile environment for any piece of computer equipment, in particular when the operator's input device is subjected to dirt and grease. While Freya could be kept in a supervisor's office, to gain maximum benefits from the system, it was clear from the outset that a machine on the factory floor would be required. For the interface device a modified tracker ball is used, these are easy to use and do not suffer from problems experienced by the mouse or touch screens.

A first full-scale pilot application has been delivered in January 1999, to enable to have the feedback of super-users. The first version has been installed in the B4 hall in February 1999 and is regularly evaluated internally and updated with respect to users' wish list (fixing bugs, updating diagnosis process and documentation).

5.1 Typical Session

A typical session starts when the operator chooses his name in the user's list. If an existing session is already opened by another operator, the current state is stored in an history file so that the previous operator can restart his session at his point of use (it should be recognised that only one PC is available in the B4 hall for Freya). An additional tool called the «wrapper» manages this part of the system. Then operator is presented with two options, to use the system as an information resource or follow a diagnostic procedure.

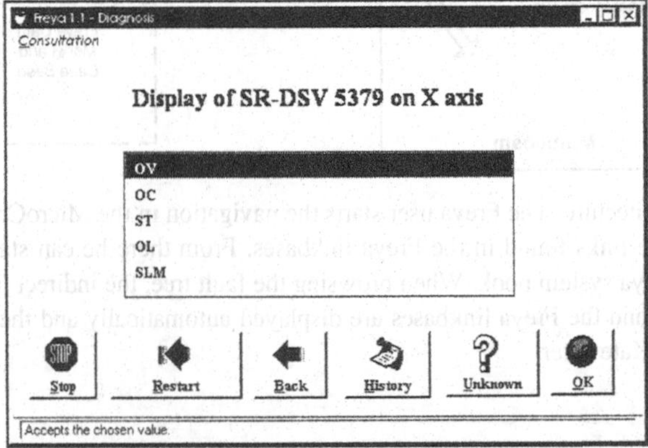

Fig. 2. Typical session during the diagnosis process. At each level of the decision process, the operator can display the list of solutions reached so far, go back and modify a previous level, select one of the proposed values or select "Unknown" to enlarge the search.

As an information resource the operator is taken to an index page, and by following links can navigate the resource to locate the information. When starting a diagnostic procedure the operator follows a question and answer dialogue session, using the user interface as that shown in Figure 2.

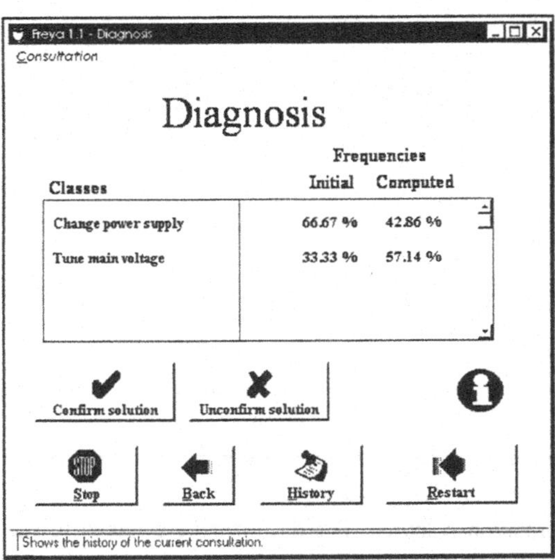

Fig. 3. Once the operator reaches a set of possible solutions, he can compare the initial probability of each solution as provided in the case base and the computed frequency based on real cases. He can confirm the solution (and hence, update the case statistics) or unconfirm it (then he has to provide the correct solution).

Once the answer is selected, selection of *'OK'* takes the user to the next stage in the case. If however the question can not be easily answered, selection of the *'?'* presents the operators with a range of option, with respective probabilities, the most probable solution based on the operator's knowledge of the problem and on case statistics can be selected (Figure 3). The operator has the opportunity to confirm the solution proposed, which changes the statistic of the case base and therefore the computed frequency of solutions, or unconfirm it. In the latter case, he is required to indicate what would be the correct solution. All operators' actions are traced into a log report, which is regularly analysed by the B4 specialist in order to update the case base.

At any place during the diagnosis process a point may be reached where information is required. A link then takes the user to the open hypermedia resource base, allowing the repair to be undertaken. The Kate filter paints automatically the active links in blue (this is not shown in the back-and-white screenshots). Figure 4 shows a typical page of information.

Remark: All the figures presented below have an English interface for the sake of clarity. In the system installed in the B4 hall, the user interface and the data model are in Danish. This does not affect the linking procedure thank to the indirect links. Additionally, this multi-language approach makes it easy to evolve to other languages in the future.

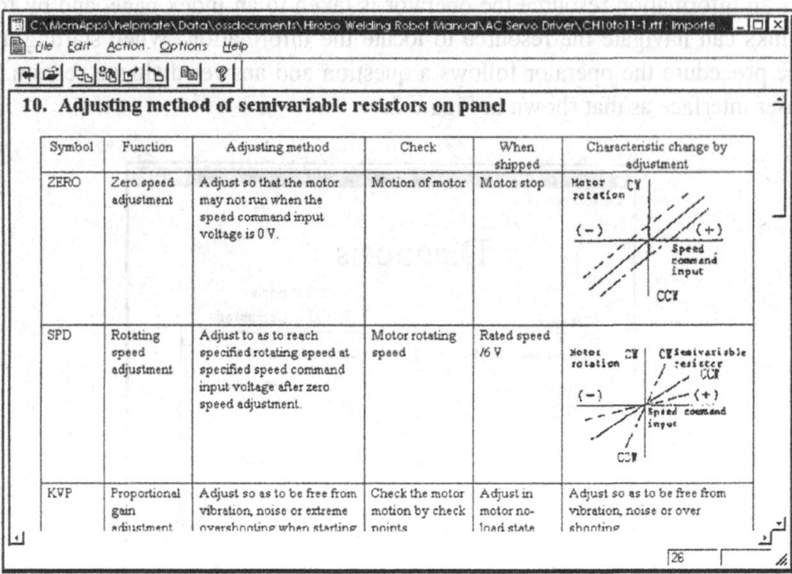

C:\McmApps\helpmate\Data\ossdocuments\Hirobo Welding Robot Manual\AC Servo Driver\CH10to11-1.rtf : Imported

File Edit Action Options Help

10. Adjusting method of semivariable resistors on panel

Symbol	Function	Adjusting method	Check	When shipped	Characteristic change by adjustment
ZERO	Zero speed adjustment	Adjust so that the motor may not run when the speed command input voltage is 0 V.	Motion of motor	Motor stop	Motor rotation CW (−) (+) Speed command input CCW
SPD	Rotating speed adjustment	Adjust to as to reach specified rotating speed at specified speed command input voltage after zero speed adjustment.	Motor rotating speed	Rated speed /6 V	Motor rotation CW CW Semivariable resistor CCW (−) (+) Speed command input CCW
KVP	Proportional gain adjustment	Adjust so as to be free from vibration, noise or extreme overshooting when starting	Check the motor motion by check points	Adjust in motor no-load state	Adjust so as to be free from vibration, noise or over shooting

26

Fig. 4. Typical information resource. The documents are linked to each other thank to the MicroCosm linkbase.

6 Evaluation

We describe in this section the current results of this on-going project, both in terms of the development efforts involved, and in term of improvement of the performance and easiness of the diagnostic process.

6.1 Main Dates and Efforts Involved

The HelpMate project started in September 1997 and will end up in November 1999. Most of the time during the first year has been spent on technical work for building the bridge, called KateCosm, between the case-based reasoning and the multimedia tools. In parallel, a pilot system was developed and delivered in June 1998 in order to collect the end-users requirements. The first version of the system has been delivered in January 1999 and installed after testing in the B4 hall on the 15th of February 1999. A second version has been delivered in April 1999. During the development process, an end-user's "wish list" has been continuously maintained in order to improve the system in the desired way.

The overall effort for the HelpMate project was estimated as follow:

- Technical integration between the case based and the hypermedia tools: 7 months
- Model building and case authoring: 6 months
- Hypermedia preparation: 7 months
- System development: 9 months
- Organisation (training, operation, tuning, evaluation…): 10 months

In practice, it appeared that the technical part (integration and system development) required more effort than expected. For the integration part, this is due to the fact that we wanted create a generic integration procedure between Kate and MicroCosm, beyond the target application. For the system development part, this is due to the two-steps approach chosen (pilot + several versions delivered). The user requirements that arose from the pilot were much more complex and difficult to complete than it was expected when we started the project. Additionally, new tools were required both for the development part (e.g., the tool for building analytical cases from fault trees) and for the application part (e.g., the wrapper, and the tool for logging the end-users actions). On the other hand, the case authoring was easier to complete, thanks to the pilot system. It was recognised that analytical cases were needed, which were available directly from the super-users under the form of fault trees. The analysis of cases provided by the end-users was eased thanks to the log facility.

6.2 Freya Users

There are a number of different types of users of Freya. Table 1 lists the various categories and indicates the number of users in each category. "Normal" users can consult the system. They can confirm or unconfirm a solution proposed by the diagnostic tool. Their actions are logged into a log file so that it is possible to create new cases or to modify existing cases by analysing the content of the log files. More generally, all actions of the users (cases used, solutions obtained, documents browsed...) are logged for further analysis. The super-users have different rights in Freya. They can create new cases or validate existing ones, modify the data model, create new links between the documents etc. Also the super-users do the initial test of a new version of Freya. Among the super-users, the service co-ordinator has a specific role: He is responsible for maintaining up to date the case base, the document base, the data model and more globally the diagnostic system.

Table 1. The type and number of Freya users

HelpMate users	Nb. of users	Reserve users	Nb. of super-users within each user type
Operators	12	5	1
Maintainers	3	2	1
Foreman	1	1	
Service co-ordinator	1	0	1

- *The operators*: As shown in the table above, there are 12 full-time operators and 5 reserve operators. The welding robot installation in hall B4 is operated 24 hours daily, by 3 separate shifts. There are 4 operators per shift. The operators main tasks are to perform daily robot welding operations, to repair minor faults and to co-ordinate major repairs.
- *The maintainer*: There are 3 (not full-time) maintainers and 1 reserve maintainer. The maintainers' main tasks are to perform routine preventive maintenance and major reparations.

- *The foreman*: There is only one foreman responsible for the robot system. The foreman's main tasks are to co-ordinate and to plan the production of assemblies at the robot station in shop B4.
- *The service co-ordinator*: There is one service co-ordinator for co-ordinating and planning the routine and emergency servicing of all robot installations in the yard. He is also responsible for helping other shipyards, using the OSS robot systems, to detect robot faults. The service co-ordinator's role has not become fully established, because the position is relatively new.

6.3 Results of the Evaluation

The main goal of the second phase of the project, which has started with the release of the first version of Freya in the B4 hall in February 1999, aims at evaluating the results of the system. This is achieved through round-table discussions between B4 robot station maintenance and production personnel, and through direct measurements of the time spent for diagnostic and documentation search tasks.

It is too early in the evaluation to have a clear measurement about the quantitative gains associated to the use of Freya. However, it is felt than Freya can contribute to reduce the expenses of maintaining complicated technological gantry systems and to reduce robot down time caused by repetitive faults and no cause found, which can affect the cost effectiveness of the gantry system. More results will be available in a later phase.

According to OSS, the results of the HelpMate application are today mainly qualitative. Freya helps:

- To involve the robot operators in the maintenance process by creating greater competence in diagnosing and repairing minor failures in the system. The robot operators do not need to refer systematically to the maintainer each time a failure occurs. This saves the maintainer's time for other tasks, and increase the availability of the robots since the failures are repaired quicker;
- To exchange and expand knowledge and experience concerning maintenance. This is particularly true for the maintainers, the foreman and the service coordinator;
- To accelerate operator training. The introduction of Freya required regular teachings by the service coordinator to the operators. As a consequence, operators working during the day shifts could share their experience with the ones working during the night shift;
- To create an on-line help system for the operators and to give the operators easy access to pertinent information.

7 Conclusion

The HELPMATE project aims to take the diagnostic capabilities of case-based reasoning and augment this with open hypermedia linking technology to provide the operator with important context information regarding the problems and solutions presented to him. This has been achieved through a seamless integration of two industrial products, Kate and MicroCosm Pro. It is a major challenge, not only to provide a single application for the specific need of the B4 robot station at OSS, but also to develop a pragmatic and repeatable processes in order to ensure that the system receives acceptance by the people tasked with robot maintenance. In the future, Freya is expected to be used for other robot stations and other types of equipment, such as cutting machines and cranes. The industrial partners of HelpMate will sell the Kate-Cosm solution as an add-on of their specific own product.

8 Acknowledgements

The authors acknowledge the European Commission for funding HELPMATE under grant number ESPRIT IV, project 25282.

9 References

1. Aamodt A. & Plaza E., "Case-based reasoning: Foundational issues, methodological variations, and system approaches". AI Communications 7, Vol. 1, 1994.
2. Quinlan J. R., "Learning Efficient Classification Procedures and their Application to Chess End Games", in Machine Learning 1: an Artificial Intelligence Approach, Michalski R.S., Carbonell J.G. & Mitchell T.M. (eds.), Morgan Kaufmann, Redwood City CA, 1983.
3. Manago M. & Auriol E., "Application of Inductive Learning and Case-Based Reasoning for Troubleshooting Industrial Machines", in Machine Learning and Data Mining – Methods and Applications, Michalski R.S., Bratko, I. & Kubat, M. (eds.), John Wiley & Sons, 1998.
4. Lenz M., Auriol E. & Manago M., "Diagnosis and Decision Support", in Case-Based Reasoning Technology – From Foundations to Applications, Lenz M., Bartsch-Spörl B., Burkhard H.-D. & Wess S. (eds.), Springer, 1998.
5. Bergmann R., Breen S., Göker M., Manago M. & Wess S. (eds.), "Developing Industrial Case Based Reasoning Applications - The INRECA Methodology", Springer, 1999 (to appear).
6. Malcolm K, Poltrock S. & Schuler D., "Industrial Strength Hypermedia: Requirements for a Large Engineering Enterprise". *Proceedings of Hypertext'91*, December 1991.
7. Crowder R. M., Hall W., Heath I., Bernard R. & Gaskall D., "A Hypermedia Maintenance Information System". *IEE Computing and Control Engineering Journal, 7(3), 1996, 109-13.*
8. Greenough R. & Fakun D., "An innovative information system to support team based maintenance". *3rd International Conference:* Managing Innovative Manufacturing, Nottingham UK, July 1998.
9. Further information on MicroCosm can be found at http://www.multicosm.com/
10. Further information on Kate can be found at http://www.acknosoft.com/

Integrating Rule-Based and Case-Based Decision Making in Diabetic Patient Management*

Riccardo Bellazzi[1], Stefania Montani[1], Luigi Portinale[2], Alberto Riva[1]

[1] Dipartimento di Informatica e Sistemistica
Università di Pavia, Pavia (Italy)
[2] Dipartimento di Scienze e Tecnologie Avanzate,
Università del Piemonte Orientale "A. Avogadro", Alessandria, (Italy)

Abstract. The integration of rule-based and case-based reasoning is particularly useful in medical applications, where both general rules and specific patient cases are usually available. In the present paper we aim at presenting a decision support tool for Insulin Dependent Diabetes Mellitus management relying on such a kind of integration. This multi-modal reasoning system aims at providing physicians with a suitable solution to the problem of therapy planning by exploiting, in the most flexible way, the strengths of the two selected methods. In particular, the integration is pursued without considering one of the modality as the most prominent reasoning method, but exploiting complementarity in all possible ways. In fact, while rules provide suggestions on the basis of a situation detection mechanism that relies on structured prior knowledge, CBR may be used to specialize and dynamically adapt the rules on the basis of the patient's characteristics and of the accumulated experience. On the other hand, if a particular patient class is not sufficiently covered by cases, the use of rules may be exploited to try to learn suitable situations, in order to improve the competence of the case-based component. Such a work will be integrated in the EU funded project T-IDDM architecture, and has been preliminary tested on a set of cases generated by a diabetic patient simulator.

1 Introduction

The interest in multi-modal approaches involving Case-Based Reasoning (CBR) as a fundamental modality is recently increasing in very different areas and tasks [1,9]. In fact, because of its "inductive" nature, CBR is well suited for integration with other reasoning paradigms grounded on more general knowledge such as Rule-Based or Model-Based systems. Particular attention has received the combination of CBR with Rule-Based Reasoning (RBR), since rules are in fact the most succesful knowledge representation formalism for intelligent systems.

Such a kind of integration has been pursued in very different tasks like planning [4], diagnosis [13], legal reasoning [18,5] and classification [21]. In such approaches, RBR and CBR can cooperate at different levels. The usual integration

* This paper is part of the EU TAP project T-IDDM HC 1047.

is represented by the Rule-Based system dealing with knowledge on standard or typical situations, letting CBR to face problems that are not typically covered by rules. In this view, RBR is usually applied first; when it fails to provide the user with a reliable solution, CBR allows one to retrieve similar cases from a library of peculiar and non-standard situations [21]. Other approaches suggest to exploit the differences in generality between rules and cases, so rules are used as an "abstract" description of a situation, while cases represent a further "specialization". Cases assist RBR by instantiating and by providing suitable contexts to rules, while rules assist CBR by permitting the extraction of more general concepts from concrete examples [5]. In this case, the resulting architecture may be more flexible than in the previous kind of approach, as it is possible to decide "a priori" which method should be applied first, or to select the most convenient one in a dynamic way, depending on the situation at hand [5, 3]. In particular, the rule base and the case memory can be searched in parallel for applicable entities. Then the best entity (i.e. rule or case) to reuse (and therefore the reasoning paradigm to apply) can be selected on the basis of its suitability for solving the current problem [3].

The common basis of all the above approaches (except perhaps the work in [5]) is that CBR and RBR are to some extent used in a quite exclusive way. In the present paper, we propose an approach combining rules and cases in a medical application, where the cooperation between RBR and CBR takes place within a general problem-solving cycle. This results in a very tight integration with cases and rules flexibly used during problem solving.

The basic philosophy underlying this work is to overcome the limitations of the two paradigms. On one side, we aim at providing a Rule-Based system with the capability to *specialize* the rules on the basis of the patient's characteristics, by trying to avoid the *qualification problem* (i.e. without highly increasing the number of rules for dealing with more specific situations); moreover we would like some rules (or part of them) to be *dynamically* adapted on the basis of the past available experience. On the other side, we would like to provide a CBR system with a module for giving suggestions based on structured prior knowledge, and not only on the case library; this can be realized in at least two ways: by using general knowledge coded into rules as the basis for adapting retrieved solutions of past cases and by "filling the competence gap" that the CBR component may have because of the specific nature of cases. This capability is particularly important for medical applications, since final decisions should be always based on established knowledge.

2 The Application Framework: IDDM Patient Management

Medical applications are a natural framework where the integration of structured general knowledge and more specific situations can be exploited; indeed, well-established knowledge is in general available in forms of rules [3], prototypes [20] or models [11] and specific knowledge may be obtained from patient case-bases.

Following the ideas outlined in section 1, we have defined a multi-modal decision support tool for the management of Insulin Dependent Diabetes Mellitus (IDDM) patients. Rather interestingly, while Rule-Based systems have been largely exploited in the context of medical problems, no examples of Case-Based Reasoning (CBR) systems for diabetes therapy can be found in the literature, although, being IDDM a chronic disease, it would be possible to rely on a large amount of patient data, coming both from periodical control visits and from home monitoring.

IDDM patients undergo control visits every 2/4 months; during these visits physicians analyze the data coming from home monitoring, in order to assess the metabolic control achieved in the period under examination. The results of such analysis are then combined with other available information, such as laboratory results and historical and/or anamnestic data, in order to revise the patient's therapeutic protocol. During this complex process, the physician may detect some problems and propose a solution relying on some **structured knowledge** (i.e. the pharmacodynamic of insulin, the main drug provided in the protocol) as well as on the specific patient behavior (i.e. young or adult patient) and on **previous experience** (i.e. the information that a certain protocol has been applied on that patient or to patients with similar characteristics in the past, with a particular outcome). When dealing with automated decision support in IDDM management, the combination of different reasoning tools seems a natural solution: the widely-recognized scientific knowledge is formalized in our system as a set of rules [7], while additional knowledge, consisting of evidence-based information, is represented through a database of past cases collected by physicians during visits. The latter kind of knowledge is very important, since information gathered from periodic visits is the ground for any therapy adjustment.

In this paper we present the overall architecture of the multi-modal reasoning system, as well as a first implementation developed within the EU-project T-IDDM. In particular, the Rule-Based system has been defined in collaboration with the Department of pediatrics of the Policlinico S. Matteo Hospital of Pavia, and has been revised on the basis of the suggestions of the medical partners of T-IDDM [14]. The case-base has been derived from the clinical records of 29 patients, for a total of 145 cases collected at the Policlinico S. Matteo Hospital in Pavia. The details of the proposed architecture are presented in the following.

3 Integrating CBR and RBR for IDDM Patient Management

3.1 The CBR System

The CBR component of our decision support tool is based on the architecture we described in [2]. A case is defined by a set of feature-value pairs, by a solution and by an outcome: formally it is the triple

$$C = \{\langle F : f\rangle, \langle S : s\rangle, \langle O : o\rangle\}$$

where f is the vector of values for the set of descriptive features F, s is the solution schemata selected from the solution space S and o is the outcome of the solution selection in the space of the possible outcomes O.
In IDDM management, we interpret a periodical control visit as a case. In this context, F summarizes the set of data collected during the visit; we have defined 27 features of which 6 are *linear (continuous)*, and 21 are *nominal (discrete)*; among them, some are abstractions of the raw visit data. The features are extracted from three sources of information: *general characterization* (e.g. sex, age, distance from diabetes onset), *mid-term information*, (e.g. weight, Glycated Hemoglobin (HbA1c) values), and *short term (day-by-day) information* (e.g. the number of hypoglycemic episodes). The solution s is the array of insulin types and doses prescribed by the physician after the analysis of the feature values, and the outcome o of the therapeutic decision is obtained by inspecting HbA1c and the number of hypoglycemic events at the following visit. Table 1 in section 4 shows a subset of an example case features. To make retrieval more flexible we have structured the case memory resorting to a taxonomy of prototypical classes, that express typical problems that may occur to patients[1].

Retrieval is hence implemented as a two-step procedure: a *classification* step, that proposes to the physician the class of cases to which the current case could belong, and a proper *retrieval* step, that effectively identifies the "closest" past cases. This will allow the actual retrieval to be focused on the most relevant part of the case library; as a consequence a very simple *flat memory* organization is sufficient to store cases inside a given class[2].

The taxonomy on which we based our classification consists of a set of mutually exclusive classes that may occur to IDDM pediatric patients (see figure 1). Root class (*Patient's problems*) represents the most general class including all the possible cases we may store into the case memory. The root's subclasses are prototypical descriptions of the set of situations they summarize. In more detail, an inner node (called *macroclass*) represents a class with certain properties that all the classes of its descending subtree have in common, while leaves (called *basic classes*) provide the most detailed description of pathologies, or clinical course conditions taken in consideration. Each case in the case memory is an instance of a unique basic class and can be retrieved through such a class. The classification process aims at limiting the search space for similar cases to the context (i.e. the class, or a small number of classes in the taxonomy), into which the problem at hand can be better interpreted. In other words, we implement the usual *situation assessment* step of the CBR cycle [10] by means of prototype classification. Classification may be performed on the leaves of the taxonomy

[1] Even if at the current stage such a taxonomy is derived a-priori by consider general medical knowledge, the possibility of automatically discovering such a structure by means of clustering algorithms is currently under investigation.

[2] Actually, cases are stored in an Oracle^{TM} relational data-base, whose table structure mirrors the classes taxonomy; each leaf of the taxonomy tree matches a table, whose columns correspond to the case features, and whose rows are instances of the class at hand (i.e. the cases).

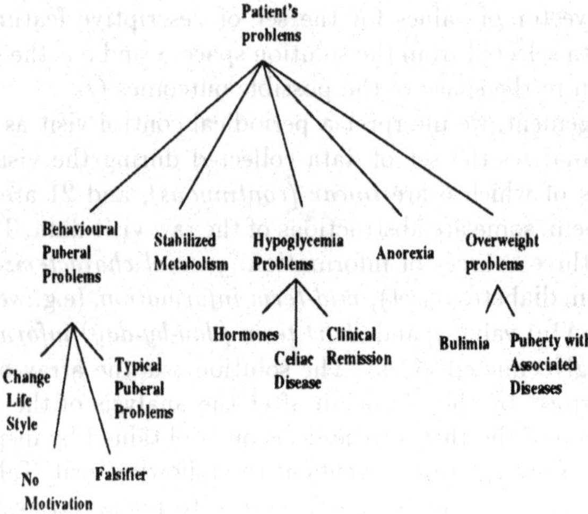

Fig. 1. Taxonomy of classes of prototypical situations that may happen during monitoring of pediatric IDDM patients

tree, to find the most probable classes to which the input case could belong; when several features in the case are missing, or when a less specific identification of the situation at hand is required, the classification step may be conducted just at the upper level of the tree, working on the more general macroclasses.

Our tool implements a Naive Bayes strategy, a method that assumes conditional independence among the features given a certain class, but that is known to be robust in a variety of situations [8], even in the presence of conditional dependencies[3]. In our application, the prior probability values were derived from expert's opinion, while posterior probabilities were learnt from the available case base (145 cases) by using a standard Bayesian updating technique [15].

The actual case retrieval takes place by exploiting the classification results. The physician is allowed to choose whether to retrieve cases belonging only to the most probable class identified by the classifier (*intra-class retrieval*), or to a set of possible classes (*inter-class retrieval*). Independently of the intra-class or inter-class choice, searching and matching procedures are based on a Nearest-Neighbor (NN) technique; what is different in the two situations is just the adopted distance metric. Indeed, if we focus our attention to just one class (the most probable one), a simple Heterogeneous Euclidean-Overlap Metric (HEOM) can be adopted; in the second hypothesis, we cannot rely on the surface similarity provided by HEOM and a metric like the Heterogeneous Value Difference Metric (HVDM) has to be considered. In this situation, differences are evaluated by explicitly considering the class of each case (see [22] for a general discussion on HEOM and HVDM and [2] for more details on the application in our system). Both methods are applicable not only for numeric and continuous variables, but

[3] See [2, 15] for details of the implementation.

also for symbolic ones. Moreover, since HVDM may be computationally inefficient when working with case-bases of relevant size[4], we have also implemented a non exhaustive search procedure, that exploits an anytime algorithm called *Pivoting-Based Retrieval* (PBR) [16]. Experimental results have shown the efficacy of PBR in our application, even for large case-bases (see [2] for evaluation on a case library containing more than 10000 cases).

3.2 The Rule-Based System

The Rule-Based system relies on a taxonomy of rule classes, that embed the domain knowledge of the application; the production rules are fired through a forward chaining mechanism.

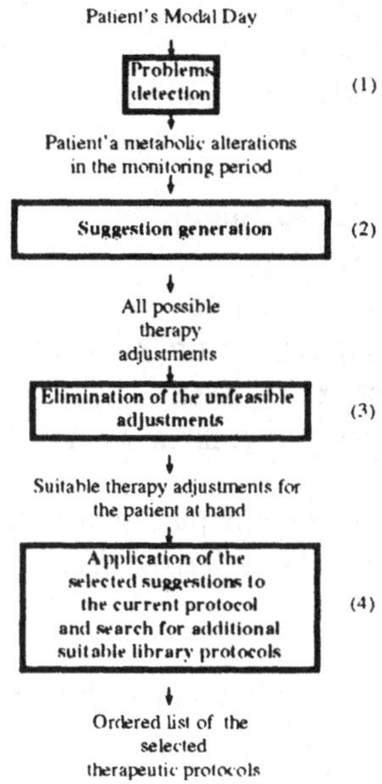

Fig. 2. Steps of the Rule-Based reasoning process.

The system performs a series of steps (see figure 2), each one relying upon a specific rule class.

Data analysis and problem identification.
In order to temporally contextualize the large amount of time-stamped data collected by patients during home monitoring (Blood Glucose Level (BGL) measurements, insulin doses and diet information), the day is subdivided into seven

[4] HVDM complexity is known to be $O(FnC)$ [22], where F is the number of features, n is the number of cases and C is the number of classes (proportional to the number of cases)

non-overlapping time-slices, centered on the injection and/or meal times. The raw data are then abstracted through a Temporal Abstractions (TA) technique [12]: in particular, STATE abstractions (e.g. low, normal, high values) are extracted and aggregated into intervals called *episodes*. From the most relevant episodes, it is possible to derive the **modal day** [12], an indicator able to summarize the average response of the patient to a certain therapy. The BGL modal day, in particular, is obtained by calculating the marginal probability distribution of the BGL state abstractions in each time slice, through the application of a Bayesian method able to explicitly take into account the presence of missing data [17].

After the BGL modal day has been calculated, the **problem detection rule class** is exploited, to identify the patient's metabolic alterations. Such rules act as follows: when the frequency (called *minimum probability*) of a certain BGL abstraction is higher then the α threshold, and when the number of missing data (called *ignorance*) is sufficiently small to rely on such information (i.e. it is smaller than the β threshold), a *problem* is detected. For example, the following rule detects a hypoglycemia problem in a generic time slice Y using the information contained in the relative modal day component X:

```
IF X IS A BGL-MODAL-DAY-COMPONENT
   AND THE TIME-SLICE OF X IS Y
   AND THE BGL-LEVEL OF X IS LOW
   AND THE MINIMUM-PROBABILITY OF X >= alpha
   AND THE IGNORANCE OF X <= beta
THEN GENERATE-PROBLEM HYPOGLYCEMIA AT Y
```

where α and β are the two threshold parameters that can be instantiated at run-time. Their default values where derived from medical knowledge, and are equal to 0.3 and 0.8 respectively.

Suggestions generation.
In order to cope with the problem it founds, the Rule-Based system generates a set of suggestions. Each rule in the **suggestion generation rule class** has a premise which is verified by the presence of a particular metabolic alteration. Rules are divided into subclasses on the basis of the advice they generate: a specific problem might be solved by adjusting the insulin doses, or by revising the diet, or the physical exercise plan. **Suggestions selection.**
Among all the generated suggestions, the system selects the most effective ones, always verifying their suitability for the patient at hand. Such a step relies upon the activation of two rule classes, the **suggestion selection rule class** and the **filtering rule class**. The premises of the *suggestion selection* rules take into account the patient's characteristics (e.g. age, associated diseases). The *filtering* rules are applied after the deletion of suggestions that resulted to be not admissible for the patient at hand, to identify just the most effective action in a single time slice.

Protocol revision.
Insulin suggestions are applied to the current insulin protocol by the **protocol**

rule class, obtaining a revised therapy for the patient at hand. If other suitable protocols are available in the system data-base, they are retrieved as well, and pushed in an ordered list. The more a protocol is similar to the current one (in terms of number of injections and of insulin doses for every injection), the higher position it takes in the list: the similarity is calculated using the HEOM method [22]. The physician is able to evaluate the system choices step by step, and finally to choose a suitable solution among the proposed ones.

3.3 Integration between CBR and RBR

As previously noted, the rule base is partitioned into a set of rule classes that perform the above outlined reasoning steps, and the order in which the rule classes are activated is determined by a set of *metarules*. The integration of CBR into this framework is achieved by defining additional metarules that guide the interaction between the results of the CBR procedures and the rule system. This corresponds to define a SUPERVISOR controlling the activation and integration of the CBR and RBR components by means of such metarules. Integration takes place by means of a *rule refinement* process involving the change of suitable rule parameters on the basis of information obtained from the case library (i.e. classification and retrieval).

Refinement affects rule parameters that without case specific information tend to deal with too general situations. This occurs as follows: rules are represented as objects characterized by an activation condition, an action and a set of parameters that influence both the activation condition and the action. In this phase, the parameters of the rules can be changed in order to obtain a more effective and more suitable definition of a therapy for the patient at hand. In particular, the behavior of two rule classes is affected.
Problem detection rules can be specialized by:

1. setting a proper value of the α *threshold* for the frequency of BGL abstractions;
2. defining the maximum admissible *number of missing data* so that the information may be relied upon (i.e. setting the β threshold).

This kind of refinement is made by considering the class of the patient to which the input case refers. This can be in principle either the most probable class pointed out by the Naive Bayes classifier, or the class of the most similar case if inter-class retrieval is required. In the latter situation, the process becomes a NN classification that may produce, in general, different results from the Naive Bayes technique[5].

For example, when dealing with patients suffering from anorexia, it is important to be able to promptly detect all hypoglycemic episodes, even when few data are available. This is motivated by the fact that such patients run a higher

[5] This should happen only if the posterior distribution on classes resulting from Bayesian classification is not significantly skewed.

risk of hypoglycemia, due to their nutritional disorder. This implies that the α threshold has to be decreased, while the β threshold has to be increased. As an example, the rule described in section 3.2 becomes:

```
IF X IS A BGL-MODAL-DAY-COMPONENT
   AND THE TIME-SLICE OF X IS Y
   AND THE BGL-LEVEL OF X IS LOW
   AND THE MINIMUM-PROBABILITY OF X >= 0.2
   AND THE IGNORANCE OF X <= 1
THEN GENERATE-PROBLEM HYPOGLYCEMIA AT Y
```

Suggestion generation rules can be specialized by modifying:

1. the *number of insulin doses* to be added or eliminated to tackle a metabolic alteration;
2. the overall *variation in daily requirement*;
3. the quantitative *variation in a single insulin dose*.

This is done by considering retrieved cases and in particular by correlating the metabolic state of the patient associated to the input case with the therapeutic actions adopted in retrieved insulin protocols.

In particular, the whole integration, summarized in figure 3, allows the physician to be provided with a suitable set of suggestions for insulin protocol adjustment, in the following way:

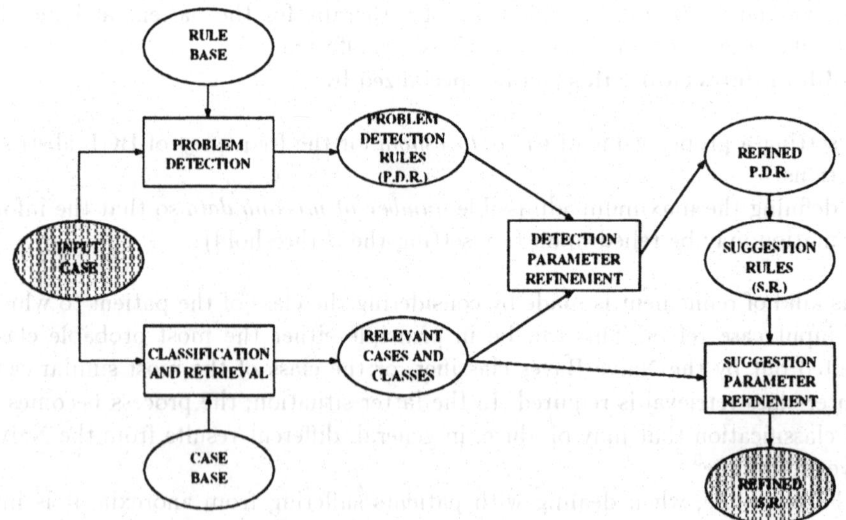

Fig. 3. CBR-RBR Integration

- The SUPERVISOR invokes the *Bayesian classifier* of the CBR module on the patient's visit data. During this step, the user of the system (i.e the physician) can choose whether to exploit only the results of the classification step, if the output is considered reliable, or to analyze the "closest" cases obtained through intra-class or inter-class retrieval.
- If the physician chooses to rely just on the Bayesian classification step, the information about the class is used to refine the α and β thresholds for the relevant problem detection rules and the rule-based system is then applied to such refined rules.
- If the physician decides to perform retrieval, a simple test on the applicability of the corresponding protocols is performed[6]. Only cases whose protocol has a positive test are considered for subsequent elaboration. If no such a case is retrieved, then RBR is applied without considering any CBR integration.
- If useful specific cases are obtained, both detection rules and suggestion rules can be in principle refined. In particular, NN classification (if different from the Bayesian one) can be exploited for detection parameter refinement. After that the relationships between the features describing the metabolic state of the patient and the therapeutic actions in the retrieved cases are evaluated. For example, the HbA1c trend and the insulin requirement trend are jointly analyzed to determine whether an increase in the former is treated with an increase in the latter. The results of retrieval will then be used only if the relationship is statistically significant (with a p-value of 0.1)[7].
- In case the previous step identifies a significant therapeutic action, the refinement of suitable suggestion rules takes place by distinguishing between cases having *positive outcome* (i.e. cases for which the applied protocol has resulted in a low number of hypoglycemic events and in a HbA1c decreasing trend) from those having *negative outcome* (all the others). Only for "positive cases" the result of the CBR process, is used to tailor the Rule-Based system according to the identified context. In particular, some descriptive statistics are used to set the *number of insulin injections* (voting strategy on the variation of injection number of retrieved positive cases or computation of the mean variation), the *variation of daily insulin requirement* (computation of mean variation) and the *variation of a single insulin dose* (computation of mean variation).
- The result of the previous step is a set of refined suggestion rules that can be used to complete the RBR cycle described in figure 2 for providing final suggestions to the physician.

To summarize, CBR influences steps (1) and (2) in figure 2, by transforming the sequence of such steps as shown in figure 3. Finally, the RBR proceeds with suggestions selection and with the definition of a list of alternative protocols, as described above. The integration, by making the system more effective in the detection of patient's problems, and in prescribing insulin modifications that can

[6] Such a test is simply based on the number of insulin doses (injections) they predict.

[7] A χ^2 test is applied to check if the conditional distribution of the insulin requirement trend given HbA1c trend is significantly different from the uniform distribution

be stronger or milder, depending on the context in which the RBR is operating, can enhance the RBR performance; in particular we expect the time needed for problem resolution to be reduced, through the definition of a therapy properly tailored on the patient's peculiar needs.

An important aspect of the above integration process concerns the fact that also CBR can take advantage of the result of RBR. In fact, if the outcome of CBR is not applicable in a given context (i.e. to a given input case and with a particular case library available), RBR is performed without integration, in order to avoid wrong specialization due to misleading cases. This situation suggests that a gap in the competence of the CBR component is present; our approach is to fill this gap by relying on the (possibly conservative) result of the RBR process. Indeed, in such a kind of situations (i.e. if no suitable case is retrieved, either because no positive outcome is found or because the retrieved therapeutic protocols are significantly different from the current one) then, as soon as the outcome of the proposed protocol is available (usually at the next periodical visit), a new case is learnt and stored in memory with the following parameters:
Descriptive features: the features of the input case;
Classification: either the class resulting from Bayesian classification if reliable or the class resulting from NN classification;
Solution: the insulin protocol suggested by the Rule-Based system;
Outcome: the resulting outcome.

4 Implementation and System Evaluation

From an implementation point of view, the RBR and the CBR systems are fully integrated in the T-IDDM architecture, a distributed, Web-based environment, where the cooperation among the different modules relies on *Lispweb*, an extended, special-purpose Web server written in Common Lisp, that makes it possible to create "intelligent" and "secure" applications while remaining in the context of Web-based systems [19]. In particular the T-IDDM service is provided by the communication between two main units: a Patient Unit (PU), meant to help patients in day by day self monitoring, and a Medical Unit (MU). The latter, devoted to assist physicians in IDDM patients management, includes the RBR and the CBR systems, and will soon be extended with the multi-modal reasoning functionality described in this paper.

In order to provide a first evaluation of multi-modal reasoning described in the previous sections, we have compared the performances of RBR with the ones of the CBR-RBR integrated approach in stabilizing the metabolic control of a simulated patient. The patient's characteristic features have been derived from a real pediatric patient case of our case memory, while her BGL measurements were generated by an IDDM patient simulator, developed in the context of the T-IDDM project [6]. The test has been carried out as an iterative procedure, consisting in simulating 7 days of monitoring data and then in revising the insulin protocol on the basis of the collected information.

Table 1 and table 2 report the most relevant features of the test patient, and the therapeutic protocol at the beginning of the experiment.

Age	19
Sex	Female
Weight	40
Height	160
HbA1c	5.1
HbA1c Trend	Decreasing
Insulin Requirement	0.6
Insulin Requirement Trend	Decreasing

Table 1. The main features defining the test case

Breakfast Regular Insulin	4
Breakfast NPH Insulin	0
Lunch Regular Insulin	4
Lunch NPH Insulin	0
Dinner Regular Insulin	4
Dinner NPH Insulin	12

Table 2. The therapeutic protocol at the beginning of the experiment

The CBR system identified the above case as an example of *anorexia*, and we used this information to refine the *problem detection rule class* (see section 3.3 for an example). By performing some statistical analyses on 20 cases retrieved through a NN technique, a significant result about the average variation of insulin doses in each injection was obtained; in particular the average variation of NPH insulin at dinner was equal to 4, while the default variation proposed by the Rule-Based system is of 1 unit. This result was used in the multi-modal approach to specialize the *suggestion generation rule class*, permitting a more aggressive action in insulin treatment. We began our study by generating 7 days of BGL data, with an average of three measurements per day and including also some post-prandial data. To introduce intra-patient variability, the data were derived adding a 10% noise on the simulation results. The obtained BGL values were analyzed both by the Rule-Based system and by the multi-modal reasoning system. The revised protocols were acquired by the simulator and used to obtain the data for the following monitoring period. Such procedure ended when the simulated patient metabolic condition was stabilized. Figure 4 shows the outcome of the Rule-Based system, while figure 5 shows the outcome of the integration approach. While the Rule-Based system, being more conservative and "cautious", took 4 weeks (i.e. 4 adjustments) to stabilize the simulated patient, the integrated approach was more effective, as 1 week was enough to produce the same result. These first validation results proved to be encouraging, although we aim at exploiting real patients' BGL measurements to get more reliable information.

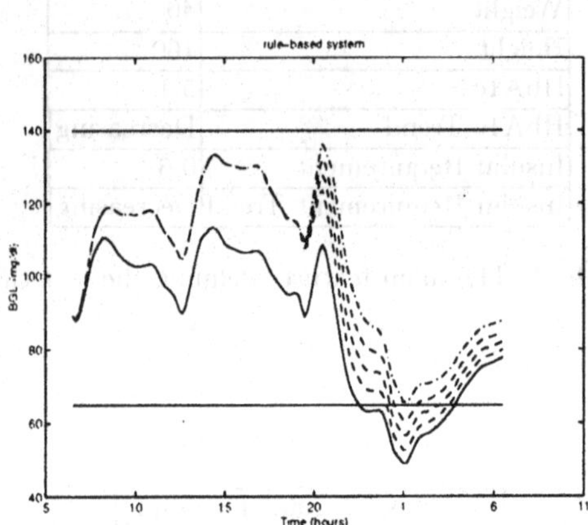

Fig. 4. The 24 hours profiles of blood glucose in response to the different therapeutic protocols proposed by the rule-based system. The patient's metabolic stabilization (within normal BGL ranges, i.e. 65-140 mg/dl), represented by the dash-dotted line, is obtained after three intermediate adjustments, represented by the dashed lines.

5 Conclusions

In this paper, we have described a reasoning approach that integrates CBR and RBR to provide suggestions on insulin therapy planning for IDDM patients. We plan to include the multi-modal reasoning system here described in the running prototype of T-IDDM. As a matter of fact, the T-IDDM project validation phase has already started, involving eight pediatric patients at the Policlinico S. Matteo Hospital in Pavia, and eight adult patients in the three other project validation sites. By making the multi-modal reasoning methodology available for the testing sites, we will be able to get a feedback of its performance directly from the end users. Moreover, in the future we will study a possible integration of CBR with other reasoning systems, such as model-based ones. Finally, from an application point of view, we will work on possible implementations of multi-modal reasoning in the context of different chronic diseases management.

Acknowledgments Dr. Stefano Fiocchi and Dr. Giuseppe d'Annunzio are gratefully acknowledged their support in the CBR and in the RBR systems definition. We thank Prof. Claudio Cobelli and Gianluca Nucci for having provided us with

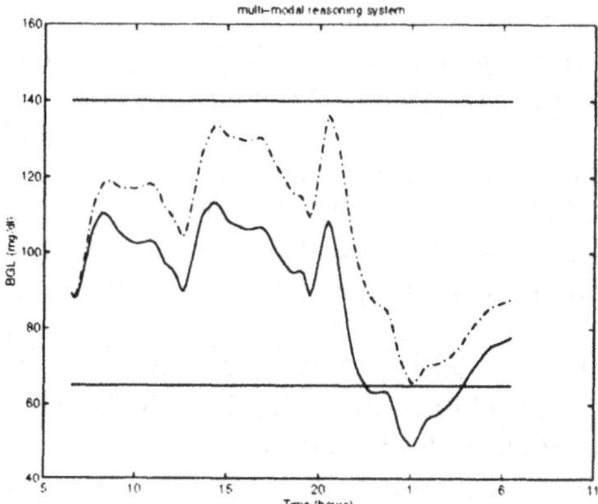

Fig. 5. The 24 hours profiles of blood glucose in response to the different therapeutic protocols proposed by the multi-modal reasoning system. The BGL values fall into the normality range just with one protocol revision (dash-dotted line).

the simulation tool. Finally we thank the T-IDDM partners for their suggestions on the Rule-Based system.

References

1. D. Aha and J. Daniels (eds.). *Proc. AAAI Workshop on CBR Integrations.* AAAI Press, 1998.
2. R. Bellazzi, S. Montani, and L. Portinale. Retrieval in a prototype-based case library: a case study in diabetes therapy revision. In *Proc. 4th EWCBR, LNAI 1488*, pages 64–75. Springer Verlag, 1998.
3. I. Bichindaritz, E. Kansu, and K.M. Sullivan. Case-based reasoning in CARE-PARTNER: gathering evidence for evidence-based medical practice. In Springer Varlag, editor, *Proc. 4th EWCBR, LNAI 1488*, pages 334–345, 1998.
4. P.P. Bonissone and S. Dutta. Integrating case-based and rule-based reasoning: the possibilistic connection. In *Proc. 6th Conf. on Uncertainty in Artificial Intelligence*, Cambridge, MA, 1990.
5. L.K. Branting and B.W. Porter. Rules and precedents as complementary warrants. In *Proc. 9th National Conference on Artificial Intelligence (AAAI 91)*, Anaheim, 1991.
6. C. Cobelli, G. Nucci, and S. Del Prato. A physiological simulation model of the glucose-insulin system in type 1 diabetes. *Diabetes Nutrition and Metabolism*, 11, 1998.
7. The Diabetes Control and Complication Trial Research Group. The effect of intensive treatment of diabetes on the development and progression of long-term complications in insulin-dependent diabetes mellitus. *The New England Journal of Medicine*, 329:977–986, 1993.
8. P. Domingos and M. Pazzani. On the optimality of the simple Bayesian classifier under zero-one loss. *Machine Learning*, 29:103–130, 1997.
9. E. Freuder (ed.). *AAAI Spring Symposium on Multi-modal Reasoning.* AAAI Press, 1998.

10. J.L. Kolodner. *Case-Based Reasoning*. Morgan Kaufmann, 1993.
11. P. Koton. Integrating causal and case-based reasoning for clinical problem solving. In *Proc of the AAAI Symposium on Artificial Intelligence in Medicine*, pages 53–54, Stanford, 1988.
12. C. Larizza, R. Bellazzi, and A. Riva. Temporal abstractions for diabetic patients management. In *LNAI 1211*, pages 319–330. Springer Verlag, 1997.
13. D. Macchion and D.P. Vo. A hybrid KBS for technical diagnosis learning and assistance. In *Lecture Notes in Artificial Intelligence 837*, pages 301–312. Springer Verlag, 1993.
14. S. Montani, R. Bellazzi, C Larizza, A. Riva, G. d'Annunzio, S. Fiocchi, R. Lorini, and M. Stefanelli. Protocol-based reasoning in diabetic patient management. *International Journal of Medical Informatics*, 53:61–77, 1999.
15. S. Montani, R. Bellazzi, L. Portinale, S. Fiocchi, and M. Stefanelli. A case-based retrieval system for diabetic patients therapy. In *Proceedings of IDAMAP 98 workshop, ECAI 98*, pages 64–70, Brighton, 1998.
16. L. Portinale, P. Torasso, and D. Magro. Selecting most adaptable diagnostic solutions through Pivoting-Based Retrieval. In *Proc. 2nd ICCBR, LNAI 1266*, pages 393–402. Springer Verlag, 1997.
17. M. Ramoni and P. Sebastiani. The use of exogenous knowledge to learn bayesian networks for incomplete databases. In *Advances in data Analysis, LNCS*, pages 537–548. Springer Verlag, 1997.
18. E.L. Rissland and D.B. Skalak. Combining case-based and rule-based reasoning: a heuristic approach. In *Proc. 11th IJCAI*, pages 524–530, Detroit, 1989.
19. A. Riva, R. Bellazzi, and M. Stefanelli. web-based system for the intelligent management of diabetic patients. *MD Computing*, 14:360–364, 1997.
20. R. Schmidt and L. Gierl. Experiences with prototype designs and retrieval methods in medical Case-Based Reasoning systems. In *Proc. 4th EWCBR, LNAI 1488*, pages 370–381. Springer Verlag, 1998.
21. J. Surma and K. Vanhoff. Integrating rules and cases for the classification task. In *Proc. 1st ICCBR, LNAI 1010*, pages 325–334. Springer Verlag, 1995.
22. D.R. Wilson and T.R. Martinez. Improved heterogeneous distance functions. *Journal of Artificial Intelligence Research*, 6:1–34, 1997.

Managing Complex Knowledge in Natural Sciences

Noël Conruyt, David Grosser

IREMIA, Institut de REcherche en Mathématiques et Informatique Appliquées
University of La Réunion
15, av. René Cassin – 97715 Saint-Denis, Messag. Cedex 9, France
{Conruyt, Grosser}@univ-reunion.fr

Abstract. In many fields dependant upon complex observation, the structuring, depiction and treatment of knowledge can be of great complexity. For example in Systematics, the scientific discipline that investigates bio-diversity, the descriptions of specimens are often highly structured (composite objects, taxonomic attributes), noisy (erroneous or unknown data), and polymorphous (variable or imprecise data). In this paper, we present IKBS, an Iterative Knowledge Base System for dealing with such complex phenomena. The originality of this system is to implement the scientific method in biology: experimenting (learning rules from examples) and testing (identifying new individuals, improving the initial model and descriptions). This methodology is applied in the following ways in IKBS: 1 - Knowledge is acquired through a descriptive model that suits the semantic demand of experts. 2 - Knowledge is processed with an algorithm derived from C4.5 in order to take into account structured knowledge introduced in the previous descriptive model of the domain. 3 - Knowledge is refined through the use of an iterative process to evaluate the robustness of the descriptive model and descriptions. The IKBS system is presented here as a life science application facilitating the identification of coral specimens of the family *Pocilloporidæ*.

1. Introduction

In the natural sciences, data to be processed may be more complex than in other fields. In Systematics, attributes that describe organisms are numerous (> 100) compared with the number of individuals by class which is mostly not representative (< 10): the domain to describe is established deterministically (empirically) rather than probabilistically (statistically) [14]. In such domains, we must take into account diversity and incompleteness, and the exception is the only valid rule.

Learning systems intended to facilitate classification (class definition) and identification of natural organisms must adapt themselves to the representation and process of such reality.

For the necessities of representation, taking into account the structuring of biological knowledge [2], [5] is a progress that allows to consider useful common sense background knowledge in order to acquire, manage and process complex knowledge in a more elegant and efficient way.

The identification procedure that is described in this paper takes care of structured descriptions intelligently by reducing the number of eligible criteria for information gain calculation and manages coherent consultations through a guide to observation (web questionnaire).

Nevertheless, the problem we are faced with in Systematics is more difficult: good identifications depend on previously good classifications from experts, and also good descriptions from other biologists. Nature is so conceived that giving a name to organisms can also be difficult for experts (synonymies' problem), especially when there is a great intra-specific variation. This is the case in coral taxonomy where the number of named species in the world is uncertain [18]. Thus, managing complex knowledge in natural sciences means to cope with such evolving knowledge.

We have designed an Iterative Knowledge Base System to build knowledge bases in natural sciences that responds to these requirements. The main goal of IKBS is to produce quality descriptions which is a key factor for getting better results in identification process [11] and avoid future revisions.

2. Methodology

In the computer sciences, knowledge is a controversial term [Kodratoff, 1997]. We thus offer a working definition for our purpose in biology that consists of three kinds of knowledge: domain, instantiated and derived.

Domain knowledge (or background knowledge) relates to the definition of what is *observable*, i.e., build a descriptive model that corresponds to the modeling of data, or metadata [6]. *Instantiated knowledge* refers to the description of *observed* instances (case descriptions). *Derived knowledge* can be compared with produced hypotheses (cluster definitions, decision trees, rules, identification) discovered from domain and instantiated knowledge. Obviously, knowledge is also grounded in expert's mind and what is "extracted" is but a minimal part of his or her experience.

Knowledge Discovery methodology views knowledge as an output of a linear process of input data handling [8]. In biological domains, our emphasis is placed on a different interpretation of knowledge which consists of both input (domain and instantiated) and output (derived). This viewpoint is more relevant to Case-Based Reasoning methodology: i.e. the CBR cycle described in [1] with an extensive use of domain knowledge in the processing phase.

In practice, knowledge is extracted with IKBS by a cyclical process, divided into three parts:

1. Knowledge acquisition:
   - Acquire a descriptive model (domain knowledge or observable facts),
   - Acquire descriptions (observed facts or cases),
2. Knowledge processing:
   - Generate classification rules with decision tree induction,
   - Identify new observations(unknown specimens) with case-based reasoning,
3. Knowledge validation and refinement:
   - Verify the origin of misidentifications by analyzing differences of interpretation between the expert and the users of the knowledge base,
   - Iterate on the definition of the descriptive model (characters), update old cases.

For experts in biology, this approach is well suited to the natural process of their knowledge acquisition (conjecture and test) [16]:

1. Observe and familiarize oneself,
2. Represent observations, i.e. make descriptions,
3. Build hypotheses from descriptions (pre-classified), i.e. generate identification keys,
4. Test and experiment them with new observations, i.e. identify new specimens,
5. Refine their initial knowledge (new characters, cases and classifications).

The last point of the method is fundamental because the building of a knowledge base in natural sciences is very difficult. This was our experience in applications such as diagnosis of plant pathologies [12]. It is hard for experts to define the best representation of reality at once in a descriptive model. The challenge is to acquire the best character definitions and illustrations leading to interpretations of observations understood by anyone consulting the knowledge base.

3. Knowledge acquisition

This part of the methodology is very important to acquire a case base with good quality descriptions, i.e. that are well structured in different dimensions with all the required information, with characters, illustrations and comments that are easily comprehensible for other biologists.

3.1 The descriptive model

The descriptive model represents all the *observable* characteristics (objects, attributes and values) pertaining to individuals belonging to a particular domain. It is organized in a structured scheme, the name of the domain being at the root of a description tree. Each node of the tree is an object (a component of the individual) defined by a list of attributes with their respective possible values. Designing a descriptive model is essentially an expert task.

For helping them, we have set up logical rules for case description covering: decomposition, viewpoint, iteration, specialization, contextual conditions, etc. [11]. These rules were constructed from the analysis of expert's process of creating monographs of organisms or diseases.

To serve as an example, we present the descriptive model of one of the world's most widespread family of corals: *Pocilloporidæ* [7] (see Fig. 1). 51 objects and 120 attributes have been defined by the expert. With them, biologists are able to describe 4 genus and 14 species (see attribute called "taxon" in Fig. 1).

There are multiple benefits in such a representation. Viewpoints divide the descriptive model into homogeneous parts, thus giving a frame of reference for describing organisms at a particular level of observation (see objects identification, context, description, macro and micro structure in Fig. 1).

Sub-components introduce modularity into the descriptions making it possible to structure the domain from most general to most particular parts. This object representation of specimens is semantically better than the flat feature-value one: in the former, local descriptions of attributes depend on the existence of parent objects, although in the latter the defined characters are independent of one another. Some of the possibly missing objects are marked with a minus sign (e.g. columella).

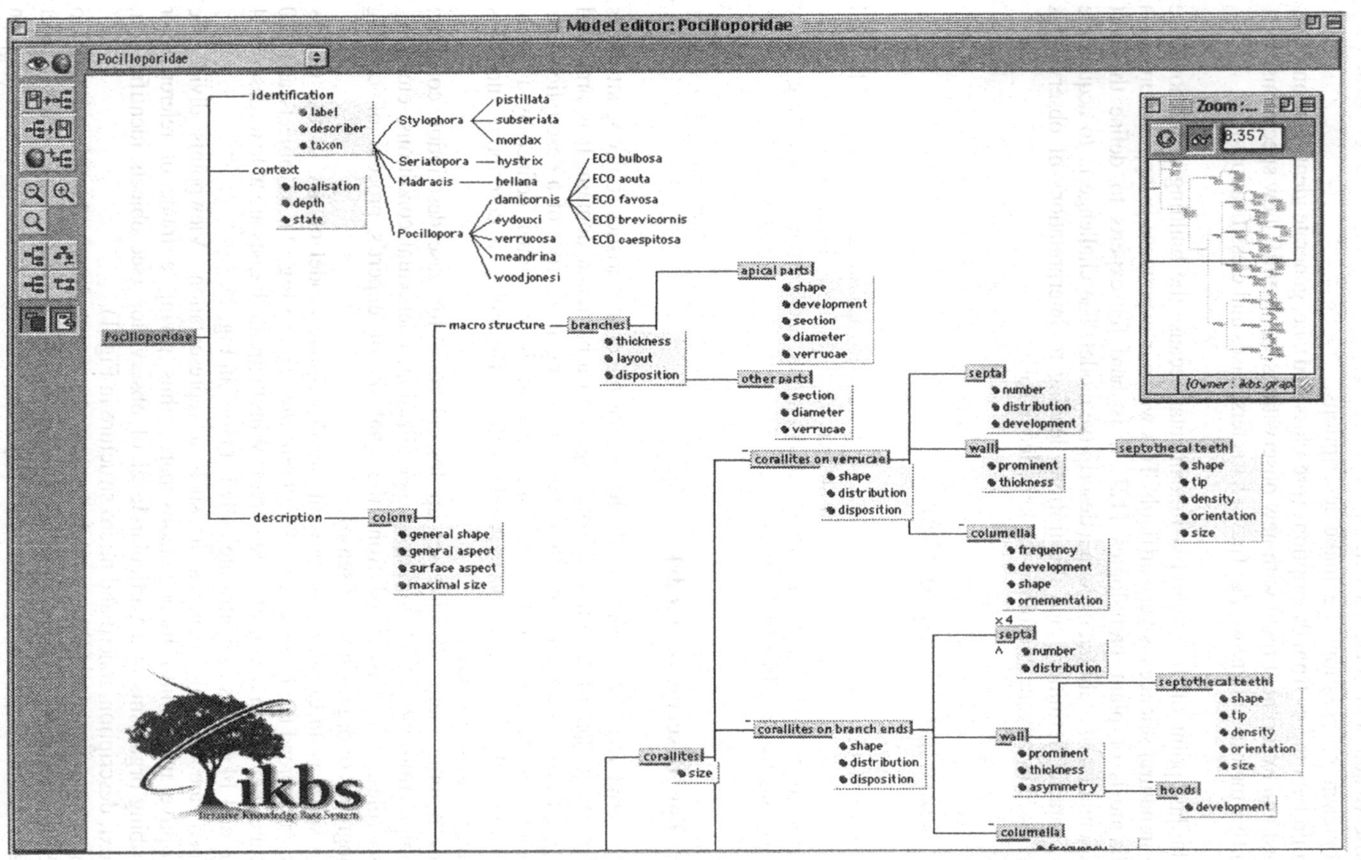

Fig. 1. Part of the descriptive model of the Family *Pocilloporidae*

Fig. 1 shows the partitioning dimension of objects (subpart links for disjoint classes). For some of them (i.e. septa), other dimensions such as multi-instantiation (x symbol) and specialization (^ symbol) of objects can be seen. The former enables users to describe several sorts of the same object by descriptive iteration (there are 4 possible instances for septa in Fig. 1) and the latter lets users name each sort with the help of the following classification tree of objects (specialization links in Fig. 2).

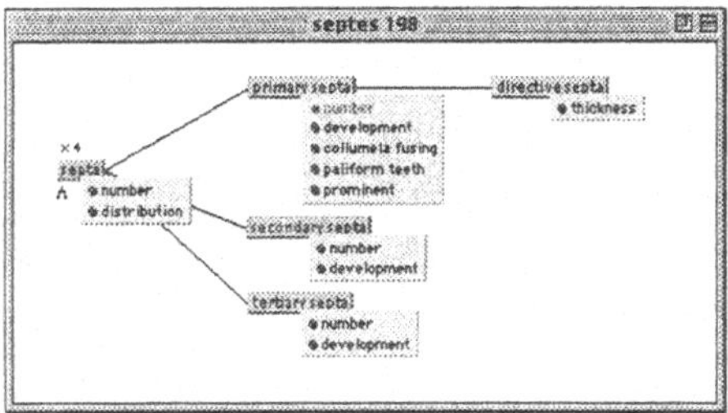

Fig. 2. Classification tree of object "septa"

In fact, one of the roles of the descriptive model is to bring an observation guide for the end-user: the objects are linked together by relations that go from the most general to the most specific (from left to right), making the next description process easier for the non specialist (see below).

3.2 The descriptions

Starting from the selection of a descriptive model, the program automatically generates a questionnaire [4]. It permits the less informed biologists, as the expert, to acquire personal descriptions and create a case base. An identification name is associated to each observation in order to form a description or a case (Fig. 3).

The description process generates sub-trees of the descriptive model (Fig. 1 and Fig. 3). Therefore, observed descriptions can be directly compared to one another by leafing through page by page: this navigation process is easier than viewing different lists of attribute-value pairs.

In Fig. 3, we illustrate possibilities of IKBS for rendering complete and comprehensive descriptions of a given sample.

Different types of attribute are used: taxonomic ones (e.g. general shape of object colony), numerical intervals (e.g. diameter of apical parts) and multi-nominal values (e.g. section of apical parts). The latter shows variation in objects displaying a set of multiple elements.

The visualization of objects differs graphically according to their status: black if present, black with a cross if absent, dimmed if unknown (see object "hood" at the bottom-right side of Fig. 1 and Fig. 3).

At last, an object can be specialized (e.g. the septa of calices from apical parts, see Fig. 1): the result is a substitution of its name by a more precise one (e.g. primary septa, see Fig. 3) with its associated attributes (inherited or not, see Fig. 2).

It is important for the user to visualize structured descriptions: so doing brings better clarity and comprehensibility to the acquisition phase. This is the most important part of our methodology for acquiring good results of classification and identification.

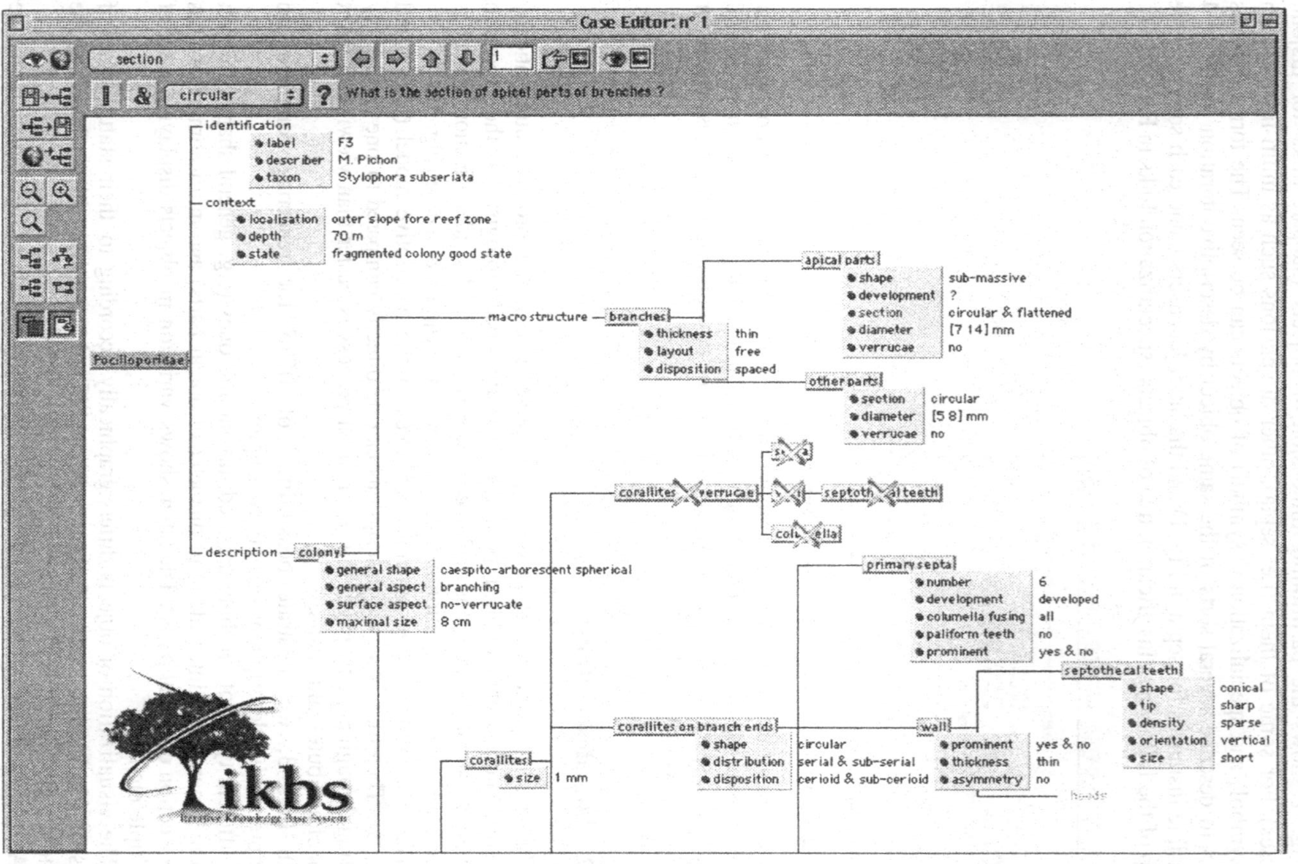

Fig. 3. Part of the description tree of a case of the Family *Pocilloporidæ*: *Stylophora subseriata*

4. Knowledge processing

This section highlights how usual inductive learning algorithms can be stretched to complex data processing by using domain knowledge to generate accurate and meaningful decision trees (from pre-classified examples).

4.1 Tree-based classification using domain knowledge

Starting from the well known decision tree builder algorithm C4.5 [17] which works on discrete and continuous attributes, IKBS extends some functionality of this algorithm for dealing with:

1. Structured objects
2. Taxonomic attribute-values
3. Multi-valued attributes:

Let $E=\{\omega_1, ..., \omega_n\}$ be a set of observed examples, $M=\{N, Y\}$, a set of observable components and attributes defined in the descriptive model with $N=\{n_1,..., n_m\}$ a set of structured components and $A = \{A_1, ..., A_p\}$ a set of attributes depending on N.

Let dom(A) be the definition domain (range) of A.

Structured objects

The algorithm for building decision trees from structured objects is the following:

```
BuildDecisionTree (E, M)
   Y = SelectClassifier (root(M))
   BuildTree(E, Y)
end BuildDecisionTree

BuildTree(E, Y)
   if stop Criterion(E, Y) then BuildLeaf(E)
   else
     A = BestTest(E, Y) // A = y(n)
     di = BuildNode(A)
     Y = FilterClassifier(A) // depending on type of A
     partitioning(di) = R(E)
          // R(E)  : ∀ ω ∈ E, Q(vi, A(ω ))=1⇔ ω ∈ Ei
     for each Ei ∈ partitioning(di)
          BuildBranch(vi)
          if (A = exist(n)) ∧ (vi = "Present"))
            Y = SelectClassifier (n)
          end if
          BuildTree (Ei, Y)
     end for each
   end if
end BuildTree
```

```
SelectClassifier (r)
   Y' = Ø
   if (possiblyAbsent(r) = "yes") then
      Y' = Y' ∪ {exist(r)}
   else
      Y' = Y' ∪ Att(r)
      for each n_f ∈ depend(r)
            SelectClassifier (n_f)
      end for each
   end if
   return Y'
end SelectClassifier
```

The original aspect of the algorithm is the classifier's selection function. The tree of the descriptive model is followed from root to leaves, component by component in depth search first. If one of it *can* be absent (e.g. calices on verrucæ of Fig. 1), an "*exist component*" test is dynamically generated and placed in the eligible classifiers' list with values "*Present*" or "*Absent*". The sub-tree of this object is not yet visited in order to avoid inapplicable sub-objects and attributes as other classifiers. On the other hand, if components are always present (e.g. septa), dependent attributes are placed in this list.

In the identification process (see further), if the test *exist* of a component is chosen as the "best" one and the user answers that it is really present, then the classifier's selection function is recursively called on the sub-tree of the descriptive model.

Taxonomic attribute-values

For attributes which values are structured by relations of hierarchical type (classified values), an extension of the discrete classifier partitioning process is proposed.

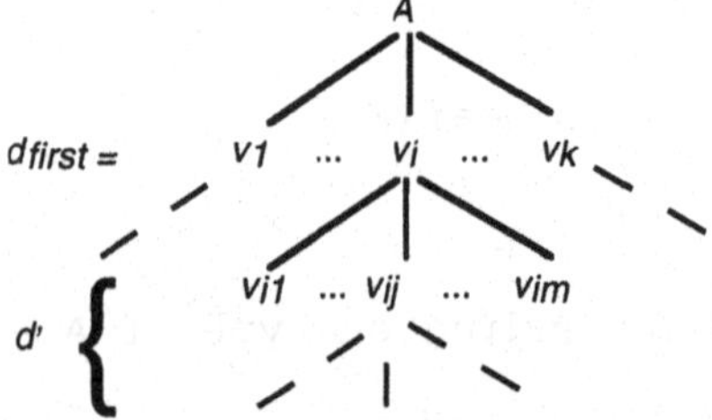

Fig. 4. Classified values of attribute A

The method consists, when such a classifier is selected, in creating a set of partitions corresponding to the first level of the hierarchy (noted $d_{first}= \{v_1,\ldots, v_i,\ldots, v_k\}$ with k elements). Each case is assigned to the partition that generalizes its value. Let A be a taxonomic attribute with the domain $d = \{v_1,\ldots,v_i,\ldots,v_n\}$ of n modalities and $d' = \{v_{i1},\ldots,v_{ij},\ldots,v_{im}\}\subset d$ is a subtree of m submodalities of v_i [Fig. 4.]:

Let Q be a Boolean application (called question) which determines if the modality v_i generalizes a value v_{ij}. Q is defined by:

$Q(v_i, v_{ij}) = 1$, if $v_{ij} \in d \cup \{v_i\}$ else $Q(v_i, v_{ij}) = 0$

Then, we can generate k partitions from d_{first}:

$$E_{A1}=\{\omega \in E_A / Q(v_1, A(\omega))=1\},\ldots, E_{Ak}=\{\omega \in E_A / Q(v_k,A(\omega))=1\}$$

In the next step, we create temporarily k attributes $\{A_1,\ldots, A_j,\ldots, A_k\}$ in each partition $E_{A1},\ldots,E_{Ak}$ with a set of modalities defined by the subvalues of $\{v_1,\ldots, v_i,\ldots,v_k\}$. These ones can be picked by the test function (information gain, gain ratio) and the method is recursively reapplied.

Multi-valued attributes

When modeling the descriptive model, a discrete attribute (nominal or taxonomic) can be defined as multi-valued. It can express doubt (disjunction of imprecision) or the simultaneous presence of states (conjunction of variation) like in the following expression:

$v = (v_{11} \&\ldots v_{1i}\ldots\& v_{1m}) \mid \ldots \mid (v_{j1} \&\ldots v_{ji}\ldots\& v_{jn})\ldots\mid (v_{k1} \&\ldots v_{ki}\ldots\& v_{kp})$

where $cf_j = (v_{j1} \&\ldots v_{ji}\ldots\& v_{jn})$

Depending on the semantic associated with a conjunctive form of a case (*cf*), IKBS can apply three processing methods:

1. If *cf* is true information (association of co-existing facts), create *k* partitions corresponding to each conjunction of *v*, and dispatch cases with such value in each partition: *cf* is seen as a new possible value of dom(A).
2. If *cf* expresses fuzzy information (the intrinsic variability of multiple objects is an adding source of noise), treat conjunctions as disjunction.
3. Allow the user to customize the degree of similarity ∂ between two conjunctive forms.

The default method is the third one with $\partial = 1$ because it gives a good compromise between the tree size (number of nodes) and the discrimination accuracy. Indeed, the first method don't generate a deep tree, but carries a major risk of misidentification: each *cf* of the selected attribute at a node of the decision tree must match exactly the *cf* of the tested case. The third method is more flexible because it makes a fuzzy matching for dispatching cases in each partition, depending on the number of differences between the two conjunctive forms and ∂.

4.2 Identification process

Given a set of examples, IKBS dynamically extracts the most efficient criteria from the ordered list of tests after each answer of the user. The cases are selected from this reply. If the answer is unknown, the second most discriminate test is proposed to the user, and so on. This procedure is the same as in KATE [13]. Nevertheless, IKBS processes cases that are in an object oriented formalism, while KATE starts from cases represented in a data table. In the former, the "exist (objects)" tests are directly exploitable at a node of the decision tree, while in the latter, these tests are deduced from the appearance of at least one not-applicable value in the object's attribute column of the table. Our approach is semantically better because it guarantees that the inapplicability of an attribute's value depends on the absence of an object and not the contrary.

An illustration of a decision tree built with 30 training cases is shown in Fig. 5. The numbers refer to previously discussed classifiers' types: taxonomic attributes (1 and 2 highlight the use of the same classifier at two different levels of the values' hierarchy), multi-valued attributes (case *bulbosa* with size of spines "short&long" goes in three branches (3)) and structured objects (4).

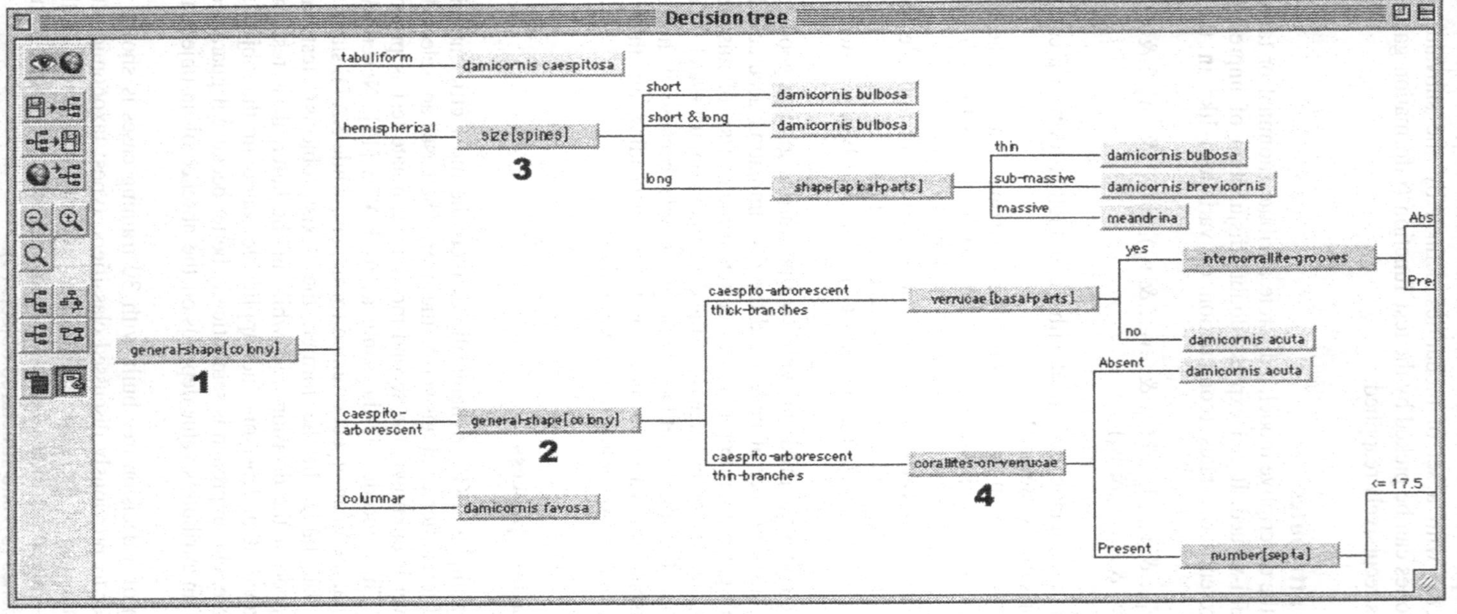

Fig. 5. Part of a decision tree that makes use of domain knowledge

5. Validation and refinement

We experimented on corals to test the reliability of IKBS identification with different users. We tested two consecutive descriptive models in a sub-domain of *Pocilloporidæ*: the genus *Pocillopora* (9 species and ecomorphs). The validation of both descriptive models was *qualitative*. It led to modification of the initial descriptive model (dm_1) and case base to the one shown in this paper (dm_2). The first test with dm_1 is called A. Later, another test B on dm_2 was carried out. The experiments were made with a sample of 15 specimens of the Genus, each one of them being described completely in both descriptive models by 3 different biologists (x_1, x_2, x_3), and the expert (E). With this training set of 60 cases, the expert added 22 other descriptions of *Pocillopora* (37 expert cases). The four experiments that were led with IKBS are the following:

- A_1: 15 cases of x_n tested against 37 cases of E.
- A_2: 15 cases of x_n tested against 67 cases (E+other x_n).
- B_1: 15 cases of x_n tested against 37 cases of E.
- B_2: 15 cases of x_n tested against 67 cases (E+other x_n).

The results on 15 consultations are shown in table 1.

Table 1. Number of good identifications with IKBS

	x_1	x_2	x_3
A_1	6	7	8
A_2	9	8	10
B_1	9	10	11
B_2	11	10	12

The results show that updating the first descriptive model and case base on *Pocillopora* brought better results. When testing the expert training set, it gave 20% (3/15) of improvement in identification process (from 46% to 66%). If we integrate other biologists' descriptions of the same specimens in the reference case base, the score goes up from 60% to 73%.

The reasons of these improvements are principally:

1. the expert was able to detect inconsistencies in the first case base (omissions or errors in descriptions) and descriptive model (misunderstood characters, faulty illustrations). He could verify the answers of other biologists in regards to decision tree questioning that lead to misidentifications. He noticed the difficulties of interpretations of observation of specimens on some noisy comparative attributes and refined them into a new descriptive model.

2. Consequently, the expert, aware of the importance of transmitting his knowledge to other biologists, postulates more precise and relevant characters that may be easier to observe and/or offer less ambiguous values (easier to interpret) in his descriptive model. For example, he will refine on the basis of mutually exclusive values, monosemic attributes, frames of reference, warning signals, enhanced illustrations.

6. Discussion

IKBS has been implemented in Java language and is fully operational on (http://www.univ-reunion.fr/~ikbs). Experts unaccustomed to computers are able to model and describe, and any non-specialists interested in the field can describe and identify new observations. IKBS is used directly by experts for creating descriptive models and filling cases without any help from a computer scientist. They find the interface very pleasant and enjoy the effectiveness of the tool.

In our methodology, it is important that the case base contains descriptions of specimens made by biologists other than the expert. This, in order to counterbalance his interpretation of observations (inter-observer variation) when consulting the knowledge base. The results of the identification process are more dependable when we mix descriptions of different users for the same specimens (shown in Table 1). As they are labeled with the correct identification name from the expert, we can integrate the noise due to misinterpretations from end-users directly into the case base.

Similarly, because of the intra-specific variability, the number of described specimens by species must be increased. Insofar as *Pocilloporidæ* is concerned, this family is one of the sixteen families of corals containing the greatest intra-variability, and its complex diversity was covered with detailed precision.

The difficulty arises due to the number of attributes applicable to each case. Thus, the building of an exhaustive knowledge base is time-consuming for describers: updating a case with the latest descriptive model on *Pocilloporidæ* requires nearly a whole day's work!

7. Related work

In other domains such as botany and zoology, some researchers have come up with solutions for coding descriptions [5]. Their programs enable to compare descriptions and facilitate identification process from databases [10], [15].

In Case-Based Reasoning methodology, IKBS can be compared with AcknoSoft's KATE, Isoft's RECALL and TecInno's CBR-Works. These decision support systems have been designed to cope with industrial fields and very large databases [3]. In the life sciences, our objective is to deal with more complex descriptions and less data (cases) by class.

8. Conclusions and future work

In collaboration with three experts, we are presently experimenting with IKBS on three other families of corals of the Mascarene archipelago (*Fungiidæ, Poritidæ, Thamnasteriidæ).* The meticulous choice of terms, drawings and images seems decisive for generating a dependable knowledge base and managing the complexity of natural objects.

This is why we are designing IKBS to build cooperative knowledge bases. The aim is to encourage experts to draw up a common thesaurus of vocabulary and illustrations (i.e. the questionnaire) on the same Family.

Collections of specimens, like experts, are distributed around the world. Thanks to satellite high-speed broadband networks, we have been able to demonstrate Telesystematics using video-conferencing and IKBS. At ATM Developments'98, experts were able to share their interpretations of observations of specimens under a microscopic examination synchronously between La Reunion (South-West of Indian Ocean) and Rennes (France).

Nowadays, expertise in natural sciences is precious (it becomes very rare). It is therefore urgent to develop tools that will ensure that expertise be collected and safeguarded for transmission to future generations. If this is not done, we will be left only with monographic descriptions and museum collections.

Acknowledgement

We would like to thank the French experts G. Faure, M. Pichon and M. Guillaume for their valuable contributions on the applications on corals. We are also grateful to Philippe Sills for English improvement. This work is supported by the Conseil Régional of La Reunion Island.

References

1. Aamodt A., Plaza E., Case-Based Reasoning: Foundational Issues, Methodological Variations, and System Approaches, AI Communications 7(1): 39-59, 1994.
2. Allkin R., Handling taxonomic descriptions by computer, In; Allkin R. and Bisby F.A. (eds.), Databases in Systematics. Systematics Association London, Academic Press, 26: 263-278, 1984.
3. Althoff K. D., Auriol E., Barletta R., Manago M., A review of Industrial Case-Based Reasoning Tools, AI Intelligence, Oxford, 1995.
4. Conruyt N., Grosser D., Faure G. Ingénierie des connaissances en Sciences de la vie: application à la systématique des coraux des Mascareignes. Journées Ingénierie des Connaissances et Apprentissage Automatique (JICAA'97), Roscoff, pages 539-566, 1997.
5. Dallwitz M.J., Paine T.A., Zurcher E.J., User's guide to the DELTA System. A general system for processing taxonomic descriptions, Canberra: CSIRO, Div. Entomol., 4th ed., 1993.
6. Diederich J.R., Milton J., Creating domain specific metadata for scientific data and knowledge bases, IEEE Trans., Knowledge Data Engineering 3(4): 421-434, 1991.

7. Faure G., Recherche sur les peuplements de scléractiniaires des récifs coralliens des Mascareignes. Thèse es sciences, Univ Aix-Marseille II, 1982.
8. Fayyad U., Piatetsky-Shapiro G., Padhraic S., From Data Mining to Knowledge Discovery in Databases, AI magazine, 17(3): 37-54, Fall 1996.
9. Kodratoff Y. L'extraction de connaissances à partir des données. Journées Ingénierie des Connaissances et Apprentissage Automatique (JICAA'97), Roscoff, pages 539-566, 1997.
10. Lebbe J., Systématique et informatique. Systématique et biodiversité, Bourgoin T. (Ed), Biosystema, 13:71-79, Paris, 1995.
11. Le Renard J., Conruyt N. On the representation of observational data used for classification and identification of natural objects. IFCS'93, Lecture notes in Artificial Intelligence, Springer-Verlag, pages 308-315, 1994.
12. Manago M., Conruyt N. Using Information Technology to Solve Real World Problems, Lecture Notes in Computer Science subseries, 622: 22-37, Springer Verlag, 1992.
13. Manago M., Althoff K.D., Auriol E., Traphoner R., Wess S., Conruyt N., Maurer F., Induction and reasoning from cases, First European workshop on case-based reasoning (EWCBR-93), MM Richter, S Wess, KD Althoff and F Maurer (Eds.), Springer Verlag, (2), 1993.
14. Mingers J. Expert Systems – Rule induction with statistical data. Journal of the operational research society. 38(1): 39-47, 1987.
15. Pankhurst R.J., Practical taxonomic computing. Cambridge Univ. Press, Cambridge, 1991.
16. Popper K.R., La logique de la découverte scientifique. Payot (Eds.) Press, Paris, 1973.
17. Quinlan J.R., C4.5: Programs for Machine Learning, Morgan Kaufmann, Los Altos, CA, 1993.
18. Veron J.E.N., Pichon M., Scleractinia of eastern australia, vol. I, Part I, Australian Institute of Marine Science Monograph Series, 1976.

ELSI: A Medical Equipment Diagnostic System

Paul Cuddihy(cuddihy@crd.ge.com),

William Cheetham (cheetham@crd.ge.com)

GE Research & Development Center,

1 Research Circle, Niskayuna, NY 12309

Abstract - A case-based reasoning system for diagnosing medical equipment, called ELSI, has been in use by the GE corporation since 1994. When a customer or field engineer calls the service center for help with a problem, the equipment's error log is automatically downloaded. In ninety seconds or less, ELSI displays a sorted list of the best-matching logs in a case base of previous known problems, shows the fix, service notes, explains which sections of the log match, and which fixes each section predicts. This diagnostic information allows the service center engineer to recommend a temporary work-around or remote fixes to a customer, or helps a field engineer show up on site with the right parts the first time.

1 Introduction

The General Electric Company (GE) is one of the worlds largest manufacturers and service providers for medical imaging equipment. GE Medical Systems is constantly advancing the state of the art in equipment availability, reliability, and service quality. One tool used to help achieve these advances is a case-based reasoning system that has been in use since 1994 to aid in diagnosing medical equipment.

GE medical equipment, including Computed Tomography, Magnetic Resonance, and X-Ray, use microprocessors that constantly monitor the status of the equipment. Machines are equipped with a telephone connection so that when a maintenance issue is detected an error log can be transferred directly to a central service facility.

A case-based reasoning system called ELSI (Error Log Similarity Index) [1] is one tool used to diagnose the issue and determine how to fix it. The diagnoses are performed by comparing the logs of the new problem to the logs of old problems with known fixes. When the most similar past cases are found, their known fixes are delivered as the most likely fixes to the new problem.

ELSI does not contain any explicit domain knowledge about the equipment that it diagnoses. The only knowledge that it has is the set of previous error logs and the fix that was done for each of those logs. It learns how best to compare error logs by itself, with very little human interaction. The more cases it has seen, the better it knows which parts of the error logs are important for diagnosis.

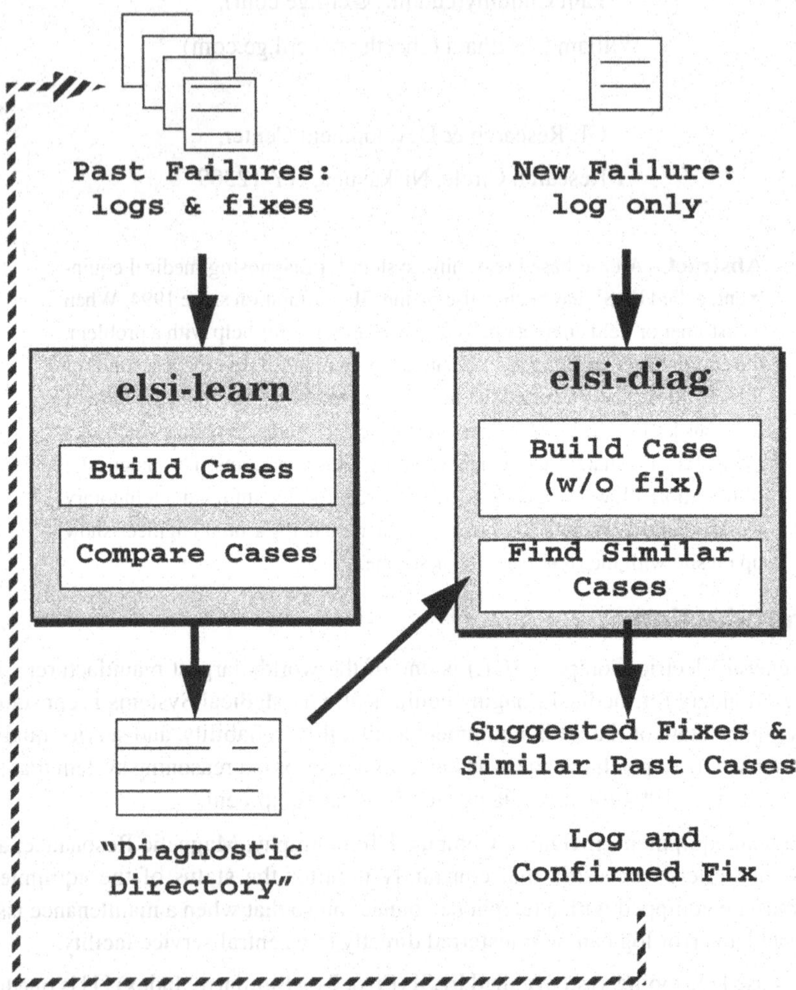

Figure 1: ELSI Overview

ELSI is designed to operate in a noisy environment, where there is no guarantee that each case's error log actually contains enough data to diagnose a fix accurately. Many fixes can be arrived at with different sets of error log entries, and many error logs do not contain enough information to diagnose a single fix.

ELSI is "glass box" approach. It show the developer and users what parts of the error logs are most useful, and precisely how useful they are. The knowledgeable user can use this information to confirm ELSI's recommendations with complete confidence, while the less knowledgeable user can actually learn about the domain from ELSI. This also allows error log design feedback and can build and standardize diagnostic knowledge.

The ELSI diagnostic system is flexible and adaptable. It grows more accurate as more cases are collected, and expands its usefulness as new versions of the equipment are released or error logs are gathered for existing equipment not previously included.

The result is a diagnostic system which operates with minimal knowledge acquisition or expert interaction--the largest obstacles of traditional expert systems. The only local expertise required is the collection of logs, removal or quantification of extraneous entries such as dates and times, and the classification of cases by fix.

Figure 1 shows the overall ELSI process. It is separated into two executable programs, one for adding new cases to the case-base (elsi-learn) and one for diagnosing fixes using the case-base (elsi-diag).The remainder of this paper will describe this ELSI process in detail. Section 2 presents the error logs used for diagnosis and the possible fixes. Section 3 goes through the ELSI process for learning new cases. Section 4 shows how to diagnose an issue. Section 5 tells how we improved the diagnostics by determining our confidence in the diagnosis performed. Section 6 describes how the case-base was maintained. And, section 7 summarizes the results obtained from using ELSI.

2 Error Logs and Fixes

The system error log is one of the most powerful tools for examining the recent state of a piece of equipment in the field, and any abnormal conditions that may have been recorded. However, the error logs often contain a complicated stream of status codes, register dumps, and other information that is hard for a human expert to quickly scan and process. Logs typically contain a mix of information relevant and irrelevant to any particular recent problem.

Most importantly, software control systems have a tendency to cascade error messages (one error causes a stream of several messages). This leaves a human reader searching backwards to find the "original" error, and often obscuring the fact that the entire group of messages and the order in which they cascaded is much more diagnostically significant than any single message by itself.

Fixes can range from as simple as resetting a circuit breaker or rebooting a sub-system, to physical replacement of parts. A significant portion of issues can be solved without physically visiting the equipment. When a repair is needed, there is often a work-around which will allow a system to run until the proper parts arrive.

All of these elements create opportunity for an automatic learning system to analyze error logs remotely and provide human experts with the information they need to quickly diagnose a problem.

3 Learning System

In the learning process, past cases with known fixes are analyzed. Sections of logs which are diagnostically significant are extracted, weighted, and stored for later use in diagnostics. This consists of three steps, which are very briefly outlined below:

- log pre-processing
- block-finding algorithm
- block-weighting

3.1 Log Pre-Processing

In order to learn without any engineering knowledge, ELSI treats all log entries as text patterns. ELSI's patented block-finding algorithm finds cascades of error logs by searching for groups of identical lines in the error logs.

Therefore, the logs need to be pre-processed in order to remove irrelevant information that changes arbitrarily (such as dates or counters), and occasionally to simplify values by rounding them or quantiling them (e.g. change both 99.9 and 99.8 to "99+" or "high" so that the text will match).

Since the pre-processed log will be shown to an expert end user, we have found it best to maintain as much of the log format and structure as possible. This is achieved by techniques like X-ing out dates and scan numbers. Figure 2 shows an example of pre-processing.

Raw Log

```
MSG: HTRTRQ 5                    LOGGED: 02/26/97 15:36:49
 AP Subprocess Failure at Bcode: 9101 status: 8
MSG: HSRTRQ 9                    LOGGED: 02/26/97 15:36:50
 Run Error of 95 in TE at Bcode: 9050

 User Specified Abort (Rstat contains req code).

 TE user specified abort code: 9101 Scan number 117
```

Pre-processed Log

```
MSG: HSRTRQ 5                    LOGGED: xx/xx/xx xx:xx:xx
 AP Subprocess Failure at Bcode: 9101 status: 8
MSG: HSRTRQ 9                    LOGGED: xx/xx/xx xx:xx:xx
 Run Error of 95 in TE at Bcode: 9050

 User Specified Abort (Rstat contains req code).

 TE user specified abort code: 9101 Scan number xxx
```

Figure 2: Pre-processing

In this example, the dates and scan numbers have been removed, since they are not diagnostically significant, and if left intact they would prevent two identical lines from occurring in different cases.

Experience has shown that it is easier to throw out information that is changing arbitrarily than it is to pre-determine which information is important extract it for processing by ELSI. It is also easier to troubleshoot: An expert can look at cases with the same fix, but which didn't match, and do a quick check to make sure the logs actually do look different. If they are nearly identical, the expert can decide whether a small tweak to the pre-processing could make them completely identical.

For log formats which are already columns of information, pre-processing consists of simply extracting the desired columns. Figure 3 shows a log in a column based format.

Raw Log

```
error_code  code    ath   bcode
----------  ------  ----  ------
LDSUMSG     1
MQERR1      1       13
LDDIDAS     1       13    300
```

Figure 3: A Simple Log Format

3.2 Block-Finding Algorithm

Once logs are pre-processed, ELSI compares all cases with the same fix to see which lines in the error logs match. Each group of matching lines is called a "block".

Figure 4 shows a simple example. Here, two parsed logs are compared. The block-finding algorithm finds the two largest blocks of consecutive matching lines possible, block A and block B. These blocks are stored by ELSI and used to find similar cases in the future.

Additional logic detects blocks which are subsets of each other but have the same diagnostic value. When found, the simplest version of the block is used, and others are discarded.

It is this block-finding algorithm (and the block-weighting algorithm that follows) which gives ELSI the capability of building up knowledge without expert intervention. Unlike traditional case-based reasoning, ELSI is not only collecting and comparing cases, but it is *learning how to compare the cases.*

3.3 Block-Weighting

The number of blocks collected during the block-finding process can be quite large. The next step has to be deciding which blocks are meaningful and which are not. ELSI performs this task through the following steps:

- grouping cases into "case sets," where a set contains all cases with the same repair (or "fix")
- searching all cases for all blocks
- counting how many case sets each block falls into
- giving a higher weight (more importance) to blocks which occur in fewer case sets

Log 1

error_code	code	ath	bcode
LDSUMSG	1		
MQERR1	1	13	
LDDIDAS	1	13	300
MGERR3	1	13	
LDDITGC	1	13	10
MGERR	1	16	
TUBECON	8	16	100
LDDITCL	65534	16	10
LDBLDA	65534	282	20
HSRVRQ	7		8010
HSRVRQ	5		9101
HSRVRQ	9		9050
RWGTSM	2	7000	700
RWGTSM	4		
RWLOOP	65534	7000	1800
RWLOOP	65534	-1	6300
HSRVRQ	7		8010
HSRVRQ	5		9101
HSRVRQ	9		9050
RWGTSM	2	7000	700
RWGTSM	4		
RWLOOP65534	7000	1800	
RWLOOP	65534	-1	6300
RWREPRI	5		
RWREPRI	6		360
HSRVRQ	7		8010
HSRVRQ	5		9101
HSRVRQ	9		9050
RWGTSM	2	7000	700

Log 2

A

B

error_code	code	ath	bcode
MQERR1	1	13	
LDDIDAS	1	13	300
MGERR3	1	13	
LDDITGC	1	13	10
MGERR	1	16	
TUBECON	8	16	100
LDDITCL	65534	16	10
LDBLDA	65534	0	20
HSRVRQ	7		8010
HSRVRQ	5		9101
HSRVRQ	9		9050
RWGTSM	2	7000	700
RWGTSM	4		
RWLOOP	65534	7000	1800
RWLOOP	65534	-1	6300
HSRVRQ	7		8010
HSRVRQ	5		9101
HSRVRQ	9		9050
RWGTSM	2	7000	700
RWGTSM	4		
RWLOOP	65534	7000	1800
RWLOOP	65534	-1	6300
RWREPRI	5		
RWREPRI	6		360
HSRVRQ	7		8010
HSRVRQ	5		9101
HSRVRQ	9		9050
RWGTSM	2	7000	700
RWGTSM	4		
RWLOOP	65534	7000	1800
RWLOOP	65534	-1	6300
HSRVR	7		8010
HSRVR	5		9101
HSRVR	9		9050
RWGTSM	2	7000	700
RWGTSM	4		

Figure 4: Block Finding Example

Through block-finding and block-weighting, ELSI has determined what to look for in future error logs, and how much power each block of error log entries has in determining which repair is needed. ELSI has performed these two steps with neither expert interaction nor domain knowledge.

These steps have also boiled a large number of complex error logs into a much smaller amount of block information. This will allow ELSI to quickly scan new logs and diagnose them without doing time-expensive comparisons to each old log in the case base.

4 Diagnostic System

In the diagnostic process, a log (or set of logs) from a new issue is searched for diagnostically significant blocks. The most similar cases in the case-base are found, and their fixes are recommended as solutions to the new issue.

4.1 Similarity Index

The similarity index is ELSI's measure of how closely the blocks on two cases' logs match. It is calculated using the following steps:

- Search each case's log(s) for all known blocks.
- Sum the weights of the matching blocks (those which occur in both cases).
- Sum the weights of all blocks in each case.
- Calculate the portion of the blocks which match, using the formula below.

$$\sqrt{\frac{\sum weights_{matching}}{\sum weights_{case1}} \times \frac{\sum weights_{matching}}{\sum weights_{case2}}}$$

Figure 5 shows similarity indices calculated for a hypothetical new case. In this example, the new case has four blocks: A, C, E, and F. Case 10 in the case base has all of these blocks, with one additional block, B. Since this block has a weight of zero, it is ignored and the two cases have a similarity of 1.000: sqrt(7/7 * 7/7). This perfect similarity means that the two cases have the same set of blocks (blocks with no weight don't count!). Notice that it does not mean that the logs are identical, only the important blocks are identical.

The next two most similar cases are case 4 and case 5. These have essentially the same blocks as the new cases, except that they do not contain block F. The similarity equation for these yields 0.76. ELSI displays the top three matching cases to the user.

5 Confidence Index

The latest version of ELSI does not display similarity, but instead computes a confidence index[2,3]. This index increased accuracy significantly over similarity scores by computing not only how many blocks of error code lines match, but how many blocks need to match before the cases should be considered similar.

Remember the original description of the problem domain stated that it can not be presumed that there is enough information in each case's error log to determine a fix.

Now consider the situation where several cases have been added with virtually identical error logs but different fixes. Presumably the error log does not contain enough information to distinguish the problems. However, using just the similarity measure, ELSI would report very high similarity with all the cases since the logs are nearly identical. This is not desirable.

With the confidence index, the most similar cases are found, then the similarity of the new case to each retrieved case is compared against other known cases' similarities to the retrieved case.

So, if a stored case has cases with five different fixes all matching it with a similarity of 0.8 or above, then when our new case matches it with 0.8 similarity, a confidence of 0.2 is reported (indicating that only 1/5 of the known cases with a 0.8 similarity actually share the same fix).

		Fix 1			Fix 2		Fix 3			Fix 4			
Block Name	wgt	1	2	3	4	5	6	7	8	9	10	11	New Case
Block A	0	A	A	A	A	A	A	A	A	A	A	A	A
Block B	0	B	B		B					B	B	B	
Block C	1				C	C	C				C		C
Block D	3						D		D			D	
Block E	3				E	E					E		E
Block F	3							F	F	F	F	F	F
Block G	9	G		G									
Block H	9	H	H	H									
Total Weight	-----	18	9	18	4	4	4	3	6	3	7	6	7
Matching Weight	-----	0	0	0	4	4	1	3	3	3	7	3	--
Similarity Index	-----	**0**	**0**	**0**	**.76**	**.76**	**.19**	**.65**	**.46**	**.68**	**1.0**	**.46**	**--**

Figure 5: Similarity Example

On the other hand, if a stored case is surrounded by matches of only 0.5 or better but all the cases share the same fix, then when our new case matches it with a 0.8 similarity, a confidence of 1.0 is reported (indicating that every case with 0.8 similarity to this case is correct).

The confidence algorithm is patented and a complete description is available in US Patent No 5,799,148 "System and Method for Estimating a Measure of Confidence in a Match Generated from a Case-Based Reasoning System."

6 Updating the Case-Base

The single feature which has allowed ELSI to be a technical success is the ease at which new cases can be added to the case base. This ease of use is a result of the combination of ELSI's tolerance noisy data, and the built in functionality for tracking cases which were run through ELSI in the past, and quickly converting them into new cases.

The case-base is updated about every six weeks. An expert raises ELSI's "Track past usage" screen, and logs into the maintenance database which contains field engineers comments on past site visits. ELSI shows past cases run through diagnostics one-by-one, and the user searches the maintenance database for comments on the actual fix. The fix information is then used to check the proper check box:

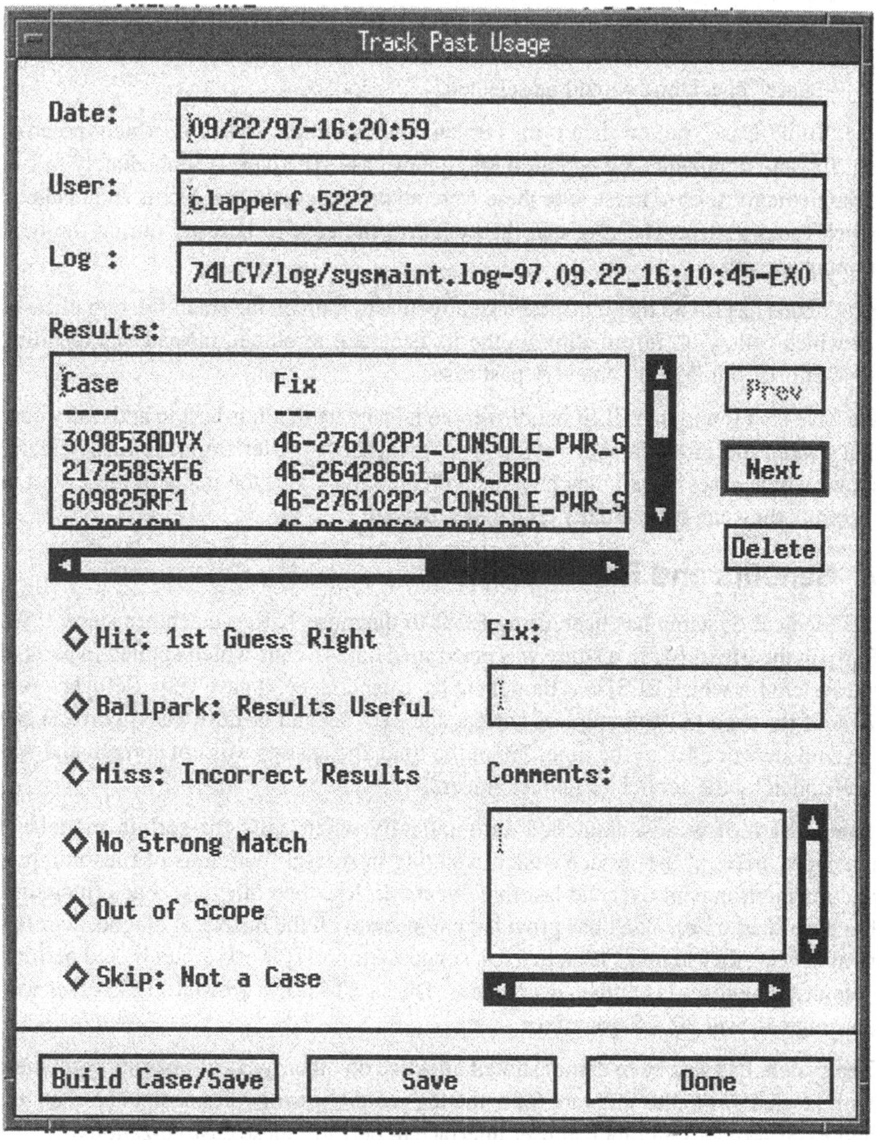

Figure 6: Tracking Past ELSI Accuracy

- If the top case suggested by ELSI was the correct fix, the "Hit: 1st Guess Right" check box selected.
- If the correct fix was the second or third case suggested by else the "Ballpark: Result Useful" check box is selected.
- If at least one case was suggested and none of the top three cases were correct then the "Miss: Incorrect Results" check box is selected.
- If there were not any confident matches then the "No Strong Match" check box is selected.

- If the issue was one that is not supposed to be covered by ELSI then the "Out of Scope" check box is selected.
- If the issue was a test, demo, or had an error in the log file the "Skip: Not a Case" check box should be selected.

The "Build Case" button then brings up an equally simple screen in which the error log, fix, and comments are captured into a new case. The case is immediately re-run through diagnostics to make sure there were no pre-processing problems and to check which cases match. The user can then confirm the case to be used during the next training session.

Experience has found that it is most cost effective to train on the small fraction of cases for which follow-up information on the fix is easiest to obtain, instead of expending large efforts to follow up on every past case.

We have also found that ELSI handles enough bad data that it is best to add every case that passes the most cursory review described above. After training, ELSI clearly shows which cases do not match others with the same fix. If too many of these start to show up, they can be manually edited or removed.

7 Benefits and Future Work

GE Medical Systems has been using ELSI to diagnose X-Ray machines since 1994. Early in the life of ELSI, a study was performed on 241 calls which applied to parts of the system for which ELSI was thought to have experience. It gave very useful answers 70% of the time (32% first guess correct and 38% second or third guess correct) and gave no answer 24% of the time. 7% of the time, the answer was not correct, and was overridden by the service or field engineers.

The ELSI tool is now launched automatically when calls for certain models of machines arrive at the service center, resulting in several thousands of runs in a production environment over the last three years. In less than ninety seconds (including log download time), ELSI has provided engineers with the historical diagnostic information necessary to make remote fixes, suggest temporary work-arounds, and perform complex diagnoses faster than ever before. The case base has grown to 1555 cases with coverage of over 50 different fixes.

The system has also been demonstrated effective on other types of imaging equipment with no changes to the software (only the log pre-processing rules need to be changed, and ELSI provides a graphical user interface to perform these customizations).

The most useful focus of future work would be help in automatically deciding which cases can be removed from the system without adversely affecting accuracy. A smaller case base is easier to maintain and has better performance.

The U.S. Patent and Trademark office has issued two patents on the algorithms described herein.

8 Acknowledgments

Special thanks to the Research and Development team, including Rasik Shah, Yumi Kim, and Alyce Stewart; and to the team of service engineers at GE Medical Systems, including Lyle Haferman, Dave Jarkins, Jon Schubert and many others.

9 References

[1] Cuddihy, P., and Shah, R., "Method and System for Analyzing Error Logs for Diagnostics"; US Patent 5463768; Oct 31,1995

[2] Cuddihy, P., and Cheetham, W.,"System and Method for Estimating a Measure of Confidence in a Match Generated from a Case-based Reasoning System"; US Patent 5799148; Aug 25, 1998

[3] Cheetham, W., Case-Based Reasoning with Confidence, Ph.D Thesis, Rensselaer Polytechnic Institute, 1996.

Case-Based Reasoning for Candidate List Extraction in a Marketing Domain

Michael Fagan, Konrad Bloor

BT Laboratories, Martlesham Heath
Ipswich, Suffolk. IP5 3RE. UK
michael.2.fagan@bt.com

Abstract. This paper describes a software tool called CALIBRE (**Ca**ndidate **Lib**rary **Re**trieval). The tool incorporates case-base reasoning to support the extraction of candidate lists for targeted marketing campaigns. The tool has been aimed at users in the marketing domain. This domain is characterised by very large databases containing many Terabytes of customer related information. Large systems such as these require careful management of the queries being submitted to optimise the use of processing and storage resources. The CBR approach encourages consistent best practice as well as cutting down on valuable negotiation time. An early prototype has been built and is currently used for experimental purposes.

1 Introduction

Extraction of candidate lists for targeted marketing campaigns is currently a time consuming and highly subjective area.

The time taken to produce a list can be measured in weeks, which in many circumstances could mean the loss of a window of opportunity.

Corporate databases are continually increasing in size and complexity, which can only magnify the problem.

Current 'candidate list' generation processes typically involve many people who, in theory at least, collaborate and negotiate to produce an optimum list within an optimum time.

Feedback, measuring the successfulness of the list (i.e. the percentage of take up) is often very limited.

An attractive goal therefore is to reduce the time spent on negotiation and increase the amount of feedback within the current process.

This paper describes the use of Case-Based Reasoning (CBR) [1,2] combined with Data Mining [3,4] as an innovative form of knowledge management to support this goal. An early prototype tool called CALIBRE (**Ca**ndidate **Lib**rary **Re**trieval) has been developed to explore initial ideas for the application of extraction and management of candidate lists for marketing campaigns.

The structure of this paper is as follows: Section 2 gives an overview of the approach taken. Section 3 describes the implementation of the tool. Section 4 discusses current issues and further work, section 5 looks at related work. Finally, Section 6 looks at the current status and plans for the tool.

2 Approach

The current process for list generation involves the production of SQL code which is constructed via negotiation through e-mail and telephony correspondence. This is inherently flawed. The resultant query could and has produced quite different outputs from what was originally envisaged.

2.1 Current Process

In large businesses, such as BT (British Telecommunications plc), there are usually many roles associated with the extraction of a candidate list. The diagram in **Fig 1** describes the typical roles involved, the arrows indicating communication. A surprising find is the apparent lack of feedback once the list has been produced. The effect of the numerous lines of communication could be analogous to a game of 'Chinese Whispers', the information being slightly changed at each step of the process making it extremely conceivable that the end product is a total opposite to what was initially requested.

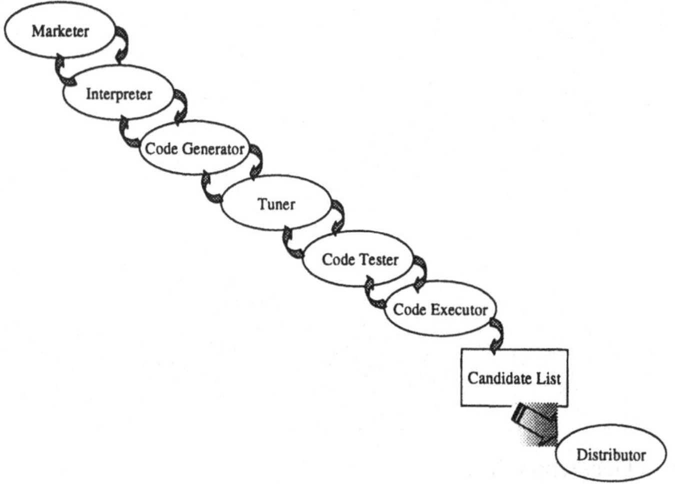

Fig 1. Typical List Generation Process

2.2 Proposed CBR enhanced Process

The advantages to a case-based approach include the following:

i. A problem does not need to be defined completely due to the use of a scoring and matching algorithm - a solution can still be found [5],

ii. The approach is simple, and easy to implement, using procedures familiar to those involved in expert systems and information retrieval,

iii. Commercial tools already exist with built-in case-based reasoning support, allowing systems to be built quickly,

iv. A case-based reasoning system will quickly capture knowledge specific to its domain; it will learn problem-solution pairs, and will, as time passes, grow more able to solve problems.

The disadvantages could include the following:

Traditionally, a case-based reasoning system is not well suited to scale, although this has been addressed [6].

A case is typically composed of a number of attributes, which have to be defined before the case-base is populated. Since they do have to be defined, the application of case-base reasoning is suited to very specific applications, that typically involve one type of recurring problem.

The Calibre list generation process reduces the number of roles and therefore, in this case, an increase in clarity and responsibility.

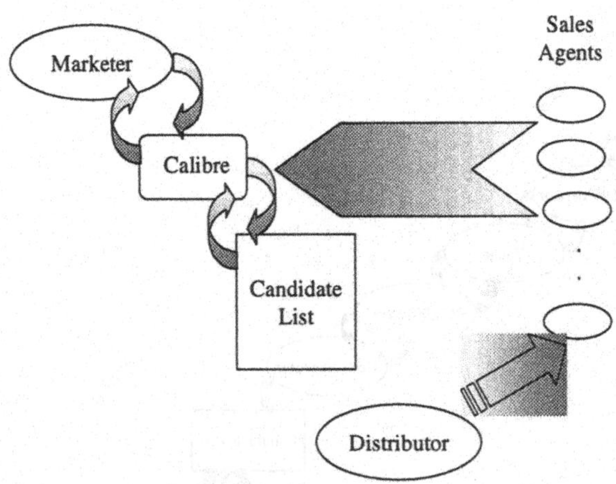

Fig 2. Calibre List Generation Process

Fig 2 illustrates that the marketer who has an initial idea of who and when to target can experiment with these ideas through an iterative approach. This is achieved by using a number of Data Mining methods to cluster customer profiles and use these as cases within a casebase. The marketer is then allowed to ask the question 'Who is similar to my ideal profile?'. The Calibre tool will return the first ten closest matches, by default, which can give the marketer a quick indication of the result.

An attempt was made previously [7] to speed up the negotiation process by managing more effectively the SQL queries used to generate the candidate list. This attempt solved only a small distinct piece of a much larger problem.

Calibre endeavors to replace the current negotiation process with a combination of Case-based Reasoning, Data Mining and Socket communication over a web client.

Calibre was built by tackling each of the disadvantages of the current process in turn, and examining the requirements of any replacement system:

- Time:
  The ability to produce mailing list in hours or days as opposed to weeks would make for a campaign effort that was much more responsive to customer and company needs.
- What-if scenarios:
  This would allow marketers to examine how the customer type and number of customers varied as they changed their requirements.
- Feedback:
  Little or no feedback means that assessment of campaign effectiveness is very difficult.
- High cost:
  A new process would have to either reduce the cost of making queries, or always return pertinent results.
- Sensitive site removal:
  The process would automatically remove sensitive addresses, or include some capability for making an address 'sensitive' so that it would not be returned by any query. This sensitive site removal could be achieved using several different approaches. Clustering [7], one cluster could contain all the sensitive addresses; matching would then not occur on that cluster. Partitioning of a case-base, which could be implemented via rules. Using a current field, or an additional field as an attribute of a case, to represent 'sensitivity' could be used. Either a case-based match giving it a lower score than any threshold possible would then use this field or a process that 'plucked' the addresses out of the final list.

It can be seen that the new process, in addition to reducing the time taken, would have to work on a faster time-scale, and eliminate the need for specialist's [9].

Case-based reasoning in tandem with other techniques can plausibly work as the mechanism that will enable the marketing requirements to be fulfilled.

3 Implementation

CALIBRE (**C**andidate **Lib**rary **Re**trieval) has been designed to give an accessible web interface in order that marketers, through iteration, can arrive at a suitable set of criteria for the selection of a marketing campaign list.

Through the use of Case-based reasoning within the ART*Enterprise product [5], the CALIBRE server is able to connect to many different database systems. An Oracle database has been used as the permanent storage for a case-base, which allows for simple updating via a data mining process, which adds new cases to the case-base when it finds them

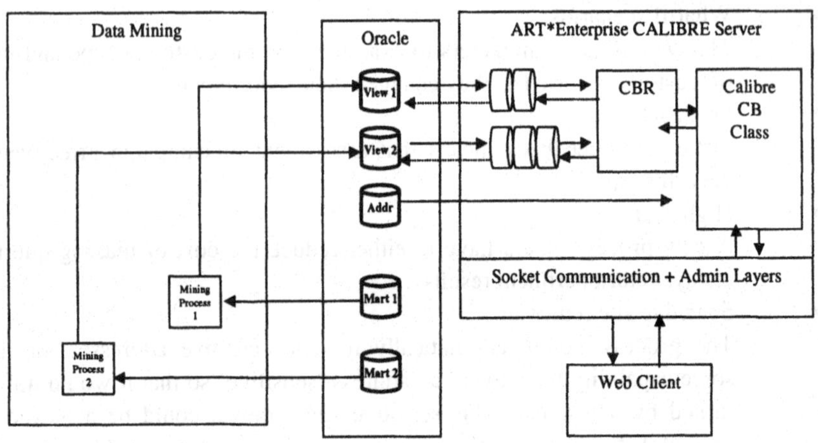

Fig 3. Calibre Architecture

3.1 The Data Mining Process

It is envisaged that the actual marketing data will be held in a vast data warehouse. Different aggregate views on this data will make up a number of data marts. To extract meaningful cases from these data marts to insert into the case-base, the data mining process has to be run.

This process is useful because it adds value to the data, by means of classifying sites as belonging to a certain cluster, that will share certain traits with the other sites in that cluster. Since this is a proof of concept, this process is run on an ad-hoc basis, using SAS[10] to cluster sample data into cases, which is then exported into Oracle, to be the case-base. This procedure speeds the process up via data abstraction.

It is envisaged that one 'sub' data mining process will exist for each data mart. Thus, different views of the main customer data will be mined, and the results put into the casebases. The data mining process has the potential of acting as an automatic maintenance advisor, which is currently a research issue within the Case-based Reasoning community.

3.2 The Server

The CALIBRE server has been created in order to give the user marketing data, by means of the client. It uses the following techniques to do this:

- Object-oriented programming
- Case-based reasoning
- The Berkeley sockets mechanism.
- A report.

3.2.1 Object-oriented Programming

The CALIBRE server uses the object-oriented capabilities of ART*Enterprise to provide an easy-to-use layer of abstraction, which uses composition (as opposed to inheritance) to perform its goal. Its primary goal is to serve the client the data required. This implies secondary goals: to overcome ART*Enterprise imposed limits, and allow for modular, simple addition of other data-marts to the system - and hence other collections of data, if they are created.

This layer of abstraction (the 'calibre-cb' class) provides methods that create, import and query a calibre-cb object, while managing a case-base as a collection of one or more actual ART*Enterprise case-bases (as these are limited in size to 65535 cases each).

The calibre-cb class also handles all administration with regard to the requirements of ART*Enterprise concerning case-bases and reporting. The exception to this, is obtaining address information (or other information, if specified in the appropriate instance of a calibre-cb object), which is a responsibility outwith the class, handled by a function.

The handling of multiple (but not concurrent) users is achieved by the use of user objects. Each of these has as attributes the user details, such as name, password, security level, etc. This allows for flexible access control. In the current system, the different marts need one level of access, that is granted to normal users, and another level of access to stop the server through software, that is granted to the administrator account.

3.2.2 Case-based Reasoning

The CALIBRE server can claim speed increases because of the way it uses data mining techniques together with case-based reasoning to give data abstraction. The case-based reasoning engine of ART*Enterprise allows CALIBRE to quickly match a presented case against a case base and return the results to the client. The procedure that the CALIBRE goes through in order to obtain addresses from matches on a presented case goes as follows:

1. On initialisation, CALIBRE loads in all case-bases that are defined, from external sources, and commences listening on a port.
2. A client connects.
3. The server obtains the presented case from the client.
4. It then instantiates a case object of the correct type, with the information it has obtained.
5. CALIBRE then executes a case-based match with the case-object in question, on the client specified data mart.
6. The attribute that is used for joining is obtained from the first n matches (where n is user specified).
7. A query is run on the data source that is defined to be for addresses. Because of the limitations of Oracle, the query is actually split up into chunks that ask for less than 255 tuples/addresses at a time. This can be executed either sequentially or in parallel
8. The address data (or other data) is sent to the client, along with a score, and a set of criteria for each address, for user perusal.

The matching used in the tool was the standard supplied in the Brightware ART*Enterprise product [5]. This consisted of two types, text and numeric.

The text matching feature score is the product of the percentage of subfeatures which match and the feature score range

$$feature-score_{f,i} = mmw_{f,i} + \frac{msf_{f,i}}{tsf_f}\left(mw_{f,i} - mmw_{f,i}\right) \text{..}equation.1$$

where

- $mw_{f,i}$ is the match weight of feature *f* for case *i*
- $mmw_{f,i}$ is the mismatch weight of feature *f* for case *i*.
- $msf_{f,i}$ is the number of matching subfeatures of feature *f* for case *i*.
- tsf_f is the total number of subfeatures of feature *f* for the presented case.

The numeric matching is based on the distance between two numbers. The equation for computing a feature score in this case is:

$$feature-score_{f,i} = mw_{f,i} - \frac{|cv_{f,i} - pcv_f|}{mdev_{f,i}}(mw_{f,i} - mmw_{f,i})..equation.2$$

where

- $cv_{f,i}$ is the numeric value of feature *f* of case *i*.
- pcv_f is the numeric value of feature *f* of the presented case.
- $mdev_{f,i}$ is the match deviation of feature *f* of case *i*.

3.2.3 The Berkeley Sockets Mechanism

The CALIBRE server uses the Berkeley sockets mechanism [11] in order to communicate with the client. This means that any client software that communicates using the protocol that the CALIBRE server expects, can extract marketing information, given the correct privileges.

3.2.4 The Report

The information is passed to the client As the report is specified in the calibre-cb class, it only contains information specified by the administrator.

The presentation of the report to the user is an interface concern; what the interface chooses to do with the raw data sent to it is arbitrary. The interface may display it in CSV (Comma Seperated Value) format for importing into a spreadsheet or DBMS, as an HTML table, or even print onto envelopes or address labels. The report is sent back to the client with three stages for every address/record that has matched within the threshold:

Several 'criteria' strings are sent. These are plain english explanations of why the address is being sent, which can be printed in some form to the user. These are sent so that the user may build up trust with the system, and for the system to be able to justify the displaying of an address.

The score is sent

The address (or other data that has been administrator specified) sent. There is some information, sometimes 'NULL' where the attribute for the tuple in question is blank. The client can strip this out. All the information is in upper case.

This simple format means that the client can ignore any of the information not applicable to its purpose. An automated client may obtain cases and weightings from a list, and create a file from which to print onto envelopes, while ignoring criteria and site number. On the other hand, the Web/CGI client that has been created allows one to examine the criteria, if a build-up of trust is required.

3.3 System Use

Outwardly, the system is to be used by those who do not necessarily have vast computing experience or skills, and are more interested in results. As such, the interface has to reflect this by being both intuitive and simple, while not getting in the way of the ministrations of an expert user. Internally, the interface between the client and the server has to be well defined, to enable for easy maintenance and alterations by administrators and programmers.

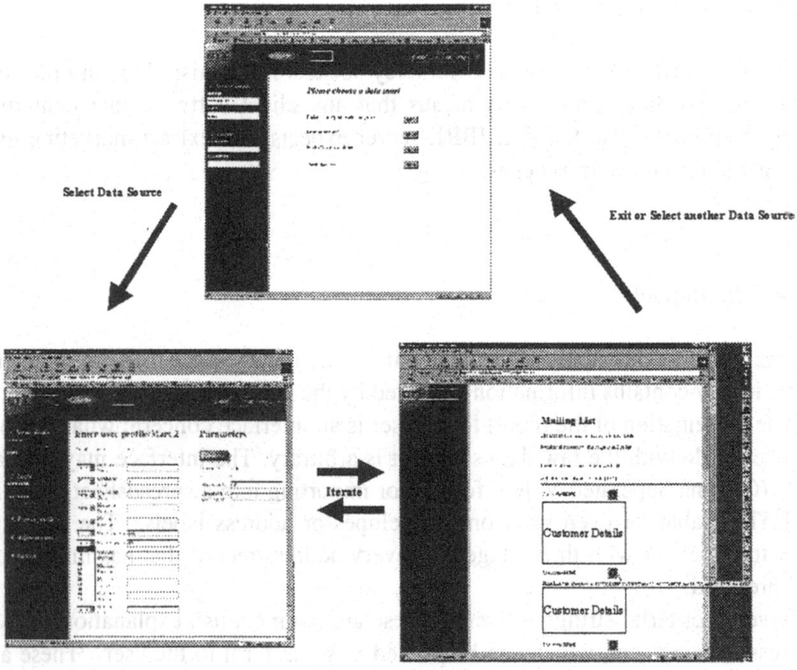

Fig 4. The User View

3.3.1 Perl/CGI

The interface has been designed to be intuitive to use, with attractive, consistent appearance and feel.

The data mart selection screen is extremely simple, requiring one to, if necessary, change the server and port number, enter username and password for the CALIBRE server, and select a data mart. Upon selection of a data mart, a screen is presented that allows one to enter a value and a weighting for each field, thus building up a prospective case. This screen also allows changing of the maximum number of addresses wanted, and a threshold; all addresses displayed will have a score allocated that is greater than, or equal to this threshold.
Once the data of a prospective profile is entered, and the weightings, threshold, and maximum matches are adjusted to the users satisfaction, then the submit button is pressed. It is here that any applicable results are displayed after a time interval that is a variable depending on the machine that the CALIBRE server is resident on, the machine the web server is resident on, and the quality of link.
The results screen displays the current time, the number of results that the query actually matched with, and the number of results displayed. Below this, is the table of addresses. This table displays the address, along with the site number, and (with a modern browser, e.g. Netscape Navigator, or Microsoft Internet Explorer) a graphical 'hotspot', that displays the criteria information for a moment, while the mouse arrow is over it. This allows the user to gradually build up trust with the information that is given them.

3.3.2 Server

The server presents the same interface to all clients. Through this interface, the client requests the services it needs in order to fulfil the objectives it has been set by its user.
The server upon receiving a username and password, processes a number of commands, ending with a 'bye', whereupon the user is disconnected and the server waits again for another connection. The finite automaton below shows this sequence:

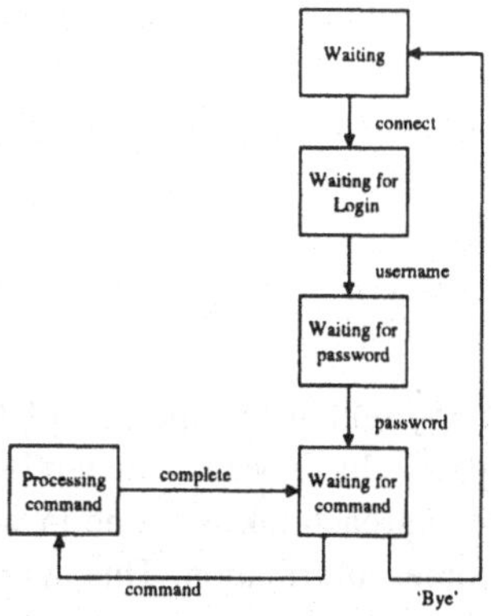

Fig 5. A Finite Automaton showing states of the Server

The command set that is allowed depends on the users security level, and may well vary. The setup of the server currently is that three security levels are used:

User accounts are easily added to the system by defining an instance of the class 'user' with the appropriate details

The commands currently allow the client to achieve objectives such as the following:

i. Change to a different data mart.
ii. Request to download a configuration file of the current mart.
iii. Query the current case-base
iv. Execute administrative commands.

The model used is not difficult to extend, and could be done so to provide extra functionality.

4 Discussion

The user may enter values for as many as the presentation case features as required. If only one feature is chosen then only that feature will be used to calculate the feature score.

The tool allows people within the marketing domain to experiment and specify exactly the type of profile they wish to target.

Further experiments are required in the following areas:

- Automating the Data Mining process to populate the data marts which in turn populate the casebases
- Negotiation between distributed casebases
- Implementation of maintenance strategies
- Addition and updating of a campaign casebase via a web interface for the inclusion of feedback from sales representatives.

It must be stressed that although the software tool is being used for experimental purpose it is still classed as 'work in progress'.

5 Related Work

An extensive search found only one paper [5] relating to the use of Case-Base Reasoning within this domain, although many papers have been written relating to the use of large scale casebases [12,13,14,15]. The approach taken is one in which SQL queries are managed and reused to extract customer information. This approach only addressed a small part of a very large problem that of the extraction process.

6 Conclusions

The techniques used and methodologies followed are tried and tested. The novelty is in the application of Case-Base Reasoning to a new domain.
We have tried to extend the boundaries of CBR by becoming removed from the typical conversational type of interaction.
Within the Marketing domain it maybe that the marketer has only an outline of an idea. This tool gives him/her the opportunity to experiment at low cost and then publish results when satisfied.

References

[1] Aamodt, A., Plaza, E.: Case-Based Reasoning: Foundational Issues, methodological Variations, and System Approaches. AI Communications 7(1), 39-52, 1994

[2] Leake, D.: Case-Based Reasoning: Experiences, Lessons, & Future Directions. AAAI Press, ISBN 0-262-62110-X LEACP, 1997

[3] Piatetsky-Shapiro, G., Frawley, W. J. (eds), Knowledge Discovery in Databases, AAAI Press, 1991.

[4] Ribeiro, J. S., Kaufmann, K. A., Kerschberg, L., 'Knowledge Discovery from Multiple Databases', in *KDD-95:* Proc. of the 1st Int'l Conf. on Knowledge Discovery and Data Mining, U. M. Fayyad, R. Uthurusamy (eds.), AAAI Press, 1995, pp240-245.

[5] Brightware Inc (1996). ARTScript Programming Guide 3, Rules & CBR

[6] Brown, M. (1993). A Memory model for Case Retrieval by Activation Passing, Department of Computer Science, Manchester University.

[7] Everitt, B.S. (1980), 'Cluster Analysis', 2d Edition, London: Heineman Educational Books Ltd

[8] Fagan, M, Corley S L, 'CBR for the Reuse of Corporate SQL Knowledge' in Advances in Case-Based Reasoning, EWCBR-98. Springer-Verlag, pp382-391.

[9] Schank, R.C., Abelson, R. (1977) Scipts, Plans; Goals and Understanding: An Inquiry into Human Knowledge Structures.

[10] SAS, http://www.sas.com/

[11] Richard Stevens, W. (1990). UNIX Network Programming, Prentice-Hall.

[12] Kitano, H., Shibata, A., Shimazu, H., Kajihara, J., & Sato, A. (1992) Building large-scale and corporate wide case-based systems In, Proceedings of AAAI-92

[13] Netten, B.D., & Vingerhoeds, R.A. (1995) Large-scale fault diagnosis for on-board train systems In, Case-Based Reasoning Research and Development

[14] Waltz, D. (1996) Large-Scale Applications of CBR In, Advances in Case-Based Reasoning

[15] Schaaf, J.W (1996) Fish and Shrink: A Next Step Towards Efficient Case Retrieval in Large-Scale Case Bases In, Advances in Case-Based Reasoning

CBR for the Reuse of Image Processing Knowledge: A Recursive Retrieval/Adaptation Strategy

Valérie FICET-CAUCHARD, Christine PORQUET & Marinette REVENU

GREYC-ISMRA - 6 Bd du Maréchal Juin - F14050 CAEN cedex FRANCE
tél: +33 (0)2-31-45-27-21 fax: +33 (0)2-31-45-26-98 e-mail: Valerie.Ficet@greyc.ismra.fr

Abstract. The development of an Image Processing (IP) application is a complex activity, which can be greatly alleviated by user-friendly graphical programming environments. Our major objective is to help IP experts reuse parts of their applications. A first work towards knowledge reuse has been to propose a suitable representation of the strategies of IP experts by means of IP plans (trees of tasks, methods and tools). This paper describes the CBR module of our interactive system for the development of IP plans. After a brief presentation of the overall architecture of the system and its other modules, we explain the distinction between an IP case and an IP plan, and give the selection criteria and functions that are used for similarity calculation. The core of the CBR module is a search/adaptation algorithm, whose main steps are detailed: retrieval of suitable cases, recursive adaptation of the selected one and memorization of new cases. The system's implementation is presently completed; its functioning is described in a session showing the kind of assistance provided by the CBR module during the development of a new IP application.

1. Introduction

We are doing research work in the design of an interactive system that can provide assistance during the working out of Image Processing (IP) applications; the system's architecture has been detailed in [5]. Our system is composed of several modules dealing with the tuning out of IP applications through interactive acquisition and representation of IP knowledge coming from IP experts, the execution of such IP applications and the reuse of applications following a Case-Based Reasoning approach (CBR). This paper is dedicated to a detailed description of the CBR module: in particular, our description of IP cases, similarity calculation between two cases and recursive search/adaptation algorithm are presented and discussed.
In section 2, the framework of our research is briefly presented along two axes: our objectives with regards to IP and our modeling of IP application. Sections 3 and 4 are entirely dealing with the CBR module: first, our definition of an IP case and the functions used for similarity calculation are given (section 3). Then the search/adaptation algorithm is described and explanations are given about the process of case selection, recursive adaptation of the selected solution and memorization of new cases (section

4). Finally, a complete session showing how to use the CBR module for developing an IP application is described in section 5.

2. Research framework: the TMT model

Our primary objective is to represent and structure the knowledge of different IP experts so as to enable knowledge share and reuse. To achieve such a goal, we are advocating for an interactive system enabling knowledge acquisition from IP experts, as it comes to the fore through the development of IP applications. In this section, our approach for the building of applications is presented; we describe our model for the representation of applications and briefly give an idea of the functioning of two essential modules of the system: the interactive creation module and the execution module.

2.1. Representation of applications by hierarchical plans

Our approach to the development of IP applications is based on the smart supervision of libraries of operators. An operator is a program that performs one basic operation on one or several images. It takes as inputs the image(s) to be processed as well as parameters and produces as outputs one or several images as well as numerical and/or symbolical results. With such libraries, the building of an application then "simply" consists in linking operators and tuning their parameters. Users can thus stand back from computer codes and perform programming at the "knowledge" level.
However, a real-size application can lead to sequences of up to tens of operators. In order to represent the reasoning associated to such sequences, we suggest to use a representation based on trees of tasks, that we call "IP plans". Such trees correspond to hierarchical decompositions of problems into sub-problems, each problem or sub-problem being related to an IP task. As is shown in figure 1, a plan not only represents the linking of IP operators corresponding to the leaves of the tree, but also all the reasoning necessary for the creation of such a linking, which is represented by IP tasks schematized as gray boxes.

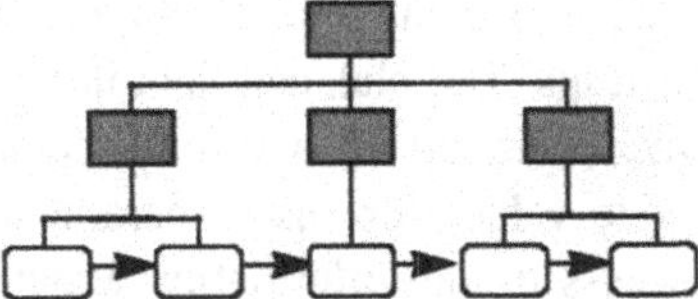

Fig. 1: representation of an IP plan

2.2. The TMT model

In our system, IP plans as well as control tasks (dealing with plan management and system control) are uniformly represented within the "task – method – tool" model. In this model, a task represents a goal or sub-goal; a method describes a know-how, it specifies how a task can be performed; a tool reifies a computer code (IP operator, Lisp or C function) in conceptual terms with a link to the code enabling to run it. There exist two types of methods: "terminal" methods (fig. 2a) that achieve a task by calling to a computer code through the medium of a tool and "complex" methods (fig. 2b) that decompose a task into sub-tasks by means of a "THEN" tree. Finally, as there may exist several strategies to solve an IP problem, a task can be associated to several methods (fig. 2c) by means of an "OR" tree, the choice of the method to be applied being made at the time of execution.

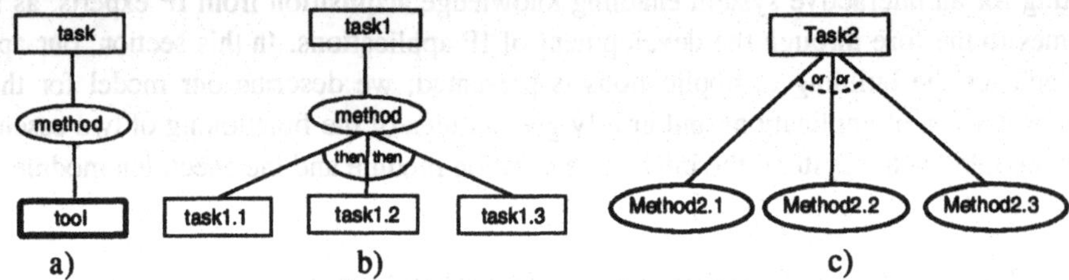

Fig. 2: various possible links between tasks, methods and tools

2.3. System's functionalities

Our system is provided with a graphical interface, in which several functionalities have been defined for the interactive construction and the interactive execution of IP applications. In particular, they include the visualization of applications as trees of tasks, so that users can study the reasoning associated to any given IP plan.
In order to create a new IP plan, the user has to define his/her tasks and tools by filling in fields in appropriate windows; he/she can link then by defining methods and data flows between tasks and sub-tasks or tasks and tools. There are three ways for specifying the way to get the values of parameters for tasks and tools: computed from another task or tool, fixed once and for all, or to be required from user.
When they want an application to be executed, users simply have to select the root task of the corresponding plan in a menu and the plan is immediately visualized on screen as a schematic tree of tasks. The plan can then interactively be executed: users are required to choose between methods when several methods exist to perform some given task, and also to provide values for "user" parameters. Once the execution is completed, they can have access to any information about tasks and tools that have actually been executed and moreover, visualize any intermediate image in order to assess critical points.
In addition to the creation and execution functionalities that have just been described, the third and most original functionality integrated into the system consists in a second mode for creating applications through CBR. The corresponding CBR module is detailed in the next two sections.

3. Case representation and similarity

A case is broadly composed of two parts: description of the solution and description of the problem. In our system, a solution is represented as a TMT tree, which can be accessed through its root task. In Case-Based Planning [9] [12] or Case-Based Design [11], a solution is generally built by combining parts of several plans coming from several cases. In order to make this kind of design possible, we have decided to associate several cases to one single plan: the first case is associated to the root task of the plan, the others to some sub-tasks of the same plan, that are considered as representative of specific IP techniques. In the example of figure 3, cases are associated to tasks Ta1, Ta2 et Ta4 that correspond to some specific strategy in IP; by contrast, no case is associated to tasks Ta3, Ta5, Ta6, Ta7 et Ta8.

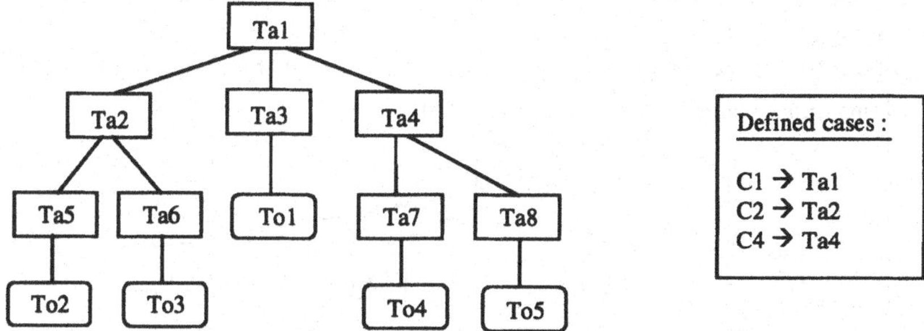

Fig.3: association of a set of cases with a TMT plan

The problem's description is made thanks to a set of discriminative criteria, which have been found out from a thorough study of the IP domain. Results of this study are presented in section 3.1; the similarity functions for comparing cases are described in section 3.2.

3.1. Criteria for case selection

The finding out of a relevant set of similarity criteria enabling to characterize an IP problem is based, on the one hand, on a study of IP systems detailed in [6] and, on the other hand on the study of books and Ph.D. dissertations dedicated to IP techniques [4] [10].

The major issue is here to choose an indexing vocabulary that can be shared and accepted by any IP programmer. Except for low-level actions (corresponding to operators from an IP library), there really exists no consensus on IP terms. In particular, this can be explained by difficulties to cut oneself off from the domain of application (most IP programmers work on one type of application at a time and thus only use terms from their current domain of application).

The criteria we put forward come from a classification of the most often encountered terms used to describe IP actions and data. We have made a distinction between two broad categories of criteria: criteria related to the task definition and criteria related to the image description.

Criteria related to the task definition
This first category includes data related to the operation performed by a task and to its position in the plan in relation to other tasks. Such criteria include IP type or phase, problem definition and abstraction level.
IP type or **phase** broadly corresponds to the type of problem that is solved by a task. According to the task's abstraction level, one can take into account:

- either the IP type: the root task of a complete plan defines a high-level processing, which belongs to an IP type (*detection, segmentation, classification,...*),
- or the IP phase: each sub-task of a plan defines one part of the complete processing, which corresponds to one specific step (*pre-processing, seed determination, region determination, ...*).

The various IP phases correspond to a vertical division of the plan (fig. 4); for some types of problems, some phases may be optional.

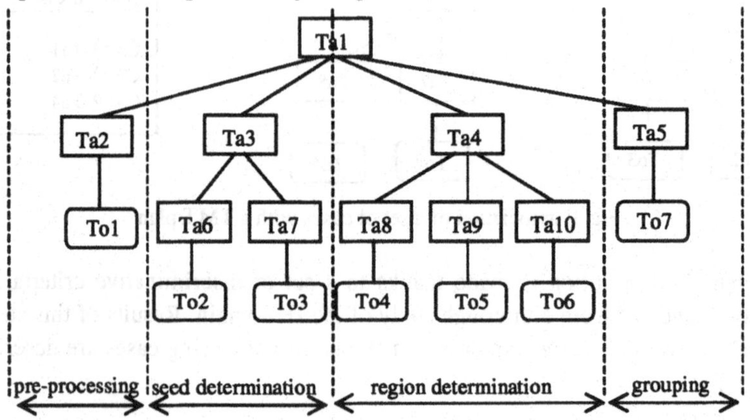

Fig.4: vertical division of a plan solving a segmentation problem

The **definition of the problem** is composed of a set of keywords selected among three pre-defined lists: 1. a list of **verbs** describing the operations performed by the task (*detect, classify, binarize, smooth, ...*), 2. a list of **nouns** corresponding, either to objects on which the action is performed (*contours, regions, image background, ...*), or to IP techniques (*region growing, region division, ...*) and 3. a list of **adjectives** qualifying, either the objects on which the action is performed (*small, local, ...*), or the action itself (*partial, strong, ...*).
As can be noticed in previous examples, the vocabulary from these three lists of keywords is completely independent from the domain of application.
Finally the **abstraction levels** that correspond to a horizontal division of the plan (fig. 5) are based on the abstraction levels of the automatic planner BORG [3].

- Tasks belonging to the *intentional level* answer question such as "what to do ?" and deal with IP objectives.

- Tasks belonging to the *functional level* answer questions such as "how to do ?" and refer to some IP technique, leaving aside technical constraints related to their implementation.
- Tasks belonging to the *operational level* answer questions such as "by means of what ?" and represent IP technical know-how that can be implemented as algorithms.

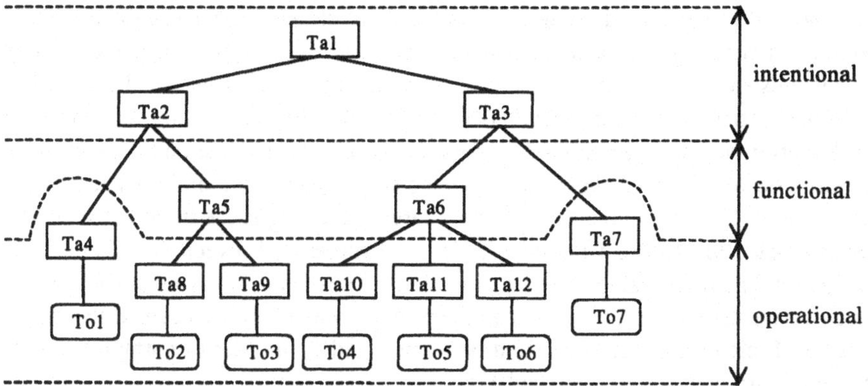

Fig.5: horizontal division of a plan

Criteria related to the image description

Among the criteria related to the context of images, some correspond to physical knowledge (related to image formation) and describe image quality (e.g. **type of noise, amount of noise** and **quality of contrast**). These criteria are of paramount importance for the choice of the pre-processing steps.

Other criteria rather correspond to perceptual knowledge (symbolic description in terms of visual primitives). They include the **presence** or **absence** of an image **background** and the **aspect of objects** (*homogeneous gray level, light color, texture, thick boundaries, ...*).

The third group of criteria corresponds to semantic knowledge (scene analysis and components of the scene) and describes the appearance of what is to be detected, but in abstract terms, independent from the domain of application. These latter criteria include the **form** of objects (*convex, concave, elongated, compact, square, round, ...*), the **relative size of objects**, their **position** (*left, middle, right, top, bottom, center)* and **inter-object relations** (*proximity, connectivity, inclusion, ...*).

3.2. Similarity calculation between two cases

One can consider two principles for the determination of similar cases, either maximize similarity [2] or minimize adaptation effort [11]. Owing to the absence of any automatic method for evaluating IP results, we have chosen the former. First the functions used for similarity calculation between a source case and a target case are described. Then comparison modes for each type of criterion are detailed. Finally, the management of missing values for a criterion is explained; in fact, as it is the case in ISAC [1], all previously enumerated criteria need not be taken into account in any application.

Similarity functions

Our first group of criteria (i.e. criteria related to the task definition) is here to characterize the action performed by a task, and is thus closely dependent on the TMT model. Such criteria define a set of tasks that can solve one "type of problem". They are "compulsory" (each criterion of the target case must have a value) and are used to reduce the search space. A first similarity function Φ_t using the criteria related to the task definition will thus be applied to reduce the set of candidate target cases. This function is defined by formula (1) as the weighted average of the similarity results for each criterion: S is the source case, T is the target case , α_{Cr} is the importance coefficient associated to criterion Cr and $\varphi_{Cr}(S,T)$ is the similarity between S et T related to criterion Cr. The result value of any φ_{Cr} function is between 0 (if values of Cr between both cases are very different from each other) and 1 (when they are deemed identical). All α_{Cr} coefficients are also comprised between 0 and 1, in order to normalize the Φ_t function (return values between 0 and 1).

$$\Phi_t(S,T) = \frac{\left(\sum \alpha_{Cr} \times \varphi_{Cr}(S,T)\right)}{\sum \alpha_{Cr}} \qquad \forall Cr \in \{\text{criteria related to the task definition}\} \qquad (1)$$

The second group of criteria (i.e. criteria related to the context of images) characterizes the objects to be detected and depends on the current image. Such criteria are not meaningful for any application: for instance, contrast quality has no sense when processing a region map. This second group of criteria are "optional" ones (all criteria of the target case need not be filled in); they enable to select the nearest cases among the candidates obtained after applying function Φ_t. The second similarity function Φ_i is thus used to reduce the set of selected cases, in order to get a list of reasonable size. This function is defined by formula (2) as the weighted average of similarity results on each criterion; notations and properties are the same as in formula (1).

$$\Phi_t(S,T) = \frac{\left(\sum \alpha_{Cr} \times \varphi_{Cr}(S,T)\right)}{\sum \alpha_{Cr}} \quad \forall Cr \in \{\text{criteria related to the image description}\} \qquad (2)$$

The definitions of functions φ_{Cr} that are in charge of similarity calculation for each category of criterion are given in the next paragraph. The use of similarity functions Φ_t et Φ_i in the selection/adaptation algorithm, as well as the adjustment of importance coefficients are explained in section 4.

Criterion comparison modes

It is clear that the list of criteria related to the context of images cannot be exhaustive: the criteria we put forward are coming from our study on IP literature and the development of our own applications. It should be completed in the course of further applications. Each criterion type is associated to a generic similarity function, in order to easily integrate new criteria. Here are the types of criteria that are presently available:

- strict numerical criterion: the value must be of integer or real type and comparison between two values returns 1 when values are strictly equal and 0 otherwise,
- strict symbolical criterion: the value is a symbol and comparison between two values returns 1 when values are strictly equal and 0 otherwise (e.g. presence of an image background),
- gradual numerical criterion: the value belongs to integer or real intervals and comparison between two values returns the difference between the two values divided by the interval length (e.g. relative size of objects),
- gradual symbolical criterion: the value belongs to an ordered set of symbols and comparison between two values returns the difference between the two values according to their order in the set, divided by the interval length (e.g. noise amount),
- multi-valued criteria: the value is defined as a non-ordered list of symbols and/or numbers and comparison between two values returns the ratio of the number of common elements in both lists to the length of the target case list (e.g. verbs used in the problem's definition).

A missing criterion value for a given case can be due to several causes (no meaning, usefulness, ...) and can be taken into account in several ways (do not take into account, consider as a specific value, ...). Our point of view on that issue differs whether one considers the source case or the target one:

- the absence of a value in a target case means that the value is considered as irrelevant for this case (either it is meaningless, or it has been judged as useless by user), that absence will have no consequence on similarity calculation ($\varphi_\alpha(S,T)=0$ and $\alpha_\alpha=0$),
- the absence of a value in a source case (while this value is present in the target one) means that one similarity condition is not respected; that absence should lower the result of similarity calculation ($\varphi_\alpha(S,T)=0$ and $\alpha_\alpha\neq0$).

Both conditions are respected by the set of generic functions that compute similarity for each criterion type.

4. Recursive selection/adaptation algorithm

In the selection/adaptation process of most CBR systems, one can notice, on the one hand, the existence of a preliminary step in the selection process, aiming at reducing the search space [1] [8], and on the other hand, the fact that the selection/adaptation cycle must be applied iteratively, in particular in CBR planning [9] [11].

Our approach (fig. 6) is also based on a selection/adaptation cycle, iteratively applied at various levels of the plan, but in addition, at each cycle loop, a reduction step of the search space has been included.

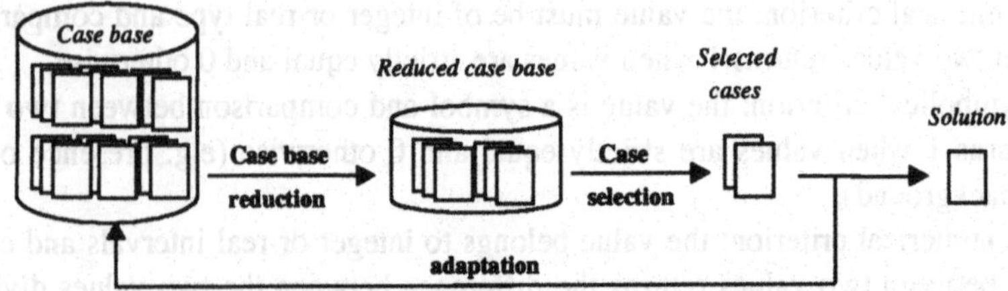

Fig. 6 : schema of our selection/adaptation process

The reduction of the search space can be achieved, either by using criteria corresponding to strict constraints, or by considering that two cases can only be compared when defined by the same set of criteria. The latter technique is not adapted to our domain. As a matter of fact, among the criteria related to the context of images, some of them bring nothing new about the target case, without disqualifying the source case. The reduction step can thus be achieved by means of function Φ_t using the "compulsory" criteria related to the task definition, while the selection step makes use of function Φ_i with the "optional" criteria related to the image description.

The objective of our CBR module is to provide some assistance to IP programmers when they are building applications, by helping them reuse solutions of previously-solved problems that are somewhat analogous to their current problem. The selection/adaptation process must thus take place in cooperation with the user, according to the following algorithm:

```
1. Ask user for values of criteria related to the task
   definition
2. Determine the set Σ of cases matching the desired cri-
   teria by means of Φt
3. Ask user for values of criteria related to the image
   description
4. While Σ is not of reasonable size do
          Modify the weight of criteria
          Reduce the set Σ by mean of Φi
5. Ask user to choose a case among the set Σ
6. Present the plan associated to the chosen case to user
   and propose him/her to modify the unsuitable sub-tasks,
   either by re-running the algorithm, or by building it
   from scratch, via the interactive creation module
```

Steps 1 and 3 correspond to the input of the description of the target case. Step 2 is the reduction step of the search space. The selection of candidate source cases is done in step 4; step 5 corresponds to the user's final choice. Finally, step 6 consists in adapting the plan associated to the selected source case to the current problem.

Principles for selection and adaptation of cases used in our algorithm are detailed in next two sections.

4.1. Selection of a source case

In the course of step 2 of the algorithm, the reduction of the search space consists in selecting source cases that solve the same type of problem as target case T. It corresponds to a selection of cases S such that Φ_t (S,T) > α_t where α_t is a threshold fixed beforehand (as function Φ_t returns a value between 0 and 1, α_t is fixed to a default-value of 0.5). The weights of each criterion in function Φ_t are also fixed: the same importance is granted to all criteria. This step provides a first set of cases Σ.
So that the user can choose a case at step 5, the set of cases resulting from step 4 must be of reasonable size. If the set is too small, the user's choice will loose importance, and if it is too large, the user's choice will be difficult. The iterative nature of step 4 enables to get a set whose size can be shown to the user as a list: he/she can then examine each case in detail, before making the final choice, which well accounts for the intuitive aspect that characterizes the way IP experts work. The modification of set Σ at each iteration is done by means of a relaxation process, by modifying the weights of criteria and/or the selection threshold. To implement this kind of relaxation, when the user enters the values of criteria for the target case, he/she must indicate whether the criterion is considered as important or not. All importance criteria are initialized with 0.5. At each iteration, the system keeps the cases S from set Σ such that Φ_i (S,T) > α_i where α_i is the selection threshold. If the size of the resulting set is too small or too large (by default between 2 and 5 cases), the coefficients of the most important criteria are raised by 0.1, whereas those of the least important ones are lowered by 0.1 for the next iteration. When it is no longer possible to modify coefficients (coefficients of the least important criteria have reached 0), if the set of source cases is still too small or too large, a second relaxation mode consisting in lowering threshold α_i is applied.

4.2. Interactive plan adaptation

Case adaptation by means of parts of other cases is particularly worthwhile in the domain of CBR planning. In our system, a case can be adapted at several levels and in several ways: locally or globally, either by means of the CBR module, or by means of the interactive creation module.
The plan solution to a case may only require minor local modifications. For instance, the parameters of an operator must be tuned, or an operator should be replaced by another one that better matches the current problem. This first type of modification can be taken into account by using the modification menu of the interactive creation module.
But a plan may also require broader modifications, i.e. necessitate the replacement of a whole sub-plan by another one. To achieve such modifications, step 5 of the selection/adaptation algorithm offers a means to adapt the solution of the current case by replacing the root task of any sub-plan of the current plan by another task. The substitution task can be obtained, either by re-running the algorithm in order to retrieve a similar case, or by building it from scratch, via the interactive creation module. In the example of figure 7, a plan is adapted along three successive steps:

- replacement of sub-plan A by sub-plan A', which is obtained by re-running the selection algorithm,
- replacement of sub-plan B by sub-plan B', which is built via the interactive creation module.
- transformation of tool C into tool C', simply by changing the operator linked to tool C.

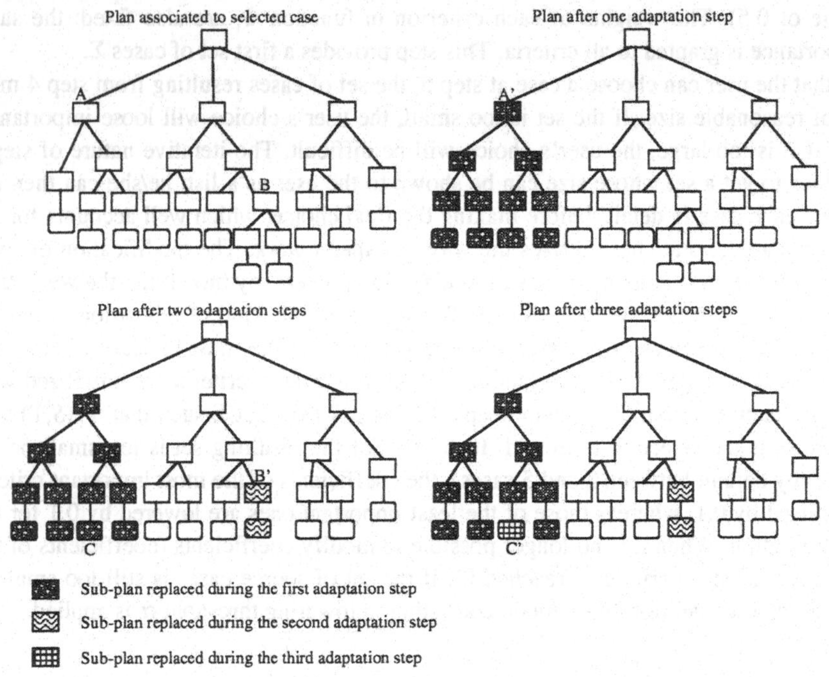

Fig. 7: adaptation of a solution plan along three steps

This example shows the interest in having a recursive algorithm: a plan can be adapted, whatever its level within the tree of tasks (A is a high-level task, B a low-level task, C an operator) and as long as necessary (A is replaced by A', then A' is adapted by replacing C by C'). Once a new plan is completed, one has to decide whether new cases associated to this plan should be added to the case library. This issue is discussed in the next section.

4.3. The memorization step

Memorizing a new case should only be considered if it brings new knowledge to the base. It implies that a case must respect two conditions in order to be integrated: the corresponding knowledge must be correct and it must bedifferent enough from the knowledge of the cases that are already in the base.

Checking the first condition consists in verifying the consistency and efficiency of the produced plan. A plan is consistent when its execution is normal and it is efficient if it

produces satisfactory results. Consistency can be checked by the correct progress of the plan execution, while its efficiency must be assessed by the user, who is the only judge of its relevancy. The integration of new cases will thus be achieved, on user's requirement, once the solution has been validated through a set of tests.
Several cases associated to one complete plan can be integrated into the base: in fact, if the complete plan represents the solution of a high-level problem, its various sub-plans represent solutions of problems at lower levels. When the integration of a case is required, a first step consists in determining the list of plans and sub-plans that are candidates to integration. This list corresponds to the plans that have been adapted, i.e. the ancestors of replaced sub-plans that are large enough (at least three levels of tasks). If the substitution plan has been built via the interactive module, it will also be inserted into the list. Figure 8 takes up again the plan adapted in figure 7; the determination of the candidates to integration is achieved by examining the three replaced sub-plans:

- sub-plan of root A': D is inserted into the list; A' is not inserted because it stems from a case of the base,
- sub-plan of root B': plans of roots E and F are inserted into the list; B' has been manually built but it is not inserted because it has only two levels.
- sub-plan of root C': plans of roots A' et G are inserted into the list, whereas H and C' are not because they have less than three levels.

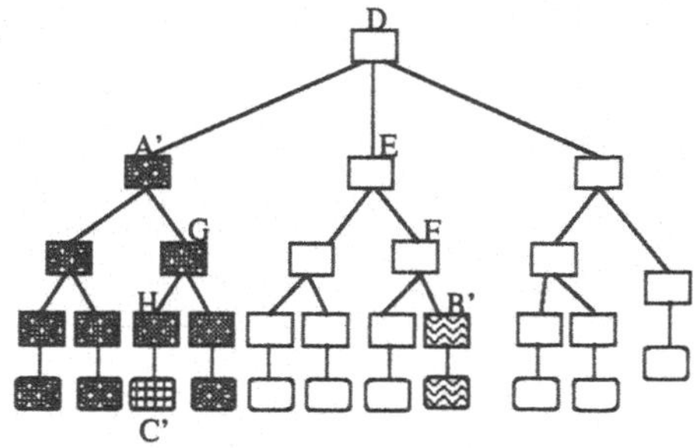

Fig. 8: determination of candidate cases to memorization

Then, for each plan in the list, the user has to provide values for the criteria of the corresponding case that have been modified. The system searches the case base for the most similar case to the new case and integrates the latter if similarity is lower than a given threshold (i.e. the new case is different enough from all base cases). The similarity here considered corresponds to the minimum between similarity on task criteria related and similarity on image criteria.

5. The CBR module at work: an example

In this section, a session showing how the CBR module can be used during the creation of a new application is described. The new problem consists here in extracting objects in an image from industrial origin (image (2), fig. 9). The user begins by defining his/her target case through an input window: **IP type** is *segmentation*, **problem** is defined as *extract* and *object*, task's **level** is *intentional*, **amount of noise** is *low*, **quality of contrast** is *medium*, there is an image **background**, objects are characterized by their *light gray level* **aspect**, *convex* **form**, **size relatively** *large* and *connectivity* **relation**. Background, aspect, form and relation are considered as important by the user.

The selection algorithm is then run and a list of four cases is returned, among which the user chooses the case that seems to be the best match for his/her problem. The plan solution to the selected case can be visualized, so as to study its strategy and it can also be executed.

The root task of the selected plan (fig. 9) is "isolate objects from background"; this plan has been built for a cytology application (images (1) and (3)), for the extraction of some categories of cells.

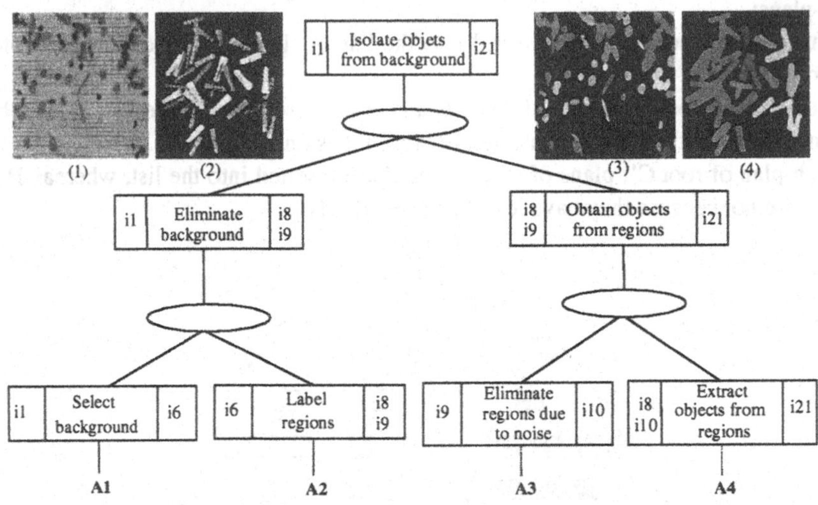

Fig. 9 : plan associated to the selected case with input and output images

The user can then start adapting the proposed plan to his/her new problem. The first modification deals with the "select background" task: in the initial plan, the problem was to isolate dark objects on a light background, whereas here, objects are light and background is dark. The first adaptation step simply consists in inverting the selection of objects (sub-plan F1, fig. 10) and is thus achieved via the interactive module. As results after execution are still unsatisfactory (imprecise localization of contours, objects not properly separated, image (4)), the user considers a second adaptation step by re-running the selection algorithm in order to find another sub-plan for the task "obtain objects from regions". A new target case corresponding to this sub-problem is thus defined, the algorithm is re-run and the user finally chooses substitution sub-plan F2 (fig. 10). After replacement, the resulting plan (fig. 10) may further be improved by local modifications (e.g. replacement of an operator by another one).

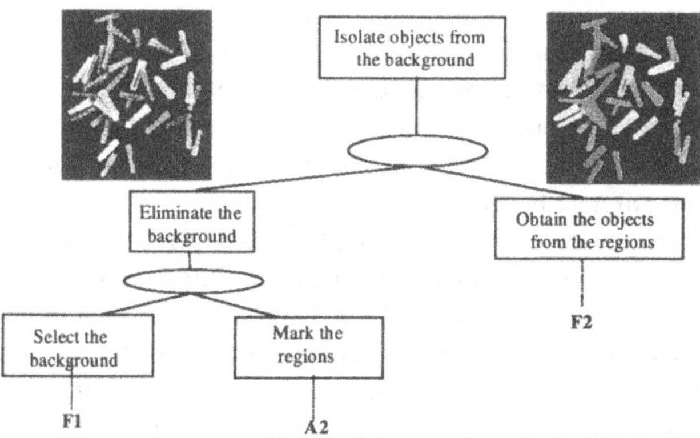

Fig. 10 : partial representation of plan after adaptation

Once all adaptations are completed, one has to define the new cases to be integrated into the base. The system produces the candidates to integration: they are the plans of roots "select background", "obtain objects from regions", "isolate objects from background" and "eliminate background". For these four tasks, the user is required to define the corresponding cases: two of these four cases are integrated into the base.
The assistance provided by the CBR module for the tuning of this plan shows the aptness of our selection criteria and the efficiency of the selection/adaptation algorithm: the interactive and recursive nature of this algorithm enables to rapidly get a satisfactory solution. However, the number of further local adaptations that must be made reveals the scarcity of our present case base, which must now be enlarged by systematically integrating all plans and cases corresponding to the applications developed within our research team.

6. Conclusions

In this paper, a CBR module providing assistance to knowledge reuse has been described. It enables an IP expert to retrieve an existing plan that solves a problem similar to his/her current problem and adapt it to the new situation. He/she can thus reuse his/her own knowledge or knowledge previously modeled by other IP experts. Our recursive selection/adaptation algorithm alternates retrieval and adaptation steps, thus enabling to build a plan by combining parts of other plans. Criteria for selecting cases are based on a definition of IP tasks and a description of images.
Similar ideas can be found in HICAP [7], a general-purpose planning architecture that is applied to the planning of military evacuation operations. It is also a CBR system that can assist users during the construction of hierarchical plans of tasks. The system integrates a user-friendly task editor conducting an interactive conversation with the user. For tasks that can be decomposed in multiple ways (i.e. problem-specific tasks), a case is associated to each available decomposition method (whereas in our system, cases are associated to tasks and not to methods). So in HICAP, the user has to define

a case in order to select each method used in the plan, which seems to be more constraining and time-consuming for the user.

The TMT system has presently been used to develop eight distinctive applications, in order to test the system along three main axes: validation of the model and architecture, experimentation of the interface by a novice and search for similarities between applications from different fields.

In order to restrain the scope of the problem, tests have presently been limited to segmentation applications. Further work will consist in diversifying the content of our libraries (plans and cases) by integrating applications dealing with more varied treatments (from image restoration to image interpretation) and applied to images from various domains. This should also enable to enrich the vocabulary used for the description of cases, and thus complete our set of criteria, so as to get a more exhaustive lists of terms.

In addition, one should consider means to alleviate the user's task in the course of the adaptation step. By using "simple" rules based on the comparison of some criterion values, the system could provide more assistance to user by indicating which parts of the plan need an adaptation.

References

[1] A. Bonzano, P. Cunningham & B. Smyth, Using introspective learning to improve retrieval in CBR: A case study in air traffic control, *ICCBR'97*, Rhode Island, USA, July 1997.

[2] P. Caulier & B. Houriez, A Case-Based Reasoning Assistance System in Telecommunications Networks Management, *XPS'95*, Kaiserslautern, Germany, 1995.

[3] R. Clouard, A. Elmoataz, C. Porquet, M. Revenu, Borg : A knowledge-based system for automatic generation of image processing programs, *IEEE Trans. on Pattern Analysis and Machine Intelligence*, Vol. 21, n. 2, pp. 128-144, February, 1999.

[4] A. Elmoataz, *Mécanismes opératoires d'un segmenteur d'images non dédié: définition d'une base d'opérateurs et implémentation*, Thèse de Doctorat, Caen, July 1990.

[5] V. Ficet-Cauchard, C. Porquet & M. Revenu, An Interactive Case-Based Reasoning System for the Development of Image Processing Applications, *EWCBR'98*, Dublin, Ireland, pp. 437-447, September 1998.

[6] V. Ficet-Cauchard, *Réalisation d'un système d'aide à la conception d'applications de Traitement d'Images: une approche basée sur le Raisonnement à Partir de Cas*, Thèse de Doctorat, Caen, January 1999.

[7] H. Munoz-Avila, D. Aha, L. Breslow & D. Nau, HICAP: An Interactive Case-Based Planning Architecture and its Application to Noncombatant Evacuation Operations. IAAI-99.

[8] B.D. Netten & R.A. Vingerhoeds, Structural Adaptation by Case Combination in EADOCS, G*WCBR'96*, Bad Honnef, Germany, March 1997.

[9] B. Prasad, Planning With Case-Based Structures, *AAAI Fall Symposium*, MIT Campus, Cambridge, Massachusetts, November 1995.

[10] Russ, John C. (1995) *The Image Processing Handbook*, second edition, CRC Press, 1995.

[11] B. Smyth, *Case-Based Design*, Doctoral Thesis of the Trinity College, Dublin, Ireland, April 1996.

[12] M. Veloso, H. Munoz-Avila & R. Bergmann, Cased-based planning: selected methods and systems, *AI Communications*, vol. 9, n. 3, September 1996.

Virtual Function Generators: Representing and Reusing Underlying Design Concepts in Conceptual Synthesis of Mechanisms for Function Generation

Younghyun Han[1], and Kunwoo Lee[2]

[1] Institute of Advanced Machinery and Design, Seoul National University,
[2] School of Mechanical & Aerospace Engineering, Seoul National University,
San 56-1, Shinlim, Kwanak, Seoul 151-742, Korea
{yhhan, kunwoo}@cad.snu.ac.kr

Abstract. This paper describes an approach to represent and reuse efficiently the underlying design concepts in the existing mechanisms in order to synthesize mechanisms for function-generation and motion-transmission. A notion of *virtual function generator* is introduced to conceptualize and represent all possible underlying design concepts in the existing mechanisms. The virtual function generators are extracted from the existing mechanisms and composed of one or more primitive mechanisms together with the involved functions. They serve as new conceptual building blocks in the conceptual synthesis of design alternatives. The whole design concept or sub-concepts of the mechanisms can be represented and reused efficiently by the notion of virtual function generator. New mechanisms are generated by extracting and combining the underlying design concepts via the virtual function generators. The capability of the proposed approach is illustrated with a design example.

1 Introduction

When designers are faced with design tasks, they usually review the existing design cases of similar tasks and generate many design concepts or alternatives by combining the relevant elements of the existing design cases [1-3]. This common activity of the design is realized in the field of mechanisms design by using atlases of mechanisms [4, 5], which is one of the typical approaches to type synthesis [6, 7]. This approach can provide direct ideas or useful design concepts for a design task because numerous design cases are classified and grouped according to their functions. Although the approach is still the typical pattern of mechanism design, it is very tedious and cumbersome to inspect all the relevant design cases even though computer-assisted tools are available. Hence, a desirable approach to the conceptual design of mechanisms requires a systematic way of reusing the previous design concepts in the existing design cases to generate design alternatives for function generation tasks.

To reuse the prior design concepts in the existing mechanisms, the essential task would be to understand how the functions of the mechanisms are realized, and to represent and store the underlying design concepts in a computerized form. To this end, some functional and/or behavior models of mechanical devices have been proposed [8-11]. Different from these model-based approaches, in the area of mechanism design, especially for function generation, one useful method conceptualizing the mechanisms is to identify and understand them by the combinations of basic building blocks [7, 12]. Since the building blocks correspond to physical artifacts in the real world and have their specific functions, the underlying design concepts can be conceptualized easily and intuitively by the designer. The whole design concepts can be represented by the combination of the constituent basic building blocks. In addition to the whole design concepts, the individual sub-concepts constituting the whole concept should be stored because new design alternatives are mostly obtained in the conceptual design phase by transferring a part of a mechanism or by combining parts from different mechanisms.

Thus, a systematic and efficient way should be provided to represent the sub-concepts as well as the whole design concepts. To this purpose, this paper proposes an efficient representation scheme for reusing the underlying design concepts and sub-concepts in the existing mechanisms using the notion of *virtual function generators*. The notion of virtual function generators is based on using the conceptual building blocks of primitive mechanisms to conceptualizing the underlying design concepts. The whole concept and sub-concepts of the existing design cases are all extracted and conceptualized as virtual function generators, which express the respective functions (motion transformations from input to output) of the extracted design concepts. New design alternatives can be synthesized by combining virtual function generators, which retain the underlying design concepts in the existing mechanisms.

2 Conceptual Synthesis of Mechanisms for Function Generation

Mechanisms and corresponding synthesis tasks can be typically classified as rigid-body guidance, path generation, and function generation [7, 12]. Function generation task which this paper addresses involves the design of mechanisms, wherein coordinated motions (or forces) between input and output links connected to ground should be satisfied. In this case, the mechanism in question should satisfy the desired motion transformation from input to output. In addition, mechanisms of this type can provide the functionality that a single input drives multiple outputs of different motion type in a complex machine.

Design specifications in the design of a mechanism for function generation can be described qualitatively or quantitatively in terms of types of input and output motions and other constraints. Here, other constraints comprise behavioral relationship between input and output (linear or nonlinear), motion characteristics (continuous or intermittent), motion direction (oscillatory/reciprocating or unidirectional), transmission characteristics (interchangeability, cycle ratio), orientation of input and output (parallel, perpendicular and skew), space requirement, cost, weight, safety, environment, etc. In the conceptual synthesis stage, not all of the specifications listed above can be considered all together. Hence, the concept generation procedure should generate design alternatives using only the critical design requirements. Then other remaining constraints can be utilized to select promising design concepts from the solution candidates generated. In the case of the function generation task, especially for the concept generation stage, the motion types of input and output, and motion characteristics can be regarded to be the critical design requirement. Thus the design problem of concept generation stage can be described as: given a set of motion types and characteristics of input and output(s), find all possible design alternatives which transform and transmit the desired motion(s) from the input to the output(s).

3 Representing Mechanisms with Conceptual Building Blocks

The notion of basic building blocks is widely used to conceptualize and represent many complicated mechanisms [7, 12]. In particular, in a mechanism for function-generation and motion-transmission, commonly called *function generator*, the notion of building blocks helps understand how the overall function is conceptualized and achieved. For example, the impact printing mechanism in an electric typewriter [12] shown in Fig. 1 can be viewed to consist conceptually of three conceptual building blocks: cam with oscillating follower, double-rocker, and type lever. The input rotation into the cam with oscillating follower is transformed to an oscillatory rotation and it is transmitted to the type-lever through the double-rocker. By identifying a mechanism as a combination of basic building blocks, we can easily understand how the overall function of the mechanism is accomplished. The constructive building blocks represent the individual subfunctions from which the overall function is achieved. Thus, the notion of building blocks allows us to understand the underlying design concepts for realizing the overall function of a mechanism.

In this work, *primitive mechanisms* are supplied to represent the existing mechanisms as a combination of conceptual building blocks. The primitive mechanisms are physical building blocks to form a resultant mechanism, which transforms and transmits motion(s) from input to output(s). An abstraction scheme is required to represent

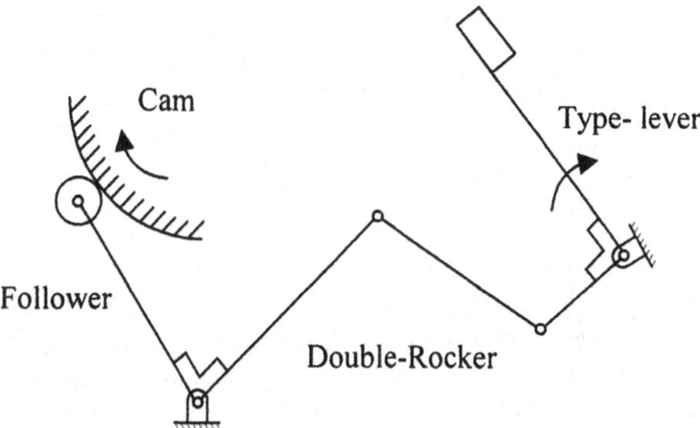

Fig. 1. Kinematic diagram of the impact printing mechanism in an electric typewriter

the primitive mechanisms in a computerized form and to use them in the computational synthesis procedure.

A primitive mechanism is abstracted and represented by a directed graph with one edge and two vertices, as shown in Fig. 2. The edge represents the abstract structure of a primitive mechanism, and two vertices of the edge indicate the input and output points, respectively. The edge has a direction from the input vertex to the output, which represents the flow of motion through the abstract structure of the mechanism.

The motions of input and output are classified as translation (T), rotation (R), and helical motion (H: coordinated T and R), following and extending the classification by Erdman [12], and Joskowicz [13]. In particular, the rotation is subdivided into shaft rotation (R_0) and pivotal rotation (R) in our approach. Shaft rotation is considered to have zero radius of rotation as in most primitive mechanisms, and pivotal rotation has conceptual radius of rotation as in crank or lever that is swiveled around an axis. In addition to the primary classification of the motion, motion qualifiers are used to represent behavioral characteristics of the motion: oscillating (o), reciprocating (r), and intermittent (i). *Reciprocating* and *oscillating* respectively qualify translation and rotation when the direction of motion changes during operation. *Intermittent* qualifies the continuity property of the motion.

Notice that a primitive mechanism can have multiple functions according to the classification of motion described above, as indicated in the figure. This is because the same primitive mechanism can be used for different motion transformations. For example, the slider-crank mechanism of an internal combustion engine is used for transforming a reciprocating motion to a shaft rotation ($rT \to R_0$), whereas it transforms a shaft rotation to a reciprocating motion ($R_0 \to rT$) in a sawing machine. This is possible because of the reversibility of the mechanism; the input and output of the mechanism are interchangeable. On the other hand, the cam with oscillating follower, as shown in the figure, can perform various functions of motion transformation ($R_0 \to oR$ or $oR_0 \to oR$) as different output points are considered. Thus, the selection for the output point of a mechanism can also give rise to different functions. These different functions, motion transformations, of a mechanism can be utilized as distinct design concepts for particular purposes in different mechanical devices.

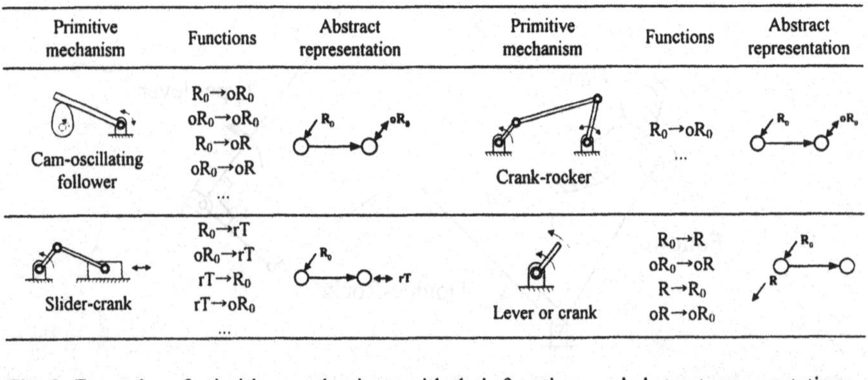

Primitive mechanism	Functions	Abstract representation	Primitive mechanism	Functions	Abstract representation
Cam-oscillating follower	$R_0 \to oR_0$ $oR_0 \to oR_0$ $R_0 \to oR$ $oR_0 \to oR$ ...	R_0, oR_0	Crank-rocker	$R_0 \to oR_0$ ...	R_0, oR_0
Slider-crank	$R_0 \to rT$ $oR_0 \to rT$ $rT \to R_0$ $rT \to oR_0$ ...	R_0, rT	Lever or crank	$R_0 \to R$ $oR_0 \to oR$ $R \to R_0$ $oR \to oR_0$	R_0, R

Fig. 2. Examples of primitive mechanisms with their functions and abstract representations

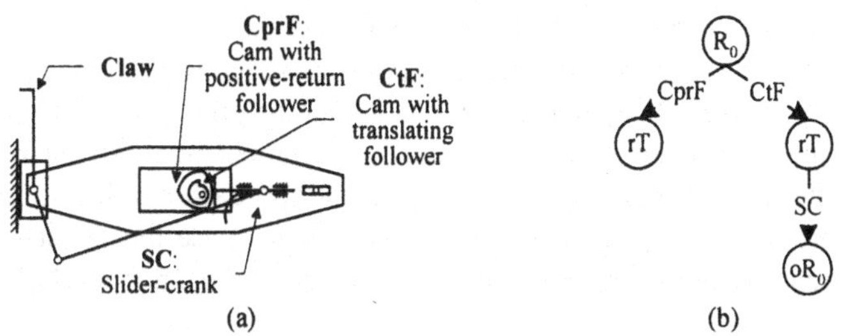

Fig. 3. Kinematic diagram and abstract representation of a film clawing mechanism

As described earlier, many complex mechanisms can actually be conceptualized and expressed by using the primitive mechanisms as the constructive building blocks. As an example, a film clawing mechanism [4] (Artobolevsky, CmL OC 3209) is illustrated with its abstract representation in Fig. 3(a). The mechanism transforms an input motion of shaft rotation (R_0) into two output motions: reciprocating translation (rT) and oscillating shaft rotation (oR_0), and transmit them respectively to the output link (claw). Two cams transform the input rotation into two separate reciprocating motions. Then a slider-crank transforms one of the reciprocating motions into an oscillating motion. Thus the mechanism can be identified conceptually to be composed of three primitive mechanisms.

The mechanism is represented as a directed graph with no cycle, as shown in Fig. 3(b). The edges of the graph represent the constituent primitive mechanisms. The root and leaf vertices indicate the input and output motions, respectively, and intermediate nodes denote type of the common motion between two concatenated primitive mechanisms. The edge label identifies the involved primitive mechanism. Thus, with the edge label and two relevant types of motion, the related primitive mechanism and its involved specific function (one of multiple functions of the primitive mechanism) can be identified.

4 Underlying Design Concepts and Virtual Function Generators

To reuse the underlying design concepts of the existing mechanisms in the conceptual synthesis of design alternatives for a new mechanism, we should first conceptualize the design concepts and then store them for later use. To this end, we introduce the notion of *virtual function generator*, using and extending the notion of building blocks [7, 12, 14] mentioned earlier.

4.1 Conceptualizing Underlying Design Concepts

In the design of function generators, the entire design space is designated basically by the overall function of motion transformation from input to output(s). Then the overall function is decomposed into several subfunctions, and then the designer tries to find physical artifacts to accomplish the individual subfunctions.

Most researches have used primarily the above approach in designing mechanisms conceptually [7, 11, 15]. They apply some technique or principles to decompose the specified design requirements and this kind of decomposition can be regarded as transforming the target cases. However, the present approach applies no explicit decomposition process by a certain principle, but tries to reuse the underlying design concepts inherent in the existing mechanisms by extracting them from the source design case.

The proposed approach to conceptualize the underlying design concepts is explained with the foregoing example of the impact printing mechanism in Fig. 1. Fig. 4(a) represents the mechanism in terms of three primitive mechanisms and their involved functions. With this example, we could infer which underlying design concepts constitute the whole mechanisms, as follows.

We could first reason that the final mechanism is obtained by the combination of three sub-mechanisms as depicted in Fig. 4(b). Each sub-mechanism consists of a primitive mechanism with a specific function; thus, in this case, a primitive mechanism and its involved function constitute a conceptual building block. The entire mechanism can be conceptualized by three conceptual building blocks, and three underlying design concepts can be recognized by the involved functions of each conceptual building block. This way of conceptualization presumes that the entire design space has been separated or discretized into three design subspace through the function decomposition or the evolution of design specifications. Each sub-mechanism or conceptual building block represents a subspace of the whole design space and account for each subfunction of motion transformation for the involved design subspace. This recognition reflects the most low-level conceptualization of the underlying design concepts for the resultant mechanisms in terms of the conceptual building blocks.

On the other hand, we could also reason that the entire mechanism is synthesized by the combination of two sub-mechanisms, as shown in Fig. 4(c) or (d). Each sub-mechanism is composed of one or two primitive mechanisms and an overall function. This way of conceptualization presumes that the entire design space has been separated into two design subspaces. One of the design subspaces is realized by a conceptual building block of a primitive mechanism, and the other by a conceptual building block consisting of two primitive mechanisms. In other words, the whole mechanism is generated by two conceptual building blocks and respective underlying design concepts

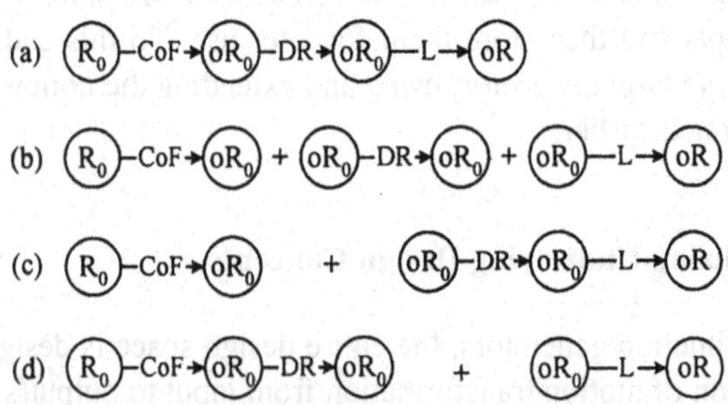

Fig. 4. Possible combinations of underlying design concepts

realizing them. From this case, we can see that a new conceptual building block can be derived from two primitive mechanisms, as a whole, as well as one primitive mechanism alone.

Conceptualizing the entire mechanism in this way provides a higher-level function decomposition than that of the case in Fig. 4(b). Of course, this kind of conceptualization can further proceed, resulting in that of Fig. 4(b) if the function decomposition is guided by a design principle or a causal model with strong domain knowledge. However, the design principles for type synthesis is not well defined in most cases and the synthesis task is usually performed by the designer's intuition. In the traditional approach depending on the designer's intuition, the design concept for a subfunction (design subspace) is sometimes realized at a time without further decomposition process. These design concepts are usually obtained by his/her own experience, or by referring to and transferring the related concepts in other mechanisms. Reflecting these intrinsic aspects of the design, the conceptualizations shown in Fig. 4(c) and (d) can be regarded as distinct underlying design concepts of the mechanism.

Similarly, the entire mechanism itself in Fig. 4(a) could also be regarded as a distinct design concept. In this case, a group of three primitive mechanisms and involved functions constitute a conceptual building block realizing the whole design concept of the mechanism. It is assumed here that the specified function has been realized by a design concept without any function decomposition process.

Because only the final artifact of a mechanism are provided in the atlases of mechanisms, and the design principles or knowledge for type synthesis of the mechanism are not available to us, we could not infer further by which way the mechanisms has been originally conceptualized. Hence, we solely presume that all possible combinations of sub-mechanisms of the entire mechanism could be distinct underlying design concepts by which the mechanism has been realized.

In summary, when conceptualizing the underlying design concepts or principles for a mechanism, we could recognize the entire mechanism by combinations of higher-level conceptual building blocks as well as by that of low-level conceptual building blocks. The conceptual building block here is composed of one or more primitive mechanisms and related functions.

4.2 Virtual Function Generators

With the assumption described earlier, we should consider, as conceptual building blocks, the combinations of primitive mechanisms appearing in all possible sub-mechanisms of a mechanism as well as the individual primitive mechanisms. Not only the individual primitive mechanisms constituting the mechanism but also all possible concatenated chains, as a whole, can be a conceptual building block.

We introduce the notion of *virtual function generator* to represent them consistently, because these building blocks are virtual entities derived from the existing mechanisms, and can perform respective functions like physical mechanisms. The notion of virtual function generator incorporates the traditional physical building blocks of primitive mechanisms and the new conceptual building blocks obtained by the combinations of the primitive mechanisms.

The virtual function generator consists of one or more primitive mechanisms with respective involved functions, and performs a specific transformation of motion from input to output. They are extracted and generated from the existing mechanisms. Several virtual function generators can be extracted from a mechanism. In the forgoing example of the impact printing mechanism in Fig. 1 and 4, a total of six virtual function generators can be derived: cam with oscillating follower + double-rocker + lever (Fig. 4(a)), cam with oscillating follower + double-rocker (left one in Fig. 4(d)), double-rocker + lever (right one in Fig. 4(c)), and three individual primitive mechanisms (Fig. 4(b)). The function generator represents the entire design concept when derived from the whole mechanism or a sub-concept if derived from a part of the mechanism.

The notion of virtual function generator introduced in the present paper has the following characteristics and advantages.

First, the virtual function generator is composed of concatenated primitive mechanisms as well as a primitive mechanism alone. This combination of primitive mechanisms shows quite different motion characteristics, spatial configuration, orientation of input and output, etc., from those of a single physical building block of a primitive mechanism even if the overall functions are equivalent. Thus it can serve as a new conceptual building block for the synthesis of mechanisms.

Second, it realizes the separation of the functional aspects from the physical building blocks, and provides flexibility in conceptualizing the usage of the traditional physical building blocks. A primitive mechanism can have multiple functions and each of the multiple functions can be used distinctly in different mechanisms. Thus the virtual function generators represent the specific usage of the individual primitive mechanisms or a combination thereof in the individual mechanisms. In addition, it can represent the common functionality that has been multiply used in several different mechanisms, which will be described later.

Third, the extraction of virtual function generators from a mechanism can be regarded to decompose the whole design space (overall function) of an existing design case into all possible combination of subspaces (subfunctions). Thus the virtual function generators play an implicit role as a previously prepared set of subfunctions that could be used in the function decomposition process, though the function decomposition is not explicitly carried out in our approach. Our approach that will be described later rather attempts to merge and combine these prepared subfunctions (virtual function generators) to satisfy the specified overall function.

5 Case Extraction and Representation

The virtual function generators are derived from all possible combinations of submechanisms of an existing mechanism. They can be obtained by extracting all possible subgraphs from the graph representation of the mechanism. For example, recall the foregoing example of a film clawing mechanism shown in Fig. 3. We can consider a total of six subgraphs from the graph structure of the film clawing mechanism in Fig. 3(b) and the extracted sub-mechanisms (subgraphs) are depicted in Fig. 5.

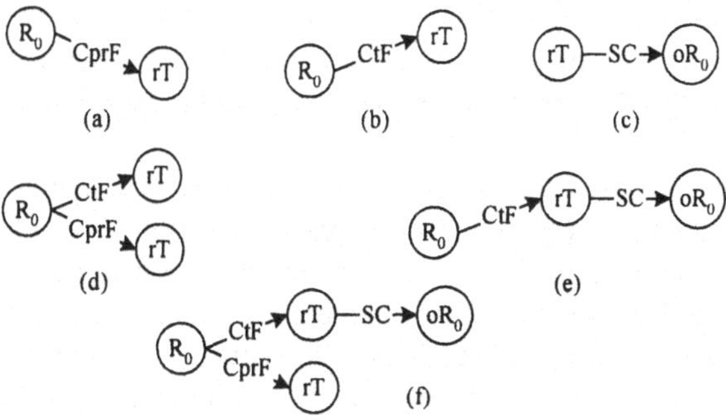

Fig. 5. Extracted sub-mechanisms of the film clawing mechanism

For the reuse of the previous design concepts in the conceptual synthesis procedure, the extracted sub-mechanisms should be stored in the form of virtual function generators. Three types of virtual function generators are defined according to the structure of the extracted sub-mechanisms; M-type is constructed from a primitive mechanism (see (a), (b), (c) in Fig. 5), C-type a concatenated chain of primitive mechanisms (see (e) in Fig. 5), and G-type a graph structure with multiple outputs (see (d), (f) in Fig. 5). The virtual function generators contain the following data.

Overall function. The overall transformation of motion from input to output(s) is stored. M-type and C-type have one input and one output. G-type has one input and multiple outputs.

Structure. The constituent primitive mechanisms and their involved functions are specified by a graph representation. The information related to the constituent primitive mechanisms is supplied by the knowledge base storing the primitive mechanisms. Since each primitive mechanism can have several functions, the function that is currently used in the mechanism should be designated accordingly.

Derivation information. A list of *parent mechanisms* and *types of derivation* is maintained for later use in the synthesis procedure. The parent mechanism is an existing mechanism stored in the case base, from which virtual function generators are derived. There can be more than one parent for a virtual function generator, because conceptually identical combination of primitive mechanisms can be used multiply in different mechanisms. The type of derivation denotes that the virtual function generator is constructed either from the entire mechanism (*complete*) or from an extracted sub-mechanism (*partial*).

6 Organization of Case Base and Indexing

In order to reuse the underlying design concepts in the existing mechanisms efficiently for the conceptual synthesis process, we should organize a case base for storing and retrieving them. That is, the virtual function generators extracted from the existing mechanisms should be indexed according to their functions. Besides, the virtual function generators consist of the primitive mechanisms stored in the knowledge base, and stem from the design cases of the existing mechanisms. Thus the organized case base should incorporate the knowledge base and the physical case base of the existing mechanisms.

Fig. 6 illustrates the case base established in our work. The case base is organized as a multi-layered structure and each layer represents different levels of abstraction.

The first layer is a functional index layer. It consists of actual indices (a primary index and auxiliary indices) to the virtual function generators stored in the next virtual case layer. The *primary index* contains indices for virtual function generators (M-type and C-type) with a single input and a single output (SISO), and is used actually for the synthesis process. The *auxiliary indices* are classified according to the number of outputs as: SI2O (single input/two outputs), SI3O, etc. Each of them is composed of indices for G-type virtual function generators and used to directly retrieve the exact-matching design cases, which will be explained later. An index in this layer is designated by the transformation of motion from input to output(s) (e.g., R→T, rT→oR, etc.). All virtual function generators performing the same function are assigned to the same index. Thus all the virtual function generators with the specified function can be accessed as a whole through the corresponding index. This layer abstracts the mechanisms in a functional point of view.

The second is a virtual case layer, wherein virtual function generators are stored as *virtual cases*. The virtual function generators are stored in separate reservoirs according to their structures. Since the virtual function generators consists of the constituent primitive mechanisms and involved functions realizing a specific overall function, this layer represents an abstraction level of mechanisms in terms of functions and physical artifacts.

The third layer is composed of the knowledge base of primitive mechanisms and the physical case base of the existing design cases (mechanisms). This layer provides physical building blocks and artifacts; thus it abstracts mechanisms from a physical point of view.

To explain the procedure of storing and indexing the virtual function generators, recall again the virtual function generators (sub-mechanisms) in Fig. 5 extracted from the film clawing mechanism in Fig. 3, and the illustrative example of the case base in Fig. 6. First, since three virtual function generators shown in Fig. 5(a), (b), and (c) are M-type, they are stored in the M-type reservoir as M0 (cam with positive return follower), M1 (cam with oscillating follower), and M2 (slider-crank) as shown in Fig. 6, and are indexed in the SISO index of the functional index layer according to their functions (R_0→rT: M0, M1; rT→oR_0: M2). The information of the *parent mechanisms* and the *types of derivation* are also shown respectively in dashed lines. Next, a C-type virtual function generator is derived from the sub-mechanism in Fig. 5(e). It is stored as C0 (cam with translating follower + slider-crank) in the C-type reservoir and indexed in the SISO index by the overall function (R_0→oR_0) as shown in Fig. 6. Finally, two G-type virtual function generators with a SI2O graph structure are derived from the sub-mechanisms in Fig. 5(d) and (f). They are stored in the G-type reservoir and indexed in the SI2O index according to their functions: G0 and G1 in Fig. 6. All of the types of derivation of the derived virtual function generators are *partial* except

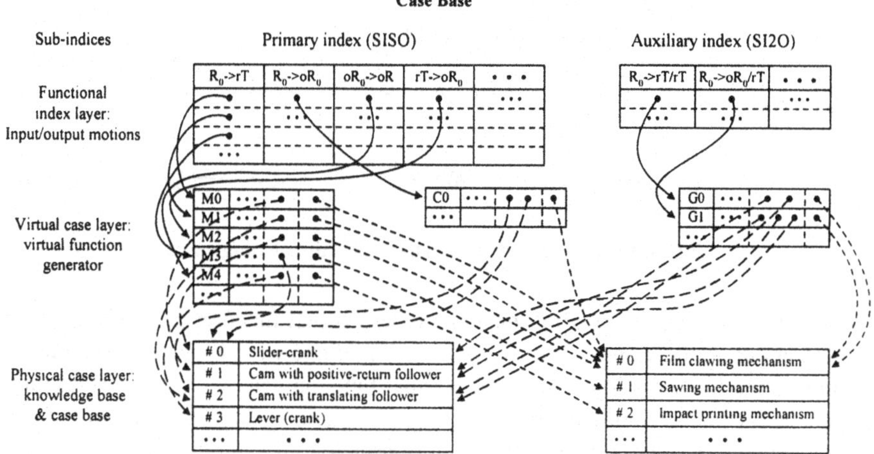

Fig. 6. Illustrative example of the organization of the case base

for the case of Fig. 5(f).

Notice that some of the virtual function generators derived from a sawing machine and the impact printing mechanism are also stored and indexed as M3 (slider-crank; $R_0 \rightarrow rT$) and M4 (lever; $oR_0 \rightarrow oR$) in the case base. They will be used in the design example later.

7 Case Reuse: Conceptual Synthesis of Mechanisms

We can consider two kinds of strategies when synthesizing design alternatives by reusing the previous design cases. The first one is searching for exact-matching source cases. Here, the exact matching means that the desired motions at input and output(s) are satisfied by the whole or a part of an existing mechanism. Since all sub-mechanisms are already extracted and stored as the virtual function generators, and they are indexed into the functional indices, we can retrieve exact-matching cases (virtual function generators) efficiently without time-consuming graph matching. Individual exact-matching cases can be chosen as design alternatives without further adaptation (synthesis) process.

The second strategy is searching for partial-matching cases that satisfy part of the specified function, and merging them to satisfy the overall function. In this case, partial-matching source cases derived from different mechanisms are combined and various new design alternatives are generated. A combination of parts of and/or the whole existing design concepts can give rise to new design concepts. It can be considered that this method shares similarity with the techniques of *combination* or *transference* which is recognized as a common method of concept generation in the systematic approach of engineering design [1, 11, 15-18].

A compatibility principle [19] is required to validate the synthesized mechanism

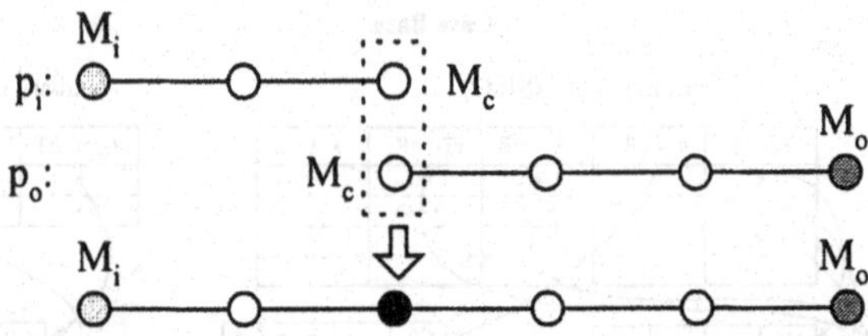

Fig. 7. Combining two compatible partial-matching cases

obtained by combining two partial-matching cases (virtual function generators). It can be stated in our application as: If the output motion of one virtual function generator is the same as the input motion of the other virtual function generator, two virtual function generators can be combined to produce a new function generator. A pair of virtual function generators satisfying the compatibility principle of combination is referred to as *compatible virtual function generators*.

The design alternatives with one input and one output are generated by incorporating two strategies of finding exact-matching cases and finding/combining partial-matching cases as follows.

Given an input motion of M_i and an output motion M_o, a set P_i of input-matching cases with the specified input motion, and a set P_o of output-matching cases with the specified output motion are retrieved from the case base using the functional indices. Then the two partial-matching cases are combined if the output motion of an input-matching case is the same as the input motion of an output-matching case. Fig. 7 illustrates that a desired mechanism with input motion of M_i and output motion of M_0 is obtained by combining two partial cases: p_i and p_o. During this process, exact-matching cases are easily obtained by searching for the same virtual function generators that exist in both the input matching and the output matching cases. This is because they satisfy both the specified input and the output motions and are already retrieved in both P_i and P_o. Thus, These virtual function generators can fulfill the specified function by themselves, and become possible design alternatives for the desired mechanism.

When the desired mechanism has multiple outputs, the foregoing procedure is applied repeatedly for each pair of the specified input motion and output motions until the synthesized mechanism for each output is merged to the previously obtained mechanism and the desired mechanism is finally synthesized. On the other hand, the exact-matching cases (virtual function generators) can also be retrieved easily by the auxiliary sub-indices that store the virtual function generators with multiple outputs. They also become possible design alternatives without further synthesis process.

Consider a sewing mechanism for an illustrative example. The input motion to the sewing machine is a shaft rotation via belt-pulley from an electric motor. From the input motion, it should transmit a reciprocating motion to the needle and two oscillating motions to the feed dog. Thus, the desired mechanism should be composed of three chains that transform and transmit the specified input motion (R_0) to individual desired output motions (rT, oR, oR). Here, we will show that the design concept for each chain can be obtained from the virtual function generators in the case base in Fig. 6.

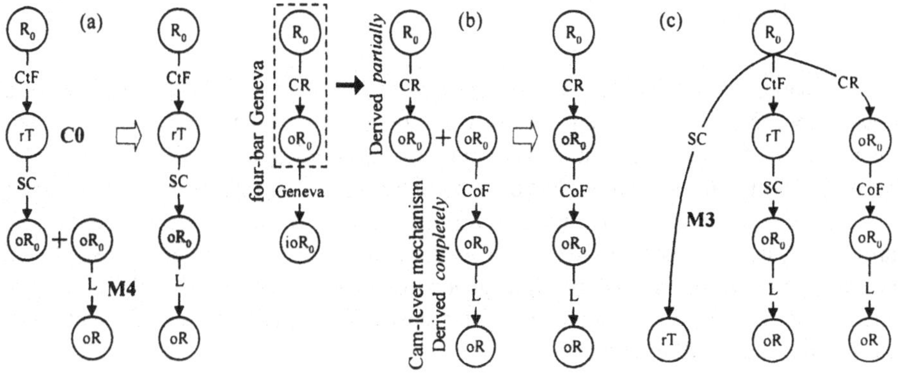

Fig. 8. Conceptual synthesis of a sewing machine

First, consider a chain that transform the input motion (R_0) into the output motion (oR) and transmit it to the feed dog; the desired function is specified by $R_0 \rightarrow oR$. From the case base in Fig. 6, the input-matching cases with the input motion of R_0 are retrieved by the functional index of $R_0 \rightarrow rT$ as M0, M1, and M3, and by the one of $R_0 \rightarrow oR_0$ as C0. The output-matching case with the output motion of oR is retrieved as M4 by the functional index of $oR_0 \rightarrow oR$. Then possible compatible virtual function generators are combined. Here, the input matching case C0 (cam with translating follower + slider-crank; $R_0 \rightarrow rT \rightarrow oR_0$) and the output matching case M4 (lever; $oR_0 \rightarrow oR$) can be merged and a chain of C0 + M4 ($R_0 \rightarrow rT \rightarrow oR_0 \rightarrow oR$) is produced as shown in Fig. 8(a). Notice that the chain is generated by two partial-matching cases derived from different parent mechanisms. The virtual function generator of C0 is derived from the film clawing mechanism in Fig. 3 and the virtual function generator M4 originates from the impact printing mechanism in Fig. 1. When the actual case base is used instead of the illustrative one in Fig. 6, many other chains can be obtained and one of them is illustrated in Fig. 8(b). These two chains transform the input motion into two oscillating motions and transmit them to the feed dog.

Next, a chain transforming the specified input (R_0) to reciprocating motion (rT) of the needle is obtained as follows; the desired function is represented by $R_0 \rightarrow rT$. The retrieved input-matching cases are the same as the foregoing example: M0 ($R_0 \rightarrow rT$), M1 ($R_0 \rightarrow rT$), M3 ($R_0 \rightarrow rT$) and C0 ($R_0 \rightarrow oR_0$). The output-matching cases are retrieved by the functional index of $R_0 \rightarrow rT$ as M0 ($R_0 \rightarrow rT$), M1 ($R_0 \rightarrow rT$) and M3 ($R_0 \rightarrow rT$). Since M0, M1, and M3 exist in both partial-matching cases, each of them can be a solution as an exact-matching case. Fig. 8(c) shows the resultant mechanism that is generated by merging the foregoing two chains and M3 (slider-crank). In this case, no chain is generated by combining two partial-matching cases because there is no compatible combination.

If the actual case base is used, more chains can be obtained for the individual motion transformations, and it gives rise to numerous final design alternatives. Notice that the sewing machine is conceptually synthesized by transferring and merging design concepts from different existing mechanisms.

8 Conclusion

This paper proposes a case-based approach to represent and reuse the underlying design concepts in the existing mechanisms for the conceptual synthesis of mechanisms in the function generation and motion transmission tasks, and illustrates its capability with a design example. The approach provides a systematic way of reusing the previous design concepts underlying in the numerous existing design cases. The previous design concepts are derived from the existing mechanisms and substantiated via the notion of the virtual function generators. The organization of the case base enables us to retrieve efficiently the prior design concepts necessary to synthesize various new design alternatives.

By conceptualizing the overall function of a mechanism in terms of subfunctions using the conceptual building blocks of virtual function generators, one can easily capture the underlying sub-concepts of design. The notion of virtual function generator is very useful in representing common functionality that is used in the design of function generators, and provides flexibility in mapping functions to structures by separating the functional aspects from the physical artifacts. With the notion of virtual function generators, new design concepts for function generators can be obtained easily and efficiently by transferring and/or combining the underlying design concepts derived from different mechanisms.

Acknowledgements

This work has been partially supported by the Turbo and Power Machinery Research Center of the Institute of Advanced Machinery and Design, Seoul National University, Korea.

References

1. Pahl, G., Beitz, W.: Engineering Design. 2nd edn. Springer-Verlag, London (1996)
2. Maher, M.L., Balachandran, M.B., Zhang, D.M.: Case-Based Reasoning in Design. Lawrence Erlbaum Associates, Mahwah New Jersey (1995)
3. Maher, M.L., Pu, P. (eds.): Issues and Applications of Case-Based Reasoning in Design. Lawrence Erlbaum Associates, Mahwah New Jersey (1997)
4. Artobolevsky, I.I.: Mechanisms in Modern Engineering Design. Vols. 1-3. MIR Publishers, Moscow (1986)
5. Chironis, N.P.: Mechanisms, Linkages, and Mechanical Controls. McGraw-Hill, New York (1965)
6. Erdman, A.G.: Computer-Aided Mechanism Design: Now and the Future. Transactions of the ASME Journal of Mechanical Design. 117 (1995) 93-100

7. Kota S., Chiou, S.-J.: Conceptual Design of Mechanisms Based on Computational Synthesis and Simulation of Kinematic Building Blocks. Research in Engineering Design. 4 (1992) 75-87
8. Shimomura, Y., Yoshioka, M., Takeda, H., Umeda, Y. Tomiyama, T.: Representation of Design Object Based on the Functional Evolution Process Model. ASME Journal of Mechanical Design. 120, (1998) 221-229
9. Goel, A.K., Bhatta, S.R., Stroulia, E.: KRITIK: An Early Case-Based Design System. In: Maher, M.L., Pu, P. (eds.): Issues and Applications of Case-Based Reasoning in Design. Lawrence Erlbaum Associates. (1997) 87-132
10. Bhatta, S.R., Goel, A.K.: From Design Experiences to Generic Mechanisms: Model-Based Learning in Analogical Design. Artificial Intelligence in Engineering Design, Analysis and Manufacturing. 10 (1996) 131-136
11. Sycara, K.P., Guttal, R., Koning, J., Narasimhan, S., Navinchandra, D.: CADET: a Case-based Synthesis Tool for Engineering Design. International Journal of Expert Systems. 4 (1992)
12. Erdman, A.G., Sandor, G.N.: Mechanism Design: Analysis and Synthesis, Vol. 1, 3rd edn. Prentice-Hall, Upper Saddle River New Jersey (1997)
13. Joskowicz, L.: Mechanism Comparison and Classification for Design. Research in Engineering Design. 1 (1990) 149-166
14. Chakrabarti, A., Bligh, T.P.: An Approach to Functional Synthesis of Solutions in Mechanical Conceptual Design. Part I: Introduction and Knowledge Representation. Research in Engineering Design. 6 (1994) 127-141
15. Madhusudan, T.N., Sycara, K.P., Navin-Chandra, D.: On Synthesis of Electro-mechanical assemblies. Proceedings of The 1996 ASME Design Engineering Technical Conference and Computers in Engineering Conference. August 18-22, 1996.
16. Pugh, S.: Total Design. Addison-Wesley (1990)
17. Voβ, A., Coulon, C.-H.: Structural Adaptation with TOPO. Proceedings of the ECAI 96 Workshop: Adaptation in Case-Based Reasoning. John Wiley & Sons (1996)
18. Bhatta, S.R., Goel, A.K.: An Analogical Theory of Creativity in Design. Proceedings of Second International Conference on Case-Based Reasoning (ICCBR-97): Case-Based Reasoning Research and Development. Providence RI USA, (1997) 565-574
19. Chakrabarti, A., Bligh, T.P.: An Approach to Functional Synthesis of Solutions in Mechanical Conceptual Design. Part II: Kind Synthesis. Research in Engineering Design. 8, (1996) 52-62

Shaping a CBR View with XML

Conor Hayes, Padraig Cunningham

Department of Computer Science
Trinity College Dublin
Conor.Hayes@cs.tcd.ie

Abstract. Case Based Reasoning has found increasing application on the Internet as an assistant in Internet commerce stores and as a reasoning agent for online technical support. The strength of CBR in this area stems from its reuse of the knowledge base associated with a particular application, thus providing an ideal way to make personalised configuration or technical information available to the Internet user. Since case data may be one aspect of a company's entire corporate knowledge system, it is important to integrate case data easily within a company's IT infrastructure, using industry specific vocabulary. We suggest XML as the likely candidate to provide such integration. Some applications have already begun to use XML as a case representation language. We review these and present the idea of a standard case *view* in XML that can work with the vocabularies or namespaces being developed by specific industries. Earlier research has produced version 1.0 of a Case Based Mark-up Language which attempts to mark-up cases in XML to enable distributed computing. The drawbacks of this implementation are outlined in this paper as well as the developments in XML that allow us to produce an XML "View" of a company's knowledge system. We will detail the benefits of our system for industry in general in terms of extensibility, ease of reuse and interoperability.

1 Introduction

Adding intelligence to Internet applications is an obvious role for Case-Based Reasoning (CBR). E-commerce sets out to sell products without the intervention of a sales-assistant and in the absence of human sales assistants there is a need for intelligent software assistants to lubricate the sales process. Since what *is* available is catalogue data and data on user behaviour and preferences CBR is an obvious technology to create these sales assistants. In this scenario, the obvious cases are descriptions of the commodities on sale and the task is to identify the case configuration that meets the user's requirements.[1] These cases might describe package holidays, hardware configurations, or real estate for instance.

The proposed standard for distributing data of this type on the Internet is XML (eXtensible Mark-up Language) so it is important that the CBR process can deal with data in this format. Indeed Shimazu (1998) and Watson & Gardingen(1998) have

[1] Several online CBR applications that conform to this secnario already exist; see http://wwwagr.informatik.uni-kl.de/~lsa/CBR/CBR-Homepage.html for some examples.

described CBR applications that receive cases in an XML format. We have already presented a proposal for CBML, a case description language based on XML (Hayes et al. 1998, Doyle et al. 1998).

XML is a description language that supports meta-data descriptions for particular domains and these meta-data descriptions allow applications to interpret data marked up according to this format. The meta-data description is the Document Type Declaration (DTD) and, for instance, a DTD for real estate will attach semantics to a document marked up in that format.

In (Hayes et al., 1998) we proposed a generic DTD for CBR called CBML that allowed cases to be marked up in an XML-based format. The major drawback of this approach was that data needed to be marked up in this CBR specific format but now the evolving potential of XML allows for an improvement on this idea. In an e-commerce situation domain specific DTDs exist and catalogue data will be marked up in this format – for instance RELML has been proposed as a standard for marking up real estate data. Any case-based assistant that would operate in this space would need to access this data. The new XML proposals for Namespaces and Schemas allow for a CBR *view* on this data and it is this approach that we describe here. This approach has the advantage that it uses existing XML data; it simply provides the appropriate CBR perspective on this data.

In section 2 we review two CBR applications that use XML as a case representation language to query a relational data base. In section 3 we examine and critique an earlier proposal for a standard case representation language in XML. We find that while the principle is still a sound one, the implementation is hampered by a failure to recognise the necessity of retaining the integrity of data marked up according to an industry specific vocabulary. The inability of the DTD to describe structured data objects such as a case base is also brought to light.

Section 4 reviews an XML standardisation project in the domain of Real Estate in the context of past CBR work in this domain. We argue that as standards such as The Real Estate Listing Mark-up Language (RELML) emerge, CBR techniques will have to integrate easily within these existing data structures. In section 5 we introduce the XML concepts of namespaces and schemas, which will allow us to integrate CBR with existing mark-up. We follow this in section 6 with our proposal for what a case namespace should look like.

2 Two XML–CBR applications

The Caret System by Hideo Shimazu is a development of earlier work on retrieving cases from a relational database (Shimazu 1998). It uses XML to mark up cases of natural language text describing technical support problems and solutions. Support staff mark up cases in XML and the documents are then parsed and stored in a relational database by the Caret system. Features either contain coded (discrete) data or textual data. However only the coded tags affect the retrieval mechanism.

The Caret system follows from work on the SQUAD system in which information retrieval using CBR is integrated with a relational database management system for reasons of security, data integrity, data standardisation and scalability (Kitano & Shimazu 1998). Indeed Kitano and Shimazu propose that CBR applications have been too narrowly focused on domain specific problems. They suggest that a case based system should be viewed as a *medium* to be used in conjunction with the mainstream corporate information system. We would share this view, and we anticipate that a standard way of marking up cases will provide an opening in this respect.

The retrieval technique used in Caret is a version of the *Many are called Few are chosen* (MAC/FAC) retrieval methods outlined by (Gentner & Forbus 1991). This algorithm is chosen in order to allow SQL retrieval from the database without having to retrieve every record to compute similarity. Since it uses only coded tags as features by which to calculate similarity, Caret returns a rude subset of the case base relying on the client case adapter to further stream the matched queries.

Since Caret doesn't use the textual parts of its cases in its retrieval mechanism, it is not quite a textual Case Base Reasoning System. Its retrieval mechanism could as easily be applied to any type of data. The second example we look at applies ideas from the Caret system to a sales support system for the installation of air conditioning units.

The HVAC air conditioning sales support system uses a similarity table to send SQL queries to an Access data base of existing installations (Gardingen & Watson 1998). A Java servlet retrieves the cases and converts them to XML. The URL addresses are sent to a Java based client adapter which issues http requests for the XML files. The client then performs nearest neighbour ranking and displays the results.

Both implementations outlined use a vocabulary of user-defined tags and a DTD that assumes a case representation consisting of a feature list and corresponding values. In each implementation, the use of XML allowed the developer to define structured domain specific data. Furthermore XML data was downloaded by issuing HTTP requests from the client end.

However, these implementations highlight some shortcomings with representing case data in this way. Data typing is not possible, nor does or is there any allowance for feature weighting. Also Since DTD creation is a difficult task, it would make sense to use the standard DTDs or schemas which emerge for industry specific data. The task in this scenario would be to use the vocabulary from these DTDs or a combination of DTDs and render them in case form. What is being proposed is a facility to create a standard case *view* of data, baring in mind that XML is suited to full integration with database technology, and that XML documents can easily be created on the fly from an existing database or from several databases. However, as we shall discuss in the following two sections the current DTD model is not powerful or flexible enough to support this task.

The next section will look at our early attempts to create a standard case representation language. The shortcomings of this implementation anticipate the new W3C namespace recommendation and the W3C schema proposal which will allow us to create a standardised case view of existing corporate data.

3 Standard Case Base Representation language

We originally designed CBML as an XML application to facilitate the storage and exchange of case data over a network. The design was motivated by the need to initiate a standard for the exchange of case data, particularly in relation to distributed computing (Hayes et al. 1998, Doyle et al 1998). Version one of CBML was influenced by the functionality of the CASUEL language specification (INRECA 1994). Casuel was developed as an interface language between all INRECA component systems. It was intended to serve as a standard for exchanging information between classification and diagnostic systems that use cases. CBML was intended to establish the ground on which the CBR community could build a standard for the exchange and storage of case data on the Internet. Several shortcomings have emerged with this early implementation and we will deal with these below.

Despite the simplicity of this early implementation, CBML required a case structure file and case base file as well as their respective DTD files to describe each case file. This implies that at least two separate documents (depending upon whether the case structure file and the case base file include their respective DTDs) need to be transmitted. This requires a minimum of two http requests for each case base.

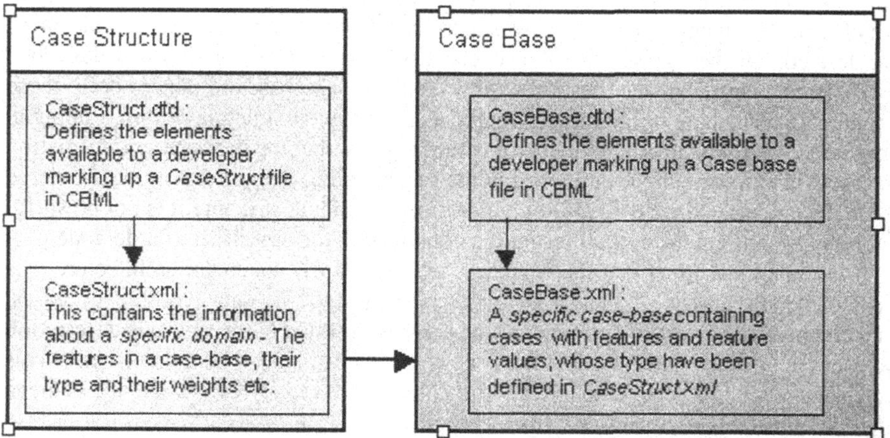

Fig. 1. The relationship between the four documents required to represent data in CBML

CBML is a flabby implementation which significantly increases the amount of data required to describe the case base. For instance, the case feature value pair `HolidayType = Bathing` is described in CBML as

```
<feature name="HolidayType">Bathing</ feature >
```

where the element `feature` and its attribute `name` are defined beforehand in the case base DTD. A less verbose way of describing the same pair would be to define the tag `<HolidayType>` thus allowing the XML feature value pair

```
<HolidayType>Bathing</HolidayType>.
```

From this example it is clear that the first implementation, as well as being over long, is not at all an intuitive representation of the feature value pair of this case. Secondly, and more importantly, in an attempt to maintain the generality of the language the portability of the data it describes has been compromised. Whereas the first example is meaningful to software that expects CBML data, it poses real problems to any software that does not expect the "feature" part of the "feature-value" pair to be represented as a value of the `name` attribute associated with the element `<feature>`.

Also, there was no way of elegantly merging elements defined according to another DTD with CBML elements without violating the readability and "meaningfulness" of the former. As in the example given earlier, a *bathing* holiday may be marked up as `<HolidayType>Bathing</HolidayType>` using a hypothetical travel agent's DTD. The CBML representation of this does not respect the mark-up for this type of data and imposes its own "case-centric" version:

```
<feature name="HolidayType">Bathing</feature>
```

Another drawback was the impossibility of having cases containing mixed data, that is, elements with tags defined according to different domains. These types of cases would occur in complex component based descriptions. Furthermore, In terms of XML document architecture, there is no logical connection between the case structure document and the case base document. (This shortcoming is dealt with in our new implementation). In this respect we were following the CASUEL syntax in which one document provides a case super-class from which a set of case instances are derived. We recognised that the super-class in our implementation was described in different parts by the casestruct.xml and the casebase.dtd since both these documents contribute to the description of a specific case structure within a domain. While the XML document architecture would suggest that the descriptive information in casestruct.xml should be contained in the casebase.dtd, it was not possible to merge these documents. Since the DTD only describes document structure it is not powerful enough to represent the extra information contained in the casestruct.xml document.

It became clear to us that the weakness of the CBML document architecture was tied to the limitations of the DTD to describe the type of data required by cases. Indeed, there is a growing opinion that the DTD is unsuited to the rigorous description demanded by data objects and that a new mechanism must be established[2]. This mechanism called a schema will support data typing, be easily extensible and achieve the inheritance requirements described earlier[3].

We will address the impact of this development in section 5.

---

[2] Connolly, D., Bray, T. W3C (1999) XML Activity Page, http://www.w3.org/XML/Activity.html

[3] Malhotra, A., Maloney, M., W3C (1999) XML Schema Requirements, http://www.w3.org/TR/NOTE-xml-schema-req

4 A Case Study

Before examining the feasibility of designing an XML based case based language, it is important to examine the situations in which such a language might be used and how it might interact with current data storage and representation techniques. We have examined already the case for Case Based Reasoning as a technology suited to the demands of internet commerce (Doyle et al. 1998). In drawing up a case based representation language, we have to examine whether we are helping or hindering the transmission of information that has been marked up in an *industry specific mark-up language*. It would seem to us that we should be looking to facilitate how data is marked up in other agreed DTDs rather than shoe-horning it into a "case-centric" mark-up language.

In the example given above, if the tag `<HolidayType>` were a standard tag for the travel industry, it would not make sense converting this to `<feature name="HolidayType">` simply to cater towards documents that store their travel data in the form of cases. We would argue that a case base document should be considered no differently that a document containing industry standard data.

A concrete example is the emergence of the Real Estate Listing Mark-up (RELML) language developed by OpenMLS and 4th World Telecom to facilitate searches on the web for real estate offered for sale from various agents through out the USA.[4] The motivation behind the RELML project is the recognition that local knowledge is important in describing and valuing property. Therefore rather than centralising this information, local real estate knowledge is marked up locally according to the publicly available RELML DTD. This data is then indexed by a crawler and from these indices searches can be performed from various web sites.

Providing a standard mark-up language allows different real estate agents list their properties in a form that can be easily searched, without losing the local knowledge which a centralised system might entail. More importantly, independent vendors are placed on a level footing with larger franchised businesses.

---

[4] OpenMLS, Real Estate Listing Management System, http://www.openmls.com
Rein, Lisa. (1998) The Business of Residential Listings. XML.com, http://www.xml.com/xml/pub/98/08/real/openmls.html

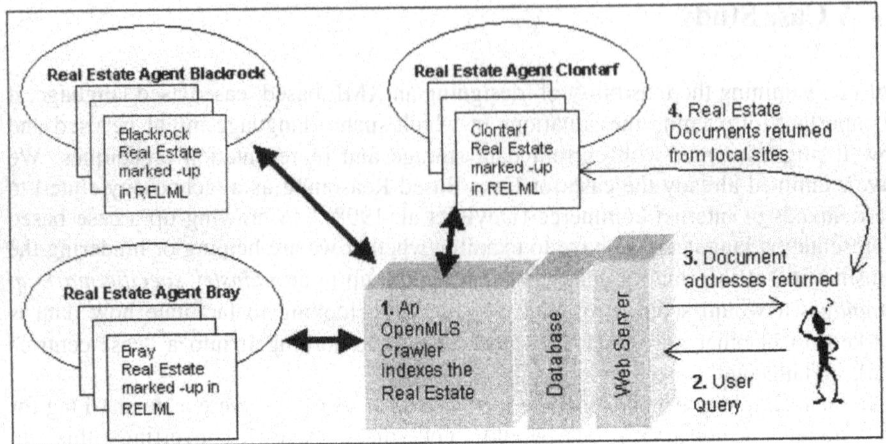

Fig. 2. The architecture proposed for the Real Estate Listings project consists of three tiers, where a crawler on the middle tier centrally indexes real estate data in XML from real estate member sites. Clients may then query this database and replies are delivered in raw XML or HTML depending on the ability of the client software.

Integrating CBR with XML and current database technology is particularly important if, as in this example, the case base is changing on a daily basis. The OpenMLS system anticipates the emergence of online brokerage facilities. Once the first wave of Internet commerce finishes, there still remains the problem of having a community of virtual shop fronts but no easy way to locate them, or compare prices and services. The next issue will be to establish an easy way to find a community of holiday vendors, for example, and be able to query their products quickly. This does not entail centralising knowledge, but exploiting the diversity of the Internet by providing a common language by which various vendors can market their goods. XML has already been suggested as a solution in this respect[5]. In the OpenMLS application the XML documents describing each property reside on the local real estate sites and are downloaded from the local site once a search at the broker end indicates a match. A better metaphor, therefore, than the virtual shopping mall would be a virtual brokerage house.

The type of scenario described by the OpenMLS system is readily amenable to the type of inexact searches suited to CBR. For instance, in a variation of the Rachmann CBR system, the indexed data from several real estate agents in a locality could be searched in order to determine a property valuation (Cunningham et al. 1994). The following example marked up in RELML is a slightly modified case taken from the property evaluation domain illustrated in Hanney's work (Hanney 1996).

[5] Microsoft Corp. (1998) Improving the Online Shopping Experience with XML http://www.microsoft.com/xml/scenario/junglee.asp

The RELML is a proposed standard which is not comprehensive enough to fully capture the details of residential real estate. However, it does give an indication of the benefits of an XML based industry standard mark up language and it certainly could be used in a case based search. The following illustrates a Dublin property marked up using pared down RELML:

```
<?XML version='1.0'?>
<RESIDENTIAL-LISTING VERSION='A1'>
<REMARKS> </REMARKS>
<GENERAL>
<IMAGE FORMAT='JPEG' WIDTH='150' HEIGHT='150'
SRC='http://www.hayesrealty.ie/search/homes/7466.jpg'/>
<TYPE>SINGLE-FAMILY</TYPE>
<PRICE>41500</PRICE>
<AGE UNITS='YEARS'>5</AGE>
<LOCATION COUNTRY='IRE' COUNTY='Dublin'>
<ADDRESS>127 Cabra road</ADDRESS>
<CITY>Dublin</CITY>
<ZIP>7</ZIP>
</LOCATION>
<STRUCTURE>
<NUM-BEDS>2</NUM-BEDS>
<NUM-BATHS>2</NUM-BATHS>
<BUILDING-AREA UNITS='SQ-FEET'>1100</BUILDING-AREA>
</STRUCTURE>
<DATES>
<LISTING-DATE>11/1/99</LISTING-DATE>
<LAST-MODIFIED>11/1/99</LAST-MODIFIED>
</DATES>
<LAND-AREA UNITS='ACRES'>0.75</LAND-AREA>
</GENERAL>
</RESIDENTIAL-LISTING>
</XML>
```

Fig. 3. A Dublin property marked up in basic RELML.

The case marked up in figure 3 gives no indication of what tags contribute to it being a case – what are its features, weighting information, which features may be constraints, what types are permissible as feature values etc. A CBR application processing this document would have to be hard coded with this information, and this coding would have to be changed every time a new feature is added or a constraint imposed, for example. This becomes a serious drawback when a product range changes or is updated.

What is required is an XML methodology that can provide a standard CBR view of data already marked up with user defined tags. This would provide searchable data to any CBR application that recognises the standard, and at the same time maintain the structural and descriptive integrity of the user-defined tags. To understand how this can be achieved we will briefly introduce the concept of XML namespaces and schemas.

5 Namespaces and Schemas

The namespace facility is an advanced feature of XML, outlined in a W3C recommendation as of January 1999.[6] Namespaces allow developers to uniquely qualify element names and relationships to avoid name collisions on elements that have the same name but are defined in different vocabularies. They allow tags from multiple name spaces to be mixed, which is essential if data is coming from multiple sources. Namespaces in XML are identified by a URI (Universal Resource Identifier) which allows each namespace to be universally unique. Every namespace is associated with a user defined prefix which allows the tags from each namespace to be distinguished even though they may in fact have the same name.

For example, an online bookstore may define the `<TITLE>` tag to mean the name of a book, contained only within the `<BOOK>` element. In a mailing list of customers, however, the `<NAME>` tag might indicate a person's position, for instance: `<TITLE>President</TITLE>`. Namespaces help define this distinction clearly.

```
<booksbought xmlns:bks="http://www.bookstore.com"
             xmlns:cst="http://www.bookstore.com/customerlist">

<book><bks:title>Fidelity in a Nutshell<bks:title><book>

<cst:name>W J Clinton<cst:title>President</cst:title></cst:name>

</booksbought>
```

Fig. 4. In this example the prefixes `cst` and `bks` denote the tag sets associated with the customerlist and book stock schemas respectively.

What is most important from the point of view of standardising a case based vocabulary is that namespaces allow us to define a unique case namespace that can be referenced by anyone wishing to mark up data in case format. Furthermore, namespaces will allow feature terms to be defined from several standard vocabularies (DTDs).

In section 5 we will present a case namespace which can be used to provide a standard case view of XML data. Before this however we wish to briefly discuss DTDs and Schemas, and the benefits adopting the latter will bring to case based data processing.

---

[6] World Wide Web Consortium 14-January-1999 Namespaces in XML, http://www.w3.org/TR/1999/REC-xml-names-19990114/

5.1 Schemas

In section 3 we acknowledged the insufficiency of our earlier implementation of a case base mark-up language. This was mainly due to two factors. Firstly, our implementation made no provision for dealing with data already marked up according to an existing DTD. Secondly, the DTD documents required by our implementation were not adequate to the task of describing case data. We began to view the caseStruct.xml document as a supplement to the case Base DTD, but a supplement that had no logical connection to the CaseBase within the standard document architecture outlined in XML 1.0[7] Its use would be limited to applications that were hard coded to recognise the CBML document structure. A better solution would have beeen to amalgamate the descriptive properties of the casestruct.xml and the DTD of the Case Base. However, the classical XML DTD is not descriptive enough to contain this additional information.

In fact, the legacy of a DTD as a descriptive syntax for document interchange makes it ill suited to the demands of data interchange (Boumphrey et al. 1998). Whereas document interchange is concerned mainly with document structure and the hierarchy of its elements, data interchange has more rigorous requirements such as an ability to constrain data types, provide easy extensions and inheritance facilities. Moreover, DTDs are unable to express the data relationships inherent in a relational database, nor do they provide support for the new W3C recommendation on namespaces.

It is unsurprising therefore that work has begun on finding an alternative to the DTD that has the descriptive powers required to adequately mark-up data. This alternative is called an XML schema and currently four such proposals are before the W3 consortium. Schema semantics constitute a superset of those provided by XML DTDs and are designed specifically for data interchange. Unlike the DTD, a schema document is itself an XML document with a mechanism somewhat analogous to but more expressive than a DTD for constraining document structure.

To date, the W3C Schema working group have published a requirements document for XML schemas and plan to deliver working drafts and proposed recommendations later this year [8]. Despite the immaturity of the Schema recommendation, we have decided in the following section to use one of the proposal notes (XML-Data)[9] as a basis for designing a case namespace[10]. While the details of the schema syntax are expected to change, the principles elucidated in the proposal note soundly reflect the issues surrounding XML data mark-up.

---

[7] W3 Consortium 10-February-1998. Extensible Mark-Up Language (XML) 1.0 http://www.w3.org/TR/REC-xml

[8] W3C XML Activity page http://www.w3.org/XML/Activity.html

[9] W3C Note 05 Jan 1998, XML-Data, http://www.w3.org/TR/1998/NOTE-XML-data/

[10] Microsoft Internet Explorer 5 provides support for a schema and data typing based on the XML-Data proposal note.

6 A Case Namespace

The XML namespace mechanism allows us to create a unique set of structured XML tags that can be referenced from within any XML document. By providing an agreed case namespace, we are essentially allowing any developer mark-up data in a standard case format. Data already marked up according to an existing DTD or schema can also be converted to case data by using the namespace facility to mix tags from different domains. We are attempting in this way to present the idea of CBR as a medium (Kitano & Shimazu 1995).

Figure 3 illustrates the document architecture for a case based view of real estate data using the namespace and schema mechanism. The real estate case schema is essentially a real estate case template created from the case namespace and the real estate namespace or tag set. Another way of visualising this is by imagining that the case namespace provides the pieces for a case wrapper around data tagged according to another namespace. The makeup of this template is determined by a domain expert using the case namespace and the real estate namespace. This is not simply a question of picking and mixing at will. Each namespace has rules that need to be complied with. For instance, within the case namespace the `case` element must contain a `featurelist` element and a `solution` element. Once the Real Estate Case Schema has been determined, an XML case base compliant with this can be created on the fly using technology such as active server pages.

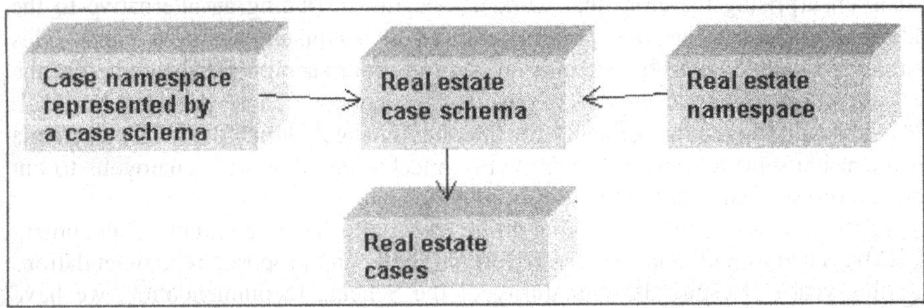

Fig. 5. The document architecture for a case-base marked up using a Real Estate namespace and a case namespace.

We have decided to use the well known travel domain[11] as a basis for comparison with CBML version 1.0. The small size of each case also allows us also demonstrate our concept with brevity. Figure 6 illustrates a simple case base in XML containing one case marked-up using the case namespace and a hypothetical travel agent namespace. Elements prefixed by the letter `c` belong to the case namespace. Since the travel agent namespace is declared first, it becomes the default namespace in this document and non-prefixed elements are understood to belong to this domain.

---

[11] Decision support in a travel agency, by Mario Lenz, GMD-FIRST, available at http://wwwagr.informatik.uni-kl.de/~bergmann/casuel/casebases.html

```
<?xml version='1.0'?>
<holidaycases xmlns:t="http://www.travelagent.com/travel"
                    xmlns:c="x-schema:caseschema.xml">
  <c:cases>
        <c:case caseid="1">
        <c:featurelist>
              <c:feature>
                    <holidayType>Bathing</holidayType>
              </c:feature>
              <c:feature><price>2498</price></c:feature>
              <c:feature>
                    <numberofPersons>2</numberofPersons>
              </c:feature>
              <c:feature><region>Egypt</region></c:feature>
              <c:feature><transport>Plane</Transport></c:feature>
              <c:feature><duration>14</duration></c:feature>
              <c:feature><season>April</season></c:feature>
              <c:feature><accomodation>2</accomodation></c:feature>
        <c:featurelist>
              <c:solution>
                    <hotel>Hotel White House, Egypt</hotel>
              </c:solution>
        </c:case>
  </c:cases>
  </holidaycases>
```

Fig. 6. A Case marked up using a case schema and a holiday schema

```
1.  <Schema name ="caseschema" xmlns="urn:schema-microsoft-com:xml-data"
2.  xmlns : dt="urn:schema-microsoft-com:datatypes">
  --
3.  <ElementType name="feature" content = "mixed" model="open"
    order="many">
4.  <AttributeType name="weight" required="no" dt:type="int"
    model="closed"/>
5.  <AttributeType name="constraint" required="no" dt:type="boolean"
    default="0"/>
6.  </ElementType>
7.  <ElementType name="featurelist" content="eltOnly" model="open"
    order=many">
8.  <element type="feature"/>
9.  </ElementType>
10. <ElementType name="solution" content="mixed" model="open"/>
11. <ElementType name="case" content="eltonly" order="one">
12. <AttributeType name="caseid" required="yes" dt:types="integer"
    model="closed"/>
13. <element type="featurelist"/>
14. <element type="solution"/>
15. </ElementType>
16. <ElementTye name="cases" content ="eltonly" model ="open"
    order="many">
17. <element type="case"/>
18. </ElementType>
  --
19. </Schema>
```

Fig. 7. An excerpt from a Case Schema based on XML-Data schema proposal.

The case namespace referenced in the holidaycases tag in figure 6 is delimited by the simple case schema shown in figure 7. This schema is easily extended and includes a facility for data-typing .

A full explanation of the syntax of the schema is outside the scope of this paper. However, a few points will make it a little clearer. The schema is an XML document itself, unlike the DTD which is defined according to EBNF notation. The `ElementType` tag (I will use *tag* in place of *element* here for purposes of clarity) defines the features that can appear in an XML document based on this particular schema. The `ElementType` tag contains a list of the elements permissible within the parent element. Constraints can be placed on these as to whether their presence is optional, their number and their type. For example, the `Featurelist` tag is defined in line 7 and it is allowed contain many Feature tags (line 8). Likewise the `AttributeType` defines an attribute associated with the element defined by an `ElementType` tag. For example, in lines 4-5 of figure 7 there are optional weight and constraint attributes associated with the feature element defined in line 3.

7 Conclusions

This paper presented the idea of a standard integrated CBR *view* of a company's information system. The ability of XML to integrate with relational database systems makes it a suitable candidate to represent this view. We have looked at two CBR systems that store cases in a database and use XML as a case representation format. These systems make use of the XML facility to create a custom tag set for each domain of use. We explain that since good DTD creation is not an easy task, and domain specific vocabularies are emerging it makes sense to find a standard way of representing case data without violating the syntax of the domain data. As an example, we look at an industry initiative in the real estate domain that uses a standard XML vocabulary, and suggest a role for CBR in such a scenario. We review CBML, an initial implementation of a standard case representation language using XML, and find it lacking for a number of reasons. Its syntax subsumes that of the domain data completely and its document architecture can only be understood by applications that have been designed to handle it. Our research into a solution has led us to the conclude that the current DTD model is inappropriate for the more rigorous requirements of data (as opposed to document) description. We then introduce two new initiatives stemming from the XML project - namespaces and schemas, which when used together allow us to create a powerful descriptive model for data which can be used as an alternative to the DTD. Arising from this we present the idea of a case namespace represented by a powerful case schema. The examples we present are taken from the holiday domain.

Further work will need to be done to refine our case namespace and explore its application in the realm of internet commerce, particularly in the area of internet brokerage. Schemas offer the advantage of easy extensibility, inheritance and data-typing support - none of which can be achieved with the current DTD model. The goal is to develop an XML case schema that fully exploits these features.

References

[1] Boumphrey, F. et al. (1998) XML Applications, Wrox Press, pgs. 97 -130

[2] Cunningham P., Finn. D., Slattery, S. (1994) Knowledge Engineering requirements in Derivational Analogy in Topics in Case Based Reasoning, Lecture notes in Artificial Intelligence, S. Wess, K-D Althoff, M.M Richter eds., pp234-245, Springer Verlag, 1994

[3] Doyle, M., Ferrario, M.A, Hayes, C., Cunningham, P., Smyth, B. (1998) CBR Net: Smart Technology Over a Network. TCD Technical Report TCD-CS-1998-07 - available at http://www.cs.tcd.ie/publications/tech-reports/tr-index.98.html

[4] Gentner, D., and Forbus, K. D. 1991. MAC/FAC: A model of similarity based access and mapping. In Proceedings of the Thirteenth Annual Conference of the Cognitive Science Society. Northvale, NJ: Erlbaum

[5] Gardingen D., Watson I. (1998). A Web based Case-Based Reasoning System for HVAC Sales Support. Proceedings of British Expert Systems conference 1998.

[6] Hanney, K 1996. Learning Adaptation Rules From Cases. MSc. Thesis. Computer Science Department, Trinity College Dublin.

[7] Hayes C., Cunningham P., Doyle M. (1998) Distributed CBR using XML in proceedings of the Workshop: Intelligent Systems and Electronic Commerce, Bremen, September 15-17 1998. Also available as TCD technical report TCD-CS-1998-06
http://www.cs.tcd.ie/publications/tech-reports/tr-index.98.html

[8] INRECA consortium.(1994). Casuel: A Common Case Representation Language, available at http://wwwagr.informatik.uni-kl.de/~bergmann/casuel/CASUEL_toc2.04.fm.html

[9] Kitano, H. & Shimazu, H. (1996) The Experience Sharing Architecture: A Case Study in Corporate-Wide Case-Based Software Quality Control. In Case-Based Reasoning: Experiences, Lessons & Future Directions. Leake, D.B. (Ed.) pp 235-268. AAAI Press/The MIT Press Menlo Park, Ca, US.

[10] Shimazu, H. (1998). Textual Case Based Reasoning using XML on the World-wide Web in Advances in Case Based Reasoning, proceedings of 4th European workshop on CBR (EWCBR),
Springer Verlag LNAI

[11] Wilke, W., Lenz, M., Wess, S. (1998). Intelligent Sales Support with CBR. In Case-Based Reasoning Technology: from foundations to applications. Lenz, M., Bartsch-Sporl, B., Burkhard. H-D & Wess, S. (Eds.). Lecture Notes in AI#1400 91-113. Springer-Verlag, Berlin.

Integrating Information Resources: A Case Study of Engineering Design Support*

David B. Leake,[1] Larry Birnbaum,[2] Kristian Hammond,[2] Cameron Marlow,[3] and Hao Yang[4]

[1] Computer Science Department, Lindley Hall, Indiana University, 150 S. Woodlawn Ave, Bloomington, IN 47405, U.S.A., leake@cs.indiana.edu
[2] Intelligent Information Laboratory, Computer Science Department, Northwestern University, 1890 Maple Avenue, Evanston, IL 60201, U.S.A., {birnbaum,hammond}@ils.nwu.edu
[3] Computer Science Department, The University of Chicago, 1100 East 58th Street, Chicago, IL 60637, U.S.A., cameron@ils.nwu.edu
[4] PDC, MD 270, GB-D68, Vehicle Operations, Ford Motor Company, 21500 Oakwood Blvd., Dearborn, MI 48124, U.S.A., hyang1@ford.com

Abstract. The development of successful case-based design aids depends both on the CBR processes themselves and on crucial questions of integrating the CBR system into the larger task context: how to make the CBR component provide information at the right time and in the right form, how to access relevant information from additional information sources to supplement the case library, how to capture information for use downstream and how to unobtrusively acquire new cases. This paper presents a set of design principles and techniques that integrate methods from CBR and information retrieval to address these questions. The paper illustrates their application through a case study of the Stamping Advisor, a tool to support feasibility analysis for stamped metal automotive parts.

1 Introduction

An experienced designer's memory of prior design experiences can be a powerful aid during the design process. When the designer who faces a new task is reminded of similar previous tasks, those remindings may suggest related solutions and warn of potential problems to avoid. Case-based design support systems leverage this process: They augment the designer's own memory by providing relevant cases from a library of prior experiences.

Case-based design has long been an active area of case-based reasoning research, and numerous case-based design aids have been implemented to support

*This research is supported by the Ford Motor Company under award No 0970-355-A200. David Leake is currently a Visiting Professor at Northwestern University, on sabbatical leave from Indiana University, and thanks the Intelligent Information Laboratory and the Northwestern Computer Science Department for their support. His research is supported in part by NASA under award No NCC 2-1035.

a wide range of design tasks (see (Kolodner, 1993) for some examples of these systems). Fully realizing the benefits of such systems, however, requires addressing additional issues beyond the case-based design support process itself. In order to maximize the usefulness of case-based design aids, they must be designed not as stand-alone systems but as integral parts of a single unified framework that supports all phases of the design process and the multiple actors that are often involved, and that draws on the multiple available information resources. Developers of such systems must address crucial questions of integrating the CBR system into the larger task context: how to make the CBR component provide information at the right time and in the right form, how to exploit other information sources in concert with case information, and how to capture information for use downstream and to unobtrusively acquire new cases. This paper presents a set of design principles and techniques addressing these questions. It illustrates their application through a case study of the Stamping Advisor, a tool to support feasibility analysis for stamped automotive parts.

2 The Stamping Advisor Domain

Automotive body design is a crucial task in automobile development. Body design has a profound impact on the vehicle's appeal and function, and the body is the most expensive component of the vehicle to manufacture. Stamped body parts, which make up the major portion of the body subsystem, are designed under constraints arising from aesthetic considerations, structural and functional requirements, cost concerns, and the availability of manufacturing resources.

Body styles are developed in an iterative process between the designers and feasibility engineers who examine the design for potential manufacturing issues. These include formability issues, which may result in splitting or wrinkling of the metal after the stamping process; manufacturing process complexity issues, such as shapes that must be stamped with a large number of dies (increasing costs), and quality concerns due to material properties and feature shapes, which may add significant cost to die testing or affect the quality or consistency of the final product.

The feasibility engineer's task is to identify potential problems, to justify why they are likely to occur, to estimate the costs that will be incurred if they are not addressed, and to propose design revisions to remedy them. Feasibility engineers report that they often base their judgments on specific experiences with prior designs. However, new engineers begin their work without this library of experiences, and even experienced engineers may not have had experience with the most relevant designs for a particular problem. Multiple information resources exist to aid the feasibility analysis task, such as records of experiences with prior designs, stored in paper and electronic forms. However, it may be difficult or excessively time-consuming for engineers to locate the needed information. Likewise, communicating their decisions and justifications is often cumbersome: The standard method for communicating their decisions downstream is to fill out and send a paper form.

Key questions for improving this process are how to provide better access to experiences and other engineering knowledge, and how to improve the usefulness of the information when it is reapplied. A collaboration was established between the Intelligent Information Laboratory at Northwestern University and the Vehicle Operations and Visteon divisions at the Ford Motor Company to investigate integrated case-based design support systems to address these questions. The company already had captured paper records of feasibility assessment issues and decisions, some of which had been placed in a database, providing a library of seed cases. The research question was how, given a set of feasibility analysis cases and the standard manuals used by feasibility engineers, to access and present them to maximize their usefulness to the design process.

Thus one goal of the project was *information integration* (Knoblock and Levy, 1998): to develop methods for satisfying the designer's information needs using cases and other information sources, for integrating the CBR system to automatically produce the information needed downstream, and for supporting unobtrusive case acquisition from available information. The Intelligent Information Laboratory developed the *Stamping Advisor* system, described in this paper, to demonstrate a framework for this design support process, and its approaches are now being applied to new systems at the Ford Motor Company.

3 Principles for Integrated Intelligent Design Support

The Stamping Advisor system embodies five general principles for the integration of case-based design support systems into the design environment. These principles are:

- **Seamless interaction**: Interaction with the combined system must parallel the feasibility engineer's own problem-solving process.
- **Just-in-time retrieval**: The system must proactively anticipate information needs and automatically provide the right information when it is needed, rather than placing the burden on the user to formulate requests.
- **Integration with other knowledge sources**: The system must link all available information resources, presenting prior cases, supplementary information to help understand the cases or apply their lessons, and additional information as appropriate to the task.
- **Integration across tasks**: The system must serve not only the immediate reasoning task but also the downstream tasks it serves. The system should automatically access information about the previous tasks to provide a context for its reasoning, and should produce products that can be used by the reasoning processes downstream.
- **Experience capture**: Each processing episode must provide new cases in a usable form.

These principles are related to basic tenets of the case-based reasoning cognitive model (Kolodner, 1994; Leake, 1998; Schank, 1982): That accessing and storing cases is a natural part of task performance and that models of knowledge access must reflect the task context. Our design support framework extends these principles to anticipate the user's needs, accessing relevant information wherever it is available, and extends the target of support beyond the current user to capture and transmit relevant information downstream.

3.1 Realizing these principles

Achieving a design support system that respects the previous principles requires addressing a number of CBR issues. Integrating the system with the feasibility engineer's reasoning and providing just-in-time support requires modeling his or her reasoning process, and especially modeling when and why particular cases and other information resources are retrieved. Integrating multiple knowledge sources depends both on appropriate task-based indexing and on methods for similarity assessment and retrieval that can be applied to preexisting documents and other information sources that differ from traditional cases. Experience capture depends on methods for case acquisition. The remainder of this paper discusses how the Stamping Advisor system addresses each of these issues.

4 Coordinating Case Presentation with the Reasoning of Feasibility Engineers

One of the goals of the Stamping Advisor project was to make case presentation fit the engineer's own reasoning. This is done in two ways: by designing the case presentation interface to fit the engineer's reasoning style, and by using knowledge of the engineer's task to anticipate the engineer's information needs and provide information proactively.

Feasibility engineers are given a computer-generated image of the part to evaluate, produced by the computer-aided design (CAD) system that the engineer used to generate the design. Interviews with feasibility engineers established that one of their reasoning styles is to sequentially scan the image, tracing around the boarder of the part looking for portions of the design that raise feasibility issues. The primary system interface provides a CAD image of a part, with different regions annotated by information about relevant cases. This makes it easy for the engineer to follow his or her normal process of scanning the design.

Given a design whose feasibility needs to be determined, the system presents a summary of the cases retrieved and the issues involved, using a graphical display of a part image with annotations concerning the number of issues found for each region of the part and their resolutions. The graphical interface organizes case information geometrically according to the regions of the part. For each region, it provides a summary of the cases found that involve issues for that region. The summaries of the issues for each area of the design are highlighted with color-coded warnings to identify the most problematic regions (green when surrogates support feasibility, yellow for limited problems, red for more serious problems). Figure 1 shows the issue summary interface for an automobile fender. In the screen display, the leftmost box, describing the headlamp opening, is highlighted in red because previous cases identified two potential issues that could not be resolved. The boxes for the nose (upper left) and wheel opening (bottom center) are highlighted in yellow, because each one includes one unresolved problem. No other problems were found, so all other boxes are highlighted in green.

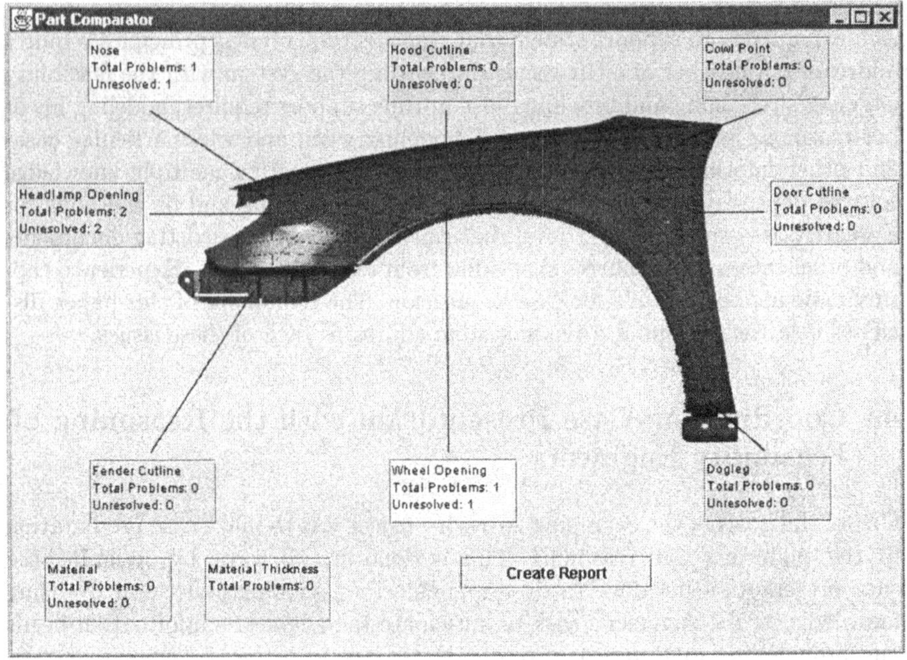

Fig. 1. Screen image from the Stamping Advisor's issue summary screen.

To see additional information for a region, the feasibility engineer clicks on the boxes for the displayed issue sets to select a region of interest. A window appears with information about problems in prior parts (called "surrogate parts") in which that region was similar. The engineer can select problems from this list to see how they were resolved. In some cases, the design will have been revised to repair the problem, suggesting a possible revision to consider. In others, the previous engineer may have detected mitigating factors that were originally overlooked, which made the problem inapplicable; these suggest factors for the engineer to check in the current design. In some cases, the prior engineer may have decided that the problematic design feature was so valuable aesthetically that it counterbalanced the extra production costs; in that situation the old case contains information about the estimated costs to consider when weighing whether to allow the potential problem to remain. The interface for this process is shown in Figure 2.

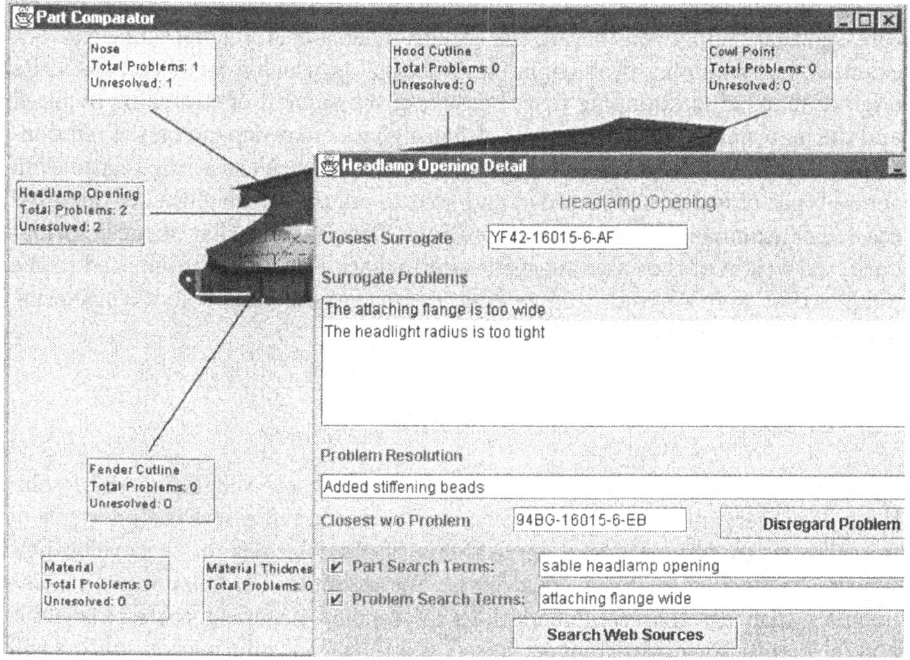

Fig. 2. Presentation of relevant surrogates, issues, and resolutions.

5 The Case Retrieval Process

In the Stamping Advisor, each part type is associated with a predefined set of classes of features to examine for feasibility. For a fender, there are ten such classes. Eight of these are associated with geometric regions of the part (e.g., the class of features involved in the headlamp opening), while two concern characteristics of the material used (e.g., stamping aluminum parts instead of steel parts involves special feasibility issues concerning sheet metal thickness).

When the system retrieves cases for potential issues, candidate cases are filtered according to the type of part being analyzed; for example, when examining the feasibility of a fender, only prior experiences with fenders are considered for retrieval. Within the cases for the given type of part, the system retrieves one set of relevant cases for each class of features to examine. For example, the system retrieves cases for fenders with similar headlamp openings to suggest feasibility issues associated with the design of the headlamp opening; it retrieves cases for fenders with similar wheel opening tabs to suggest feasibility issues associated with the design of the wheel opening tabs, and so forth. After cases have been filtered by the part and the type of part feature under consideration, the basic matching process is a nearest-neighbor algorithm using feature weightings developed for the domain.

In some instances, relationships may exist between distinct classes of features, so that simply considering the regions independently is not sufficient. For example, one stamping problem is "springback," in which a panel returns to its original shape after stamping (e.g., because of the amount of stretching required and the material used). The amount of "springback" may depend on the relationships between the shapes of two adjacent regions. In such cases, the relationship across types of features is recorded and used to adjust the weighting of retrieved cases. For example, if both adjacent regions have features that suggest springback, the weight of the cases suggesting springback is increased compared to the weights that were derived from looking at each region alone before considering the supporting relationship between them.

6 Integrated Information Access

Cases are helpful for warning of potential problems and suggesting prior solutions. However, additional information may be needed to assess the relevance of prior issues, to determine the applicability of old solutions, or to develop new solutions reflecting changed constraints. For example, Ford maintains on-line manuals with design recommendations for keeping stamping costs reasonable and for maintaining consistent styling. Given that these information sources will often be required to supplement retrieved cases, access to this information is important.

Keeping with the philosophy of integrating the CBR system, our goal was to use knowledge of the user's task and task context to automatically guide the search for this information: to automatically present the engineer with the supplementary information that is useful, given the knowledge that it is being retrieved in response to specific issues in a specific case. To provide this support, the Stamping advisor uses tracking information about the current task to automatically formulate targeted queries that can go against documents indexed by standard search engines. The delivered system demonstrates this capability by automatically generating queries to retrieve relevant style guidelines from the Ford Advanced Feasibility Guidelines for Styling.

6.1 Query Generation and Document Retrieval

As a product of the manual feasibility analysis process, textual information such as part names, part numbers, problem descriptions, feature names, and the vehicle name are recorded in a paper description. This information has been encoded into the database from which the cases are retrieved, and consequently is available for every part handled by the Stamping Advisor. This text is sufficient to distinguish parts at a textual level.

The Stamping Advisor uses this descriptive information, combined with its model of task relevance, to form queries to other information resources. Specifically, when a feasibility engineer is considering a feature, the system automatically forms queries to gather additional information about related features or problems from on-line resources. Four pieces of information establish the context for this query: the names of the vehicle, part, and problematic feature, and the textual description of the problem in question. These are extracted form the record of the current design. The system removes words contained in a standard stop list and makes a query from the remaining terms.

For example, when the feasibility engineer examines the headlamp opening problems highlighted in Figure 1, one of the issues is that the attaching flange is too wide. The Stamping Advisor generates a query containing "Sable headlamp opening" for the part under consideration, and "attaching flange wide" for the problem. Upon the feasibility engineer's request, this query is used to search for relevant guidelines in on-line manuals. Before initiating search, the engineer can request that the query be focused on only similar parts or similar problems, and can edit the query text as desired (e.g., to replace "Sable" to compare the styling on a different line of car). The query presentation interface is shown at the bottom right of Figure 2.

Once created, this query can be passed to any typical Internet search engine to search selected resources. In our implementation, we use the document indexing system Verity to index documents such as the on-line Ford Style Guide illustrated in Figure 3. Verity processes queries by stemming each of the given words, broadening the search to other possible forms of the terms, and assigning a numerical score. This score is based first on the number of word matches and then on the density of those matches within a given document. The list of matches is presented to the feasibility engineers, who can select documents to retrieve.

7 Integration Across Tasks

Previous case-based design support tools have a natural goal: aiding a designer in his or her task. However, in industrial settings, the designer's task is only one step in an extended process. For example, in stamping design, one or more designers initially formulate the design, a feasibility engineer critiques the design and makes suggestions, and the design is refined though an iterative cycle of changes and critiques. When a design is finalized, downstream design team members may need to evaluate the design, its potential issues and the designers' justifications for why they matter (or do not matter), and how they were resolved. Ideally, design aids should support this entire *process* rather than supporting only one individual step. This requires the sharing of information across tasks.

A tenet of our design support principles is that the design support system for any particular task should automatically access information about the previous tasks to provide a context for its reasoning, and should produce products that can be used by the reasoning processes downstream. Work is under way on augmenting the CAD system used for initial design to automatically capture the specification information used in feasibility analysis cases (e.g., to capture the part number, part type, vehicle, and a pointer to the CAD file), to be passed

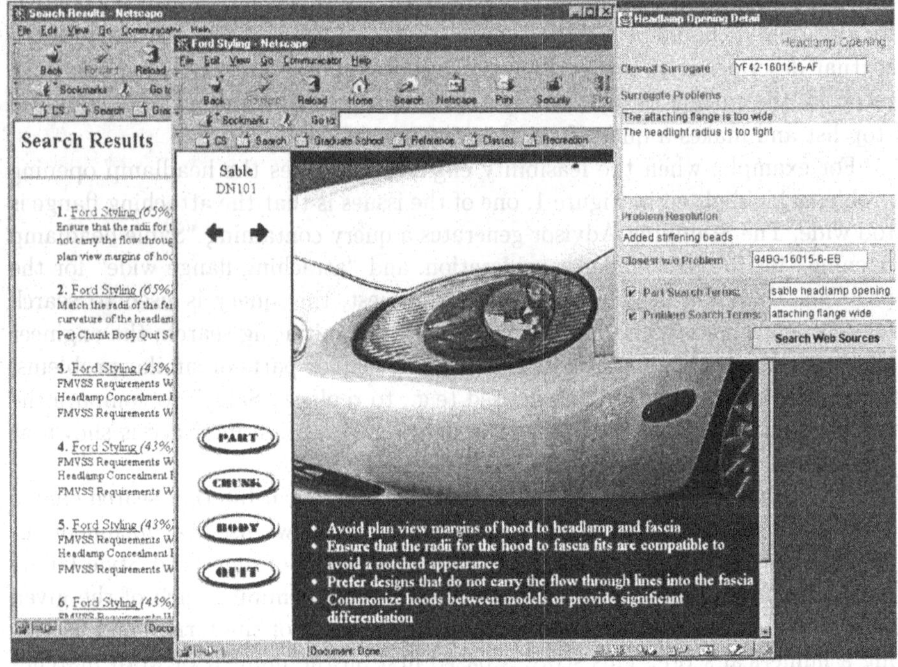

Fig. 3. Style guide page retrieved as relevant to the problem of headlamp opening being too tight.

automatically to the Stamping Advisor at the start of feasibility analysis. This will provide additional integration between the task of the initial designer and the feasibility engineer.

At the close of the feasibility assessment process, the system generates a Final Report Document to aid upstream or downstream design team members who need to understand or evaluate the feasibility engineer's work, replacing documentation generated by hand. In our model of the evaluation task, the information needed is: (1) the part being examined, (2) the issues considered, (3) how they were disposed of, and (4) the surrogates providing evidence relevant to the issues and decisions. A sample Final Report Document is shown in Figure 4.

8 Case Capture

Ford maintains an extensive library of reports of feasibility analysis problems and solutions in paper form. However, as is often the case in applying CBR, there is a bottleneck in translating this information into a usable case form. The ability of the Stamping Advisor to create Final Report Documents suggests a way to alleviate this bottleneck. In the Stamping Advisor, a user's decisions about appropriate surrogates, the problems they predict, and the ultimate disposition

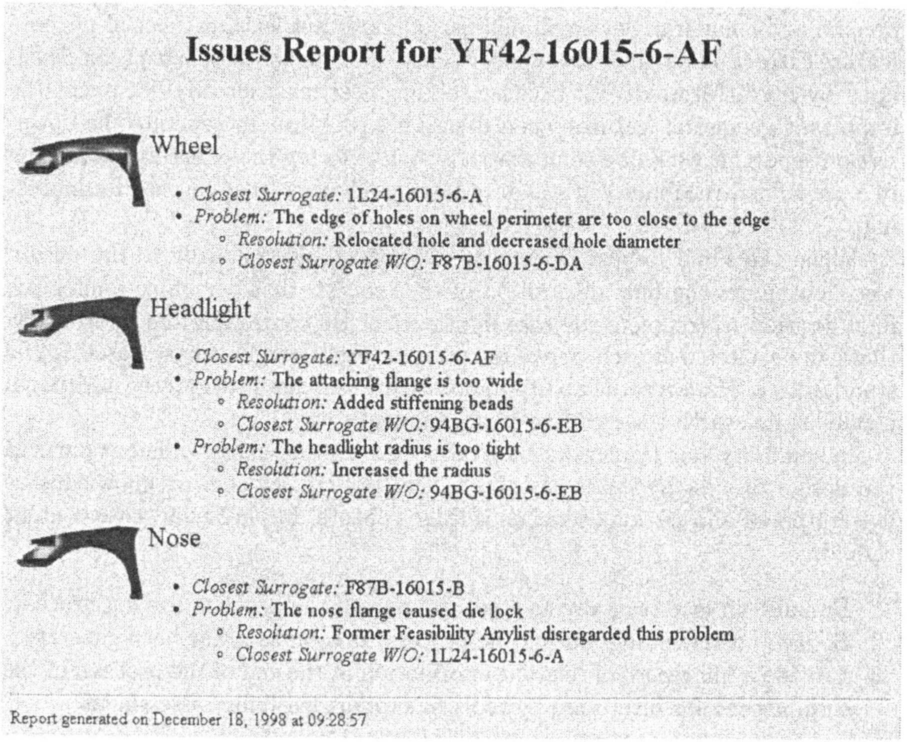

Issues Report for YF42-16015-6-AF

Wheel

- *Closest Surrogate:* 1L24-16015-6-A
- *Problem:* The edge of holes on wheel perimeter are too close to the edge
  - *Resolution:* Relocated hole and decreased hole diameter
  - *Closest Surrogate W/O:* F87B-16015-6-DA

Headlight

- *Closest Surrogate:* YF42-16015-6-AF
- *Problem:* The attaching flange is too wide
  - *Resolution:* Added stiffening beads
  - *Closest Surrogate W/O:* 94BG-16015-6-EB
- *Problem:* The headlight radius is too tight
  - *Resolution:* Increased the radius
  - *Closest Surrogate W/O:* 94BG-16015-6-EB

Nose

- *Closest Surrogate:* F87B-16015-B
- *Problem:* The nose flange caused die lock
  - *Resolution:* Former Feasibility Anylist disregarded this problem
  - *Closest Surrogate W/O:* 1L24-16015-6-A

Report generated on December 18, 1998 at 09:28:57

Fig. 4. Final report document.

of the problems are captured by the system during the feasibility assessment process. These are used to create the Final Report Document. This document is produced as the by-product of the user's decision-making and does not require additional effort on his or her part beyond that already required to convey the needed information downstream. This document automatically combines information captured from the user with other background information, gathering all the information needed to generate a new feasibility assessment case.

This case capture framework gathers data when they are available at each phase of the design process, not just during feasibility analysis. The growing record is made available to each downstream process for reasoning from existing data and addition to the record. In particular, information is built up during initial part design, feasibility analysis, and final decision-making on how to proceed on a part.

Information used to characterize part designs in the CAD system (e.g., (model, year, and part number, and a pointer to the CAD file) provide an initial record of the design. Current seed cases include geometric features, and work is ongoing to support the addition of geometric features to new cases. Ideally, general-purpose automatic geometric matching procedures (e.g., (Coulon and

Steffens, 1994)) could be applied to the designs. However, given the specialized domain and comparatively small number of important features, special-purpose feature extraction routines also appear practical. Some of these have been developed by Ford. Alternatively, because the engineer must already document the important geometric features when describing problems to generate the downstream report, it would be comparatively simple to tag these features according to a predefined vocabulary of standard features that can then be used for matching.

When the Final Report Document is provided electronically to the person who determines the final disposition of the request, that person can enter the final decision to complete the case information. By controlling the information that can be entered at each step of the process (e.g., though menus), cases can be standardized. However, the ability to do textual searches provides the additional capability to search through free-form comments, etc.

In summary, our framework integrates case capture across different parts of the design process and uses cases as a vehicle both for sharing knowledge as it is gathered and for long-term knowledge capture. In particular, case content should:

1. Be built up incrementally as a natural part of the problem solving process.
2. Be used incrementally during the process, as soon as it has been generated.
3. Provide a full record of relevant information at the end of the process, in the form needed for future use by tools to support feasibility assessment.

This supports rapid growth of case information and the standardization of provided information.

9 Relationship to Previous Work

9.1 Case-Based Design Support

A wide range of case-based design support tools has been developed for numerous tasks such as architectural design (Gebhardt *et al.*, 1997; Goel *et al.*, 1991; Hua and Faltings, 1993; Maher *et al.*, 1995; Smith *et al.*, 1995), conceptual design of aircraft subsystems (Domeshek *et al.*, 1994; Leake and Wilson, 1999), autoclave layout design (Hinkle and Toomey, 1995), device design (Goel, 1989; Sycara *et al.*, 1991), and circuit design (Vollrath, 1998). The Stamping Advisor's task is most closely related to that of the load validator in the system Clavier (Hinkle and Toomey, 1995), which warns users about potential problems in new autoclave layouts by presenting users with similar prior layouts and their outcomes. A crucial issue in autoclave layout design is the interacting effects of components of the layouts, and these interactions are hard to explain and separate. Consequently, Clavier based its predictions on the similarity of the previous layouts, taken as a whole, with entire current designs. In the Stamping Advisor domain, problems can be localized by the feasibility engineer. Consequently, Stamping Advisor cases represent problems at the level of the individual regions they affect (with additional checks for interactions that span multiple regions), which facilitates transfer of problem information to new contexts (for example, headlamp opening problems can be predicted based on prior experiences with the headlamp openings in very different styles of fenders). The Stamping Advisor also differs in using cases not only to advise, but also to capture and communicate the rationale underlying design decisions taken in response to its advice.

The Stamping Advisor demonstrates a number of principles for integrating CBR into the engineering design process. First, the system brings CBR into the feasibility engineer's normal reasoning process by integrating case-based support with the CAD tools already used to create and examine designs for stamped parts. This approach is similar to those taken by the FABEL (Gebhardt *et al.*, 1997) and CADRE (Hua *et al.*, 1996) projects, both of which integrate the CBR system with existing CAD systems. It differs, however, in using a very specific task model to automatically determine the types of information to provide and when to provide it with just-in-time retrieval. In contrast, FABEL provides a "virtual construction site" that the engineer can navigate, and a tool kit from which the designer selects tools to perform particular types of retrievals. The Stamping Advisor uses its model of how the feasibility analysis task is done to anticipate specific information needs and proactively determine what information is needed and how to retrieve it.

9.2 Integrating CBR and IR

The Stamping Advisor also goes beyond case-based support to integrate multiple knowledge sources. There is considerable current interest in the use of CBR for textual cases, and in the use of information retrieval methods to access them (Lenz and Ashley, 1998). A challenging question is how to maintain the strengths of CBR—the pragmatic focus that traditional CBR provides—while exploiting the generality of IR methods for assessing the similarity of documents. This depends on bridging the gap between task-relevant indexing used in CBR and methods that can be applied to unstructured textual data. (Rissland and Daniels, 1996) present one method for this integration in the retrieval of legal cases. Their system first performs a feature analysis to do a traditional CBR retrieval of the most relevant cases from a case library represented in a carefully structured form. It then uses the textual descriptions of those cases as seed examples for the relevance feedback mechanism of a text-based information retrieval system, which generates queries to retrieve similar texts from a larger library of textual case descriptions. The Stamping Advisor uses task-based characterizations more directly: it directly generates a search engine query from relevant problem features. Because the role of each component in the query is readily apparent, the Stamping Advisor also provides the user with the capability to revise this query before search to reflect additional information goals that may not be known to the system.

9.3 Case Capture

A crucial issue for scaling up CBR applications is knowledge capture. The Stamping Advisor system is designed to facilitate this through knowledge capture during use. Feasibility analysis is a "natural" CBR domain (Mark *et al.*, 1996), in that the manual feasibility analysis process includes extensive paper documentation for each design case. However, the primary case acquisition mode we envision is from system use itself. Even if *no* cases were available in the system case library, the system would be useful as a convenient interface for recording feasibility information (now recorded on paper) and aiding search through online resources. Thus feasibility engineers have the incentive to use the system, and their use provides cases that will increase its usefulness as sufficient data is gathered to take full advantage of the CBR component.

10 Conclusions

The Stamping Advisor project illustrates a set of principles for integrating case-based reasoning systems into the larger task context. The system was designed to provide an open architecture for case and other information retrieval based on features of the current design, and to exploit and support the flow of information from successive steps of the design process. To make the system natural to use, the interaction is designed to parallel the feasibility engineer's own problem-solving process and to automatically provide just-in-time access to the right cases, rather than placing the burden on the user to formulate requests. The system uses its task model to generate focused IR queries to access additional knowledge sources, retaining the capability for the user to adjust those queries to explore additional topics. The system does automatic knowledge capture, gathering information about each interaction and using it for a dual purpose: to provide the information needed downstream of the reasoning task and package new cases for future use.

The central lesson of this work is that the development of successful case-based design aids must depend not only on the CBR processes themselves but on crucial questions of integrating CBR system into the larger task context: making the system automatically provide information when it is needed and in the right form, accessing relevant information from additional information sources, and communicating and capturing information. We are continuing to strengthen this integration as the current system is refined. One goal, for example, is to fully integrate the Stamping Advisor into the initial CAD design process, to immediately warn the original designer of potential problems while the design is being generated. We believe that CBR fits naturally into a new mode of knowledge management that not only tracks where documents *are*, but tracks *how they are used* and *where they are needed* to access multiple information sources to provide the right information at the right time.

References

[Coulon and Steffens, 1994] C.-H. Coulon and R. Steffens. Comparing fragments by their images. FABEL Report 13, Gesellschaft für Mathematik und Datenverarbeitung mbH, 1994. Pages 36–44.

[Domeshek *et al.*, 1994] E. Domeshek, M. Herndon, A. Bennett, and J. Kolodner. A case-based design aid for conceptual design of aircraft subsystems. In *Proceedings of the Tenth IEEE Conference on Artificial Intelligence for Applications*, pages 63–69, Washington, 1994. IEEE Computer Society Press.

[Gebhardt *et al.*, 1997] Friedrich Gebhardt, Angi Voß, Wolfgang Gräther, and Barbara Schmidt-Belz. *Reasoning with complex cases.* Kluwer Academic Publishers, Boston, 1997.

[Goel *et al.*, 1991] A. Goel, J. Kolodner, M. Pearce, and R. Billington. Towards a case-based tool for aiding conceptual design problem solving. In R. Bareiss, editor, *Proceedings of the DARPA Case-Based Reasoning Workshop*, pages 109–120, San Mateo, 1991. DARPA, Morgan Kaufmann.

[Goel, 1989] A. Goel. *Integration of Case-Based Reasoning and Model-Based Reasoning for Adaptive Design Problem Solving.* PhD thesis, The Ohio State University, 1989.

[Hinkle and Toomey, 1995] D. Hinkle and C. Toomey. Applying case-based reasoning to manufacturing. *AI Magazine*, 16(1):65–73, Spring 1995.

[Hua and Faltings, 1993] K. Hua and B. Faltings. Exploring case-based design - CADRE. *Artificial Intelligence in Engineering Design, Analysis and Manufacturing*, 7(2):135–144, 1993.

[Hua *et al.*, 1996] K. Hua, B. Faltings, and I. Smith. CADRE: Case-based geometric design. *Artificial Intelligence in Engineering*, 10:171–183, 1996.

[Knoblock and Levy, 1998] K. Knoblock and A. Levy, editors. *Proceedings of the AAAI-98 workshop on AI and information integration.* AAAI Press, Menlo Park, CA, 1998.

[Kolodner, 1993] J. Kolodner. *Case-Based Reasoning.* Morgan Kaufmann, San Mateo, CA, 1993.

[Kolodner, 1994] J. Kolodner. From natural language understanding to case-based reasoning and beyond: A perspective on the cognitive model that ties it all together. In R. Schank and E. Langer, editors, *Beliefs, Reasoning, and Decision Making: Psycho-Logic in Honor of Bob Abelson*, pages 55–110. Lawrence Erlbaum, Hillsdale, NJ, 1994.

[Leake and Wilson, 1999] D. Leake and D. Wilson. Integrating CBR with interactive tools for acquiring, manipulating and reusing design knowledge. In *Proceedings of the Third International Conference on Case-Based Reasoning*, Berlin, 1999. Springer Verlag. In press.

[Leake, 1998] D. Leake. Cognition as case-based reasoning. In W. Bechtel and G. Graham, editors, *A Companion to Cognitive Science*, pages 465–476. Blackwell, Oxford, 1998.

[Lenz and Ashley, 1998] M. Lenz and K. Ashley, editors. *Proceedings of the AAAI-98 workshop on textual case-based reasoning.* AAAI Press, Menlo Park, CA, 1998.

[Maher *et al.*, 1995] M. Maher, B. Balachandran, and D. Zhang. *Case-based reasoning in design.* Erlbaum, Hillsdale, NJ, 1995.

[Mark *et al.*, 1996] William Mark, Evangelos Simoudis, and David Hinkle. Case-based reasoning: Expectations and results. In D. Leake, editor, *Case-Based Reasoning: Experiences, Lessons, and Future Directions*, pages 269–294. AAAI Press, Menlo Park, CA, 1996.

[Rissland and Daniels, 1996] E. Rissland and J. Daniels. The synergistic application of CBR to IR. *Artificial Intelligence Review*, 10:441–475, 1996.

[Schank, 1982] R.C. Schank. *Dynamic Memory: A Theory of Learning in Computers and People.* Cambridge University Press, Cambridge, England, 1982.

[Smith *et al.*, 1995] I. Smith, C. Lottaz, and B. Faltings. Spatial composition using cases: IDIOM. In *Proceedings of First International Conference on Case-Based Reasoning*, pages 88–97, Berlin, October 1995. Springer Verlag.

[Sycara *et al.*, 1991] K. Sycara, R. Guttal, J. Koning, S. Narasimhan, and D. Navinchandra. CADET: a case-based synthesis tool for engineering design. *International Journal of Expert Systems*, 4(2):157–188, 1991.

[Vollrath, 1998] I. Vollrath. Reuse of complex electronic designs: Requirements analysis for a CBR application. In P. Cunningham, B. Smyth, and M. Keane, editors, *Proceedings of the Fourth European Workshop on Case-Based Reasoning*, pages 136–147, Berlin, 1998. Springer Verlag.

A Hybrid Case-Based Reasoner for Footwear Design

Julie Main and Tharam S. Dillon

Dept of Computer Science and Computer Engineering
La Trobe University, Bundoora 3083, Australia.
Ph: +61 3 9479-2393, Fax: +61 3 9479-3060
and Expert and Intelligent Systems Laboratory,
Applied Computing Research Institute
Email: main@cs.latrobe.edu.au

Abstract. This paper details the way case-based reasoning has been used to aid footwear designers in creating new designs while maximizing component reuse. A hybrid system was created which uses an object-oriented memory model, neural networks for retrieval and fuzzy feature vectors to augment the basic case-based reasoning model. One of the main tasks involved in the design of any case-based system is determining the features that make up a case and finding a way to index these cases in a case-base for efficient and correct retrieval. This paper looks at the components of this footwear design system and how the various elements join together to create a useful system, in particular, how the use of fuzzy feature vectors and neural networks can improve the indexing and retrieval steps in case-based systems.

Background

As early as 3700 BC the ancient Egyptians wore sandals made of plant fibers or leather. Most civilizations since then have made and worn some type of foot covering either as protection or decoration. Although people have made footwear for thousands of years, it was only in the mid 1800s with the invention of Howe's sewing machine and more specialist footwear manufacturing equipment that the mass production of shoes in factories started. From this time on there has been a growing desire to reduce the cost of manufacture by using components across various styles and streamlining production. Starting with the move away from be-spoke footwear (the individual making of a pair of shoes where a person would order a pair of shoes for themselves and an individual last[1] would be made on which to create this shoe) to the use of standardized lasts (to make multiple pairs of the same style for the general public), component and tool reuse has now become essential for today's mass production.

It is not hard to understand why. Looking at some of the development costs of shoes it becomes obvious why there is a need to minimize pre-production and tooling-up costs. In creating a ladies' fashion shoe in the late 20th century there

[1] A last is a form, shaped like a foot, on which shoes are made.

are many costs involved in creating a new design, even before reaching the stage of volume production (see Appendix A).

To give an estimate of how much these pre-production or tooling-up costs contribute to the cost of an item we can specify the minimum number of pairs needed, using each tool, to make it worthwhile producing it. To make it cost effective the tooling-up costs need to be no more than 10% of the wholesale cost of the shoe. The minimum pairing to be sold before creating the following tools is shown in Table 1.

Table 1. Pairages to justify volume production

Sole moulds:	
Injection moulded PVC-nitrile rubber	- 200,000 pair over 2-3 years
Thermoplastic rubber	- 20,000 pair over 1 season
Polyurethane	- 10,000 pair over 1 season

lasts:	
Minimum run of 30 pair of lasts	- 2,000 pair over 1 season

knives:	
minimum set of metal clicking knives	- 1,000 pair over 1 season

These figures are hard to achieve especially in an isolated country such as Australia where the consumer base is small. As soon as large runs of any item occur it becomes cheaper to source the goods in a country with a lower labor rate. Therefore, if large pairages are needed but cannot be obtained on individual items, tool and mould reuse becomes vital.

Component and Tool Sharing

There are many different ways that components and tools can be shared between styles in the footwear manufacturing area (Figure 1 shows some of these).

Increasing the drive for component reuse in the ladies fashion footwear domain is the way fashions change from season to season, and even mid-season. Fashion trends tend to have a cyclic behavior, in that a fashion 'look' will often go 'out' and a number of years later make another appearance. Another factor in women's fashion is its diversity. Even within a single trend, there are a multitude of variations. Customers usually want something that is up to date, but a little different, or a little better than the other shoes on the market.

Fig. 1. Some types of component and tool reuse in footwear designs

In a company that produces women's fashion shoes there are hundreds of designs produced each year and a designer forgets all but a few of the key designs in a relatively short span of time. Thus, when a fashion trend makes a second (or third) appearance, or when a designer wants to reuse parts of existing designs, the previous designs have been forgotten and the new shoes are re-designed from scratch. This forgetting and starting over procedure is a problem that, if overcome, could not only increase the number of parts reused, but could lead to a faster design stage and also to the input of a wider variety of ideas than the designer has access to at that time.

To address this problem we designed a case-based reasoning system that stores the past shoe designs and retrieves a number of designs that are close to a design specification that the designer inputs. The output from this system is a set of previous designs that most closely approximate the desired design. From these designs most importantly we can determine as many components for reuse as possible and through adaptation adapt the design to use components from other designs to make up for any discrepancies between the retrieved designs and the desired designs.

It is of course impossible to always adapt and reuse. Fashion styling is such that new parts frequently have to be made but there are also often parts that are able to be reused. The more components and tools that can be shared between styles, the lower the tooling-up costs. While it was indicated above that the maximum that tooling-up costs should contribute to the cost of a shoe was 10% of the wholesale cost, sharing parts can push down the tooling-up costs to a more desirable 0.5%.

A CBR to Maximize Reuse

The type of system we set out to create was an intelligent knowledge-based system, that would retrieve design specifications and provide lists of the components that could be reused and adaptation suggestions. It is primarily for standardizing components across styles and reducing pre-production costs. What we were not trying to achieve was a CAD/CAM design package. There are other excellent footwear specific systems for doing that. We are not providing a tool for designing at the lower level of patterns, lasts and moulds, such as these, but rather a complementary pre-manufacturing system for the higher level design including the identification of possible common or standard parts.

Case Base Creation

There were two very distinct components of knowledge available to create a case based reasoner, both of which had to be used together to determine the required solution. These were:

1. The large collection of previously existing designs. To create a case base for Main Jenkin Pty. Ltd, a Melbourne-based footwear manufacturer, we

needed their previous designs with descriptive attributes as well as the lists of components composing each design.

2. The expertise of footwear designers to classify, analyze and provide adaptation rules.

Cases include two components:

1. Their design feature description by which they are indexed and retrieved.
2. Their technical description including the components and manufacturing techniques needed for production.

An Object-Oriented Memory Model

The initial structuring of the domain was carried out manually. Some designs were so similar that we felt it was best to group these designs together. Further combining of similar groups created a hierarchical structure incorporating all designs. Although the hand grouping of cases is not really desirable for large case bases it was an initial solution that has worked well. To apply this system to other manufacturers or other types of goods, it would be better to apply an automated solution. The best way of determining the structure of the domain is still being refined.

When it came to determining how cases would be represented for storage and organized in memory, a number of factors had to be taken into account. As the shoes are divided into larger and smaller groups in a hierarchy and the lowest level groups consist of individual designs, it emerged that an object-oriented representation was a possible solution. Particular shoe designs could be represented as objects, being instances of particular classes. Groupings such as 'sandals' could be represented as subclasses with every subclass or individual object as a division of the superclass of shoes.

Individual shoes could then be attached statically to the lowest level classes in the hierarchy to be easily retrieved when the lowest sub-class to which the current input can be associated has been determined. The possible number of objects that can be attached to a sub-class is large, but it needs to be limited to a small number so that only the most relevant cases are retrieved. Each sub-class can have varying numbers of instance objects associated with it depending on how many cases are associated with it. This may range from as little as 1 to as many as 20 depending on the popularity of the type of design.

The actual creation of the hierarchy of classes was a significant task. Each class (except the lowest level) had to be divided into component sub-classes, and at the lowest level, instances (particular designs) had to be attached to the appropriate sub-classes.

In each layer of classification, the division is not clear cut. For each class there is more than one way of sub-dividing that class. The super class can be said to consist of the union of the instances contained in its subclasses. This corresponds to Union type of inheritance [9].

The desired classification was the one in which the cases that are retrieved most closely match the problem specification and in which those retrieved cases in the class will be useful in the new shoe design. Therefore, design of the class structure for the system was carried out in a way that divided cases into groups that are similar from a design and conceptual perspective.

It is not possible in a domain such as footwear to arrive at a definitive solution. However it is possible that in the majority of cases the class hierarchy will group the cases in a useful way.

Neural Networks in Retrieval

After considering numerous retrieval methods from the nearest neighbor, inductive and knowledge guided approaches to case retrieval, and comparing them to the retrieval capabilities of neural networks, we decided that neural networks would best satisfy the retrieval problem in our system.

The benefits of neural networks for retrieval include the following: essentially Case Retrieval is the matching of patterns, a current input patterns (case) with one or more stored patterns or cases. Neural networks are very good at matching patterns. They cope very well with incomplete data and the imprecision of inputs which is of benefit in the footwear design domain, as sometimes some portion of a footwear design is important for a new case while some other part is of little relevance.

The use of neural networks for case retrieval presents some problems of its own. In the system described shortly, over 400 cases are contained in the case base. It is impractical that a single neural network be expected to retrieve a single case from hundreds of possible cases. As a hierarchy of cases has already been created, grouping similar designs together, we can use a number of neural networks to determine at each level in which sub-class it is most likely that we would find a case similar to the current input. Therefore one neural network can be used to classify all the cases into the highest level classes. For each of those high level classes, a further neural network will be used to divide the cases in that class into its sub-classes. This is repeated for each sub-class until the lowest level sub-classes are reached.

Domains that use the case-based reasoning technique are usually complex. This means that the classification of cases at each level is normally non-linear and hence, for each classification a single-layer network is insufficient and a multi-layered network is required. Therefore, for the footwear design system, three layered networks (i.e. with one hidden layer) were used at each level to determine the classification. The use of a three layered network allowed the networks to build their own internal representation of the inputs and determine the best weightings.

As it is was known how each particular case was classified into its classes and sub-classes, supervised learning was to take place. In other words because the input features and the output goals were provided, a teacher can be said to be training the network, hence 'supervised' as opposed to 'unsupervised' learning is taking place.

The next step was to define the learning algorithm that was used to determine changes in weights during training. Taking into account the use of multi-layer networks and supervised learning, we chose to use the back-propagation algorithm for training the neural networks.

Features as Inputs to the Neural Networks

The determination of the features that are important in the classification of cases into each class was a major knowledge engineering task. For example, to determine the features that should be used as inputs into the highest level neural network we had to look at the classes into which the super-class was divided, and how the cases in each of those sub-classes differed from each other.

Distinguishing these features is not easy. If it were, we could easily construct rules to do the classification. Determining the correct features involved looking at the cases, seeing the major differences between them, and using these features to attempt to successfully train a network. When a network learnt the input patterns to give a low sum of squared error, then the features we had determined were correct. If there were patterns that this network could not classify, we needed to add new features that would distinguish between these cases. For example, sometimes the inputs to a neural network were the same for cases in more than one output class. When this occurred, obviously there was a difference between these cases that the attributes defined had not captured.

It was still helpful when the networks did not train successfully as the cases that were not learnt led us to distinguishing important features that were previously undetected. Once the additional features had been determined, the input patterns for the neural network needed to be modified to include the additional attributes and the networks retrained. This training and testing cycle continued until all the networks had negligible error rates. While it would be possible to input all features into each network and let the neural network dismiss some features by giving them a low rating, we agreed it was better to eliminate those features of little importance. This was to minimize the number of case descriptors that had to be input by the user, and reduce the number of input nodes and therefore the size of the network.

Representation of Features

The features that define a case and index that case in a case base can be of a number of different types which all must be represented in different ways. What follows is a number of actual features that had to be represented and what types they were:

Does the shoe have an open toe?

This can only be true or false so it was represented as a Boolean type. Boolean data values are needed to represent factors of a case that can be present or absent, true or false.

How much is the shoe open or cut out?

As this is best defined as a percentage it is represented as a continuous type. Such a value could be 7%, 8% or 9%. It can be 8.5%, 7.11% or 6.976%. Hence, the representation of this type of data will be a decimal number with any number of decimal places.

What is the toe shape? What degree of toe shape does this shoe have?

Multi-valued data can have several different yet deterministic values. There are a number of different types of multi-valued variables that can be distinguished.

The first of these types is interval data. Interval data can take a number of different values, for instance w, x, y, z and these values have two conditions upon them; that $w < x < y < z$ and that the intervals between the values are the same, i.e. that $x - w = y - x = z - y$.

Ordinal data is similar but has only one of the above conditions. The data must still be ordered: $w < x < y < z$, however $x - w$ does not necessarily equal $z - y$. Degree of toe shape is an example of ordinal data as it can take the valuse minimal, average, large and extreme.

Finally nominal data values have no relationships between them. Toe shape above is an example of a nominal data type as we do not say for example that *round < chiselled < square*.

How high is the shoe? Is the footwear item a sandal, shoe, short boot or long boot?

This was represented as a Fuzzy data type: perhaps the most interesting type of data encountered in the footwear domain. It is best explained by our example. The height of a shoe can be small (sandal), medium (shoe), high (short boot) or very high (long boot). If we have to classify actual data into these four ranges of values, we have to determine which values fit into each category. This is a problem as values can be considered to be between groups or in more than one group. A pair with an inside back height of 30 cm would be considered very high (a long boot) and likewise a pair with an inside back height of 5 cm would be considered medium (a shoe), and 10 cm high (a short boot). When it comes to a value of 7 cm, is that average or high? What about 8 cm or 9 cm? What is the boundary between a shoe and a short boot? A large number of the features that characterize cases frequently consist of linguistic variables which are best represented using fuzzy feature vectors.

When determining the features and the type of features of the cases we had the following criteria. Firstly, as far as the user is concerned, the number of properties that had to be defined should not be large, and the values of the properties were relevant to the shoe domain, not requiring any conversion for the computer to accept them. For example, values for toe shape are 'pointed', and 'chiseled'. These are both the terms used by the designers and also what is input into the system making the system accessible for designers. Most importantly the features and their characterization had to be accurate and produce the desired outcomes of retrieving cases that were similar to the desired case.

Fuzzy Representation

As was detailed above the inside-back height of a shoe can be classified as very high (a long boot), high (a short boot), medium (a shoe) or low (a type of sandal), but some shoes will not fit into the crisp separations of categories. If a shoe has a height of 7 cm we want to represent that it is partly a shoe and partly a boot.

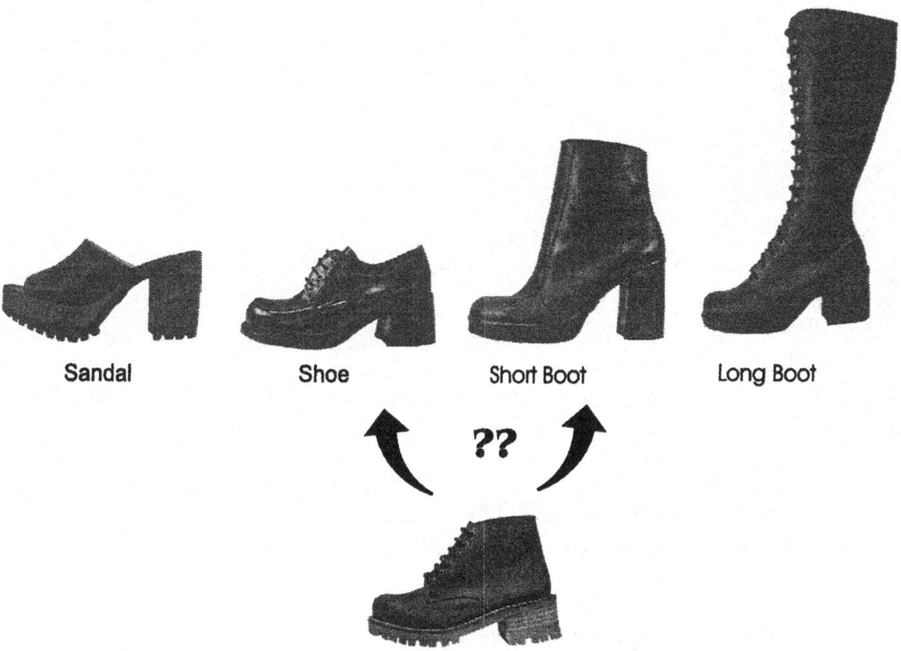

Fig. 2. A Footwear item between height categories

This can be represented for input to the neural network by using 4 attributes: 'low', 'medium', 'high' and 'very high'. Each shoe would have a value for each of these four variables. A low shoe (e.g. a mule) would have attributes with these values:

$$low : 1 \; medium : 0 \; high : 0 \; veryhigh : 0$$

A long boot with a large inside-back height would have the following:

$$low : 0 \; medium : 0 \; high : 0 \; veryhigh : 1$$

A traditional shoe (of 5 cm) would have the following values:

$$low : 0 \; medium : 1 \; high : 0 \; veryhigh : 0$$

This is straightforward for the instances that fall exactly into one of the main categories. However, for those cases that do not fit so nicely (e.g. the 7 cm case), we needed to define a function that determines the value for in-between cases.

This function can take many forms, but as an initial function we used straight line functions. The actual function to determine the values associated with the height of the shoe is shown in Figure 3. In this case the values for the shoe with height 7 cm can be seen to be:

$$low : 0 \; medium : 0.6 \; high : 0.4 \; veryhigh : 0$$

Fuzzy data can be represented using two or more functions. They do not have to be straight or continuous functions.

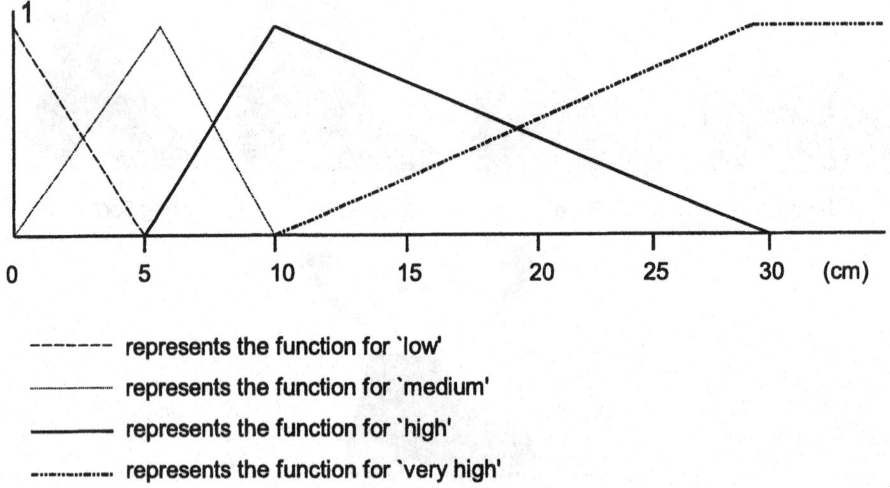

Fig. 3. Fuzzy representation of shoe height

Case Adaptation

After retrieval of the best case we can modify the design (or do case adaptation) by searching individually for components to see if we can make up the parts where the retrieved design does not meet the required design from components from other designs.

Learning

Every time a new design was created, whether through the CBR system or completely independently by a footwear designer, the new design (assuming it is successful) had to be added to the case base as every design that can be made increases the likelihood of finding components to reuse. Every time a case is added, the system 'learns' a little. By adding a case the CBR system may now be able to retrieve a design with more components to reuse than it could before the case was added.

To add a new case to the footwear design system, the case must first be classified or grouped as best possible with similar designs. This may involve some change to the hierarchical structure of the case base. Once the case has been classified, the neural networks used in its classification must be retrained. This is a simple matter assuming the normal case where new features are not needed for the classification. If the addition of a new case requires the addition of some new input to a neural network then a new neural network has to be created and trained.

Application to Other Industries

The problems encountered in the manufacture of footwear, as outlined in the Background section, are found in many other industries. Other fashion industries, such as clothing, would have similar tooling-up costs, similar problems and similar numbers of styles in a season. We believe the techniques we applied to obtain our solution for Main Jenkin could easily be applied to these other industries with comparable results.

Conclusion

This paper describes the development of a case based reasoning system for shoe design that maximizes reuse. The special features of the system include an object memory model, use of several genre of features including binary, continuous, discrete ordinal, discrete categoric, discrete interval and fuzzy linguistic. To carry out case retrieval, multi-level supervised neural nets were used.

The use of neural networks and fuzzy logic was found to be a useful means of retrieval. In testing, the retrieved cases were the closest match of the cases in the case base in 95% of tests carried out. In the other 5% the retrieved case was still useful for adaptation, though not the closest possible match.

Acknowledgments

The management and staff of Main Jenkin Pty. Ltd. provided essential domain expertise for which we would like to thank them.

References

1. Ashley, K.D.: Modeling Legal Argument: Reasoning with Cases and Hypotheticals. MA, MIT Press, 1990.
2. Beale, R. and Jackson, T.: Neural Computing: An Introduction. Hilger, Bristol, 1990
3. Dillon, T.S. and Tan, P.L.: Object-Oriented Conceptual Modeling. Australia, Prentice Hall, 1993.
4. Hammond, K.J.: CHEF: A Model of Case-Based Planning. Proc. Fifth National Conference. on Artificial Intelligence (AAAI-86). 1986:267-271.
5. Hennessey, D. and Hinkle, D.: Applying Case-Based Reasoning to Autoclave Loading. IEEE Expert. 7(5):21-26, October 1992.
6. Kolodner, J.: Case Based Reasoning. CA, Morgan Kaufmann, 1993.
7. Main, J., Dillon T.S. and Khosla R.: Use of Neural Networks for Case-Retrieval in a System For Fashion Shoe Design. Proc. Eighth International Conference on Industrial and Engineering Applications of Artificial Intelligence and Expert Systems (IEA/AIE 95: Melbourne, Australia; June 1995). Gordon and Breach, pp. 151-158.
8. Riesbeck, C. K. and Schank, R.C.: Inside Case-based Reasoning. New Jersey, Lawrence Erlbaum, 1989.
9. Rahayu, W. and Chang E.: A Methodology for Transforming an Object-Oriented Data Model into a Relational Database Design. Proceedings of the 12th International Conference on Technology Object-Oriented Languages and Systems, Melbourne, 1993, pp 99 - 115.

Appendix A

Table 2. Tooling up and Other Pre-production costs

Costs from the conception of design to creation of pullovers (trials)	
consultation	- stylist's time and labor
styling costs	- pattern design and cutting
manufacture of pullovers	- making of initial trials

Costs from the pullover to sample stage (for sales department)	
designer	- time and labor for the development of specifications
sample lasts	- single sample size last creation
sample patterns	- usually a metal pattern for hand cutting samples
sample materials	- samples are tried in various materials
sample soles or heels	- may include creation of sole or heel moulds
costings	- for establishing wholesale and retail pricing

Selling in of the range	
mass samples	- creation of mass samples for sales representatives
presentation of range	- sales representative's time and labor
taking orders	- reception and entry of orders
order compilation	- collation of orders and determination of sufficient sales volume of styles to justify their production

Costs for tooling-up for volume production	
production lasts	- right and left foot lasts for each size and half size and width fitting(s) required
grAding for knives and soles	- professional scaling up and down from sample to all sizes required
production knives	- metal knives for each pattern piece in every size
production sole or heel moulds	- left and right foot sole/heel moulds for each size required
production dies and punches	- metal punches and cut out knives if required
sourcing of materials	- materials must be sourced at required costs and be available to meet delivery requirements

Fault Management in Computer Networks Using Case-Based Reasoning: DUMBO System

Cristina Melchiors and Liane M. R. Tarouco

PPGC, Universidade Federal do Rio Grande do Sul
Av. Bento Gonçalves, 9500. Bloco IV. Porto Alegre, Brazil
cristina@inf.ufrgs.br, liane@penta.ufrgs.br

Abstract. Nowadays, the complexity involved in computer network fault management demands a great amount of information about the involved technologies and their associated problems. Besides, Trouble Ticket Systems have been used to store the occurred problems, actuating as an historical memory of the network. Thus, a correct approach to consolidate the network historic memory is the development of an expert system that takes in account the knowledge accumulated in the Trouble Ticket Systems to propose solutions for an average problem. This work presents a system that uses Case-Based Reasoning paradigm applied to a Trouble Ticket System to suggest solutions for a new problem occurred. This system aims to aid diagnosis and resolution stages of network management problems. Typical problems of this domain, the proposed solution and results reached with the developed prototype are described.

1 Introduction

With the growth of the number and heterogeneity of equipments and involved technologies in computer networks, the number of potential problems and the complexity required in the diagnosis of them become critical. Because of that, the networks are usually controlled by experts entrusted with maintaining the availability and the quality of the network services through network management.

In order to aid the management of faults occurred in the network, Trouble Ticket Systems (TTS) have been used in the network management [15]. Such systems aid the managers in the task of monitoring problems occurring in a network, maintaining a registration of their life cycle and storing the historical memory of the faults of network.

In view of the knowledge accumulated in such systems, derived from the troubleshooting of the previous problems, these systems can be used to aid the diagnosis of a new problem. Thus, a correct solution to consolidate the network historical memory is the development of an expert system that uses the knowledge stored in a TTS to help the managers in the diagnosis of a new similar situation, proposing solutions using the stored tickets.

This paper presents a system that incorporates Case-Based Reasoning (CBR) paradigm in a traditional TTS, aiming to use the knowledge stored in these tickets to propose solutions for a new problem. This system is called *DUMBO* [10].

2 Using Case-Based Reasoning in Network Management

There are several paradigms that have been used in the development of expert systems in network management field, being Rule-Based Reasoning the more used [5]. Systems with this paradigm, however, can show some drawbacks [8], such as (*i*) the bottleneck in knowledge acquisition [5] and (*ii*) the brittleness when a novel situation is presented. These drawbacks are intensified when applied for the network management domain, in which just a little number of tasks involve a well understood and relatively steady situation — the networks are constantly incorporating new technologies, what imposes an overload to the managers and increases the difficulty of building expert systems using rules for network problem diagnosis, since these systems may become obsolete quickly [9].

Another paradigm that can be used for the diagnosis of such problems is Model-Based Reasoning. This use for network management domain suffers, however, for the difficulty in modeling a complete network, with its interactions in an application [5].

Thus, an interesting approach for expert systems in network management is Case-Based Reasoning, that brings benefits as the capacity to learn naturally with the experience and to avoid the excessive maintenance [8]. When, however, it is used with TTS, where the ticket structure is already similar the one of a case, it is added to these advantages the fact of trouble ticket systems already represent a consolidated technology in the area and are usually used in network operation centers. This provides a more natural use and learning of the system, since the paradigm is integrated into the collaboratives features inherent of ticket systems.

3 DUMBO System

DUMBO System [10] consists in a case-based reasoning system that was developed upon the architecture and technology of traditional TTS. A trouble ticket can be easily conceived as a case and the trouble ticket base conceived as the case base of the system. It remains, so, to add to the architecture of such systems the reasoning processes, and to add about the additional information in traditional tickets, so that, these processes can be performed. These topics will be commented in the next sections.

3.1 Particularities about Domain

The knowledge acquisition of the system was accomplished using interviews with experts, analysis of trouble tickets stored in the base used by the network operation center POP/RS (CINEMA [14]), and bibliography (troubleshooting books and network equipments manuals, network computer theoretical references and projects of expert systems developed to the domain, such as [3], [6], [11], [15]). The network environment, for which, the model was conceived and validated is characterized by TCP/IP network in Unix environment, with presence of Ethernet and serial lines.

From analysis performed over the domain, the problems found were classified as (*i*) for network connection problems: *connectivity*, communication *performance* and *high traffic* in the channels; (*ii*) user application; (*iii*) for system services: *naming resolution*, *authentication* and *file sharing*. By virtue of the manifold situations of connectivity problems, it was still identified two different subtypes: problems of *physical connectivity and hardware configuration* and problems of *addressing and routing*. These problems are not mutually exclusive: some problems found in networks can be in more than one of the types presented [10].

The knowledge derived from the knowledge acquisition was represented in this system through semantic nets [13].

Besides the problem classification and features related to them, the analysis allowed to identify the relation between features and probable problem types, the relation between some features and relevance of others, and the relation of some features to the automatic elaboration of other important features in order to better describe the problem. From these relations, production rules were manually developed to be used in the reasoning processes.

3.2 System Architecture

DUMBO System was structured in order to maintain the functions of traditional TTS, inserting the reasoning procedures in the stages of creation, closing and appending the notes of a ticket [10]. DUMBO architecture can be seen in fig. 1.

At the moment of ticket's creation, *context setting module* is activated and it obtains problem description information. The problem type and other features reported are used to identify some additional information that should be acquired.

Then the trouble ticket/case goes trough the *search module*. This module retrieves in the library the cases whose problem type matches some of those types selected for search. The retrieved cases are ranked by the *selector module* and the best cases are shown to the user.

The user can accept these cases directly or request a refine process. For that, he provides all or some of the requested information (*specific features*), and the retrieval process is restarted using now also these information. Situations where the system was not able to propose similar cases are learned by the system at the moment of ticket's closing. These procedures are controlled by the *learner module*.

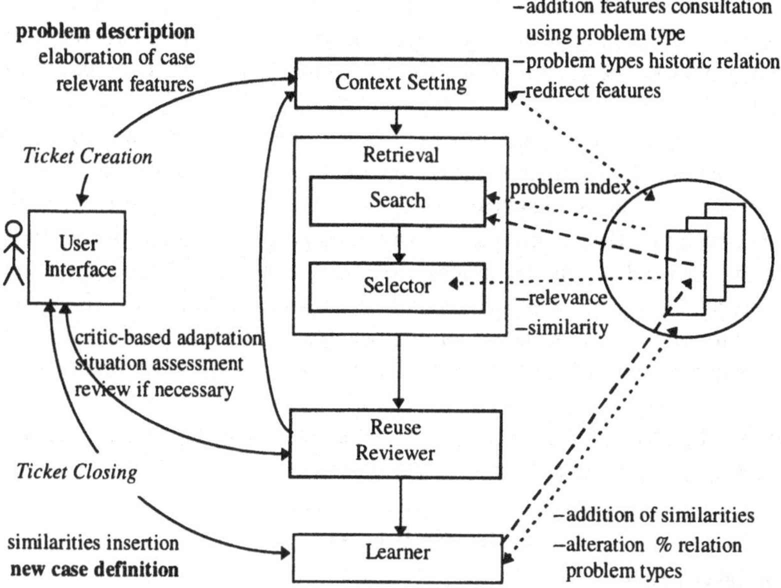

Fig. 1. DUMBO Architecture

3.3 Knowledge Base

For a traditional trouble ticket to be conceived as a case, it is necessary some additional information about the problem so that it can be used in an efficient way in reasoning processes. These information represent important aspects about the problem, that are identified for the expert as features that can contribute to the problem solution, indicating a specific symptom or indicating a condition of the network environment that can be related to the problem.

From the knowledge acquisition stage, it was noted that different problem types show different symptoms and they own different relevant information to solve the problem. To cope with this, a list of typical problems types of the domain was elaborated (commented previously), as proposed in [9], and for each problem type it was identified a roll of information that contributes to reach the problem solution, being called *additional features.*

However, gaps would remain in the system if just these information was used. In first place, there are a large variation and complexity in the problems of the domain. If each problem had all its important data used in this stage, this would carry to a very extensive and exhaustive questionnaire. Besides, a case structure just composed by the *additional features* would become excessively structured, and it wouldn't allow, neither any other way to report additional data, nor the evolution of the language. Finally, a third gap says respect to the absence of manners of incorporating in the system information originated from the diagnosis actions performed for the insulation of a problem. Such action are chosen for the experts using the problem initial description and they are fundamental for the evolution of the diagnosis. Therefore, it is very important that the system could represent the obtained results of these actions so that these one can be used for the reasoning processes.

It was conceived, so, a refine process applied after first retrieval. This approach uses the content of information presented in the retrieved cases to identify new important information for the current case, denominated *specific features*. With such features, new important additional information can be registered in the cases and used in the retrieval to identify a subset of cases more similar among the selected cases, letting the result of diagnosis actions be used in this stage. Besides, they contribute to the increase of the system knowledge and they make the case language flexible, since now new features can be added to the system in the moment of case learning.

The system cases are formed by two main parts: the *description* part and the *solution* part, as shown in fig. 2.

Trouble Ticket - Case

Problem Description
- Ticket Creation Information
  - Initial Information (problem type, short description, message, probable causes, data with only management purpose)
  - Addition Information, in agreement with context situation (problem type, problem location, what the problem includes, network interface, application,...)
- Information Through Specific Features
  - Each Feature: name and value
- Notes
  - Each Note: data with only management purpose, relation with specific features

Problem Solution
- Information with only management purpose (closing date, user, ...)
- Causes, Affected Component, Component Fault
- End Problem Type
- Adopt Solution

Fig. 2. Trouble Ticket/Case Components

Further the cases, the knowledge base of DUMBO system also includes a general knowledge model of the domain. This general model comprehends several kinds of information: historical relation among the problem types, relation among some characteristics with the probable problem types, similarity of the features, the influence of some features over the relevance of others.

3.4 Reasoning Cycle Processes

3.4.1 Context Setting. The context setting process is sensitive to the context, being suitable for the different problem types so that the features elaborated for each one of them are important for the situation. Further problem type, another information, such as the *problem location* (i.e., if the problem occurs in a serial line, among hosts of the same IP subnet, etc) and *what the problem includes*, are also used for define the situation better.

After discovering which are the additional features that should be elaborated in the situation, the system implements mechanisms to obtain these information. This mechanism can be automatic or not (requesting to user). The automatic ways are done (*i*) using a combination of features already elaborated and the domain knowledge present in system (such as the *probable components with physical fault*), (*ii*) using the network topologic knowledge obtained with the use of the system and (*iii*) using operations over SNMP objects or data from integrated network management platforms (such as *rate of collisions* in a Ethernet network).

Among the features elaborated automatically by the system, two of them deserve special attention: the *probable components with physical faults* and the *probable problem types*.

The feature *probable components with physical faults* was conceived so that the *affected component* feature of the solution part of the case could be used in the matching of the stored cases whose faults were physical. As this information is part of the case solution, when the situation is well understood, its comparison can contribute in a special way to the similarity of the current case. Furthermore, the occurrence of a certain element in this feature can help to better define the relevance of another information in the current context.

The elements defined for this feature were: *cabling*, *data link interconnection equipments, network interconnection equipments* and *source and destination hosts*. The elaboration of the probable components is made by the exclusion of those elements that, in agreement with the information already supplied for the problem, cannot be involved with physical faults. This elaboration is made through production rules (11 rules), like show fig. 3.

```
IF 'problem_location' = 'among_host_of_the_same_IP_subnet' AND
   'what_problem_includes_in_source_hosts_of_involved_segments' = 'all' AND
   'what_problem_includes_in_destination_hosts_of_involved_segments' = 'all' AND
   'alteration' = 'worked_previously_without_recent_alteration'
THEN 'probable_component_with_physical_fault' don't own
        'source_and_destinantion_hosts'
```

Fig. 3. Example of rule to elaboration of *probable components with physical faults* feature

The feature regarding to *probable problem types*, for its time, aid to identify which of the other types are related to the situation and should be used during the search. That is necessary by virtue of the division of problems in types, it demands that two cases are classified in the same category to be matched. However, the problems in networks are sometimes extremely complex, and a problem that is detected initially as a type can be caused, in fact, for a problem type correlate. With that, depending of development stage of the situation when the ticket is created, this feature can be reported as different classifications, what would prevent the retrieval of a similar case registered in a different development stage.

Thus, not just the problem type used in the ticket creation must be considered but, also, the problem type identified after its closing (using this information to identify the other related problem types). That is reached through the feature *probable problem types*, whose elaboration is made automatically based on the combination of two different points: (*i*) rules associated to the features already elaborated that aid address the case for another probable types and (*ii*) the historical relationship among the problem types.

The first point helps the analysis of the situation using the information already available, in order to elaborate other problem types that should be used also for search. It is implemented through production rules. Two rules of the system are presented in fig. 4.

```
IF 'problem_maintains_using_IP' = 'no'
THEN problem_type 'servers-resolution of names' grade 3
IF 'lack_of_access' = 'intermittent' AND 'problem_type' is not 'performance'
THEN problem_type 'performance' grade 3
```

Fig. 4. Example of system rules to elaboration of *probable problem types* feature

The second point, for its time, aids to attain of those cases where the real problem type of the situation will only be identified in the final stage of diagnosis, where its initial data point to a superficial problem type that is, in fact, caused by another. An example of that is a situation where a problem with file sharing in a host went, at the end stage, diagnosed as an authentication problem, or a situation where a high traffic in communication channels is caused in fact by routing problems.

The historical relationship is processed using the relation of previous cases between the problem type reported in the moment of ticket creation and the real problem type identified after the solution, showing the percentile of times that each initially reported type was caused in fact by another one. These relationships are updated for each learned case. The system can thus improve its knowledge for each particular network.

The final probability of each problem type is accomplished using both mentioned points, giving, however, larger importance to the historical relationship (at the moment, degree 3). Finally, it's selected as probable problem types, that will be used for the search, those whose probability to exceed a predefined threshold (0,2).

3.4.2 Retrieval: Search and Ranking. The retrieval process begins with the search in the knowledge base for the cases that belong to each one of the types identified as probable in context setting. Those cases are then submitted to a detailed evaluation of the degree of matching with the current, through the ranking process, that involves two main stages: (*i*) the determination of the similarity type being considered for the matching among each feature that should be compared and, (*ii*) the identification of the relevance of each feature in the final calculation.

The DUMBO *similarity evaluation* supports six types of features and similarity, that can assume the following degrees of matching *total* (1,0), *high* (0,75), *medium* (0,5), *low* (0,3) *and no matching* (0) (table 1).

Table 1. System Features Similarity Types

Similarity Type	Possible Values	Partial Matching Calculation	Examples
numeric	positive real numbers	attribution for areas, calculation using the number of areas among values	collision rate, rate of network load
boolean	*yes, no*	allow only exact matching	is many traffic, environment has many protocols
qualitative to fixed terms	pre defined terms to the feature	similarity of terms pre defined	what problem includes in source network segment
qualitative to variable terms	registered terms, with possibility of new terms	similarity of terms registered, with possibility of aid new relations to new terms	operation system, product
exact to variable terms	registered terms, with possibility of new terms	allow only exact matching	equipment IP number
textual	free text	matching of expressions registered	short problem description

The *assignment of relevance degrees*, for its time, is accomplished for each one of the features, in order to emphasize those information that own better potential to indicate similar cases. In the presented system, was established five degrees of importance for the case features: (*i*) filter (degree 5 in ranking); (*ii*) with excessive importance (degree 5, without filter); (*iii*) very important (degree 3); (*iv*) important (degree 1) and (*v*) without importance (degree 0).

However, the attribution of a simple static degree for all case features is not suitable for this system, seeing that, depending of the current situation, the importance of some information have large variability. So, it was necessary to assign to some of them (*additional features*) the degrees of importance that are relative to the context of the current situation.

This particularity was implemented in two ways, depending on the information being considered. The first of them assigns different degrees of relevance in agreement with the problem type — used for features as *lack of access, there is high traffic*. The second way was conceived because it was noted that the combination of some values for certain features influences the relevance for others. These relationships among features were implemented through production rules, as shows the example in the figure below.

```
IF 'problem_type' = 'connectivity-generic' OR 'problem_type' = 'high traffic' OR
   'problem_type' = 'connectivity-physical and config HW' OR
   'problem_type' = 'performance' AND
   'probable_component_with_physical_fault' own 'cabling'
THEN 'interface_network_type' grade 5
```

Fig. 5. Example of rule to attribution of relevance

The process of similarity's degree evaluation between two cases begins with the matching of the *specific features* of the current case and of the retrieved cases, being eliminated from the group if they own a common specific feature that has essential degree, and the *similarity* among them is inferior to the minimum defined for it. The following stage consists in the calculation of the similarity degree among the cases using all the important features, as it shows the formula (1).

$$Similarity(Cr,R) = \frac{\sum_{i=1}^{n} W_i \times sim\left(f_i^C, f_i^R\right) \times C_i}{\sum_{i=1}^{n} W_i \times C_i} . \quad (1)$$

$$Reliability(Cr,R) = \frac{\sum_{i=1}^{n} W_i \times C_i}{\sum_{i=1}^{n} W_i} . \quad (2)$$

$$OrderingFactor(R) = \frac{I \times Similarity(Cr,R) + Reliability(Cr,R)}{I+1} . \quad (3)$$

$Similarity(Cr,R)$	similarity between cases
$Reliability(Cr,R)$	reliability in the matching
W_i	relevance of feature i
$sim()$	similarity function to feature i
C_i	confidence in the similarity of feature i
I	importance of similarity upon reliability
f_i^C, f_i^R	values to feature i in current and retrieved case

When a feature was not elaborated, it's not used in the calculation of case similarity degree, that takes in account just those features that can be compared. By virtue of that, it was created another factor that takes into account how much of similarity calculated between two cases is reliable, that was called reliability. The reliability function can be seen in formula (2).

Finally, it is done an ordering of cases (3) considering the result of similarity and reliability of each one. In this, the similarity is twice more important than the reliability.

3.4.3 Reuse and Review. After the best cases be selected among the ones retrieved from base, the experience of those cases can be reused in the current situation or the user can requested a refine process.

The refine process takes place in a dynamic way, defining new useful elaborations based on the content of the retrieved cases. For that, is extracted from the retrieved cases the features (*specific features*) that contributed in the previous situation for the evolution of the problem diagnosis. The selection about what features should be elaborated and in which order among the whole group of extracted features is accomplished according four factors: (*i*) the cost of obtaining the information by user; (*ii*) the probability of this feature to contribute in the problem, identified by the degree of similarity of the best retrieved case that contains it; (*iii*) the possibilities of this feature to influence a larger number of cases, obtained by the number of times that it appears in the selected cases and (*iv*) the order in which this information was stored in the previous case.

Once elaborated the specific features, the current case description is refined with the new features and a new retrieval is done. With these new features, the solutions proposed previously through the retrieved cases can be validated or not by the system, selecting new cases and be eliminated cases selected previously or changes the degree of similarity of the cases already retrieved.

3.4.4 Learning. A case is learned by system when it represents a new experience, for which the system was not able to propose an appropriate solution. If, however, the proposal solution was correct, it is stored as a simple ticket, so that, the functions of traditional TTS are still maintained in the system (such as statistical analysis of the network equipments, etc), and it won't be used in the next retrieval. The only update executed in the system is concerning to the historical relationship among the types of problems.

The closing of a ticket that will be learned, however, demands some additional stages, such as, the elaboration of the additional features related to the final problem type that were not still elaborated and the learning of new terms still not registered (such as a new operating system or application). The definition of what additional features should be elaborated is accomplished by the system using the final problem type and problem description information. The defined features are requested to user, as well as some information about the terms not registered informed previously (such as operation system family and group). This approach allows an increasing of the domain's knowledge. However, if it was not used, the system would present a gradual loss of performance, even with the adding of new cases, since the system would not allow the computation of the similarity of its terms.

The second stage in learning consists in the indication of which specific features among the ones already reported wouldn't be necessary to diagnosis. Those features will be marked in order of not be considered in the refine process. Besides, this stage allows that new important information be supplied that are not still registered in case. This can be done adding in the case specific features already registered in system, or registering this new features in the system.

4 Results

The developed prototype was implemented in Unix environment, using the C language and the POSTGRES database, with interface through WWW.

For the evaluation of the prototype, was inserted in the system the group of cases collected and defined during the modeling of system. In this version of prototype, only the problems that involve faults in the connection were focused — problems in applications and services were treated in the model but they were not implemented in this version.

The inserted cases represent faults stored in CINEMA TTS [14] (10 cases). These faults occurred in the real environment acquired from the interviews with experts (6 cases) and faults extracted of the bibliography (8 cases). These cases are distributed in the following way: *Connectivity - Physical and HW Config*, 11 cases; *Routing and Addressing*, 12 cases; *High Traffic*, 1 case.

Initially, a first stage of tests aimed a tuning in the relevance and similarity degree of the system features conceived during modeling stage. For that, several retrievals were performed in the system, and the analysis of the relevance defined for each feature in agreement with the current situation context was accomplished as well as, the analysis of the equivalence among the values attributed in the similarity for the several features.

The second test stage had as goal to evaluate if the retrieved cases own information with potential to contribute in the problem's solution, including the own retrieved cases and the specific features selected by the system. Thus, several retrievals were performed in the system, using as new situations (current) some cases removed from the system or adapted cases from situations mentioned in interviews and that had not still been included in the case base.

In follow, an example of a retrieval performed for a problem in a serial line is shown. Initially, some information of the ticket creation can be visualized, and soon after, the performed retrievals are presented (formed by the retrieved cases and by the specific information requested by the system). The specific information answered are shown, as well as the results of the new retrieval. Finally, it is shown the solution data, the specific features registered and the specific features maintained after the case learning.

```
Case 134
Initial Problem Type: Performance
Short Description: High error rate in the communication
between POA-SP, POA-DF.
No Access: Intermittent   Bad Performance: Intermittent

Case 134 - First Retrieval Results
Search: Connectivity-Generic. Connectivity-Physical and HW
Config. Performance
[0.69]  Similarity [0.63], Reliability [0.82] - Case 103
Description: The 64kb line from Unisinos isn't working well,
big datagrams are lost.
```

```
[0.64]  Similarity [0.56], Reliability [0.80] - Case 108
Description: User can't access extern network.
[0.63]  Similarity [0.54], Reliability [0.82] - Case 102
Description: The UCS have not access to world network.

Addition Information Requested:
[0.63]  (Id 3) Contact telecommunication line provider
company.
[0.56]  (Id 6) Is there lose of big datagrams in ping test?
[0.45]  (Id 1) Putting remote interface in loop (in the
remote router), what is the local interface status?

Answered Information:
(Id 3) Contact telecommunication line provider company.
(Id 6) Is there lose of big datagrams in ping test? Answer:
YES

Case 134 - Second Retrieval Results
[0.73]  Similarity [0.67], Reliability [0.84] - Case 103
[0.64]  Similarity [0.56], Reliability [0.80] - Case 108
[0.63]  Similarity [0.54], Reliability [0.82] - Case 102

Addition Information Requested:
[0.45]  (Id 1) Putting remote interface in loop (in the
remote router), what is the local interface status?
[0.45]  (Id 8) Use show interfaces command in the remote
router. Is the configuration ok?
[0.45]  (Id 2) Doing loop test to intermediary node of link,
what is the local interface status?

Case 134 Solution:
Causes: Link 34, that interconnect CRC equipments inside
Embratel building was defective.
Adopted Solution: CRT correct fault.
Final Problem Type: Connectivity - Physical and HW Config

Specific Features Registered in System:
Id: 22  Description: Is there high CRC error rate? Degree: 5
Type: boolean
Id: 5   Description: Contact remote node. Are in this center
another links with problems? Degree: 5  Type: boolean

Final Specific Features of Case 134:
Id: 6   Value: "YES",  Order: 1
Id: 5   Value: "NO",   Order: 1
Id: 3
Id: 22  Value: "YES",  Order: 1
```

Fig. 6. Retrieval Example

The example above presents a problem caused by an intermittent fault in a link provided by the telecommunication company. Immediately in the first retrieval, the first selected case (case 103) represents a similar problem that can be reused for the solution of the current. The first two specific features proposed are also important for some problems like this: they suggest to contact the telecommunications company (Id 3), and they suggest a *ping* test asking if there is a big lose of packets (Id 6). In fact, in the original trouble ticket registered in CINEMA TTS [14] that gave origin to the case 103, these actions had been really used by the experts, and the result of the *ping* test was already described in the remarks of the ticket, so the system was able to propose appropriate actions.

One of the drawbacks found in this stage for the evaluation of the system accuracy in the several contexts was caused by the number of registered cases represent just a initial collected group and don't correspond to the learning with the normal use of the system. Thus, sometimes, the cases selected in a retrieval are *the best cases among the cases of base*, although they don't represent *the most similar situation inside all the possible situations of the management domain.*

However, the performed tests allowed to verify that the system has the ability of retrieval similar cases for a current situation, and it is able to be applied to a wider real environment. In this environment, the system learning — through new cases learned and through the improvement of the historical relationship — will increase its knowledge for the specific management domain for which it is applied and will allow that situations more and more similar to the current can be retrieved.

The search of another case-based reasoning approaches applied to network management resulted in just a little number of references found: some systems applied to the telecommunications domain (3 approaches); a system applied for routing; and the systems CRITTER [8], [9] and MASTER [4] applied for fault management in computer networks, also using association of CBR in trouble ticket systems.

In relation to these, DUMBO system interface for ticket creation is quite difficult and complex when compared the one of MASTER. Besides, its way of request actions and present solutions is less structured than CRITTER, and its adaptation is based on the mechanism of context refinement, while in CRITTER it acquires adaptation strategies for the exactly solution. Among the positive points of DUMBO, we can point out its flexibility, whose problem types were defined in order to include most of the situations that can be found in the domain, besides the maintenance and learning simplified, what makes possible the system being applied in several management domains. A comparison of the results among the systems was not able by the absence of information in the references that allow the comparison with the results obtained in the DUMBO tests.

5 Conclusion and Future Work

The presented approach was developed aiming to help network managers in fault diagnosis, being defined a model to the system, implemented a prototype and performed groups of tests for the approach evaluation, seeking to treat the wide range of problems from the network management domain.

The best results were obtained with physical and hardware configuration faults. The routing and addressing faults presented results less exact in the first retrieval. That was caused by the small number of additional features in the system with specific information of routing. This aspect was outlined by the use of specific features for these data.

Characteristic of the developed approach include treatment to an environment with large variety of problems with different singularities, that can be confused one with the other ones in the initial problem stages. Besides, the possibility to identify diagnosis actions further the cases is also part of the positive aspects. In troubleshooting activities, the use of diagnosis actions is indispensable in the several stages of the problem, and the integration of its results in the system contributes to improve situation assessment dynamically.

The proposal approach can also be applied for other domains where there is the need of treatment of a large diversity of situations, and where information along the evolution of the problem can contribute to best to describe it, including medical diagnosis and troubleshooting activities of engineering domain and of another fields of computer science.

Among the goals established for future development, can be mentioned the implementation of the additional features modeled but still not included in the prototype and the integration of the system in management platforms (just as HP OpenView, of Hewlett Packard), in order to supply more specific and automatic data for the additional and specific features. Besides, would be desired the identification of ways in implanting automatic adaptation techniques to the reasoning cycle, as well as means of integrating to the system applications that have free text interpretation capacities, in a similar way of the used in MASTER [4]. This applications could, using the problem description in free text, to fill some of the features that are requested to the user.

References

1. Aamodt, A., Plaza, E.: Case-Based Reasoning: Foundational Issues, Methodological Variations, and System Approaches. *AI Communications*, Vol.7(1) (1994) 39-59
2. Brandau, R., Lemmon, A., Lafond, C.: Experience with Extended Episodes: Cases with Complex Temporal Structure In: Bareiss, E. R. (ed.): *Proceedings DARPA Workshop on Case-Based Reasoning*. Morgan Kaufmann, San Francisco (1991)
3. Cisco Systems, Inc: Internetwork Troubleshooting Guide. 1997. Reference available in *http://www.cisco.com/univercd/cc/td/doc/cisintwk/itg_v1/index.htm*.
4. Dreo, G., Valta, R.: Using master tickets as a storage for problem-solving expertise. In: Sethi, A., Raynaud, Y., Faure-Vincent, F. (eds.) *Proceedings of Integrated Network Management IV* Chapman & Hall, London (1995) 328-340
5. Goyal, S.: Knowledge technologies for evolving networks. In: Krishnan, I., Zimmer, W. (eds.): *Proceedings of Integrated Network Management II*. Elsevier Science, Amsterdam (1991)
6. Hunt, C.: TCP/IP Network Administration. 2nd edn. O'Reilly, Sebastopol (1998)
7. Kolodner, J.: Case-Based Reasoning. Morgan Kaufmann, San Mateo (1993)

8. Lewis, L.: A Case-Based Reasoning Approach to the Management of Faults in Communications Networks. *Conference on Computer Communications*. IEEE, San Francisco, Vol 3 (1993) 1422-1429
9. Lewis, L.: Managing Computer Networks: A Case-Based Reasoning Approach. Artech House, Norwood (1995)
10. Melchiors, C.: Raciocínio Baseado em Casos Aplicado ao Gerenciamento de Falhas em Redes de Computadores. Master of Science Thesis PGCC/UFRGS (1999). In evaluation stage.
11. Miller, M.: Troubleshooting TCP/IP. M&T Books, New York (1996)
12. Simoudis, E.: Using Case-Based Retrieval for Customer Technical Support. *IEEE Expert*, Vol.7(5) (1992) 7-12
13. Stefik, M.: Introduction to Knowledge Systems. Morgan Kaufmann, San Francisco (1995)
14. Tarouco, L. et al.: Um ambiente para gerenciamento integrado e cooperativo. In: *Proceedings of Workshop sobre Administração e Integração de Sistemas*. UFC, Fortaleza (1996) 235-246
15. Udupa, D.: Network Management Systems Essentials. McGraw-Hill, New York (1996)
16. Watson, I.: Applying Case-Based Reasoning: Techniques for Enterprise Systems. Morgan Kaufmann, San Francisco (1997)

An Architecture for a CBR Image Segmentation System

Petra Perner

Institute of Computer Vision and Applied Computer Sciences
Arno-Nitzsche-Str. 45, 04277 Leipzig, Germany
e-mail: ibaiperner@aol.com fax: +49 341 8665 636

Abstract. Image Segmentation is a crucial step if extracting information from a digital image. It is not easy to set up the segmentation parameter so that it fits best over the entire set of images, which should be segmented. In the paper, we propose a novel architecture for image segmentation method based on CBR, which can adapt to changing image qualities and environmental conditions. We describe the whole architecture, the methods used for the various components of the systems and show how it performs on medical images.

1 Introduction

Image Segmentation is a crucial step in extracting information from a digital image. It is not easy to set up the segmentation parameter so that it fits best over the entire set of images. Most segmentation techniques contain numerous control parameters, which must be adjusted to obtain optimal segmentation performance. The parameter selection is usually done on a large enough test data set, which should represent the entire domain well enough in order to be able to built up a general model for the segmentation. However, often it is not possible to obtain a large enough data set so that the segmentation model doesn't fit well to the data and needs to be adjusted to new data. Besides that, a general model doesn't guarantee the best segmentation for each image rather than it guarantees an average best fit over the entire set of images.

Another aspect goes along with changes in image quality caused by variations in environmental conditions, image devices, etc. Then the segmentation performance needs to be adapted to these changes in image quality. All that suggests using CBR for image segmentation. We already successfully used CBR framework for the high-level unit of an image interpretation system [1][2] and could show the extraordinary good performance of this approach for image interpretation compared to other approaches.

In the paper, we propose a novel image segmentation scheme based on case-based reasoning. CBR is used to select the segmentation parameter according to the current image characteristics. By taking into account the non-image and image information we break down our complex solution space to a subspace of relevant cases where the variation among the cases is limited. It is assumed that images having similar image characteristics will show similar good segmentation results when the same segmentation parameters were applied to these images.

We evaluate our method on a set of medical images (CT scans of the brain) where the variations among the images and objects in the images are naturally very high. The complexity of the brain CT-scans is due to partial volume effects, which disturb the edges and produce contrast degradation by spatial averaging, and to the typical problems such as patient movements, beam hardening, and reconstruction artifacts. These image characteristics are responsible for the over- and undersegemented results observed when unsupervised segmentation is applied.

We use the proposed method for labeling brain and liquor areas in CT slices. Based on this we calculate brain/liquor ration which is a parameter to determine the degree of degenerative brain disease [3].

In Section 2 of the paper, we describe the overall architecture. The case description is presented in Section 3. The similarity measure for the non-image information and the image information is described in Section 4. Results are given in Section 5. Finally, we give conclusions in Section 6.

2 Overall Architecture

We will divide the overall architecture into the image segmentation unit based on case-based reasoning (see Fig. 1) and in the unit for the casebase management part (see Fig.2).

2.1 Case-Based Reasoning Unit

The case-based reasoning unit for image segmentation consists of a case base, in which formerly processed cases are stored by their original images, their non-image information (e.g. image acquisition parameters, object characteristics and so on), and their image segmentation parameters. The task is now to find the best segmentation for the current image by looking up the case base for similar cases. Similarity determination is done based on non-image information and image information. The evaluation unit will take the case with the highest similarity score for further processing. In case there are two or more cases with the same similarity score the first appeared case will be taken. After the closest case has been chosen, the image segmentation parameter associated with the selected case will be given to the image segmentation unit and the current image will be segmented, see Fig. 1. It is assumed that images having similar image characteristics will show similar good segmentation results when the same segmentation parameters were applied to these images.

In the following we will understand for segmentation: the definition of regions based on constant local image features, and for labeling: the classification of regions into the object classes: brain and liquor.

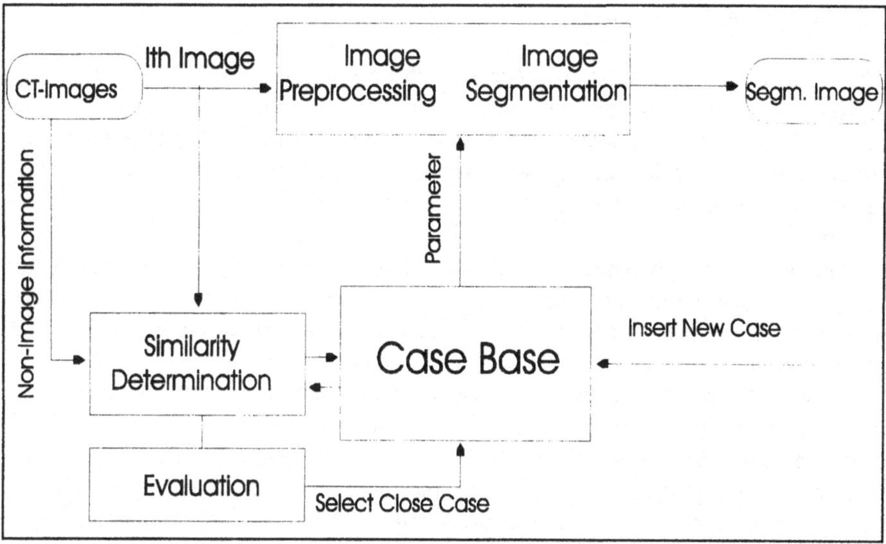

Fig. 1. Case-Based Reasoning Unit

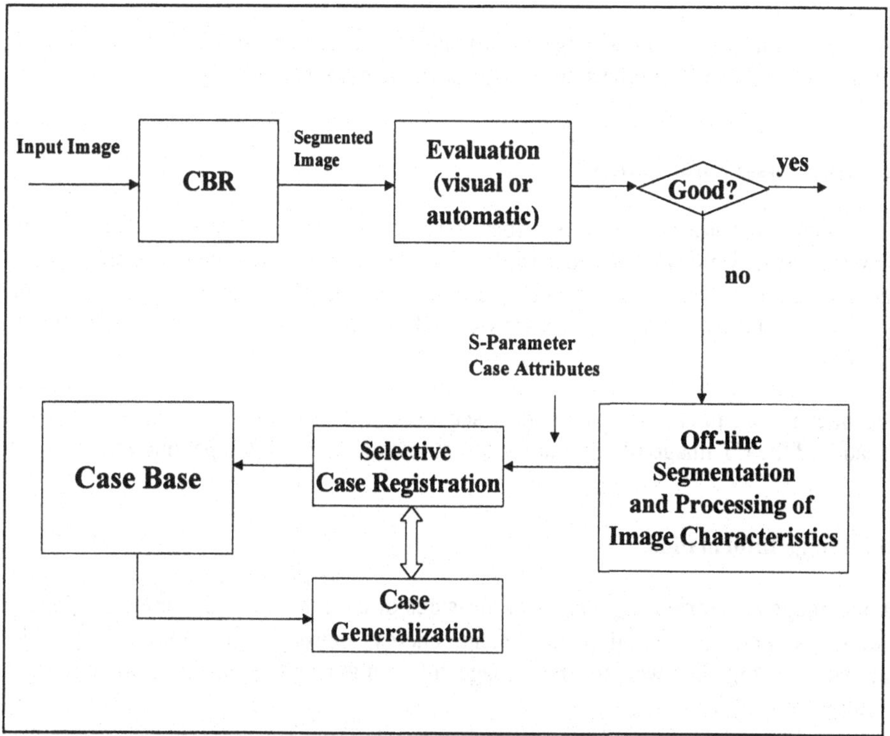

Fig. 2. Management of Casebase

2.2 Management of Casebase

The result of the segmentation process is observed by the user. He compares the original image with the labeled image on display. If he detects deviations of the marked areas in the segmented image from the objects area in the original image, which should be labeled than he will evaluate the result as bad result and casebase management will start. This will also be done if no similar case is available in the casebase.

The evaluation procedure can also be done automatically [4]. However, the drawback is that there is no general procedure available. It can only be done domain dependent. Therefore, an automatic evaluation procedure would constrain the usage of the system.

In an off-line phase, the best segmentation parameters for the image are determined and the attributes, which are necessary for similarity determination, are calculated from the image. Both, the segmentation parameters and the attributes calculated from the image, are stored into the casebase as new case. During storage, case generalization will be done to ensure that the casebase will not become too large.

3. Case Structure and Case Base

A case consists of non-image information, parameters describing the image characteristics itself, and the solution (the segmentation parameters).

3.1 Non-Image Information

The non-image information's described here are necessary to describe our medical application. If we deal with other applications, then other non-image information are contained in the case. For example, motion analysis [5], where we have camera position, relative movement of the camera and the object category itself as non-image information.

For our brain/liquor determination in CT-images, we use patient specific parameter, slice thickness and scanning sequence. This information is contained in the header of the CT image file so that we can automatic access these parameters.

3.2 Image Information

Each image is described by statistical measures of the gray level like: mean, variance, skewness, kurtosis, variation coefficient, energy, entropy, and centroid [6]. This information together with the non-image information and segmentation parameters comprises a case.

4. Segmentation Algorithm

The gray level histogram is calculated from the original image. This histogram is smoothed by some numerical functions and heuristic rules [7][8][9] to find the cut points for the liquor and brain gray level area. The parameters of the function and rules are stored with the cases and given to the segmentation unit if the associated case is selected.

The following steps are performed: The histogram is smoothed by a numerical function. There are two parameters to select: the complexity of the interpolation function and the interpolation width. Then the histogram is segmented into intervals such that each begins with a valley, contains a peak and ends with a valley. The peak to shoulder ratio of each interval is tested first: An interval is merged with the neighbor sharing the higher of its two shoulders if the ratio of peak height to the height of it's higher shoulder, is greater than or equal to a threshold. Finally, the number of the remaining intervals is compared to a predefined number of intervals. If more than this have survived, the intervals with the highest peaks are selected. The number of intervals depends on the number of classes the image should be segmented. The cut points are calculated and then applied to the image. Fig. 3 shows a histogram for an original image and the histogram after it was processed by the algorithm. The original image and the resulting labeled images are shown in Fig. 4.

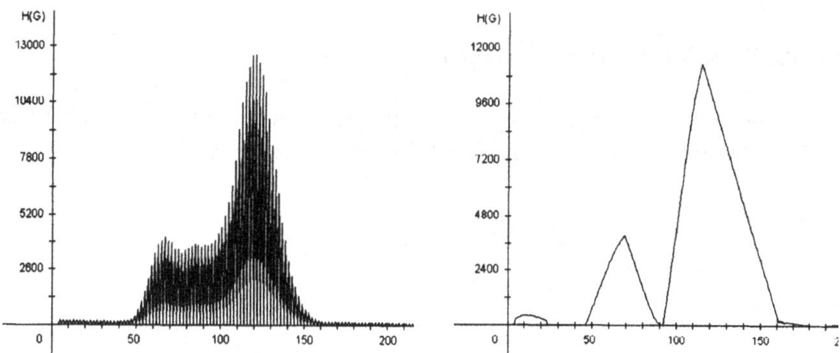

Fig. 3. Histogram of a CT-Image and refined Histogram

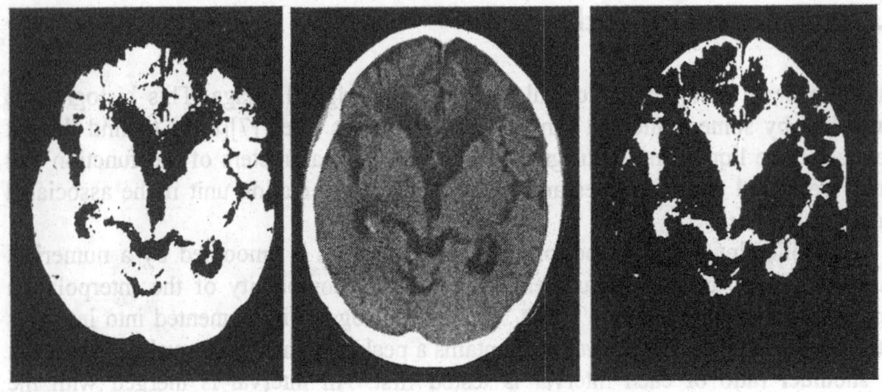

Fig. 4. Original Image, Labeled Images for Brain, and Labeled Image for Liquor

5 Similarity Determination

5.1 Similarity Measure for Non-Image Information

We use Tversky's similarity measure for the non-image information [10]. The similarity between a Case C_i and a new case b presented to the system is:

$$S(C_i, b) = \frac{|C_i|}{\alpha|A| + \beta|D| + \gamma|M|} \tag{1}$$

$$\alpha = 1, \beta, \gamma = \frac{1}{2}$$

where $|C_i|$ is the set of attributes in case C_i, A is the set of corresponding attributes in case C_i and *b*, *D* is the set of attributes having different values, and M is the set of attributes having missing values.

5.2 Similarity Measure for Image Information

For the numerical data, we use:

$$dist_{AB} = \sum_{i=1}^{I+J} W_i \left| \frac{C_{iA} - C_{iMIN}}{C_{iMAX} - C_{iMIN}} - \frac{C_{iB} - C_{iMIN}}{C_{iMAX} - C_{iMIN}} \right| \tag{2}$$

C_{IA} and C_{IB} are ith feature values of image A and B, respectively. C_{iMIN} is the minimum value of the ith numeric or symbolic feature. C_{iMAX} is the maximum value of the ith feature, and W_i is the weight attached to the ith feature. For the first run, W_i is set to one. Further studies will deal with learning of feature weights.

6 Results

A hardcopy of the recent system is shown in Fig. 5. The original images are shown at the top of the display and the labeled images are shown at the bottom of the display, so that the user can also compare the images visually. The system is used in practical use by the medical department at the university of Halle. The system contains 130 cases in casebase.

We compared the performance of the system with manual labeled images by the physicians and automatic labeled images by our system. Some of these images are contained in the casebase others are not contained. In a BMFT study [11], one physician from the university of Leipzig labeled the images of 30 patients by hand. For each patient we have approx. 20 images that give a total of 600 images for evaluation. We also used images labeled by another physician from the university of Halle. This physician labeled the images twice so that we got an understanding of measurement error done by a human.

Case	in CaseBase	Brain (ccm)		Liquor (ccm)		Brain/Liquor Ratio	
		manual	autom.	manual	autom.	manual	autom.
NNA	contain	1331,5	1197,89	287,76	316,98	4,63	3,78
WFH	contain	1211,2	1123,75	201,2	243,58	6,02	4,91
MRG	contain	1381,5	1078,2	314,51	346,13	4,39	3,12
HNH	part_cont	1097,3	1080,48	213,51	274,5	5,14	3,94
MRR	part_cont	1152,8	1212,08	144,92	145,01	7,95	8,36
TRM	part_cont	1420	1232,88	248,34	284,45	5,72	4,33
MEI	not_cont	983	986,31	147,95	180,27	6,64	5,47
MNH	not_cont	846,7	833,23	165	189,22	5,13	4,4
....	...	...	...	...	...	...	...

Table 1. Manual and Automatic Measures for Brain/Liquor for 9 Patients

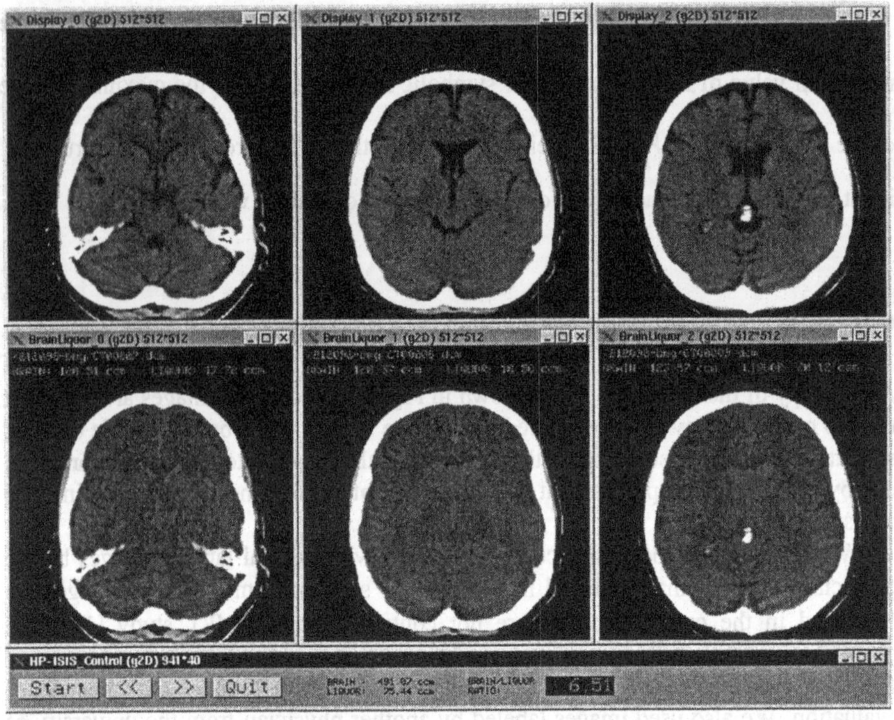

Fig. 5. Hardcopy of the Case-based Brain/Liquor System

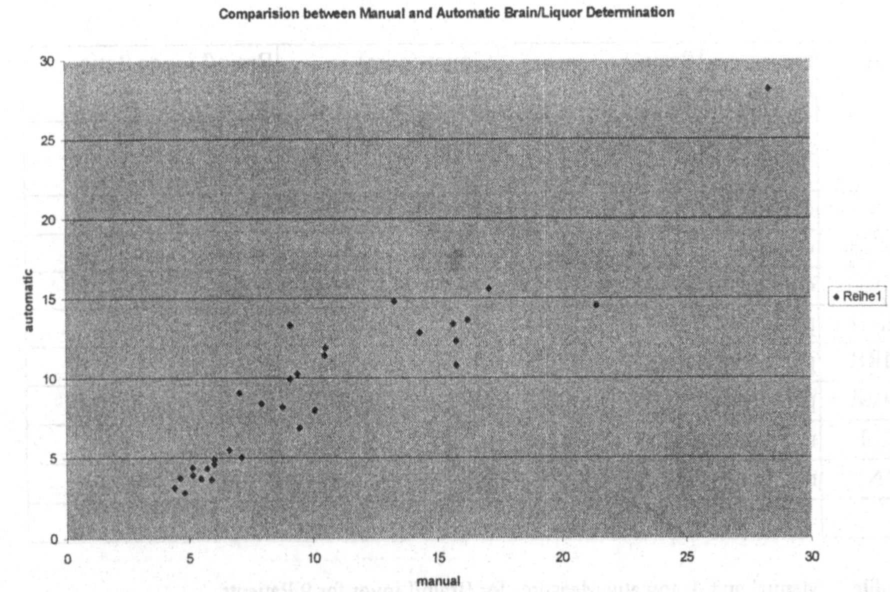

Comparision between Manual and Automatic Brain/Liquor Determination

automatic

0 5 10 15 20 25 30

manual

0 5 10 15 20 25 30

Reihe1

Fig. 6. Diagram Manual versus Automatic Results

Table 1 compares the manual results and the automatic results. Our algorithm labels more liquor area than a human expert does. However, Figure 6 shows a strong linear correlation between our results and the results of a human expert (r=0,85). This is a very good result.

For the first time, a system automatically delivers to the physicians a measure for the brain/liquor ratio. The only thing what the physician has to do is that he tells the systems what images should be examined. No human interaction is necessary like it is required for other volumetric image analysis systems [12]. The system automatically delivers a measure back to the physician. In opposition to the recent qualitative examination of the CT images, a quantitative examination is possible which gives a valid measure and allows a graduation between different stages of a disease and a control of a patient over time.

7 Conclusion

We have presented our concept for a CBR based image segmentation system. The system performs image segmentation by looking up a case base for similar formerly processed images and takes the segmentation parameters associated to the similar image in order to do segmentation of the current image. We examined our system by comparing manually labeled images with automatic labeled images. The results show that by our method good results for the brain/liquor ratio can be obtained. Since it is well know that also a physician doesn't always know what he should take as brain and liquor object we are not seriously concerned about the difference in labeling between a human and the system. A good evaluation of the system would only be possible if there would exists a true gold standard which might be available if the work on simulation of the brain CT-images will show good results.

With our system, we have given to the user a fully automatic system, which needs no user interaction when calculating the brain/liquor ratio. Such a system gives the opportunity to overcome the qualitative measure based on a subjective judgement to a quantitative measure, which is reproducible.

Further work will be done on generalizing cases and segmentation parameters and how to learn feature weights.

Acknowledgment

We like to thank Prof. Heywang-Köbrunner and Dr. Beck from the medical department of the university of Halle for the cooperation on this work. For providing us the results of the BMFT study, we like to thank Prof. Dietrich from the medical department of the university of Leipzig. For technical help, we thank Mr. Kraft.

References

1. P. Perner, Different Learning Strategies in a Case-Based Reasoning System for Image Interpretation, Advances in Case-Based Reasoning, B. Smith and P. Cunningham (Eds.), LNAI 1488, Springer Verlag 1998, S. 251-261.
2. P. Perner, Case-Based Reasoning For Image Interpretation in Non-destructive Testing, 1st European Workshop on Case-Based Reasoning, Otzenhausen Nov. 1993, Proc. SFB 314 Univ. Kaiserslautern, Hrsg. M. Richter, vol. II, pp. 403-410
3. Bettin, J. Dietrich, C. Dannenberg, H. Barthel, D. Zedlick, K. Jobst, W.H. Knapp, "Früherkennung von Hirnleistungstörungen – Vergleich linearer und volumetrischer Parameter (CT) mit Ergebnissen der Perfusions-SPET," 78. Deutscher Röntgenkongreß Wiesbaden 1997
4. S. Zhang, "Evaluation and Comparision of different Segmentation Algorithm," Pattern Recognition Letters, v. 18, No. 10, pp. 963-968, 1997.
5. G. Kummer and P. Perner, Motion Analysis, IBaI Report January 1999, ISSN 1431-2360
6. H. Dreyer and W. Sauer, Prozeßanalyse, Verlag Technik Berlin 1982
7. R. Ohlander, K. Price, and D.R. Reddy, "Picture Segmentation using recursive region splitting method," Comput. Graphics and Image Processing, 8: 313-333, 1978
8. C.H. Lee, "Recursive region splitting at the hierarchical scope views," Computer Vision Graphics, and Image Processing, 33, 237-259, 1986
9. P. Perner, Similarity-Based Image Segmentation, IBaI Report 1996 ISSN 1431-2360
10. A. Tversky, „Feature of Similarity", Psychological Review, vol. 84, No. 4, pp. 327-350, 1977.
11. Alzheimer Study "Degenerative Erkrankungen des zentralen und peripheren Nervensystems - Klinik und Grundlage", BMFT Study, Abschlußbericht der medizinische Fakultät der Uni Leipzig 1996
12. A. Tschammler et. al,"Computerized tomography volumetry of cerebrospinal fluid by semiautomatic contour recognition and gray value histogram analysis", Rofo Fortschr. Geb. Roentgenstr. Neue Bildgeb. Verfahren 1996, Jan: 164(1): 13-1

Supporting Reusability in a System Design Environment by Case-Based Reasoning Techniques [1]

Herbert Praehofer and Josef Kerschbaummayr

Johannes Kepler University Linz
Department of Systems Theory and Information Technology
A-4040 Linz, Austria
{hp|kj}@cast.uni-linz.ac.at

Abstract. *CASA (computer aided systems architecting)* is a methodology and tool to support the design of complex technical systems. It combines approaches from systems and requirement engineering and AI. System design in CASA is requirement-driven and works by a hierarchical stepwise top-down refinement of designs and a hierarchical decision making process. One important task in CASA deals with reusability of existing design artifacts and is supported by case-based reasoning techniques. Based on given structural specifications and formal requirements, a search procedure finds the best inexact match in a design base and computes an estimated degree of fulfillment for requirements. The approach employs efficient graph matching and indexing scheme for case retrieval and structural similarities and has adapted usual similarity measures to compute degree of fulfillment of requirements. It has been show by different example projects that the developed methods can be of great practical assistance for a designer.

Keywords. case-based design, system design, requirement engineering, structural similarity, graph matching algorithm

1. Introduction

Systems analysis and design is gaining increasing importance in the development of complex technical systems. On one side systems' complexity is increasing constantly, on the other side development time (*time to market*) has to be lowered in order to be competitive. Requirements on technical systems become harder and not only concern function, performance, and realizations costs, but also other aspects such as user friendliness, maintainability, security, environmental issues, disposal and so on.

CASA (computer aided systems architecting) [16, 17, 12, 13, 14] is a methodology and tool, which supports the design of complex technical systems. The method combines approaches from systems and requirement engineering and AI. Essential tasks in CASA are (1) the formal specification of functional and non-functional requirements,

[1] Work supported by Siemens AG Munich, ZT SE 2, application for patent submitted

(2) the refinement of the system design by a hierarchical, multi-level approach [9], (3) a strict separation of functional specification and physical design (4) the traceability of the requirements over the entire design process, (5) the automatic verification of the requirements, and (6) the reuse of design artifacts from earlier designs.

System design in CASA is requirement-driven and works by hierarchical stepwise top-down refinement and a hierarchical decision process. Design starts with initial user requirements in user documents and proceeds by extracting, classifying, breaking up, formulating, and assigning requirements to design components. Requirements assigned to design components guide their design. The design of a component should occur so that all the requirements assigned to it are fulfilled. Evaluation of requirements is done automatically by a hierarchical decision making process where properties in architectures are computed based on properties of their subcomponents and checked against requirements.

One important task in CASA deals with the reuse of existing design artifacts and is supported by case-based reasoning techniques. When requirements are assigned to components and a refinement of the component is desired, one preferable approach is to look if an appropriate artifact already exists which fulfills the requirements at least partly. We have developed and realized case-based reasoning techniques to search and check for design artifacts in an design database and compute inexact measures for fulfillment of requirements. This paper presents the principal approach and the methods developed as well as prototypical applications of those techniques in CASA.

In sections 2 and 3 we review the principal concepts of CASA – the design representations and the design process. In chapter 4 and 5 we present the methods developed to support reusability. In chapter 6 and 7 we show application of the approach by two test projects.

Many projects investigated usage of CBR techniques in design, e.g. [4, 18, 15, 3, 1, 2, 8, 5, 20] and others. Our work has been stimulated by many of them, in particular by KRITIK [4] which uses a model-based approach with functional specifications of designs, Julia [7] with its hierarchical structuring concepts for cases, KDSA [20] which is outstanding for its multilayer design representation, and FABEL [3] which employs structural similarity concepts.

Our work differs from those approaches as follows:

- CASA first of all is not a CBR system but a system design environment. CBR techniques are integrated as a fundamental mechanisms in an overall design process to support reusability.
- CASA adopts a requirement driven design approach. Therefore, usual similarity concepts are adapted to estimate the fulfillment of requirements by design artifacts.
- CASA's search for reusable cases not only is done based on functional specifications but also is able to care for non-functional requirements.
- In our system structural comparison plays a dominant role not only in computing similarity but also for indexing.

2. Capturing Designs in CASA

In the following we want to give a review of the main design representations in CASA. These representations serve as a basis to introduce our reusability approach in the following sections.

Architectures

An *architecture* in CASA is the means to represents any design artifact at different levels of granularity and from different aspects (called *strata*) [9]. Architectures are used to capture the functional specification of the system (*functional stratum*) and the physical design (*physical stratum*). Architectures are configured hierarchically, i.e., components of an architectures can be configured by subarchitectures to support a design with stepwise refinement.

An architecture in CASA as depicted in Fig. 1 consists of [17]:

- a set of ports for the architecture to be coupled in a superior architecture
- a set of properties of the architecture
- a set of component specifications
- coupling structure in the form of port to port connections
- property calculators to compute property values based on the values of its components
- causality rules to define dependencies between components in the form of constraints.

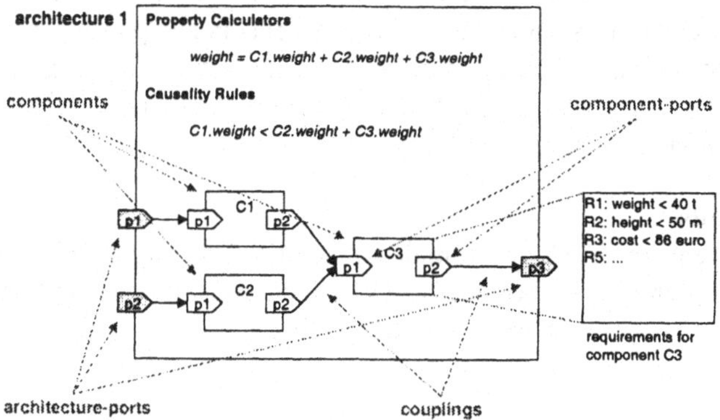

Fig. 1. CASA architecture

An architecture represents a design artifact with some degree of freedom. The unique and essential feature in CASA is that a component of an architecture is a *specification* for the subarchitectures which can serve as realizations (called *configurations*) of this component [17]. It specifies which ports and properties the subarchitecture must have and which requirements it has to fulfill. The set of allowed subarchitectures is principally open. Therefore, each component specification defines the

- ports to be used in the coupling of the architecture
- properties used in the component
- requirements which the architectures for this component have to fulfill.

Properties, property definitions, and property calculators

An *architecture property* is used to describe any relevant property of an architecture, e.g., physical properties, costs, performance, etc. Properties are also used for the formal definition of non-functional requirements. Non-functional requirements are checked against architectures' properties to determine if an architecture fulfills the requirement (see below).

Property definitions are used to define the types of properties in use in a particular application domain. Any architecture property must be derived from an associated property definition. A property definition defines:

- the name for the property, e.g. *total weight*,
- the range of property values, e.g. 10 to 1000,
- the unit of measurement, e.g. *kg* of m^2.

A property in architectures then is an instantiation of a property definition in the domain and can define

- the *value* of the property if known exactly,
- a *property calculator* to compute the value of the property from values of the architectures' components,
- a subset or range of *feasible values* for the properties.

An important feature for reusability are feasible values of properties. Architectures allow for some degree of freedom in that their components are not fixed but configurable. Depending on the concrete configuration the property value may vary, but possibly in certain bounds. For example, a *total weight* of an architecture computes as the sum of the weight of its components. Requirements in components may constraint the weight to be within certain bounds. So the architecture knows in advance that its weight will lay in certain bounds. To express this is the purpose of feasible values and important feature to support reusability.

Requirements

Requirements in CASA are formulated based on property definitions as logical expressions. A grammar has been defined which contains the usual arithmetic, relational and logical operators [12]. An interactive syntax editor then is available as a user interface to support the application engineer in requirement formulation in a convenient way.

3. Design Process and Reusability in CASA

Design process:

System design in CASA [17] proceeds by formulating and assigning requirements to existing design components. In each phase of the hierarchical stepwise top-down refinement process, the goal is to find an architecture for a component which fits best the assigned requirements. In a refinement step the designer has several possibilities:

- he can design a new architecture from scratch,
- he can reuse an existing architecture from the architecture base,

- a combination of both, where an existing architecture is selected and adapted to the new needs, and
- making a sketch of an architecture by fixing some essential components and couplings and searching for an existing one which best matches this structure.

As a next step, the component is *configured* with the designed architecture (Figure 2), that means, that ports of the architecture are assigned to ports of the component and properties of the architecture are matched with those in the component. After configuration of a component the design process can proceed with the next level in the hierarchy to design and configure the components of the just configured architecture.

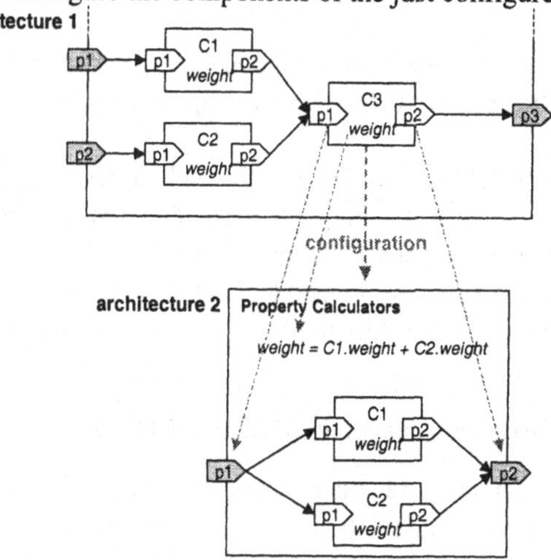

Fig. 2. Configuration of component by a subarchitecture

In course of configuration of a component, two steps are important. First, when the architecture has defined values or feasible values for properties, it is possible to test the requirement for fulfillment. Thereby, an exact property value will allow to definitely determine if a requirement is fulfilled, whereas a feasible value will only allow to estimate an inexact *degree of fulfillment*. We use methods similar to similarity measures [7, 19] to compute degree of fulfillment as explained in the following section.

Second, by availability of property values or feasible values of components' architectures, property calculators can compute property values or feasible subsets for the architecture itself. Those values will facilitate checking of requirements posted on the architecture. Therefore, hierarchical configuration of components in architectures will successively fix property values allowing to check more and more requirements in upper architectures of the hierarchy enabling the hierarchical decision making process.

Search procedure

Reusability works by finding an architecture which matches best the component specification. Searching for a configurable architecture for a component is accomplished in the following steps:

- Starting with the component specification which contains properties and ports of the components, requirements assigned to the component, and, eventually, partly specified component and coupling structure,
- an index structure is employed to make a first search for feasible architectures in the architecture base,
- a structural similarity is computed based on a match of the structural elements, that is, the properties, ports and partly given component and coupling structure,
- then, if possible, the degrees of fulfillment for the requirements are computed,
- the found architectures are ranked based on structural similarity and degree of fulfillment, and, finally,
- the architectures together with structural similarities and degree of fulfillment are presented to the designer for further investigation and final selection, configuration, and adaption.

In the following sections we present the techniques employed. We first show the methods we have developed to compute inexact degree of fulfillment of requirements, then we show the method for computing structural similarities for which we employed a graph matching algorithm developed by [10]. It is further shown how the same graph matching approach is beneficially used for hierarchical index structures.

4. Determining Degree of Fulfillment (DOF)

Recall that requirements are logical expressions (Fig 3) formulated based on property definitions and arithmetic, relational and logical operators. Requirement serve the purpose to restrict the values of an architectures' properties. In evaluating an architecture against a requirement, exact property values will result in a Boolean decision saying that the requirement is fulfilled or not. However, this statement is often unsatisfactory for a designer. He might also want to know how far the value is from the required. Also recall that, besides exact values, properties in architectures may alternatively define a subset of feasible values for that architecture. Feasible values, however, represent an uncertainty and no definite statement about the fulfillment can be made. We express both, distance of a value from a required and the uncertainty in requirement fulfillment due to feasible values by a *degree of fulfillment* (DOF) measure similar to similarity measures.

In our approach the DOF for a requirement is a value between -1 and 1 with the following interpretation:

- A DOF equal to 1 means that the requirement is definitely fulfilled.
- a positive DOF value (]0 .. 1[) means that it is possible that the requirement can eventually be fulfilled when the architecture is configured appropriately. A higher value thereby gives estimate that it is more likely that an architecture can be found which fulfills the requirement.
- A negative DOF ([-1 .. 0]) means that the requirement cannot be fulfilled. The value gives estimate of the distance for fulfillment of the requirement, i.e., a value close to 0 means that the requirement is almost fulfilled whereas a value of –0.5 and less says that architecture is far from fulfilling the requirement.

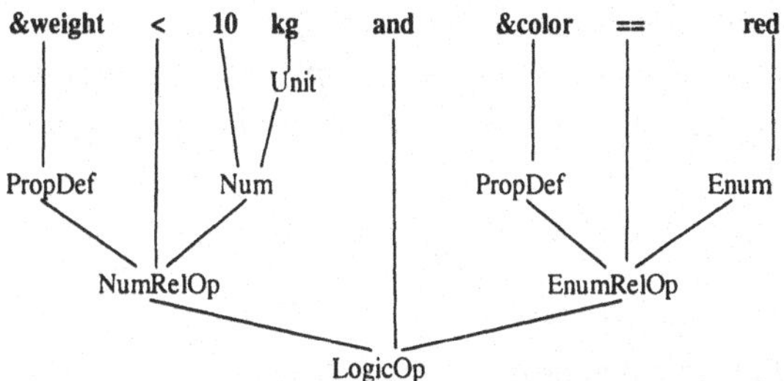

Fig. 3. Requirement expression

Parsing logical expressions

A requirement expression is formulated based on property definitions defined in the domain, constant expressions, and arithmetic, relational, and logical operators. Fig 3 shows a requirement expression together with its syntax tree. The leaf nodes of a requirement expression are properties and constant expressions. They may be combined first by arithmetic operators, then relational operators, and finally logical operators.

Determining the DOF for a requirement expression is done in the following steps:

- The property in the expression is matched with the properties in the architecture. This is accomplished through the common property definition.
- Values and feasible value ranges of properties in the architecture are combined by the arithmetic expressions and lead to new values or feasible value ranges.
- A DOF is computed for each relational expression based on the formula presented below.
- The DOFs from the relational operators are combined for the logical expressions as shown below.

Computing DOF for relational operators

Feasible value subsets of properties are interpreted to emerge from the union of the property values of all possible configurations of this architecture. As a simplification we assume that obtaining a particular property value by a specific configuration is uniformly distributed. Positive values for degree of fulfillment then are computed as the probability to select a configuration which fulfills the requirement. It computes as the number of feasible values which fulfill the requirement divided by the whole number of feasible values. Formula (1) depicts the computation of positive DOF based on subsets of feasible property values p and the subset r defined by the requirement. Is the intersection of p and r not-empty, then we will obtain a positive degree by the size of the intersection of p and r divided by the size of subset p.

$$DOF(p,r) = \frac{|p \cap r|}{|p|} \quad \text{if } p \cap r \neq \emptyset \tag{1}$$

In case that the intersection of p and r is empty the requirement cannot be fulfilled and we are supposed to obtain a negative DOF (2). We compute the minimal distance of values in p and r and divide this by a normative scaling factor n. The scaling factor n is computed based on the requirement subset r and differs if the subset is bounded or not as follows

- *r* has finite *lower bound* and *upper bound* : *n* = *upper bound* – *lower bound*
- *r* has finite *lower bound* only: $n = \max\{x \mid x \in p \cup r\}$ – *lower bound*
- *r* has finite *upper bound* only: *n* = *upper bound* – $\min\{x \mid x \in p \cup r\}$.

$$DOF(p,r) = -\frac{\min |x-y|, x \in p, y \in r}{n} \quad \text{if } p \cap r = \emptyset \tag{2}$$

Combining DOFs for logical operators

DOFs obtained through the relational operators have to be combined by the logical operators to obtain total estimates. As we have interpreted positive degrees as probabilities we can use the usual combination of probabilities, that is the sum of independent events for the disjunction (2), the multiplication of independent events for the conjunction (3) and the complement for the negation (4). For negative probabilities we take the obvious choice to take the minimal distance (greater negative value) for the disjunction (2) and the maximal distance for the conjunction. The negation needs special treatment. The negation of a not-fulfilled requirement always becomes fulfilled. Therefore, a negative DOF becomes 1. A fully fulfilled requirement (DOF = 1) might still be fulfilled to some extend after negation. Therefore we compute the negation of a DOF by computing the DOF of the complement *r*' of the requirement *r* (4).

$$DOF(x \text{ or } y) = \begin{cases} x + y - x * y & \text{if} \quad x \geq 0, y \geq 0 \\ \max(x,y) & \text{if} \quad x < 0 \text{ or } y < 0 \end{cases} \tag{3}$$

$$DOF(x \text{ and } y) = \begin{cases} x * y & \text{if} \quad x \geq 0, y \geq 0 \\ \min(x,y) & \text{if} \quad x < 0 \text{ or } y < 0 \end{cases} \tag{4}$$

$$DOF(not\ x) = not\ DOF(p,r) = \begin{cases} 1-x & \text{if} \quad 0 \leq x < 1 \\ DOF(p,r') & \text{if} \quad x = 1 \qquad \text{r': complement of subset r} \\ 1 & \text{if} \quad x < 0 \end{cases} \tag{5}$$

5. Structural Similarity and Indexing

Structural similarity measures are used to determine the match between properties and ports defined in a component to those defined in the architecture, the match between partly specified architectures and architectures in the architecture base, and the match between two architectures, here especially between functional specifications (see chapter 7). We use graph matching algorithms to determine structural similarity. We represent properties, ports, and components as nodes and couplings as edges. Our graph matching algorithm is based on the concepts and we use the implementation of Messmer [10].

Graph matching algorithms in general work by transforming one graph into the other until they are isomorphic. For transformation different operations – like adding and removing nodes and links and transforming dissimilar nodes and links – are used.

Different costs can be associated with different operations. The total of the costs for the operations needed to transform one graph into the other represents a similarity measure for the graphs.

Graph matching algorithms can be adapted to different needs by defining different costs for the different operations. For example, a transformation of a node into a similar node should cost less than transforming it into a completely different one. In some applications, adding a node should cost nothing but deleting one should cost. For example, when matching an architecture against a component specification, the architecture should at least have the ports and properties of the component specification but can and normally will have much more. Therefore, adding a node should cost but deleting should not.

The graph matching algorithm presented in [10, 11] use a hierarchical lattice of subgraphs to find fast matches. The graphs – in our application the architectures – are inserted as leaves into a hierarchical lattice of subgraphs. The lattice is organized that at the top there are all most primitive subgraphs, i.e., those with one node, and that descendents of a lattice element are the graphs which contain this element as subgraph. At the bottom are the leaves of the lattice which represent the architectures. In that, the lattice of subgraphs very much functions like a hierarchical index structure in the sense of CBR [7].

For more detail of the algorithm the reader is referred to [10]. We adopted the GUB implementation of the approach of [10] for indexing and determining structural similarity. Currently we are investigating how those CBR-techniques are best applied in CASA. We have identified two basic qualities of application:

1. Searching for configurable architectures based on properties and ports. This is a general form of search which can be applied in all stages and all strata of a design.
2. Searching for *reusable* architectures based on functional specifications and non-functional requirements.

In the following two sections we will illustrate those approaches by two test applications.

6. Searching in CASA based on Structural Similarity

In CASA we use the above described indexing mechanism to efficiently search for architectures similar to an initial component specification. Architectures are ranked based on a structural match. The fulfillment of non-functional requirements will be used to rank architectures with the same structural similarity.

Figure 4 shows a component with two ports, four properties and one non-functional requirement. This component serves as an initial specification for the subsequent search.

The result of a search for suitable architectures can be seen in Figure 5. Two architectures have the same ports and properties indicated by a structural error 0. The second value shows the DOF of the non-functional requirements. The value of property *Weight* of *GearUnit* is 17,6 and therefore fulfills requirement *R2*, while property *Weight* of architecture *PlanetaryGear* has a value of 22,1 kg resulting in a negative

DOF, however, the value is close to 0 and therefore the designer sees that the requirement is almost fulfilled.

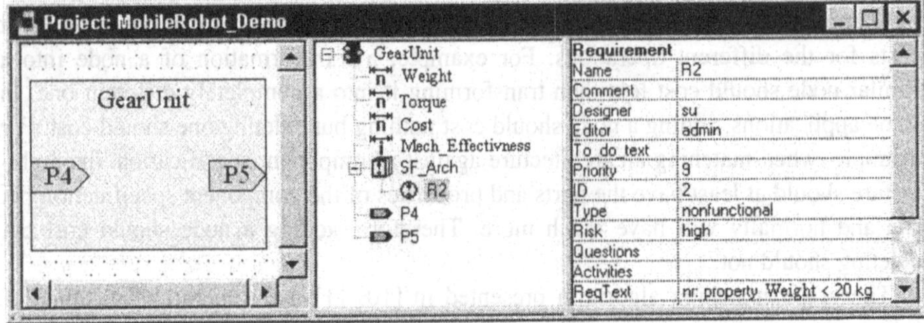

Figure 4 Component specification

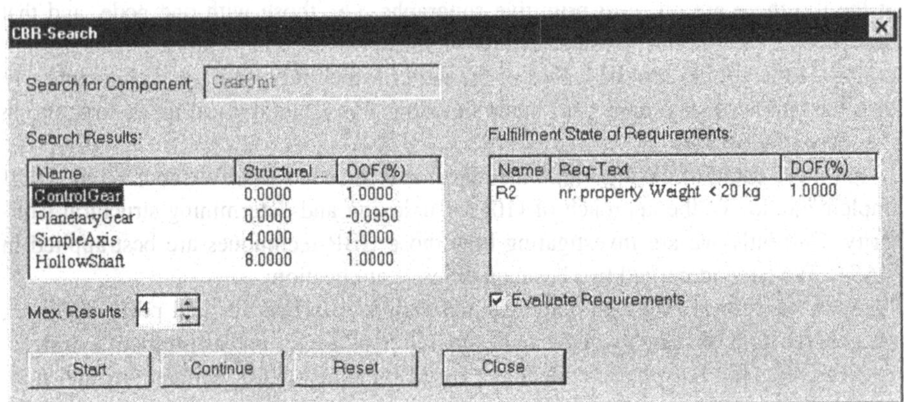

Figure 5 Result of the search with ranked architectures

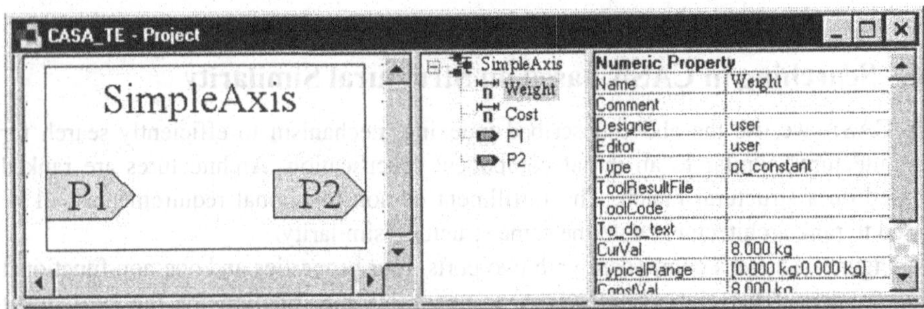

Figure 6 Architecture *SimpleAxis* with error 4

Comparison of the structure of architecture *SimpleAxis* shown in Figure 6 with the search specification results in an structural error of 4, which represents the costs to insert the properties *Torque* and *Mech_Effectivness* into architecture *SimpleAxis*.

7. Prototypical Application in the Transportation Domain

Transportation and material handling system design [6] is our favorable application domain to test our approach. Transportation system design is mainly based on standard components and therefore is suitable for a reuse-based approach.

In the transportation and material handling domain it is common to use *function plans* for functional specification of transportation systems. CASA provides architectures with components and couplings as a means for functional specification. The most important indicator for reusability of components in a specific design situation is the fulfillment of a desired function. So we use functional specifications to guide the search for reusable components.

Reusable Architecture – Case representation

In Figure 7 you see an example of a reusable architecture. A reusable architecture not only contains the component and coupling but also specifies functional *services* it can fulfill. Its description is divided into two strata, namely function and topology. Mappings from strata function to strata topology are called *realize-mappings* and assign functions to physical components. In the example component *BC1* has two functions assigned, *transmit* and *store*, which represent the functional services of *BC1*. The architecture *BC1* is further described by a set of properties. Next to the property name you can see the exact value (? if not known), its unit of measurement, and its feasible value range. For example, *PR: TotalWeight : ? kg – [1200 kg; 1500 kg]* has the meaning property *TotalWeight* has no exact value, has unit *kg*, and the feasible values are known to lie within 1200 kg and 1500 kg.

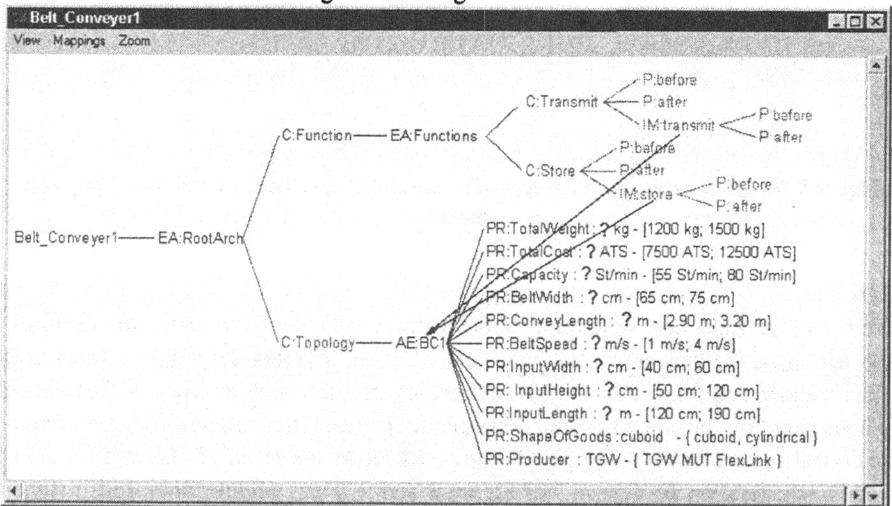

Figure 7 Reusable architecture with functional services and properties

System design typically proceeds by first defining a functional specification, then defining an initial physical structure, and then assigning functional components to physical components, meaning that physical component should overtake this functions. Figure 8 shows a design situation with a functional specification at the top, an initial physical structure at the bottom part and realize-mappings from functions to physical components (crosslinks, e.g., *transmit* and *collect* to component *Collector*).

Besides functional requirements for a component you will have assigned a set of non-functional requirements and define a set of properties and ports. Figure 9 depicts a detailed specification of component *InpConvey1* with its 11 properties (*PR*) and 10 non-functional requirements (*R1* to *R10*).

In this design situation, the designer will preferable search in the database for reusable architectures to fulfill the assigned functions and non-functional requirements.

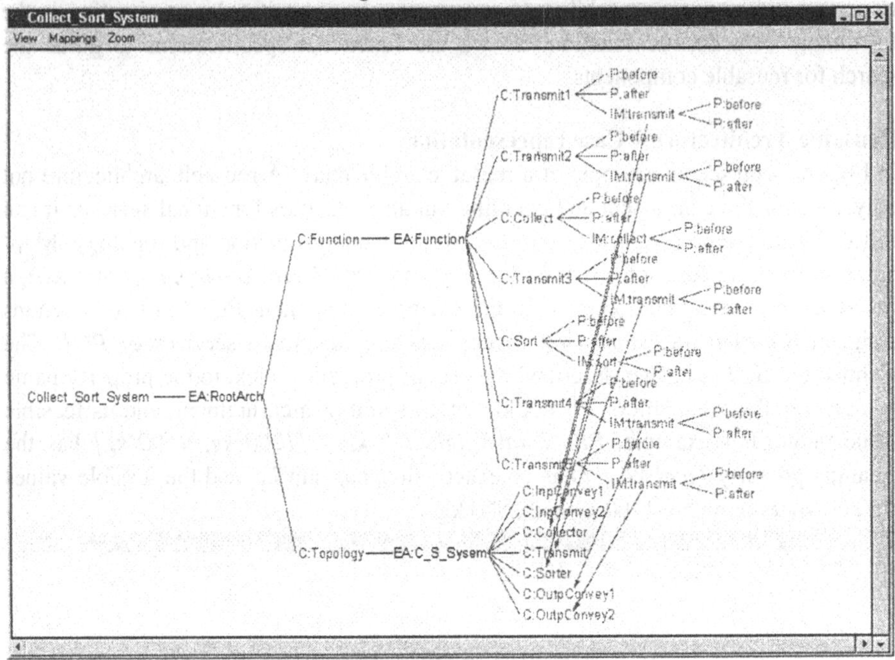

Figure 8 Design situation with functional requirement specification and initial physical structure

Retrieve

We see in the functional requirements the primary indicator to reusable architectures. We use the described graph-matching and indexing schemes to compare functional specifications and functional services defined by reusable architectures. A first match is done based on fulfillment of functional requirements. Afterwards fulfillment of non-functional requirements is computed. Figure 10 shows the result of a search for component specification *InpConvey1* of Figure 8 and 9. Three architectures fulfill (functional error 0) the functional requirements. *Belt_Conveyer3* has the best DOF for the non-functional requirements.

In the next step the designer can do a detailed investigation of each architecture and see which of the requirements are fulfilled, configure the component with the architecture of his choice, and adapt it to its special needs.

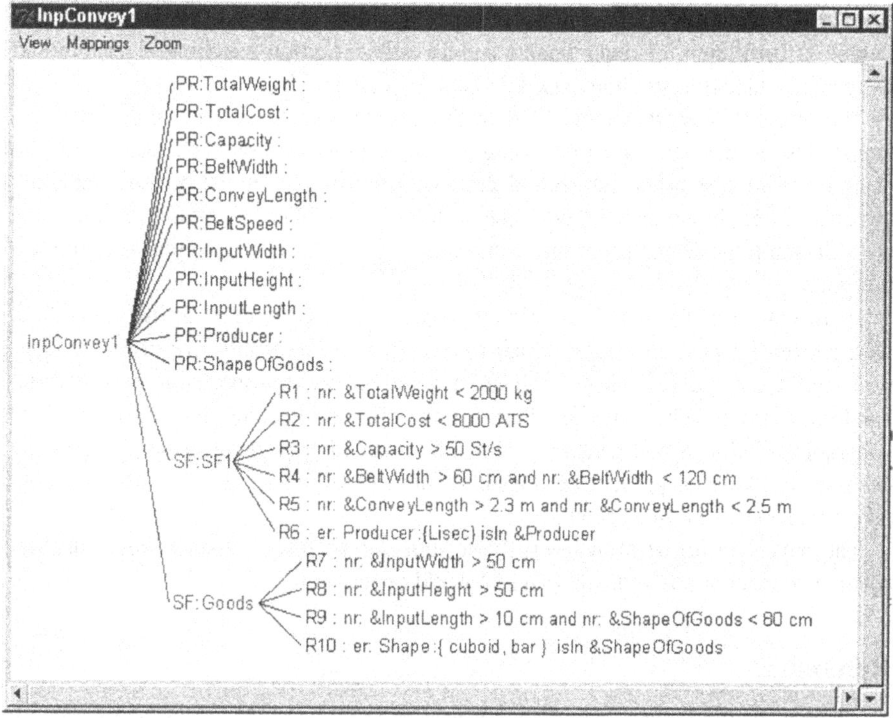

Figure 9 Details of component specification *InpConvey1* with properties and requirements

Result of Search for InpConvey1

Name of CompArch	Function error	DOF
Belt_Conveyer3	0.0	0.88
Belt_Conveyer1	0.0	0.26
Belt_Conveyer2	0.0	0.07
Collector2	6.0	0.23
Distributor1	6.0	0.16
Distributor2	6.0	0.14
Collector1	6.0	0.02

Figure 10 Result of search for *InpConvey1* with ranking of found architectures

8. Summary

In this paper we have shown how CBR techniques can successfully be applied to support reusability in a system design environment. The approach is based on a formal specification and verification of functional and non-functional requirements and a hierarchical design representation in form of configurable architecture specifications.

The CBR techniques adopted and developed are a method to determine an inexact degree of fulfillment of requirements and an efficient graph matching algorithm and hierarchical indexing structure based on lattices of subgraphs.

The reusability approach and CBR methods have been tested by two different example design projects. The first, using a basic reusability approach, dealt with the design of a mobile robot, the second dealt with transportation and material handling systems. It has shown that, although the projects and number or reusable architectures are still small, the search procedure works very well and is a very helpful feature for a designer.

Performance of the search algorithms have been tested with an artificial database with a size of 500 architectures which we regard as a reasonable size of an architecture base for a medium sized application domain, e.g., transportation and material handling systems. The index structure for the 500 architectures has a size of 4000 subgraphs. Finding a best match is within a few seconds and therefore acceptable for a designer (looking up product catalogs certainly takes longer). Further matches only take a fraction of the first search.

The next step in the project will be to look for an design domain and industrial partners to test our environment in a real world application.

References

1. Börner, K. (Ed.): Modules for Design Support, FABEL-Report 35, GMD, St. Augustin (1995)
2. Flemming, U.: Case-based Design in the SEED System, Automation and Construction, (1994)
3. Gebhardt, F.: Methods and systems for case retrieval exploiting the case structure, FABEL-Report 39, GMD, St. Augustin, Germany (1995)
4. Goel, A. K.: Integration of case-based and model-based reasoning for adaptive problem solving, PhD Thesis, The Ohio State University (1989)
5. Hua, K., Falting, B., Smith, I.: CADRE: case-based geometric design, Artificial Intelligence in Engineering 10 (1996)171-183.
6. Kettner, H., Schmidt, J., Greim, H.R.: Guidelines for a systematic manufacturing system planning, Hanser Verlag (1984) (in German)
7. Kolodner, J.: Case-Based Reasoning, Morgan Kaufmann (1993)
8. Maher, M.L., de Silva Garza, G.:Developing CaseBased Reasoning for Structural Design, IEEE Expert. Vol. 11 (1996)
9. Mesarovic, M.D., Macko, D., Takahara, Y.: Theory of Hierarchical, Multilevel, Systems, Academic Press, New York (1970)
10. Messmer, B.T.: Efficient Graph Matching Algorithms for Preprocessed Model Graphs, Dissertation, University Bern, Switzerland (1996)
11. Messmer, B.T., Bunke, H.: A network based approach to exact and inexact graph matching, Institut für Informatik und angewandte Mathematik, University Bern, Switzerland (1993)
12. Mittelmann, R., Kogler, M.: CASA-TE: Representation of Requirements, Technical Report 154-97, Johannes Kepler University, Dept of Systems Theory and Information Technology, Linz, Austria (1997) (in German)

13. Praehofer, H.: Reusability in CASA, Technical Report 144-96, Johannes Kepler University, Dept of Systems Theory and Information Technology, Linz, Austria, (1997) (in German)
14. Praehofer, H. and Kerschbaummayr, J.: Concepts for Reusability in CASA, Technical Report 160-97, Johannes Kepler University, Dept. Systems Theory, Linz, Austria (1997) (in German)
15. Reich, Y.: The Development of Bridger: A Methodological Study of Research on Machine Learning in Design, Artificial Intelligence in Engineering, 8 (1993) 217-231
16. Schaffer, C.: CASA – Computer Aided Systems Architecting, Technical Report 141-96, Johannes Kepler University, Dept of Systems Theory and Information Technology, Linz, Austria (1997) (in German).
17. Schaffer, C.: Computer Aided System Architecting (CASA): Requirement-Driven Design of Multi-Disciplinary Systems, PhD Thesis, Johannes Kepler University, Linz, Austria (1999) (in German).
18. Sycara, K. Guttal, R., Koning, J., Narasimhan, S., Navinchandra, D.: CADET: A Case-based Synthesis Tool for Engineering Design, International Journal of Expert Systems, Vol. 4 (1992)
19. Voß A. (Ed.): Similarity concepts and retrieval methods, FABEL-Report 13, GMD, St. Augustin, Germany (1994)
20. Wolverton, M., Hayes-Roth, B.: Finding analogues for innovative design, Techn. report KSL 95-32, Knowledge System Laboratory, Stanford University, CA (1995)

Case-Based Reasoning for Antibiotics Therapy Advice

Rainer Schmidt [a)], Bernhard Pollwein [b)], Lothar Gierl [a)]

a) Institut für Medizinische Informatik und Biometrie, Universität Rostock
Rembrandtstr. 16 / 17, D-18055 Rostock, Germany
Email: {rainer.schmidt , lothar.gierl} @medizin.uni-rostock.de
b) Institut für Anästhesiologie, Ludwig-Maximilians Universität München
Marchioninistr. 15, D-81377 München, Germany

Abstract

In this paper, we describe case-based techniques in a medical application. We have developed a prototype of an antibiotics therapy adviser within the ICONS project, where the main advantage of applying CBR techniques is to speed-up the process of computing advisable therapies. However, some adaptations do not really belong to the Case-Based Reasoning paradigm though information from former cases is considered. They deal with rather typical medical tasks, namely modifications due to information updates. In our incrementally working system we have attempted to solve the problem of the continuously increasing number of stored cases by generalising from specific single cases to more general prototypes and by subsequently erasing redundant cases. Here we present results of experiments with threshold settings for our prototype architecture. The results show that the chosen design, which has mainly been founded on experiences with diagnostic applications, is not only advantageous for this therapeutic task, but that it contains a slight drawback as well.

1. Introduction

Severe bacterial infections are still a life threatening complication in intensive care medicine correlated with a high mortality [1]. Identification of bacterial pathogens is often difficult. It normally requires at least 24 hours to identify the pathogen that is responsible for an infection and at least another 24 hours to find out which antibiotics have therapeutic effects against the identified pathogen. To not endanger the patient, physicians often have to start an antimicrobial therapy before the responsible pathogen and its sensitivities are determined. This sort of antibiotic therapy is called "calculated" in contrast to a "selective" therapy, which is used when microbiological results are already available.

The main task of our adviser is to present suitable calculated antibiotics therapy advice (Fig. 4.) for intensive care patients, who have developed a bacterial infection as an additional complication. As for such critical patients physicians cannot wait for the laboratory results, we use an expected pathogen spectrum based on medical background knowledge. This spectrum should be completely covered by each advisable antibiotics therapy. Furthermore, as advice is needed very quickly we speed-up the process of computing advisable antibiotics therapies by using Case-Based Reasoning methods (the right path in Fig. 1.). We search for a similar previous patient and transfer the suggested therapies made for his situation to the current patient. These previous suggestions are adapted to be applicable to the new medical situation of the current patient.

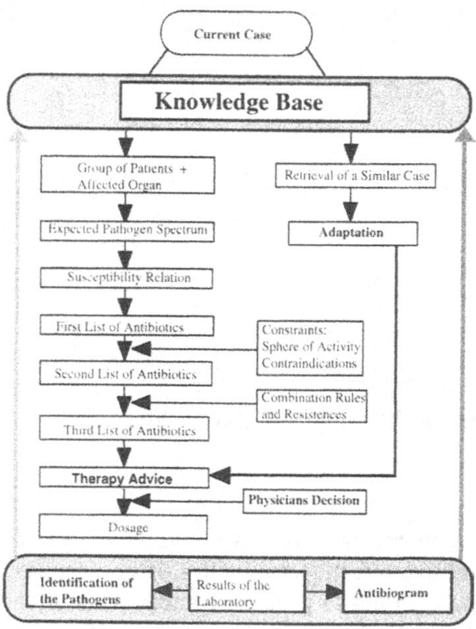

Fig. 1. Overview of ICONS

1.1. Strategy for Selecting Advisable Antibiotic Therapies

As ICONS is not a diagnostic system, we do not attempt to deduce evidence for diagnoses based on symptoms, frequencies or probabilities, but instead pursue a strategy that can be characterised as follows (Fig. 2.): Find all possible solutions and reduce them using the patient's contraindications and the complete coverage of the calculated pathogen spectrum (establish-refine strategy).

First, we distinguish among different groups of patients (infection acquired in- or outside the ward resp. the hospital, immuncompromised patients). A first list of antibiotics is generated by a susceptibility relation, that for each group of pathogens provides all antibiotics which usually have therapeutic effects. This list contains all those antibiotics that can control at least a part of the potential pathogen spectrum. We obtain a second list of antibiotics by reducing the first one by applying two constraints: The patient's contraindications and the desired sphere of activity. Using the antibiotics of this second list, we try to find antibiotics which under consideration of the expected susceptibility cover the whole pathogen spectrum individually.

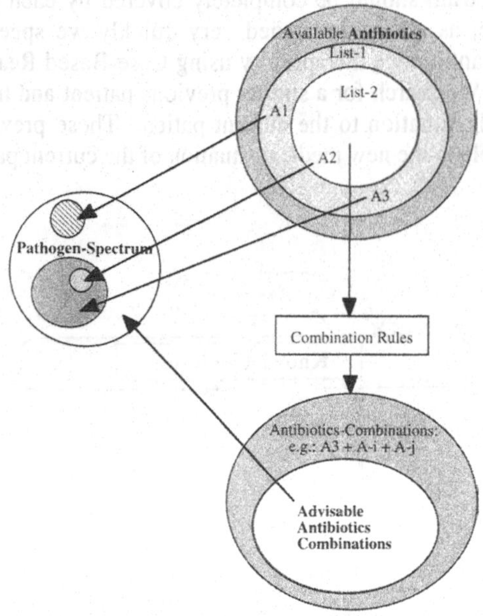

Fig. 2. Antibiotics Selection Strategy

Except for some community acquired infections, monotherapies have to be combined with synergistic or additive effecting antibiotics. If no adequate single therapy can be found, we use combination rules to generate combinations of antibiotics. Each possible combination must be tested for the ability to cover the whole expected spectrum.

2. Retrieval

In this application the main argument for using CBR methods is to speed-up the process of finding adequate therapies. We shorten the above described strategy of selecting advisable antibiotic therapies by searching for a similar case, retrieving it's suggested therapies and by adapting them concerning the contraindications of the current patient. The retrieval consists of three steps (Fig. 3.).

First we select that part of the case base, in which all cases share two attributes with the current patient: The group of patients and the infected organ system. This means a selection of the appropriate prototype tree (see chapter 4.1.). Subsequently, we apply the Hash-Tree-Retrieval-Algorithm of Stottler, Henke, and King [2] for nominal valued contraindications and the similarity measure of Tversky [3] for few integer valued contraindications. Furthermore, we use an adaptability criterion, because not every case is adaptable [4]. As the attributes used for the retrieval are the contraindications, which work as constraints for the set of possible antibiotics suggestions, it is obvious, that a former case who has contraindications which the current patient does not share should not be used. To guarantee this condition the adaptability criterion has to be checked during the retrieval. This can be considered as an example to support the ideas of Smyth and Keane

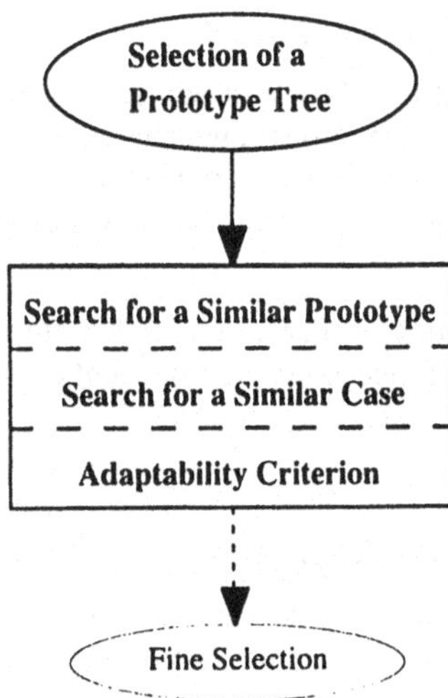

Fig. 3. Retrieval steps in ICONS

that the similarity assumption alone is often inappropriate and that the retrieval should take the adaptation into account [5].

3. Adaptations

In the antibiotics therapy adviser three different sorts of adaptations occur: A CBR adaptation to obtain sets of calculated advisable therapies for current patients (Fig. 4. shows the presentation of such a set), an adaptation of chosen therapies to laboratory findings and a periodical update of laboratory information used by the system.

Restrictions Pathogen Spectrum Additional Therapies Own Creation

ADVISABLE THERAPIES:		Price (DM/Day)
LINCOSAMIDE	+ GYRASEHEMMER :	
☐ CLINDAMYCIN	+ CIPROFLOXACIN	92 to 205
PENICILLINE	+ AMINOGLYKOSIDE :	
☐ PIPERACILLIN	+ GENTAMICIN	48 to 119
☐ PIPERACILLIN	+ TOBRAMYCIN	65 to 146
☐ PIPERACILLIN	+ AMIKACIN	166 to 233
☐ AUGMENTAN	+ TOBRAMYCIN	66 to 122
☐ AUGMENTAN	+ AMIKACIN	168 to 209
☐ TAZOBAC	+ GENTAMICIN	11 to 15
☐ TAZOBAC	+ TOBRAMYCIN	28 to 42
☐ TAZOBAC	+ AMIKACIN	129
☐ MEZLOCILLIN	+ TOBRAMYCIN	75 to 140
☐ MEZLOCILLIN	+ AMIKACIN	177 to 228
CARBAPENEME	+ AMINOGLYKOSIDE :	
☐ IMIPENEM	+ AMIKACIN	237 to 349
☐ IMIPENEM	+ TOBRAMYCIN	136 to 261
☐ IMIPENEM	+ GENTAMICIN	119 to 234
GYRASEHEMMER	+ AMINOGLYKOSIDE :	
☐ CIPROFLOXACIN	+ AMIKACIN	186 to 246
☐ CIPROFLOXACIN	+ TOBRAMYCIN	85 to 159
☐ CIPROFLOXACIN	+ GENTAMICIN	68 to 132

Fig. 4. Presentation of advisable antibiotics combinations

3.1. Case-Based Reasoning Adaptation

Each contraindication restricts the set of advisable therapies. As already mentioned above we use a criterion during the retrieval which guarantees that the retrieved case does not have any additional contraindications in comparison to the current case. Otherwise the solution set for the current case would be inadmissibly reduced by additional contraindications of a previous case.

The adaptation of a previous similar case is rather simple. It is just a transfer of the set of advisable therapies and if necessary a subsequent reduction of this set by additional contraindications of the current case.

3.2. Adaptations of Chosen Therapies to Laboratory Findings

Adaptations of laboratory findings do not really belong to the Case-Based Reasoning paradigm, but they are based on information about cases. The goal of the main part of the therapy adviser is to present advisable therapies before the results of the laboratory are known. When later on these results are known, the already started therapy has to be adapted to them. There are two sorts of findings, after 24 hours the identification of the pathogen which is responsible for the infection and after another 24 hours the sensitivity test results (antibiogram) of this pathogen against the various antibiotics. If the identified pathogen does not belong to the considered calculated pathogen spectrum and if this pathogen is according to the systems sensitivity information not sensitive against the already started therapy, new specific advisable therapies against this pathogen have to be computed. If the laboratory sensitivity test results show that the identified pathogen is in contrast to the systems sensitivity information not sensitive against the already started therapy, it leads to the same task: New "selective" advisable therapies which have therapeutic effects against the identified pathogen have to be computed.

It might seem to be a contradiction that laboratory tests can show that a pathogen is not sensitive against an antibiotic although the current sensitivity information says it should be. However, as pathogens are never exactly alike, but always slight mutations, the sensitivity information is based on a percentage value. For example, most of the problematic pathogens are nowadays only in slightly more than 80% of the cases sensitive against the strongest antibiotics. So an observed sensitivity higher than 66% is usually already considered as sensitive.

When new cases are incorporated into the system, the sensitivity information has to be updated, the laboratory findings for these new cases must be taken into account. Additionally, the used expected pathogen spectra might change on time too. For both laboratory information sources used by the system we have implemented a periodical update. This can be seen as another form of adaptation which is not founded on single cases, but on statistical evaluation of specific information of a number of cases.

4. Prototypes

As in an incrementally working system the number of cases increases continuously, storing each case would slow down the retrieval time and exceed any space limitations. So we decided to structure the case base by prototypes and to store only those cases that differ from their prototype significantly. Though the general use of prototypes was early introduced in the CBR field [6, 7], it is still mainly applied in the medical domain [e.g. 8,

9, 10, 11]. Our prototype architecture is mainly based on experience with a diagnostic application [12], where we create prototypes that share most features with most of their cases. This idea is founded on empirical research [13], which indicates that people consider cases to be more "typical" when the number of features between the presented case and the "normal" case increases.

In diagnostic applications prototypes correspond to typical diseases or diagnoses. So, for antibiotic therapies prototypes are expected to correspond to typical antibiotic treatments associated with typical clinical features of patients. However, as the attributes are contraindications which are not responsible for the generation but the restriction of the solution set, this is only partly true. We have investigated the growth of a hierarchical prototype structure built up from a randomly ordered stream of cases.

4.1. Selection of a Prototype Tree

We do not have just one prototype tree, but a wood of trees which are independent from each other. For each affected organ combined with each group of patients an own tree can be generated. That means, for nearly 20 organ systems and 5 patient groups nearly 100 prototype trees are possible. We generate them only if required dynamically. For example a tree for "community acquired kidney infections" will be generated as soon as the first data input of a patient occurs who has a kidney infection which he acquired outside the hospital.

So, all cases within the same prototype tree belong to the same group of patients, the same organ system is affected and therefore the same expected pathogen spectrum deduced from background knowledge has to be covered. The cases within a prototype tree are only discriminated from each other by their different contraindications. These are antibiotic allergies, reduced organ functions (e.g. kidney and liver), specific diagnoses (e.g. acoustic distortion or diseases of the central nervous system), special blood diseases, pregnancy and the patient's age.

4.2. Generating Prototypes

First, all cases are stored below the prototypes they belong to. If after storing a new case below a prototype the threshold "number of cases" is reached, the prototype will be "filled". This means, that every contraindication which occurs in the cases belonging to this prototype at least as often as the second threshold "minimum frequency" will be included into the prototype. Subsequently, the "filled" prototype can be treated like a case. The same as for cases holds for prototypes: Each contraindication restricts the set of advisable therapies. The contraindications of a prototype are those that occur most often within its cases. So from the viewpoint of frequency they are the typical ones. Those cases that have no additional contraindications in comparison with their prototypes are erased. Only information about their occurred contraindications are saved in the frequency table of their prototype.

When later on a new case is added to an already filled prototype, its frequency table, which contains information about the frequency of the contraindications of its cases, has to be updated and if necessary the contraindications of the prototype have to be recomputed. If the (re-) computed contraindications of the prototype change, the suggested antibiotic therapies have to be recomputed too. All cases must be inspected again for their need to be stored.

Below an already existing prototype we create an "alternative" prototype if for the latter enough cases exist (that means the threshold "number of cases" is reached), that have at least one contraindication in common which the already existing prototype does not include. We construct this new alternative prototype from those cases that share at least one from the already existing prototype deviating contraindication. We place this new prototype in the hierarchy directly below the existing prototype (a part of a possible prototype hierarchy is shown in Fig. 5.). New "alternative" prototypes differ from their superior prototypes by their contraindications and therefore by their sets of advisable antibiotic therapies too.

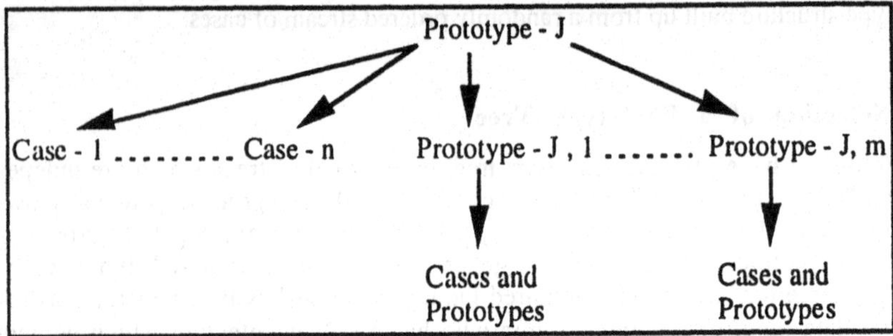

Fig. 5. Possible relationships of a prototype

Even the adaptation of an "empty case", that is a case without any contraindication and therefore with an unrestricted set of advisable therapies, works faster than the normal program flow. The most time-consuming step of the program flow without CBR is the computation of advisable antibiotic combinations, because a lot of conditions have to be checked, e.g. the current sensitivity situation for each pathogen in the expected pathogen spectrum has to be considered for each antibiotic of each possible therapy combination. So, when the first prototype of a tree is filled, we additionally generate an artificial "empty case", which can be retrieved if no adaptable case can be found in this tree.

4.3. Results of our Experiments with Threshold Settings

For testing our prototype design, we used data of 21 postoperative lung infected patients who on average had almost 1.5 contraindications. We varied the two threshold parameters. For each variation the cases were entered in the same randomly chosen order. Each time after entering all 21 cases we inspected the current system state. We looked at the number of created prototypes, stored cases and realised adaptations of previous cases or of prototypes. Though it must be considered that the state of our system is always subject to the influence of random patient data, the sequence of their data input into the system, and the choice of the inspection time, we believe that it is possible to make some general statements on favourable settings of the two threshold parameters from the results of our tests (Table 1.). Of course these statements depend on two desired goals: To increase the number of adaptations and to decrease the number of stored cases and prototypes. As the number of possible adaptations obviously increases with the number of stored cases and prototypes, both goals are contrasting.

Table 1. Settings and consequences of threshold parameters

"minimum frequency" (in %)	"number of cases"	created prototypes	stored cases	realised adaptations
33	2	5	7	3
33	3	5	14	7
33	4	4	15	7
33	5	2	17	6
25	2	4	3	1
25	3	3	8	4
25	4	3	15	6
25	5	1	18	4
20	3	2	5	2
20	4	1	10	2
20	5	1	14	4
-	> 21	-	21	6

The effects of the two threshold parameters are as follows:

(1) The parameter "minimum frequency" determines how (relatively) often a contraindication has to occur in the set of cases to be incorporated into the prototype. Should for example just three cases form a prototype, then a "minimum frequency" of 34% means, that only those contraindications are included in the prototype, which exist in more than one case, while a lower "minimum frequency" value would lead to the effect of "initial amnesia": All contraindications of the three cases are included in the prototype, none of the three cases still shows any additional contraindication in comparison with the prototype, and all three cases will therefore be erased.

(2) The parameter "number of cases" determines the required number of cases that are necessary to fill a prototype or to create an alternative prototype. The lower this threshold the more prototypes are created and the less cases are stored.

When new cases are added to an already filled prototype, the observed contraindication frequencies and therefore the filling of the prototype might change. One underlying idea is to update the prototype, another idea is that a prototype should contain the typical (most frequent) attributes of its cases. As a case forgotten once is lost forever, it may happen that a case is assimilated (with the consequence of getting lost) by a prototype, but that this prototype later changes in such a manner, that the case would have at least one additional contraindication and would therefore be kept.

It can be seen, that the goal of increasing the number of adaptations can mainly be achieved by a high "number of cases" value (so, many cases will be stored) and additionally by a high "minimum frequency" percentage value. The goal of reducing the number of stored cases can be achieved by the opposite strategy. And for a well balanced compromise both parameter values should be set to a moderate intermediate value.

5. Conclusions

We have presented case-based techniques that are used in our antibiotics therapy adviser. Some of them do not really belong to the CBR paradigm, but are rather typical for the medical domain where information about diseases, pathogens, resistances etc. often changes on time.

To solve the problem of the incremental growth of the case base we adopted ideas for the prototype design from our diagnostic experiences. However, for this therapeutic application they are not only advantageous, but have a slight drawback. Because on the one hand, we accumulate typical characteristics of several cases into one single general prototype, and on the other hand, we reduce the number of solutions using constraints, we are confronted with two conflicting goals. A case is well adaptable if it shows as few contraindications as possible. However, a case is deleted when it does not show additional contraindications with respect to its prototype. Both opposing goals to increase the number of adaptations and to decrease the storage amount can individually be achieved by strategies to set the threshold parameter values.

So far only few CBR approaches to therapeutic tasks are known. Some of them use prototypes as well [e.g. 10], some apply schemata [e.g. 14]. However, the uniqueness of our prototype architecture results from the fact that the attributes, which are used to determine similarity, are not responsible for the generation, but the restriction of solutions.

5.1. Evaluation

First, we have evaluated the expected pathogen spectra and the resistance situation the system starts with. We analysed the microbiological results of the last two years provided by the microbiological laboratory. In addition to the information from literature and publications only few pathogens had become resistant against some antibiotics. So a few resistances had to be added. For testing the correctness and the quality of the proposed therapies, we asked some experienced intensive care physicians to assess ICONS's proposals. As the interobserver variability among the physicians concerning the assessments of ICONS's therapy advice and concerning their own proposed therapies was tremendous (some physicians thought very highly of ICONS's advice while others assessed some proposed therapies as unsuitable), it is impossible to define any "golden standard".

5.2. Future Work

In a new project we are going to improve the antibiotic therapy adviser mainly concerning the visualisation of additional information such as the current sensitivity drift on time. Furthermore, we will extend the system by a pharmacological component, which should use CBR methods too, to optimise the individual dosage recommendation during the whole therapy. So far ICONS provides only general initial dosage guidelines.

References

1. Bueno-Cavanillas, A., Delgado-Rodriguez, M., Lopez-Luque, A., Schaffino-Cano, S., Galvez-Vargas, R.: Influence of nosocomial infection on mortality rate in an intensive care unit. *Crit Care Med 22* (1994) 55-60
2. Stottler, R.H., Henke, A.L., King, J.A.: Rapid Retrieval Algorithms for Case-Based Reasoning. International Joint Conference on Artificial Intelligence 11 (1989) 233-237
3. Tversky, A.: Features of Similarity. *Psychological Review 84* (1977) 327-352
4. Smyth, B., Keane, M.T.: Retrieving Adaptable Cases: The Role of Adaptation Knowledge in Case Retrieval. In: Richter, M.M., Wess, S., Althoff, K.-D., Maurer, F. (eds.): First European Workshop on Case-Based Reasoning, University of Kaiserslautern (1993) 76-81
5. Smyth, B., Keane, M.T.: Adaptation-guided retrieval: questioning the similarity assumption in reasoning. *Artificial Intelligence 102* (1998) 249-293
6. Schank, R.C.: Dynamic Memory: A Theory of Learning in Computer and People. Cambridge University Press, New York (1982)
7. Bareiss, R.: Exemplar-based Knowledge Acquisition. Academic Press, San Diego (1989)
8. Evans, C.D.: A case-based for diagnosis and avalying of dysmorphic syndromes. In: van Bemmel, J.H., McCray, A.T. (eds.): Yearbook of Medical informatics, Schattauer-Verlag, Stuttgart (1996), 473-483
9. Turner, R.: Organizing and Using Schematic Konwledge for Medical Diagnosis. In: Kolodner J.L. (ed.): Proceedings Case-Based Reasoning Workshop, Morgan Kaufmann Publishers, San Mateo (1988) 435-446
10. Bichindaritz, I.: From Cases to Classes: Focusing on Abstraction in Case-Based Reasoning. In: Burkhard, H.-D., Lenz, M. (eds.): 4th German Workshop on Case-Based Reasoning, Humboldt University Berlin (1996) 62-69
11. Bellazzi, R., Montani, S., Portinale, L.: Retrieval in a Prototype-Based Case Library: A Case Study in Diabetes Therapy Revision. In: Smyth, B., Cunningham, P. (eds.): 4th European Workshop on Case-Based Reasoning, Lecture Notes in Artificial Intelligence Vol. 1488, Springer Verlag, Berlin Heidelberg New York (1998) 64-75
12. Gierl, L., Stengel-Rutkowski, S.: Integrating Consultation and Semi-automatic Knowledge Acquisition in a Prototype-based Architecture: Experiences with Dysmorphic Syndromes. *Artificial Intelligence in Medicine 6* (1994) 29-49
13. Rosch, E., Mervis, C.B.: Family resemblances: studies in the structure of categories. *Cognitive Psychologie 7* (1975) 573-605
14. Schwartz, A.B., Barcia, R.M., Martins, A., Weber-Lee, R.: PSIQ - A CBR Approach to the Mental Health Area. In: Bergmann, R., Wilke, W. (eds.): 5th German Workshop on Case-Based Reasoning, University of Kaiserslautern (1997) 217-223

Surfing the Digital Wave

Generating Personalised TV Listings using Collaborative, Case-Based Recommendation

Barry Smyth & Paul Cotter

Department of Computer Science
University College Dublin
Belfield, Dublin 4, Ireland
{Barry.Smyth, Paul.Cotter}@ucd.ie

Abstract. In the future digital TV will offer an unprecedented level of programme choice. We are told that this will lead to dramatic increases in viewer satisfaction as all viewing tastes are catered for all of the time. However, the reality may be somewhat different. We have not yet developed the tools to deal with this increased level of choice (for example, conventional TV guides will be virtually useless), and viewers will face a significant and frustrating information overload problem. This paper describes a solution in the form of the PTV system. PTV employs user profiling and information filtering techniques to generate web-based TV viewing guides that are personalised for the viewing preferences of individual users. The paper explains how PTV constructs graded user profiles to drive a hybrid recommendation technique, combining case-based and collaborative information filtering methods. The results of an extensive empirical study to evaluate the quality of PTV's case-based and collaborative filtering strategies are also described.

1 Introduction

With the advent of new cable and satellite services, and the next generation of digital TV systems, we will soon be faced with an unprecedented level of programme choice. Where we have tens of TV channels today, tomorrow we will have hundreds, and soon after that it will be thousands. If we believe the hype, we are entering a new age of television viewing, an age of incredible choice and unprecedented viewing satisfaction. However, while increased programme choice does offer the *potential* for improved viewing satisfaction, the reality may be somewhat different. We have not yet developed the tools to deal with this new level of choice, and it will become increasingly difficult to find out what programmes are on in a given week, never mind locating a small set of relevant programmes for a quiet evening's viewing.

Consider for example the traditional TV guide, listing programming information on local channels for up to a week in advance. The days of a slim, easy to digest 30 page volume are essentially gone. Looking to the US for a sign of things to come we notice, with some consternation, that the current issue of the TV Guide (that weekly bible for American channel surfers) runs to nearly 400 pages of indigestible schedule charts. Moreover, the way that we interact with our TV sets will also have to change. Those rapid "remote-controlled surfs", that prove so effective (and so irritating to your partner) for 10 or 20 channels, will no longer be a viable means of finding out what is on at a given time. A 10 second per channel surf over even a modest 200 channel service will take about 35 minutes to complete! The digital TV vendors do recognise this as a serious information overload problem, and in response they are now offering electronic programme guides to help users to navigate this digital maze. However, these guides are relatively crude and offer little more than a static category based view of the evenings programming; the burden of search remains with the user.

This paper describes the PTV system (http://ptv.ucd.ie), which offers a working solution to the problem of locating relevant programme information quickly and easily. PTV combines user profiling and case-based reasoning (CBR) techniques to generate electronic TV viewing guides that are carefully personalised for the viewing preferences of individual users ([2, 6, 7]). At the present time, these electronic guides are Web based and delivered over the Internet to desktop PCs, but of course the advent of WebTV and cable-internet services will allow PTV to deliver personalised programme information directly to the TV set.

The remainder of this paper is organised in the following way. The next section provides an overview of the PTV system, describing its various sources of knowledge and main functional components. Section 3 focuses on PTV's user profiling and case-based recommendation strategy. Before concluding, section 4 reports the results of an extensive empirical study to evaluate the quality of the personalised programme guides that are produced, and the effectiveness of the case-based and collaborative recommendation strategies. Finally, a new appendix has been added to indicate the current state of the PTV system including the results of a recent online survey that add further support to the PTV concept and, we believe, paves the way for the use of collaborative, case-based recommendation methods in a wide range of personalised media service in the future.

2 The PTV System

PTV is a client-server system operating over the Web, allowing users to register, login, and view their personalised TV guides as specially customised Web pages. The architecture of PTV is shown in Figure 1. A standard Web browser provides the required client functionality, and all user interaction is handled via the HTML Forms interface. The heart of PTV lies with its server-side components, which handle all the main information processing functions such as user registration and authentication, user profiling, guide compilation, and the all-important programme recommendation and grading.

In the following sections we will concentrate on user profiling in PTV, focusing on how these profiles are used to deliver personalised content and, in particular, how PTV can make intelligent recommendations to PTV subscribers. However, in this section we will provide a suitable backdrop for these future discussions by taking a broad look at the form and function of PTV's main components.

Profile Database & Profiler: The key to PTV's personalisation facility is an accurate database of user profiles. Each user profile encodes the TV preferences of a given user, listing channel information, preferred viewing time, liked and disliked programmes, subject preferences, etc (see Figure 1). Preliminary profile information is collected from the user at registration time in order to bootstrap the personalisation process. However, the majority of information is learned from grading feedback provided by the user; each recommended programme is accompanied with grading icons allowing the user to explicitly evaluate the proposed recommendation (see also section 3.1).

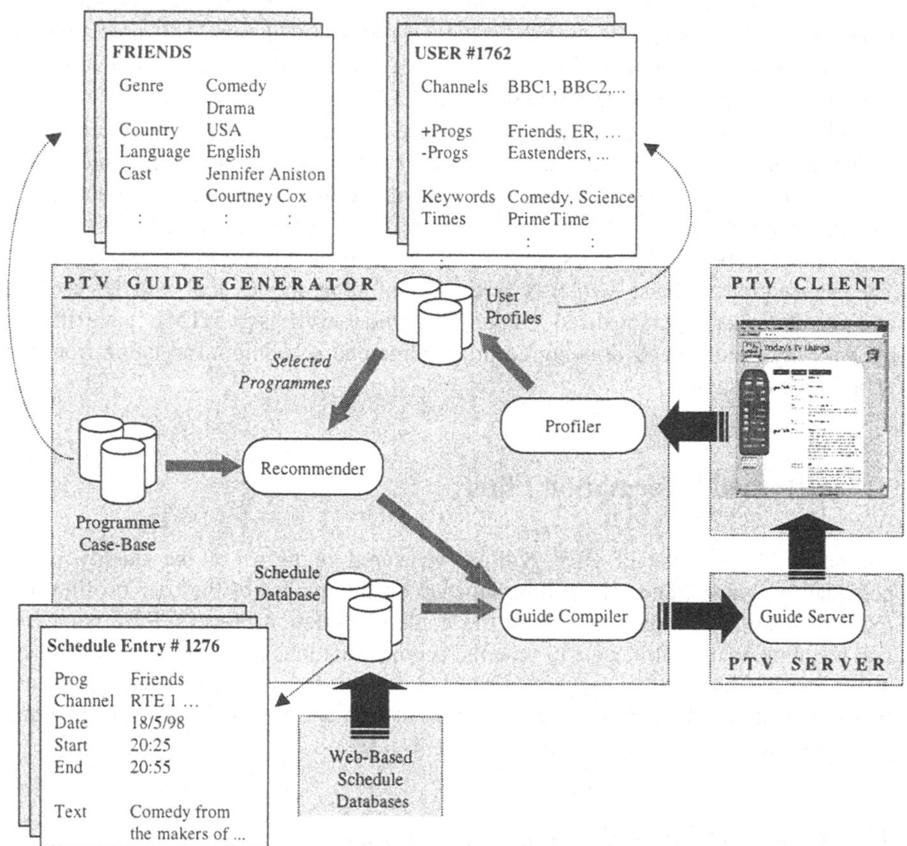

Fig. 1. An overview of the PTV system.

Programme Case-Base: This database contains the programme content descriptions (programme cases). Each entry describes a particular programme using features such as the programme title, genre information, the creator and director, cast or presenters, the country of origin, and the language; an example programme case for the comedy

'Friends' is shown in Figure 1. This information repository is crucial for the case-based recommendation component of PTV (see Section 3.2).

Schedule Database: This database contains TV listings for all supported channels. Each listing entry includes details such as the programme name, the viewing channel, the start and end time, and typically some text describing the programme in question (see the schedule entry example in Figure 1). The schedule database is constructed automatically from online schedule resources (e.g., online teletext pages and static entertainment guides) by PTV's schedule agents. Each agent is designed to mine a particular online resource for relevant schedule information and the results of these many parallel searches is the compilation of a rich schedule database.

Recommender: The recommendation component is the intelligent core of PTV. Its job is to take user profile information and to select new programmes for recommendation to a user. In the next section we will explain how PTV uses a hybrid recommendation approach that combines case-based and collaborative recommendation strategies (see section 3.2 and 3.3).

Guide Compiler: To compile a personalised TV guide for a given date and user, PTV constructs two programme lists: (1) a list consisting of those programmes listed as positive in the user's profile, along with those programmes selected for recommendation (which of course do not occur in the profile); (2) a list of all programmes to be aired on the specified date by a channel listed in the user's profile. The intersection of these two lists is the set of programmes that will be used to compile the user's personalised guide. The guide itself is a HTML page that is dynamically produced by drawing on programme and schedule information from the appropriate databases.

3 A Hybrid Information Filter

Ultimately the success of PTV will be measured in terms of the quality of its personalised guides, and this in turn depends on the quality of the user profiles and recommendation strategies that drive the guide compilation process. PTV harnesses two recommendation strategies to base its recommendations on the programmes that a given user has liked in the past (case-based or content-based) and on the programmes that similar users like (collaborative). In this section we look at PTV's profiling and recommendation components in more detail.

3.1 User Profiling for Programme Recommendation

In PTV each user profile contains two types of information, domain preferences and programme preferences. The former describe general user preferences such as a list of available channels, preferred viewing times, subject keywords, in addition to guide preferences such as whether guide programmes are to be sorted according to viewing time or channel. Programme preferences are represented as two lists of programme titles, a positive list containing programmes that the user has liked in the past, and a negative list containing programmes that the user has disliked.

At registration time a new user is invited to provide basic information including domain and programme preferences. This initial profile is needed to bootstrap the recommendation process, but usually only constitutes a restricted snapshot of a user's preferences. The left-hand screen shot of Figure 2 shows part of the user profile input screen used to gather explicit user information during registration time; indeed users can also use this facility to display and manually edit their own profile.

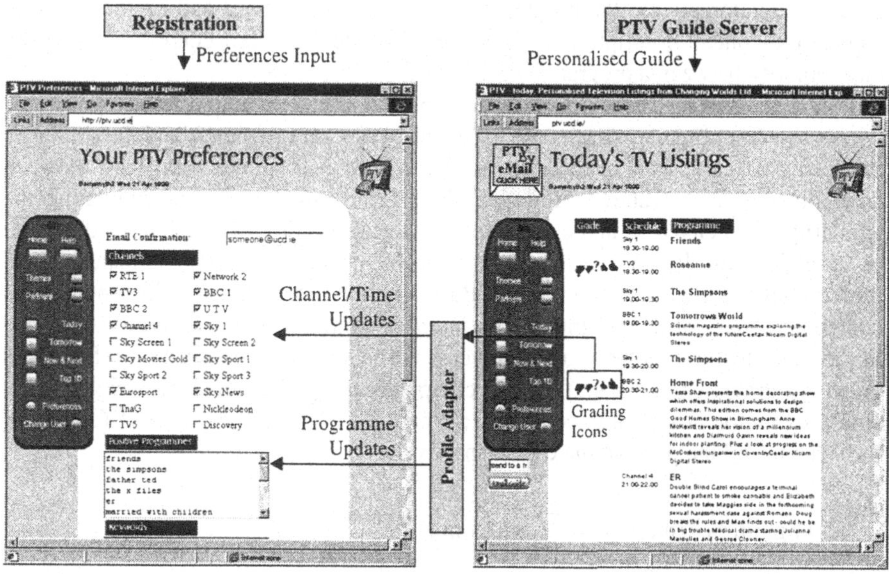

Fig. 2. User profiles and feedback

Of course while manual profile editing has its advantages (usually in terms of profile accuracy) it is a burden for users. In particular, we have found that users are happy to provide complete domain preferences but tend to provide only limited programme preferences. For this reason, PTV includes an automatic profile update facility that is driven by direct user feedback through a set of grading icons listed beside recommended guide programmes. PTV's profiler can use this feedback information to automatically alter a user's profile in a number of ways. The simplest modification is to update the programme preference lists by adding positively or negatively graded programmes to the appropriate list. However, the domain preferences can also be altered. For example, viewing time preferences can be adjusted if a user frequently prefers prime-time programmes to morning shows. This long-term feedback connection between user and system is vital if PTV is to maintain an accurate picture of each user over time.

3.2 Case-Based Recommendation

The basic philosophy in case-based recommendation is to recommend items that are similar to those items that the user has liked in the past (see also [1, 5, 11]). For PTV, this means recommending programmes that are similar to the programmes in the positive programme list and dissimilar to those in the negative programme list. Three components are needed for case-based-recommendation: (1) content descriptions for all TV programmes (see the programme case-base in section 2 and Figure 1); (2) a compatible content description of each user's profile; (3) a procedure for measuring the similarity between a programme and a user.

PTV's programme case-base has already been outlined in section 2 and an example case is shown in Figure 1. Each case is described as a set of features and the similarity between two cases can be defined as the weight sum of the similarity between corresponding case features. However, there is no direct means of computing the similarity between a case and a user profile, as user profiles are not described as a set of case features. Instead each raw user profile is converted into a feature-based representation called a *profile schema*. Basically, the profile schema corresponds to a content summary of the programme preferences contained in a user profile, encoded in the same features as the programme cases. The similarity between a profile and a given programme case can then be computed using the standard weighted-sum similarity metric as shown in equation 1; Where $f_i^{Schema(u)}$ and $f_i^{\,p}$ are the ith features of the schema and the programme case respectively.

$$1.\quad \Pr gSim(Schema(u),p) = \sum w_i \bullet sim\left(f_i^{Schema(u)},\ f_i^{p}\right)$$

The main problem associated with case-based methods is the knowledge-engineering effort required to develop case representations and sophisticated similarity models. In addition, because case-based methods make recommendations based on item similarity, the newly recommended items tend to be similar to the past items leading to reduced diversity. In the TV domain this can be a significant problem as we may find that all a user's recommendations are, for example, comedies if the majority of profile programmes are comedies.

3.3 Collaborative Recommendation

Collaborative recommendation methods such as automated collaborated filtering are an alternative to case-based techniques. Instead of recommending new programmes that are similar to the ones that the user has liked in the past, we recommend programmes that other *similar users* have liked ([1, 3, 4, 8 ,9, 10]). Rather than compute the similarity between items, we compute the similarity between users, or more precisely the similarity between user profiles. Note that we have opted for a lazy-approach to collaborative filtering rather than the more traditional eager approach where the user-base is pre-processed in to virtual communities prior to recommendation. So the recommendations for a target user are based on the viewing preferences of k similar users.

PTV computes user similarity by using a simple graded difference metric shown in equation 2; where p(u) and p(u') are the ranked programmes in each user's profile, and $r(p_i^u)$ is the rank of programme p_i in profile u. The possible grades range from –2 to +2 and missing programmes are given a default grade of 0. Of course this is just one possible similarity technique that has proved useful in PTV, and any number of techniques could have been used, for example statistical correlation techniques such as Pearson's correlation coefficient (see eg., [3, 10]).

$$2.\quad PrfSim(u,u') = \frac{\sum_{p(u)\cup p(u')} \left| r(p_i^u) - r(p_i^{u'}) \right|}{4 \bullet \left| p(u) \cup p(u') \right|}$$

$$3.\quad PrgRank(p,u) = \sum_{u' \in U} PrfSim(u,u')$$

Once PTV has selected k similar user profiles for a given target user, a recommendation list is formed from the programmes in these similar profiles that are absent from the target profile. This list is then ranked and the top r programmes are selected for recommendation. The ranking metric is shown in equation 3; U is the subset of k nearest profiles to the target that contain a programme p. This metric biases programmes according to their frequency in the similar profiles and the similarity of their recommending user. In this way popular programmes that are suggested by very similar users tend to be recommended.

Collaborative filtering is a powerful technique that solves many of the problems associated with case-based methods. For example, there is no need for content descriptions or sophisticated case similarity metrics. In fact, high quality recommendations, that would ordinarily demand a rich content representation, are possible. Moreover, recommendation diversity is maintained as relevant items that are dissimilar to the items in a user profile can be suggested.

Collaborative filtering does suffer from a number of shortcomings. There is a startup cost associated with gathering enough profile information to make accurate user similarity measurements. There is also a latency problem in that new items will not be recommended until these items have found their way into sufficiently many user profiles. This is particularly problematic in the TV domain because new and one-off programmes occur regularly and do need to be considered for recommendation even though these programmes will not have made it into any user profiles.

The key to PTV's success is the use of a combined recommendation approach. For a given guide, a selection of programmes is suggested, some are case-based recommendations (including new or one-off programmes) while others are collaborative recommendations. In particular, recommendation diversity is ensured through the use of collaborative filtering and the latency problem can be solved by using case-based methods to recommend new or one-off programmes.

4 Experimental Studies

PTV's normal mode of operation involves the generation of daily personalised TV guides containing a list of programme recommendations predicted to be of interest to each user. Guides contain, on average, 3 new recommendations per day. The hope is that all of these recommendations will be relevant, but of course the reality will inevitably be somewhat different. In this experiment we look at the gradings that users provided for the programme recommendations that they received in their daily guides. The primary question to be answered is whether or not users consider PTV's recommendations to be useful; that is, how often are the recommendations graded as relevant? In addition we are interested in comparing the recommendation quality of collaborative and case-based techniques.

4.1 Setup

The following results are based on an online evaluation by PTV users (mostly students and staff from University College Dublin and Trinity College Dublin) during March 1998. At this time the PTV system contained a population of approximately 200 users and a case-base of 400 programmes, which provided about 30% coverage of a typical week of television, and about 60% coverage of the prime-time viewing slots. During the experimental period a total of 2000 individual programme guides were requested. Each guide contained 3 new programme suggestions generated using either a collaborative approach or a case-based approach. This allows us to independently assess the relative competence of the collaborative filtering and case-based approaches. In addition, we generated guides by picking programme suggestions at random. These guides provide us with a basic benchmark against which to judge the quality of our two recommendation strategies.

4.2 Method

Each time a new programme is recommended as part of a personalised guide, the user is invited to grade the recommendation on a 5 point scale ranging from –2 (terrible) through 0 (no comment) to +2 (an excellent suggestion). These gradings are the raw data for the experiment; each grading encodes the username, the programme name, the date, the grade itself, and whether the recommendation was a case-based one or a collaborative filtering one. Over the experimental period a total of approximately 1000 individual gradings were saved from 100 different users; on average each user was submitting 10 grades over the test period. This provided us with three sets of data: (1) the grades associated with case-based recommendations; (2) the grades associated with collaborative filtering recommendations; (3) the grades associated with random recommendations.

4.3 Results

The quality of PTV's suggestions could be measured in any number of ways. For example, we could simply calculate the average grade assigned to collaborative, case-based, and random recommendations. However, we feel a better approach is to look at recommendation quality in the context of individually generated guides. For this reason our approach is to take each guide in turn, and to count the percentage of users that received 'n' or more good recommendations per day. This allows us to count the number of users that received at least 1, 2, or 3 good recommendations per day, which to our minds is a far better way of evaluating recommendation success in this setting. The results are displayed in Figure 3. Clearly, the results for PTV are very positive with 96% and 78% of users receiving at least one good new programme suggestion per day, depending on whether the guide was generated using collaborative filtering techniques or case-based methods. By comparison only 27% of users found one of the random recommendations to be worth watching. In fact, the results show that PTV recommended 3 good programmes a day more often than the random method recommended 1 good programme (42% or 32% versus 27%).

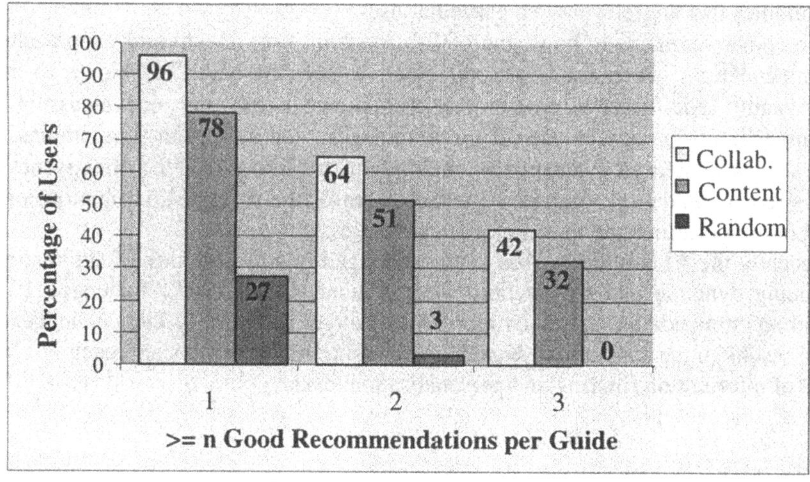

Fig. 3. PTV Guide Quality Results

TV programme recommendation is a difficult task. Viewers display extremely varied, and often inconsistent, viewing preferences and patterns. In addition, recommendations for a given guide on a given day are drawn from a limited set. There may be very few programmes scheduled for a particular day that suit a given user. Therefore, the results presented here bode extremely well for PTV's long-term recommendation prospects. Both collaborative and case-based methods have been shown to perform extremely well, and form an ideal partnership in PTV to ensure the recommendation of a diverse range of regular and new programmes.

These experiments represent an initial attempt at evaluation and admittedly the use of random recommendations as an evaluation benchmark is quite limited – it is easy to imagine more sophisticated benchmarks. However, in the Appendix we provide additional support in favour of PTV compiled from an extended user trial during March 1999.

5 Conclusions

As the latest satellite and digital TV services beam hundreds (and soon, thousands) of TV channels into our homes, we are faced with a significant choice problem, and the job of finding the right TV programme at the right time becomes increasingly difficult. In fact, instead of witnessing an increase in viewer satisfaction, some commentators have predicted quite the opposite, as viewers fail to come to grips with the new range of channels and fall into channel-hopping oblivion. In this paper we have described one possible solution to the problem, a solution that involves automatically generating personalised TV guides for individuals based on their learned viewing preferences, each guide containing information about a select set of programmes that are relevant to a particular user.

We have explained how the PTV system uses a hybrid approach to recommendation, which combines collaborative and case-based techniques to make high quality and diverse programme recommendations, and encompassing the recommendation of new or one-off programmes as well as regular programmes. We have also presented an evaluation of the system to demonstrate the effectiveness of PTV's recommendation components and to examine the separate contributions of the collaborative filtering and the case-based strategies.

Recently the AI community has been challenged to solve the task of automatically producing dynamic and personalised Web content (IJCAI-1997 Challenge). PTV's hybrid recommendation approach represents a direct response to this challenge. The initial results in the TV domain suggest a promising future for this approach in a wide range of information filtering and personalisation tasks.

Appendix

Initially the PTV project started life as a demonstration of what we saw as an important idea, namely that, in general, Internet content could be effectively personalised for the needs of individuals, and more specifically that users could receive accurate personalised TV guides to help them cope with the onslaught of digital TV. Since going live, and without significant advertising or marketing, the PTV system has attracted and profiled over 5000 registered users (growing by 500 - 1000 users per month) and over 15,000 personalised TV guides per month.

The following charts summarise the relevant results of a recent user survey carried out during March 1999. In particular they indicate that the recommendation approach is producing good quality guides at an acceptable speed thus supporting the claim that collaborative, case-based recommendation provides an effective and efficient personalisation technique.

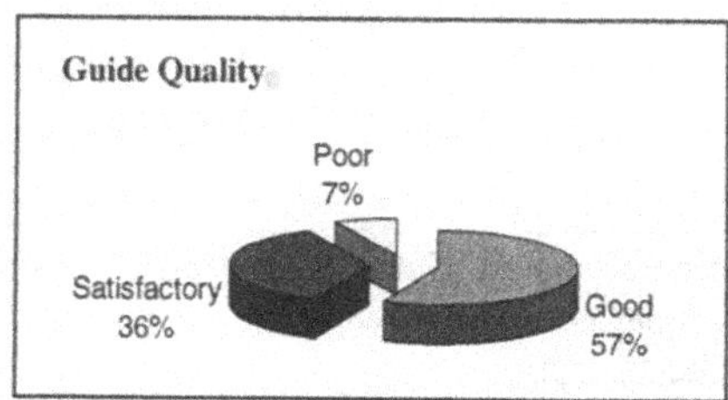

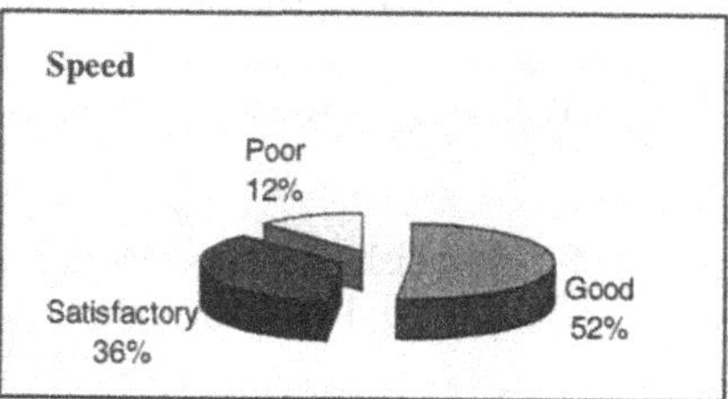

References

1. Balabanovic M., Shoham Y.: FAB: Content-Based Collaborative Recommender. Communications of the ACM, **40**(3) (1997) 66-72
2. Baudisch, P.: Recommending TV Programs: How far can we get at zero effort. In: Proceedings of the AAAI-98 Workshop on Recommender Systems, Wisconsin, USA, (1998) 16-19
3. Billsus, D. & Pazzani, M. J.: Learning collaborative Information Filters. In: Proceedings of the International Conference on Machine Learning, Wisconsin, USA, (1998)
4. Goldberg D., Nichols D., Oki B. M., Terry D.: Using Collaborative Filtering to Weave an Information Tapestry. Communications of the ACM, **35**(12) (1992) 61-70
5. Hammond, K. J., Burke, R., and Schmitt, K.: A Case-Based Approach to Knowledge Navigation. In: (Leake, D.B, ed.) Case-Based Reasoning Experiences Lessons and Future Directions, MIT Press, (1996) 125-136
6. Jennings, A. & Higuchi, H.: A user model neural network for a personal news service. User Modeling and User-Adapted Information, **3**(1) (1993).1-25
7. Kay J.: Vive la Difference! Individualised Interaction with Users. In: Proceedings IJCAI '95, Montréal, Canada, (1995). 978-984
8. Konstan J. A., Miller B. N., Maltz D., Herlocker J. L., Gordan L. R., Riedl J.: Grouplens: Applying Collaborative Filtering to Usenet News. Communications of the ACM, **40**(3) (1997) 77-87
9. Maltz D., Ehrlich K.: Pointing the Way: Active Collaborative Filtering. In: Proceedings of the ACM Conference on Human Factors in Computing Systems (CHI '95) ACM Press, New York, N.Y., (1995). 202-209
10. Shardanand, U. & Maes, P.: Social Information Filtering:Algorithms for Automating 'Word of Mouth'. In: Proceedings of the Conference on Human Factors in Computing Systems (CHI95), ACM Press, New York, N.Y., (1995). 210-217
11. Watson, I., Applying Case-Based Reasoning: Techniques for Enterprise Systems, Morgan-Kaufmann, (1997)

Case-Based Quality Management System Using Expectation Values

Hirokazu Taki[1], Satoshi Hori[2], and Norihiro Abe[3]

[1] Wakayama University, Systems Engineering Department, 930 Sakae-dani, Wakayama, Japan
taki@sys.wakayama-u.ac.jp
[2] Mitsubishi Electric Corporation, Manufacturing Technology Center, 8-1-1 Tsukaguchi-Honmachi, Amagasaki Hyogo, Japan
hori@int.mdl.melco.co.jp
[3] Kyushu Institute of Technology, Information Engineering Department, 680-4 Kawazu, Iizuka-Shi, Fukuoka, Japan
abe@sein.mse.kyutech.ac.jp

Abstract. This paper describes a quality management system (called CBQM: Case-Based Quality Management) using the case-based reasoning mechanism which is based on a cost expectation value. The cost expectation value is calculated from objective and subjective values. We developed a quality management system that employs a stochastic method. However, in some cases, this stochastic-based system failed to select good cases. Therefore, we have integrated some expectation values into the case selection mechanism. The CBQM has an expectation measurement. Its case selection criteria use not only similarity, but also some expectation values. If unforeseen malfunctions may occur due to inappropriate design, manufacturing condition and/or unsuitable usage, the similarity is not enough to select useful cases from a casebase. That is because the similarity is mainly based on products themselves. The CBQM adopts the cost expectation value in order to pick up useful cases. The CBQM's selection criteria is based on the quality of cases, which considers repair time, repair part cost, trouble recurrence, the confidence of diagnosis and repair difficulty. We validated this system in real product repair problems which field service engineers repair home appliances.

1 Introduction

The case-based reasoning, CBR, is very suitable for diagnosis of home appliances. However, the similarity function of the conventional CBR is not enough in order to select appropriate repair cases from a casebase. It is necessary to enable the case selection mechanism to consider not only the symptom similarity but also repair time, trouble recurrence and so on. This section describes why the CBR is useful for the field service domain and the necessity of introducing the cost expectation value.

1.1 Field service and CBR

Field service is now recognized as one of the most important corporate activities for manufacturing industries in order to improve customer satisfaction and to successfully take on global competition[7][9]. Competitive field service ought to have well-trained service technicians, service parts, and technical information. The demand for technical information, with which service technicians troubleshoot and repair, has especially been increasing because home electrical appliances are becoming more complicated in their functions and the number of models is increasing. Therefore an intelligent information system that can support service technicians to diagnose and repair efficiently has been keenly demanded. We developed a diagnostic intelligent system[14] , which infers possible defects in a home electrical appliance and lists up necessary service parts. This system employed CBR, case-based reasoning mechanism. The case selection mechanism of its CBR is based on the similarity of symptoms and the case frequency, i.e., how many times this case occurred[15][16]. The CBR is suitable to build a diagnostic system for field service because the CBR imitates how a experienced service technician infers and is able to learn defect trends and novel repair cases from the database of service reports.

1.2 Benefits of using CBR techniques

A complete, accurate and updated knowledge base is essential for an expert system to conduct accurate diagnosis. However making a good knowledge base is a time consuming and difficult process. Therefore the knowledge acquisition has been recognized as a bottleneck of conventional expert systems which adopt a production rule base. Model-based reasoning[6], rule induction[8]and case-based reasoning [3] have been proposed to overcome this bottleneck. The CBR has been employed for several diagnostic systems[1][5], because previous troubleshooting experience is often available in the field of diagnosis.

The major advantages of employing the CBR to the field service diagnosis are:

1. Avoid the knowledge acquisition bottleneck of the rule-based expert systems.
2. Mimic the diagnostic ability of experienced service technicians who can infer a malfunction cause accurately from their diagnostic knowledge and experience.
3. Exploit computer files of tens of thousands of repair reports. We can learn defect trends and novel repair cases from the repair report database.

1.3 Cost Expectation Value for CBR

There are some successful CBR systems[10][11][12] that employs a stochastic method. The stochastic method utilizes the similarity and probabilistic measurements in the case selection. However, it has turned to be necessary to utilize background knowledge, e.g., repair cost, loss cost of a broken product. These factors are considered in a cost expectation value in our new quality management system (called CBQM: Case-Based Quality Management). The CBQM adopts the cost expectation value in order to pick up useful cases. We have integrated some expectation values into the case selection mechanism. Its case selection criteria use not only similarity, but also some expectation values. If unforeseen malfunctions may occur due to inappropriate design, manufacturing condition and/or unsuitable usage, the similarity is not enough to select useful cases from a casebase. That is because the similarity is based mainly on product design. The CBQM adopts the cost expectation value in order to pick up useful cases. The CBQM's selection criteria is based on the quality of cases, which considers repair time, repair part cost, trouble recurrence, the confidence of diagnosis and repair difficulty.

2 Overview of CBQM

The CBQM, Case-based Quality Management, retrieves the most suitable repair cases from a casebase that stores previous service incidents. Its retrieval mechanism is the CBR integrating with the cost expectation values. Diagnostic CBR systems usually computes the similarity of symptoms and target products. Retrieved cases are listed up according to the similarity and the case frequency. However, the first case is not necessarily the most appropriate solution for a service technician to carry out. The first case is often a more expensive solution or results in trouble recurrence. This is because the CBR ignores the likelihood of trouble recurrence, repair fee, and repair difficulty. Our method takes these factors into account as expectation values. The expectation values are classified into two categories, objective (quantitative) values and subjective (qualitative) values. We employ AHP[13], Analytical Hierarchical Process, a decision making algorithm, in order to combine the similarity, frequency, and the expectation values.

2.1 Case representation

Each service incident has the following attributes:

- Service Facts: *End-user's name & address, Service date, Service technician's name*
- Repair Facts: *Product model, Symptoms, Cause of malfunction, Replaced parts*
- Objective Values: *Repair time, Repair fee*
- Subjective Values: *Confidence of diagnosis, Repair difficulty*

Diagnostic CBR systems generally utilize the repair facts and compute the similarity. And the retrieved cases, which have the higher similarity, are listed up as candidates to solve the target case. However, the objective and subjective values should be considered in selecting the most appropriate solution from these retrieved cases, because the biggest quantity of the objective and subjective values means maximizing the user's benefit. The first three attributes, service facts, repair facts, and objective values, are recorded in a service report. The subjective values need to be afterwards input by a service technician. Each subjective value is a category attribute. For example, the confidence of diagnosis has three categorical values: *{uncertain, almost certain, certain}*, and the repair difficulty has one of *{easy, average, difficult}*.

2.2 Case selection

Our method firstly selects cases that have higher possibility than a threshold. Then the expectation values of the retrieved cases are computed. The case with the highest expectation value is picked up to solve the target problem. The case selection procedure is as follows:

Step-1. Compute the similarity of the repair facts.

$$Similarity = \begin{cases} 0 & \text{if } S_0, S_i \text{ has an exclusive value.} \\ m/n & \text{otherwise} \end{cases}$$

where m is size of same items between ones of S_0 and S_i,
n is size of items of S_i respectively,
S_0, S_i are sets of the repair facts of C_0 the target case and C_i a case in a casebase.

Step-2. Compute the possibility from the similarity and case frequency. The possibility denotes how much possible a case likely solves the target problem.

$$\text{Possibility of } C_i = \text{Similarity} \times \text{Freq. of } C_i$$

Step-3. Select cases that have the possibility bigger than a threshold.
Step-4. Compute the cost expectation value for the retrieved cases. The maximum expectation value denotes the greatest customer satisfaction. The detail of the algorithm is described in the next section.
Step-5. Apply the selected case to the target problem.

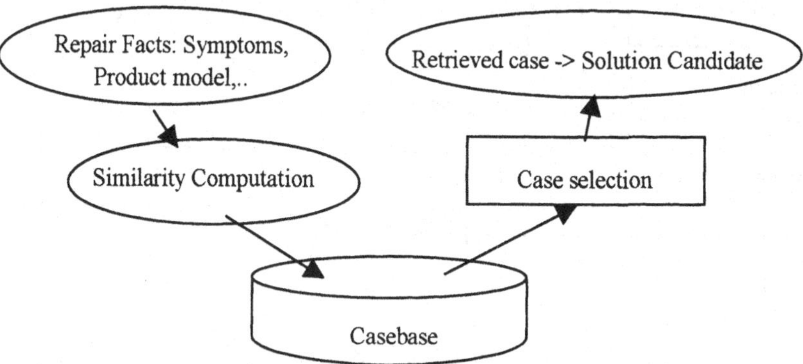

Fig. 1. Conventional CBR mechanism

3 Expectation Value Model

This section explains the algorithm of computing the cost expectation value. Fig. 1 is a typical CBR system using only similarity for selecting cases. Fig. 2 shows a CBR system that uses similarity, stochastic information and objective and subjective measurement for selecting cases. The rule base contains questions of limitations of symptoms and expectation value criteria. Fig. 3 depicts the hierarchical structure of the expectation value model. This model firstly calculates the expected repair cost from the objective values, repair fee and time, and so on. These are combined with the subjective values. And the cost expectation value of each case is finally computed so that the maximum expectation value denotes the greatest customer satisfaction.

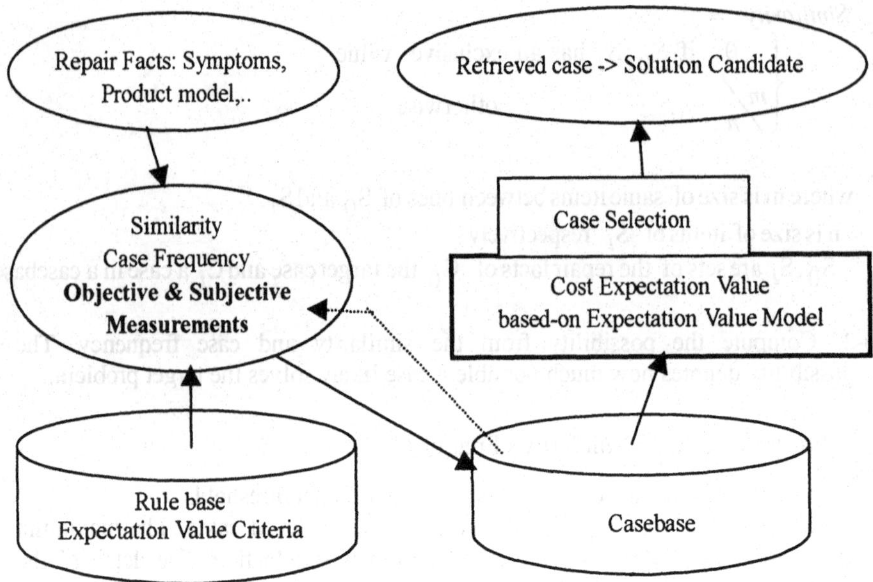

Fig. 2. Case Selection Mechanism Using Expectation Value Model

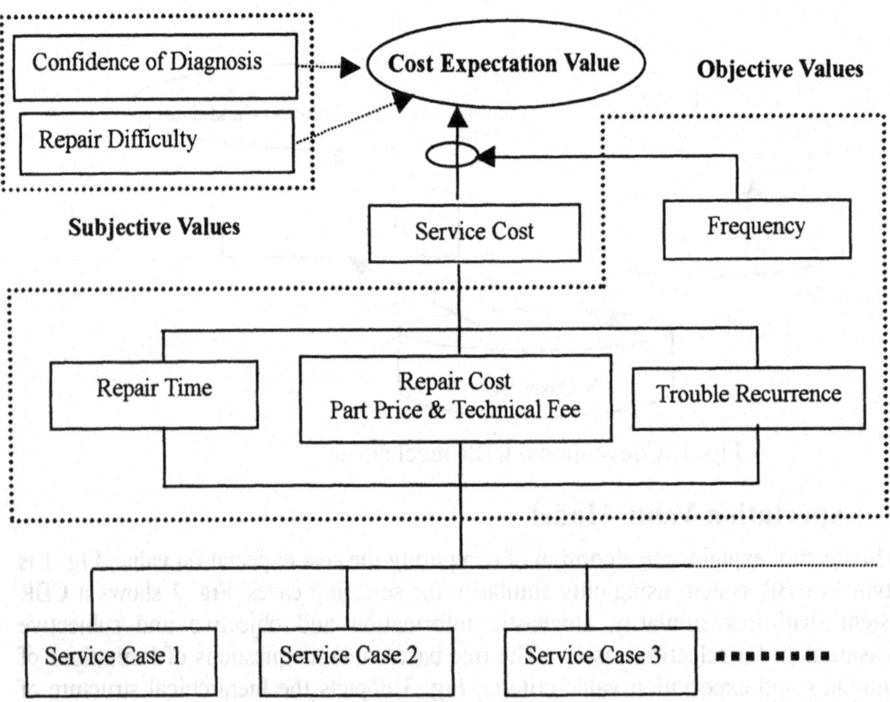

Fig. 3. Cost Expectation Value Model

This evaluation method is based on the AHP algorithm. Table 1(a) shows the importance comparison among the repair time, fee, and trouble recurrence. Its importance measurement has the range from 1 (equal importance) to 9 (absolute importance), and its diagonal element is represented in its reciprocal number in the matrix of Table 1(a). Its element, $e_{k,l}$ denotes the importance of attribute k over attribute l. For example, $e_{3,1} = 3$ denotes that "Repair Time" is weakly important compared with "Reccurence". This importance matrix may vary depending on target products. The importance matrix is converted into the weighting matrix as shown in Table 1(b) according to the following steps:

Table 1 (a). Importance Comparison Matrix

	Repair Time	Repair Fee	Recurrence
Repair Time	1	1/4	1/3
Repair Fee	4	1	2
Recurrence	3	1/2	1

Table 1 (b). Weighting Matrix

	Repair Time	Repair Fee	Recurrence
Repair Time	**0.122**	0.140	0.107
Repair Fee	0.488	**0.558**	0.640
Recurrence	0.366	0.279	**0.320**

Step-1. Prepare the importance matrix M. Its size is $n \times n$. $m_{k,l}$ denotes an element of M.

Step-2. Compute its geometrical average $\lambda_k = \sqrt[n]{\prod_k^n m_{k,l}}$ for each row of the important matrix M.

Step-3. Normalize the average $\eta_k = \lambda_k \Big/ \sum_q^n \lambda_q$.

Step-4. Compute the weighting matrix W by $w_{k,l} = m_{k,l} \times \eta_k$.

In this case, the weighting coefficients of "repair time", "repair fee", and "trouble recurrence" are 0.122, 0.558, 0.320 respectively.

The expected repair cost $Ev(C_i)$ is computed from the objective values by the following equation:

$$Ev(C_i) = \sum_j P(C_i) \times r_j V_j(C_i)$$

Where

$\mathrm{P}(C_i)$: Frequency of $C_i, \sum_i \mathrm{P}(C_i) = 1$ r_j: Weight Coefficient

$V_j(C_i)$: Value of Repair fee, time and trouble recurrence. Range is (1,2,..,10).
Next, the subjective values are combined with the expected repair cost $Ev(C_i)$.
The value of each attribute is categorized as following:

- Repair difficulty $RD(C_i)$ has the value of
  {1 (difficult), 2 (average), 3 (easy)}.
- Confidence of diagnosis $CD(C_i)$ has the value of
  {0 (uncertain), 1 (almost certain), 2 (certain)}.

The cost expectation value $V(C_i)$ is computed by the following equation:

$$V(C_i) = RD(C_i) \times CD(C_i) / Ev(C_i)$$

The case with the biggest $V(C_i)$ is finally selected. The bigger $V(C_i)$ is, the better the case C_i is.

4 Experimental Results

The CBQM, utilizes both of the similarity and the cost expectation value in selecting appropriate cases from a casebase. We applied our method to a field service casebase that contains 20,916 service reports. This casebase is build for a product. One report has 16 items. The varieties of symptoms are more than 300. Fig. 4 shows the most frequently-occurred service cases, whose product model and symptoms are similar to those of a target case. The conventional CBR in Fig. 1 selects these 15 cases. They should be promising candidates to solve the target problem. However, there exist five cases, N1,...N5, which a service technician cannot carry out. The contents of these cases are displayed in Table 2. The reason why these cases are selected is that the CBR mechanism ignores "repair difficulty", "repair cost", and "confidence of diagnosis".

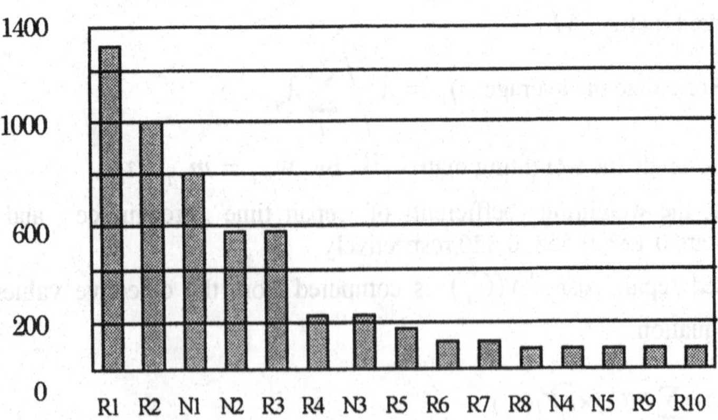

Fig. 4. Service Reports ordered by Frequency.

However, our method evaluates these useless cases at very low points as shown in Fig. 5. According to our experiments, 60% of the conventional CBR's output are useful solutions. On the contrary, 93% of the CBQM's output are effective solutions.

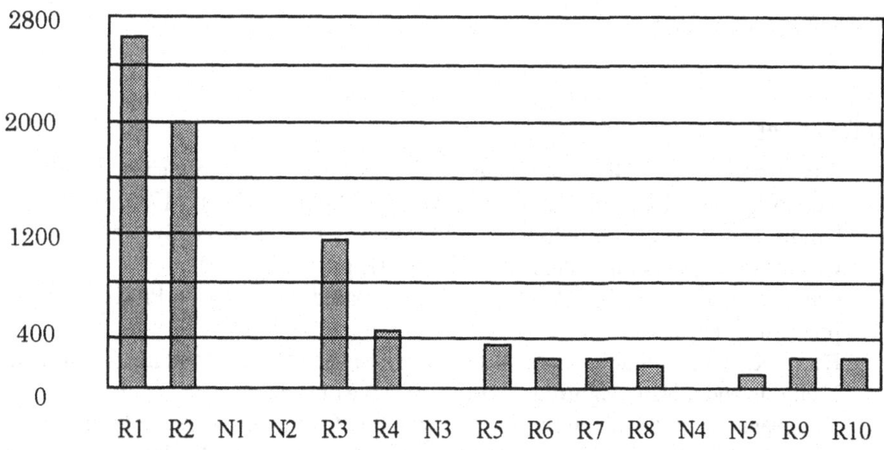

Fig. 5. Expectation value $V(C_i)$ of Service

Table 2. Cases which Service Technicians cannot carry out.

Case	Description
N1	Confidence of diagnosis is low. The service technician didn't observe malfunction. This might be an intermittent defect. This case cannot be applied to solve the target case because the case doesn't contain confirmed cause and remedy.
N2	Repair time is long. Various causes result in this malfunction so that the frequency of this case becomes large. However, this case doesn't contain a single remedy to solve the malfunction.
N3	Repair cost is high. Inappropriate design is the cause of defect. Not a service technician but Design section ought to take an action to solve this problem.
N4	User's insufficient understanding of product operation resulted in the service call. This call should not be solved by a service technician.

5 Conclusion

The CBQM (Case-Based Quality Management) employs the case-based reasoning mechanism which is based on the cost expectation value $V(C_j)$. The cost expectation value enables the CBR mechanism to consider not only similarity, but also some expectation values, e.g., repair difficulty, confidence of diagnosis. As the experimental results shows that information stored in cases is not sufficient to evaluate the their usefulness. Therefore it is necessary to add subjective evaluation to each case. This kind of knowledge is difficult to elicit and write them as rules. Our mechanism utilizes the subjective judgement of human experts through the cost expectation value $V(C_j)$.

References

1. Casadaban, C.E.: "DEB: A Diagnostic Experience Browser using Similarity Networks", NASA Conf. Publication, Vol.NASA-CP-3073, pp.517-524 (1990).
2. Golding, A.R. and Rosenbloom, P.S.: "Improving Rule-Based Systems through Case-Based Reasoning", Proc. of AAAI 1991, pp.22-27 (1991).
3. Hammond, K.J.: "CHEF:A Model of Case-based Planning", Proc. AAAI86, pp267-271 (1986).
4. Kira, K. and Rendell, L.A.: "The Feature Selection Problem: Traditional Methods and a New Algorithm" , Proc. of AAAI (1992).
5. Kobayashi, S. and Nakamura, K.: "Knowledge Compilation and Refinement for Fault Diagnosis", IEEE Expert, Vol.6, No.5, pp.39-46, Oct. (1991).
6. Kuiper, B.: "Qualitative Simulation" Artificial Intelligence Vol.2 pp.289- 338 (1986).
7. Nguyen, T., et. al.: "Compaq Quicksource Providing the Consumer with the Power of AI" AI magazine pp.48-60 (Fall 1993).
8. Quinlan, J.R.: "Decision Trees and Decision making", IEEE Trans. on Systems, Man and Cybernitics, Vol.20,No.2, pp.339-346 (1990).
9. Rewari, A. ed.: "AI in Corporate Service and Support", IEEE Expert, Vol.8, No.6, pp.5-38 (1993).
10. Shinmori, A.: "A Proposal to Combine Probabilistic Reasoning with Case-Based Retrieval for Software Troubleshooting", AAAI Technical Report WS-98-15, 1998 Workshop Case-based Reasoning Integration, pp149-154 (1998).
11. Tsatsouli, C., Cheng, Q. and Wei, H-Y: "Integrating Case-Based Reasoning and Decision Theory", IEEE Expert, Vol.12, No.4, pp.46-56 (1997).
12. Yang, Q., Kim, E. and Racine, K.: CaseAdvisor: "Supporting Interactive Problem Solving and Case Base Maintenance for Help Desk Applications", IJICAI97 practical Use of CBR Workshop, pp.31-40 (1997).
13. Saaty, T.L.: "Multicriteria Decision Making - The Analytic Hierarchy Process", RWS publications, (1990).
14. Hori, S., Shugimatsu, K., Furukawa, S. and Taki, H.: Utilizing Repair Cases of Home Electrical Appliances, Proc. of Practical Use of Case-Based Reasoning IJICAI-97 Workshop, pp.41-52 (1997)
15. Aamodt, A. and Plaza, E.: Case-Based Reasoning: Foundational Issues, Methodological Variations, and System Approaches. AI Communications 7(1): 39-59 (1994)
16. AcknoSoft: http://www.acknosoft.com/fTechnology.html

ICARUS: Design and Deployment of a Case-Based Reasoning System for Locomotive Diagnostics

Anil Varma[1]

[1]Information Technology Laboratory,
General Electric Corporate Research and Development,
Niskayuna, NY 12301
varma@crd.ge.com

Keywords : Case-based reasoning, locomotive, diagnosis, feature extraction, feature weighing, fault codes

Abstract. Locomotives, like many modern complex machines, are equipped with the capability to generate on-board fault messages indicating the presence of anomalous conditions. Such messages tend to generate in large quantities and difficult and time consuming to interpret manually. This paper presents the design and development of a case-based reasoning system for diagnosing locomotive faults using such fault messages as input. The process of using historical repair data and expert input for case generation and validation is described. An algorithm for case matching is presented along with some results on pilot data.

1 Introduction

There is a recent move in industry towards supporting equipment servicing as a means of augmenting traditional revenue sources such as those generated by equipment sales with limited warrenties and subsequent parts supply. This is especially applicable in the case of heavy machinery which due to its design complexity is often best serviced by the manufacturer. Examples in case include gas turbines, aircraft engines and locomotives. With the emergence of long-term service contracts for such equipment, it is essential that the manufacture minimize its cost of service by proactive on-board and off-board monitoring and diagnosis. Within this context, this paper describes the development of ICARUS (Intelligent Case-based Analysis for Railroad Uptime Support) - a case-based reasoning tool for off-board locomotive diagnosis for use by GE Transportation Systems.

Locomotives are complex electromechanical systems and are equipped with the capability to monitor their state and generate fault messages in response to anomalous conditions of varying severity. Since removing a locomotive from a track for repair (or powering down a gas turbine or removing an airplane engine from wing) is an extremely expensive and disruptive procedure, it is desirable that

1. Problems occurring on the equipment while in operation are accurately identified so the repair can be scheduled best keeping with the severity of the problem.
2. Problems with the equipment are completely identified so the time in the repair shop is utilized at not merely fixing one problem but releasing an overall healthy machine.

ICARUS was designed to reason with the fault codes generated by locomotives during operation. In addition, it was a requirement ICARUS be able to build up it's information base quickly for rapid deployment and have the capability to learn as new information became available. It was also required that the tool be applicable across locomotive models and fleets with little modification.

This project presented three challenges that are typical of the real-world requirements deviating from textbook theory. First, diagnostic cases for the case base were not readily available and had to be reconstructed by mining historical repair records. Their accuracy was thus not guaranteed and case validation became an essential activity in itself. Very limited expert knowledge and time was available to fully validate the cases. Association of fault codes to specific repairs was difficult due to the standard railroad practice of multiple repairs on the same visit as well as some uncertainty about the accuracy of the date of repair. Finally, the continual nature of the fault logs made casting the case as a finite feature vector almost impossible.

This paper first presents the current operating scenario and the nature and availability of the data. We then present details of the process for generating meaningful cases. A new feature extraction and weighing algorithm is described as well as the results obtained from its implementation. This work is then related to prior activity in the literature. Finally some lessons learned from the project about CBR design and deployment are discussed.

2 Overview of Current Process

Locomotive fault logs are accumulated on-board the locomotive and are periodically uploaded to a database for access in case a diagnostic need arises. Highly skilled field engineers at General Electric Transportation Systems have acquired expert knowledge over time that enables accurate diagnosis of locomotive problems from an examination of the fault log. While this provides positive evidence for the diagnostic significance of fault logs, the volume of logged data makes it impossible to rely on human examination alone for reliable and consistent identification of locomotive problems on many hundred locomotives on a daily basis.

A case-based approach was considered as this appeared to be cognitively closest to the procedure used by the experts during diagnosis. It was desirable to move away from a rule based approach for several reasons. Some of these may be outlined as :

1. Accurate rules only existed for a small percentage of the locomotive's failure modes. The rest apparently happened in a manner too varied to capture in rules.
2. Frequent configuration changes and upgrades make rule based approaches hard to maintain.
3. Capturing knowledge as cases appeared to be the best approach for maintaining knowledge in a remote diagnostics environment where the diagnostic personnel were not necessarily all experts.
4. There was a realization that many more patterns may exist in the fault log data then anyone was aware of or could create rules for. There was a push for a learning approach for identifying these from case data.
5. It was desirable to deploy a functional system fairly rapidly, from concept to pilot operation in less than a year. However, experts had severe time constraints while there was considerable historical data that could be potentially mined for cases.

The objective of the project, thus was to build a tool that could take the fault log shown in Fig. 1 as input and output the top n repair codes with associated confidence values.

2.1 Historical Fault log and Repair Data

A sample fault log is shown in Fig. 1 . While the actual data constituting the log has been changed or masked, the essential features of the log are present. The first two columns identify the company that is operating the locomotive and the specific locomotive ID respectively. The next column indicates the date on which the fault occurred. The fault itself is identified by a 'fault code' a unique alphanumeric label associated with that fault. Next , a time stamp indicates the beginning and end of the fault message. The next few columns marked with 'X' represent a 'snapshot' of some important operating parameters of the locomotive at the time the fault occurred. Representative examples of such parameters would be speed, operating temperatures, pressure readings, whether certain switches are on or off etc. Finally a short text description associated with the fault code is displayed.

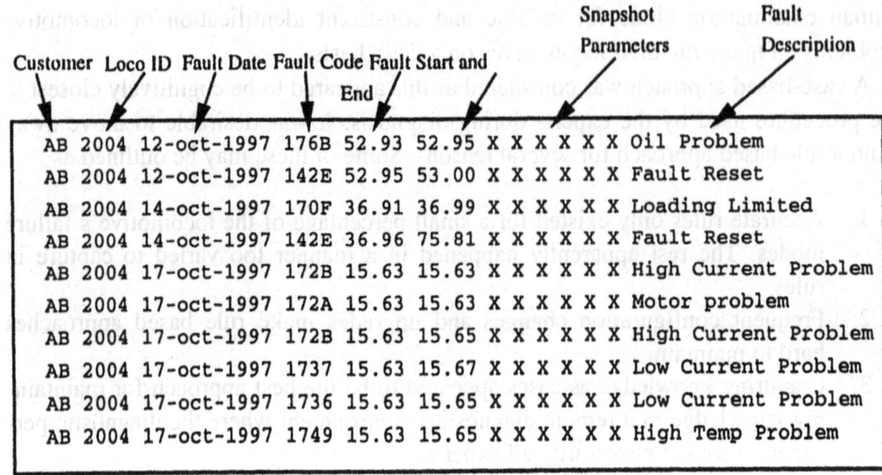


```
AB 2004 12-oct-1997 176B 52.93 52.95 X X X X X X Oil Problem
AB 2004 12-oct-1997 142E 52.95 53.00 X X X X X X Fault Reset
AB 2004 14-oct-1997 170F 36.91 36.99 X X X X X X Loading Limited
AB 2004 14-oct-1997 142E 36.96 75.81 X X X X X X Fault Reset
AB 2004 17-oct-1997 172B 15.63 15.63 X X X X X X High Current Problem
AB 2004 17-oct-1997 172A 15.63 15.63 X X X X X X Motor problem
AB 2004 17-oct-1997 172B 15.63 15.65 X X X X X X High Current Problem
AB 2004 17-oct-1997 1737 15.63 15.67 X X X X X X Low Current Problem
AB 2004 17-oct-1997 1736 15.63 15.65 X X X X X X Low Current Problem
AB 2004 17-oct-1997 1749 15.63 15.65 X X X X X X High Temp Problem
```

Fig 1. Sample Locomotive Fault Log

The fault log represents an arbitrarily long data stream with new data flowing in every day. Locomotive experts intimately familiar with the engineering specifics of the locomotive are able to look at the log alone and usually identify patterns that may indicate problems. It is worthwhile noting that multiple problems may be occurring simultaneously in the locomotive that will register a presence in the fault log. However, not all problems are critical enough to stop the basic operation of the locomotive and these accumulate till they are attended to during a regular service visit.

Since there was no direct association from individual fault codes to actual locomotive problems requiring repair, this information was sought to be implicitly acquired. A source of data used for this purpose was the repair database maintained by the manufacturer. The nature of the repair log was as shown in Fig. 2.

Customer	Loco ID	Repair Code	Repair Date	Repair Description
AB	1101	5013	24-FEB-1997	Fixed Component A
AB	1101	6105	27-MAY-1997	Scheduled Maintenance
AB	1101	4105	27-MAY-1997	Fixed Component B
AB	1101	5405	27-MAY-1997	Replaced Component D

Fig. 2.Sample Locomotive Repair Log

The basic operation of the tool required taking the fault log as input and recommending a repair action with associated confidence. For reference, there were about 600 distinct faults that could be logged and 700 repair actions that could be taken. In addition, the repair actions could be logged in the database up to a week later than the actual physical repair.

An approach was defined wherein, candidate cases would be generated to 'seed' the case base by mining historical fault log and repair records. These cases would then be minimally validated by format checking and checking for missing data. It was acknowledged that many of these cases could be diagnostically partially or completely incorrect. This may be due to the fact that either an incorrect repair was performed that did not actually address the problem that was causing activity in the fault logs or that the repair was incorrectly dated, or that there were multiple problems not all of which were addressed.

3 Process for defining and acquiring cases

The first task was to build candidate cases from historical fault log and repair records. A program was written to interleave the repair log with the fault log. A two year data window was chosen for prototype case generation with data gathered for over 200 locomotives. The process of raw case generation was as follows :

1. A particular repair type (diagnosis) was chosen for case collection.
2. All locomotives repair records were sequentially scanned for occurrence of that repair.
3. Every time that repair was encountered on a locomotive, a case was generated that contained the fault log contents for the N days preceding that repair.

This process is shown graphically in Fig. 3.

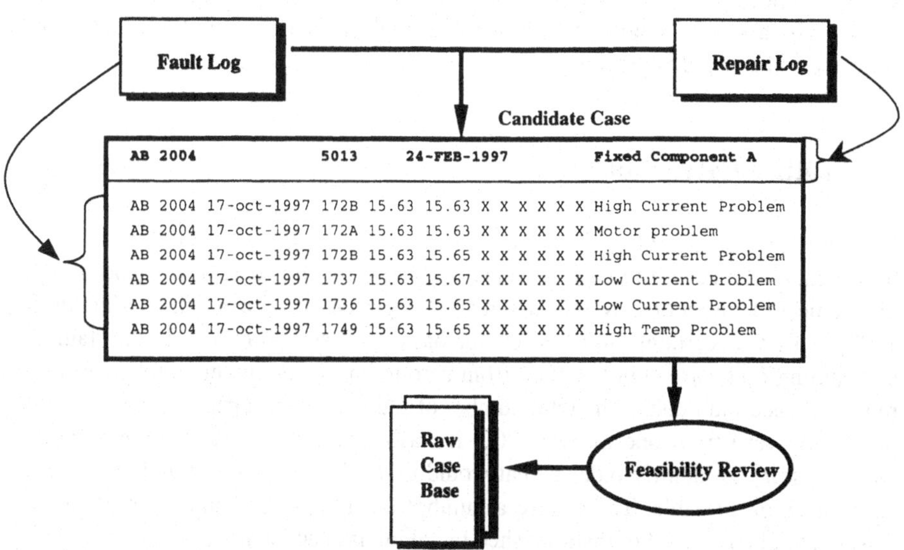

Fig. 3. Process for Case Acquisition

Each case was labeled by the repair code – the intended diagnosis. Multiple cases were collected for each repair code to capture the different fault code scenarios leading to that repair being the diagnosis. This process was repeated for many repair codes for which case-base coverage was required.

Each case so produced was still beset with certain problems. These included

1. Insufficient or missing fault log data : Since the fault log is fairly continual in nature, gaps of many days in the log indicated missing data rather than absence of faults.
2. Multiple repairs on the same day : There were many instances of 3-5 repairs performed on the same day. By our process, this resulted in many cases with identical fault logs but associated with different repairs.
3. Overlapping fault logs for repairs : If there were multiple repairs within N days of each other, they shared a common portion of the fault log for those N days.

For the above 3 conditions, heuristics were used to weed out cases that could possible 'contaminate' the case base. Cases with missing fault log were eliminated. Due to large quantities of historical data available, it was possible to restrict case selection to only those instances where there was only one repair on a given day. Nothing was done to correct for situation 3 since it was reasoned that the effect of overlapping fault log would be reduced with appropriate case feature weighing if sufficient cases for each of the overlapping repairs were collected.

Each case thus collected was subjected to a feasibility review by an experienced field engineer. The task of the field engineer was to review and eliminate any case in which the fault log was obviously **not** related to the repair performed. This task of saying yes or no placed a lower cognitive burden on the experts as compared to verifying each case as a 'gold' standard for that kind of repair. About 500 cases were collected following this procedure.

4 Feature Extraction

Much CBR work has implicitly assumed the availability of a finite number of indices by which to characterize a case. This is not always true, however as evidenced by the ultrasonic rail inspection system application reported in (Jarmulak & Kerckhoffs, 1997). This was certainly not true of our basic case structure. The N day fault log constituting each case could contain from zero to an indeterminate number of occurrences of each fault code. The total number of fault codes occurring in the case could potentially vary from one to over 700. It was evident that some feature extraction was necessary to identify indexes that would unify the case representation and make case matching possible. There were a number of options for feature representation. Cases could be matched or distinguished by taking into account

1. Presence/Absence of fault codes.
2. Fault code frequency
3. Combinations of fault codes

4. Time based trends in fault code occurrences i.e. if fault code frequency increased leading up to the repair.
5. Anomalous indicators in the parameter data i.e. if any of the continuous parameters were out of specification.
6. Sequence information in fault code occurrence i.e. if fault codes repeatedly occurred in a certain sequence .

However, there was another consideration constraining the choice of features. This was the fact that our cases were constructed by assuming that a certain causal relationship existed between fault logs and repairs data when their time line was overlaid. There was no initial evidence as to the degree of error associated with the assumptions underlying this approach. For this reason, it was decided to keep feature extraction fairly basic till such a determination could be made.

4.1 Fault Cluster Generation

Fault combinations were selected as the feature of choice for case representation. A variety of tests were carried out on historical fault log data to determine the maximum number of fault codes that appeared to occur repeatedly in combination on a given day. The analysis appeared to indicate that more than four faults seldom occurred repeatedly in combination in test data. As a result, the following approach was adopted. Each case was polled for a list of distinct fault codes occurring before the repair with which it was associated. The list of distinct faults was used to generate combinations (or fault clusters, as we termed them) as follows :

Distinct faults contained in case 1 : A,B,C,D
1-Clusters : A, B,C,D
2-Clusters : AB, AC,AD,BC,BD,CD
3-Clusters : ABC,ABD,ACD,BCD
4-Clusters : ABCD

This process was carried out for all the cases. A master list of fault clusters of each size was maintained. Each case was now indexed in terms of its features – namely Diagnosis + fault clusters. An example is shown in Fig. 4.

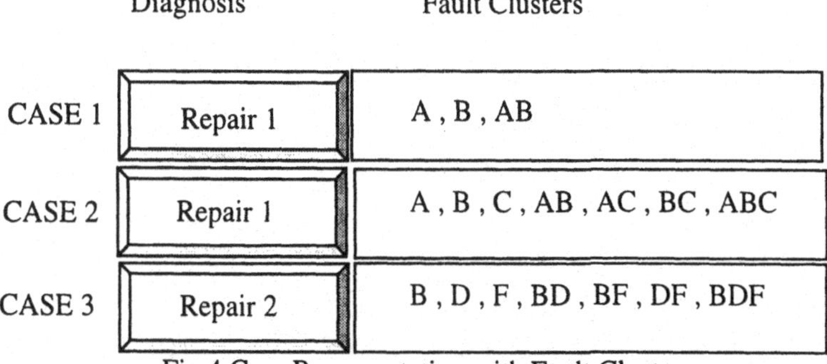

Fig 4 Case Representation with Fault Clusters

The objective of this exercise was to generate a complete list of candidate fault clusters of size four or less. Using this list, the next step was to determine which of this exhaustive list of clusters represented valuable repetitive patterns with diagnostic significance. This computer-intensive approach was adopted since there was virtually no expert opinion available to guide the selection of diagnostically useful fault patterns. Considering all possibilities of size four and under let the weighing algorithm consider a wide variety of cluster candidates in a reasonable time period.

4.2 Fault Cluster Weighing

Due to the inexact case creation procedure as well as the knowledge that there was not a one-to-one mapping between faults in the fault log and repairs, a process was created to assign weights to fault clusters based upon the cases in the case base. As new cases were continually being added, the system was designed to operate in two modes. In the learn mode, it calibrated the significance of available fault clusters based upon all the cases in the case base. During the diagnose mode, it used the weighted clusters as indicators to match the features of the incoming case with the most appropriate stored case.
The learn mode involves learning a weight value $\in [0,1]$ for each fault cluster. The weight is intended to be representative of each cluster's ability to isolate a specific repair code. If a cluster only appears in cases of a specific repair code, it has a weight of 1. On the other hand, if that cluster occurs with an evenly distributed frequency in cases of multiple repair codes, it's weight is appropriately lowered. A cluster is required to repeat a certain number of times before it is assigned a non-zero weight. After weight assignment, a clusters below a certain weight threshold are assigned a weight of zero. The process is shown in pseudo code below.

```
Program Calculate_cluster_weights

for each target repair code I (where repair code is a
categorization of a repair action)

 {
select distinct fault codes where (incident date -
fault date) < N days.

Store as case.

Delete from cases where #fault codes < min or > max.
}
for each case C_I
{  from  distinct fault list F_i belonging to C_I
for (j = Maxclustersize ; j=1; j=j-1)

 [ Maxclustersize = 4 in our application]

     create distinct Fault clusters of size j .
}

For each fault cluster F_cluster_I
{
count total # of cases it occurs in
count # incident codes it occurs in with what frequency.
Cluster significance = f(#cases,#distinct repair codes
it occurs in cases of,discriminating power)

If total # of cases < case_threshold : delete cluster
```

Generating [1-4] sized combinations of all faults in a case results in generating a lot of candidate fault clusters. In practice, thresholding resulted in only a small percentage of fault clusters emerging as significant in that they had non-zero weights. This was consistent with our approach of examining a wide variety of options to learn the features that were significant. In general, the number of single and double fault clusters that emerged as significant was larger that the number for three and four sized clusters. The average weight though followed the inverse relation. Three and Four sized clusters had higher average weights that one and two sized clusters. When faults appeared repeatedly in three and four sized combination they were usually strong indicators of diagnostic significance. The weight assignment can simply recognized as the maximum conditional probability of any repair for a given fault cluster over all the repairs it occurrs before.

$$\text{Weight of Fault Cluster } F\_cluster_i = \text{Max}_j \,[\, P(\text{Repair}_j \,/\, F\_cluster_i) \,]$$

5 Case Matching

Once weights for fault clusters were acquired, case matching was straightforward. New diagnosis was requested by identifying the locomotive that was experiencing problems. The fault log database was queried for fault codes occurring in the N days preceding the diagnosis request.

Degree of match between a new and stored case was calculated as

$$\frac{[\sum \text{Weights of common clusters between stored and new case}]^2}{[\sum \text{Weights of Clusters in stored case}] \times [\sum \text{Weights of Clusters in new case}]}$$

The repair code associated with the case with the highest degree of match was the diagnosis returned by the system.

6 Case Validation

The case base currently contains cases for diagnosing over 50 repair codes. The number of cases associated with each repair code varies from three to seventy. Leave-one-out testing was performed to test the performance of the case base. In this process, one case was removed from the case base and formed the testing set. All other cases, as part of the training set were used to learn fault cluster weights. The case-base was then used to match and retrieve the top three repair codes in response to the left-out case. If the repair code associated with the testing case was in the top-3 set, the diagnosis was declared a success. This process was repeated with every case in the case base being the testing set once.

The accuracy of the case base was then tabulated as success % by repair code. There were a few repair codes where the case-base was consistently unable to correctly diagnose even in top 3 predictions more than 10-15% of the time. The cases associated with these repair codes were referred back to the domain experts. In most cases it was discovered that the repair codes were such that the fault codes could not be expected to predict them. In other instances, the same repair situation was classified under three different repair codes. Once these were unified, the accuracy of diagnosis on that repair code increased.

This process of case validation was a necessary closure to our initial approach of gathering cases that were approximately accurate. This allowed us to avoid requiring the time of domain experts to verify each case in the beginning. Now only a focused number of cases were required to be examined that did not appear to be consistent with each other.

7 Results of Experiments

Accuracy was measured only for repair codes that had over 10 cases associated with them. After removing repair codes deemed undiagnosable through the process in the previous section, accuracy on repair codes ranged from 23% to 94%. Overall accuracy was around 80% , assuming that the correct diagnosis appearing in the top three diagnoses given by the system was regarded as a success. In general the following trends were observed.

1. Repair codes associated with a greater number of cases had a higher diagnosis accuracy rate.
2. Accuracy increased as fault clusters of increasing size were used. The relative increase in accuracy was small but significant. Accuracy using fault clusters of size 1 was about 60 - 65%.

8 Related Work

There are quite a few examples of CBR being applied to diagnosis. We discuss a few that have addressed problems similar to ours both from an application as well as design viewpoint. Jarmulak et al. (1997) present a system that uses CBR for a rail inspection application. Their system uses image data as input and shares the limitation in that it is not easily expressed as a feature vector. They use a hybrid rule + case-based system for image classification with no adaptation. They also mention the need to periodically identify cases in the case base that never match well as possibly 'bad' cases or noisy images. Acorn and Walden (1992) report on SMART – a CBR help-desk system developed for COMPAQ. In contrast to our semi-automated, mining approach to creating cases, this describes a more conventional case-population process wherein senior engineers were designated as case-builders with a daily review process. Correctness of the cases is not an issue. However, their observations that they could go live before having a complete and correct knowledge base is in agreement with our experience as well. Hennessy and Hinkle (1992) report on CLAVIER – one of the early commercial CBR applications. A key aspect motivating its development is described as the inability of the operators to articulate good rules. This, again, is consistent with our experience. CLAVIER's role as corporate memory that increases in quality and quantity with use very much in line with the role expected of ICARUS. Kitano et al. (1993) with their SQUAD system highlight the role of CBR systems as maintainers of corporate knowledge. Since they report dealing with over 20,000 cases, they describe a well managed human intensive process for case collection, filtering and quality control. They use a system of abstraction hierarchies to create neighborhood relationships between attributes. Interestingly, they also appear to use a system of combination generation. The motivation however seems to be to enumerate a sql type query for each type of attribute value below in the hierarchy from where the user has specified the attributes. Bonzano et al. describe an approach towards 'introspective' learning of feature weights in CBR, recognizing that standard CBR matching functions can be extremely sensitive to noise and irrelevant features and suitable weight vectors are not always available. While this concept is recognized in our approach, we do not make an effort to adjust feature weights in response to incorrect retrieval. This arises from our understanding that the error could lie with the case itself, and consequently consistent incorrect retrieval is used as an indication of a defective case rather than incorrect feature weighing.

CBR applications in similar domains have been reported under the INRECA project (Klaus-Dieter et al., 1995). INRECA uses induction to extract a decision tree to guide the user but uses CBR to handle unknown values. An application of INRECA to robot diagnosis uses a combination of causal rules, decision trees and weight factors for knowledge representation. This seems consistent with future development plans for ICARUS where a hybrid rule/case based system is eventually envisaged. In another application to CFM56 engines, use of legacy data to create initial cases with ongoing integration of model based knowledge is described. A concurrent benefit of the case building activity mentioned here is creation of a knowledge management process that helps highlight high occurrence failure modes through a systematic cleaning and analysis of data. This has been the case with ICARUS as cost-benefit analysis of fault generation from a diagnostic point of view is being revisited with a goal of generating more meaningful faults on the locomotive.

9 Institutional deployment and Cost-Benefit Analysis

ICARUS development was started in early 1997. A first prototype was deployed on pilot fault log data from 35 locomotives in October of the same year. A team of five diagnostics experts independently examines the fault logs daily and arrive at a diagnosis. These conclusions are compared with the output of ICARUS. This constituted the validation phase of the tool. An integrated recommendation was delivered to the railroad based on this activity. The primary benefit of identifying problems is that the locomotive can be better scheduled for repair and unscheduled failures leading to a mission loss are avoided. In most instances, a recommendation is kept open until feedback is obtained from the repair shop as to the actual work done. If this feedback corresponds to the top 3 repair recommendations of the CBR tool, the case is closed and declared as a success. If not, then it is classified as a failure. One field engineer at GE Transportation systems has been assigned the primary responsibility of running and validating the tool each day.

Both successful and failed attempts at diagnosis are examined in greater detail by the tool design team including the author. In many cases, experts point out that certain problems are not well manifested in fault logs and cases relating to these repairs are removed from the case-base. The primary driver for seeking expert input is when the case base is unable to predict a repair code at a > 50% accuracy despite having > 10 cases for it. This focused approach helps minimize expert time requirements.

Some early successes in diagnosing problems in the pilot program have helped management allocate increasing resources to the project. The biggest benefit is that new incoming cases (that are not mined from historical data but based upon daily analysis) are of much higher quality due to expert validation and have contributed to increasing the accuracy of the tool. It is estimated that a savings of a few thousand dollars could be realized per locomotive per year just by optimizing its repair actions based upon an accurate understanding of the failures occurring on board. Over 350 locomotives expected to be monitored in 1999-2000, this adds up to a considerable sum. There is a considerable productivity benefit as well as a limited staff of upto ten experts will be required to monitor the 350 locomotive fleet and tools like ICARUS can considerably reduce the effort required for diagnosis.

10 Discussion

A number of lessons were learned in the course of this project. Some of these may be listed as

1. The availability of high quality cases cannot be taken for granted. In complex domains specially, it becomes increasingly difficult to find expertise that will certify cases as fully correct. In this application we were specially mandated not to rely on 'preconceived' expert knowledge to guide the case base development – rather to learn from the data. Many experts freely acknowledged that there was possibly much more hidden in the data than they had expertise over.

2. Case representation can be a design issue. In most case-based applications, the identification of a case feature vector arises naturally from the way the case exists. Out of many possible features that could characterize the cases in this application, fault combinations were one of the features identified as being potentially significant and were chosen for case representation. Feature weighing was able to consider and eliminate a majority of fault clusters as being diagnostically insignificant.

3. The assumption that each case contained data associated with only one diagnosis was not valid in this case. The extent that multiple simultaneous problems were being manifested in the fault codes was not known. Again, this was addressed partly by choosing candidate cases carefully and subsequently by feature weighing. Only fault clusters that consistently occurred in cases of a particular repair code were assigned high weights by the feature weighing algorithm.

4. Commonly recognized advantages of a case-based reasoning approach like quick deployment, capability for continuous learning, low knowledge elicita-

tion needs and a measure of explanation stood true in this application. The system was developed in about eight months and is currently running on live pilot data. While the initial case seeding was based on historically mined cases, future cases that are being added are of much higher quality since the final resolution of problems will are accurately tracked and verified from the field.

The portability of the case-based approach was vividly demonstrated once the system was developed. Business focus required that ICARUS be applied to a model of locomotives different from the data on which the system was developed. In less than a month, new seeding cases were acquired, feature weights were recomputed and another version of ICARUS was released. This was in comparison to a rule-based approach which would have required development from scratch. For reference, previous rule-based approaches for locomotive models had taken few years to develop.

Incremental learning was specially important in this application. Locomotives undergo frequent hardware and software changes. A case-based approach could adapt to this, given sufficient quantity of cases.

5. Learning weights for case features can help make implicit knowledge explicit. In many cases, a physical explanation could be attached to particular faults occurring together. This provided an additional means to occasionally check the knowledge in the case base.

6. As yet, there is no concept of adaptation in the working of ICARUS.

7. Finally, the ability to come up with a working albeit incomplete system early on was vital in maintaining management and user involvement in the application.

11 Conclusions and Future Work

ICARUS will be deployed for providing monitoring support to over 350 locomotives in 1999. As more cases are added to the system, we are exploring additional features by which to characterize cases to sustain and improve the system's accuracy. Preliminary results incorporating fault occurrence trends as case features have shown evidence of positively impacting diagnostic accuracy. As can be expected, this too has a stronger effect on certain repair codes as compared to others.

In conclusion, we have presented a case-based application for diagnosis that employs a variety of pre and post-processing techniques to transform historical data into a format suitable for a case-based approach. We present an 'propose and verify' approach towards case generation where candidate cases of approximate diagnostic accuracy are generated and case performance metrics are used to isolate cases that may need expert validation. Feature weights are learned from the data. The application is such that a complete and accurate diagnostic formulation with any approach is practically impossible. Our experience has shown that a case-based approach has been able to contribute significantly towards capturing a tractable amount of knowledge even if approximately, and consequently reducing the load of the diagnostics expert.

Acknowledgements

The author would like to acknowledge and thank Nicholas Roddy for developing the CBR software as well as running validation tests. Thanks are due to Tom Shaginaw for motivating the Case-Based approach. Special thanks to David Gibson for supporting our efforts with business and data support and domain expertise.

References

1. Jarmulak, J., Kerckhoffs, E.,Veen, P. : Case-Based Reasoning in an Ultrasonic Rail-Inspection System. In: Leake, D., Plaza, E.(eds.): Case-Based Reasoning Research and Development. Lecture Notes in Computer Science, Vol 1266. Springer-Verlag New York (1997) ,43–52.

2. Acorn,T., and Walden, S. : SMART: Support Management Automated Reasoning Technology for Compaq Customer Service. In Proceedings of AAAI-92. Cambridge, MA: AAAI Press, MIT Press.(1992)

3. Hennessy, D., and Hinkle, D. : Applying Case-Based Reasoning to Autoclave Loading. IEEE Expert,(1992), 7(5), 21-26.

4. Kitano, H., Shimazu, H. and Shibata, A. : Case-Method: A Methodology for Building Large-Scale Case-Based Systems. In Proceedings of the Eleventh National Conference on Artificial Intelligence, (1993), 303-308.

5. Bonzano, A., Cunningham, P. and Smyth, B. : Using Introspective Learnng to Improve Retrieval in CBR : A Case Study in Air Traffic Control. In: Leake, D., Plaza, E.(eds.): Case-Based Reasoning Research and Development. Lecture Notes in Computer Science, Vol 1266. New York (1997) ,291–302.

6. Klaus-Dieter, A., Auriol, E., Bergmann, R., Breen, S., Dittrich, S., Johnston,R. Manago, M., Traphoener, R., Wess, Stefan : Case-Based Reasoning for Decision Support and Diagnostic Problem Solving: The INRECA Aproach. In B. Bartsch-Sporl, D. Janetzko & S. Wess (eds.), Proceedings of the 3rd workshop of the German special interest group on CBR , (1995), 63-72.

List of Authors

Lecture Notes in Artificial Intelligence (LNAI)

Vol. 1489: J. Dix, L. Fariñas del Cerro, U. Furbach (Eds.), Logics in Artificial Intelligence. Proceedings, 1998. X, 391 pages. 1998.

Vol. 1495: T. Andreasen, H. Christiansen, H.L. Larsen (Eds.), Flexible Query Answering Systems. Proceedings, 1998. IX, 393 pages. 1998.

Vol. 1501: M.M. Richter, C.H. Smith, R. Wiehagen, T. Zeugmann (Eds.), Algorithmic Learning Theory. Proceedings, 1998. XI, 439 pages. 1998.

Vol. 1502: G. Antoniou, J. Slaney (Eds.), Advanced Topics in Artificial Intelligence. Proceedings, 1998. XI, 333 pages. 1998.

Vol. 1504: O. Herzog, A. Günter (Eds.), KI-98: Advances in Artificial Intelligence. Proceedings, 1998. XI, 355 pages. 1998.

Vol. 1510: J.M. Zytkow, M. Quafafou (Eds.), Principles of Data Mining and Knowledge Discovery. Proceedings, 1998. XI, 482 pages. 1998.

Vol. 1515: F. Moreira de Oliveira (Ed.), Advances in Artificial Intelligence. Proceedings, 1998. X, 259 pages. 1998.

Vol. 1527: P. Baumgartner, Theory Reasoning in Connection Calculi. IX, 283 pages. 1999.

Vol. 1529: D. Farwell, L. Gerber, E. Hovy (Eds.), Machine Translation and the Information Soup. Proceedings, 1998. XIX, 532 pages. 1998.

Vol. 1531: H.-Y. Lee, H. Motoda (Eds.), PRICAI'98: Topics in Artificial Intelligence. XIX, 646 pages. 1998.

Vol. 1532: S. Arikawa, H. Motoda (Eds.), Discovery Science. Proceedings, 1998. XI, 456 pages. 1998.

Vol. 1534: J.S. Sichman, R. Conte, N. Gilbert (Eds.), Multi-Agent Systems and Agent-Based Simulation. Proceedings, 1998. VIII, 237 pages. 1998.

Vol. 1535: S. Ossowski, Co-ordination in Artificial Agent Societies. XVI, 221 pages. 1999.

Vol. 1537: N. Magnenat-Thalmann, D. Thalmann (Eds.), Modelling and Motion Capture Techniques for Virtual Environments. Proceedings, 1998. IX, 273 pages. 1998.

Vol. 1544: C. Zhang, D. Lukose (Eds.), Multi-Agent Systems. Proceedings, 1998. VII, 195 pages. 1998.

Vol. 1545: A. Birk, J. Demiris (Eds.), Learning Robots. Proceedings, 1996. IX, 188 pages. 1998.

Vol. 1555: J.P. Müller, M.P. Singh, A.S. Rao (Eds.), Intelligent Agents V. Proceedings, 1998. XXIV, 455 pages. 1999.

Vol. 1562: C.L. Nehaniv (Ed.), Computation for Metaphors, Analogy, and Agents. X, 389 pages. 1999.

Vol. 1570: F. Puppe (Ed.), XPS-99: Knowledge-Based Systems. VIII, 227 pages. 1999.

Vol. 1571: P. Noriega, C. Sierra (Eds.), Agent Mediated Electronic Commerce. Proceedings, 1998. IX, 207 pages. 1999.

Vol. 1572: P. Fischer, H.U. Simon (Eds.), Computational Learning Theory. Proceedings, 1999. X, 301 pages. 1999.

Vol. 1574: N. Zhong, L. Zhou (Eds.), Methodologies for Knowledge Discovery and Data Mining. Proceedings, 1999. XV, 533 pages. 1999.

Vol. 1582: A. Lecomte, F. Lamarche, G. Perrier (Eds.), Logical Aspects of Computational Linguistics. Proceedings, 1997. XI, 251 pages. 1999.

Vol. 1585: B. McKay, X. Yao, C.S. Newton, J.-H. Kim, T. Furuhashi (Eds.), Simulated Evolution and Learning. Proceedings, 1998. XIII, 472 pages. 1999.

Vol. 1599: T. Ishida (Ed.), Multiagent Platforms. Proceedings, 1998. VIII, 187 pages. 1999.

Vol. 1609: Z. W. Raś, A. Skowron (Eds.), Foundations of Intelligent Systems. Proceedings, 1999. XII, 676 pages. 1999.

Vol. 1611: I. Imam, Y. Kodratoff, A. El-Dessouki, M. Ali (Eds.), Multiple Approaches to Intelligent Systems. Proceedings, 1999. XIX, 899 pages. 1999.

Vol. 1612: R. Bergmann, S. Breen, M. Göker, M. Manago, S. Wess, Developing Industrial Case-Based Reasoning Applications. XX, 188 pages. 1999.

Vol. 1617: N.V. Murray (Ed.), Automated Reasoning with Analytic Tableaux and Related Methods. Proceedings, 1999. X, 325 pages. 1999.

Vol. 1620: W. Horn, Y. Shahar, G. Lindberg, S. Andreassen, J. Wyatt (Eds.), Artificial Intelligence in Medicine. Proceedings, 1999. XIII, 454 pages. 1999.

Vol. 1621: D. Fensel, R. Studer (Eds.), Knowledge Acquisition Modeling and Management. Proceedings, 1999. XI, 404 pages. 1999.

Vol. 1632: H. Ganzinger (Ed.), Automated Deduction – CADE-16. Proceedings, 1999. XIV, 429 pages. 1999.

Vol. 1634: S. Džeroski, P. Flach (Eds.), Inductive Logic Programming. Proceedings, 1999. VIII, 303 pages. 1999.

Vol. 1638: A. Hunter, S. Parsons (Eds.), Symbolic and Quantitative Approaches to Reasoning and Uncertainty. Proceedings, 1999. IX, 397 pages. 1999.

Vol. 1640: W. Tepfenhart, W. Cyre (Eds.), Conceptual Structures: Standards and Practices. Proceedings, 1999. XII, 515 pages. 1999.

Vol. 1650: K.-D. Althoff, R. Bergmann, L.K. Branting (Eds.), Case-Based Reasoning Research and Development. Proceedings, 1999. XII, 598 pages. 1999.

Lecture Notes in Computer Science

Vol. 1603: V. Vitek, C.D. Jensen (Eds.), Secure Internet Programming. X, 501 pages. 1999.

Vol. 1605: J. Billington, M. Diaz, G. Rozenberg (Eds.), Application of Petri Nets to Communication Networks. IX, 303 pages. 1999.

Vol. 1606: J. Mira, J.V. Sánchez-Andrés (Eds.), Foundations and Tools for Neural Modeling. Proceedings, Vol. I, 1999. XXIII, 865 pages. 1999.

Vol. 1607: J. Mira, J.V. Sánchez-Andrés (Eds.), Engineering Applications of Bio-Inspired Artificial Neural Networks. Proceedings, Vol. II, 1999. XXIII, 907 pages. 1999.

Vol. 1608: S. Doaitse Swierstra, P.R. Henriques, J.N. Oliveira (Eds.), Advanced Functional Programming. Proceedings, 1998. XII, 289 pages. 1999.

Vol. 1609: Z. W. Raś, A. Skowron (Eds.), Foundations of Intelligent Systems. Proceedings, 1999. XII, 676 pages. 1999. (Subseries LNAI).

Vol. 1610: G. Cornuéjols, R.E. Burkard, G.J. Woeginger (Eds.), Integer Programming and Combinatorial Optimization. Proceedings, 1999. IX, 453 pages. 1999.

Vol. 1611: I. Imam, Y. Kodratoff, A. El-Dessouki, M. Ali (Eds.), Multiple Approaches to Intelligent Systems. Proceedings, 1999. XIX, 899 pages. 1999. (Subseries LNAI).

Vol. 1612: R. Bergmann, S. Breen, M. Göker, M. Manago, S. Wess, Developing Industrial Case-Based Reasoning Applications. XX, 188 pages. 1999. (Subseries LNAI).

Vol. 1613: A. Kuba, M. Šámal, A. Todd-Pokropek (Eds.), Information Processing in Medical Imaging. Proceedings, 1999. XVII, 508 pages. 1999.

Vol. 1614: D.P. Huijsmans, A.W.M. Smeulders (Eds.), Visual Information and Information Systems. Proceedings, 1999. XVII, 827 pages. 1999.

Vol. 1615: C. Polychronopoulos, K. Joe, A. Fukuda, S. Tomita (Eds.), High Performance Computing. Proceedings, 1999. XIV, 408 pages. 1999.

Vol. 1617: N.V. Murray (Ed.), Automated Reasoning with Analytic Tableaux and Related Methods. Proceedings, 1999. X, 325 pages. 1999. (Subseries LNAI).

Vol. 1619: M.T. Goodrich, C.C. McGeoch (Eds.), Algorithm Engineering and Experimentation. Proceedings, 1999. VIII, 349 pages. 1999.

Vol. 1620: W. Horn, Y. Shahar, G. Lindberg, S. Andreassen, J. Wyatt (Eds.), Artificial Intelligence in Medicine. Proceedings, 1999. XIII, 454 pages. 1999. (Subseries LNAI).

Vol. 1621: D. Fensel, R. Studer (Eds.), Knowledge Acquisition Modeling and Management. Proceedings, 1999. XI, 404 pages. 1999. (Subseries LNAI).

Vol. 1622: M. González Harbour, J.A. de la Puente (Eds.), Reliable Software Technologies – Ada-Europe'99. Proceedings, 1999. XIII, 451 pages. 1999.

Vol. 1625: B. Reusch (Ed.), Computational Intelligence. Proceedings, 1999. XIV, 710 pages. 1999.

Vol. 1626: M. Jarke, A. Oberweis (Eds.), Advanced Information Systems Engineering. Proceedings, 1999. XIV, 478 pages. 1999.

Vol. 1627: T. Asano, H. Imai, D.T. Lee, S.-i. Nakano, T. Tokuyama (Eds.), Computing and Combinatorics. Proceedings, 1999. XIV, 494 pages. 1999.

Col. 1628: R. Guerraoui (Ed.), ECOOP'99 - Object-Oriented Programming. Proceedings, 1999. XIII, 529 pages. 1999.

Vol. 1629: H. Leopold, N. García (Eds.), Multimedia Applications, Services and Techniques - ECMAST'99. Proceedings, 1999. XV, 574 pages. 1999.

Vol. 1631: P. Narendran, M. Rusinowitch (Eds.), Rewriting Techniques and Applications. Proceedings, 1999. XI, 397 pages. 1999.

Vol. 1632: H. Ganzinger (Ed.), Automated Deduction – Cade-16. Proceedings, 1999. XIV, 429 pages. 1999. (Subseries LNAI).

Vol. 1633: N. Halbwachs, D. Peled (Eds.), Computer Aided Verification. Proceedings, 1999. XII, 506 pages. 1999.

Vol. 1634: S. Džeroski, P. Flach (Eds.), Inductive Logic Programming. Proceedings, 1999. VIII, 303 pages. 1999. (Subseries LNAI).

Vol. 1636: L. Knudsen (Ed.), Fast Software Encryption. Proceedings, 1999. VIII, 317 pages. 1999.

Vol. 1638: A. Hunter, S. Parsons (Eds.), Symbolic and Quantitative Approaches to Reasoning and Uncertainty. Proceedings, 1999. IX, 397 pages. 1999. (Subseries LNAI).

Vol. 1639: S. Donatelli, J. Kleijn (Eds.), Application and Theory of Petri Nets 1999. Proceedings, 1999. VIII, 425 pages. 1999.

Vol. 1640: W. Tepfenhart, W. Cyre (Eds.), Conceptual Structures: Standards and Practices. Proceedings, 1999. XII, 515 pages. 1999. (Subseries LNAI).

Vol. 1644: J. Wiedermann, P. van Emde Boas, M. Nielsen (Eds.), Automata, Languages, and Programming. Proceedings, 1999. XIV, 720 pages. 1999.

Vol. 1649: R.Y. Pinter, S. Tsur (Eds.), Next Generation Information Technologies and Systems. Proceedings, 1999. IX, 327 pages. 1999.

Vol. 1650: K.-D. Althoff, R. Bergmann, L.K. Branting (Eds.), Case-Based Reasoning Research and Development. Proceedings, 1999. XII, 598 pages. 1999. (Subseries LNAI).

Vol. 1653: S. Covaci (Ed.), Active Networks. Proceedings, 1999. XIII, 346 pages. 1999.